Scott Foresman

Glenview, Illinois
Boston, Massachusetts
Chandler, Arizona
Upper Saddle River, New Jersey

ISBN-13: 978-0-328-47640-4
ISBN-10: 0-328-47640-4
7 8 9 10 V011 15 14 13

CC1

Contents

Part 1
English Language Learners: Professional Development Articles

Contents

Resources on Reading Street for English Language Learner Support

All the support you need for your ELL instruction

The teacher's edition has ELL instructional strategies built into the lesson plans at point of use. The lessons provide guidance in using sheltered techniques and routines for teaching academic vocabulary, listening comprehension, phonics, vocabulary, reading comprehension, grammar and conventions, and writing.

Teacher's Edition

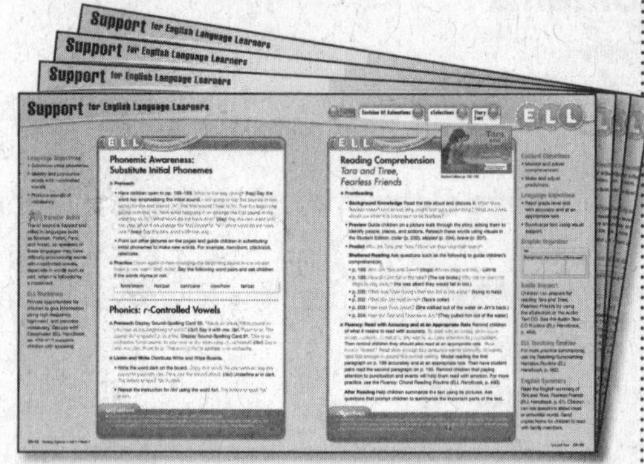

ELL Support pages

ELL Posters contain high-quality illustrations and five days of activities to support key oral vocabulary, selection vocabulary, and lesson concepts.

ELL Poster

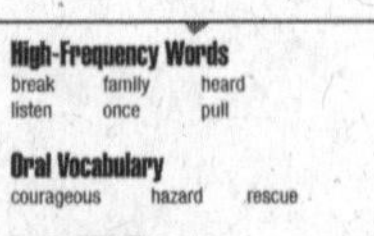

High-Frequency Words
break family heard
listen once pull

Oral Vocabulary
courageous hazard rescue

Poster Talk-Through
This **family's** cat is stuck in the tree. The family **heard** the cat meowing loudly. They came out to see what was wrong. The mother went back inside and called 911. Then she came out to wait for help with her family. Courageous firefighters came to rescue the cat. They started to work at **once**. They did not wait. Now one fireman **pulls** the cat from the tree as the branch is about to **break**! The family **listens** as the fireman talks gently to the cat. When they listen, they feel calm. Everything is going to be all right. The hazard is gone.

DAY 1

Check Prior Knowledge
Read the Poster Talk-Through aloud, pointing to images in the art. Check children's knowledge by asking questions.

Beginning Ask children to point to items they recognize on the poster and say what they are. Help them name items if necessary.

Intermediate Have children use short sentences to describe what is happening in the poster.

Advanced/Advanced High Ask children to describe the dangerous situation shown in the poster. Have them explain why it is dangerous.

Develop Concepts and Oral Vocabulary
Reread the Poster Talk-Through to introduce the Oral Vocabulary words. Give visual support by pointing to items on the poster that illustrate courageous, hazard, and rescue. Work with the class on a list of ideas that exemplify the words. Generate examples of hazards, ways to rescue something or someone, and courageous acts. Relate these concepts to the Question of the Week by asking children how they can help each other in dangerous situations.

DAY 2

Use the poster art and question to help children briefly discuss the lesson concept.

Teach High-Frequency Words
Share the Poster Talk-Through again, this time to introduce the tested High-Frequency Words. Label the poster with the High-Frequency Words. Then have the children, one at a time, act out one of the words for the others to guess.

DAY 3

Expand Vocabulary
Give the class examples of possible dangerous situations, such as: *Somebody gets hurt on the playground. Your friend is lost on a busy street.* As you name each situation, give pairs time to discuss and write down or sketch an appropriate way to help. Have pairs share their responses with the class at the end of the allotted time. Tell children that when there is real danger, they should tell an adult or call 911.

DAY 4

Produce Oral Language
Have the class pretend that they are in the poster scene. Have groups act out a television interview with the poster characters. Write *Who?*, *What?*, *When?*, *Where?*, *Why?*, and *How?* on the board to guide questions.

Beginning/Intermediate Have children act as reporters and ask simple questions of people on the scene.

Advanced/Advanced High Have them play the parts of family members or firefighters.

DAY 5

Check Concepts and Language
Read the Question of the Week aloud. Monitor children's understanding of the lesson concept.

Beginning Provide the children with this sentence prompt: *In a dangerous situation, we can help by ______.* Ask each child to come up with one or two ways to complete the sentence.

Intermediate Ask: *What are two things that we can do to help in dangerous situations?* Have children write a simple sentence for each response.

Advanced/Advanced High Have children write a very brief paragraph that answers the Question of the Week, *How can we help each other in dangerous situations?*

The ELL Handbook includes phonics and grammar transition lessons, comprehension skill practice, selection vocabulary word cards, study guides for ELL Readers, and multilingual selection summaries and vocabulary charts. Weekly planners provide daily instructional plans.

ELL Handbook

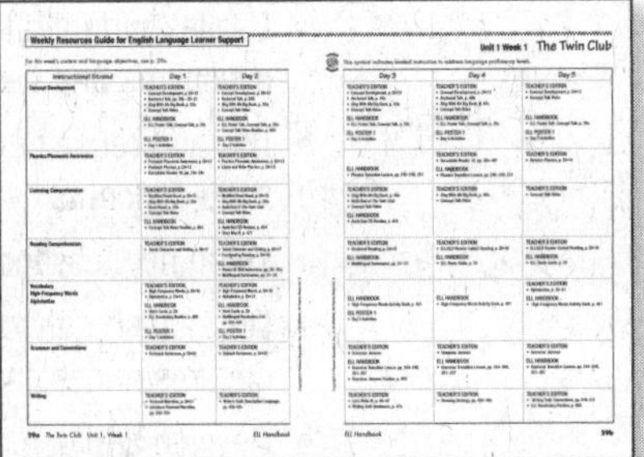
Weekly Planner

Instructional-level fiction and nonfiction books are provided for readers at all proficiency levels. The ELL, ELD, and Concept Literacy Readers relate to weekly concepts and offer children opportunities to read texts and practice target skills and strategies.

ELL/ELD Reader Teaching Guide

ELD Reader

ELL Reader

Concept Literacy Reader

Technology

Concept Talk Video

Use the Concept Talk Video to activate an engaging discussion about the weekly concept. Use the Concept Talk Video Routine found in the ELL Handbook to guide students' understanding.

AudioText CD

Use the AudioText CD and the AudioText CD Routine in this ELL Handbook to help children build fluency and comprehension and prepare for reading the main selection.

Grammar Jammer

Grammar Jammer provides additional practice with weekly grammar skills. For suggestions on how to use this learning tool, see the Grammar Jammer Routine in the ELL Handbook.

Language Development Student Outcomes

Language Learning Strategies	• Use prior knowledge and experiences to understand English. • Self-monitor oral or written language to recognize and correct errors or to seek help. • Use strategic learning techniques (such as concept mapping, drawing, memorizing, comparing, contrasting, or reviewing) to learn vocabulary. • Use learning strategies when speaking (request assistance, employ non-verbal cues, or use synonyms and descriptions in place of unknown English words). • Use and reuse newly acquired English words and expressions to improve proficiency and to build concepts. • Learn new essential language by using familiar or accessible language. • Distinguish between formal and informal English and use each language register in appropriate circumstances, in accord with grade-level expectations. • Develop and use language-learning strategies (such as looking for patterns in language or analyzing sayings and expressions), in accord with grade-level expectations.
Listening Skills	• Distinguish sounds and intonation patterns in English words and expressions with increasing clarity. • Distinguish phonetic sounds of English during word learning. • Learn English language structures, expressions, and vocabulary by listening to instruction and talking with peers and teachers. • Self-monitor for understanding of language during instruction and conversations, and seek clarification as needed. • Use visual resources, context, and familiar language to better understand unfamiliar spoken English. • Listen to a variety of media, paying attention to language meaning, to build concepts and acquire language. • Understand the meaning, main points, and important details of spoken language about familiar or unfamiliar topics. • Understand information and implied ideas in complex spoken language, in accord with grade-level expectations. • Demonstrate listening comprehension by following directions, responding to questions and requests, collaborating with peers, taking notes, or retelling and summarizing spoken messages.
Speaking Skills	• Produce phonetic sounds in newly acquired words and expressions in order to pronounce English words in an understandable manner. • Learn and use high-frequency English words to identify and describe people, places, animals, and objects. • Learn English vocabulary by retelling simple stories and information represented or supported by pictures. • Learn and use English words and expressions needed for classroom communication. • Speak using a variety of English grammatical structures, sentence lengths, sentence types, and connecting words with increasing accuracy and ease. • Speak using grade-appropriate content-area vocabulary in context to learn new English words and build academic language proficiency. • Share information interactively with peers and teachers. • Ask for and give information, using high-frequency, concrete words and expressions for basic communication and using abstract and content-based vocabulary during extended speaking assignments.

	• Express opinions, ideas, and feelings, ranging from using words and short phrases to participating in discussions about various grade-appropriate topics. • Explain, narrate, and describe with increasing specificity and detail as more English is acquired. • Adapt spoken language appropriately for formal and informal purposes. • Respond orally to information in print, electronic, audio, and visual media to build concepts and acquire language.
Reading Skills	• Learn relationships between sounds and letters in English, and decode words by recognizing sound-letter relationships and identifying cognates, affixes, roots, and base words. • Recognize the directionality of written English: left to right and top to bottom. • Develop basic English sight vocabulary. • Derive meaning of environmental print. • Comprehend English used routinely in grade-level texts. • Use before-reading strategies such as previewing graphic organizers and illustrations or learning topic-related vocabulary to enhance comprehension of written text. • Read adapted content-area material with a decreasing need for linguistic accommodations as more English is learned. • Use visual resources and context to read grade-appropriate text with understanding and to acquire vocabulary including academic language. • Use support from peers and teachers to read grade-appropriate text with understanding and to acquire vocabulary including academic language. • Demonstrate comprehension of increasingly complex grade-appropriate texts in English by participating in shared reading, retelling, or summarizing; responding to questions; and taking notes. • Read silently with increasing ease and comprehension for sustained periods. • Demonstrate English comprehension by employing and expanding basic reading skills (such as summarizing, understanding supporting ideas and details in text and graphic sources, and distinguishing main ideas from details) in accord with grade-level needs. • Demonstrate English comprehension by employing and expanding inferential skills (such as predicting, making connections between ideas, drawing conclusions from text and graphic sources, and finding supporting text evidence) in accord with grade-level needs. • Demonstrate English comprehension by employing and expanding analytical skills (such as evaluating written information and critically examining texts) in accord with grade-level needs.
Writing Skills	• Represent the sounds of the English language with letters when writing words in English. • Write using newly acquired basic English vocabulary and grade-level academic vocabulary. • Spell common English words with increasing accuracy, and use spelling patterns correctly as more English is acquired. • Edit writing for standard grammar and usage, including subject-verb agreement, pronoun agreement, and appropriate verb tenses, in accord with grade-level expectations as more English is acquired. • Use grammatical structures (such as verbs in different tenses, pronouns, possessive nouns, contractions, and negatives) correctly in writing, in accord with grade-level expectations. • Write using a variety of grade-appropriate sentence lengths, patterns, and connecting words to combine phrases, clauses, and sentences in increasingly accurate ways. • Narrate, describe, and explain with increasing detail to fulfill grade-appropriate writing needs as more English is acquired.

Grade 2 Readers on Reading Street

Every week there are a variety of readers to choose from to target instruction and meet the language development needs and reading levels of all learners. Every reader supports weekly grade-level concept development and the Question of the Week.

Leveled Readers

Weekly fiction and nonfiction readers are provided for children at the On-Level, Strategic Intervention, and Advanced levels.

On-Level

Strategic Intervention

Advanced

Build Concepts

The Concept Literacy Reader builds concepts and language.

Concept Literacy

Build Language

Scaffolded versions build vocabulary and comprehension skills each week at different proficiency levels.

ELD Reader

ELL Reader

Beginning • Intermediate
• Contains the same high-quality art as the ELL Reader.
• Text adapted for Beginning and Intermediate proficiency levels.
• High-frequency and concept words are emphasized.
• Graphic elements are simplified.
• Captions for photos are simple, then progress to either phrases or short sentences.

Intermediate • Advanced • Advanced High
• Contains the same high-quality art as the ELD Reader.
• Text adapted for Intermediate to Advanced High proficiency levels.
• Concept words that students need to know to understand the text are highlighted and defined.
• Graphic elements such as captions, diagrams, maps, flow charts, and signs are included.
• Captions for photos are complete sentences.

Scott Foresman ELL Authors

Elena Izquierdo, Ph.D.
Associate Professor
University of Texas at El Paso

Jim Cummins, Ph.D.
Professor
Department of Curriculum, Teaching and Learning
University of Toronto

Lily Wong Fillmore, Ph.D.
Professor Emerita
Graduate School of Education
University of California, Berkeley

Georgia Earnest García, Ph.D.
Professor
Language and Literacy Division
Department of Curriculum and Instruction
University of Illinois at Urbana-Champaign

George A. González, Ph.D.
Professor (Retired)
School of Education
University of Texas-Pan American, Edinburg

The Three Pillars of English Language Learning

Dr. Jim Cummins, the University of Toronto

In order to understand how English learners develop second-language literacy and reading comprehension, we must distinguish between three different aspects of language proficiency:

Conversational fluency This dimension of proficiency represents the ability to carry on a conversation in face-to-face situations. Most native speakers of English have developed conversational fluency by age 5. This fluency involves use of high-frequency words and simple grammatical constructions. English learners generally develop fluency in conversational English within a year or two of intensive exposure to the language in school or in their neighborhood environments.

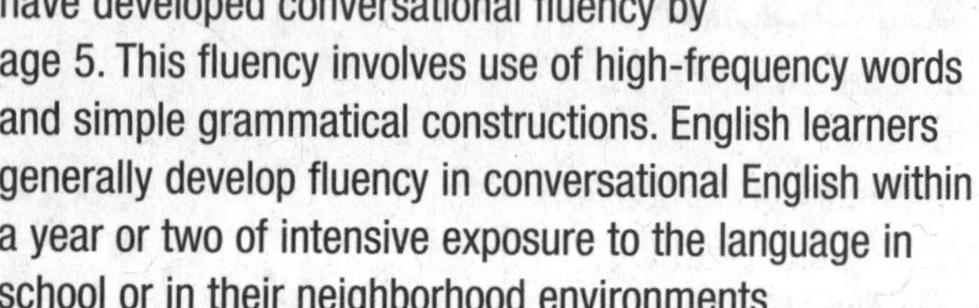

Discrete language skills These skills reflect specific phonological, literacy, and grammatical knowledge that students can acquire in two ways— through direct instruction and through immersion in a literacy-rich and language-rich environment in home or in school. The discrete language skills acquired early include:

- knowledge of the letters of the alphabet
- knowledge of the sounds represented by individual letters and combinations of letters
- the ability to decode written words

Children can learn these specific language skills concurrently with their development of basic English vocabulary and conversational fluency.

Academic language proficiency This dimension of proficiency includes knowledge of the less frequent vocabulary of English as well as the ability to interpret and produce increasingly complex written language. As students progress through the grades, they encounter:

- far more low-frequency words, primarily from Greek and Latin sources
- complex syntax (for example, sentences in passive voice)
- abstract expressions

Acquiring academic language is challenging. Schools spend at least 12 years trying to teach all students the complex language associated with academic success. It is hardly surprising that research has repeatedly shown that English language learners, on average, require *at least* 5 years of exposure to academic English to catch up to native-speaker norms.

Effective instruction for English language learners is built on three fundamental pillars.

English Language Learners

Activate Prior Knowledge/ Build Background	Access Content	Extend Language

Activate Prior Knowledge/ Build Background

No learner is a blank slate. Each person's prior experience provides the foundation for interpreting new information. In reading, we construct meaning by bringing our prior knowledge of language and of the world to the text. The more we already know about the topic in the text, the more of the text we can understand. Our prior knowledge enables us to make inferences about the meaning of words and expressions that we may not have come across before. Furthermore, the more of the text we understand, the more new knowledge we can acquire. This expands our knowledge base (what cognitive psychologists call *schemata*, or underlying patterns of concepts). Such comprehension, in turn, enables us to understand even more concepts and vocabulary.

It is important to *activate* students' prior knowledge because students may not realize what they know about a particular topic or issue. Their knowledge may not facilitate learning unless that knowledge is brought to consciousness.

Teachers can use a variety of strategies to activate students' prior knowledge:	
Brainstorming/Discussion	Visual stimuli
Direct experience	Student writing
Dramatization	Drawing

When students don't already have knowledge about a topic, it is important to help them acquire that knowledge. For example, in order to comprehened texts such as *The Midnight Ride of Paul Revere,* students need to have background knowledge about the origin of the United States.

Access Content

How can teachers make complex academic English comprehensible for students who are still in the process of learning English?

We can *scaffold* students' learning by modifying the input itself. Here are a variety of ways of modifying the presentation of academic content to students so that they can more effectively gain access to the meaning.

Using Visuals Visuals enable students to "see" the basic concepts we are trying to teach much more effectively than if we rely only on words. Among the visuals we can use are:

- pictures/diagrams
- vocabulary cards
- real objects
- graphic organizers
- maps

Dramatization/Acting out For beginning English learners, *Total Physical Response,* in which they follow commands such as "Turn around," can be highly effective. The meanings of words can be demonstrated through *gestures* and *pantomime.*

Language clarification This category of teaching methods includes language-oriented activities that clarify the meaning of new words and concepts. *Use of dictionaries,* either bilingual or English-only, is still the most direct method of getting access to meaning.

Making personal and cultural connections We should constantly search for ways to link academic content with what students already know or what is familiar to them from their family or cultural experiences. This not only validates children's sense of identity, but it also makes the learning more meaningful.

Extend Language

A systematic exploration of language is essential if students are to develop a curiosity about language and deepen their understanding of how words work. Students should become *language detectives* who investigate the mysteries of language and how it has been used throughout history to shape and change society.

Students also can explore the building blocks of language. A large percentage of the less frequently heard academic vocabulary of English derives from Latin and Greek roots. Word formation follows predictable patterns. These patterns are very similar in English and Spanish.

When students know rules or conventions of how words are formed, it gives them an edge in extending vocabulary. It helps them figure out the meanings of words and how to form different parts of speech from words. The exploration of language can focus on meaning, form, or use:

Focus on meaning Categories that can be explored within a focus on meaning include:

- home language equivalents or cognates
- synonyms, antonyms, and homonyms
- meanings of prefixes, roots, and suffixes

Focus on form Categories that can be explored within a focus on form include:

- word families
- grammatical patterns
- words with same prefixes, roots, or suffixes

Focus on use Categories that can be explored within a focus on use include:

- general uses
- idioms
- metaphorical use
- proverbs
- advertisements
- puns and jokes

The Three Pillars

- Activate Prior Knowledge/ Build Background
- Access Content
- Extend Language

The Three Pillars establish a solid structure for the effective instruction of English language learners.

English Learners and Literacy: Best Practices

Dr. Georgia Earnest García, the University of Illinois at Urbana-Champaign

Like other children, English language learners come to school with much oral language knowledge and experience. Their knowledge and experience in languages other than English provide skills and world knowledge that teachers can build on.

Making literacy instruction comprehensible to English language learners is essential. Many of the teaching strategies developed for children who are proficient in English can be adapted for English learners, and many strategies from an English as a Second Language curriculum are also useful in "mainstream" reading education.

Building on Children's Knowledge

It is vital to learn about each student's literacy development and proficiency in the home language. School personnel should ask parents:

- How many years of school instruction has the child received in the home language?
- Can the child read and write in that language?
- Can the child read in any other language?

Students can transfer aspects of home-language literacy to their English literacy development, such as phonological awareness and reading (or listening) comprehension strategies. If they already know key concepts and vocabulary in their home languages, then they can transfer that knowledge to English. For the vocabulary concepts they already know in their home languages, they only need to learn the English labels. Not all English learners automatically transfer what they have learned in the home language to their reading in English. Teachers can help facilitate relevant transfer by explicitly asking English learners to think about what they have learned about a topic in the home language.

A teacher need not speak each student's home language to encourage English language learners to work together and benefit from one another's knowledge. Students can communicate in their home languages and English, building the content knowledge, confidence, and English skills that they need to participate fully in learning. Devising activities in which students who share home languages can work together also allows a school to pool resources, such as bilingual dictionaries and other books, as well as home-language tutors or aides.

Sheltering Instruction in English

Often, beginning and intermediate English language learners may not understand what their classroom teachers say or read aloud in English. These students benefit when teachers shelter, or make comprehensible, their literacy instruction.

Sheltered techniques include using:

- consistent, simplified, clearly enunciated, and slower-paced oral language to explain literacy concepts or activities
- gestures, photos, illustrations, drawings, real objects, dramatization, and/or physical action to illustrate important concepts and vocabulary
- activities that integrate reading, writing, listening, and speaking, so students see, hear, read, and write new vocabulary, sentence structures, and content

When it is clear from students' actions and responses that they understand what is being said, teachers can vary their strategies. As students' comprehension expands, teachers can gradually curtail their use of adapted oral language and of gestures, illustrations, and dramatizations.

Adapting Literacy Activities

Teachers can use many instructional activities developed for native English speakers with English language learners. For example, teacher read-alouds, shared reading, and paired reading can allow an English learner to follow the text during a reading. Such techniques greatly improve students' learning skills and comprehension.

Similarly, interactive journal writing, in which the teacher and student take turns writing entries, allows students to explore topics and ask questions. It also allows teachers to engage in ongoing authentic assessment of student proficiency and to pinpoint areas of misunderstanding.

Small group instruction and discussion also are helpful. Beginning English language learners benefit from the repeated readings of predictable texts with illustrations, especially when the teacher has provided a brief preview of each text to introduce the topic of the story and preview new vocabulary.

Repeated reading aloud of such predictable, patterned, illustrated texts provides English language learners with multiple opportunities to match the text they read with the words they hear. When students participate in shared reading and echo the spoken text or read the words aloud chorally, anxiety about pronunciation or decoding errors is reduced. When teachers choose texts that are culturally familiar and ask English language learners personal questions related to the text, the result is a lower-risk learning environment and an increased opportunity for students to make accurate inferences.

Examples of Teaching Strategies

Before students read content material, provide them with hands-on or visual experience directly related to the content. Then, have them use a graphic organizer to map what they have learned or seen about the topic. Let pairs or small groups of students brainstorm for words that are related to the concept. Then introduce other related words, including vocabulary from the reading. Illustrate new concepts or vocabulary with drawings, photographs, or artifacts that represent the concepts. The hands-on experience and graphic organizer that precede the reading help introduce students to new concepts. Students will thus be familiar with the selection's subject before they begin to read.

Semantic Mapping Working with graphic organizers can help teach vocabulary and concepts in subject areas.

For example, before a reading on the subject of baby animals, have students help you to complete a semantic map showing pictures of animals and the names of baby animals. Ask them to volunteer the names for animal babies in their home language and transcribe their responses. Then, show students examples of the different forms of writing. Ask students to meet in small groups to identify the examples. They may do this in English or their home language. If they use the home language, the teacher needs to write the English labels on the board for each form of writing. Then, students need to enter the words for the different forms of writing, with drawings or home language equivalents, into a vocabulary notebook.

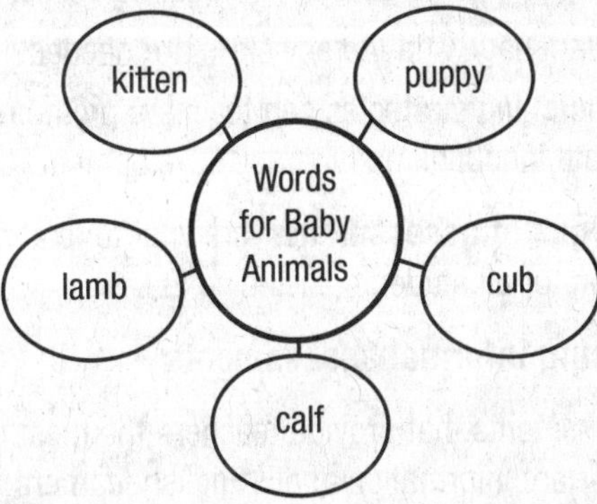

Summarizing After reading, students can dictate what they remember from their reading to the teacher. Students can then illustrate their summaries, and label the illustrations with vocabulary from the reading.

Preparing English Language Learners for Assessment

Dr. Lily Wong Fillmore, the University of California, Berkeley

Under federal and state law, all students—including English learners—must be assessed annually on their progress toward mastery of academic standards in reading, math, and science. Many questions arise when certain assessments are used with ELLs, because their test scores are never easy to interpret when they are assessed in English. The most critical question is this: What do test scores mean when they are based on instruction and assessments given in a language students have not yet mastered? Although difficult to interpret, assessments are required of all students, so we must consider how to help ELLs perform as well as possible.

Addressed in this essay

- What can teachers do to fast-track their ELL students' mastery of the language and content needed to perform as well as possible in required assessments?
- What language and literacy skills are needed?
- What learning strategies can teachers promote to facilitate language and literacy development?

Three types of assessments are vital to reading instruction for all students, including ELLs.

1. Ongoing informal assessments

The assessments that provide teachers the most useful and important information about English learners are those used as part of the instructional process. How well do children understand the materials they are working with, and what needs adjustment or modification in instruction? These are built into these instructional materials and help teachers keep an ongoing record of student progress over time. Such assessments do not need to be elaborate.

Asking children what they think is happening in a text can reveal how well they comprehend what they are reading. Asking children what they think words or phrases mean can show whether they are trying to make sense of text. These types of questions are highly useful to teachers since they allow them to monitor participation levels and help them discover who understands the materials and who needs more attention and support.

2. Diagnostic assessments

A second type of assessment that some ELLs may require is diagnostic, and it is needed when individuals are not making the progress expected of them. The school must determine where student problems lie (e.g., skill development, perception or awareness of English sounds, vocabulary, or grammar) before teachers can provide the corrective help needed.

3. Standardized assessments

The type of assessments that cause teachers of ELLs the greatest concern are the standards-based tests of English Language Arts and content area tests (especially in Math). These state tests are required of all students and are recognized as "high stakes" tests for students and for schools. They are often used to evaluate the effectiveness of a curriculum, the teacher, or the instructional approach used.

What's involved in reading?

Reading skills are built on several types of knowledge: linguistic, symbolic, experiential, and strategic. Each is crucial and is linked with the others. *Language is fundamental;* it is the medium through which meaning—information, story, knowledge, poetry, and thought—is communicated from writer to reader. Unlike speech, what is communicated by written language is indirect and *encoded in symbols* that must be deciphered before access to meaning is possible.

But reading goes beyond mere decoding. Texts call for readers to apply what they know about how language is used to convey thought and ideas to interpret what they are reading. Having *experienced reading as a sense-making activity,* readers will seek meaning as they learn to read. This calls for *special strategies:* they look for meaning if they assume it is to be found in texts. If they do not know

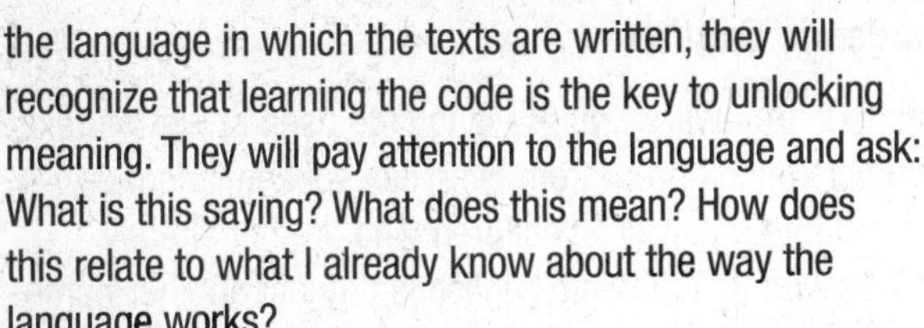

the language in which the texts are written, they will recognize that learning the code is the key to unlocking meaning. They will pay attention to the language and ask: What is this saying? What does this mean? How does this relate to what I already know about the way the language works?

English learners have an easier time learning to read in English if they have already learned to read in their first language. Without question, a language barrier makes learning to read a more difficult task. But if students have already learned to read in their primary language, they know what is involved, what to expect, and thus they are in a better position to deal with learning to read in the new language in order to access meaning.

Can children learn to read in a language before they are fully proficient in that language?

Can they in fact learn the language through reading? *Yes, but only with ample instructional assistance that supports the development of both.* Ideally, reading instruction in English comes after ELLs have gained some familiarity with the sounds and patterns of spoken English. Children need to hear the sounds of the new language before they can connect symbols to those sounds. For example, in order for children to gain confidence relating the many vowel sounds of English to the 5 vowel symbols used to "spell them" they need help hearing them and differentiating them in words.

Similarly, many ELLs need help dealing with the ways consonants pile up at the beginning and at the ends of syllables and words in English, which may be quite different than the way consonants are used in their primary language. Most crucially, ELLs need help in connecting the words they are learning to decode from the text to their referents. Using pictures, demonstrations, diagrams, gestures, and enactments, teachers can help ELLs see how the words, phrases, and sentences in the reading selections have meaning that can be accessed through the language they are learning.

Helping ELLs become successful readers

The most important way to help ELLs perform well in mandated reading assessments is by giving them the instructional support they need to become successful readers. This involves help in:

- Learning English
- Discovering the purpose of reading
- Becoming active learners
- Gaining access to academic language

Learning English

The more proficient children are in the language they are reading, the more readily they learn to read. For ELLs, support for learning English is support for learning to read. The most effective kind of help comes in content-focused language instruction, where learners are engaged in grade-level-appropriate instructional activities and their participation is scaffolded and supported as needed.

The most effective activities provide ELLs ample opportunity to hear English and to use it productively in meaningful communication. Teachers play a vital role in creating a supportive classroom environment. ELLs must be able to participate to the extent possible (again, with as much support as needed) in discussions with classmates who are more proficient in English. Peers can offer practice and support, but only teachers can ensure that ELLs get access to the kind of language needed for literacy development.

Purpose of reading

The greatest dangers ELLs face in learning to read in English before they are proficient in that language is that the effort involved in decoding takes precedence in their minds over all else. Connections between words and referents, between words and structures, and between text and meaning are overlooked when children focus on sounding out, figuring out symbols, and figuring out sounds. This is especially likely to happen when there is too little emphasis placed on reading as a sense-making activity in instructional programs. If meaning—no matter how difficult it is to come by—is not constantly emphasized in reading instruction, children end up believing that decoding is reading, and that there is nothing missing when they read without understanding.

Decoding becomes an end in itself, and the real purpose of reading is lost. Unfortunately, this is the outcome for many ELLs, who even after having learned English do not perform well in reading assessments.

Literacy in English begins as deciphering for ELLs—they must first figure out how the code in which the text is written works. It is not until the reader engages in an interpretive process in which the thoughts, information, concepts, situations, and relations encoded in the texts are manifested as meanings that there is real reading. This is true for both ELLs and for native English speakers. ELLs, however, will need a lot of guidance and instructional support from teachers to do that. Once children have gained enough familiarity with English to participate even at a rudimentary level in discussions about reading selections and content, they begin to learn that the materials they are reading have something to say to them and that hearing what they have to say is the real purpose of learning to read.

Active readers

Helping children become active learners of English and users of the literacy skills they are acquiring is a key to their becoming successful students and performing well in the assessments they have to take. This is accomplished by encouraging children to take an active role in instructional activities, asking questions, seeking answers, and trying to make sense of what they are studying in school.

Both teachers and students can have many preconceived ideas about the roles they play as teachers and learners. Children sometimes come to school believing that learning is something that will be done to them, rather than something they must take an active role in doing. In their view, the role of the teacher is active and the role they play as learners is passive. When teachers share that belief, there is little likelihood of active or independent learning. Instruction is most effective when teachers are knowledgeable about the subject matter they are teaching and they create a classroom environment in which learners can take an active role in discovering how things work, what things mean, and how to get and make sense of information.

Academic English

Teachers are aware that the language used in written texts is sufficiently different from everyday spoken language to constitute a barrier to children who are not already familiar with it. Academic English is not just another name for "standard English." It is, instead, the special forms of standard English used in academic discourse and in written texts. It makes use of grammatical constructions, words, and rhetorical conventions that are not often used in everyday spoken language.

Paradoxically, academic language is both a prerequisite for full literacy and the outcome of it. Some children arrive at school with a running start in acquiring it. Children who come from homes where family members engage in frequent discussions of books and ideas are already familiar with it, and thus have an advantage learning to read.

It should be noted that the language used at home does not have to be English for children to benefit from such experiences. Teachers can provide their students, irrespective of background, experiences with academic language by reading to them and discussing readings, instructional activities, and experiences. By drawing children into instructional conversations focused on the language they encounter in their school texts and other materials, teachers get children to notice language itself and to figure out how it works.

Supporting language and literacy development for ELLs

Teachers support language development by engaging children as active participants in making sense of the texts they are working on. They do it by drawing the English learners into discussions relating to the texts. Even relative newcomers are able to participate in these discussions as long as ample scaffolding is provided:

It says here, "Her teacher picked up the paper and studied it carefully."

Hector, what does the text tell us Vashti's teacher did first?

Yes, she picked up the paper first.

Take a look at the picture. Marta, can you show us which part of the sentence tells us what the teacher is doing?

Can you tell us what she is doing?

Yes! She is studying the paper carefully.

Teachers draw attention to words, phrases, and sentences, asking: "Let's see if we can figure out what that means!" By relating language to meaning, they help students gain access to meaning by demonstrating, referring to illustrations and diagrams, and paraphrasing in simpler language.

Instructional conversations about the texts they are reading are as essential for newcomers as they are for ELLs who have already gained some proficiency in English. It is vital to their literacy development to realize that what they are "reading" can be understood, even if its meaning is not immediately available to them as it would be to readers who are fully proficient in English. Without such help, ELLs sometimes come to believe that decoding without access to meaning is an empty exercise one does in school, and except for that, it has little relevance to their lives.

Teachers can help students discover how the language works and how to extract meaning from texts by considering how the language they encounter can convey information, ideas, stories, feelings, and images. This cannot wait until the learners are fully proficient in the language they are reading. It can enhance language development if done from the start, as soon as ELLs are introduced to English reading.

Strategies for supporting language and literacy development and preparing ELLs for assessment

The most effective support comes in the form of instructional conversations in which ELLs are drawn into discussions of reading selections and content. By hearing their teachers and other classmates discuss the materials they are reading, they gradually learn how the language works in texts and in conversation.

- Draw attention to the language used in reading selections and other text materials—words, phrases, and sentences—and relate them to meaning that is discussed and commented on, both locally and globally, to help ELLs learn how to get at meaning in texts.
- Provide students ample opportunity to use the language of texts in speaking (during discussions of the reading selections, for example) and in writing (in response to writing prompts).
- Teach English learners to be strategic readers by guiding them to assume that the text should make sense and that meaning can be accessed by figuring out what the words, phrases, and sentences mean.
- Teach students to ask questions about meaning as it unfolds in the text. Help them recognize that some parts of texts provide background knowledge while other parts reveal new information.
- Teach children how to relate new information presented in a text to what is already known. Train students to make inferences about meaning based on the words and phrases used in a text.
- Expect ELLs to make progress, and then ensure it by providing ample grade level discussion of content. At the same time, recognize that it takes time to learn English, and that learners may differ in the amount and kind of help they need in order to make progress.
- Recognize that the most crucial kind of preparation for assessment is in helping children develop the **language and literacy skills** that are essential to successful performance in tests and for academic progress itself.
- Call children's attention to words, phrases, and constructions that often figure in text items. For example, words such as *both, not,* and *best* may not seem to be noteworthy, but their uses in test questions prove otherwise. ELLs need help in seeing how such words frame and constrain the ideas expressed in sentences in which they appear.
- Teach children the logic of test questions. Use released test items or models of test items (both of which are likely to be available online from your state department of education or district web sites). Show children, for example, that the question, "Which of the following is NOT a sentence?" entails that all of the listed options except one *are* sentences.
- Teach children to read carefully. Children who are fully proficient in English may occasionally benefit

from test-taking strategies such as reading the test question and answer options first and then skimming the test passage to find information that will aid in the selection of the correct answer to the question. This tactic does not serve English learners well. They need to read and understand the passage carefully, and then consider how to answer the questions asked.

- Teach children when the text calls for activation of prior knowledge. All children have such knowledge, but English learners need help in deciding where it is called for and how they should bring what they already know to interpret the texts they are reading.
- Expand children's horizons by reading them texts that may be too difficult to handle on their own. Help them make sense of such materials by commenting on meaning, drawing attention to how language is used in them, and engaging children in discussions about aspects of the texts.

The texts that are read to children, and the ones they read themselves, provide reliable access to the academic language they need for literacy and for assessment, provided teachers call their attention to language, and help children see how it works. Teachers do this by identifying interesting (not just new) phrases and commenting on them, inviting children to try using the phrases, and providing scaffolds as needed; they model the uses of language from texts in subsequent instructional activities; they encourage children to remember and keep records of words they learn from texts; they remind them when words and phrases encountered earlier show up again in different contexts.

The Concept of Transfer

Dr. Elena Izquierdo, the University of Texas at El Paso

Research continues to support the critical role of the child's first language (L1) in literacy development and its effect on literacy in (L2) English. Strong L1 literacy skills facilitate the transfer into English literacy, and students ultimately progress rapidly into learning in English. In reality, the concept of transfer refers to the child's facility in appropriating knowledge from one language to the other. Children do not know they know, but they know. They are constantly and indirectly, unconsciously and automatically, constructing the knowledge that is inherent in the contexts for which each of these languages can function. Reasearch by Jim Cummins has shown that the effective transfer of skills transpires as students develop their metalinguistic and metacognitive skills and as they engage in a contrastive analysis of the two languages.

Matters of transfer occur within essentials of language that are (1) common to L1 and L2; (2) similar, but not exact in both languages; and (3) specific to each language and not applicable to the other language. In essence, children develop a special awareness of language and its function; learn that some sounds are the same in both languages; and also learn that there are certain boundaries for specific sounds depending on the language.

Children who have developed an awareness for phonemes, phonics, vocabulary building, and reading comprehension skills, can transfer these skills to English. They develop an enhanced awareness of the relationship between their L1 and English, which leads them to successfully appropriate strategies of transfer in similar types of word recognition processing; searching for cognates; making reference to prior knowledge, inferencing, questioning, and monitoring. Facilitating these cognitive skills in children will support their success in English literacy and their learning in English.

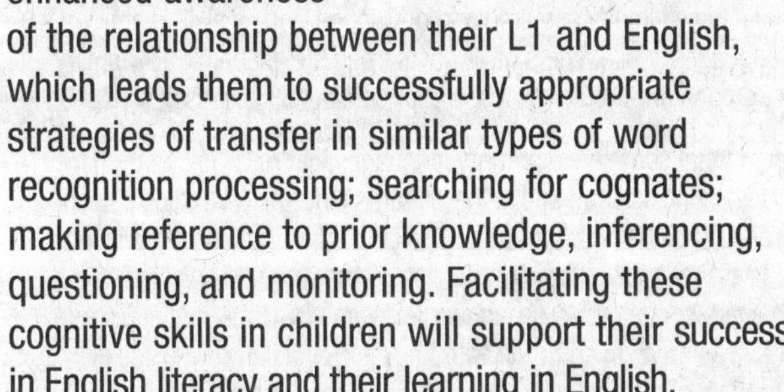

English Language Learner Profiles

English Language Learners—ELLs—are a quickly growing population in U.S. schools. While some are children of recent immigrants, many more were born in the United States but have spoken other languages in their homes. ELLs may come to classrooms with knowledge of other places as well as diverse cultures and customs. As you work with ELLs, you will want to consider how proficient your students are and how you can make the academic content accessible. You will be integrating language and content instruction, most likely within the context of a classroom of students with many abilities and proficiencies. As you consider how to best meet the needs of ELLs in your classroom, think about their characteristics, patterns of development, and literacy challenges.

General Characteristics of English Language Learners

- ELLs have a first language—also called a home language, primary language, or native language—other than English and are in the process of acquiring English.
- Some ELLs have newly arrived in the United States, while others were born in the United States but have lived for many years in households where family members do not speak English.
- Some ELLs have already acquired and developed literacy skills in their native languages, while others have not learned the academic vocabulary and background knowledge necessary for continued success in school.
- ELLs vary in that some have primary languages that resemble English in word order, sound system, and in the patterns of forming words. Spanish, French, and Portuguese, for example, are languages that share alphabets and left-to-right directionality with English. Some words in English and Spanish share cognates. Some languages, such as Swahili or Vietnamese, do not have as much in common with English. For children who speak these languages, initial learning of English is more difficult.

Types of English Language Learners

- **Newly Arrived English Language Learners** may come with adequate or limited schooling. Those with adequate schooling will make steady academic progress, although they may have difficulty on standardized tests in English. Those with limited formal schooling may lack a sense of school culture and routines. Their limited literacy development may lead to poor academic achievement until both their background knowledge and English proficiency grow.
- **Long Term English Language Learners** have been in the United States for some time, but they have had limited exposure to English in their communities and little reason to learn or know English. As they begin to acquire English, they may lose proficiency in their native languages and have difficulty grasping new content.
- **Older English Language Learners** may be more capable of quickly learning academic concepts even though they have not developed the language proficiency of other students their age. Curriculum challenges will help these students bridge their academic gaps while they gain English proficiency. Provide scaffolds for instruction and organize collaborative activities to help these students gain success.

Literacy Challenges for ELLs

1. **Phonemic Awareness** ELLs may find it difficult to differentiate between certain phonemes in English. Some children may find it difficult to separate groups of phonemes into words.
2. **Phonics** ELLs need to be able to match sounds to letters and letters to sounds in order to read and write English successfully. They need to develop both oral vocabularies of frequently used words and written vocabularies of sight words.
3. **Vocabulary Development** Some ELLs are able to repeat, pronounce, decode, and produce words in English without really knowing what these words mean. ELLs need opportunities to link vocabulary words to meaning through routines, concrete objects, pictures and gestures, physical movement, and experiences. These students need multiple exposures to words through explanation, discussion, and repeated readings.
4. **Fluency** Fluent reading involves reading quickly, accurately, and expressively. This can be challenging for ELLs, who need many opportunities to listen and speak English before they can feel comfortable and successful with fluent reading. In large groups, ELLs may be reluctant to read orally. They need opportunities to listen and follow along with read-alouds.
5. **Comprehension** Help ELLs gain comprehension in reading by choosing reading materials with familiar topics, settings, and concepts. Use nonfiction materials, such as photographs and science experiments. Use anticipation guides and graphic organizers to prepare ELLs for reading and allow them to comprehend more of what they read.

Best Practices

Scaffolding instruction for ELLs allows them to access content while gaining proficiency in English. Most strategies that help ELLs access content and language are appropriate for struggling readers in your classroom whose native language is English, so these strategies can be used with the whole class. Some best practices for teaching ELLs include:

- using questioning techniques to elicit experiences that relate to students' native cultures;
- using visual aids, including photographs, graphic organizers, and real objects;
- linking learning to a physical response, such as raising hands, doing a "thumbs up," nodding, and moving to a different part of the room;
- actively engaging students in the lesson by including less teacher talk and down time and keeping students involved;
- using scaffolding techniques, such as think-alouds, paraphrasing, partnering, and reciprocal teaching; and
- building background with such activities as cloze sentences, creating word walls, and working with students to make personal dictionaries.

English language learners are generally divided into proficiency levels. The chart below describes what you might expect from students at each level, and it compares different proficiency levels used across the United States. It also includes teaching strategies for your classroom. *Reading Street* provides systematic leveled support to meet the needs of all students.

	LEVELS OF PROFICIENCY		BEHAVIORS	TEACHING STRATEGIES
I	Beginning		• may be unfamiliar with sounds, rhythms, or patterns in English • respond by pointing, gesturing, or drawing • can use simple yes/no responses or one- to two-word answers • read simple language that they have already heard • write labels, patterned sentences, or short cloze sentences	• provide opportunities for active listening and visuals • model language with songs and chants • pair students with more proficient speakers • ask yes/no questions; require responses of one or two words • use manipulatives and pictures • provide writing frames
II	Early Intermediate	Intermediate	• may understand more details in spoken English • use longer phrases and sentences with better grammar • write for a variety of purposes using models • can read independently after oral previews	• allow students to make personal connections with the material • structure group discussion time • ask open-ended questions and then model, expand, restate, and enrich student language • allow students opportunities to create language for a variety of purposes and audiences
III	Intermediate		• participate in discussions about academic content • can use higher-order language to describe or persuade • write narratives and expository text • use vocabulary with more accuracy and correctness	• use graphic organizers to prepare students for reading and to discuss selections • promote academic concepts and vocabulary with nonfictional texts, magazines, newspapers, and so on • conference with students about writing to point out areas of progress and areas for improvement
IV	Early Advanced	Advanced	• have a deeper understanding of everyday language, including idioms • use more extensive vocabulary and produce language with fewer grammatical errors • use standard forms when writing • produce writing about varied topics	• structure discussion for the group • provide reference materials for students and guide them with the research • introduce more variety of literary forms • provide opportunities for more variation in writing assignments
V	Advanced	Advanced High	• use more complex and varied grammatical structures and vocabulary • read texts appropriate for grade level • write about a variety of topics on grade level • begin to self-monitor and correct as they read and write	• provide opportunities for students to publish their writing for others to read • increase students' production of language through drama and music • continue to make strong links between content-area materials and literacy activities

Essentials of ELL Instruction in *Reading Street*

Imagine children from diverse language backgrounds communicating in English on the playground. It's easy to think that they are fluent English speakers, but they may still be at the beginning stage of using English for learning purposes. Research proves that it takes at least five years of exposure to academic English to catch up with native-speaker proficiency in school.

How Do English Language Learners Differ from Other Learners?

ELLs face challenges because they have not acquired academic English. Children's reading and language skills may seem deficient because their language experiences have lacked academic instruction. ELLs need targeted instruction to participate fully in reading/language arts lessons with their peers. Helping ELLs achieve academically is critically important because they must meet the same state and federal grade-level standards as other children. Their academic success depends on learning to read well, and this depends on rich language knowledge.

Academic Language is the language of the classroom. It's used for academic purposes, not social or personal ones.

Essentials of ELL Instruction

These five essential practices take into account language and academic needs of English language learners. They are incorporated into *Reading Street* as common-sense, everyday strategies that help you build an effective learning relationship between you and your ELL children.

Identify and Communicate Content Objectives and Language Objectives English language learners need instruction for the same grade-level skills and strategies as children whose first language is English. Deliver your instruction with clear, simple language. Provide extra support for academic vocabulary. Provide direct instruction for the academic language that children need to use to complete classroom tasks successfully.

Frontload the Lesson When new information arrives as a blur to ELL children, they are lost at the beginning of a lesson. Taking time to frontload, or preteach lesson elements, will bring them into mainstream instruction. Activating prior knowledge, building background, previewing, and setting a purpose for reading are frontloading methods that remove learning obstacles. Asking children to make personal connections helps them see relationships and gives you insight into their experiences and backgrounds.

Provide Comprehensible Input The instruction and content you present to ELL children may be unclear because of language barriers. Using visual supports, multimedia, examples of real items, and demonstrations are a few ways to provide comprehensible instruction. Communicating with methods such as gestures, props, and dramatization can be an effective approach. Hands-on activities and multiple exposures to new concepts can lessen confusion.

Enable Language Production The listening, speaking, reading, and writing ELLs do for school is different from the language they use in everyday conversation. In school, ELLs need ample opportunities to demonstrate their use of English. Two critical methods for enabling children's English language production are direct instruction and modeling the use of a skill in a comprehensible way. Create scaffolds so that children can read and hear English language patterns and build on them to express their own thoughts. Paraphrasing, restatements, cloze sentences, writing prompts, and templated forms for note-taking are other useful supports. Responding to children's strengths and needs by modifying instruction gives them opportunities to express themselves in an academic setting and gain proficiency in English.

Assess for Content and Language Understanding ELLs are required to achieve the same high standards as mainstream children. Keep in mind that children are at different stages for learning English language and literacy skills. Asking these questions frequently and using assessments will help you determine how to modify your instruction for different proficiency levels.

- Where are ELL children in their acquisition of English language proficiency?
- Where are they in their acquisition of literacy skills?

Just as for all children, you will rely on diagnostic, formative, and summative assessments for ELLs. Consistently integrate informal assessment into your lessons to target specific problem areas for learning, adapt your instruction, and intervene earlier rather than later.

You can modify both formal and informal assessments so that ELLs show their proficiency in literacy skills with a minimal amount of negative impact. These modifications include time extensions, use of bilingual dictionaries and glossaries, repeated readings of listening passages, use of dual-language assessments, and allowing written responses in the first language.

To meet ELLs at their own levels of English acquisition, teachers use instructional supports and tools. Through scaffolding and modifying instruction you can lead ELLs to achieve the same instructional goals that mainstream children do. The ELL strategies and supports in *Reading Street* have the five essential principles of ELL as their foundation. Use them throughout your instruction to modify or scaffold core instruction. With *Reading Street* ELL Leveled Support activities, you meet children where they are—from beginning to advanced levels of English proficiency.

Other English language learner resources include:

Student Edition The Student Edition builds every child's reading and language skills.

Teacher's Edition The Teacher's Edition has ELL instructional strategies built into the lesson plans. The ELL weekly lessons have pacing plans to help you carefully integrate instruction. The ELL Support lessons guide you in using sheltered techniques and routines for teaching academic vocabulary, listening comprehension, phonics, vocabulary, comprehension, and writing.

ELD/ELL Readers ELD/ELL Readers develop English learners' vocabulary and comprehension skills. Study guides support comprehension and provide writing and take-home activities.

ELL Posters ELL Posters contain high-quality illustrations and five days of activities supporting key oral vocabulary, selection vocabulary, and lesson concepts.

Essentials of ELL Instruction in *Reading Street*

- Identify and Communicate Content Objectives and Language Objectives
- Frontload the Lesson
- Provide Comprehensible Input
- Enable Language Production
- Assess for Content and Language Understanding

ELL Handbook The ELL Handbook supports teachers' professional development and children's transition to advanced levels of proficiency. The Handbook contains comprehension skill practice, selection vocabulary word cards, multilingual summaries of Student Edition literature, study guides for ELL readers, and multilingual vocabulary charts. The English selection summaries and vocabulary charts are accompanied by translations in Spanish and in several other languages. The flexible bank of Phonics and Grammar Transition Lessons provides differentiated practice.

Ten Important Sentences The Ten Important Sentences reproducibles help children focus on comprehension while they expand their English proficiency.

English Language Proficiency—What, Why, and How The next section, English Language Proficiency—What, Why, and How, provides ideas for how to use *Reading Street* across language proficiency levels and instructional strands. Using research from Dr. Jim Cummins, this section explains why and how *Reading Street* promotes literacy attainment for English language learners at all levels.

English Language Proficiency—What, Why, and How

Concept Development

"No learner is a blank slate. The more we know about the topic in the text, the more of the text we can understand."—Dr. Jim Cummins

Why

Organizing concept development around big question themes is essential for English language learners. Through the use of themes, it is easier to connect the curriculum to children's lives and backgrounds. Themes help to make sense of the curriculum because children know what the topic is, even if the instruction is in English. By learning more about the topic through concept development, children will increase their social and academic vocabulary production and be more engaged when reading the text.

How

Reading Street promotes literacy attainment through the daily Concept Development activities in the core instruction along with a full page of leveled Concept Development activities in the ELL Support lessons. These engaging activities activate prior knowledge, build background, scaffold meaning, affirm identity, and extend language for all proficiency levels.

Activate Prior Knowledge/Build Background

Frontload the lesson Use the Concept Development section of the ELL Support pages and the Poster Talk Through in a small group prior to the core lesson to build background and scaffold meaning to prepare for the core daily Concept Talk lesson.

Access Content

Provide Comprehensible Input Use the linguistically accommodated questions in the Concept Development section of the ELL Support pages to reach all language proficiency levels and make personal and cultural connections that validate identity and link academic content with what children already know. Ideas for using the Concept Talk Video from the digital path further develop the concepts throughout the week.

Scaffold Meaning Give visual support that children need to access academic content with the photographs in the Let's Talk About sections in the Student Edition, the concept graphic organizer created during the week's discussion, the Concept Talk Video from the digital path, the *Sing with Me* Big Book, and the daily Poster activities. The activities on the ELL Support pages for Concept Development and the ELL Support notes throughout the Teacher Edition give ideas to scaffold meaning for all language proficiency levels.

Extend Language

Enable Language Production Use the daily activities on the ELL Poster and the Anchored Talk questions in the core to build concept attainment and encourage oral language production. The Team Talk Routine in the core instruction and the Poster Talk, Concept Talk activities from the *ELL Handbook* provide nonthreatening small group oral practice with social and academic vocabulary related to the concept. The Concept Development page in the ELL Support lessons gives ideas for extending oral and written production for all levels of language proficiency. The Concept Literacy Reader builds concepts and language.

	Child Behaviors	Teacher Behaviors	Examples
Beginning	• Actively listens • Responds nonverbally • Can follow one-step oral directions. • Can match oral statements to illustrations or objects • Answers in one- to two-word phrases • May not seek clarification if he or she doesn't understand Child can: point, move, choose, match, mime, draw.	• Use gestures, repetition, slower speech, visuals, and simple language. *Point to the __________.* *Find the __________.* *Is this a __________?*	Concept Talk What can we learn by exploring the desert? Use the Let's Talk About It photographs in the Student Edition to activate prior knowledge and build background. *Point to the desert. Is a desert wet or dry?* *Is this a cactus?* *Find the turtle.*
Intermediate	• Actively listens with greater understanding • Needs processing time • Uses short phrases • Identifies people and objects • Begins to seek clarification if he or she doesn't understand Child can: name, list, say, tell, restate.	• Model correct responses. • Don't call attention to grammar errors. • Ask general questions to encourage production. • Ask questions for two-word responses. *What is this?* *Is this a ________ or a ________?*	*Is this a desert or a rain forest?* *What do you see in the desert?* *What is the weather like in a desert?*
Advanced	• Actively listens to longer questions and directions • Uses language more freely • Sometimes needs processing time; depends on visuals • Will seek clarification Child can: describe, restate, compare, contrast.	• Ask open-ended questions to encourage language production. • Check comprehension frequently. *Why?* *How?* *Tell me about ________.* *Describe ________.*	*Describe the desert.* *Tell me about the animals that live in the desert.* *How can animals and plants live in the desert?* *Tell me how the desert is the same as the place you live. How is it different?*
Advanced High	• Understands longer, elaborated discussions • Occasionally needs processing time • Understands details and information comparable to a native speaker • Rarely seeks clarification • Produces a variety of sentence lengths Child can: explain, define, support, describe, summarize.	• Make lessons interactive and comprehensible. • Structure group discussions. *Describe/compare ________.* *How are these similar or different?* *What would happen if ________?* *What is your opinion of ________?*	*Describe the desert in the picture.* *Describe the weather in a desert.* *Compare the desert to the place you live. How is it the same or different?*

Listening Comprehension

"How can teachers make complex academic English comprehensible for children who are still in the process of learning English? We can scaffold students' learning by modifying the input itself." –Dr. Jim Cummins

Why

English language learners must be able to comprehend newly acquired language in all content areas. They must listen to a variety of speakers, including teachers and peers, along with understanding the language they hear in electronic media. In order for English language learners to meet grade-level learning expectations and have access to the core curriculum, all instruction delivered in English must be linguistically accommodated for all levels of English language proficiency.

How

Reading Street promotes literacy attainment with listening comprehension activities in the core lessons and ELL Support lessons that encourage literacy engagement. These activities activate prior knowledge, build background, scaffold meaning, affirm identity, and extend language.

Activate Prior Knowledge/Build Background

Frontload the Lesson Each adapted Read Aloud in the Listening Comprehension section of the ELL Support pages covers the same concept and information as the Read Aloud in the core curriculum. Use it with a small group to build background and scaffold meaning before listening to the core Read Aloud. Each adapted Read Aloud has frontloading activities that build background to improve comprehension before listening to the selection. In the core Teacher Edition, ELL Notes give ideas for frontloading the regular Read Aloud at point of use.

Access Content

Provide Comprehensible Input For Beginning and Intermediate levels, use the grade-appropriate adapted Read Aloud in place of the regular Read Aloud until children no longer need the linguistic support and modification.

First Listening: Listen to Understand gives children a purpose for listening. The questions are designed to generate interest and help children get the gist of the adapted Read Aloud so that all proficiency levels can achieve success without cognitive overload.

Language Clarification Second Listening: Listen to Check Understanding allows children to clarify what they have heard. Once children have understood the main idea of the adapted Read Aloud, they can listen again on subsequent days to clarify understanding of important details of spoken language. The graphic organizers provide visual support for organizing information.

Extend Language

Enable Language Production Discussing the adapted Read Aloud in a small group setting provides a nonthreatening environment, lowering the affective filter and facilitating increased language production.

The *Sing with Me* Big Book, the Audiotext CD of the main reading selection, and the digital products provide more opportunities for listening practice throughout each week, building and reinforcing children's concept and language attainment.

	Child Behaviors	Teacher Behaviors	Examples
Beginning	• Needs accommodations to understand grade-appropriate stories • Responds nonverbally • Can follow one-step oral directions • Answers in one or two words • Can match oral statements to illustrations or objects Child can: point, move, choose, match, mime, draw, label.	• Use gestures, repetition, slower speech, visuals, and simple language. *Point to the __________.* *Find the __________.* *Is this a __________?*	In a small group, use the modified Read Aloud. Build background and scaffold comprehension by reviewing the concept or showing a visual. Read the text clearly. Stop at intervals to check for understanding and clarify language. Use gestures to scaffold meaning. Children may need to hear the text repeated multiple times.
Intermediate	• Need accommodations to understand grade-appropriate stories. • Actively listens with greater understanding • Uses short phrases • Understands simple directions • Identifies people and objects • Identifies key words and phrases • Begins to seek clarification if he or she doesn't understand Child can: name, list, say, tell, restate, describe.	• Model correct responses. • Use visuals, gestures, and preteaching to preview topic-related vocabulary. • Don't call attention to grammar errors. • Ask general questions to encourage production. • Ask questions that elicit two-word responses. *(Where did he go? To work.)* *Is this a ______ or a ______?* *What is this?*	In a small group, use the modified Read Aloud. Preview topic-related vocabulary, then read the text clearly. Stop at intervals to check for understanding and clarify language. Then use the Anchored Talk! photographs to build vocabulary and concepts and encourage more discussion.
Advanced	• Actively listens and understands longer questions • Understands multistep oral directions • Understands main points and most important details • Uses language more freely • Can categorize or sequence oral information using objects or pictures • Can analyze and apply oral information • Will seek clarification Child can: describe, restate, compare, contrast, retell.	• Ask open-ended questions to encourage language production. • Check comprehension frequently. • Give more time to process information and provide visual support as needed. *Why?* *How?* *Tell me about ________.* *Describe ________.*	In a small group, use the modified Read Aloud to prepare for listening to the oral reading in the core text. Stop at intervals to check for understanding. Then have partners restate some of the important points and share with the class.
Advanced High	• Understands longer, elaborated discussions • Understands details and information comparable to a native speaker • Can draw conclusions from oral information • Rarely seeks clarification • Produces a variety of sentence lengths Child can: explain, define, support, describe, summarize.	• Make lessons interactive and comprehensible. • Structure group discussions. • Give more processing time if needed. *Describe/compare _______.* *How are these similar or different?* *What would happen if ____?* *What is your opinion of ______?*	In a small group, use the modified Read Aloud to prepare for listening to the oral reading in the core text. Then have children summarize the selection and explain something new that they learned.

Phonics, Spelling, and Word Analysis

"A systematic exploration of language is essential if students are to develop a curiosity about language and deepen their understanding of how words work. Students should become language detectives who investigate the mysteries of language and how it has been used throughout history to shape and change society."—Dr. Jim Cummins

Why

Discrete language skills that English language learners need to develop second language literacy and comprehension include:

- knowledge of the letters of the alphabet
- knowledge of the sounds represented by individual letters and combinations of letters
- the ability to decode words
- knowledge of the rules and conventions of how words are formed

Children can learn these skills at the same time they are developing basic English vocabulary. While letter-sound correspondences in numerous languages are relatively simple, the relationships of letters to sounds in English can be complicated. The challenges of written English affect spelling, word recognition, comprehension of text, and confidence in language learning. *Reading Street* addresses these challenges in both the core curriculum and the ELL Support pages.

How

Reading Street promotes literacy attainment through engaging phonemic awareness, phonics, spelling, and vocabulary skill activities in the core lessons and ELL Support lessons. These activities activate prior knowledge and build background, scaffold meaning, affirm identity, and extend language.

Activate Prior Knowledge/Build Background

Frontload the Lesson Use the Phonemic Awareness, Phonics/Spelling, and Vocabulary Skill lessons in the ELL Support pages with a small group to preteach the skill before the core lesson, and then use the Reteach and Practice activities from the ELL Support pages to provide more practice and to internalize language.

Affirm Identity The Transfer Skills Notes throughout the core Teacher Edition, in the ELL Support pages, and in the Phonics Transition Lessons in the ELL Handbook activate prior knowledge about a phonics, phonemic awareness, or vocabulary skill before the core lesson.

Access Content

Provide Comprehensible Input Use the Let's Listen for Sounds spread, the Sound-Spelling Cards, and the Envision it! Words to Know from the Student Edition to provide visual support and scaffold meaning for the phonics, phonemic awareness, and spelling lessons at all proficiency levels. Choose appropriate Phonics Transition Lessons and reproducible practice pages from the bank of lessons in the ELL Handbook to provide instruction and more practice on phonics challenges for all proficiency levels. The Decodable Practice Readers help children to internalize language by providing additional practice with the weekly target phonics skill in context.

The *Words! Vocabulary Handbook* in the Student Edition provides visual support for explaining the Vocabulary Skill. Use the Preteach and Practice and the leveled Vocabulary Skill practice sections of the ELL Support pages to differentiate instruction and reach all children.

Extend Language

Enable Language Production Use the leveled Phonics lessons from the ELL Support pages to guide oral and written production. Help small groups of children to explore words and expand vocabulary with the leveled Vocabulary Skill lessons from the ELL Support pages. When children learn the patterns of English word formation, they are more engaged in literacy activities, and oral and written production will increase.

Focus on Meaning and Form Use the Vocabulary Skill lessons from the ELL Support pages to engage children in figuring out meanings of new words to increase their comprehension and language production.

	Child Behaviors	Teacher Behaviors	Examples
Beginning	• Actively listens and responds nonverbally • Can follow one-step oral directions • Answers in one- to two-word phrases • Uses high-frequency words, concrete words, and phrases Child can: point, move, choose, match, mime, draw, label.	• Use gestures, repetition, slower speech, visuals, and simple language. *Point to the ________.* *Find the ________.* *Is this a ________?*	Prefix *un-* and *in-* Give children a piece of cloth and model the difference between *cover* and *uncover.* Use Student Edition *Words! Vocabulary Handbook* to provide more visual support for meaning. Have children draw and label pictures to show *lock/unlock* and *happy/unhappy.*
Intermediate	• Actively listens with greater understanding • Uses short phrases • Understands simple directions • Identifies people and objects • Begins to seek clarification if he or she doesn't understand Child can: name, list, say, tell, restate.	• Model correct responses. • Don't call attention to grammar errors. • Use visuals, gestures, and preteaching to preview. • Ask general questions to encourage production. *Is this a ________ or a ________?* *What is this?*	Use the Student Edition *Words! Vocabulary Handbook* to provide visual support for meaning. Ask questions about the picture to clarify understanding. Use the handbook reproducible pages to provide more practice with prefixes.
Advanced	• Actively listens to longer questions • Understands multistep directions • Uses language more freely • Understands main points and details • Will seek clarification Child can: describe, restate, compare, contrast.	• Ask open-ended questions to encourage language production. • Check comprehension frequently. • Give time to process information; provide visual support. *Why? How?* *Tell me about ________.* *Describe ________.*	Use the Student Edition *Words! Vocabulary Handbook* to provide visual support for meaning. Write the words *lock, happy, complete, and action* on the board. Have pairs add the appropriate prefix, then write sentences using the words.
Advanced High	• Understands longer, elaborated discussions • May need processing time • Understands information comparable to a native speaker • Rarely seeks clarification • Produces a variety of sentences Child can: explain, define, support, describe, summarize.	• Make lessons interactive and comprehensible. • Structure group discussions. • Give more processing time. *Describe/compare ________.* *What would happen if ________?* *What is your opinion of ________?*	Use the Student Edition *Words! Vocabulary Handbook* to provide visual support for meaning. Write the words *lock, happy, complete,* and *action* on the board. Have pairs add the appropriate prefix, then write sentences using the words.

Vocabulary

"We should constantly search for ways to link academic content with what students already know or what is familiar to them from their family or cultural experiences. This not only validates children's sense of identity, but it also makes the learning more meaningful."—Dr. Jim Cummins

Why

Vocabulary development is critically important for English language learners, even more so than for their English-speaking peers. English learners need explicit instruction to acquire both social and academic language for literacy attainment. Research indicates that a broad knowledge of academic vocabulary is critical to student achievement and distinguishes students who experience academic success from those who struggle in school. Instruction in social and academic vocabulary should be explicit and systematic. Children need multiple exposures to new vocabulary through frequent listening, reading, writing, and oral language activities.

How

Reading Street promotes literacy attainment through interactive vocabulary activities in the core lessons and ELL Support pages that encourage literacy engagement. These activities activate prior knowledge, build background, scaffold meaning, affirm identity, and extend language.

Activate Prior Knowledge/Build Background

Frontload the Lesson The Concept Development activities from the ELL Support Lessons, the Vocabulary Routines in the core and in the ELL Support pages, the Poster illustrations, and the word card activities using the cards in the ELL Handbook can be used to activate prior knowledge and build background for reading the selection. Use them in a small group to preteach, practice, and reinforce the grade-level lesson vocabulary. By using and reusing the words in meaningful interactions, children internalize the words and are more engaged in reading the selection.

Access Content

Provide Comprehensible Input The High-Frequency Words and Vocabulary Activities in the ELL Support Lessons provide ideas for giving visual, contextual, and linguistic support so children can access grade-level lesson vocabulary. The activities are designed so children reuse the vocabulary using different modalities, confirming and enhancing understanding. Give visual support that children need to access academic vocabulary in the core instruction with the Let's Talk About spread, Envision It! Words to Know, *Sing with Me* Big Book, Let's Listen for Sounds visuals in the Student Edition, the Poster illustrations, and the digital vocabulary activities.

Affirm Identity Multilingual vocabulary lists in the ELL Handbook translate the selection vocabulary words from English into Spanish, Chinese, Vietnamese, Hmong, and Korean. Use the lists to preview the words and to check understanding.

Language Clarification Throughout the core and ELL Support pages, there are a variety of ideas for teachers to use to help children clarify meaning of vocabulary in listening, speaking, reading, and writing activities. In the core Teacher Edition, helpful ELL Notes are located at point of use. These notes give language transfer support and various ideas for clarifying meaning.

Extend Language

Enable Language Production Use the Concept Talk and the High-Frequency Words/Vocabulary activities on the ELL Support pages and the daily activities on the ELL Poster to give repeated exposure to social and academic vocabulary to build concept and language attainment.

The leveled high-frequency words and vocabulary activities in the ELL Support lessons, along with the reproducible word cards in the ELL Handbook, actively engage children in producing and reusing grade-level vocabulary in different contexts through spoken and written communication so that vocabulary becomes internalized.

	Child Behaviors	Teacher Behaviors	Examples
Beginning	• Responds nonverbally and follows one-step oral directions • Answers in one or two words • Matches words to pictures/ objects • Uses/reads high-frequency words/ concrete words and understands phrases represented by pictures Child can: point, move, choose, match, mime, draw, label.	• Activate prior knowledge. • Use gestures, repetition, slower speech, visuals, and simple language. *Point to the* ________. *Find the* ________. *Is this a* ________?	Word Cards Pair Activity: High-Frequency Words Give each pair two copies of the word cards at their level. Model how to identify and match identical words. Use visuals and gestures to clarify meaning of the words. Children can spread the word cards face up on their desks; then take turns finding pairs of matching words.
Intermediate	• Actively listens with greater understanding and seeks clarification • Uses short phrases and understands simple directions • Identifies people, objects, key words, and phrases Child can: name, list, say, tell, restate, describe.	• Model correct responses. • Use visuals, gestures, and preteaching to preview. • Ask general questions and questions that elicit two-word responses. *Is this a* ______ *or a* ______? *What is this?*	Give each pair two copies of the word cards at their level. Model how to identify and match identical words. Use visuals to clarify meaning of the words. Children can spread the word cards face down on their desks; then take turns turning over two cards at a time. When the cards match, children can say the words.
Advanced	• Actively listens and understands longer questions • Understands multistep directions • Understands main points and details • Categorizes/sequences information with objects or pictures • Analyzes/applies oral information Child can: describe, restate, compare, contrast, retell.	• Ask open-ended questions. • Check comprehension frequently. • Give time to process information; provide visual support. *Why? How?* *Tell me about* ________. *Describe* ________.	Give each pair two copies of the word cards at their level. Model how to identify and match identical words and clarify meaning. Children can spread the word cards face down and turn over two cards at a time. When the cards match, children say them and use the words in a sentence.
Advanced High	• Understands longer, elaborated discussions • Understands information comparable to a native speaker • Can draw conclusions from oral information • Rarely seeks clarification • Produces a variety of sentences Child can: explain, define, support, describe, summarize.	• Make lessons interactive and comprehensible. • Structure group discussions. • Give more processing time. *Describe/compare* ______. *How are these similar or different?* *What would happen if* ______? *What is your opinion of* ______?	Give each pair two copies of the word cards. Model how to identify and match identical words. Children can spread the word cards face down on their desks, then take turns turning over two cards at a time. When the cards match, children can use the words in a sentence.

Reading Comprehension

"The more of the text we understand, the more new knowledge we can acquire. This expands our knowledge base, what cognitive psychologists call schemata, or underlying patterns of concepts. Such comprehension, in turn, enables us to understand even more concepts and vocabulary."—Dr. Jim Cummins

Why

English language learners need guidance to become active readers who engage with texts on multiple levels before, during, and after reading. Comprehension instruction in *Reading Street* focuses on *metacognition*, a good reader's ability to independently reflect on the purpose of reading, select appropriate approaches to texts, ask questions as he or she reads, and actively resolve areas of confusion.

How

Guide Comprehension: Core Comprehension Skill

Activate Prior Knowledge/Build Background

Frontload the Lesson Use the Preteach and Practice activities in the Guide Comprehension section of the ELL Support lessons with a small group to build background for the main Comprehension Skill. The Envision It! pictures in the Student Edition and Envision It! Animations from the digital path provide visual support to fully engage children in the core skill.

Access Content and Scaffold Meaning

Provide Comprehensible Input The leveled Reteach and Practice activities in the Guide Comprehension section of the ELL Support pages provide visual, contextual, and linguistic support for the grade-level comprehension skill. The interactive activities are designed so that children reuse the academic vocabulary to enhance understanding. Topics range from basic reading skills, such as understanding supporting ideas, to expanded skills, such as making inferences.

Language Clarification The leveled support notes in the Reteach activities of the Guide Comprehension section of the ELL Support pages provide ideas for clarifying meaning.

Extend Language

Enable Language Production and Affirm Identity The mini-lessons in the Guide Comprehension section of the ELL Support pages focus on the comprehension strategy. Use them to encourage children to express ideas and participate in discussions using social and academic language.

Comprehension of Core Selection: Sheltered Reading

Activate Prior Knowledge/Build Background

Frontload the Lesson Use the Before Reading activities in the Sheltered Reading section in the ELL Support pages for ideas to preview the text and set a purpose for reading. The Multilingual Summaries in the ELL Handbook activate prior knowledge, affirm identity, and build background before reading the main selection. Children can take them home to read with family members.

Access Content and Scaffold Meaning

Provide Comprehensible Input Use the Sheltered Reading questions in the ELL Support pages to guide comprehension and clarify understanding of the selection. The graphic organizers provide visual support for organizing the information.

Extend Language

Enable Language Production The Sheltered Reading section in the ELL Support pages has questions that encourage children to use oral language during reading to demonstrate understanding of supporting ideas and details in text and to employ inferential skills such as predicting, connecting ideas, drawing conclusions, and finding supporting text evidence. The Fluency and the After Reading sections have ideas for shared reading, summarizing, and extending oral production.

ELD and ELL Readers

There is an ELD and an ELL Reader for each week of instruction. Each Reader has a topic that supports grade-level concept development, tying into the Key Question of the Week. The ELD Readers are written for Beginning and Intermediate language proficiency levels, and the ELL Readers are designed for Intermediate to Advanced High levels. The rich language and information, sentence patterns, repetition, and visual support will unlock new words for children and give them models for using English words, phrases, and sentence structures.

Activate Prior Knowledge/Build Background

Frontload the Lesson Use the Before Reading section in the ELL Support pages for the ELL and ELD Readers for ideas to preview the text and set a purpose for reading.

Access Content and Scaffold Meaning

Provide Comprehensible Input Use the During Reading Routine along with the sheltered questions in the ELL/ELD Reader Support pages and visuals in the Readers to build background, model, and guide comprehension.

Extend Language

Enable Language Production and Affirm Identity Use the Anchored Talk! and Let's Write About It activities on the inside back cover of each ELL Reader to have children apply the lesson's target comprehension skill. The reproducible Study Guide found in the ELL Handbook supports comprehension and provides writing and take-home activities.

	Child Behaviors	Teacher Behaviors	Examples
Beginning	• Uses vocabulary that includes environmental print, some high-frequency and concrete words represented by pictures • Depends on visuals and prior knowledge • Able to apply comprehension skills when reading texts at his or her level • May recognize a few letter-sound relationships • Reads word by word	• Use gestures, repetition, slower speech, visuals, and simple language. • Assess prior knowledge, build background, and frontload extensively before reading text. • Make sure text is linguistically accommodated for level.	Use gestures to explain *first, next,* and *last.* Hold up a finger as you say *first* and put on a shoe. Hold up two fingers as you say *next* and tie the shoe. Hold up three fingers as you say *last* and take a step forward. Then use the Envision It! picture in the Student Edition to identify sequence words *first, next,* and *last.* Use the Picture It! activity from the ELL Handbook and the ELD Reader to practice and assess understanding of sequence.
Intermediate	• Reads some everyday oral language; knows literal meanings of common words and routine academic language • Comprehends texts on familiar topics • Reads in short phrases and may need to reread to clarify meaning • Can locate and classify information • Understands simple sentences but is dependent on visual cues, topic familiarity, prior knowledge, and pretaught vocabulary • Can apply basic and higher-order thinking skills in texts that are linguistically accommodated for level	• Use gestures, repetition, slower speech, visuals, and simple language. • Assess prior knowledge, build background, and frontload extensively before reading text. • Make sure text is linguistically accommodated for level or provide teacher/peer support for grade-level text.	Use gestures to explain *first, next,* and *last.* As you tie your shoe, have children describe what you do first, next, and last. Then use the Envision It! picture in the Student Edition to have children identify sequence words *first, next,* and *last* to describe the sequence in the pictures. Use the Picture It! activity from the ELL Handbook to practice and assess sequence.
Advanced	• Reads with greater ease • Uses a variety of comprehension strategies • Can understand words and phrases beyond their literal meanings • Able to apply basic and higher-order comprehension skills • Occasionally depends on visuals and needs assistance with unfamiliar topics, concepts, or vocabulary	• Frontload text and build background before reading. • Preteach unfamiliar concepts and related vocabulary. • Use visuals to clarify meaning of new topics. • Provide support for grade-level text.	Use the Envision It! picture in the Student Edition to preteach sequence. Children can describe what is happening in each picture and identify sequence words. After using the Routine to frontload the ELL Reader, guide children to find words that show sequence. Use the graphic organizer to fill in the sequence of events. Children can use the organizer to retell the sequence of events with a partner and with the class.
Advanced High	• Reads and understands vocabulary nearly comparably to native English-speaking peers • Can infer meaning, draw conclusions, and use context to infer meanings of new words • Can interpret information and find details that support main ideas	• Frontload text and build background before reading. • Preteach unfamiliar concepts and related vocabulary. • Use visuals to clarify meaning of new topics. • Provide peer/teacher support for grade-level text as needed.	Use the Envision It! picture in the Student Edition to preteach sequence. Children can describe what is happening in each picture and identify other sequence words. After using the Routine to frontload the ELL Reader, pairs can find words that show sequence. They can use a graphic organizer to fill in the sequence of events and then retell the story using the organizer if needed.

Conventions and Writing

"Writing helps solve problems, affirms students' identities, and generates linguistic feedback from teachers that can increase language awareness and academic language proficiency."— Dr. Jim Cummins

Why

Research shows that children acquire language most readily when they are fully involved in all learning activities in the classroom. Activities should integrate listening, speaking, reading, and writing, since these language skills develop interdependently. Teachers can facilitate language learning and literacy development by ensuring that children hear language in natural ways—in real and practical contexts—and write it in structured formats.

Each English language learner comes from a unique background of language, literacy, and culture. Because children are at varying levels of English proficiency, it is important that each child has challenging work, appropriate for his or her level of English proficiency and literacy. The grammar and writing lessons in the ELL Support pages of *Reading Street* provide the systematic instruction that children need at each language proficiency level to scaffold use of increasingly complex grammatical structures in content area writing.

How

Reading Street promotes literacy attainment through engaging Conventions and Writing activities in the core Teacher Edition and ELL Support lessons. These activities activate prior knowledge, build background, scaffold meaning, affirm identity, and extend language.

Activate Prior Knowledge/Build Background

Frontload the Lesson Use the Preteach activities in the Conventions and Writing sections of the ELL Support pages with a small group of children before the lesson to introduce the concepts. Each Conventions lesson contains a helpful chart to convey grammatical forms and has ideas for addressing the functions of the grammatical structure to children. The Writing section contains a simple model to use when guiding instruction for beginning and intermediate levels.

Affirm Identity Use the Language Transfer notes in the core Teacher Edition, the Language Transfer Charts in *First Stop,* and the *ELL Handbook* Grammar Transition Lessons to lead children in transferring knowledge from their home languages to English.

Access Content and Scaffold Meaning

Provide Comprehensible Input Use the leveled Conventions practice activities in the ELL Support pages for contextual and linguistic support for each grade-level grammar skill. The interactive activities are designed so children reuse the language related to each core convention using different modalities to enhance understanding. For more practice on a core skill, or to meet the needs of beginners and intermediate children, use the Grammar Transition bank of flexible activities in the ELL Handbook or the Grammar Jammer from the digital path during small group time. Use the leveled writing ideas and the simplified writing models in the ELL Support pages to scaffold meaning for all children.

Language Clarification The leveled support notes throughout the Teacher Edition pages and the Grammar Transition Lessons in the ELL Handbook contain ideas for clarifying meaning for all proficiency levels.

Extend Language

Enable Language Production The Conventions and Writing sections of the ELL Support pages have practice activities for children to actively use grammar and writing skills. The sentence frames and leveled writing prompts guide and encourage oral and written language production for all levels of English proficiency. Use the ELL Notes throughout the core Teacher Edition Language Arts pages for ideas to support all levels of English language learners in prewriting, editing, revising, and publishing writing pieces.

References for English Language Proficiency—What, Why, and How

Gottlieb, Margo, M. Elizabeth Cranley, and Andrea R. Oliver (2007). *The WIDA English Language Proficiency Standards and Resource Guide, Pre-Kindergarten through Grade 12.* Board of Regents of the University of Wisconsin on behalf of the WIDA Consortium.

Peregoy, Suzanne F., and Owen F. Boyle (2008). *Reading, Writing, and Learning in ESL: A Resource Book for Teaching K–12 English Learners.* New York: Pearson.

	Child Behaviors	Teacher Behaviors	Examples
Beginning	• Can label, list, copy, use basic punctuation and capitalization • Uses some standard word order • Uses high-frequency words, phrases and short sentences • Primarily uses present tense and may use primary language features such as spelling patterns, word order, and literal translation • May recognize a few letter-sound relationships	• Allow extra time for prewriting. • Use language experience stories. • Help children turn words and phrases into sentences. • Accept phonetic spelling, but show correct spelling, capitalization, and punctuation. • Give a visual revising checklist. • Allow child to correct errors. • Build background before writing.	Descriptive paragraph about things in the neighborhood .... Display a T-chart with *I see* in one column and *Description* in the other. Children can draw pictures of things in their neighborhood in the first column. Guide children to tell about their pictures. Supply words children need, and they can copy them in the second column.
Intermediate	• Communicates best when topics are familiar and concrete • Produces simple, original messages consisting of short phrases and simple sentences • Future and past tenses may be used inconsistently • Has difficulty expressing abstract ideas and using cohesive devices • Descriptions, explanations, and narrations have limited details	• Allow extra time for prewriting. • Use language experience stories. • Help children turn phrases into sentences. • Accept phonetic spelling, but show correct spelling and punctuation. • Give a written revising checklist. • Help child use a dictionary or word wall to find correct spellings. • Allow child to correct errors.	Display the T-chart on the board with *I see* in one column and *Exact Description* in the other column. Pairs can list things they see in their neighborhoods in the first column. As children share their lists, guide them in making their language more vivid and exact. Children can use the sentence starter *I see* ________ and the words on the T-chart to scaffold oral and written production.
Advanced	• Can express ideas in writing and engage in grade-appropriate tasks • Can write sentences and paragraphs with some errors • Understands basic verb tenses, grammar and sentence patterns • Uses common cohesive devices and adds more detail • Can edit and revise writing using a checklist, a dictionary, word bank, or word wall	• Allow extra time for prewriting. • Use brainstorming, concept mapping, peer conferencing, interviewing, and reading. • Help children with correct spelling, capitalization, and punctuation. • Clarify error correction by peer or teachers to make changes and help children incorporate suggestions.	Display the T-chart on the board with *I see* in one column and *Exact Description* in the other column. Pairs can list things they see in their neighborhood in the first column. As children share their lists, guide them in making their language more vivid and exact. Children can use the sentence starter *In my neighborhood I see* _______ and the words on the T-chart to scaffold oral and written production of three or four sentences. Share sentences with the class.
Advanced High	• Can express ideas and engage meaningfully in grade-level assignments with minimal support • Writing is comparable to that of a native English speaker • Has occasional difficulty with expression and phrasing • Errors are minor and rarely interfere with communication	• Use brainstorming, concept mapping, peer conferencing, interviewing, and reading. • Help children with correct spelling, capitalization, and punctuation if needed. • Clarify error correction by peers or teachers to help children incorporate suggestions.	Use the graphic organizer for prewriting. Have children use their completed organizers to share things they see in the neighborhoods. Guide them to make language more vivid and exact. Have children use the T-chart to scaffold oral and written production of four or more sentences.

ELL Language Development Routine

See It! Say It! Use It!

Use this flexible routine with all levels of English language learners to guide their language development as they learn new basic and academic vocabulary, increase conceptual knowledge, and improve their reading comprehension. The following instructional sequence will encourage production and guide language development.

Start with choral work (Whole Group), and then move to partners or small groups, followed by "on your own" activities. Because choral, partner, and small group practice activities are nonthreatening, the affective filter is lowered, increasing language production.

Academic Vocabulary Routine

Model the word so that students can hear the correct pronunciation. Provide a student-friendly definition and relate it to something that students know, affirming their identity.

Display the word, and use a picture or pantomime to visually clarify meaning. Ask questions and have students respond to show their understanding of the word.

Say It!

Have students repeat the word chorally and then with a partner. Students will be able to use the word with more confidence and accuracy.

Use It!

Engage students in a variety of activities that encourage language production. Have them create their own definitions and use the word multiple times orally and in writing to internalize vocabulary and concept knowledge.

ELL Use the Academic Vocabulary Routine

This example shows how to use the Academic Vocabulary Routine to pre-teach the word *noun*.

How to Teach the Word *Noun*

Hear It!	Say the word **noun**. *A **noun** is a naming word for people, places, animals, or things.* Point to a desk. Say *this is a desk. A desk is a thing, so the word* desk *is a **noun**.*
See It!	Write the word **noun** on the board and word wall. To clarify meaning, point to other items in the classroom. Ask: *What is this?* (a chair) *Is this a person?* (no) *Is this a place?* (no) *Is this a thing?* (yes) *So, the word* chair *must be a **noun**.*
Say It!	Have students repeat the word **noun**. In pairs, have them say the word **noun** and the definition, *a **noun** is a naming word for people, places, animals, or things.*
Use It!	Have partners work together to identify more **nouns** for people and things they see in the classroom. Then have them write and illustrate their own definition of ***noun***. Partners can then share their definitions orally with the class.

Leveled Support

Beginning Pair students with more proficient speakers or students who speak the same language. Use more gestures and repetition. Allow students to answer by pointing, gesturing, or giving one-word responses.

Intermediate Continue to use visuals and gestures. Model correct responses. Ask questions that elicit two-word responses.

Advanced Continue to provide visual support. Give students more time to process information. Questions can be more open-ended, but be sure to check comprehension frequently.

Advanced High Provide visual support as needed. Have students work with beginners who speak the same language to clarify meaning.

Contents

Professional Development

Introduction: How to Use This Book

Across the United States, teachers are welcoming increasing numbers of English language learners (ELLs) into their classrooms. English language learners make up the fastest growing K-12 student population in the United States.

While English language learners share many characteristics with other students, they need support and scaffolding specific to their needs. They represent a highly diverse population. They come from many home language backgrounds and cultures, and they have a wide range of prior educational and literacy experiences acquiring in their home languages.

This Handbook is designed to help you identify and support the needs of ELLs in your classroom. The strategies and activities will allow you to scaffold and support instruction so that all students can learn in ways that are comprehensible and meaningful, and in ways that promote their academic success and achievement.

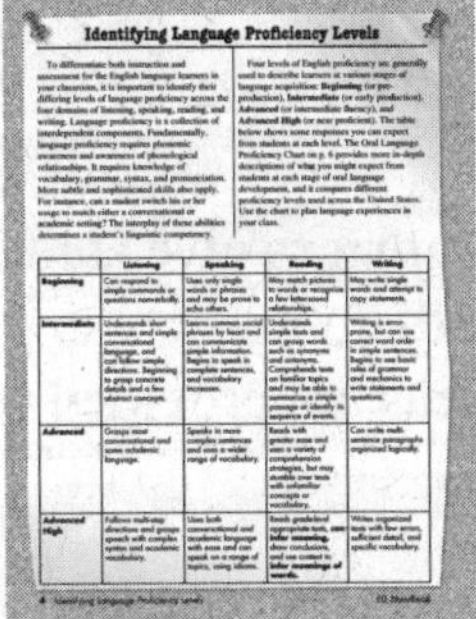

Carefully crafted **professional development articles** assist you in understanding and planning for the unique needs of English language learners in your classroom.

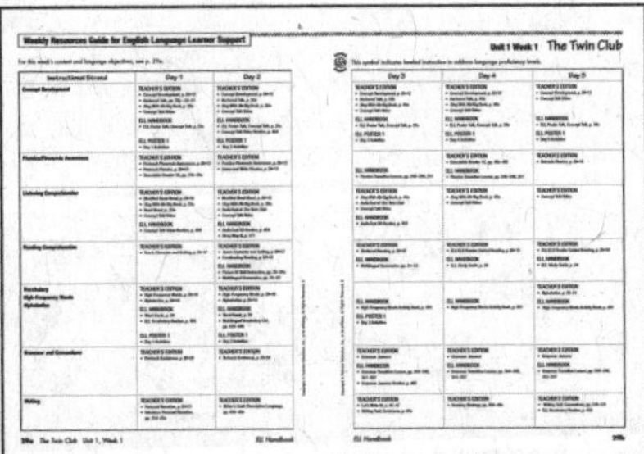

Weekly Planners outline all activities in a "week at a glance" format and include objectives for each instructional strand.

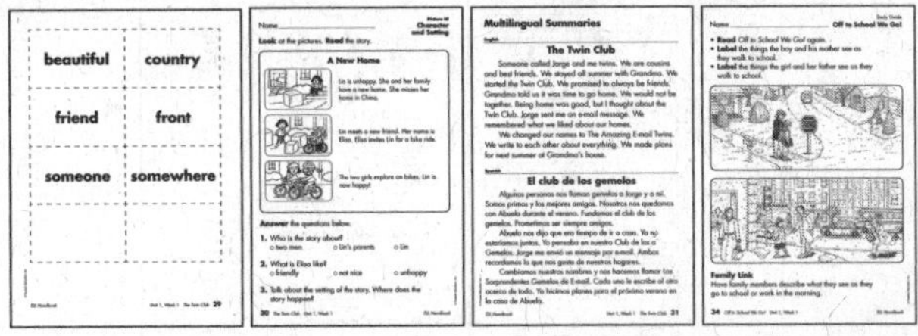

Each reading selection is supported by a set of reproducibles. **Word Cards** allow students to use key vocabulary for speaking, writing, and content acquisition. Each **Picture It!** focuses on a reading comprehension skill with instruction targeted to English language learners. **Multilingual Selection Summaries,** in English, Spanish, Chinese, Vietnamese, Korean, and Hmong, allow students to access selection content and share their reading with their families. **Study Guides** for ELL Readers allow you to assess comprehension of content and the use of key reading strategies. All of these resources provide access to core content material, each unit and week of the year. Detailed instructions for using these resources are provided in the ELL Support pages of the Teacher's Edition.

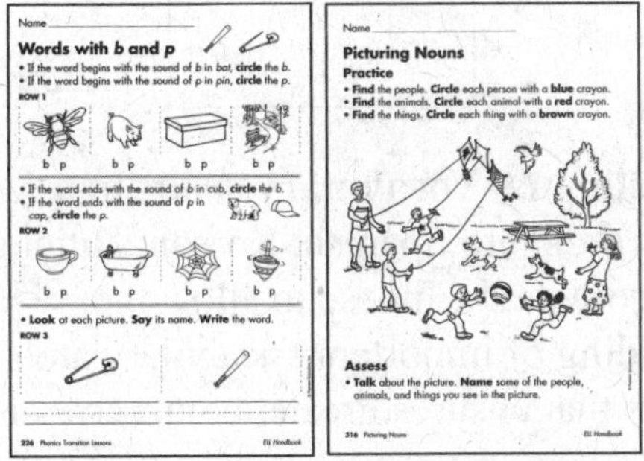

Phonics pages target instruction with consonants, vowels, and syllable patterns that may be challenging for English language learners. **Grammar** lessons supplement core instruction in speaking and writing. Use these lessons as students need additional support.

English Language Learner Workshops provide direct and explicit instruction in such topics as using transactional language, retelling or summarizing in English, asking for assistance, giving and following directions, and using formal and informal English. A teacher-driven lesson as well as a student worksheet is provided for a model/teach/practice/assess progression as students gradually master these skills.

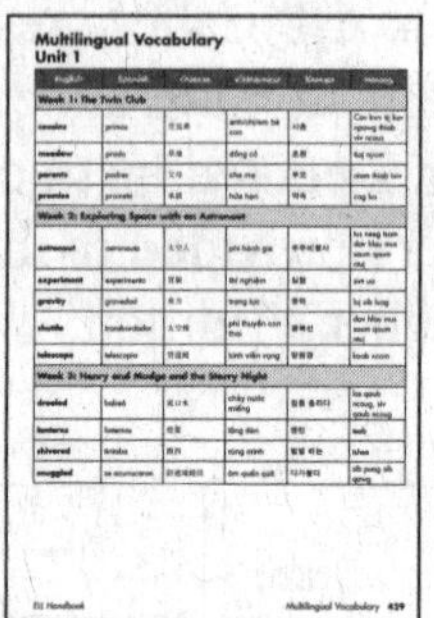

Multilingual Vocabulary charts translate the lesson words into Spanish, Korean, Hmong, Vietnamese, and Chinese to allow the frontloading of important vocabulary and concepts that ensures greater comprehension.

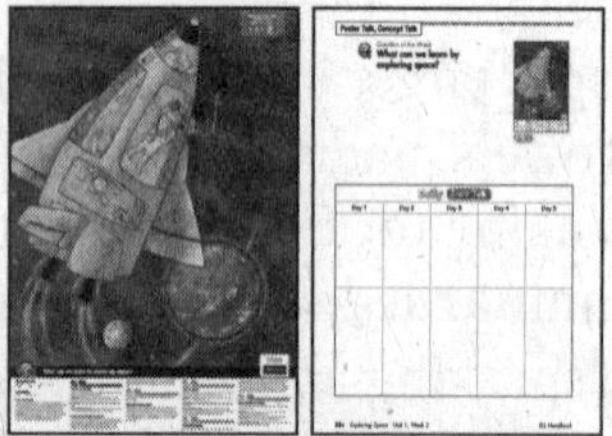

Poster Talk, Concept Talk leveled activities encourage language production using the poster visuals and vocabulary related to the weekly concept.

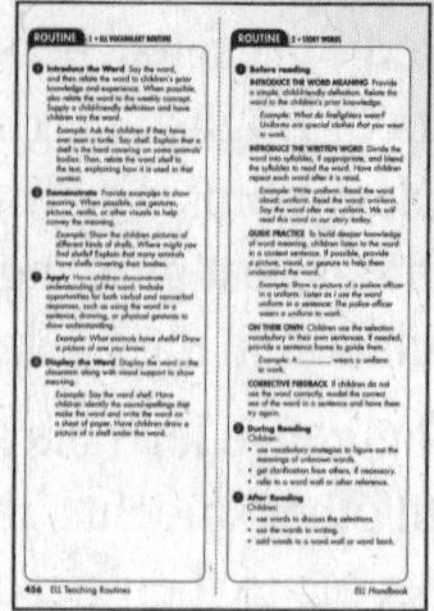

Teaching Routines for English language learners allow for a systematic approach to learning that yields results. Routines are tied to instruction, allowing students to master the skills needed to succeed.

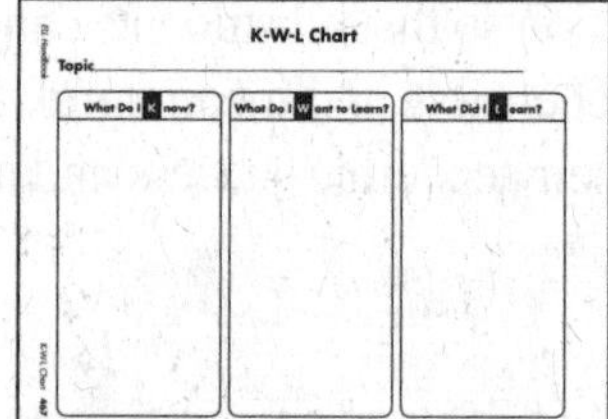

Graphic Organizers give students visual support to assist them in accessing the content. ELL teaching ideas are provided for each Graphic Organizer.

Identifying Language Proficiency Levels

To differentiate both instruction and assessment for the English language learners in your classroom, it is important to identify their various levels of language proficiency across the four domains of listening, speaking, reading, and writing. Language proficiency is a collection of interdependent components. Fundamentally, language proficiency requires phonemic awareness and awareness of phonological relationships. It requires knowledge of vocabulary, grammar, syntax, and pronunciation. More subtle and sophisticated skills also apply. For instance, can a student switch his or her usage to match either a conversational or academic setting? The interplay of these abilities determines a student's linguistic competency.

Four or five levels of English proficiency are generally used to describe learners at various stages of language acquisition: **Beginning** (or pre-production), **Intermediate** (or early production), **Advanced** (or intermediate fluency), and **Advanced High** (or near proficient). The table below shows some responses you can expect from students at each level. The Comparative Oral Language Proficiency Chart on p. 6 provides more in-depth descriptions of what you might expect from students at each stage of oral language development, and it compares different proficiency levels used across the United States. Use the chart to plan instruction for your class.

	Listening	**Speaking**	**Reading**	**Writing**
Beginning	Can respond to simple commands or questions nonverbally.	Uses only single words or phrases and may be prone to echo others.	May match pictures to words or recognize a few letter-sound relationships.	May write single words and attempt to copy statements.
Intermediate	Understands short sentences and simple conversational language and can follow simple directions. Beginning to grasp concrete details and a few abstract concepts.	Learns common social phrases by heart and can communicate simple information. Begins to speak in complete sentences, and vocabulary increases.	Understands simple texts and can group words such as synonyms and antonyms. Comprehends texts on familiar topics and may be able to summarize a simple passage or identify its sequence of events.	Writing is error-prone, but can use correct word order in simple sentences. Begins to use basic rules of grammar and mechanics to write statements and questions.
Advanced	Grasps most conversational and some academic language.	Speaks in more complex sentences and uses a wider range of vocabulary.	Reads with greater ease and uses a variety of comprehension strategies, but may stumble over texts with unfamiliar concepts or vocabulary.	Can write multi-sentence paragraphs organized logically.
Advanced High	Follows multi-step directions and grasps speech with complex syntax and academic vocabulary.	Uses both conversational and academic language with ease and can speak on a range of topics, using idioms.	Reads grade-level appropriate texts, can infer meaning, draw conclusions, and use context to infer meanings of words.	Writes organized texts with few errors, sufficient detail, and specific vocabulary.

How can you differentiate instruction for the different proficiency levels?

You can use a variety of instructional techniques, activities, and assessment tools to support English language learners at different levels of proficiency—all within the same lesson. For example, to teach sequence of events, you might choose to adapt your instruction as follows:

Teach/Model

Read a short passage to the whole class, showing pictures of each event in the story as you do so. When you have finished reading, review the events in the story. Model using sequence words.

- Use gestures to explain "first," "next," and "last" to students at the **Beginning** level. For example, hold up one finger as you say "first" and put on a shoe. Hold up two fingers as you say "next" and lace up the shoe. Hold up three fingers as you say "last" and take a step.
- Have students at the **Intermediate** level echo you as you say "first," "next," and "last" and then add a detail to each to make a phrase or short sentence.
- Have students at the **Advanced** level answer questions about sequence of events as you read aloud.
- Have students at the **Advanced High** level answer questions about the sequence of inferred events as you read aloud. (For example, "What must have happened before Jack slipped in the paint?" "The paint can fell.")

Practice

- After you read, have students at the **Beginning** level arrange the pictures in the story in the correct order.
- Have students at the **Intermediate** level answer the questions, "What happened first?" "What happened next?" "What happened last?"
- Have students at the **Advanced** level verbally describe the events in the story using sequence words.
- Have students at the **Advanced High** level write the sequence of events in the story using complete sentences.

Assess

- Have students at the **Beginning** level arrange a new series of pictures in the correct order.
- Have students at the **Intermediate** level look at a new series of pictures and then answer the questions, "What happened first?" "What happened next?" "What happened last?"
- Have students at the **Advanced** level read a new passage and then verbally describe its events using sequence words.
- Have students at the **Advanced High** level read a new passage and answer questions about the sequence of inferred events.

Comparative Oral Language Proficiency Chart

Levels of Proficiency	Level I Entering	Level II Beginning	Level III Developing	Level IV Expanding	Level V Bridging
	Beginning	Early Intermediate	Intermediate	Early Advanced	Advanced
	Beginning	Intermediate		Advanced	Advanced High
Characteristics of the English Language Learner	• Minimal comprehension • May be very shy • No verbal production • Non-English speaker • Silent period (10 hours to 3 months) • Uses gestures and actions to communicate	• Limited comprehension • Gives one- or two-word responses • May use two- or three-word phrases • Stage may last 6 months to 2 years	• Comprehension increases • Errors still occur in speech • Simple sentences • Stage may last 2 to 4 years	• Good comprehension • Sentences become more complex • Engages in conversation • Errors in speech are more complex	• Few errors in speech • Orally proficient • Near-native vocabulary • Lacks writing skill • Uses complex sentences
What They Can Do: Performance Indicators	• Listen • Point • Illustrate • Match • Choose	• Name • List and group • Categorize • Label • Demonstrate	• Compare and contrast • Recall and retell • Summarize • Explain	• Higher-order thinking skills • Analyze, debate, justify	• All performance indicators
Instructional Ideas for Teachers	• Visual cues • Tape passages • Pair students • Total Physical Response activities • Concrete objects • Graphic organizers	• Short homework assignments • Short-answer quizzes • Open-ended sentences	• Graphs • Tables • Group discussions • Student-created books • Cloze activities	• Group panels • Paraphrasing • Defending and debating	• Lessons on writing mechanics • Free reading of appropriate books • Cooperative learning groups

What Reading Teachers Should Know About Language

Why do reading teachers need to know about the structure of language?

English language learners are entering U.S. classrooms in steadily increasing numbers. The demands on teachers are also surging. To communicate effectively with these students, teachers need to know how to make their instructional talk more comprehensible. All teachers need to better understand their students' attempts at written and spoken language. To improve students' literacy skills in English, teachers must understand how language works *in education.* What should we know about English and other languages? What truths about language help teachers as communicators, as guides, and as evaluators?

Knowledge about the structure of languages—and particularly of English—is vital not only to linguists and ELL teachers. Reading and content-area teachers, too, can make practical, everyday use of the concepts that are posed and explored by the following questions.

What are the basic units of language?

Spoken language consists of units of different sizes:

Phonemes

Phonemes are the individual sounds in a word that affect meaning. The word *cat* consists of these three phonemes: /k/ /a/ /t/.

Different languages use different sets of phonemes. English language learners may not be familiar with some English phonemes and may need help recognizing and producing these sounds.

Phonemes signal different word meanings. For example, the different vowel sounds in the words *hit* and *heat* indicate that these are two different words.

Morphemes

Morphemes are the smallest units of meaning in a language. Some morphemes are **free** (or independent) units. Words such as *dog, jump,* and *happy* are free morphemes. Other morphemes are **bound** (or attached), such as inflected endings, prefixes, and suffixes:

- the noun ending *-s* in *dogs*
- the verb ending *-ed* in *jumped*
- the prefix *un-* in *unhappy*
- the adjective ending *-er* in *happier*
- the suffix *-ness* in *happiness*

These bound morphemes add meaning and, in fact, form new words.

Words

A word consists of one or more morphemes. A word also can be defined as a meaningful group of morphemes. Native English speakers may pronounce words in ways that make it difficult for English language learners to hear word boundaries. For example, in conversation, an English speaker may ask, "Did you eat?"—but pronounce it like "Jeet?"

Some languages use bound morphemes (for example, word endings) to convey the meanings of certain functional English words such as the prepositions *in, on,* and *between.* English language learners may need explicit instruction in order to use these functional words correctly. On the other hand, an English word such as *in* may seem familiar to a Spanish speaker who uses the similar preposition *en.*

Phrases

A phrase is a group of words that have meaning together but do not include a subject and a predicate. Since some languages allow the subject or verb to be understood, students may believe that certain phrases in English are equivalent to sentences.

Sentences

A sentence is a meaningful group of words that includes a subject and a predicate. English language learners may understand the concept of sentences, but they may apply word order conventions from their home languages. They also may struggle with the dense sentence structures of academic English.

Discourses

Discourses include speeches, essays, and many other kinds of communication made up of sentences. One kind of discourse frequently heard in U.S. classrooms involves the teacher asking questions and students responding aloud. Depending on their home cultures, some English language learners may find the question-and-answer form of discourse unfamiliar.

Why do English language learners need to learn about basic units of language?

It helps teachers to understand that units, such as bound and free morphemes, words, phrases, and sentences or clauses, operate differently in different languages. For example:

- In Chinese, the past tense is not expressed with verb endings, but by separate words that indicate the time of the action (similar to *yesterday* and *already*).
- In Spanish, verb endings indicate the person and number of sentence subjects, so the subject may not be stated in some sentences.
- In Arabic, related words share three-consonant roots. Speakers form related verbs, nouns, and adjectives by applying fixed patterns to these roots and sometimes adding prefixes and suffixes.

English language learners are working mentally to determine how units of English work—as they also try to understand texts and acquire content knowledge.

What is academic English?

Academic English might be described as the language of teachers, literature, textbooks, and content areas, such as science and social studies. Unlike conversational English, academic English is language of a cognitively demanding register, or range. Academic English does not depend as much upon the gestures and circumstances of speech as conversational English does.

Academic English includes content-area vocabulary embedded in complex grammatical structures. It features words about abstract ideas. Understanding this language requires knowledge of content, as well as experience with written materials and classroom discussions. Many English language learners can carry on conversations in English with their native-English-speaking classmates. But they still struggle with reading and writing English—and even understanding their teachers in class. They have acquired social English skills used in personal communication, but they have not yet mastered the academic English used at their grade level.

How do English language learners learn vocabulary?

English language learners must learn much more than the selected vocabulary words in a lesson. They also must make sense of the other unfamiliar words in the lesson—and thousands of other words they continually encounter in school.

Knowing a word involves much more than hearing it and learning its definition. Students must learn how each word relates to its other forms. They gradually learn how it relates to other words and concepts. Knowledge of a word grows during many encounters.

Students learn words in meaningful groups more effectively than in unrelated lists. Look for opportunities to group words in meaningful ways. For example, as students learn the word *invite*, they also can learn *invited, uninvited, invitation, inviting,* and other words in this family.

What is "regular" to English language learners?

Proficient English speakers often take for granted irregularities in English that can puzzle younger and less fluent learners.

For example, a student who learns the plural forms *dogs, cats,* and *turtles* may wonder why *mouses, mooses,* and *childs* meet with disapproval. A student who masters these past tense forms—*jumped, walked,* and *stopped*—may try to use *throwed, catched,* or *taked.* In both cases, the child demonstrates an awareness of English conventions, and a teacher should acknowledge this in a positive way. The teacher also should gradually help each student master the many exceptions to the rules. Teachers who are aware of the principles of word formation in English can help students acquire vocabulary. English has many helpful patterns for new speakers, readers, and writers to learn. Savvy teachers break up the instruction into manageable chunks so that students are not overwhelmed by the many English word patterns they encounter.

What characteristics of written words might challenge English language learners?

- Written English is an alphabetic language, and letters represent sounds in words. Languages such as Chinese and Japanese are not alphabetic; written symbols can represent larger parts of words than just individual sounds. For students whose home languages are not alphabetic, learning the alphabetic system is an early and continuing challenge.
- The home languages of many English language learners—including Spanish, Vietnamese, Hmong, Haitian Creole, and others—are alphabetic. Yet the letter-sound correspondences in these languages are different from those of English. Students can use literacy skills they may have in their home languages, but much new learning is needed to master English.
- While letter-sound correspondences in numerous languages are relatively simple, the relationships of letters to sounds in English can be complicated. In Spanish, for example, the vowel *a* has one sound. In English, *a* can represent many different sounds.
- Even in related English words, the same letters can stand for different sounds. Consider *c* in the words *electric, electricity,* and *electrician.* The spellings of these words may challenge English language learners.
- The challenges of written English affect not only spelling but also word recognition, comprehension of text, and confidence in language learning.

Welcoming Newcomers to the Mainstream Classroom

The teacher's first concern when welcoming newcomers to the mainstream classroom must be to help each student learn the basic concepts and vocabulary needed to participate in school life.

Prepare

Learn as much as possible about your newcomer students in order to tailor instruction to their individual needs.

Find out from parents or other sources about educational practices in the student's home country or culture. For example, if the student is accustomed to memorizing and reciting material in a group, he or she may feel anxious about independent work or homework, particularly if the family is not able to help the child in English.

Newcomers who are acquiring English may experience identifiable stages of adjustment and adaptation.

- **A Silent Period** For a student quite new to an English-language environment, a "silent period" is normal. The student may be learning classroom routine and acquiring basic vocabulary by watching and listening.
- **Culture Shock** In this phase, newcomers may prefer to spend much of their time with family or friends from the home culture and to temporarily reject the new language and culture. Help children to cope with this phase by providing extra help and attention when possible. A bilingual friend or classroom aide can help to make the environment feel more navigable to the child and can help to alleviate any feelings of anxiety or sadness.

Getting Started in the Classroom

Before classes begin, you may wish to plan a small reception for newcomers. Invite the students' parents or other family members and include someone who can translate.

- **Orient the newcomer to the classroom.** Have students help you to label the classroom and the objects in it with self-stick notes. Pronounce the name of each item as you do, and use the word in a short sentence. "*Desk. This is your desk.*"
- **Show interest in and respect for each child's home culture.** Create opportunities for the class to learn more about the newcomer's home country and culture. Learn a few phrases in the student's home language. Correctly pronounce the student's name.
- **Demonstrate crucial skills.** Have students tour the school with older students who speak the same home language. Post seating charts and go through assigned textbooks with newcomers to help them understand what content is presented in each.
- **Try to provide a risk-free learning environment.** Create opportunities for students to practice speaking English in small groups or with a partner without worrying about errors they may make. Accept errors in speech without comment and model the correct phrasing.
- **Provide a "buddy."** A buddy system helps students feel more secure in their environment. Buddies need not speak the same home language, but pairing up buddies with the same home language can allow buddies to serve as tutors.
- **Include newcomers in classroom routines.** Assign newcomers their share of regular classroom chores. Such responsibilities can help them feel they are part of the group. Students can be shown how to successfully carry out routine tasks without using or needing extensive English.

Teaching Strategies

Educational strategies should assist students to learn in content areas at the same time that they acquire the new language. Remember that students' skills in the home language can be transferred to English learning. Encourage students to continue to speak and read in the home language.

- **Build on students' prior knowledge.** Newcomers often have knowledge bases that are much greater than their skill levels in English. Find ways to gauge students' familiarity with the topics of upcoming lessons. Regularly using visual aids, such as semantic maps, K-W-L charts, or time lines, can help you determine how much each student already knows or needs to learn about a topic.
- **Encourage students to use learning resources.** Teach students how to use a picture dictionary or a children's dictionary, and encourage them to use it frequently to find the words they need. Ask them to start their own word banks by listing frequently used vocabulary in a notebook. Provide bilingual dictionaries for extra support.
- **Use environmental print to teach.** Put up posters and other materials from periodicals and magazines. If possible, provide students with parallel texts about the same topic in English and in the home language.
- **Invite the families of newcomers to participate in school life.** Find ways to communicate information about homework and class projects in English and the home language. Make families aware that literacy skills in the home language can help students transfer those skills to English.
- **Build a support network.** Bilingual tutors or classroom aides can clarify assignments or lesson content for English language learners without disrupting the day's activities. Similarly, family members who volunteer to help in the classroom can greatly lessen students' anxiety levels.
- **Help students transfer their writing skills.** For English language learners who have developed any emergent writing skills in their home languages, build on these skills by occasionally having them write in both languages. Short sentences and picture labels written in a home language and English help students with writing and English acquisition.
- **Include culturally relevant assignments.** Try to find readings for students that refer to their home cultures. If writing skills are limited, encourage learners to show their understanding by talking about the stories and creating illustrations.

While it may take some time for English language learners to gain proficiency in academic English, newcomers need not feel like outsiders for very long.

Sheltering Instruction for English Language Learners

What is sheltered instruction?

Sheltered instruction is a combination of strategies for teaching academic content to English language learners at the same time that they are developing proficiency in the English language. This approach to instruction is called *sheltered* because it offers a haven, or refuge, for students who must comprehend subject matter presented in a language they are still learning. Sheltered instruction supports English language learners who do not have grade-level academic vocabulary or the familiarity with the American school system that their English speaking classmates have. It provides extended English language support that English language learners receive as they learn subject-area concepts.

How does sheltered instruction help students and teachers?

Sheltered instruction offers practical, easy-to-implement strategies that teachers can use in a mainstream classroom to extend and scaffold instruction about the English language. Sheltered instruction helps English language learners find the keys they need to make sense of instruction in English about the concepts and processes they need to perform grade-level work in all subjects.

Teachers can help students build mental bridges to new concepts and learning in English by encouraging them to connect their prior knowledge—the diverse skills, experiences, language, and cultural knowledge that they bring to the classroom—to their new learning activities. Finding ways for students to draw on their home language, cultural background, and prior experience can facilitate each English language learner's ability to grasp and retain abstract ideas and grade level vocabulary. Finding connections between what they are learning and what they already know in their home language can motivate students to read, write, listen, and speak in English. As comprehension and vocabulary increase, students can transfer more and more concepts from their home languages into English.

This knowledge transfer can work for teachers, too. As teachers tap into students' prior knowledge, the teachers will discover when they need to supply background about American events, customs, and idioms that may be new to English language learners. At the same time, they will be expanding their knowledge about English language learners' backgrounds and traditions.

Some Basics

1. Use Appropriate Speech (Comprehensible Input)
   - ✓ **Enunciate.** Speak slowly and clearly, especially when introducing new content and vocabulary.
   - ✓ **Provide wait time.** English language learners often need extra time to process questions in English and to formulate responses.
   - ✓ **Explain and demonstrate the meanings of complex terms.** Use activities that help students practice speaking, hearing, writing, and reading key words and phrases.

Complex term	Activities to clarify meaning
weather	Write and say: weather Write and say: hot, cold Say: The weather is hot today. (Fan yourself to show you are hot.) Then say: The weather is cold today. (Hug yourself and shiver to show you are cold.) Have volunteers repeat each sentence with gestures. Then fan yourself and ask: What is the weather like today? (hot) Hug yourself and shiver and ask: Is the weather hot or cold today? (cold) Have partners take turns using gestures and asking and answering the questions. Start a wall chart of weather words with pictures.

✓ **Allow students to show comprehension at their levels of language proficiency.** Ask questions that can be answered with "yes" or "no," by choosing one of two words as the answer ("Is ice hot or cold?"), by pointing to a picture or object ("Point to the tree."), or by following simple oral directions.

2. Develop Academic Concepts

✓ **Link concepts explicitly to students' prior knowledge and background.** For example, if you introduce a unit on weather, ask students to describe, illustrate, and share what they know about weather. Create and display a class chart that tells about weather in places where students have lived.

✓ **Use hands-on activities to build background for new information.** For example, introduce the idea of touch (The Five Senses) by having students touch objects with different textures and learn a word or words to describe how each object feels.

✓ **Use supplementary materials.** Picture books can clarify and support concept learning. Use picture books that show terms that are hard to explain, such as *covered wagons, rations,* or the *Pony Express.*

3. Emphasize and Develop Key Vocabulary

✓ **Repeat key words, phrases, and concepts, and have students practice using them.**

✓ **Provide feedback on students' language use.** Use gestures to indicate understanding, as well as supportive questions to prompt students to provide more details.

✓ **Make the development of proficiency in English an explicit goal in all of your teaching. To learn new academic vocabulary, students need to use it.** Provide situations that challenge students to push themselves to a higher level of proficiency.

4. Connect Written and Oral Language

✓ **Say and write new vocabulary.** When teaching new words or phrases, such as idioms, write the word or phrase where everyone can see it. Say it slowly as you point to it. Have students repeat the word or phrase. Use gestures, role play, or drawings to demonstrate what the word means. Have students practice saying, reading, and writing the word or phrase in sentences.

✓ **Use word and picture cards to explain vocabulary and content.**

✓ **Have students build personal word files.** Have them write a word on one side of a card and draw a picture to represent its meaning on the other side. The files can include target words for different content areas as well as words that students find interesting or important. Have students use the cards for sorting and categorizing activities (*e.g.,* color words, animal names, weather words, math words, action words).

✓ **Provide letter and phoneme cards for phonics activities.** Pair English language learners with native English speakers to use cards in order to build and say words that contain target sounds and spelling patterns. Give English language learners extra time and support to hear, say, and practice sounds and to build words using those sounds

5. Use Visuals, Dramatization, and Realia (Real Things)

✓ **Use picture walks to preview text, concepts, and vocabulary—and to build background knowledge.** Use pictures to introduce characters and the setting and to give a simple summary of a story. You can use this same strategy with nonfiction text, having students preview illustrations, captions, boldfaced words, and other text features.

✓ **Use realia and graphic organizers.** Whenever possible, show objects and pictures that will help students understand concepts and speak about them in English. Use graphic organizers, diagrams, drawings, charts, and maps to help students conceptualize abstract information.

✓ **Use Total Physical Response (TPR) for active learning, so that students can show comprehension through physical movement.** For example, have students hear and follow instructions: "Clap your hands for Carla." "Go to the board, and circle the noun in red."

✓ **Use role play, drama, rhymes, songs, and movement.** All students need opportunities to be active learners. For English language learners, participating in a small group re-enactment of a story, for example, can allow them to show comprehension and personal responses beyond what their language abilities may allow them to express.

6. Ongoing Formal and Informal Assessment

✓ **Assess early to understand a student's language level and academic preparedness. Use your assessment to plan and guide instruction.**

✓ **Set personal goals for each student and monitor progress regularly.** A student who uses phrases might be pushed to say and write complete sentences. A student who uses simple sentences might be pushed to add clauses to the sentences.

✓ **Provide various ways to demonstrate knowledge, including acting, singing, retelling, demonstrating, and illustrating.**

✓ **Use a variety of formal assessments such as practice tests, real tests, and oral and written assessments.** Use multiple choice, cloze, and open-response formats to help students become familiar with various assessment formats. Sheltered instruction provides English language learners with opportunities to understand and access content-area learning. Within this framework, teachers provide activities that integrate reading, writing, listening, and speaking. Teachers can address the range of cultural, linguistic, and literary experiences that English language learners bring to the classroom. Sheltered instruction provides English language learners with many opportunities to understand and access content-area learning. Within this kind of instruction, teachers support English language learners by providing activities that integrate reading, writing, listening, and speaking. Teachers use students' experiences and prior knowledge as the key to unlock doors to content and language learning.

Vocabulary Knowledge and Strategies

Knowing how to organize vocabulary instruction around a few key areas will go a long way toward ensuring that students achieve both language proficiency and overall academic success. The new vocabulary that you teach should be carefully selected. As you consider the vocabulary you will teach in your classroom, you'll need to be aware of both survival language and academic language.

Survival Language

Think of survival language as a useful toolkit for new English language learners—a practical store of words and phrases that can be used to navigate new environments and accomplish everyday tasks in the classroom and at home. Survival language not only involves teaching students labels for common objects, places, and people, but includes giving students instruction in how to understand and follow directions, ask for help, and function appropriately in social situations. While it is valuable to reinforce this type of vocabulary acquisition throughout the day, as spontaneous interactions with students arise, it is also important to offer structured and intentional instruction in survival language. Consider organizing related words and phrases under the heading of a topic such as "School," as in the following table.

People	Places	Objects	Phrases
principal teacher nurse student coach	cafeteria classroom bathroom library gym	desk chair chalkboard worksheet ruler	May I have...? Please show me.... I want to.... What is a ...? I need help with....

Teachers Support Vocabulary Learning

English language learners come to school with a wide range of home language literacy, English language proficiency, and previous educational experiences. All of these factors impact their learning in English.

Teachers can use various strategies to support vocabulary development. Students need multiple exposures to words. Understanding deepens over time through gradually increased and varied experiences with the words.

English language learners need opportunities to learn vocabulary through activities that integrate reading, writing, speaking, and listening skills in the context of meaningful literacy experiences. Language learning is an exploration. Students have a curiosity about learning, and effective teachers nurture this quality through engaging and meaningful activities. Teachers can use what students already know to help them extract meaning from text by teaching them ways to learn and think about words.

Strategies for Exploring Words

Use these strategies to build vocabulary.

Related Words

Provide opportunities for English language learners to learn new words by grouping words that are related to a specific theme, quality, or activity. Help students classify English words in meaningful categories.

Use word walls, graphic organizers, and concept maps to group related words and create visual references that can be used in future lessons. Teachers can help students group and relate words in different ways, depending on what they can notice and understand, as well as how students will use the vocabulary.

Color names are one example of related words that can be the focus of a lesson.

- ✓ Write the word *colors* at the top of a wall chart.
- ✓ With colored markers, make a column of squares under the heading: red, blue, yellow, green.
- ✓ Point to the word *colors* and tell students they are going to learn the names of colors.
- ✓ Point to the first square and say, "This color is red." Write *red* and repeat it clearly as you underline it with your finger.

✓ Show a familiar red object, such as a block, and say: "This is a red block. The color of this block is red. What color is this block?" (red)

Repeat this process with the other colors, making sure that students hear, say, and read each color name, and connect it to the color itself.

Have students create other sections in their personal word card files such as "family names," "numbers," "days and months," "weather," and "time."

Whenever you introduce a new topic or concept, take time to teach English language learners words they will need to understand the lesson. Keep in mind that they may need to learn some words and phrases in the lesson—including idioms and background references—that may already be common knowledge to native speakers. Encourage native speakers to act as resources for English language learners when they encounter a word, phrase, or concept that puzzles them.

Charts such as the one here can help students learn how words change form, depend-ing on their function.

Naming Word	Describing Word	Action Word
rain	rainy	rain, rains, rained, raining
dance, dancer	dancing	dance, dances, danced, dancing
sleep, sleeper	sleepy	sleep, sleeps, slept, sleeping

Cognates

When students hear or see a word that looks or sounds similar to a word they know in their home language, encourage them to explore the conne-ction. For example, a Russian speaker hearing the word *music* may recognize its connection to the Russian word *musika.* Many words that sound similar in two or more languages are cognates—they have the same or similar meaning in both languages. Record cognates on a wall chart and add to it during the year.

Multiple-meaning Words

Many English words have multiple meanings. Illustrating and creating examples of the ways words are used can build English language learners' experiences and understanding of the multiple meanings that words may have. Teachers can help students expand their understanding of multiple meanings by sharing sentences, definitions, and pictures that demonstrate the different meanings. For example, contrasting *The pitcher is full of water* with *The pitcher threw the ball,* with illustrations, will help English language learners remember the two meanings of *pitcher.*

Academic Language

Research indicates that acquiring a strong grasp of academic vocabulary is perhaps the most vital factor that distinguishes successful students from those who struggle in school. Becoming fluent in academic language will enable English language learners to understand and analyze texts, write clearly about their ideas, and comprehend subject-area material. Academic vocabulary differs from conversational English. It is the language of classroom discourse, and it is used to accomplish academic, not social or personal, purposes. Academic vocabulary also includes words, phrases, and sentence structures not commonly found in oral language but used frequently in academic texts such as textbooks, reports, essays, articles, and test materials. Instruction in academic vocabulary should be explicit and systematic. Give students multiple exposures to academic terms through frequent reading, writing, and oral language activities. Because academic vocabulary involves the use of language that is not commonly encountered in conversational contexts, English language learners need structured opportunities to practice this vocabulary in formal settings where teachers and peers are modeling the use of effective academic language.

Below is a partial list of types of academic vocabulary to which students should be exposed

- **Transition words**

  therefore; thus; however; similarly; alternatively
- **Content-specific words**

  cell (science); *era* (social studies); *graph* (math)
- **Difficult verb and tense forms**

  was written by (passive voice); *have voted* (present perfect); *had ended* (past perfect)
- **The language of written instructions**

  compare; define; analyze; calculate; summarize

<u>Home Language Activities</u>

Teachers can use home language activities to help students reinforce their learning of the concepts and meanings of vocabulary and literacy activities. English language learners can participate in a variety of activities such as discussion, telling or reading stories, listening to songs and music, hearing radio or television weather or sports reports, and interviewing family members, and then use those experiences as topics for discussion and sharing in the classroom. Students can transfer their understanding of a word or concept from their home language to English when they have experiences that illustrate meaning. Teachers can find ways to use the home environment as an educational resource by planning activities that involve reading, writing, listening, and speaking about students' family histories, cultures, and experiences.

<u>Technology</u>

Teachers can use various forms of technology (computer, Internet, audio, video recording) to meet the specific and varied needs of English language learners.

For example, you might choose target words and have students use computers to find images that illustrate their meanings.

Creating and Adapting Strategies

A great deal of reading in English, listening to selections read aloud, and conversing in English will help learners acquire thousands of words per year if they are engaged in learning. Continue using the instructional strategies that work, adapt (or discontinue) the ones that are not effective, and try new approaches as needed.

References

August, Diane (Principal Investigator), and T. Shanahan (Panel Chair) (2006). *Developing Literacy in Second-Language Learners: Report of the National Literacy Panel on Language-Minority Children and Youth.* Mahwah, New Jersey: Lawrence Erlbaum Associates.

Blachowicz, Camille L. Z., and Peter Fisher. *Teaching Vocabulary in All Classrooms.* Upper Saddle River, NJ: Prentice Hall, 2002.

Vocabulary Development for Reading Success. Scott Foresman Professional Development Series, Module 6. Glenview, IL: Scott Foresman, 2004.

Effective Comprehension Instruction for English Language Learners

Clear and explicit comprehension instruction is a key component of successful English language development. Traditionally, the main purpose of comprehension instruction has been limited to having students answer assigned questions related to a passage they have read. As a result, what can and should be a complex, analytical process has been diminished by a narrow focus on products. A greater benefit to English language learners, as for all students, is guidance in becoming active readers who are engaged in texts on multiple levels before, during, and after reading.

Jim Cummins identifies conditions that promote engaging with literacy for English language learners and, in fact, for all students. To attain literacy, students must be fully engaged in their reading and writing. Students need to read a variety of texts that reflect children's cultures and languages. Teachers must use strategies that promote a deep understanding of the text. Through engaging students by activating prior knowledge, frontloading to build background, affirming identity, scaffolding the language, and extending language through various experiences, students move from engagement in literacy to achievement in literacy.

Comprehension instruction that will achieve this more sophisticated goal focuses on *meta-cognition*, the name we give to a good reader's ability to independently reflect on the purpose of reading, select appropriate approaches to texts, ask questions as he or she reads, and actively resolve areas of confusion. Metacognitive strategies such as predicting, questioning, self-monitoring, summarizing, and making inferences should be transferable from one type of text to another. For this reason it is important to introduce these strategies to students using a variety of fiction and nonfiction texts. The following comprehension instruction techniques will help you encourage literacy engagement and the development of metacognition in your students.

What Is Frontloading?

Imagine that you are teaching someone how to bake a cake. If you knew that your pupil had no experience in the kitchen, you would not jump right into the recipe and instructions. Instead, you would start by naming and explaining the key ingredients in the cake—the flour, sugar, baking powder, eggs, and so on. You would demonstrate how to use measuring cups. You might explain how baking differs from frying or boiling. In other words, you would anticipate the knowledge that your budding baker requires in order to be successful at this new task and make sure to introduce that knowledge first. This is the essence of frontloading.

Frontloading for English language learners involves preteaching the vital vocabulary, background concepts, and sometimes the text structures that students need to know before they can understand an upcoming lesson. Prior to a lesson in which students will be reading a story from *Aesop's Fables*, for example, you might choose to frontload the following vocabulary using a graphic organizer.

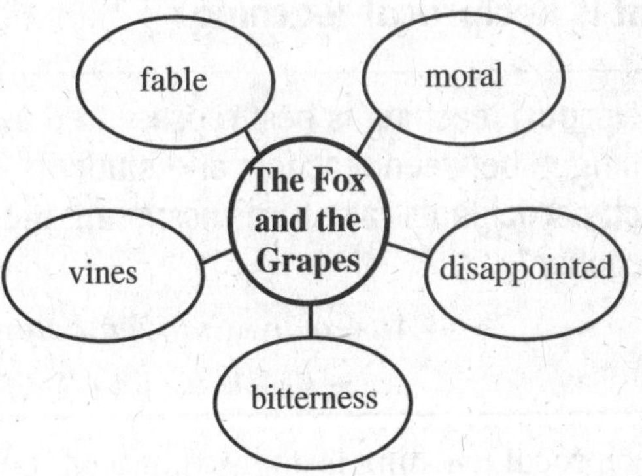

What Is Shared Reading?

Shared reading is reading that is rich with interactions between teacher and students. When using the shared reading model, the goal is to invite students to actively participate in the reading process. This is an excellent opportunity to encourage English language learners to use oral language in a relaxed and informal setting. Use an enlarged text as the central focus as you conduct a shared reading session, so that everyone in the group can clearly see the text. The basic elements of shared reading include:

✓ **Think Alouds:** Model making predictions, asking questions, and drawing conclusions about the text by thinking aloud as you read.

✓ **Guided Discussions:** Using open-ended questions, encourage students to respond to, analyze, and summarize the text.

✓ **Active Participation:** Students can contribute to the reading of the text by chorusing repetitive words or phrases or reading sight words that you point to.

✓ **Multiple Readings:** Return to the same text several times over a few days. Set a focus for each reading such as enjoyment, decoding, comprehension, or vocabulary.

What Is Reciprocal Teaching?

> **"Reciprocal teaching is best represented as a dialogue between teachers and students in which participants take turns assuming the role of teacher."**
>
> — *Annemarie Sullivan Palincsar, instructional researcher*

Reciprocal teaching is an instructional model that focuses on four key comprehension strategies: predicting, question generating, clarifying, and summarizing. First, you explain, discuss, and model the strategies. Then, while working in small groups, students gradually take responsibility for strategies while making their way through a text.

- **Predicting:** Make predictions about what an author will discuss next.
- **Question Generating:** Pose "teacher-like" questions about main ideas in the text.
- **Clarifying:** Notice potential areas of confusion and take steps to clarify them (e.g., reread, identify the definition of a word).
- **Summarizing:** Identify and recap the most important information.

Reciprocal teaching has proven to be of great help in developing the skills of English language learners. Although it can be used with a variety of text types, this technique is especially useful for deepening comprehension of expository text.

References

Cummins, Jim. *Reading Instruction and Reading Achievement Among EL Students* (Research Into Practice monograph). Glenview, IL: Pearson, 2009.

Drucker, M. J. "What Reading Teachers Should Know About ESL Learners." *The Reading Teacher,* 57(1) (2003), pp. 22–29.

Francis, D. J., et al. "Practical Guidelines for the Education of English Language Learners: Research-Based Recommendations for Instruction and Academic Interventions." Houston, TX: Center on Instruction, 2006.

Institute of Education Sciences, National Center for Educational Evaluation and Regional Assistance. "Effective Literacy and English Language Instruction for English Learners in the Elementary Grades." IES Practice Guide, 2007.

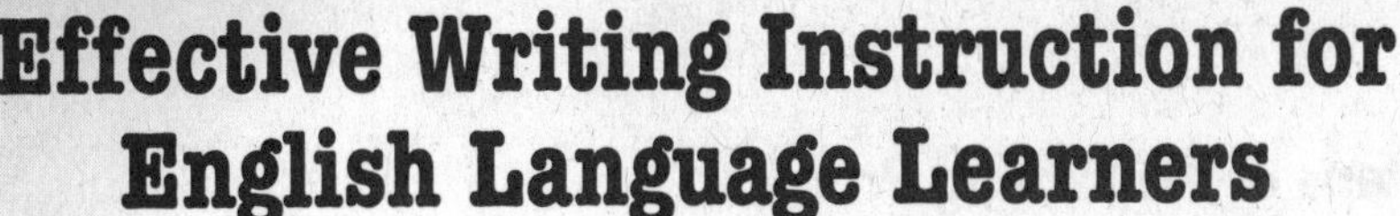

Effective Writing Instruction for English Language Learners

The Role of Writing in Language and Literacy Development

Research shows that students acquire language most readily when they are fully involved in all learning activities in the classroom. Classroom activities should integrate reading, writing, listening, and speaking, as these language skills develop interdependently. This approach supports English language development in the context of meaningful instructional content. That is, students will learn to write (in English) about real ideas and things.

Teachers can facilitate students' language learning and literacy development by ensuring that:

- students hear language in natural ways, in real and practical contexts—and write it in structured formats
- activities in which students participate regularly provide opportunities for listening and speaking so students can internalize the language
- opportunities for acquiring new vocabulary are always present in reading activities and environmental print, and are related to the content areas of the curriculum
- opportunities are always available for interesting conversations with English-speaking peers
- mistakes are accepted as part of learning
- students understand why they are being asked to complete various oral communication, reading, and writing tasks

English language learners who are already literate, or are emergent readers and writers in their home languages, no doubt have been influenced by their backgrounds and experiences with writing genres, writing styles, and cultural discourse. By learning more about the characteristics of English language learners' literacy experiences, teachers can recognize when students are transferring what they already know to their new, early literacy learning in English, and teachers can support these efforts. It is helpful to seek information about students in sensitive ways, appropriately respecting families' privacy and regarding home languages and cultures with respect.

Such efforts to find out students' strengths and needs are worthwhile. For example, teachers who compare spelling patterns between a home language and English will better understand the efforts students make to acquire and write English words. Teachers can point out the differences and similarities so that students can learn to compare the languages and develop metalinguistic understanding about how both languages work. This will help them sort out the ways they can use language in their writing.

ENGLISH	rose
SPANISH	rosa

Young English language learners also are emergent writers. For most children, the line between emergent writing and drawing (that is, art) is not a bold border. It helps learners to write in both words and pictures. Experts in English language learning advise, however, that English language learners who draw too often without writing any words are missing vital opportunities to practice writing in English. Encourage students to write about their pictures.

Scaffolding the Steps of the Writing Process

Writing, whether in a home language or especially in a new language, is the most difficult mode of language use to master (Collier and Ovando, 1998). Each English language learner has a unique background and set of experiences with language, literacy, and culture. Students access writing instruction at varying levels of English proficiency. It is important for teachers to provide each student with challenging work that is appropriate for his or her level of English proficiency and literacy.

By understanding the specific kinds of support English language learners need at each stage of the writing process, teachers can tailor their instruction to fit individual needs. The chart below provides suggestions to help you do this.

	Level I	Level II & III	Level IV & V
	Beginning (little experience in English)	**Intermediate** (conversational but not academic English)	**Advanced/ Advanced High** (gaining skills in academic English)
Prewrite	Allow extra time for prewriting. Use brainstorming. Have student draw or act out ideas. Map, or illustrate and label, words that the student needs.	Allow extra time for prewriting. Use brainstorming. Have student draw and label, or act out and describe, ideas. Help student learn and write the words he or she needs.	Allow extra time for prewriting. Use brainstorming, drawing, word mapping, and story mapping. Help student learn and write the words he or she needs.
Draft	Allow student to dictate, as appropriate. As skills emerge, student writes words and phrases. Accept phonetic invented spelling, but model correct spelling, capitalization, and punctuation.	Student writes words, phrases, and simple sentences. Help student turn phrases into sentences. Accept phonetic invented spelling, but show correct spelling, capitalization, and punctuation.	Student writes words, phrases, and simple sentences. Help student add details to sentences and create paragraphs. Accept phonetic invented spelling, but show correct spelling, capitalization, and punctuation.
Revise	With help, student revises work with the aid of a checklist that has visual clues about each task.	Student revises work with the aid of a checklist that has visual and written clues about each task. Help student incorporate written or oral commentary from teacher in revisions.	Student revises work with the aid of a checklist that has visual and written clues about each task—and asks for clarification. Help student incorporate written or oral comments from teacher in revisions.
Edit	Student sees teacher model how to correct errors and begins to correct errors.	Student corrects errors with help from the teacher.	Student corrects errors with help from the teacher and incorporates teacher's suggestions into writing.
Publish	Student creates final product of writing with teacher's guidance.	Student creates final product of writing with teacher's guidance.	Student creates final product of writing with teacher's guidance.

Structured Writing

Teachers can use **structured writing** to scaffold writing instruction. Structured writing aids include writing/sentence frames and graphic organizers, which help students record and organize their ideas.

Writing Assignments for English Language Learners

There are various kinds of assignments and activities that encourage English language learners to use their background knowledge and previous experiences to connect with the writing process. Establishing a daily or weekly **routine** for these assignments and activities helps cue students about what to expect and provides extra support for participating in classroom instruction.

Teachers can compile a **writing portfolio** to show progress and to facilitate home communication and teacher/student dialogue about writing.

Writing Products

While there are varieties of authentic writing assignments that encourage students to write about their interests and experiences, there are specific genres with which students must become familiar in order to build an understanding of text structures that reflect district and state standards/ curriculum frameworks. The following examples suggest ways to approach each genre in relation to English language learners' needs.

Language Experience Approach
Students dictate stories to the teacher (or aide), who writes them down. Students then copy the words that the teacher wrote. In this way, reading and writing become processes directly related to children's experiences. They read and write to express themselves and communicate their experiences.

Dialogue Journals
Dialogue journals develop writing skills and provide authentic communication between a student and teacher. This writing is informal and may include pictures. It allows students to choose topics for writing. The teacher may suggest topics, but the choice is the writer's. The student writes as in conversation with the teacher. The teacher responds to the content of the writing, also in a conversational manner. Writing errors are not explicitly corrected, but the teacher's writing serves as a model (Collier and Ovando, 1998).

Home Literacy Activities
Home literacy activities encourage conversation between students and their families as they read together in their home language and/or in English. If parents are not literate, students can practice reading aloud and discussing stories with them. Teachers can plan activities such as interviewing family members in the home language and then sharing the responses with the class in English.

Students learning to write will benefit from writing in their home language as well as the new language, English. Bilingual parents, staff members, and students can help children write in home languages.

Rubrics to Evaluate Writing

Teachers can use school, district, state, or national standards for English language learners (which are aligned with English Language Arts standards) to create rubrics that adjust expectations for English language learners based on their individual English proficiency levels.

The sample rubric on the following page focuses on one of the traits of good writing: rules (or conventions) of English. It describes what English language learners at various levels (beginning, intermediate, advanced, and advanced high) would be expected to write. Teachers can develop similar evaluation forms that reflect the needs of the school, the grade, and the students involved. Other examples of traits of good writing may include Focus/Ideas, Order, Writer's Voice, Word Choice, and Sentences.

Traits of Good Writing: Rules (English Language Learners)

	Level	Capitalization	Punctuation	Sentence Structure and Grammar	Spelling
Beginning (little experience in English)	1	Uses capitalization when writing one's own name.	Adds a period to the end of a sentence and a question mark to the end of a question.	Begins to use some standard word order, with mostly inconsistent grammatical forms (for example, subject/verb agreement).	Produces some independent writing that includes inconsistent spelling.
Intermediate/ Advanced (conversational but not academic English)	2–4	Uses capitalization to begin sentences and proper nouns.	Produces independent writing that may include some inconsistent use of periods and question marks.	Uses standard word order but may use inconsistent grammatical forms.	Produces independent writing that includes some misspellings.
Advanced High (gaining skills in academic English)	5	Produces independent writing with consistent use of correct capitalization.	Produces independent writing with generally consistent use of correct punctuation.	Uses complete sentences and generally correct word order.	Produces independent writing with consistent use of correct spelling.

References

August, Diane (Principal Investigator), and T. Shanahan (Panel Chair) (2006). *Developing Literacy in Second-Language Learners: Report of the National Literacy Panel on Language-Minority Children and Youth.* Mahwah, New Jersey: Lawrence Erlbaum Associates.

Collier, V. P., and C. J. Ovando (1998). *Bilingual and ESL Classrooms: Teaching in Multicultural Contexts.* Boston, MA: McGraw Hill.

Echevarria, J.; M. Vogt; and D. Short (2004). *Making Content Comprehensible for English Learners: The SIOP Model.* Boston: Allyn & Bacon.

Fillmore, L. W., and C. E. Snow (2000). "*What Teachers Need to Know About Language.*" Washington, DC: ERIC Clearinghouse on Languages and Linguistics.

English Language Learners and Assessment

Assessment Needs of Diverse Learners

Because English language learners make up a dynamic group of learners who enter school with a wide range of linguistic, cultural, and learning experiences, it is important for teachers to learn about the unique background of each individual learner. Overall, assessment can provide important information about students' learning that can be used to plan appropriate and meaningful instruction. However, the kinds of assessment, the purposes for which they are used, and how the results are evaluated can directly impact how meaningful the assessments are (Cummins, 1981).

High-stakes Testing vs. Authentic Assessment

While so-called "high-stakes" testing has become increasingly influential, high-profile tests can be difficult for English language learners because they require proficiency in academic English, understanding of grade-level subject matter, and an understanding of cultural contexts. While high-stakes test results in the United States influence instructional decisions made in schools, these results often do not reflect what English language learners know. Consequently, the instructional decisions based on test results often do not reflect the specific learning needs of English language learners (Bielenberg and Fillmore, 2005).

It is important to find a variety of ways to assess English language learners that show what each learner is able to do. Focusing on what students already know—and what they are learning but have not mastered—helps teachers identify specific educational needs and enables educators to build their ongoing instruction upon all the resources, experiences, and abilities that English language learners bring to school. Authentic assessment, or ongoing classroom-based (often informal) assessment of students by teachers, allows students to show their strengths. Ongoing assessment also provides teachers with an accurate, dynamic picture of how to plan instruction and provide feedback in ways that meet the changing learning needs of each student (García, 1994).

Outcome-based/norm-referenced tests are different from ongoing authentic assessment because they evaluate, or make a judgment about, the performance of a student at a given time, while authentic assessment informs both teachers and students about day-to-day learning and provides feedback about how to proceed in order to meet the needs of individual learners.

English language learners must be taught test-taking strategies and must build background about the language and procedures of test taking. Use the suggestions below when preparing English language learners, who may not be experienced with the specialized language and implications of standardized tests. (Bielenberg and Fillmore, 2005):

- Point out text structures and conceptual references used in tests.
- Point out difficult language structures, and provide sufficient practice before the test.
- Preteach basic and content-area vocabulary.
- Build background and knowledge about test taking and procedural language.

Preteach Vocabulary and Question Types

- Make a T-chart to show examples of the question types students will find on tests. Explain what the structures mean and what they ask test-takers to do.
- Make a short list of test vocabulary, phrases, and instructions found on tests—such as *choose, write, fill in the circle, less than,* and *greater than.* Illustrate what these expressions ask students to do.

English Language Learners and Assessment, continued

Example:

TEST DIRECTIONS	WHAT SHOULD I DO?
<u>Choose</u> the word that goes in the <u>blank</u>. **<u>Mark</u> your answer.** 1. Nancy rides her ____. O book O bike O store O gloves	• **Choose** = pick, decide on one • **Blank** = the line 1. Nancy rides her ____. • **Mark** = use pencil to fill in the circle

Example:

INSTRUCTIONS	WHAT SHOULD I DO?		
Find the **<u>sum</u>.**	Add numbers, + 10 + 1 = 11		
Compare the numbers using **>** , **<** , or **=**	<	less than	1 < 10
	>	greater than	9 > 2
	=	equals	3 = 3

Reading Fluency and Comprehension Assessment

Authentic assessment focuses on teachers making informed decisions based on authentic literacy tasks within the classroom context that reflect individual student's progress and learning (García, 1994). Finding ways to help English language learners develop reading fluency means finding out if students really comprehend what they read, rather than just decode words.

Student's English language proficiency levels, the kinds of literacy and learning experiences students have had, and how familiar they are with the topic of the reading passage will affect how much they struggle with understanding what they read. Literature also can be challenging for English language learners because of the use of figurative language, including metaphors, similes, and symbolism. Check students' reading comprehension and understanding of concepts such as *setting, characters, plot, beginning, middle,* and *end.*

When assessing fluency and comprehension, it is helpful for teachers to learn how students' home literacy and languages affect their learning in English. English language learners may draw on what they already know; for example, an English language learner whose home language is Spanish may use Spanish spelling patterns and/or phonetics when reading or writing words in English. Recognizing the influence of the home language, and the student's reliance upon the literacy skills and strategies he or she knows in the home language, will help teachers not only assess more accurately, but know how to point out similarities and differences between English and the home language as a way to develop awareness about how different languages are related. This helps develop metalinguistic awareness, or thinking about how language works.

Teachers must ultimately use all they know about each student's English proficiency and literacy skills in order to:

- monitor progress
- organize students in groups for effective learning
- differentiate instruction

Assessing English language learners and learning about their cultural, linguistic, and learning experiences can help teachers plan instruction that is comprehensible and challenging.

Scaffolding High-stakes Testing

While "high-stakes" testing presents various challenges for English language learners, there are various test-taking strategies that teachers can use to support students in preparing for eventual mastery of standardized testing. Showing students ways in which they can recognize test formats and decode the questions of a test will help them figure out what each question is asking them to do.

Assessment Accommodations for English Language Learners

While English language learners need time to acquire the academic language necessary to be able to practice and perform well on standardized tests in English, there are some accommodations that may support their attempts at extracting meaning from test language, questions, and passages. Accommodations for English language learners may include the following:

- Provide English language learners with extra time to complete the test.
- Allow the use of a bilingual dictionary or a picture dictionary to clarify words that may hinder comprehension.
- Read the question aloud in some cases.

References

August, D., and K. Hakuta. *Improving Schooling for Language Minority Children: A Research Agenda*. Washington, DC: National Academy Press, 1997.

Bielenberg, B., and L. W. Fillmore. "The English They Need for the Test." *Educational Leadership,* 62(4) (2004/2005), pp. 45–49.

Cummins, J. "The Role of Primary Language Development in Promoting Educational Success for Language Minority Students." *Schooling and Language Minority Students: A Theoretical Framework.* Sacramento, CA: California Department of Education, 1981.

García, G. E. "Assessing the Literacy Development of Second Language Students: A Focus on Authentic Assessment." K. Spangenbergk-Urbschat and R. Pritchard, eds. *Kids Come in All Languages: Reading Instruction for ESL Students,* pp. 180–205. Newark, DE: International Reading Association, 1994.

Scott Foresman Reading Street

Overview of Weekly Support for English Language Learners

The ELL Handbook provides weekly lesson materials to support English language learners with scaffolded and leveled comprehension and vocabulary instruction for language development. It builds on the Student Edition and on literacy instruction in the Teacher's Edition. Each strand contains a wide variety of activities that promote literacy attainment for your English language learners.

Weekly Planners offer a quick reference to the ELL support materials for each lesson of the year.

Weekly Resources Guide for English Language Learner Support

Unit 2 Week 1 Tara and Tiree, Fearless Friends

For this week's content and language objectives, see p. 59e.

This symbol indicates leveled instruction to address language proficiency levels.

Instructional Strand	Day 1	Day 2	Day 3	Day 4	Day 5
Concept Development	TEACHER'S EDITION • Concept Development, p. DI•12 • Anchored Talk, pp. 186j—186–187 • *Sing With Me* Big Book, p. 188a • Concept Talk Video ELL HANDBOOK • ELL Poster Talk, Concept Talk, p. 59c ELL POSTER 6 • Day 1 Activities	TEACHER'S EDITION • Concept Development, p. DI•12 • Anchored Talk, p. 192b • *Sing With Me* Big Book, p. 192a • Concept Talk Video ELL HANDBOOK • ELL Poster Talk, Concept Talk, p. 59c • Concept Talk Video Routine, p. 464 ELL POSTER 6 • Day 2 Activities	TEACHER'S EDITION • Concept Development, p. DI•12 • Anchored Talk, p. 208b • *Sing With Me* Big Book, p. 208a • Concept Talk Video ELL HANDBOOK • ELL Poster Talk, Concept Talk, p. 59c ELL POSTER 6 • Day 3 Activities	TEACHER'S EDITION • Concept Development, p. DI•12 • Anchored Talk, p. 212b • *Sing With Me* Big Book, p. 212a • Concept Talk Video ELL HANDBOOK • ELL Poster Talk, Concept Talk, p. 59c ELL POSTER 6 • Day 4 Activities	TEACHER'S EDITION • Concept Development, p. DI•12 • Concept Talk Video ELL HANDBOOK • ELL Poster Talk, Concept Talk, p. 59c ELL POSTER 6 • Day 5 Activities
Phonics/Phonemic Awareness	TEACHER'S EDITION • Preteach Phonemic Awareness, p. DI•13 • Preteach Phonics, p. DI•13 • Decodable Reader 6A, pp. 190b–190c	TEACHER'S EDITION • Practice Phonemic Awareness, p. DI•13 • Listen and Write Phonics, p. DI•13	ELL HANDBOOK • Phonics Transition Lesson, pp. 270, 272	TEACHER'S EDITION • Decodable Reader 6C, pp. 212e–212f ELL HANDBOOK • Phonics Transition Lesson, pp. 270, 272	TEACHER'S EDITION • Reteach Phonics, p. DI•14
Listening Comprehension	TEACHER'S EDITION • Modified Read Aloud, p. DI•15 • *Sing With Me* Big Book, p. 188a • Read Aloud, p. 191b • Concept Talk Video ELL HANDBOOK • Concept Talk Video Routine, p. 464	TEACHER'S EDITION • Modified Read Aloud, p. DI•15 • *Sing With Me* Big Book, p. 192a • AudioText of *Tara and Tiree* • Concept Talk Video ELL HANDBOOK • AudioText CD Routine, p. 464 • Story Map A, p. 470	TEACHER'S EDITION • *Sing With Me* Big Book, p. 208a • AudioText of *Tara and Tiree* • Concept Talk Video ELL HANDBOOK • AudioText CD Routine, p. 464	TEACHER'S EDITION • *Sing With Me* Big Book, p. 212a • Concept Talk Video	TEACHER'S EDITION • Concept Talk Video
Reading Comprehension	TEACHER'S EDITION • Teach Cause and Effect, p. DI•17	TEACHER'S EDITION • Teach Cause and Effect, p. DI•17 • Frontloading Reading, p. DI•18 ELL HANDBOOK • Picture It! Skill Instruction, pp. 60–60a • Multilingual Summaries, pp. 61–63	TEACHER'S EDITION • Sheltered Reading, p. DI•18 ELL HANDBOOK • Multilingual Summaries, pp. 61–63	TEACHER'S EDITION • ELL/ELD Reader Guided Reading, p. DI•19 ELL HANDBOOK • ELL Study Guide, p. 64	TEACHER'S EDITION • ELL/ELD Reader Guided Reading, p. DI•19 ELL HANDBOOK • ELL Study Guide, p. 64
Vocabulary **High-Frequency Words** **Unfamiliar Words**	TEACHER'S EDITION • High-Frequency Words, p. DI•16 • Unfamiliar Words, p. DI•14 ELL HANDBOOK • Word Cards, p. 59 • ELL Vocabulary Routine, p. 456 ELL POSTER 6 • Day 1 Activities	TEACHER'S EDITION • High-Frequency Words, p. DI•16 • Unfamiliar Words, p. DI•14 ELL HANDBOOK • Word Cards, p. 59 • Multilingual Vocabulary List, pp. 429–440 ELL POSTER 6 • Day 2 Activities	ELL HANDBOOK • High-Frequency Words Activity Bank, p. 491 ELL POSTER 6 • Day 3 Activities	ELL HANDBOOK • High-Frequency Words Activity Bank, p. 491	TEACHER'S EDITION • Unfamiliar Words, p. 216–217 ELL HANDBOOK • High-Frequency Words Activity Bank, p. 491
Grammar and Conventions	TEACHER'S EDITION • Preteach Nouns, p. DI•20	TEACHER'S EDITION • Reteach Nouns, p. DI•20	TEACHER'S EDITION • Grammar Jammer ELL HANDBOOK • Grammar Transition Lesson, pp. 312, 316, 317 • Grammar Jammer Routine, p. 465	TEACHER'S EDITION • Grammar Jammer ELL HANDBOOK • Grammar Transition Lesson, pp. 312, 316, 317	TEACHER'S EDITION • Grammar Jammer ELL HANDBOOK • Grammar Transition Lesson, pp. 312, 316, 317
Writing	TEACHER'S EDITION • Narrative Nonfiction, p. DI•21 • Introduce Narrative Nonfiction, pp. 191d–191e	TEACHER'S EDITION • Writer's Craft: Sequence, pp. 207c–207d	TEACHER'S EDITION • Let's Write It!, p. 210–211 • Writing Trait: Voice, p. 211a	TEACHER'S EDITION • Revising Strategy, pp. 215c–215d	TEACHER'S EDITION • Writer's Craft: Nouns, pp. 217h–217i

Copyright © Pearson Education, Inc., or its affiliates. All Rights Reserved. 2

59a *Tara and Tiree* Unit 2, Week 1 *ELL Handbook* *ELL Handbook* Unit 2, Week 1 *Tara and Tiree* **59b**

Weekly Planner

The daily Concept Development activities activate prior knowledge and build background, scaffold meaning, affirm identity, and develop and extend language.

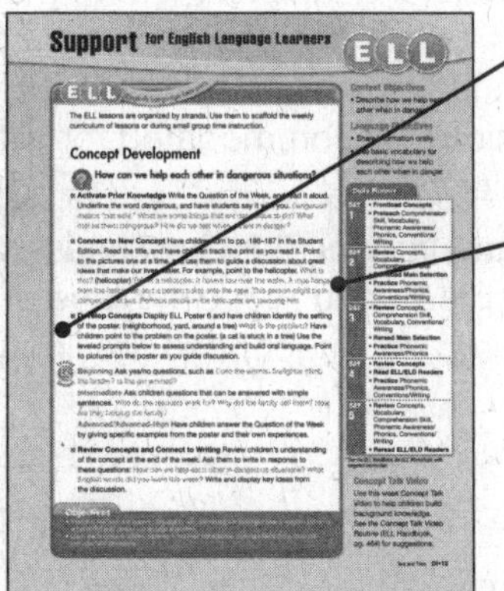

- Use the linguistically accommodated questions to reach all language proficiency levels and make personal and cultural connections that validate identity and link academic content with what children already know.
- Use the Concept Development section and the Poster in a small group prior to the core lesson to build background and scaffold meaning.

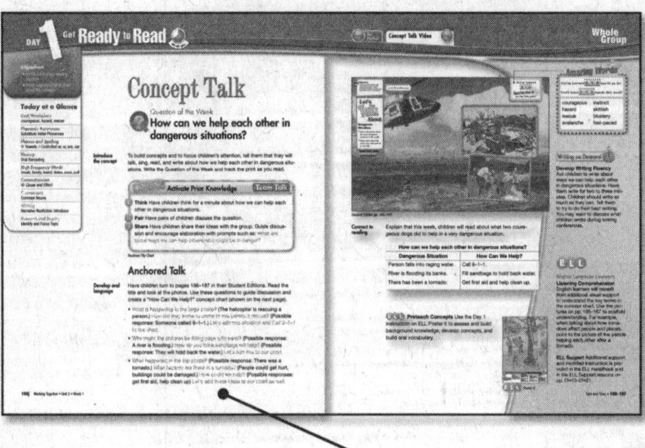

- Use the daily activities on the ELL Poster and the Anchored Talk questions in the core lesson to build concept attainment and encourage oral language development and production.

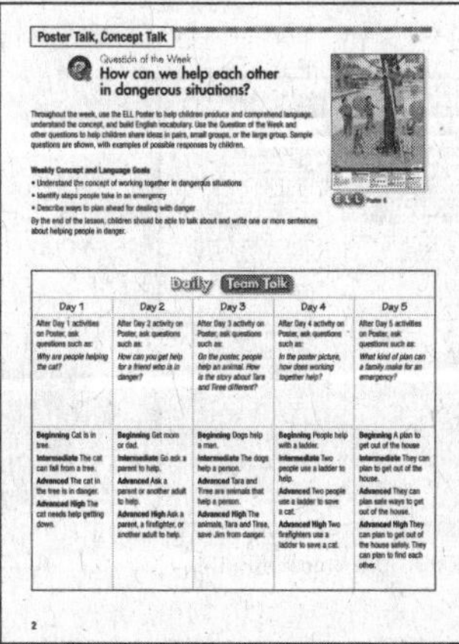

- Use the daily, leveled Poster Talk, Concept Talk in the ELL Handbook and the Team Talk activities in the core lesson to encourage oral language production.

Listening Comprehension

The adapted Read Aloud in the Listening Comprehension section of the ELL Support pages covers the same concept and information as the Read Aloud in the core curriculum.

In order for English language learners to meet grade-level learning expectations, have access to the core curriculum, and develop language, all instruction delivered in English must be linguistically accommodated for all levels of English language proficiency.

For Beginning and Intermediate levels, use the grade-appropriate adapted Read Aloud in place of the regular Read Aloud until children no longer need the linguistic support and modification.

- **First Listening: Listen to Understand** gives children a purpose for listening. The questions are designed to generate interest and help children get the gist of the adapted Read Aloud, so all proficiency levels can achieve success.
- **Second Listening: Listen to Check Understanding** Once children understand the main idea of the adapted Read Aloud, they can listen on subsequent days to clarify understanding of important details of spoken language.

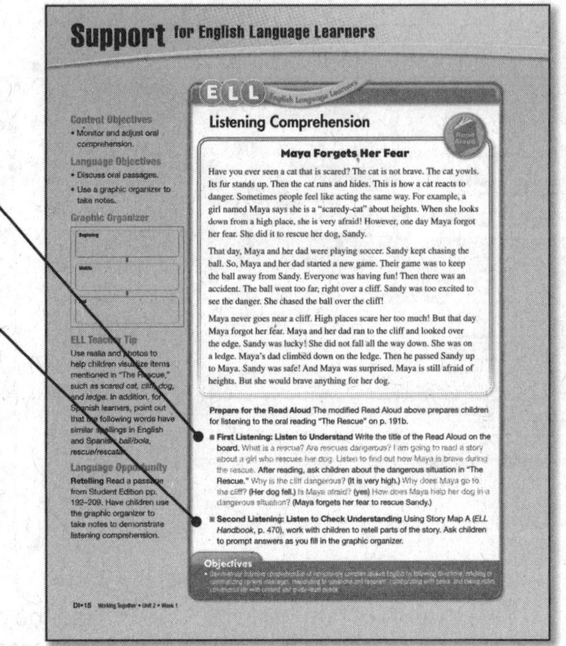

Support for English Language Learners

ELL English Language Learners

Content Objectives
- Monitor and adjust oral comprehension.

Language Objectives
- Discuss oral passages.
- Use a graphic organizer to take notes.

Graphic Organizer

ELL Teacher Tip
Use realia and photos to help children visualize items mentioned in "The Rescue," such as *scared cat, cliff, dog,* and *ledge*. In addition, for Spanish learners, point out that the following words have similar spellings in English and Spanish: *ball/bola, rescue/rescatar.*

Language Opportunity
Retelling Read a passage from Student Edition pp. 192–209. Have children use the graphic organizer to take notes to demonstrate listening comprehension.

Listening Comprehension

Maya Forgets Her Fear

Have you ever seen a cat that is scared? The cat is not brave. The cat yowls. Its fur stands up. Then the cat runs and hides. This is how a cat reacts to danger. Sometimes people feel like acting the same way. For example, a girl named Maya says she is a "scaredy-cat" about heights. When she looks down from a high place, she is very afraid! However, one day Maya forgot her fear. She did it to rescue her dog, Sandy.

That day, Maya and her dad were playing soccer. Sandy kept chasing the ball. So, Maya and her dad started a new game. Their game was to keep the ball away from Sandy. Everyone was having fun! Then there was an accident. The ball went too far, right over a cliff. Sandy was too excited to see the danger. She chased the ball over the cliff!

Maya never goes near a cliff. High places scare her too much! But that day Maya forgot her fear. Maya and her dad ran to the cliff and looked over the edge. Sandy was lucky! She did not fall all the way down. She was on a ledge. Maya's dad climbed down on the ledge. Then he passed Sandy up to Maya. Sandy was safe! And Maya was surprised. Maya is still afraid of heights. But she would brave anything for her dog.

Prepare for the Read Aloud The modified Read Aloud above prepares children for listening to the oral reading "The Rescue" on p. 191b.

- **First Listening: Listen to Understand** Write the title of the Read Aloud on the board. What is a *rescue*? Are *rescues* dangerous? I am going to read a story about a girl who rescues her dog. Listen to find out how Maya is brave during the rescue. **After reading, ask children about the dangerous situation in "The Rescue."** Why is the cliff dangerous? **(It is very high.)** Why does Maya go to the cliff? **(Her dog fell.)** Is Maya afraid? **(yes)** How does Maya help her dog in a dangerous situation? **(Maya forgets her fear to rescue Sandy.)**
- **Second Listening: Listen to Check Understanding** Using Story Map A (*ELL Handbook*, p. 470), work with children to retell parts of the story. Ask children to prompt answers as you fill in the graphic organizer.

Objectives

DI•15 Working Together • Unit 2 • Week 1

Additional Products

Sing with Me Big Book

Concept Talk Video

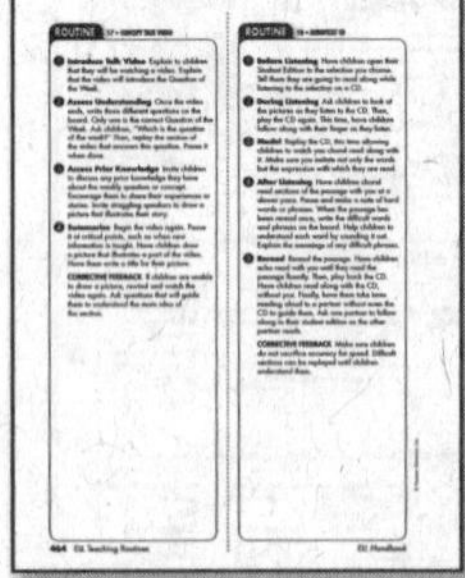
Concept Talk Video Routine

AudioText CD

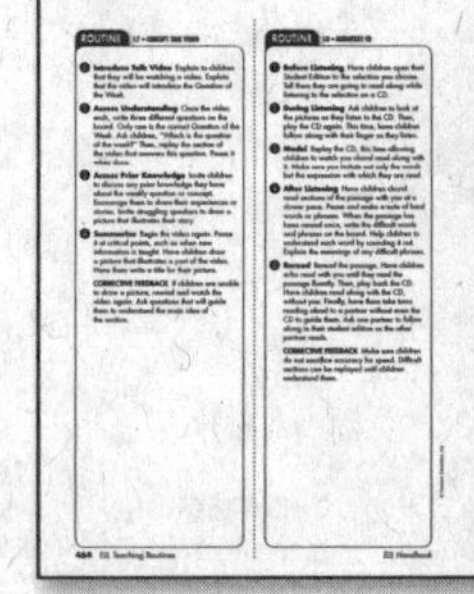
AudioText Routine

Discrete language skills that English language learners need include knowledge of the letters of the alphabet, familiarity with the sounds represented by letters, the ability to decode words, and the rules and conventions of how words are formed.

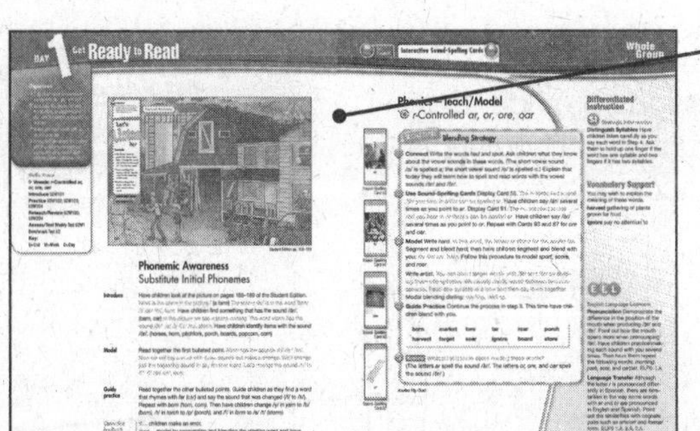

- The Let's Listen for Sounds illustration provides visual support and scaffolds meaning for the core phonemic awareness lesson.

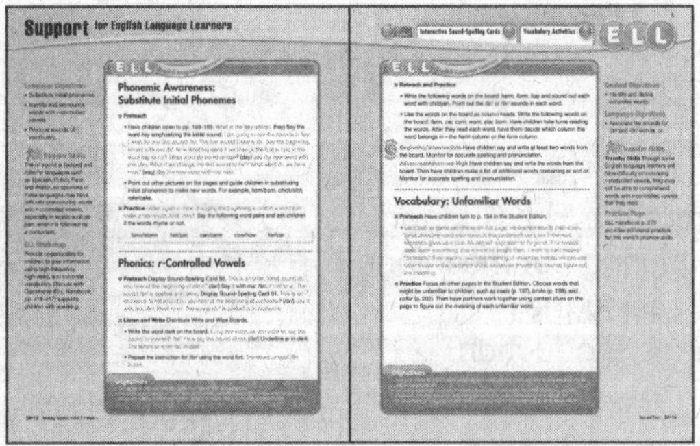

- The Phonics and Phonemic Awareness support lessons work along with the core lessons to help children learn these skills at the same time they are developing basic English vocabulary.

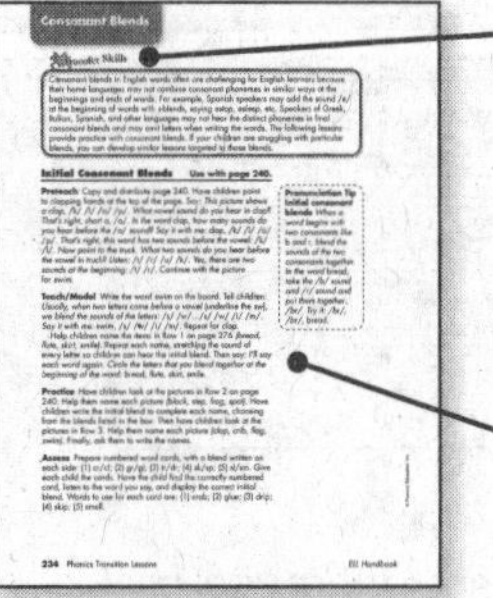

- Language Transfer Notes activate prior knowledge about a phonics or phonemic awareness skill and affirm children's identity.
- The flexible bank of Phonics Transitions Lessons provides practice for developing and internalizing language at all proficiency levels.

- The Decodable Readers help children internalize language by providing additional practice with phonics skills in context.
- Differentiate instruction to meet the needs of all teachers using the leveled support notes in the core Teacher's Edition.

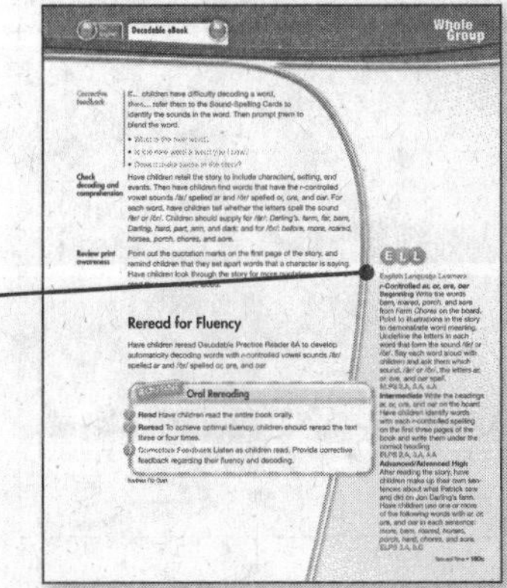

Vocabulary

English learners need explicit and systematic instruction to acquire both social and academic language for literacy attainment. Children need multiple exposures to new vocabulary through frequent listening, reading, writing, and oral language activities.

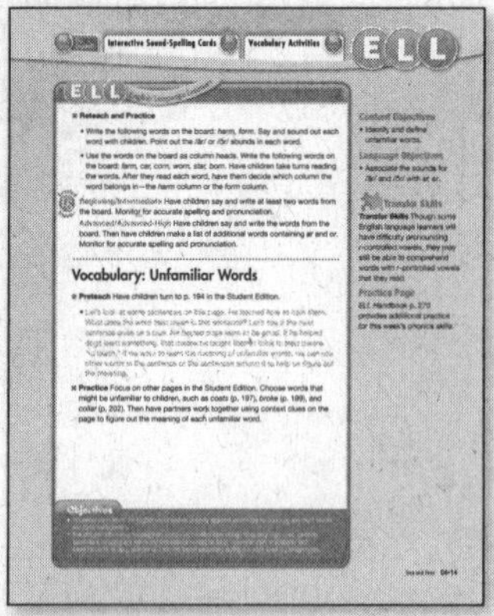

- Vocabulary activities in the ELL Support pages and in the core lessons provide ideas for giving visual, contextual, and linguistic support so children can access grade-level lesson vocabulary.

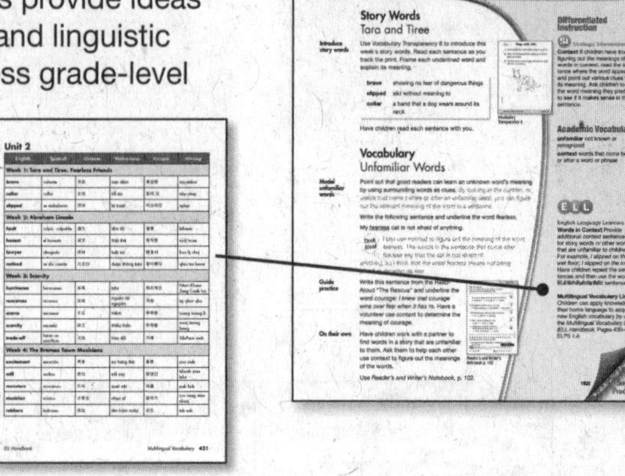

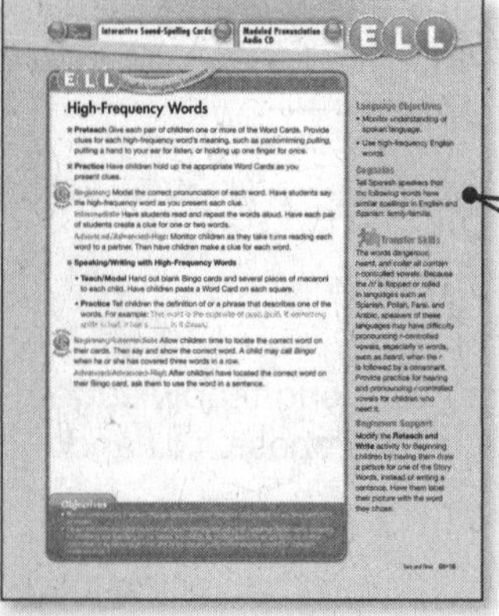

- Vocabulary Skill lessons from the ELL Support pages engage children in figuring out meanings of new words, thereby increasing their comprehension and language production.

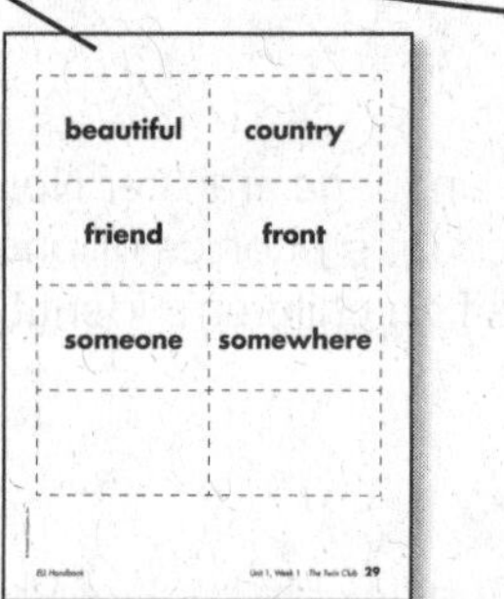

beautiful	country
friend	front
someone	somewhere

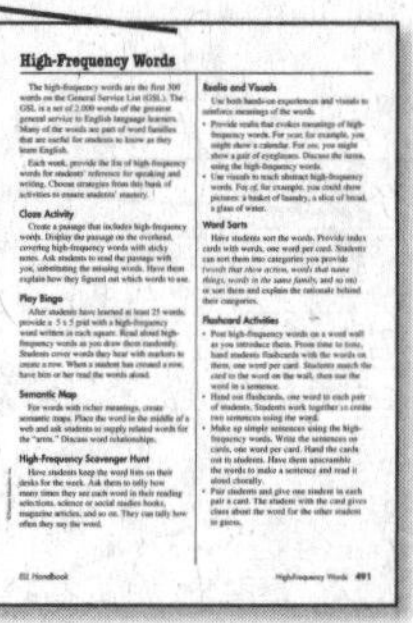

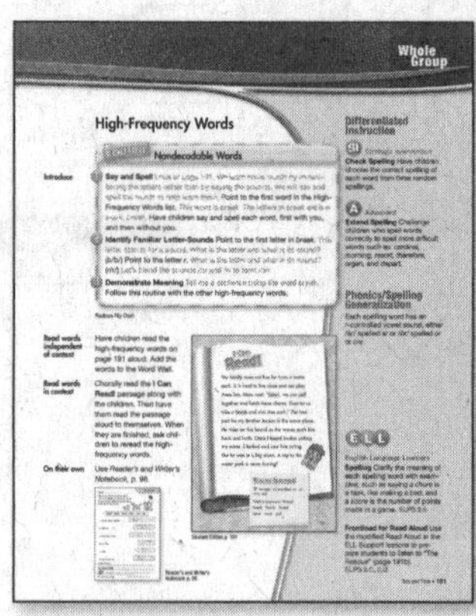

- Daily activities in the Poster increase oral and written production of newly acquired vocabulary.
- The Poster Talk, Concept Talk provides leveled support to meet the needs of all students.

Engaging activities in the core lessons, the ELL Handbook, and the three Comprehension sections of the ELL Support lessons activate prior knowledge, build background, scaffold meaning, affirm identity, and develop and extend language.

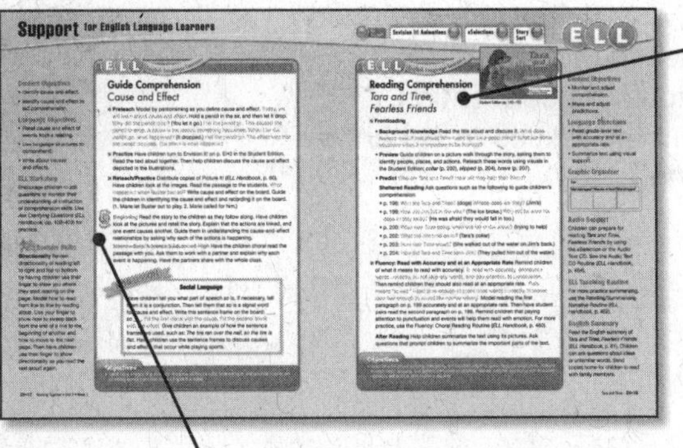

- Comprehension activities provide questions that encourage children to use oral language during reading to demonstrate understanding of text and to employ inferential skills.

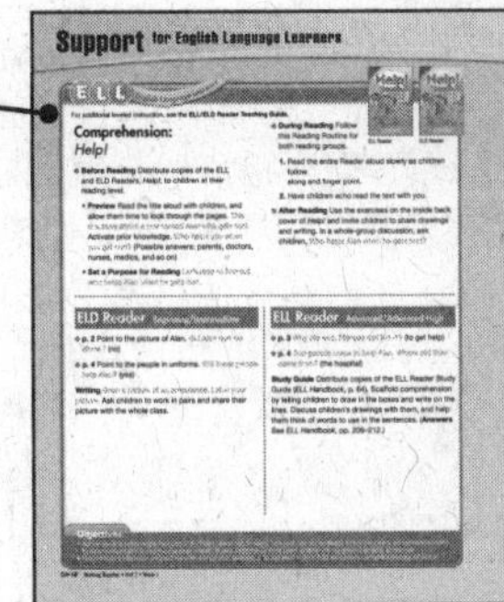

- The leveled notes in the ELL Support and Picture It! instruction pages provide ideas for differentiating instruction at all proficiency levels.

- The ELD Readers are written for Beginning and Intermediate language proficiency levels, and the ELL Readers are designed for Advanced to Advanced High levels, allowing you to meet the needs of a diverse classroom.

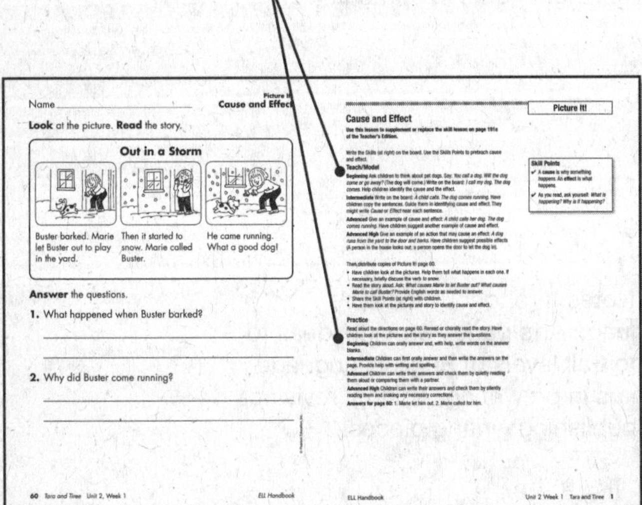

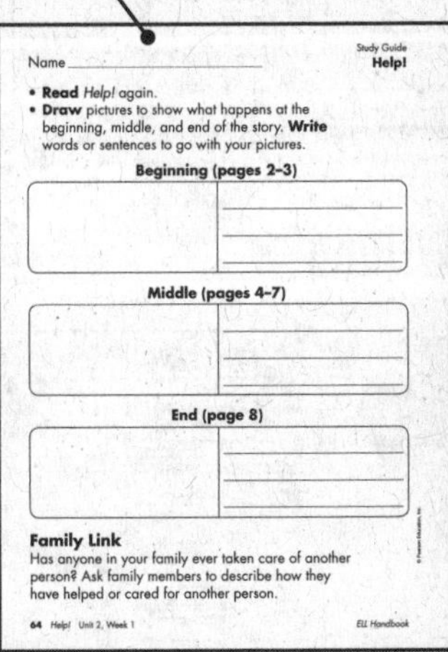

Additional Products

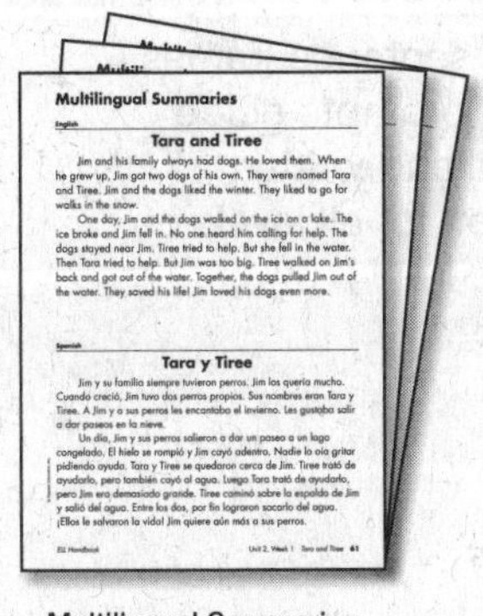

Multilingual Summaries

AudioText CD

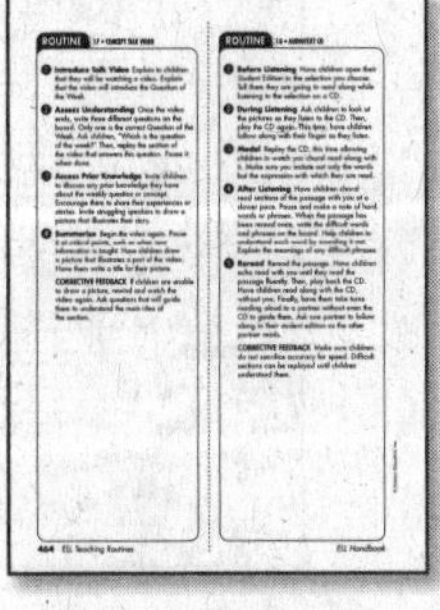

AudioText CD Routine

Language Arts

The Grammar and Conventions and Writing lessons provide the systematic instruction that children need at each language proficiency level to scaffold use of increasingly complex grammatical structures in content area reading and writing.

Grammar and Conventions

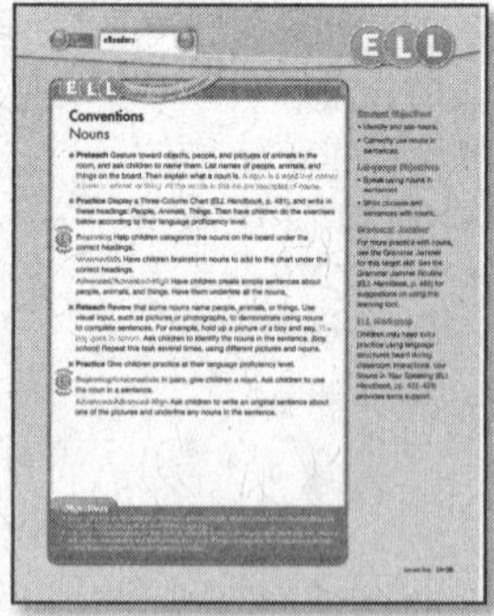

- The interactive activities are designed so children reuse the language related to each core convention, using different modalities to enhance understanding.

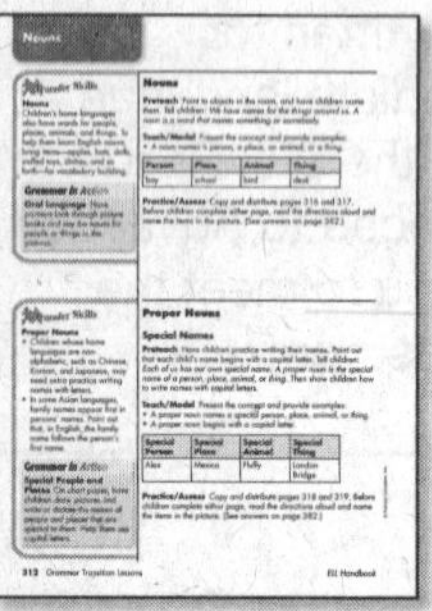

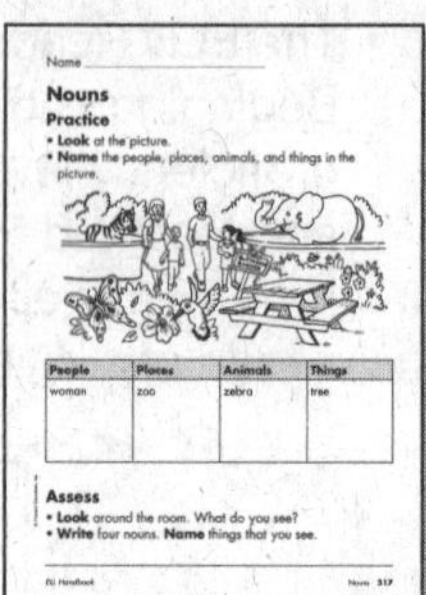

- The flexible bank of Grammar Transition Lessons leads children in transferring knowledge from their home languages to English and guides language development.

Writing

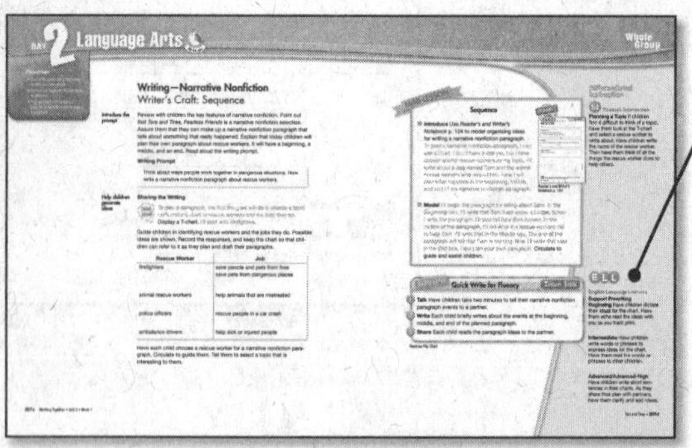

- ELL Notes throughout the core Language Arts pages provide ideas to support all levels of English language learners in prewriting, editing, revising, and publishing writing pieces.

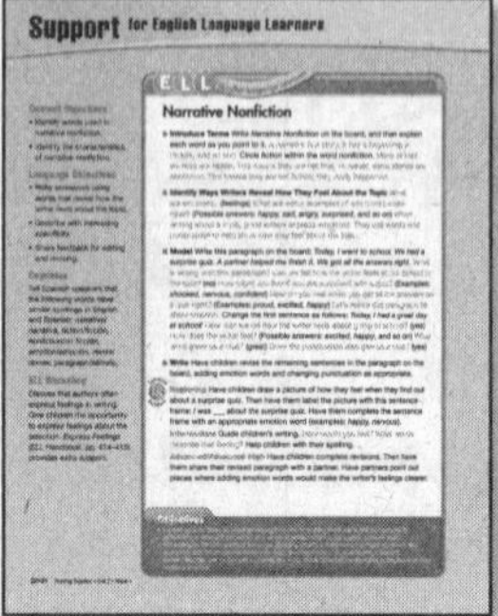

- The writing model, sentence frames, and leveled writing prompts guide and encourage oral and written language production for all levels of English proficiency.

Concept Talk Video

- Use the Concept Talk Video to activate an engaging discussion about the weekly concept. Use the Concept Talk Video Routine found in the ELL Handbook to guide students' understanding.

AudioText CD

- Children can build fluency and comprehension and prepare for reading the main selection by using the AudioText CD and the AudioText CD Routine.

Grammar Jammer

- Use the Grammar Jammer for additional practice with the target skill. For suggestions on how to use this learning tool, see the Grammar Jammer Routine in the ELL Handbook.

Sing with Me Big Book

- Use the *Sing with Me* Big Book to build and reinforce children's concept and language attainment.

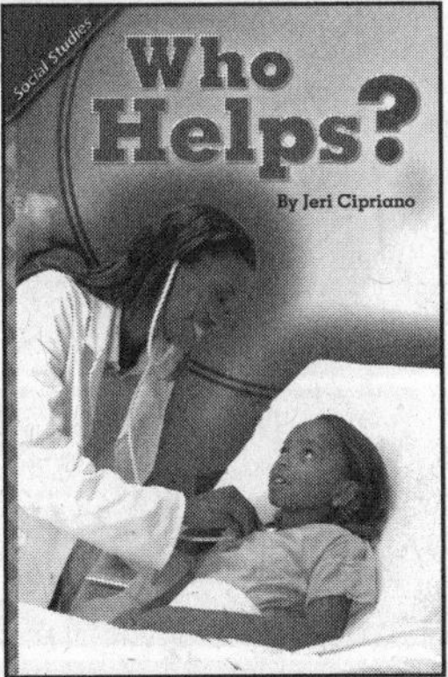

Concept Literacy Reader

- Use the Concept Literacy Reader for additional support to develop the weekly concept.

Sound Spelling Cards

- Provide visual support and scaffold meaning for the weekly phonics skill.

Part 2
English Language Support

Contents

Weekly Resources Guide for English Language Learner Support

For this week's content and language objectives, see p. 29e.

Instructional Strand	Day 1	Day 2
Concept Development	TEACHER'S EDITION • Concept Development, p. DI•12 • Anchored Talk, pp. 20j—20–21 • *Sing With Me* Big Book, p. 22a • Concept Talk Video ELL HANDBOOK • ELL Poster Talk, Concept Talk, p. 29c ELL POSTER 1 • Day 1 Activities	TEACHER'S EDITION • Concept Development, p. DI•12 • Anchored Talk, p. 26b • *Sing With Me* Big Book, p. 26a • Concept Talk Video ELL HANDBOOK • ELL Poster Talk, Concept Talk, p. 29c • Concept Talk Video Routine, p. 464 ELL POSTER 1 • Day 2 Activities
Phonics/Phonemic Awareness	TEACHER'S EDITION • Preteach Phonemic Awareness, p. DI•13 • Preteach Phonics, p. DI•13 • Decodable Reader 1A, pp. 24b–24c	TEACHER'S EDITION • Practice Phonemic Awareness, p. DI•13 • Listen and Write Phonics, p. DI•13
Listening Comprehension	TEACHER'S EDITION • Modified Read Aloud, p. DI•15 • *Sing With Me* Big Book, p. 22a • Read Aloud, p. 25b • Concept Talk Video ELL HANDBOOK • Concept Talk Video Routine, p. 464	TEACHER'S EDITION • Modified Read Aloud, p. DI•15 • *Sing With Me* Big Book, p. 26a • AudioText of *The Twin Club* • Concept Talk Video ELL HANDBOOK • AudioText CD Routine, p. 464 • Story Map B, p. 471
Reading Comprehension	TEACHER'S EDITION • Teach Character and Setting, p. DI•17	TEACHER'S EDITION • Teach Character and Setting, p. DI•17 • Frontloading Reading, p. DI•18 ELL HANDBOOK • Picture It! Skill Instruction, pp. 30–30a • Multilingual Summaries, pp. 31–33
Vocabulary **High-Frequency Words** **Alphabetize**	TEACHER'S EDITION • High-Frequency Words, p. DI•16 • Alphabetize, p. DI•14 ELL HANDBOOK • Word Cards, p. 29 • ELL Vocabulary Routine, p. 456 ELL POSTER 1 • Day 1 Activities	TEACHER'S EDITION • High-Frequency Words, p. DI•16 • Alphabetize, p. DI•14 ELL HANDBOOK • Word Cards, p. 29 • Multilingual Vocabulary List, pp. 429–440 ELL POSTER 1 • Day 2 Activities
Grammar and Conventions	TEACHER'S EDITION • Preteach Sentences, p. DI•20	TEACHER'S EDITION • Reteach Sentences, p. DI•20
Writing	TEACHER'S EDITION • Personal Narrative, p. DI•21 • Introduce Personal Narrative, pp. 25d–25e	TEACHER'S EDITION • Writer's Craft: Descriptive Language, pp. 43d–43e

This symbol indicates leveled instruction to address language proficiency levels.

Day 3	Day 4	Day 5
TEACHER'S EDITION • Concept Development, p. DI•12 • Anchored Talk, p. 44b • *Sing With Me* Big Book, p. 44a • Concept Talk Video ELL HANDBOOK • ELL Poster Talk, Concept Talk, p. 29c ELL POSTER 1 • Day 3 Activities	TEACHER'S EDITION • Concept Development, p. DI•12 • Anchored Talk, p. 48b • *Sing With Me* Big Book, p. 48a • Concept Talk Video ELL HANDBOOK • ELL Poster Talk, Concept Talk, p. 29c ELL POSTER 1 • Day 4 Activities	TEACHER'S EDITION • Concept Development, p. DI•12 • Concept Talk Video ELL HANDBOOK • ELL Poster Talk, Concept Talk, p. 29c ELL POSTER 1 • Day 5 Activities
ELL HANDBOOK • Phonics Transition Lesson, pp. 246–248, 251	TEACHER'S EDITION • Decodable Reader 1C, pp. 48e–48f ELL HANDBOOK • Phonics Transition Lesson, pp. 246–248, 251	TEACHER'S EDITION • Reteach Phonics, p. DI•14
TEACHER'S EDITION • *Sing With Me* Big Book, p. 44a • AudioText of *The Twin Club* • Concept Talk Video ELL HANDBOOK • AudioText CD Routine, p. 464	TEACHER'S EDITION • *Sing With Me* Big Book, p. 48a • Concept Talk Video	TEACHER'S EDITION • Concept Talk Video
TEACHER'S EDITION • Sheltered Reading, p. DI•18 ELL HANDBOOK • Multilingual Summaries, pp. 31–33	TEACHER'S EDITION • ELL/ELD Reader Guided Reading, p. DI•19 ELL HANDBOOK • ELL Study Guide, p. 34	TEACHER'S EDITION • ELL/ELD Reader Guided Reading, p. DI•19 ELL HANDBOOK • ELL Study Guide, p. 34
ELL HANDBOOK • High-Frequency Words Activity Bank, p. 491 ELL POSTER 1 • Day 3 Activities	ELL HANDBOOK • High-Frequency Words Activity Bank, p. 491	TEACHER'S EDITION • Alphabetize, p. 50–51 ELL HANDBOOK • High-Frequency Words Activity Bank, p. 491
TEACHER'S EDITION • Grammar Jammer ELL HANDBOOK • Grammar Transition Lesson, pp. 344–346, 351–357 • Grammar Jammer Routine, p. 465	TEACHER'S EDITION • Grammar Jammer ELL HANDBOOK • Grammar Transition Lesson, pp. 344–346, 351–357	TEACHER'S EDITION • Grammar Jammer ELL HANDBOOK • Grammar Transition Lesson, pp. 344–346, 351–357
TEACHER'S EDITION • Let's Write It!, p. 46–47 • Writing Trait: Sentences, p. 47a	TEACHER'S EDITION • Revising Strategy, pp. 49d–49e	TEACHER'S EDITION • Writing Trait: Conventions, pp. 51h–51i • ELL Vocabulary Routine, p. 456

Poster Talk, Concept Talk

Question of the Week

What can we learn by exploring different communities?

ELL Poster 1

Throughout the week, use the ELL Poster to help children produce and comprehend language, understand the concept, and build English vocabulary. Use the Question of the Week and other questions to help children share ideas in pairs, small groups, or the large group. Sample questions are shown, with examples of possible responses by children.

Weekly Concept and Language Goals

- Know that communities can be different
- Identify what the city and the country are like
- Describe their own communities

By the end of the lesson, children should be able to talk about and write one or more sentences about life in the city and in the country.

Daily Team Talk

Day 1	Day 2	Day 3	Day 4	Day 5
After Day 1 activities on Poster, ask questions such as *What kind of community does this picture show?*	After Day 2 activity on Poster, ask questions such as *How is an urban community different from a rural community?*	After Day 3 activity on Poster, ask questions such as *In* The Twin Club, *Juan lives on a farm. How is his community like yours? How is it different?*	After Day 4 activity on Poster, ask questions such as *In the poster picture, we see a busy city street. What sounds will you hear in this urban community?*	After Day 5 activity on Poster, ask questions such as *What things do you see and hear in your community?*
Beginning A city. **Intermediate** It shows a city. **Advanced** It shows a city or urban community. **Advanced High** It shows a busy city street in an urban community.	**Beginning** Many people. **Intermediate** There are lots of people. **Advanced** An urban community has big buildings and lots of people. A rural community has farms. **Advanced High** An urban community has bigger buildings and more people than a rural community.	**Beginning** More people. **Intermediate** My community has more people. **Advanced** Juan's community has barns and farm animals. My community has tall buildings and pets. **Advanced High** My community is more urban because it has more people and tall buildings.	**Beginning** Cars, people. **Intermediate** Cars, people, and animals. **Advanced** We will hear cars, people, and dogs. **Advanced High** We will hear the sounds of cars beeping, people talking, and dogs barking.	**Beginning** People and animals. **Intermediate** I see people, bugs, animals. **Advanced** I see people and hear crickets. **Advanced High** I see children playing in the park and hear people talking.

This Week's Materials

Teacher's Edition pages 20j–51k

See the support for English language learners throughout the lesson, including ELL strategies and scaffold activities at points of use.

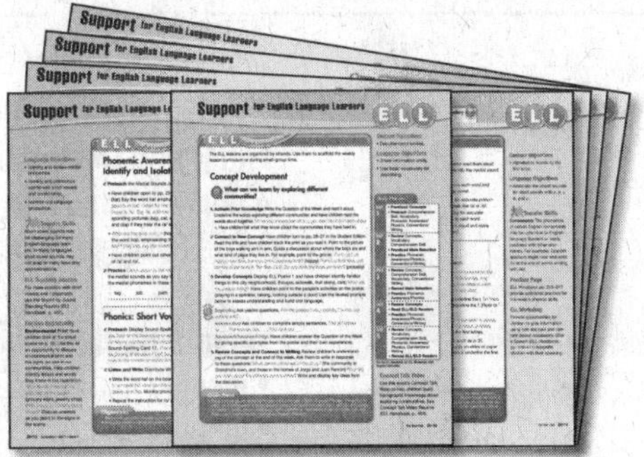

Teacher's Edition pages DI•12–DI•21

Differentiated Instruction for English language learners provides daily group activities that "frontload," or preteach, core instruction.

ELL Handbook pp. 29a–34

Find additional lesson materials that support the core lesson and the ELL instructional pages.

ELL Poster 1

ELD Reader 2.1.1

ELL Reader 2.1.1

Concept Literacy Reader

ELD, ELL Reader Teaching Guide

Concept Literacy Reader Teaching Guide

Technology

Online Teacher's Edition Use the digital version of the core teacher's edition for planning and instruction.

eReaders
This Week's ELL and ELD Readers and Concept Literacy Reader are also available in digital format.

This Week's Content and Language Objectives by Strand

Concept Development What can we learn by exploring different communities?	**Content Objective** • Describe how communities are different. **Language Objectives** • Share information orally. • Use basic vocabulary for describing.
Phonics/Phonemic Awareness Short Vowels and Consonants; Identify and Isolate Medial Phonemes	**Language Objectives** • Identify and isolate medial phonemes. • Identify and pronounce words with short vowels and consonants. • Monitor oral language production.
Listening Comprehension Modified Read Aloud: "Making Friends"	**Content Objective** • Monitor and adjust oral comprehension. **Language Objectives** • Discuss oral passages. • Use a graphic organizer to take notes.
Reading Comprehension Character and Setting	**Content Objectives** • Identify character and setting. • Explain how characters and setting influence a story. **Language Objectives** • Discuss details of a story setting. • Describe character traits. • Write about characters and setting.
Vocabulary High-Frequency Words	**Language Objectives** • Understand and use basic vocabulary. • Internalize new basic vocabulary through writing.
Vocabulary Alphabetize	**Content Objective** • Alphabetize words by the first letter. **Language Objective** • Associate the vowel sounds for short vowels with *a, e, i, o,* and *u.*
Grammar and Conventions Sentences	**Content Objectives** • Write sentences correctly. • Edit writing for usage. **Language Objective** • Speak in complete sentences.
Writing Personal Narrative	**Content Objectives** • Identify complete sentences that contain correct capitalization and punctuation. • Identify the characteristics of personal narrative. **Language Objectives** • Write complete sentences with correct capitalization and punctuation. • Share feedback for editing and revising.

Word Cards for Vocabulary Activities

beautiful	country
friend	front
someone	somewhere

Teacher Note: Beginning Teach two to three words. **Intermediate** Teach three to four words. **Advanced** Teach five to six words. **Advanced High** Teach all words.

Name ______________________________

Picture It!
Character and Setting

Look at the pictures. **Read** the story.

A New Home

Lin is unhappy. She and her family have a new home. She misses her home in China.

Lin meets a new friend. Her name is Elisa. Elisa invites Lin for a bike ride.

The two girls explore on bikes. Lin is now happy!

Answer the questions below.

1. Who is the story about?

o two men o Lin's parents o Lin

2. What is Elisa like?

o friendly o not nice o unhappy

3. Talk about the setting of the story. Where does the story happen?

Character and Setting

Use this lesson to supplement or replace the skill lesson on page 25a of the Teacher's Edition. Display the Skill Points (at right) and share them with children.

Skill Points

✔ A **character** is a person or animal in a story. The author tells you what characters are like, what they think, and what they say and do.

✔ The **setting** is where and when a story takes place. The setting can be a real place or an imaginary one.

Use the Skill Points to preteach character and setting.

Teach/Model

Review a familiar story such as *Goldilocks and the Three Bears.*

Beginning Point to pictures of the characters as you ask: *Who is this?* (Goldilocks) *Goldilocks is a character.* Guide children to identify other characters in the story. Repeat this process with setting.

Intermediate Display the following and read aloud: *Three bears walk in the woods. A girl goes into their home.* Guide children in drawing circles around the words for the story's characters and boxes around the words for the story's settings.

Advanced Give an example of a character and setting: *Goldilocks goes into the three bears' house.* Have children identify the characters and settings of other familiar stories.

Advanced High Say: *Look at what characters say, think, and do.* Have children suggest words that tell about Goldilocks. List the words on the board. Have children copy and complete this sentence frame with one of the words: *Goldilocks is* ___. Continue by asking children to suggest words that describe the setting.

Then distribute copies of Picture It! page 30.

- Have children look at the pictures and tell what is happening in each one.
- Read the story aloud. Ask: *What character is the story about? Why is she unhappy? Who else is in the story?*
- Review the Skill Points with children.
- Have children look at the pictures and words to identify the characters and setting of the story.

Practice

Read aloud the directions on page 30. Reread or chorally read the story. Have children look at the pictures and the story as they answer the questions.

Beginning Children can orally answer and, with help, mark the correct answers.

Intermediate Children can first orally answer and then mark the answers on the page. Provide help with writing and spelling.

Advanced Children can mark their answers and check them by quietly reading them aloud or comparing them with a partner's.

Advanced High Children can mark their answers and check them by silently reading them and making any necessary corrections.

Answers for page 30: 1. Lin; 2. friendly; 3. Possible answers: It takes place in front of Lin's new home. It takes place on the street where Lin lives.

Multilingual Summaries

English

The Twin Club

Someone called Jorge and me twins. We are cousins and best friends. We stayed all summer with Grandma. We started the Twin Club. We promised to always be friends. Grandma told us it was time to go home. We would not be together. Being home was good, but I thought about the Twin Club. Jorge sent me an e-mail message. We remembered what we liked about our homes.

We changed our names to The Amazing E-mail Twins. We write to each other about everything. We made plans for next summer at Grandma's house.

Spanish

El club de los gemelos

Algunas personas nos llaman gemelos a Jorge y a mí. Somos primos y los mejores amigos. Nosotros nos quedamos con Abuela durante el verano. Fundamos el club de los gemelos. Prometimos ser siempre amigos.

Abuela nos dijo que era tiempo de ir a casa. Ya no estaríamos juntos. Yo pensaba en nuestro Club de los a Gemelos. Jorge me envió un mensaje por e-mail. Ambos recordamos lo que nos gusta de nuestros hogares.

Cambiamos nuestros nombres y nos hacemos llamar Los Sorprendentes Gemelos de E-mail. Cada uno le escribe al otro acerca de todo. Ya hicimos planes para el próximo verano en la casa de Abuela.

Multilingual Summaries

Chinese

雙人組

有人說喬治和我是雙胞胎， 但我們並不是雙胞胎。 我們是堂兄弟，也是最好的朋友。 我們整個夏天都待在奶奶家。 我們成立了「雙人組」。我們說好要永遠做好朋友。

奶奶說我們該回家了。 我們不能在一起玩了。我想到了「雙人組」的事。 喬治寄了一封電子郵件給我。 我們都記得我們喜歡家的哪些地方。

我們把我們的名字改成了「超炫電子郵件雙人組」。 我們使用電子郵件來互相分享所有的事情。 我們已經想好明年夏天要在奶奶家做哪些事情了。

Vietnamese

Câu Lạc Bộ Sanh Đôi

Vài người gọi Jorge và tôi là anh em sanh đôi. Chúng tôi không phải sanh đôi. Chúng tôi chỉ là họ hàng và bạn thân. Chúng tôi ở chung trong suốt mùa hè với Bà. Chúng tôi mở Câu Lạc Bộ Sanh Đôi. Chúng tôi hứa với nhau lúc nào cũng là bạn.

Bà cho chúng tôi biết đã đến lúc phải trở về nhà. Chúng tôi không thể ở chung với nhau nữa. Tôi nghĩ về Câu Lạc Bộ Sanh Đôi. Jorge gởi điện thơ cho tôi. Cả hai chúng tôi nhớ lại những gì chúng tôi thích về gia đình mình.

Chúng tôi đổi tên lại là Đôi Điện Thơ Kỳ Lạ. Chúng tôi viết cho nhau về tất cả mọi việc. Chúng tôi đặt kế hoạch cho mùa hè năm sau tại nhà của Bà.

Multilingual Summaries

Korean

쌍둥이 클럽

호르헤라는 아이와 나는 마치 쌍둥이와 같다. 우리는 진짜 쌍둥이는 아니다. 우리는 사촌이고 제일 친한 친구이다. 우리는 온 여름을 할머니 댁에서 함께 보냈다. 그리고 쌍둥이 클럽을 만들었다. 우리는 항상 친구가 되자고 약속했다.

할머니가 이제 집에 갈 시간이라고 말씀하셨다. 그러면 함께 지내지 못하게 될 것이다. 나는 쌍둥이 클럽에 대해 생각했다. 호르헤가 내게 이메일로 편지를 보냈다. 우리는 둘 다 각자의 집에서 좋았던 점들을 떠올렸다.

우리는 클럽의 이름을 '위대한 이메일 쌍둥이'로 바꾸었다. 우리는 서로에게 거의 모든 것에 대해 알려준다. 우리는 할머니 댁에서 보낼 내년 여름 계획을 짰다.

Hmong

Koom Huam Me Nyuam Ntxaib

Muaj neeg hu Jorge thiab kuv ua me nyuam ntxaib. Wb tsis yog me nyuam ntxaib. Wb yog kwv tij thiab phooj ywg zoo xwb. Peb nrog niam Pog nyob tas lub caij ntuj sov. Peb pib lub koom haum Me Nyuam Ntxaib. Peb cog lus tseg hais tias peb yuav ua phooj ywg mus tas li.

Niam Pog hais rau peb hais tias txog caij mus tseg lawm. Peb yuav tsis tau ua ke ntxiv lawm. Kuv xav txog lub koom haum Me Nyuam Ntxaib. Jorge xa ib daim E-mail tuaj rau kuv. Wb ob leeg nco ntsoov txog hais tias nyob tom tsev nws zoo licas.

Wb hloov peb cov npe mus rau The Amazing E-mail Twins. Peb sib sau ntawv hais txog txhua yam. Peb npaj tswv yim txog qhov peb yuav rov mus nyob tom niam Pog tsev rau lwm lub caij ntuj sov.

Name ______________________ **Off to School We Go!**

- **Read** *Off to School We Go!* again.
- **Label** the things the boy and his mother see as they walk to school.
- **Label** the things the girl and her father see as they walk to school.

Family Link

Have family members describe what they see as they go to school or work in the morning.

Weekly Resources Guide for English Language Learner Support

For this week's content and language objectives, see p. 35e.

Instructional Strand	Day 1	Day 2
Concept Development	TEACHER'S EDITION • Concept Development, p. DI•33 • Anchored Talk, pp. 52j—52–53 • *Sing With Me* Big Book, p. 54a • Concept Talk Video ELL HANDBOOK • ELL Poster Talk, Concept Talk, p. 35c ELL POSTER 2 • Day 1 Activities	TEACHER'S EDITION • Concept Development, p. DI•33 • Anchored Talk, p. 58b • *Sing With Me* Big Book, p. 58a • Concept Talk Video ELL HANDBOOK • ELL Poster Talk, Concept Talk, p. 35c • Concept Talk Video Routine, p. 464 ELL POSTER 2 • Day 2 Activities
Phonics/Phonemic Awareness	TEACHER'S EDITION • Preteach Phonemic Awareness, p. DI•34 • Preteach Phonics, p. DI•34 • Decodable Reader 2A, pp. 56b–56c	TEACHER'S EDITION • Practice Phonemic Awareness, p. DI•34 • Listen and Write Phonics, p. DI•34
Listening Comprehension	TEACHER'S EDITION • Modified Read Aloud, p. DI•36 • *Sing With Me* Big Book, p. 54a • Read Aloud, p. 57b • Concept Talk Video ELL HANDBOOK • Concept Talk Video Routine, p. 464	TEACHER'S EDITION • Modified Read Aloud, p. DI•36 • *Sing With Me* Big Book, p. 58a • AudioText of *Exploring Space* • Concept Talk Video ELL HANDBOOK • AudioText CD Routine, p. 464 • Problem and Solution, p. 477
Reading Comprehension	TEACHER'S EDITION • Teach Main Idea and Details, p. DI•38	TEACHER'S EDITION • Teach Main Idea and Details, p. DI•38 • Frontloading Reading, p. DI•39 ELL HANDBOOK • Picture It! Skill Instruction, pp. 36–36a • Multilingual Summaries, pp. 37–39
Vocabulary **High-Frequency Words** **Position Words**	TEACHER'S EDITION • High-Frequency Words, p. DI•37 • Position Words, p. DI•35 ELL HANDBOOK • Word Cards, p. 35 • ELL Vocabulary Routine, p. 456 ELL POSTER 2 • Day 1 Activities	TEACHER'S EDITION • High-Frequency Words, p. DI•37 • Position Words, p. DI•35 ELL HANDBOOK • Word Cards, p. 35 • Multilingual Vocabulary List, pp. 429–440 ELL POSTER 2 • Day 2 Activities
Grammar and Conventions	TEACHER'S EDITION • Preteach Subjects, p. DI•41	TEACHER'S EDITION • Reteach Subjects, p. DI•41
Writing	TEACHER'S EDITION • Expository Nonfiction, p. DI•42 • Introduce Expository Nonfiction, pp. 57d–57e	TEACHER'S EDITION • Writer's Craft: Supporting Main Idea, pp. 71d–71e

Unit 1 Week 2 Exploring Space with an Astronaut

Leveled Support (LS)

This symbol indicates leveled instruction to address language proficiency levels.

Day 3	Day 4	Day 5
TEACHER'S EDITION • Concept Development, p. DI•33 • Anchored Talk, p. 72b • *Sing with Me* Big Book, p. 72a • Concept Talk Video ELL HANDBOOK • ELL Poster Talk, Concept Talk, p. 35c ELL POSTER 2 • Day 3 Activities	TEACHER'S EDITION • Concept Development, p. DI•33 • Anchored Talk, p. 76b • *Sing with Me* Big Book, p. 76a • Concept Talk Video ELL HANDBOOK • ELL Poster Talk, Concept Talk, p. 35c ELL POSTER 2 • Day 4 Activities	TEACHER'S EDITION • Concept Development, p. DI•33 • Concept Talk Video ELL HANDBOOK • ELL Poster Talk, Concept Talk, p. 35c ELL POSTER 2 • Day 5 Activities
ELL HANDBOOK • Phonics Transition Lesson, pp. 254, 258–259	TEACHER'S EDITION • Decodable Reader 2C, pp. 76e–76f ELL HANDBOOK • Phonics Transition Lesson, pp. 254, 258–259	TEACHER'S EDITION • Reteach Phonics, p. DI•35
TEACHER'S EDITION • *Sing with Me* Big Book, p. 72a • AudioText of *Exploring Space* • Concept Talk Video ELL HANDBOOK • AudioText CD Routine, p. 464	TEACHER'S EDITION • *Sing with Me* Big Book, p. 76a • Concept Talk Video	TEACHER'S EDITION • Concept Talk Video
TEACHER'S EDITION • Sheltered Reading, p. DI•39 ELL HANDBOOK • Multilingual Summaries, pp. 37–39	TEACHER'S EDITION • ELL/ELD Reader Guided Reading, p. DI•40 ELL HANDBOOK • ELL Study Guide, p. 40	TEACHER'S EDITION • ELL/ELD Reader Guided Reading, p. DI•40 ELL HANDBOOK • ELL Study Guide, p. 40
ELL HANDBOOK • High-Frequency Words Activity Bank, p. 491 ELL POSTER 2 • Day 3 Activities	ELL HANDBOOK • High-Frequency Words Activity Bank, p. 491	TEACHER'S EDITION • Position Words, p. 80–81 ELL HANDBOOK • High-Frequency Words Activity Bank, p. 491
TEACHER'S EDITION • Grammar Jammer ELL HANDBOOK • Grammar Transition Lesson, pp. 345, 352–353 • Grammar Jammer Routine, p. 465	TEACHER'S EDITION • Grammar Jammer ELL HANDBOOK • Grammar Transition Lesson, pp. 345, 352–353	TEACHER'S EDITION • Grammar Jammer ELL HANDBOOK • Grammar Transition Lesson, pp. 345, 352–353
TEACHER'S EDITION • Let's Write It!, p. 74–75 • Writing Trait: Sentences, p. 75a	TEACHER'S EDITION • Revising Strategy, pp. 79c–79d	TEACHER'S EDITION • Writing Trait: Subjects in Sentences, pp. 81h–81i

Poster Talk, Concept Talk

Question of the Week

What can we learn by exploring space?

Poster 2

Throughout the week, use the ELL Poster to help children produce and comprehend language, understand the concept, and build English vocabulary. Use the Question of the Week and other questions to help children share ideas in pairs, small groups, or the large group. Sample questions are shown, with examples of possible responses by children.

Weekly Concept and Language Goals

- Understand that the job of an astronaut is to explore space
- Identify the tools astronauts use and the things they explore
- Describe what makes exploring space hard

By the end of the lesson, children should be able to talk about and write one or more sentences about exploring space.

Daily Team Talk

Day 1	Day 2	Day 3	Day 4	Day 5
After Day 1 activities on Poster, ask questions such as *In the poster picture, we see three astronauts. What do astronauts do?*	After Day 2 activity on Poster, ask questions such as *In the poster picture, what tools do the astronauts use to explore space?*	After Day 3 activity on Poster, ask questions such as *What things are the astronauts in the poster picture exploring?*	After Day 4 activity on Poster, ask questions such as *Why is it hard for people to explore space?*	After Day 5 activity on Poster, ask questions such as *Imagine you are on a shuttle going into space. What will you explore?*
Beginning Go to space. **Intermediate** They go into space. **Advanced** Astronauts explore space. **Advanced High** Astronauts travel in a shuttle and explore things in space.	**Beginning** Machines. **Intermediate** They have machines. **Advanced** They use a robot arm and machines with buttons. **Advanced High** The astronauts use computers, spacesuits, and a machine with a robot arm.	**Beginning** The shuttle and space. **Intermediate** Stars, moon, Earth. **Advanced** They are exploring things in space. **Advanced High** They are exploring things in space, such as stars, the moon, and Earth.	**Beginning** Space is far away. **Intermediate** They have to go a long way in a shuttle. **Advanced** People travel a long way from home. **Advanced High** People have to wear spacesuits and travel in a shuttle.	**Beginning** The moon. **Intermediate** I will go to the stars. **Advanced** I will explore other planets. **Advanced High** My shuttle will go to Mars. I will land there and explore the planet.

This Week's Materials

Teacher's Edition pages 52j–81k

See the support for English language learners throughout the lesson, including ELL strategies and scaffold activities at points of use.

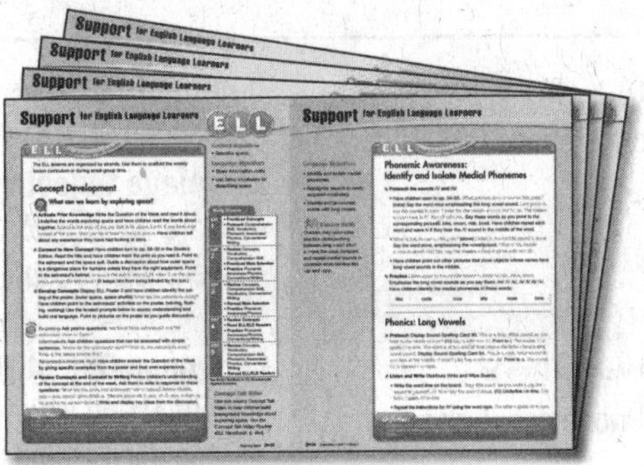

Teacher's Edition pages DI•33–DI•42

Differentiated Instruction for English language learners provides daily group activities that "frontload," or preteach, core instruction.

ELL Handbook pp. 35a–40

Find additional lesson materials that support the core lesson and the ELL instructional pages.

ELL Poster 2

ELD Reader 2.1.2

ELL Reader 2.1.2

Concept Literacy Reader

ELD, ELL Reader Teaching Guide

Concept Literacy Reader Teaching Guide

Technology

Online Teacher's Edition Use the digital version of the core teacher's edition for planning and instruction.

eReaders
This Week's ELL and ELD Readers and Concept Literacy Reader are also available in digital format.

This Week's Content and Language Objectives by Strand

Concept Development What can we learn by exploring space?	**Content Objective** • Describe space. **Language Objectives** • Share information orally. • Use basic vocabulary for describing space.
Phonics/Phonemic Awareness Identify and Isolate Medial Phonemes; Long Vowels	**Language Objectives** • Identify and isolate medial phonemes. • Recognize sounds in newly acquired vocabulary. • Identify and pronounce words with long vowels.
Listening Comprehension Modified Read Aloud: "Space Food"	**Content Objective** • Monitor and adjust oral comprehension. **Language Objectives** • Discuss oral passages. • Use a graphic organizer to take notes. • Use contextual support to enhance understanding.
Reading Comprehension Main Idea and Details	**Content Objectives** • Identify the main idea. • Explain how to find the main idea of a story. • Monitor and adjust comprehension. **Language Objectives** • Discuss the main idea of a story. • Write about main ideas and details in a story. • Monitor understanding of story. • Read grade level text with appropriate reading accuracy.
Vocabulary High-Frequency Words	**Language Objectives** • Understand and use basic vocabulary. • Use high-frequency words to describe people.
Vocabulary Position Words	**Content Objective** • Identify and use position words. **Language Objectives** • Associate the vowel sounds for short vowels with *a, e, i, o,* and *u.* • Learn academic vocabulary heard during classroom instruction.
Grammar and Conventions Subjects	**Content Objectives** • Understand sentence parts. • Identify a sentence subject. **Language Objectives** • Speak in complete sentences. • Edit writing for subject-verb agreement.
Writing Expository Nonfiction	**Content Objectives** • Understand how sentence variety improves expository nonfiction. • Identify the characteristics of expository nonfiction. **Language Objective** • Write expository nonfiction using sentence variety.

Word Cards for Vocabulary Activities

everywhere	**live**
machines	**move**
woman	**work**
world	

Teacher Note: Beginning Teach two to three words. **Intermediate** Teach three to four words. **Advanced** Teach five to six words. **Advanced High** Teach all words.

Name ______________________________

Main Idea and Details

Look at the picture. **Read** the paragraph.

- What are the sentences and picture mostly about? **Write** the main idea in the middle oval.
- What are some smaller pieces of information? **Write** details in the other ovals.

Astronauts

Astronauts are people who go into space. Sometimes they live in space for many months. They wear special clothes and use special tools. These astronauts are on a space shuttle. Each of them has an important job to do.

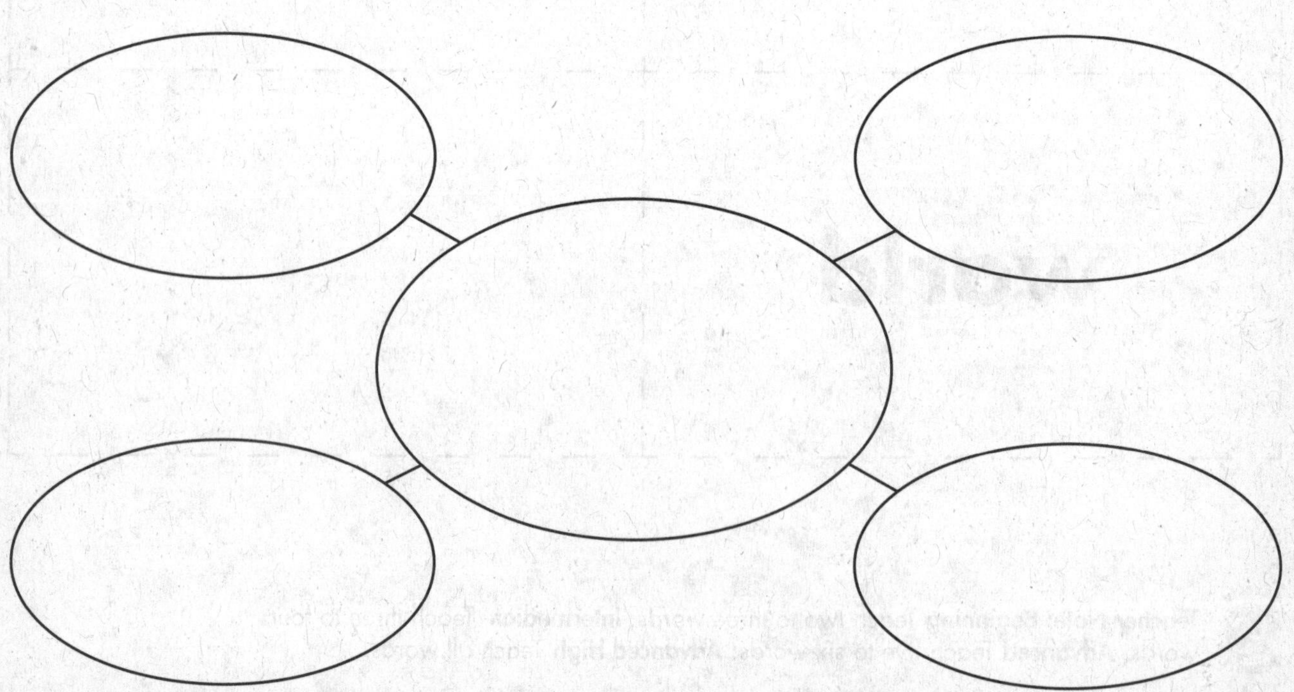

Main Idea and Details

Use this lesson to supplement or replace the skill lesson on page 57a of the Teacher's Edition. Display the Skill Points (at right) and share them with children.

Use the Skill Points to preteach main idea and details.

Teach/Model

Beginning Show a picture of carrots and oranges. Say: *We need to eat fruits and vegetables. Carrots are good for our eyes. Oranges have many vitamins.* Guide children in identifying the main idea. Ask: *What details tell about our main idea?*

Intermediate Display the following and read aloud: *Vegetables help us stay healthy. They are low in fat. They give us energy.* Guide children in circling the main idea. Help them think of another detail to support the main idea.

Advanced Write on the board: *We need healthy food to live and grow.* Read the sentence and say: *I am writing a report. This is my main idea. What details can I use to tell about this main idea?* Guide children in suggesting details that support the main idea.

Advanced High Give several details that support this idea: *Healthy food is important for a healthy body.* Ask children to suggest the main idea of an article with these details. Write their suggestions on the board and use them to compose a main-idea sentence.

Then distribute copies of Picture It! page 36.

- Have children look at the picture and describe what they see.
- Read the paragraph aloud. Ask: *What is the paragraph mostly about?* (astronauts in space)
- Review the Skill Points with children.
- Have children tell you which sentence contains the main idea. Then ask them to find the details.

Practice

Read aloud the directions on page 36. Reread or chorally read the story. Have children look at the pictures and the story as they answer the questions.

Beginning Children can orally answer and, with help, write words on the graphic organizer.

Intermediate Children can first orally answer and then write the answers on the page. Provide help with writing and spelling.

Advanced Children can write their answers and check them by quietly reading them aloud or comparing them with a partner's.

Advanced High Children can write their answers and check them by silently reading them and making any necessary corrections.

Answers for page 36: Main Idea: Astronauts are people who go into space. Details: wear special clothes; use special tools; live in space for months; travel on a space shuttle

Skill Points

- ✔ The topic is what a selection is about. The **main idea** is the most important idea about the topic.
- ✔ Small pieces of information tell more about the main idea. These small pieces of information are called **details.**

Multilingual Summaries

English

Exploring Space with an Astronaut

Astronauts fly shuttles into space. A shuttle is like a rocket. Eileen Collins was the shuttle's first woman pilot. She worked on a team with other astronauts. In space, astronauts float inside the shuttle. Their sleeping bags are tied to the wall. Astronauts exercise to stay strong.

Astronauts do experiments. They fix problems in the shuttle. They have many tools. Eileen's crew tested telescopes. They also took X-ray photographs of stars. The astronauts studied plants.

If you want to be an astronaut, you should study math and science. You should enjoy going to new places. You should also enjoy working with people on a team.

School + Home

Spanish

Explorar el espacio con un astronauta

Los astronautas vuelan al espacio en transbordadores. Un transbordador es como un cohete. Eileen Collins fue la primera mujer piloto de un transbordador. Ella trabajaba en un equipo con otros astronautas. En el espacio, los astronautas flotan dentro del transbordador. Los sacos de dormir están amarrados a la pared. Los astronautas hacen ejercicios para mantenerse fuertes.

Los astronautas hacen experimentos. Arreglan problemas en el transbordador. Tienen muchas herramientas. La tripulación de Eileen probaba telescopios. También les hacía fotografías de rayos X a las estrellas. Los astronautas estudiaban las plantas.

Si quieres ser astronauta, debes estudiar matemáticas y ciencias. Te debe gustar ir a lugares nuevos. También te debe gustar trabajar en equipo con otras personas.

Multilingual Summaries

Chinese

跟太空人一起探索太空

太空人乘坐太空梭進入太空，太空梭的樣子有點像火箭。愛林˙柯林斯是太空梭上的第一名女船長，她和其他太空人在同一個小組裡面工作。在太空中，太空艙裡的太空人是飄浮著的，因此睡袋必須固定在牆上。太空人還要運動，以維持強壯的體格。

太空人要做實驗，太空梭故障時也要負責修理，他們有很多工具。愛林的組員會測試望遠鏡，也會幫星星拍 X 光照片，以及研究植物。

假如你想當太空人，必須要唸數學和科學、喜歡到新的地方探險，還要喜歡團隊工作。

Vietnamese

Thám Hiểm Không Gian Với Một Phi Hành Gia

Các phi hành gia bay những chiếc phi thuyền con thoi vào không gian. Phi thuyền con thoi giống như một hỏa tiễn. Eileen Collins là nữ phi công đầu tiên của phi thuyền con thoi. Cô cùng làm việc với các phi hành gia khác trong nhóm. Trong không gian, các phi hành gia lơ lửng bên trong phi thuyền. Túi ngủ của họ được cột vào tường. Các phi hành gia tập thể dục để giữ cho khỏe mạnh.

Phi hành gia thi hành các cuộc thí nghiệm. Họ sửa chữa những hư hỏng trong phi thuyền. Họ có nhiều dụng cụ. Phi hành đoàn của Eileen thử nghiệm các kính viễn vọng. Họ cũng chụp ảnh của các vì sao bằng tia X. Phi hành gia nghiên cứu thực vật.

Nếu em muốn trở thành một phi hành gia, em nên học toán và khoa học. Em phải thích đi đến những nơi mới lạ. Em cũng phải thích làm việc với những người khác trong một nhóm.

Multilingual Summaries

Korean

우주 비행사와 우주 탐사를

우주 비행사들은 로켓 같은 우주 왕복선을 타고 우주를 비행한다. 에일린 콜린스는 우주 왕복선을 타는 첫 번째 여성으로 다른 우주 비행사들과 한 팀이 되어 일을 한다. 우주에서 비행사들은 왕복선 안을 떠다니기 때문에 이들의 침낭은 벽에 묶여 있다. 이들은 건강을 유지하기 위해 운동을 한다.

우주 비행사들은 실험도 하고 우주 왕복선 안의 고장난 부분도 수리한다. 이들은 기구들도 많이 가지고 있다. 에일린의 팀은 망원경을 시험해 보고 별의 X선 사진을 찍으며 식물에 대한 공부도 한다.

우주 비행사가 되고 싶으면 수학과 과학을 공부해야 하며 새로운 곳에 가는 것, 그리고 사람들과 팀을 이뤄 일하는 것을 좋아해야 한다.

Hmong

Mus Xyuas Nruab Ntug Nrog Ib Tug Tibneeg Kawm Txog Nruab Ntug

Cov tibneeg kawm txog nruab ntug caij dav hlau mus rau saum nruab ntug. Lub dav hlau no zoo li lub hoob pob tawg rhe. Thawj thawj tug pojniam uas tsav yam dav hlau no yog Eileen Collins. Nws ua haujlwm nrog ib pab kawm txog nruab ntug. Thaum nyob saum nruab ntug, cov tibneeg no ya sab hauv lub dav hlau. Lawv muab cov hnab pw khi rau ntawm phab ntsa. Cov tibneeg kawm txog nruab ntug siv zog ua haujlwm kom lawv muaj zog ntxiv.

Cov tibneeg kawm txog nruab ntug xyaum kawg txog tej txujci. Lawv kho tej teebmeem hauv lub dav hlau. Lawv muaj ntau yam cuabyeej siv. Cov ua haujlwm nrog Eileen lawv kawm txog lub looj qhovmuag tsom saum nruab ntug. Lawv muab cov hnub qub los yees dua xoo faim faj. Cov tibneeg kawm txog nruab ntug kuj kawm txog tej xyoob tej ntoo.

Yog koj xav ua ib tug tibneeg kawm txog nruab ntug, koj yuav tau kawm txog lej thiab tej txujci. Koj nyiam thiab txaus siab mus xyuas tej qhov chaw tshiab. Koj nyiam ua haujlwm nrog lwm cov tibneeg ua ib pab ib pawg.

Name ______________________________

- **Read** *The First Trip to the Moon* again.
- **Draw** a picture that shows what the book is about.
- **Write** a sentence that goes with your picture.

____

____

Family Link

Ask family members to tell you what they know about the first time astronauts walked on the moon.

Weekly Resources Guide for English Language Learner Support

For this week's content and language objectives, see p. 41e.

Instructional Strand	Day 1	Day 2
Concept Development	TEACHER'S EDITION • Concept Development, p. DI•54 • Anchored Talk, pp. 82j—82–83 • *Sing with Me* Big Book, p. 84a • Concept Talk Video ELL HANDBOOK • ELL Poster Talk, Concept Talk, p. 41c ELL POSTER 3 • Day 1 Activities	TEACHER'S EDITION • Concept Development, p. DI•54 • Anchored Talk, p. 88b • *Sing with Me* Big Book, p. 88a • Concept Talk Video ELL HANDBOOK • ELL Poster Talk, Concept Talk, p. 41c • Concept Talk Video Routine, p. 464 ELL POSTER 3 • Day 2 Activities
Phonics/Phonemic Awareness	TEACHER'S EDITION • Preteach Phonemic Awareness, p. DI•55 • Preteach Phonics, p. DI•55 • Decodable Reader 3A, pp. 86b–86c	TEACHER'S EDITION • Practice Phonemic Awareness, p. DI•55 • Listen and Write Phonics, p. DI•55
Listening Comprehension	TEACHER'S EDITION • Modified Read Aloud, p. DI•57 • *Sing with Me* Big Book, p. 84a • Read Aloud, p. 87b • Concept Talk Video ELL HANDBOOK • Concept Talk Video Routine, p. 464	TEACHER'S EDITION • Modified Read Aloud, p. DI•57 • *Sing with Me* Big Book, p. 88a • AudioText of *Henry and Mudge* • Concept Talk Video ELL HANDBOOK • AudioText CD Routine, p. 464 • Web, p. 473
Reading Comprehension	TEACHER'S EDITION • Teach Character and Setting, p. DI•59	TEACHER'S EDITION • Teach Character and Setting, p. DI•59 • Frontloading Reading, p. DI•60 ELL HANDBOOK • Picture It! Skill Instruction, pp. 42–42a • Multilingual Summaries, pp. 43–45
Vocabulary **High-Frequency Words** **Synonyms**	TEACHER'S EDITION • High-Frequency Words, p. DI•58 • Synonyms, p. DI•56 ELL HANDBOOK • Word Cards, p. 41 • ELL Vocabulary Routine, p. 456 ELL POSTER 3 • Day 1 Activities	TEACHER'S EDITION • High-Frequency Words, p. DI•58 • Synonyms, p. DI•56 ELL HANDBOOK • Word Cards, p. 41 • Multilingual Vocabulary List, pp. 429–440 ELL POSTER 3 • Day 2 Activities
Grammar and Conventions	TEACHER'S EDITION • Preteach Predicates, p. DI•62	TEACHER'S EDITION • Reteach Predicates, p. DI•62
Writing	TEACHER'S EDITION • Realistic Fiction, p. DI•63 • Introduce Realistic Fiction, pp. 87d–87e	TEACHER'S EDITION • Realistic Fiction, pp. 103c–103d

Unit 1 Week 3 Henry and Mudge

This symbol indicates leveled instruction to address language proficiency levels.

Day 3	Day 4	Day 5
TEACHER'S EDITION • Concept Development, p. DI•54 • Anchored Talk, p. 104b • *Sing with Me* Big Book, p. 104a • Concept Talk Video ELL HANDBOOK • ELL Poster Talk, Concept Talk, p. 41c ELL POSTER 3 • Day 3 Activities	TEACHER'S EDITION • Concept Development, p. DI•54 • Anchored Talk, p. 108b • *Sing with Me* Big Book, p. 108a • Concept Talk Video ELL HANDBOOK • ELL Poster Talk, Concept Talk, p. 41c ELL POSTER 3 • Day 4 Activities	TEACHER'S EDITION • Concept Development, p. DI•54 • Concept Talk Video ELL HANDBOOK • ELL Poster Talk, Concept Talk, p. 41c ELL POSTER 3 • Day 5 Activities
ELL HANDBOOK • Phonics Transition Lesson, pp. 234–236, 240–242	TEACHER'S EDITION • Decodable Reader 3C, pp. 108e–108f ELL HANDBOOK • Phonics Transition Lesson, pp. 234–236, 240–242	TEACHER'S EDITION • Reteach Phonics, p. DI•56
TEACHER'S EDITION • *Sing with Me* Big Book, p. 104a • AudioText of *Henry and Mudge* • Concept Talk Video ELL HANDBOOK • AudioText CD Routine, p. 464	TEACHER'S EDITION • *Sing with Me* Big Book, p. 108a • Concept Talk Video	TEACHER'S EDITION • Concept Talk Video
TEACHER'S EDITION • Sheltered Reading, p. DI•60 ELL HANDBOOK • Multilingual Summaries, pp. 43–45	TEACHER'S EDITION • ELL/ELD Reader Guided Reading, p. DI•61 ELL HANDBOOK • ELL Study Guide, p. 46	TEACHER'S EDITION • ELL/ELD Reader Guided Reading, p. DI•61 ELL HANDBOOK • ELL Study Guide, p. 46
ELL HANDBOOK • High-Frequency Words Activity Bank, p. 491 ELL POSTER 3 • Day 3 Activities	ELL HANDBOOK • High-Frequency Words Activity Bank, p. 491	TEACHER'S EDITION • Synonyms, pp. 112–113–113a ELL HANDBOOK • High-Frequency Words Activity Bank, p. 491
TEACHER'S EDITION • Grammar Jammer ELL HANDBOOK • Grammar Transition Lesson, pp. 345, 354–355 • Grammar Jammer Routine, p. 465	TEACHER'S EDITION • Grammar Jammer ELL HANDBOOK • Grammar Transition Lesson, pp. 345, 354–355	TEACHER'S EDITION • Grammar Jammer ELL HANDBOOK • Grammar Transition Lesson, pp. 345, 354–355
TEACHER'S EDITION • Let's Write It!, p. 106–107 • Writing Trait: Organization, p. 107a	TEACHER'S EDITION • Writer's Craft: Time-order Words, pp. 111c–111d	TEACHER'S EDITION • Revising Strategy, pp. 113h–113i

Poster Talk, Concept Talk

Question of the Week

What can we discover by exploring nature?

Poster 3

Throughout the week, use the ELL Poster to help children produce and comprehend language, understand the concept, and build English vocabulary. Use the Question of the Week and other questions to help children share ideas in pairs, small groups, or the large group. Sample questions are shown, with examples of possible responses by children.

Weekly Concept and Language Goals

- Know that nature includes animals and plants and the places where they live
- Identify what natural environments are like
- Describe plants and animals in different environments

By the end of the lesson, children should be able to talk about and write one or more sentences about exploring nature.

Daily Team Talk

Day 1	Day 2	Day 3	Day 4	Day 5
After Day 1 activities on Poster, ask questions such as *What kinds of animals do you see in the poster picture?*	After Day 2 activity on Poster, ask questions such as *What kinds of plants are in the poster picture?*	After Day 3 activity on Poster, ask questions such as *In the poster picture, where does the bird live?*	After Day 4 activity on Poster, ask questions such as *The poster picture shows a natural environment. What does this environment look like?*	After Day 5 activity on Poster, ask questions such as *What plants and animals can we see in our natural environment?*
Beginning Deer and bear. **Intermediate** There are some deer and birds. **Advanced** I see two deer, a bear, and birds. **Advanced High** I see deer, birds, butterflies, a bear, a turtle, and a frog.	**Beginning** Trees. **Intermediate** There are trees and flowers. **Advanced** The picture has trees, flowers, and grass. **Advanced High** The plants in the picture are trees, grass, bushes, and blue flowers.	**Beginning** In a tree. **Intermediate** It has a nest in a tree. **Advanced** The bird builds a nest in a tree. **Advanced High** The bird will live in the nest it is building in the tree.	**Beginning** It has a river and animals. **Intermediate** Many animals and plants live there. **Advanced** The natural environment has plants, animals, a river, and hills. **Advanced High** The natural environment has a river and hills. Many plants and animals live in this place.	**Beginning** Trees and dogs. **Intermediate** We see flowers and trees and birds. **Advanced** We can see trees, flowers, birds, and squirrels. **Advanced High** We can see plants such as trees and grass. We can see animals such as birds, squirrels, and bugs.

This Week's Materials

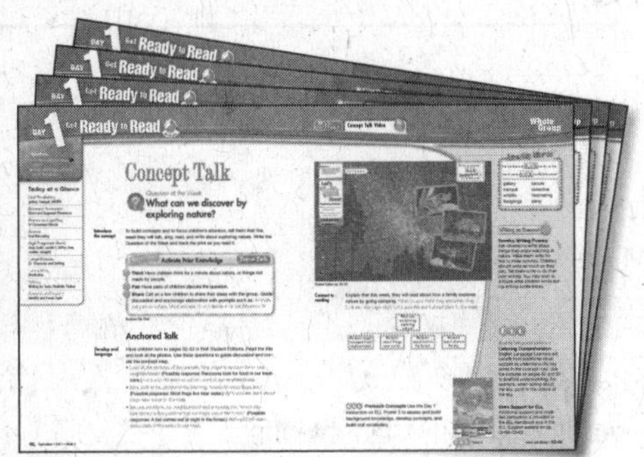

Teacher's Edition pages 82j–113k

See the support for English language learners throughout the lesson, including ELL strategies and scaffold activities at points of use.

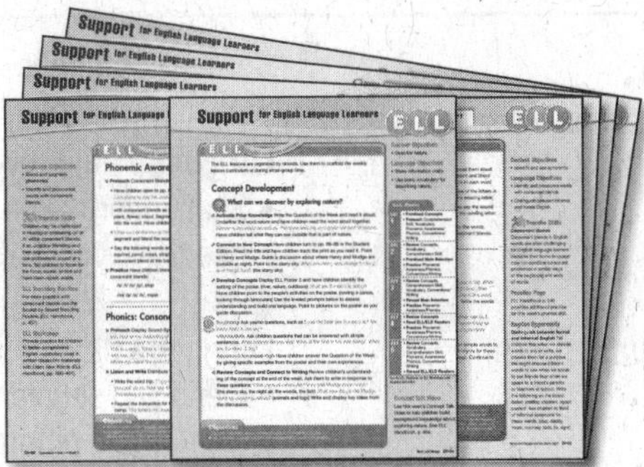

Teacher's Edition pages DI•54–DI•63

Differentiated Instruction for English language learners provides daily group activities that "frontload," or preteach, core instruction.

ELL Handbook pp. 41a–46

Find additional lesson materials that support the core lesson and the ELL instructional pages.

ELL Poster 3

ELD Reader 2.1.3

ELL Reader 2.1.3

Concept Literacy Reader

ELD, ELL Reader Teaching Guide

Concept Literacy Reader Teaching Guide

Technology

Online Teacher's Edition Use the digital version of the core teacher's edition for planning and instruction.

eReaders
This Week's ELL and ELD Readers and Concept Literacy Reader are also available in digital format.

This Week's Content and Language Objectives by Strand

Concept Development What can we discover by exploring nature?	**Content Objective** • Describe nature. **Language Objectives** • Share information orally. • Use basic vocabulary for describing nature.
Phonics/Phonemic Awareness Consonant Blends; Blend and Segment	**Language Objectives** • Blend and segment phonemes. • Identify and pronounce words with consonant blends.
Listening Comprehension Modified Read Aloud: "Animals in Nature"	**Content Objective** • Monitor and adjust oral comprehension. **Language Objectives** • Discuss oral passages. • Use a graphic organizer to take notes.
Reading Comprehension Character and Setting	**Content Objectives** • Identify the characters and setting. • Monitor and adjust comprehension. **Language Objectives** • Discuss characters and setting of a story. • Internalize vocabulary by retelling. • Read grade level text with appropriate reading accuracy.
Vocabulary High-Frequency Words	**Language Objectives** • Understand and use basic vocabulary. • Understand and read story words. • Ask and give information using high-frequency words.
Vocabulary Synonyms	**Content Objective** • Identify and use synonyms. **Language Objectives** • Identify and pronounce words with consonant blends. • Distinguish between informal and formal English.
Grammar and Conventions Predicates	**Content Objectives** • Understand sentence parts. • Identify a sentence predicate. **Language Objective** • Speak in complete sentences.
Writing Realistic Fiction	**Content Objectives** • Understand how stories have a beginning, middle, and end. • Identify the sequence in realistic fiction. **Language Objectives** • Write realistic fiction using a beginning, middle, and end. • Share feedback for editing and revising.

Word Cards for Vocabulary Activities

bear	**build**
couldn't	**father**
love	**mother**
straight	

Teacher Note: Beginning Teach two to three words. **Intermediate** Teach three to four words. **Advanced** Teach five to six words. **Advanced High** Teach all words.

Name ________________________________

Picture It!
Character and Setting

Look at the pictures. **Read** the story.

A Camping Trip

Ana and Pedro hike with their dad. It is a beautiful summer day at the lake.

They find a good place to camp. Dad and Pedro put up the tent. Ana makes a place for the fire.

"What a great day," says Ana. Pedro smiles and nods.

Answer the questions below.

1. Where are Ana, Pedro, and their father?
o in the city   o at their house   o by a lake

2. What time of year is it?
o summer   o fall   o winter

3. Talk about how Ana and Pedro feel about camping. Tell how you know.

Character and Setting

Use this lesson to supplement or replace the skill lesson on page 87a of the Teacher's Edition. Display the Skill Points (at right) and share them with children.

Use the Skill Points to preteach character and setting.

Skill Points

✔ A **character** is a person or an animal in a story. The author tells you what characters look like, how they act, and how they think and feel.

✔ The **setting** is where and when a story takes place.

Teach/Model

Beginning Draw a simple picture as you tell children this story: *Mom and Tim walk in the woods. Mom takes pictures. They sing songs.* Ask: *Who are the characters in the story? What is the setting of the story?*

Intermediate Display the following and read aloud: *Mom and Tim hike in the woods. They look for animals.* Guide children in circling the characters and drawing a box around the setting.

Advanced Write on the board: *Tim sits on a log. It is quiet in the woods. Tim is happy.* Have volunteers circle words that tell about the setting. Ask children to tell what Tim does and how he feels.

Advanced High Help children compose a group story. Have them suggest ideas for the characters and setting. List their suggestions on the board and use them to write simple sentences. Have each child copy and illustrate a sentence for the story.

Then distribute copies of Picture It! page 42.

- Have children look at the picture story and tell what is happening.
- Review the Skill Points with children.
- Read the sentences aloud. Ask: *Who are the characters in the story?* (Ana, Pedro, and their dad)
- Have children look at the pictures and sentences to find clues about the characters and setting.

Practice

Read aloud the directions on page 42. Reread or chorally read the story. Have children look at the pictures and the story as they answer the questions.

Beginning Children can orally answer and mark and share their answers. Provide help with filling in circles and discussing ideas.

Intermediate Children can first orally answer and then mark and discuss their answers.

Advanced Children can mark and discuss their answers and check them by quietly reading them aloud or comparing them with a partner's.

Advanced High Children can mark and discuss their answers and check them by reviewing the story and making any necessary corrections.

Answers for page 42: 1. by a lake; 2. summer; 3. Guide children to talk about how Ana and Pedro feel about camping. Sample answer: *They like to camp. I can tell because they are smiling, Ana says it was a great day, and Pedro agrees with her.*

Multilingual Summaries

English

Henry and Mudge

Henry's family was going camping. They took Henry's big dog, Mudge, with them. Henry's mother knew how to camp. Henry thought about animals that they might see. He was excited.

The family drove to the lake. They went hiking. Henry saw a fish jump. He saw deer. Mudge smelled many things. The family set up the tent. Mudge ate some of the food. Henry's father played the guitar.

At night, the family lay on a blanket. They looked at the stars. Mudge chewed a log. The family sang songs. They got in the tent. They went to sleep. Everything was quiet.

Spanish

Henry y Mudge

La familia de Henry se preparaba para ir de campamento. Llevaban con ellos al perro grande de Henry, Mudge. La mamá de Henry sabía acampar. Henry pensaba en los animales que verían. Estaba emocionado.

La familia condujo hasta el lago. Salieron a hacer una caminata. Henry vio saltar un pez. Vio un oso. Mudge olía muchas cosas. La familia armó la carpa. Mudge comió un poco. El papá de Henry tocó la guitarra.

Por la noche, la familia se acostó sobre una manta a mirar las estrellas. Mudge mordisqueaba un tronco. La familia cantaba canciones. Después, se metieron en la carpa para dormir. Todo quedó muy silencioso.

Multilingual Summaries

Chinese

星空下的亨利與馬奇

亨利一家人去露營，他們把亨利的大狗「馬奇」也一起帶去玩。亨利的媽媽知道怎樣露營，亨利在想他們可能會看到哪些動物，越想越興奮。

他們一家人開車到了湖邊，然後開始步行。亨利看到一條魚跳出湖面，還看到野鹿，馬奇也聞到很多東西的氣味。他們把帳篷搭起來，馬奇吃了一些食物，亨利的爸爸在彈吉他。

到了晚上，一家人躺在毯子上看星星，馬奇在一旁啃樹枝，大家唱著歌。後來累了，所以進帳篷睡覺。四周很安靜。

Vietnamese

Henry và Mudge

Gia đình của Henry đi cắm trại. Họ đem con chó to của Henry, Mudge, với họ. Mẹ của Henry biết cách cắm trại. Henry đang nghĩ về những con thú họ có thể thấy. Cậu ta nôn nao.

Gia đình lái xe đến một hồ. Họ đi bộ. Henry thấy một con cá nhảy. Cậu thấy một con nai. Mudge đánh mùi được nhiều thứ. Gia đình dựng lều. Mudge ăn một số thức ăn. Ba của Henry chơi đàn ghita.

Đêm đến, gia đình trải chăn ra. Họ ngắm sao trời. Mudge gặm một khúc gỗ. Gia đình ca hát. Họ vào lều. Họ đi ngủ. Mọi vật yên tĩnh.

Multilingual Summaries

Korean

헨리와 머지, 그리고 별이 빛나는 밤

헨리의 가족은 큰 개 머지를 데리고 캠핑을 간다. 헨리의 엄마는 야영하는 방법을 안다. 헨리는 동물들을 보게 된다는 생각에 들떠 있다.

헨리 가족은 차를 타고 강가로 가서 하이킹을 한다. 헨리는 물고기가 뛰어오르는 것도 보고 사슴도 본다. 머지는 주변의 냄새를 맡는다. 헨리 가족은 텐트를 치고 머지는 음식을 먹는다. 헨리의 아버지는 기타를 친다.

밤이 되자 헨리 가족은 담요 위에 누워 별을 바라보고 머지는 통나무를 씹는다. 가족은 노래를 부르고 텐트 안으로 들어가 잠을 잔다. 세상이 온통 고요하다.

Hmong

Henry thiab Mudge

Henry tsevneeg mus pw pem havzoov. Lawv coj nws tus dev loj, Mudge, nrog lawv mus. Henry niam paub kev mus pem havzoov yuav zoo li cas. Henry xav txog tej yam tsiaj uas lawv yuav mus pom. Nws zoo siab heev.

Lawv tsevneeg tsav lub tsheb mus txog nram ib lub pas dej. Lawv mus nce roob. Henry pom ib tug ntses dhia. Nws pom ib tug mos lwj. Mudge hnov ntau yam ntxhiab. Lawv tsevneeg tsa lawv lub tsev ntaub. Mudge noj lawv ib co zaum mov. Henry txiv ntaus lub kis ta.

Thaum ntsaus ntuj, lawv tsevneeg muab ib daim pam coj los pua pw. Lawv saib cov hnub qub. Mudge noj ib ya ntoo. Lawv tsevneeg hu nkauj. Ces lawv mus rau hauv lub tsev ntaub. Lawv mus pw tsaug zog. Txhua yam nyob ntsiag twb to.

Name ______________________

- **Read** *The Nature Walk* again.
- **Draw** a picture of the characters in the woods.
- **Label** each character in the scene.

Family Link

Share your drawing with your family. Invite a family member to go for a walk. Make a list of things you see, hear, smell, or touch.

Weekly Resources Guide for English Language Learner Support

For this week's content and language objectives, see p. 47e.

Instructional Strand	Day 1	Day 2
Concept Development	TEACHER'S EDITION • Concept Development, p. DI•75 • Anchored Talk, pp. 114j—114–115 • *Sing With Me* Big Book, p. 116a • Concept Talk Video ELL HANDBOOK • ELL Poster Talk, Concept Talk, p. 47c ELL POSTER 4 • Day 1 Activities	TEACHER'S EDITION • Concept Development, p. DI•75 • Anchored Talk, p. 120b • *Sing With Me* Big Book, p. 120a • Concept Talk Video ELL HANDBOOK • ELL Poster Talk, Concept Talk, p. 47c • Concept Talk Video Routine, p. 464 ELL POSTER 4 • Day 2 Activities
Phonics/Phonemic Awareness	TEACHER'S EDITION • Preteach Phonemic Awareness, p. DI•76 • Preteach Phonics, p. DI•76 • Decodable Reader 4A, pp. 118b–118c	TEACHER'S EDITION • Practice Phonemic Awareness, p. DI•76 • Listen and Write Phonics, p. DI•76
Listening Comprehension	TEACHER'S EDITION • Modified Read Aloud, p. DI•78 • *Sing With Me* Big Book, p. 116a • Read Aloud, p. 119b • Concept Talk Video ELL HANDBOOK • Concept Talk Video Routine, p. 464	TEACHER'S EDITION • Modified Read Aloud, p. DI•78 • *Sing With Me* Big Book, p. 120a • AudioText of *A Walk in the Desert* • Concept Talk Video ELL HANDBOOK • AudioText CD Routine, p. 464 • Web, p. 473
Reading Comprehension	TEACHER'S EDITION • Teach Main Idea, p. DI•80	TEACHER'S EDITION • Teach Main Idea, p. DI•80 • Frontloading Reading, p. DI•81 ELL HANDBOOK • Picture It! Skill Instruction, pp. 48–48a • Multilingual Summaries, pp. 49–51
Vocabulary **High-Frequency Words** **Alphabetize**	TEACHER'S EDITION • High-Frequency Words, p. DI•79 • Alphabetize, p. DI•77 ELL HANDBOOK • Word Cards, p. 47 • ELL Vocabulary Routine, p. 456 ELL POSTER 4 • Day 1 Activities	TEACHER'S EDITION • High-Frequency Words, p. DI•79 • Alphabetize, p. DI•77 ELL HANDBOOK • Word Cards, p. 47 • Multilingual Vocabulary List, pp. 429–440 ELL POSTER 4 • Day 2 Activities
Grammar and Conventions	TEACHER'S EDITION • Preteach Declarative and Interrogative Sentences, p. DI•83	TEACHER'S EDITION • Reteach Declarative and Interrogative Sentences, p. DI•83
Writing	TEACHER'S EDITION • Brief Report, p. DI•84 • Introduce Brief Report, pp. 119d–119e	TEACHER'S EDITION • Writing Trait: Word Choice, pp. 139c–139d

A Walk in the Desert

This symbol indicates leveled instruction to address language proficiency levels.

Day 3	Day 4	Day 5
TEACHER'S EDITION • Concept Development, p. DI•75 • Anchored Talk, p. 140b • *Sing With Me* Big Book, p. 140a • Concept Talk Video ELL HANDBOOK • ELL Poster Talk, Concept Talk, p. 47c ELL POSTER 4 • Day 3 Activities	TEACHER'S EDITION • Concept Development, p. DI•75 • Anchored Talk, p. 144b • *Sing With Me* Big Book, p. 144a • Concept Talk Video ELL HANDBOOK • ELL Poster Talk, Concept Talk, p. 47c ELL POSTER 4 • Day 4 Activities	TEACHER'S EDITION • Concept Development, p. DI•75 • Concept Talk Video ELL HANDBOOK • ELL Poster Talk, Concept Talk, p. 47c ELL POSTER 4 • Day 5 Activities
ELL HANDBOOK • Phonics Transition Lesson, pp. 276–277, 280–281	TEACHER'S EDITION • Decodable Reader 4C, pp. 144e–144f ELL HANDBOOK • Phonics Transition Lesson, pp. 276–277, 280–281	TEACHER'S EDITION • Reteach Phonics, p. DI•77
TEACHER'S EDITION • *Sing With Me* Big Book, p. 140a • AudioText of *A Walk in the Desert* • Concept Talk Video ELL HANDBOOK • AudioText CD Routine, p. 464	TEACHER'S EDITION • *Sing With Me* Big Book, p. 144a • Concept Talk Video	TEACHER'S EDITION • Concept Talk Video
TEACHER'S EDITION • Sheltered Reading, p. DI•81 ELL HANDBOOK • Multilingual Summaries, pp. 49–51	TEACHER'S EDITION • ELL/ELD Reader Guided Reading, p. DI•82 ELL HANDBOOK • ELL Study Guide, p. 52	TEACHER'S EDITION • ELL/ELD Reader Guided Reading, p. DI•82 ELL HANDBOOK • ELL Study Guide, p. 52
ELL HANDBOOK • High-Frequency Words Activity Bank, p. 491 ELL POSTER 4 • Day 3 Activities	ELL HANDBOOK • High-Frequency Words Activity Bank, p. 491	TEACHER'S EDITION • Alphabetize, p. 148–149 ELL HANDBOOK • High-Frequency Words Activity Bank, p. 491
TEACHER'S EDITION • Grammar Jammer ELL HANDBOOK • Grammar Transition Lesson, pp. 347, 358–359 • Grammar Jammer Routine, p. 465	TEACHER'S EDITION • Grammar Jammer ELL HANDBOOK • Grammar Transition Lesson, pp. 347, 358–359	TEACHER'S EDITION • Grammar Jammer ELL HANDBOOK • Grammar Transition Lesson, pp. 347, 358–359
TEACHER'S EDITION • Let's Write It!, p. 142–143 • Writer's Craft: Supporting Details, p. 143a	TEACHER'S EDITION • Revising Strategy, pp. 147c–147d	TEACHER'S EDITION • Writer's Craft: Sentence Variety, pp. 149h–149i

Poster Talk, Concept Talk

Question of the Week

What can we learn by exploring the desert?

Poster 4

Throughout the week, use the ELL Poster to help children produce and comprehend language, understand the concept, and build English vocabulary. Use the Question of the Week and other questions to help children share ideas in pairs, small groups, or the large group. Sample questions are shown, with examples of possible responses by children.

Weekly Concept and Language Goals

- Know that you have to plan before exploring
- Tell about how to plan and what to pack
- Tell how different items help keep people safe as they explore

By the end of the lesson, children should be able to talk about and write one or more sentences about preparing to explore.

Daily Team Talk

Day 1	Day 2	Day 3	Day 4	Day 5
After Day 1 activities on Poster, ask questions such as *In the poster picture, what do the girl and her father have that helps them explore the desert?*	After Day 2 activity on Poster, ask questions such as *Why is it important to plan ahead before going to a place such as the desert?*	After Day 3 activity on Poster, ask questions such as *Imagine you are going to explore in the desert. What will you bring with you?*	After Day 4 activity on Poster, ask questions such as *Why should explorers always have a hat and sunscreen?*	After Day 5 activity on Poster, ask questions such as *Why is a flashlight important to explorers?*
Beginning Water. **Intermediate** A bottle of water. **Advanced** They have hats to keep the sun off and a canteen of water. **Advanced High** The girl and her father have mules, binoculars, hats, and a canteen filled with water to help them explore the desert.	**Beginning** No people. **Intermediate** There are no people around. **Advanced** There is no easy way to get help. **Advanced High** It is important to have everything you need in case you have a problem.	**Beginning** Water. **Intermediate** I will have water. **Advanced** I will bring water, a hat, and a phone. **Advanced High** I will bring water, a hat, and a map. I will wear the right kind of clothes.	**Beginning** It's hot. **Intermediate** They don't want to burn. **Advanced** They can use them so they don't get a sunburn. **Advanced High** Explorers should have a hat and sunscreen to protect them from the sun.	**Beginning** To see. **Intermediate** They can use it to see. **Advanced** People can use the flashlight if it gets dark. **Advanced** High A flashlight can keep explorers safe in dark places.

This Week's Materials

Teacher's Edition pages 114j–149k

See the support for English language learners throughout the lesson, including ELL strategies and scaffold activities at points of use.

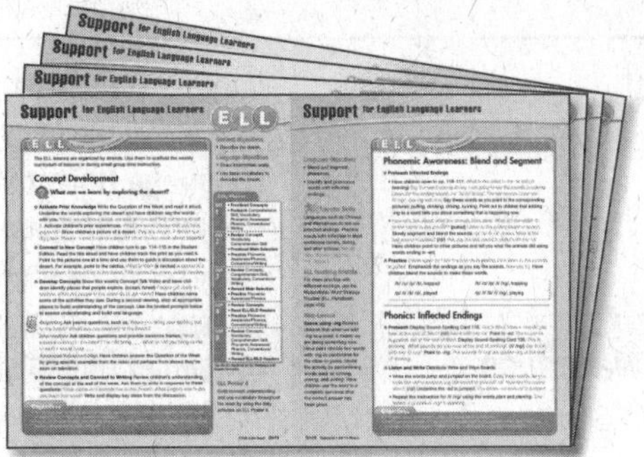

Teacher's Edition pages DI•75–DI•84

Differentiated Instruction for English language learners provides daily group activities that "frontload," or preteach, core instruction.

ELL Handbook pp. 47a–52

Find additional lesson materials that support the core lesson and the ELL instructional pages.

Poster 4

ELD Reader 2.1.4

ELL Reader 2.1.4

Concept Literacy Reader

ELD, ELL Reader Teaching Guide

Concept Literacy Reader Teaching Guide

Technology

Online Teacher's Edition Use the digital version of the core teacher's edition for planning and instruction.

eReaders
This Week's ELL and ELD Readers and Concept Literacy Reader are also available in digital format.

This Week's Content and Language Objectives by Strand

Concept Development What can we discover by exploring the desert?	**Content Objective** • Describe the desert. **Language Objectives** • Share information orally. • Use basic vocabulary to describe the desert.
Phonics/Phonemic Awareness Inflected Endings; Blend and Segment	**Language Objectives** • Blend and segment phonemes. • Identify and pronounce words with inflected endings.
Listening Comprehension Modified Read Aloud: "A Desert Plant"	**Content Objective** • Monitor and adjust oral comprehension. **Language Objectives** • Discuss oral passages. • Use a graphic organizer to take notes.
Reading Comprehension Main Idea	**Content Objectives** • Identify main ideas and details. • Differentiate between main ideas and details. • Monitor and adjust comprehension. **Language Objectives** • Discuss main ideas and details that support them. • Retell main ideas and details from a reading. • Write main ideas and support them with details.
Vocabulary High-Frequency Words	**Language Objectives** • Understand and use basic vocabulary. • Use linguistic support to enhance understanding of new language.
Vocabulary Alphabetize	**Content Objective** • Alphabetize words by the first letter. **Language Objective** • Associate the sounds and letters for inflected endings.
Grammar and Conventions Declarative and Interrogative Sentences	**Content Objectives** • Recognize and use periods and question marks in sentences. • Use correct punctuation in declarative and interrogative sentences. **Language Objectives** • Ask questions and make statements. • Distinguish intonation patterns of English. • Write declarative and interrogative sentences.
Writing Brief Report	**Content Objectives** • Identify vivid and exact descriptive words in a report. • Identify the characteristics of a brief report. **Language Objectives** • Write report sentences using vivid and exact descriptive words. • Share feedback for editing and revising.

Word Cards for Vocabulary Activities

animals	**early**
eyes	**full**
warm	**water**

Leveled Support

Teacher Note: Beginning Teach two to three words. **Intermediate** Teach three to four words. **Advanced** Teach five to six words. **Advanced High** Teach all words.

Name ______________________________

Look at the picture. **Read** the story.

What is the story mostly about? **Write** that idea in the Main Idea box below.

A Day at the Beach

Trung's family goes to the beach. It takes some planning. First, the family packs a picnic lunch and plenty of water.

Then, they pack sunscreen, towels, and toys. They carry the items across the sand until they get to a spot by the water.

Finally, they can enjoy the nice, cold water. It takes planning to go to the beach. It is always fun!

Answer the questions.

1. What is the passage mostly about?

____

____

2. Which title would best show the main idea of the story?

a. Summer Fun
b. Planning for the Beach
c. A Surprise Trip

Main Idea

Use this lesson to supplement or replace the skill lesson on page 119a of the Teacher's Edition. Display the Skill Points (at right) and share them with children.

Use the Skill Points to preteach main idea.

Teach/Model

Beginning Say and pantomime: *I like to play in sand. I dig in the sand at the beach. I have sand at home. I dig in that sand too.* Guide children in identifying the main idea. (I like to play in sand.)

Intermediate Say and pantomime: *I have fun at the beach. I run with my dog. I swim with my friends. I dig in the sand.* Have children identify and copy the sentence that tells the main idea of the story.

Advanced Say: *Listen to my story.* Tell children a story with details that support this main idea: *Our class goes to the beach.* Help children identify the main idea.

Advanced High Give several details that support this main idea: *There are many ways to play at the beach.* Ask children to suggest the main idea of a passage with these details. Write their suggestions on the board and use them to compose a main-idea sentence. Have children copy and illustrate the sentence.

Then distribute copies of Picture It! page 48.

- Have children look at the pictures and describe what they see.
- Read the story aloud. Ask: *What is the main idea of the story?* (getting ready to go to the beach)
- Review the Skill Points with children.
- Have children look at the pictures and words to understand the main idea.

Practice

Read aloud the directions on page 48. Reread or chorally read the story. Have children look at the pictures and the story as they answer the questions.

Beginning Children can orally answer and, with help, write and mark their answers. Provide help with writing and spelling.

Intermediate Children can first orally answer and then write and mark the answers on the page.

Advanced Children can write and mark their answers and check them by quietly reading their writing aloud or comparing their circles with a partner's answers.

Advanced High Children can write and mark their answers and check them by silently rereading the story and making any necessary corrections.

Answers for page 48: 1. planning a trip to the beach; 2. b

Skill Points

- ✔ The **main idea** is the most important idea in a story.
- ✔ The title of a story usually gives you a clue about the main idea of a story.

Multilingual Summaries

English

Read Together

A Walk in the Desert

The desert is very dry. But many plants and animals live there. The cactus is a plant that grows in the desert. It stores water in its stem. The saguaro is a tall cactus. Many desert animals live in the saguaro.

Some animals have special ways to live in the desert. Some have ways to protect themselves from the hot sun. Some have ways to hunt for food. Some also have ways to escape from enemies. Some desert animals hunt for food at night.

The desert can be exciting to visit. There are deserts all over the world.

Spanish

Un paseo por el desierto

El desierto es muy seco, pero hay muchas plantas y animales. El cacto es una planta del desierto. Acumula agua en su tallo. El saguaro es muy alto. Muchos animales viven.

Algunos animales tienen habilidades para vivir en el desierto. Unos se protegen del Sol. Algunos tienen maneras particulares de cazar o de escapar de sus enemigos. Algunos cazan de noche.

El desierto puede ser un lugar divertido. Hay desiertos en todo el mundo.

Multilingual Summaries

Chinese

在沙漠里漫步

沙漠很干燥，但其实沙漠里有很多动植物。

仙人掌是一种在沙漠里生长的植物，它把水存在茎里。巨人柱是很高的仙人掌，很多沙漠动物都住在里面。

沙漠动物都有特殊的生存方法：它们能防止被猛烈的太阳晒伤，能寻找食物，能逃避敌人，有些能在夜里寻找食物。

沙漠是一个很有趣的地方；这个世界到处都有沙漠。

Vietnamese

Đi Bộ Trên Sa Mạc

Sa mạc rất khô. nhưng có nhiều cây và thú vật sinh sống nơi đó.

Cây xương rồng là một loại thảo mộc mọc trên sa mạc. Nó lưu giữ nước trong cuống lá. Tử kinh là một loại xương rồng lớn. Có nhiều loài thú sa mạc ở trong cây tử kinh.

Một số loài thú có lối sống đặc biệt trên sa mạc. Có loài thú có lối tự bảo vệ chống sức nóng của mặc trời. Có loài có cách săn lùng thức ăn. Có loài có cách trốn tránh kẻ thù. Một số loài thú sa mạc săn lùng thức ăn ban đêm.

Sa mạc có thể gây hứng thú để viếng thăm. Sa mạc có trên khắp thế giới.

Multilingual Summaries

Korean

사막에서 걷기

사막은 매우 건조하다. 하지만 많은 식물과 동물들이 그 곳에 산다.

선인장은 사막에서 자라는 식물이다. 선인장은 줄기 안에 물을 저장한다. 사과로 선인장은 키가 크다. 많은 사막 동물들은사과로 선인장 안에서 산다.

동물들은 사막에서 사는 특별한 방법을 가지고 있다. 어떤 동물을은 뜨거운 태양으로부터 자신을 보호하는 방법을 가지고 있다. 어떤 동물들은 먹이를 찾는 방법을 가지고 있다. 또 어떤 동물은 적으로부터 도망치는 법을 알고 있다. 어떤 사막 동물들은 밤에 먹이를 찾아 나선다.

사막은 방문하기에 신나는 곳이다. 세상 여기 저기에 사막이 있다.

Hmong

Taug Kev Hauv Thaj Chaw Moj Siab Qhua

Thaj chaw moj siab qhua mas qhuav heev. Tiamsis tseem muaj ntau yam nrojtsuag thiab tsiaj nyob ntawd.

Ntoo pos yog ib hom nrojtsuag uas loj hlob hauv thaj chaw moj siab qhua. Nws muaj dej nyob hauv tej cag ntoo. Saguaro yog ib tsob ntoo pos siab siab. Muaj ntau tus tsiaj ua tsev rau tsob saguaro.

Tej cov tsiaj muaj tswvyim nyob taug hauv thaj chaw moj siab qhua. Ib txhia txawj tiv thaiv lawv thaus lub nub kub kub. Ib txhia txawj mus tua nrhiav mov noj. Ib txhia txawj nrhiav kev tsiv ntawm lawv cov yeeb ncuab. Ib txhia tsiaj nrhiav mov noj taus mo ntuj.

Thaj chaw moj siab qhua yog ib thaj chaw lomzem mus saib. Cov chaw moj siab qhua muaj ntau nyob thoob ntiajteb.

Name ____________________

- **Read** *The Saguaro Cactus* again.
- **Answer** the questions.

Pages	Question	Answer
2–3	**1.** What is a saguaro?	
2–3	**2.** When does a saguaro look fat?	
4–5	**3.** What happens to some saguaro seeds?	
6–7	**4.** What do spines have?	
8	**5.** What do saguaros help?	

Family Link

Has anyone in your family ever been to a desert? Ask family members to tell you what they know about the desert.

Weekly Resources Guide for English Language Learner Support

For this week's content and language objectives, see p. 53e.

Instructional Strand	Day 1	Day 2
Concept Development	TEACHER'S EDITION • Concept Development, p. DI•96 • Anchored Talk, pp. 150j—150–151 • *Sing with Me* Big Book, p. 152a • Concept Talk Video ELL HANDBOOK • ELL Poster Talk, Concept Talk, p. 53c ELL POSTER 5 • Day 1 Activities	TEACHER'S EDITION • Concept Development, p. DI•96 • Anchored Talk, p. 156b • *Sing with Me* Big Book, p. 156a • Concept Talk Video ELL HANDBOOK • ELL Poster Talk, Concept Talk, p. 53c • Concept Talk Video Routine, p. 464 ELL POSTER 5 • Day 2 Activities
Phonics/Phonemic Awareness	TEACHER'S EDITION • Preteach Phonemic Awareness, p. DI•97 • Preteach Phonics, p. DI•97 • Decodable Reader 5A, pp. 154b–154c	TEACHER'S EDITION • Practice Phonemic Awareness, p. DI•97 • Listen and Write Phonics, p. DI•97
Listening Comprehension	TEACHER'S EDITION • Modified Read Aloud, p. DI•99 • *Sing with Me* Big Book, p. 152a • Read Aloud, p. 155b • Concept Talk Video ELL HANDBOOK • Concept Talk Video Routine, p. 464	TEACHER'S EDITION • Modified Read Aloud, p. DI•99 • *Sing with Me* Big Book, p. 156a • AudioText of *The Strongest One* • Concept Talk Video ELL HANDBOOK • AudioText CD Routine, p. 464 • Main Idea, p. 474
Reading Comprehension	TEACHER'S EDITION • Teach Facts and Details, p. DI•101	TEACHER'S EDITION • Teach Facts and Details, p. DI•101 • Frontloading Reading, p. DI•102 ELL HANDBOOK • Picture It! Skill Instruction, pp. 54–54a • Multilingual Summaries, pp. 55–57
Vocabulary **High-Frequency Words** **Synonyms**	TEACHER'S EDITION • High-Frequency Words, p. DI•100 • Synonyms, p. DI•98 ELL HANDBOOK • Word Cards, p. 53 • ELL Vocabulary Routine, p. 456 ELL POSTER 5 • Day 1 Activities	TEACHER'S EDITION • High-Frequency Words, p. DI•100 • Synonyms, p. DI•98 ELL HANDBOOK • Word Cards, p. 53 • Multilingual Vocabulary List, pp. 429–440 ELL POSTER 5 • Day 2 Activities
Grammar and Conventions	TEACHER'S EDITION • Preteach Imperative and Exclamatory Sentences, p. DI•104	TEACHER'S EDITION • Reteach Imperative and Exclamatory Sentences, p. DI•104
Writing	TEACHER'S EDITION • Play Scene, p. DI•105 • Introduce Play Scene, pp. 155d–155e	TEACHER'S EDITION • Writer's Craft: Developing Characters, pp. 173d–173e

Unit 1 Week 5 The Strongest One

This symbol indicates leveled instruction to address language proficiency levels.

Day 3	Day 4	Day 5
TEACHER'S EDITION • Concept Development, p. DI•96 • Anchored Talk, p. 174b • *Sing With Me* Big Book, p. 174a • Concept Talk Video ELL HANDBOOK • ELL Poster Talk, Concept Talk, p. 53c ELL POSTER 5 • Day 3 Activities	TEACHER'S EDITION • Concept Development, p. DI•96 • Anchored Talk, p. 178b • *Sing With Me* Big Book, p. 178a • Concept Talk Video ELL HANDBOOK • ELL Poster Talk, Concept Talk, p. 53c ELL POSTER 5 • Day 4 Activities	TEACHER'S EDITION • Concept Development, p. DI•96 • Concept Talk Video ELL HANDBOOK • ELL Poster Talk, Concept Talk, p. 53c ELL POSTER 5 • Day 5 Activities
ELL HANDBOOK • Phonics Transition Lesson, pp. 237, 243	TEACHER'S EDITION • Decodable Reader 5C, pp. 178e–178f ELL HANDBOOK • Phonics Transition Lesson, pp. 237, 243	TEACHER'S EDITION • Reteach Phonics, p. DI•98
TEACHER'S EDITION • *Sing With Me* Big Book, p. 174a • AudioText of *The Strongest One* • Concept Talk Video ELL HANDBOOK • AudioText CD Routine, p. 464	TEACHER'S EDITION • *Sing With Me* Big Book, p. 178a • Concept Talk Video	TEACHER'S EDITION • Concept Talk Video
TEACHER'S EDITION • Sheltered Reading, p. DI•102 ELL HANDBOOK • Multilingual Summaries, pp. 55–57	TEACHER'S EDITION • ELL/ELD Reader Guided Reading, p. DI•103 ELL HANDBOOK • ELL Study Guide, p. 58	TEACHER'S EDITION • ELL/ELD Reader Guided Reading, p. DI•103 ELL HANDBOOK • ELL Study Guide, p. 58
ELL HANDBOOK • High-Frequency Words Activity Bank, p. 491 ELL POSTER 5 • Day 3 Activities	ELL HANDBOOK • High-Frequency Words Activity Bank, p. 491	TEACHER'S EDITION • Synonyms, p. 182–183 ELL HANDBOOK • High-Frequency Words Activity Bank, p. 491
TEACHER'S EDITION • Grammar Jammer ELL HANDBOOK • Grammar Transition Lesson, pp. 348, 360–361 • Grammar Jammer Routine, p. 465	TEACHER'S EDITION • Grammar Jammer ELL HANDBOOK • Grammar Transition Lesson, pp. 348, 360–361	TEACHER'S EDITION • Grammar Jammer ELL HANDBOOK • Grammar Transition Lesson, pp. 348, 360–361
TEACHER'S EDITION • Let's Write It!, p. 176–177 • Writing Trait: Conventions, p. 177a	TEACHER'S EDITION • Revising Strategy, pp. 181c–181d	TEACHER'S EDITION • Writing Trait: Conventions, pp. 183h–183i

Poster Talk, Concept Talk

Question of the Week

How does exploration help us find answers?

ELL Poster 5

Throughout the week, use the ELL Poster to help children produce and comprehend language, understand the concept, and build English vocabulary. Use the Question of the Week and other questions to help children share ideas in pairs, small groups, or the large group. Sample questions are shown, with examples of possible responses by children.

Weekly Concept and Language Goals

- Know that exploring helps us find answers
- Tell about how exploring helps us learn

By the end of the lesson, children should be able to talk about and write one or more sentences about learning through exploration.

Daily Team Talk

Day 1	Day 2	Day 3	Day 4	Day 5
After Day 1 activities on Poster, ask questions such as *In the poster picture, why did the woman explore the forest?*	After Day 2 activity on Poster, ask questions such as *What do you think the woman learned by exploring the forest?*	After Day 3 activity on Poster, ask questions such as *Imagine you move to a new neighborhood. How will you explore it?*	After Day 4 activity on Poster, ask questions such as *In* The Strongest One, *what answer does Little Red Ant find by exploring?*	After Day 5 activity on Poster, ask questions such as *How can exploring your library help you find answers to your questions?*
Beginning To build a house. **Intermediate** To get trees to build her house. **Advanced** She wanted to find trees for her house. **Advanced High** The woman explored the forest to find trees she could use to build her new house.	**Beginning** About trees. **Intermediate** She learned about trees and other things in the forest. **Advanced** She learned about plants and animals that live in the forest. **Advanced High** I think the woman learned about how the forest could help her.	**Beginning** With friends. **Intermediate** Ask a neighbor to show me around. **Advanced** Make new friends and let them show me the neighborhood. **Advanced High** I will talk to the neighborhood kids and ask them what I should explore.	**Beginning** Who is strong. **Intermediate** Ants are strong. **Advanced** Everyone is strong. **Advanced High** Everything is stronger than something else.	**Beginning** I get books. **Intermediate** I can look in books. **Advanced** Books and the librarian can help me find answers. **Advanced High** I can use books, magazines, and computers in the library to find answers to my questions.

This Week's Materials

Teacher's Edition pages 150j–183k

See the support for English language learners throughout the lesson, including ELL strategies and scaffold activities at points of use.

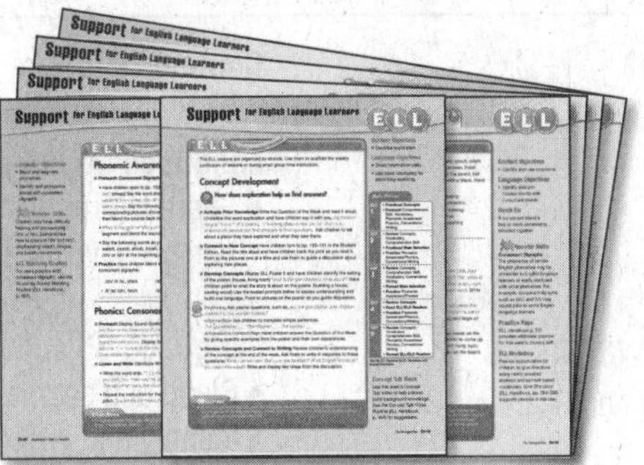

Teacher's Edition pages DI•96–DI•105

Differentiated Instruction for English language learners provides daily group activities that "frontload," or preteach, core instruction.

ELL Handbook pp. 53a–58

Find additional lesson materials that support the core lesson and the ELL instructional pages.

ELL Poster 5

ELD Reader 2.1.5

ELL Reader 2.1.5

Concept Literacy Reader

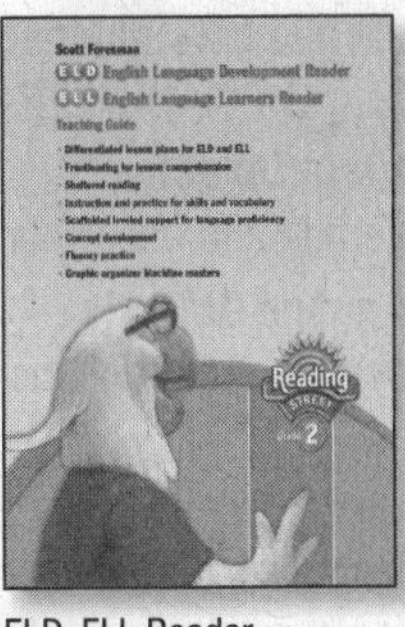

ELD, ELL Reader Teaching Guide

Concept Literacy Reader Teaching Guide

Technology

Online Teacher's Edition Use the digital version of the core teacher's edition for planning and instruction.

eReaders
This Week's ELL and ELD Readers and Concept Literacy Reader are also available in digital format.

This Week's Content and Language Objectives by Strand

Concept Development How does exploration help us find answers?	**Content Objective** • Describe exploration. **Language Objectives** • Share information orally. • Use basic vocabulary for describing exploring.
Phonics/Phonemic Awareness Consonant Digraphs; Blend and Segment	**Language Objectives** • Blend and segment phonemes. • Identify and pronounce words with consonant digraphs.
Listening Comprehension Modified Read Aloud: "All About Ants"	**Content Objective** • Monitor and adjust oral comprehension. **Language Objectives** • Discuss oral passages. • Use a graphic organizer to take notes.
Reading Comprehension Facts and Details	**Content Objectives** • Identify facts and details. • Monitor and adjust comprehension. **Language Objectives** • Discuss facts and details. • Find facts and details in text. • Learn academic vocabulary spoken in classroom. • Write facts and details. • Summarize text using visual support.
Vocabulary High-Frequency Words	**Language Objectives** • Understand and use basic vocabulary. • Ask and give information using high-frequency words.
Vocabulary Synonyms	**Content Objective** • Identify and use synonyms. **Language Objective** • Identify and pronounce words with consonant blends.
Grammar and Conventions Imperative and Exclamatory Sentences	**Content Objectives** • Recognize punctuation used in imperative and exclamatory sentences. • Use correct punctuation in imperative and exclamatory sentences. **Language Objectives** • Give commands and make exclamations. • Write imperative and exclamatory sentences. • Distinguish intonation patterns of English.
Writing Play Scene	**Content Objectives** • Recognize capitalization in parts of a play. • Identify characteristics of a play. **Language Objectives** • Write parts in a play using correct capitalization. • Share feedback for editing and revising.

Word Cards for Vocabulary Activities

gone	**learn**
often	**pieces**
though	**together**
very	

Teacher Note: Beginning Teach two to three words. **Intermediate** Teach three to four words. **Advanced** Teach five to six words. **Advanced High** Teach all words.

Name ______________________________

Look at the picture. **Read** the story.

A Rainy Day

Great-Grandmother was an amazing woman. She could lift heavy things and make plants grow. One day it was raining so hard that the rain soaked through the roof. Everyone was wet. Great-Grandmother took a very deep breath and blew as hard as she could. She blew the clouds away, and the sun came out.

Answer the questions.

1. What is something Great-Grandmother could do?

a. talk to animals
b. bake cookies
c. make plants grow
d. make it rain

2. Why was the rain a problem?

a. It made a flood.
b. It soaked through the roof.
c. It broke the plants.
d. It froze into ice.

Facts and Details

Use this lesson to supplement or replace the skill lesson on page 155a of the Teacher's Edition. Display the Skill Points (at right) and share them with children.

Use the Skill Points to preteach facts and details.

Teach/Model

Beginning Ask children to think about rain. Say: *Rain is wet. Is this a fact or opinion?* Say: *A fact is something that is true. This sentence tells a fact.*

Intermediate Display the following and read aloud: *Rain falls from the sky. Rain makes plants grow. Rain is made of milk.* Ask: *Which sentences tell facts?* Have children underline the facts.

Advanced Give an example of a fact: *Rain comes from clouds.* Have children suggest another fact about the same topic, rain. If they offer opinions or untrue statements, remind them that they must be able to prove that the information is true for it to be a fact.

Advanced High Ask children to write one fact about the weather. Then have them write one (false) silly statement on the same topic. Read aloud one sentence from each child. Have the group decide whether the statement tells a fact.

Skill Points

✔ A **fact** is information. It can be proven true or false. You can check a book, ask someone who knows, or see for yourself.

✔ **Details** are small pieces of information. They help you understand what you read.

Then distribute copies of Picture It! page 54.

- Have children look at the pictures and describe what they see.
- Read the paragraph aloud. Ask: *Can you find a fact in the paragraph?*
- Review the Skill Points with children.
- Have children look at the picture and paragraph to find facts and details.

Practice

Read aloud the directions on page 54. Reread or chorally read the story. Have children look at the picture and the story as they answer the questions.

Beginning Children can orally answer and, with help, mark their answers.

Intermediate Children can first orally answer and then mark their answers on the page.

Advanced Children can mark their answers and check them by comparing them with a partner's answers.

Advanced High Children can mark their answers and check them by reviewing the paragraph and making any necessary corrections.

Answers for page 54: 1. c; 2. b

Multilingual Summaries

English

The Strongest One

Little Red Ant wants to know who is the strongest. Little Red Ant asks Snow. Snow says Sun is the strongest. Sun says Wind is the strongest. Wind says House is the strongest. House says Mouse is the strongest. Mouse says Cat is the strongest. Cat says Stick is the strongest. Stick says Fire is the strongest. Fire says Water is the strongest. Water says Deer is the strongest. Deer says Arrow is the strongest. Arrow says Big Rock is the strongest. Big Rock says Ants are the strongest.

What did Little Red Ant learn? Little Red Ant learned that everything can be stronger than something else!

Spanish

El más fuerte

Pequeña Hormiga Roja quiere saber quién es más fuerte. Ella le pregunta a Nieve. Nieve dice que Sol es el más fuerte. Sol dice que Viento es el más fuerte. Viento dice que es Casa. Casa dice que es Ratón. Ratón dice que es Gato. Gato dice que es Palo. Palo dice que es Fuego. Fuego dice que Agua es el más fuerte. Agua dice que es Venado. Venado dice que es Flecha. Flecha dice que es Piedra Grande. Piedra Grande dice que Pequeña Hormiga es la más fuerte.

¿Qué aprendió hormiga Roja? Aprendió que ¡cada cosa puede ser más fuerte que otra!

Chinese

最强壮的一个

小红蚁想知道谁是最强壮的，所以他就问雪人，雪人说太阳最强壮，太阳却说风最强壮，风却说房子最强壮，房子却说耗子最强壮，耗子却说猫最强壮，猫却说棍子最强壮，棍子却说火最强壮，火却说水最强壮，水说却说鹿子最强壮，鹿子却说箭最强壮，箭却说大石最强壮，大石却说蚂蚁最强壮。

小红蚁学到什么呢？他学到所有东西都可能强过别的。

Vietnamese

Kẻ mạnh nhất

Kiến Lửa nhỏ muốn biết ai là kẻ mạnh nhất Kiến lửa nhỏ hỏi bác Tuyết. Bác Tuyết bảo Mặt Trời mạnh nhất. Ma9.t Trời bảo Gió mạnh nhất. Gió bảo Cái Nhà mạnh nhất Cái Nhà bảo Chuột mạnh nhất. Chuột bảo Mèo mạnh nhất. Mèo bảo Cây Gậy mạnh nhất. Cây Gậy bảo Lửa mạnh nhất. Lửa bảo Nước mạnh nhất. Nước bảo Hươu mạnh nhất. Hươu bảo Mũi Tên mạnh nhất. Mũi Tên bảo Tảng Đá mạnh nhất. Tảng Đá bảo Kiến mạnh nhất.

Kiến Lửa nhỏ biết được điều gì? Kiến Lửa nhỏ biết được rằng mọi vật đều có thể mạnh hơn một vật gì khác.

Multilingual Summaries

Korean

가장 힘센 자

꼬마 빨간 개미는 누가 가장 힘이 센지 알고 싶었다. 꼬마 빨간 개미는 눈에게 물었다. 눈은 해가 가장 힘이 세다고 했다. 해는 바람이 가장 힘이 세다고 했다. 바람은 집이 가장 힘이 세다고 했다. 집은 쥐가 가장 힘이 세다고 했다. 쥐는 고양이가 가장 힘이 세다고 했다. 고양이는 막대기가 가장 힘이 세다고 했다. 막대기는 불이 가장 힘이 세다고 했다. 불은 물이 가장 힘이 세다고 했다. 물은 사슴이 가장 힘이 세다고 했다. 사슴은 화살이 가장 힘이 세다고 했다. 화살은 큰 돌이 가장 힘이 세다고 했다. 큰 돌은 개미가 가장 힘이 세다고 했다.

꼬마 빨간 개미는 무었을 배웠을까? 꼬마 빨간 개미는 이 세상 모든 것은 다른 것보다 상대적으로 더 힘이 셀 수 있다는 것을 배웠다.

Hmong

Tus Muaj Zog Tshaj

Ntsaum Liab Me xav paub leej twg muaj zog tshaj. Ntsaum Liab Me nus Te. Te hais tias Nub yog tus muaj zog tshaj. Nub has tias Cua yog tus muaj zog tshaj. Cua hais tias Tsev yog tus muaj zog tshaj. Tsev hais tias Nastsuag yog tus muaj zog tshaj. Nastsuag hais tias Tshwsmiv yog tus muaj zog tshaj. Tshwsmiv haiv tias Cagntoo yog tus muaj zog tshaj. Cagntoo hais tias Hluavtaws yog tus muaj zog tshaj. Hluavtaws hais tias Dej yog tug muaj zog tshaj. Dej hais tias Muaslwj yog tus muaj zog tshaj. Muajlwj has tias Xibxub yog tus muaj zog tshaj. Xibxub hais tias Pobzeb Loj yog tus muaj zog tshaj. Pobzeb Loj hais tias Ntsaum yog cov muaj zog tshaj.

Ntsaum Liab Me xyaum tau dabtsi? Ntsaum Liab Me xyaum tau tias txhua yam yeej muaj peevxwm muaj zog dua lwm yam.

Name ______________________________

- **Read** *Bear and Squirrel* again.
- **Draw** a picture that shows how a bear gets food.
- **Draw** a picture that shows how a squirrel gets food.
- **Write** a sentence that goes with each picture.

A Bear Gets Food

____

A Squirrel Gets Food

____

Family Link

Ask family members to tell you about when they went grocery shopping for the first time.

Weekly Resources Guide for English Language Learner Support

For this week's content and language objectives, see p. 59e.

Instructional Strand	Day 1	Day 2
Concept Development	TEACHER'S EDITION • Concept Development, p. DI•12 • Anchored Talk, pp. 186j—186–187 • *Sing With Me* Big Book, p. 188a • Concept Talk Video ELL HANDBOOK • ELL Poster Talk, Concept Talk, p. 59c ELL POSTER 6 • Day 1 Activities	TEACHER'S EDITION • Concept Development, p. DI•12 • Anchored Talk, p. 192b • *Sing With Me* Big Book, p. 192a • Concept Talk Video ELL HANDBOOK • ELL Poster Talk, Concept Talk, p. 59c • Concept Talk Video Routine, p. 464 ELL POSTER 6 • Day 2 Activities
Phonics/Phonemic Awareness	TEACHER'S EDITION • Preteach Phonemic Awareness, p. DI•13 • Preteach Phonics, p. DI•13 • Decodable Reader 6A, pp. 190b–190c	TEACHER'S EDITION • Practice Phonemic Awareness, p. DI•13 • Listen and Write Phonics, p. DI•13
Listening Comprehension	TEACHER'S EDITION • Modified Read Aloud, p. DI•15 • *Sing With Me* Big Book, p. 188a • Read Aloud, p. 191b • Concept Talk Video ELL HANDBOOK • Concept Talk Video Routine, p. 464	TEACHER'S EDITION • Modified Read Aloud, p. DI•15 • *Sing With Me* Big Book, p. 192a • AudioText of *Tara and Tiree* • Concept Talk Video ELL HANDBOOK • AudioText CD Routine, p. 464 • Story Map A, p. 470
Reading Comprehension	TEACHER'S EDITION • Teach Cause and Effect, p. DI•17	TEACHER'S EDITION • Teach Cause and Effect, p. DI•17 • Frontloading Reading, p. DI•18 ELL HANDBOOK • Picture It! Skill Instruction, pp. 60–60a • Multilingual Summaries, pp. 61–63
Vocabulary **High-Frequency Words** **Unfamiliar Words**	TEACHER'S EDITION • High-Frequency Words, p. DI•16 • Unfamiliar Words, p. DI•14 ELL HANDBOOK • Word Cards, p. 59 • ELL Vocabulary Routine, p. 456 ELL POSTER 6 • Day 1 Activities	TEACHER'S EDITION • High-Frequency Words, p. DI•16 • Unfamiliar Words, p. DI•14 ELL HANDBOOK • Word Cards, p. 59 • Multilingual Vocabulary List, pp. 429–440 ELL POSTER 6 • Day 2 Activities
Grammar and Conventions	TEACHER'S EDITION • Preteach Nouns, p. DI•20	TEACHER'S EDITION • Reteach Nouns, p. DI•20
Writing	TEACHER'S EDITION • Narrative Nonfiction, p. DI•21 • Introduce Narrative Nonfiction, pp. 191d–191e	TEACHER'S EDITION • Writer's Craft: Sequence, pp. 207c–207d

Unit 2 Week 1 Tara and Tiree, Fearless Friends

This symbol indicates leveled instruction to address language proficiency levels.

Day 3	Day 4	Day 5
TEACHER'S EDITION • Concept Development, p. DI•12 • Anchored Talk, p. 208b • *Sing With Me* Big Book, p. 208a • Concept Talk Video **ELL HANDBOOK** • ELL Poster Talk, Concept Talk, p. 59c **ELL POSTER 6** • Day 3 Activities	**TEACHER'S EDITION** • Concept Development, p. DI•12 • Anchored Talk, p. 212b • *Sing With Me* Big Book, p. 212a • Concept Talk Video **ELL HANDBOOK** • ELL Poster Talk, Concept Talk, p. 59c **ELL POSTER 6** • Day 4 Activities	**TEACHER'S EDITION** • Concept Development, p. DI•12 • Concept Talk Video **ELL HANDBOOK** • ELL Poster Talk, Concept Talk, p. 59c **ELL POSTER 6** • Day 5 Activities
ELL HANDBOOK • Phonics Transition Lesson, pp. 270, 272	**TEACHER'S EDITION** • Decodable Reader 6C, pp. 212e–212f **ELL HANDBOOK** • Phonics Transition Lesson, pp. 270, 272	**TEACHER'S EDITION** • Reteach Phonics, p. DI•14
TEACHER'S EDITION • *Sing With Me* Big Book, p. 208a • AudioText of *Tara and Tiree* • Concept Talk Video **ELL HANDBOOK** • AudioText CD Routine, p. 464	**TEACHER'S EDITION** • *Sing With Me* Big Book, p. 212a • Concept Talk Video	**TEACHER'S EDITION** • Concept Talk Video
TEACHER'S EDITION • Sheltered Reading, p. DI•18 **ELL HANDBOOK** • Multilingual Summaries, pp. 61–63	**TEACHER'S EDITION** • ELL/ELD Reader Guided Reading, p. DI•19 **ELL HANDBOOK** • ELL Study Guide, p. 64	**TEACHER'S EDITION** • ELL/ELD Reader Guided Reading, p. DI•19 **ELL HANDBOOK** • ELL Study Guide, p. 64
ELL HANDBOOK • High-Frequency Words Activity Bank, p. 491 **ELL POSTER 6** • Day 3 Activities	**ELL HANDBOOK** • High-Frequency Words Activity Bank, p. 491	**TEACHER'S EDITION** • Unfamiliar Words, p. 216–217 **ELL HANDBOOK** • High-Frequency Words Activity Bank, p. 491
TEACHER'S EDITION • Grammar Jammer **ELL HANDBOOK** • Grammar Transition Lesson, pp. 312, 316, 317 • Grammar Jammer Routine, p. 465	**TEACHER'S EDITION** • Grammar Jammer **ELL HANDBOOK** • Grammar Transition Lesson, pp. 312, 316, 317	**TEACHER'S EDITION** • Grammar Jammer **ELL HANDBOOK** • Grammar Transition Lesson, pp. 312, 316, 317
TEACHER'S EDITION • Let's Write It!, p. 210–211 • Writing Trait: Voice, p. 211a	**TEACHER'S EDITION** • Revising Strategy, pp. 215c–215d	**TEACHER'S EDITION** • Writer's Craft: Nouns, pp. 217h–217i

Poster Talk, Concept Talk

Question of the Week

How can we help each other in dangerous situations?

Poster 6

Throughout the week, use the ELL Poster to help children produce and comprehend language, understand the concept, and build English vocabulary. Use the Question of the Week and other questions to help children share ideas in pairs, small groups, or the large group. Sample questions are shown, with examples of possible responses by children.

Weekly Concept and Language Goals

- Understand the concept of working together in dangerous situations
- Identify steps people take in an emergency
- Describe ways to plan ahead for dealing with danger

By the end of the lesson, children should be able to talk about and write one or more sentences about helping people in danger.

Daily Team Talk

Day 1	Day 2	Day 3	Day 4	Day 5
After Day 1 activities on Poster, ask questions such as: *Why are people helping the cat?*	After Day 2 activity on Poster, ask questions such as: *How can you get help for a friend who is in danger?*	After Day 3 activity on Poster, ask questions such as: *On the poster, people help an animal. How is the story about Tara and Tiree different?*	After Day 4 activity on Poster, ask questions such as: *In the poster picture, how does working together help?*	After Day 5 activities on Poster, ask questions such as: *What kind of plan can a family make for an emergency?*
Beginning Cat is in tree. **Intermediate** The cat can fall from a tree. **Advanced** The cat in the tree is in danger. **Advanced High** The cat needs help getting down.	**Beginning** Get mom or dad. **Intermediate** Go ask a parent to help. **Advanced** Ask a parent or another adult to help. **Advanced High** Ask a parent, a firefighter, or another adult to help.	**Beginning** Dogs help a man. **Intermediate** The dogs help a person. **Advanced** Tara and Tiree are animals that help a person. **Advanced High** The animals, Tara and Tiree, save Jim from danger.	**Beginning** People help with a ladder. **Intermediate** Two people use a ladder to help. **Advanced** Two people use a ladder to save a cat. **Advanced High** Two firefighters use a ladder to save a cat.	**Beginning** A plan to get out of the house. **Intermediate** They can plan to get out of the house. **Advanced** They can plan safe ways to get out of the house. **Advanced High** They can plan to get out of the house safely. They can plan to find each other.

This Week's Materials

Teacher's Edition pages 186j–217k

See the support for English language learners throughout the lesson, including ELL strategies and scaffold activities at points of use.

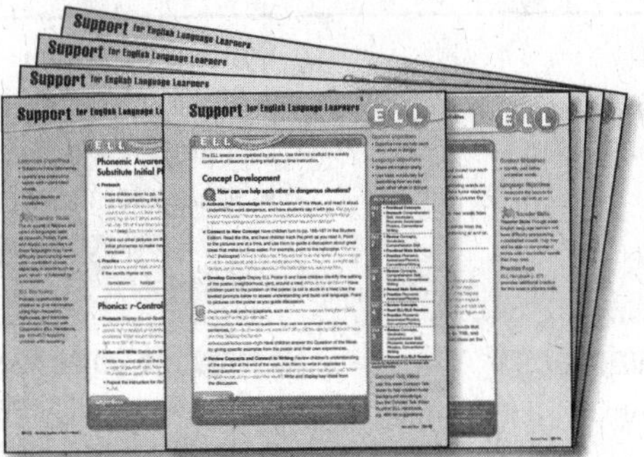

Teacher's Edition pages DI•12–DI•21

Differentiated Instruction for English language learners provides daily group activities that "frontload," or preteach, core instruction.

ELL Handbook pp. 59a–64

Find additional lesson materials that support the core lesson and the ELL instructional pages.

ELL Poster 6

ELD Reader 2.2.1

ELL Reader 2.2.1

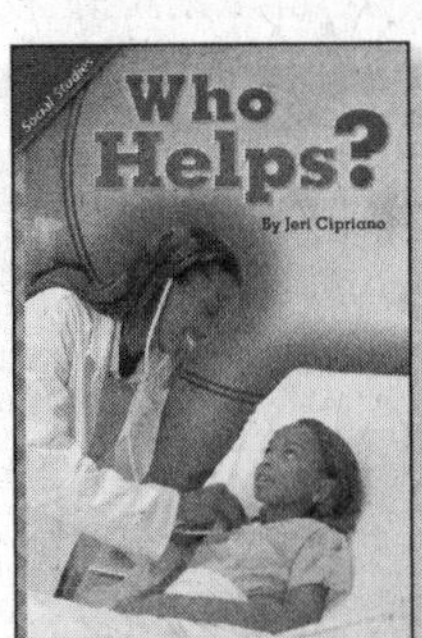

Concept Literacy Reader

ELD, ELL Reader Teaching Guide

Concept Literacy Reader Teaching Guide

Technology

Online Teacher's Edition Use the digital version of the core teacher's edition for planning and instruction.

eReaders
This Week's ELL and ELD Readers and Concept Literacy Reader are also available in digital format.

This Week's Content and Language Objectives by Strand

Concept Development How can we help each other in dangerous situations?	**Content Objective** • Describe how we help each other when in danger. **Language Objectives** • Share information orally. • Use basic vocabulary for describing how we help each other when in danger.
Phonics/Phonemic Awareness r-Controlled Vowels; Substitute Initial Phonemes	**Language Objectives** • Substitute initial phonemes. • Identify and pronounce words with *r*-controlled vowels. • Produce sounds of vocabulary.
Listening Comprehension Modified Read Aloud: "Maya Forgets Her Fear"	**Content Objective** • Monitor and adjust oral comprehension. **Language Objectives** • Discuss oral passages. • Use a graphic organizer to take notes.
Reading Comprehension Cause and Effect	**Content Objectives** • Identify cause and effect. • Identify cause and effect to aid comparison. • Monitor and adjust comprehension. **Language Objectives** • Retell cause and effect of events from a reading. • Use language structures to comprehend. • Write about causes and effects. • Summarize text using visual support.
Vocabulary High-Frequency Words	**Language Objectives** • Monitor understanding of spoken language. • Use high-frequency English words.
Vocabulary Unfamiliar Words	**Content Objective** • Identify and define unfamiliar words. **Language Objective** • Associate the sounds for /ar/ and /or/ with *ar, or.*
Grammar and Conventions Nouns	**Content Objectives** • Identify and use nouns. • Correctly use nouns in sentences. **Language Objectives** • Speak using nouns in sentences. • Write phrases and sentences with nouns.
Writing Narrative Nonfiction	**Content Objectives** • Identify words used in narrative nonfiction. • Identify the characteristics of narrative nonfiction. **Language Objectives** • Write sentences using words that reveal how the writer feels about the topic. • Describe with increasing specificity. • Share feedback for editing and revising.

Word Cards for Vocabulary Activities

break	**family**
heard	**listen**
once	**pull**

Leveled LS Support

Teacher Note: Beginning Teach two to three words. **Intermediate** Teach three to four words. **Advanced** Teach five to six words. **Advanced High** Teach all words.

Name ______________________________

Picture It!
Cause and Effect

Look at the picture. **Read** the story.

Out in a Storm

Buster barked. Marie let Buster out to play in the yard.

Then it started to snow. Marie called Buster.

He came running. What a good dog!

Answer the questions.

1. What happened when Buster barked?

____

____

2. Why did Buster come running?

____

____

Cause and Effect

Use this lesson to supplement or replace the skill lesson on page 191a of the Teacher's Edition. Display the Skill Points (at right) and share them with children.

Use the Skill Points to preteach cause and effect.

Teach/Model

Beginning Ask children to think about pet dogs. Say: *You call a dog. Will the dog come or go away?* (The dog will come.) Write on the board: *I call my dog. The dog comes.* Help children identify the cause and the effect.

Intermediate Write on the board: *A child calls. The dog comes running.* Have children copy the sentences. Guide them in identifying cause and effect. They might write *Cause* or *Effect* near each sentence.

Advanced Give an example of cause and effect: *A child calls her dog. The dog comes running.* Have children suggest another example of cause and effect.

Advanced High Give an example of an action that may cause an effect: *A dog runs from the yard to the door and barks.* Have children suggest possible effects (A person in the house looks out; a person opens the door to let the dog in).

Then distribute copies of Picture It! page 60.

- Have children look at the pictures. Help them tell what happens in each one. If necessary, briefly discuss the verb *to snow.*
- Read the story aloud. Ask: *What causes Marie to let Buster out? What causes Marie to call Buster?* Provide English words as needed to answer.
- Share the Skill Points (at right) with children.
- Have them look at the pictures and story to identify cause and effect.

Practice

Read aloud the directions on page 60. Reread or chorally read the story. Have children look at the pictures and the story as they answer the questions.

Beginning Children can orally answer and, with help, write words on the answer blanks.

Intermediate Children can first orally answer and then write the answers on the page. Provide help with writing and spelling.

Advanced Children can write their answers and check them by quietly reading them aloud or comparing them with a partner's.

Advanced High Children can write their answers and check them by silently reading them and making any necessary corrections.

Answers for page 60: 1. Marie let him out. 2. Marie called him.

Skill Points

✔ A **cause** is why something happens. An **effect** is what happens.

✔ As you read, ask yourself: *What is happening? Why is it happening?*

Multilingual Summaries

English

Tara and Tiree

Jim and his family always had dogs. He loved them. When he grew up, Jim got two dogs of his own. They were named Tara and Tiree. Jim and the dogs liked the winter. They liked to go for walks in the snow.

One day, Jim and the dogs walked on the ice on a lake. The ice broke and Jim fell in. No one heard him calling for help. The dogs stayed near Jim. Tiree tried to help. But she fell in the water. Then Tara tried to help. But Jim was too big. Tiree walked on Jim's back and got out of the water. Together, the dogs pulled Jim out of the water. They saved his life! Jim loved his dogs even more.

Spanish

Tara y Tiree

Jim y su familia siempre tuvieron perros. Jim los quería mucho. Cuando creció, Jim tuvo dos perros propios. Sus nombres eran Tara y Tiree. A Jim y a sus perros les encantaba el invierno. Les gustaba salir a dar paseos en la nieve.

Un día, Jim y sus perros salieron a dar un paseo a un lago congelado. El hielo se rompió y Jim cayó adentro. Nadie lo oía gritar pidiendo ayuda. Tara y Tiree se quedaron cerca de Jim. Tiree trató de ayudarlo, pero también cayó al agua. Luego Tara trató de ayudarlo, pero Jim era demasiado grande. Tiree caminó sobre la espalda de Jim y salió del agua. Entre los dos, por fin lograron sacarlo del agua. ¡Ellos le salvaron la vida! Jim quiere aún más a sus perros.

Multilingual Summaries

Chinese

泰拉與泰利

吉姆和他的家人一直都有養狗，吉姆很喜歡狗，長大以後，他自己也養了兩隻狗，他們的名字叫泰拉和泰利。吉姆和狗狗都喜歡冬天，因為冬天可以在雪地上散步。

有一天，吉姆和狗狗走在結冰的湖面上，冰突然破了，吉姆掉進湖裡，沒有人聽到他的求救聲。狗狗留在吉姆附近，泰利想幫忙，可是也掉進水裡去。泰拉也試著要幫忙，可是吉姆太重了，拉不上來。泰利爬到吉姆的背上，跳出水面。兩隻狗狗同心協力把吉姆救了出來。狗狗救了吉姆一命！吉姆比以前更愛狗了。

Vietnamese

Tara và Tiree

Jim và gia đình lúc nào cũng có nuôi chó. Cậu bé yêu thương chó. Khi cậu lớn lên, Jim có hai con chó. Tên của chúng là Tara và Tiree. Jim và hai con chó đều thích mùa đông. Họ thích đi dạo khi có tuyết.

Ngày nọ, Jim và chó đi trên mặt hồ đóng băng. Băng vỡ và Jim bị rơi xuống nước. Không ai nghe tiếng Jim kêu cứu. Hai con chó ở quanh quẩn bên Jim. Tiree cố giúp. Nhưng nó bị rơi xuống nước. Kế đến Tara cố giúp. Nhưng Jim to quá. Tiree đi trên lưng của Jim và thoát ra khỏi hồ. Hai con chó cùng kéo Jim ra khỏi hồ nước. Chúng đã cứu sống Jim! Jim càng thương yêu hai con chó của mình nhiều hơn.

Multilingual Summaries

Korean

타라와 타이리

짐의 가족은 항상 개를 키워왔기 때문에 짐도 개를 사랑한다. 짐은 자라서 자기 개 두 마리를 얻어 타라와 타이리라고 이름 짓는다. 짐과 개들은 겨울과 눈 속에서 걷기를 좋아한다.

어느 날 짐은 개들과 호수의 얼음 위를 걷다가 얼음이 깨지면서 물에 빠진다. 아무도 그가 도와달라고 외치는 말을 듣지 못하는데 마침 개들이 가까이에 있다. 타이리가 짐을 도우려 하지만 물에 빠지고 타라가 이들을 구하려 하지만 그러기엔 짐의 덩치가 너무 크다. 타이리가 짐의 등 위로 기어올라가 물 밖으로 나와 타라와 함께 짐을 물 밖으로 끌어낸다. 개들이 짐의 생명을 구하게 되면서 짐은 개들을 더욱 사랑하게 된다.

Hmong

Tara thiab Tiree

Jim thiab nws tsevneeg yeej ib txwm muaj ib co dev. Nws hlub lawv. Thaum nws loj lawm, Jim kuj muaj ob tug dev uas yog nws tug. Nkawd ob lub npe yog Tara thiab Tiree. Jim thiab nws cov dev nyiam lub caij no. Lawv nyiam mus taug kev saum cov te.

Muaj ib hnub, Jim thiab nws cov dev mus taug kev tom ib lub pas dej uas khov tag. Cov naj kheem tawg ua rau Jim poob rau hauv lub pas dej. Tsis muaj leejtwg hnov nws hu. Cov dev kuj tseem nyob ze ze ntawm Jim. Tiree kuj pab nws. Tiamsis ua rau nws poob rau hauv lub pas dej. Ces Tara thiaj tau pab thiab. Tiamsis Jim nws loj heev. Tiree tau caij Jim lub nrob qaum kom nws tawm tau hauv lub pas dej. Ob tug dev ntawm thiaj uake rub Jim tawm hauv lub pas dej los. Nkawd cawm tau nws txojsia. Jim haj yam hlub nws ob tug dev ntxiv xwb.

Name ____________________

- **Read** *Help!* again.
- **Draw** pictures to show what happens at the beginning, middle, and end of the story. **Write** words or sentences to go with your pictures.

Beginning (pages 2–3)

Middle (pages 4–7)

End (page 8)

Family Link

Has anyone in your family ever taken care of another person? Ask family members to describe how they have helped or cared for another person.

Weekly Resources Guide for English Language Learner Support

For this week's content and language objectives, see p. 65e.

Instructional Strand	Day 1	Day 2
Concept Development	TEACHER'S EDITION • Concept Development, p. DI•33 • Anchored Talk, pp. 218j—218–219 • *Sing With Me* Big Book, p. 220a • Concept Talk Video ELL HANDBOOK • ELL Poster Talk, Concept Talk, p. 65c ELL POSTER 7 • Day 1 Activities	TEACHER'S EDITION • Concept Development, p. DI•33 • Anchored Talk, p. 224b • *Sing With Me* Big Book, p. 224a • Concept Talk Video ELL HANDBOOK • ELL Poster Talk, Concept Talk, p. 65c • Concept Talk Video Routine, p. 464 ELL POSTER 7 • Day 2 Activities
Phonics/Phonemic Awareness	TEACHER'S EDITION • Preteach Phonemic Awareness, p. DI•34 • Preteach Phonics, p. DI•34 • Decodable Reader 7A, pp. 222b–222c	TEACHER'S EDITION • Practice Phonemic Awareness, p. DI•34 • Listen and Write Phonics, p. DI•34
Listening Comprehension	TEACHER'S EDITION • Modified Read Aloud, p. DI•36 • *Sing With Me* Big Book, p. 220a • Read Aloud, p. 223b • Concept Talk Video ELL HANDBOOK • Concept Talk Video Routine, p. 464	TEACHER'S EDITION • Modified Read Aloud, p. DI•36 • *Sing With Me* Big Book, p. 224a • AudioText of *Abraham Lincoln* • Concept Talk Video ELL HANDBOOK • AudioText CD Routine, p. 464 • Time Line, p. 478
Reading Comprehension	TEACHER'S EDITION • Teach Author's Purpose, p. DI•38	TEACHER'S EDITION • Teach Author's Purpose, p. DI•38 • Frontloading Reading, p. DI•39 ELL HANDBOOK • Picture It! Skill Instruction, pp. 66–66a • Multilingual Summaries, pp. 67–69
Vocabulary **High-Frequency Words** **Homophones**	TEACHER'S EDITION • High-Frequency Words, p. DI•37 • Homophones, p. DI•35 ELL HANDBOOK • Word Cards, p. 65 • ELL Vocabulary Routine, p. 456 ELL POSTER 7 • Day 1 Activities	TEACHER'S EDITION • High-Frequency Words, p. DI•37 • Homophones, p. DI•35 ELL HANDBOOK • Word Cards, p. 65 • Multilingual Vocabulary List, pp. 429–440 ELL POSTER 7 • Day 2 Activities
Grammar and Convention	TEACHER'S EDITION • Preteach Proper Nouns, p. DI•41	TEACHER'S EDITION • Reteach Proper Nouns, p. DI•41
Writing	TEACHER'S EDITION • Biography, p. DI•42 • Introduce Biography, pp. 223d–223e	TEACHER'S EDITION • Writing Trait: Focus/Ideas, pp. 239c–239d

This symbol indicates leveled instruction to address language proficiency levels.

Day 3	Day 4	Day 5
TEACHER'S EDITION • Concept Development, p. DI•33 • Anchored Talk, p. 240b • *Sing With Me* Big Book, p. 240a • Concept Talk Video ELL HANDBOOK • ELL Poster Talk, Concept Talk, p. 65c ELL POSTER 7 • Day 3 Activities	TEACHER'S EDITION • Concept Development, p. DI•33 • Anchored Talk, p. 244b • *Sing With Me* Big Book, p. 244a • Concept Talk Video ELL HANDBOOK • ELL Poster Talk, Concept Talk, p. 65c ELL POSTER 7 • Day 4 Activities	TEACHER'S EDITION • Concept Development, p. DI•33 • Concept Talk Video ELL HANDBOOK • ELL Poster Talk, Concept Talk, p. 65c ELL POSTER 7 • Day 5 Activities
ELL HANDBOOK • Phonics Transition Lesson, pp. 283, 286	TEACHER'S EDITION • Decodable Reader 7C, pp. 244e–244f ELL HANDBOOK • Phonics Transition Lesson, pp. 283, 286	TEACHER'S EDITION • Reteach Phonics, p. DI•35
TEACHER'S EDITION • *Sing With Me* Big Book, p. 240a • AudioText of *Abraham Lincoln* • Concept Talk Video ELL HANDBOOK • AudioText CD Routine, p. 464	TEACHER'S EDITION • *Sing With Me* Big Book, p. 244a • Concept Talk Video	TEACHER'S EDITION • Concept Talk Video
TEACHER'S EDITION • Sheltered Reading, p. DI•39 ELL HANDBOOK • Multilingual Summaries, pp. 67–69	TEACHER'S EDITION • ELL/ELD Reader Guided Reading, p. DI•40 ELL HANDBOOK • ELL Study Guide, p. 70	TEACHER'S EDITION • ELL/ELD Reader Guided Reading, p. DI•40 ELL HANDBOOK • ELL Study Guide, p. 70
ELL HANDBOOK • High-Frequency Words Activity Bank, p. 491 ELL POSTER 7 • Day 3 Activities	ELL HANDBOOK • High-Frequency Words Activity Bank, p. 491	TEACHER'S EDITION • Dictionary/Glossary: Guide Words, p. 246–247 ELL HANDBOOK • High-Frequency Words Activity Bank, p. 491
TEACHER'S EDITION • Grammar Jammer ELL HANDBOOK • Grammar Transition Lesson, pp. 312, 318 • Grammar Jammer Routine, p. 465	TEACHER'S EDITION • Grammar Jammer ELL HANDBOOK • Grammar Transition Lesson, pp. 312, 318	TEACHER'S EDITION • Grammar Jammer ELL HANDBOOK • Grammar Transition Lesson, pp. 312, 318
TEACHER'S EDITION • Let's Write It!, p. 242–243 • Writer's Craft: Know Your Purpose, p. 243a	TEACHER'S EDITION • Revising Strategy, pp. 245d–245e	TEACHER'S EDITION • Writer's Craft: Proper Nouns, pp. 247h–247i

Poster Talk, Concept Talk

Question of the Week

How has working together changed history?

Poster 7

Throughout the week, use the ELL Poster to help children produce and comprehend language, understand the concept, and build English vocabulary. Use the Question of the Week and other questions to help children share ideas in pairs, small groups, or the large group. Sample questions are shown, with examples of possible responses by children.

Weekly Concept and Language Goals

- Understand the concept of working together to change history
- Name steps people take to clean up after a storm

By the end of the lesson, children should be able to talk about and write one or more sentences about working together to make changes.

Daily Team Talk

Day 1	Day 2	Day 3	Day 4	Day 5
After Day 1 activity on Poster, ask questions such as *How did trash get on the beach?*	After Day 2 activity on Poster, ask questions such as *How did working together change the beach?*	After Day 3 activity on Poster, ask questions such as *Why should people work together to solve a problem?*	After Day 4 activities on Poster, ask questions such as *What is one thing you can do to clean up a beach after a storm?*	After Day 5 activity on Poster, ask questions such as *What does the beach have today that it didn't have long ago?*
Beginning From people. **Intermediate** People put it there. **Advanced** People left their trash. **Advanced High** People threw their trash on the beach.	**Beginning** It's clean. **Intermediate** The beach is clean. **Advanced** People worked together and cleaned the beach. **Advanced High** People working together made the beach a clean and fun place.	**Beginning** It is easy. **Intermediate** It is easy with more people. **Advanced** It is easy and better when people work together. **Advanced High** A problem is easier to solve when people work together.	**Beginning** Get help. **Intermediate** Ask friends to help. **Advanced** I can ask some friends to help me clean the beach. **Advanced High** My friends and I could bring garbage bags to the beach.	**Beginning** A building. **Intermediate** There is a place for a lifeguard. **Advanced** People built a tower for a lifeguard. **Advanced High** People built a lifeguard tower and added a recycling can.

This Week's Materials

Teacher's Edition pages 218j–247k

See the support for English language learners throughout the lesson, including ELL strategies and scaffold activities at points of use.

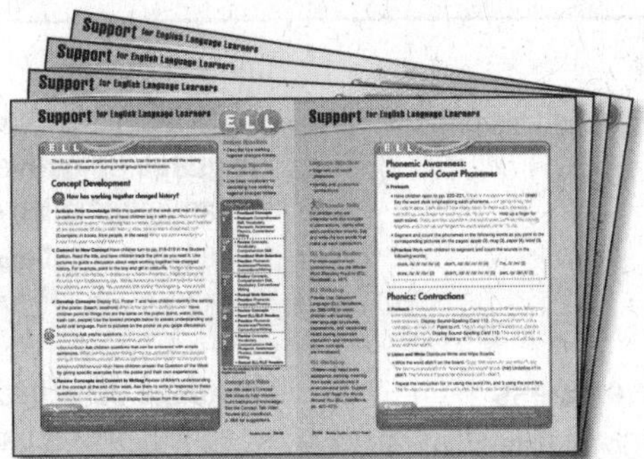
Teacher's Edition pages DI•33–DI•42

Differentiated Instruction for English language learners provides daily group activities that "frontload," or preteach, core instruction.

ELL Handbook pp. 65a–70

Find additional lesson materials that support the core lesson and the ELL instructional pages.

ELL Poster 7

ELD Reader 2.2.2

ELL Reader 2.2.2

Concept Literacy Reader

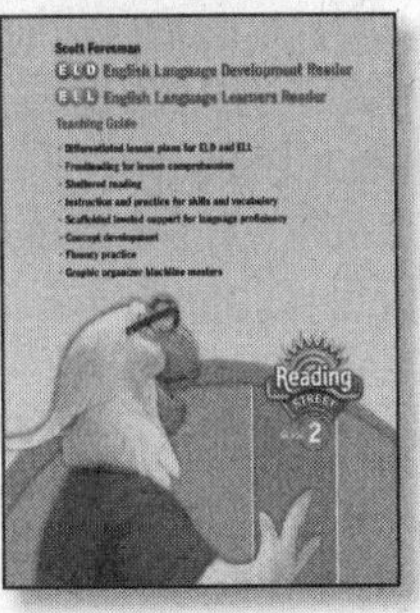
ELD, ELL Reader Teaching Guide

Concept Literacy Reader Teaching Guide

Technology

Online Teacher's Edition Use the digital version of the core teacher's edition for planning and instruction.

eReaders
This Week's ELL and ELD Readers and Concept Literacy Reader are also available in digital format.

This Week's Content and Language Objectives by Strand

Concept Development How has working together changed history?	**Content Objective** • Describe how working together changed history. **Language Objectives** • Share information orally. • Use basic vocabulary for describing how working together changed history.
Phonics/Phonemic Awareness Contractions; Segment and Count Phonemes	**Language Objectives** • Segment and count phonemes. • Identify and pronounce contractions.
Listening Comprehension Modified Read Aloud: "Coretta Scott King: Important Leader"	**Content Objective** • Monitor and adjust oral comprehension. **Language Objectives** • Discuss oral passages. • Use a graphic organizer to take notes.
Reading Comprehension Author's Purpose	**Content Objectives** • Identify author's purpose. • Identify author's purpose to aid comprehension. • Monitor and adjust comprehension. **Language Objectives** • Discuss evidence of author's purpose. • Retell author's purpose from a reading. • Write about author's purpose.
Vocabulary High-Frequency Words	**Language Objectives** • Understand and use high-frequency vocabulary. • Use high-frequency words to describe.
Vocabulary Homophones	**Content Objective** • Identify and define homophones. **Language Objectives** • Read and write contractions. • Distinguish between formal and informal English.
Grammar and Conventions Proper Nouns	**Content Objectives** • Identify and use proper nouns. • Correctly use proper nouns in sentences. **Language Objectives** • Speak using proper nouns in sentences. • Write phrases and sentences with proper nouns.
Writing Biography	**Content Objectives** • Identify words used in a biography. • Identify the characteristics of a biography. **Language Objectives** • Write sentences that communicate a strong idea about a person. • Share feedback for editing and revising.

Word Cards for Vocabulary Activities

certainly	**either**
great	**laugh**
second	**worst**
you're	

Teacher Note: Beginning Teach two to three words. **Intermediate** Teach three to four words. **Advanced** Teach five to six words. **Advanced High** Teach all words.

Name ______________________

Look at the pictures. **Read** the story.

An Exciting Game

What a great soccer game! There are only ten seconds left in the game. The score is tied. Each team has one goal.

Marta is trying to score another goal. Her team members work together. They pass the ball to her. Marta kicks the ball hard. She scores!

Answer the questions below.

1. What is the story about?
 ○ a basketball game ○ a soccer game
 ○ a baseball game

2. How does Marta's team help her?

____

____

3. Why do you think the author wrote the story?

____

____

Author's Purpose

Use this lesson to supplement or replace the skill lesson on page 223a of the Teacher's Edition. Display the Skill Points (at right) and share them with children.

Use the Skill Points to preteach author's purpose.

Teach/Model

Beginning Read aloud an age-appropriate comic strip. Ask: *Why did the author write this? Does the author want to explain something or make us laugh?* (to make us laugh) *To make us laugh is the author's purpose.*

Intermediate Read to children: *Goalkeepers stay by the goals. They keep the soccer ball out of the nets. Goalkeepers can use their hands.* Have children identify the author's purpose. (to explain what goalkeepers do)

Advanced Read aloud parts of a children's nonfiction book. Ask: *How can you tell that this author's purpose is to inform?* Read aloud parts of a fictional book. Ask: *How can you tell that this author's purpose is to entertain?*

Advanced High Draw a T-chart on the board with the headings *To Inform* and *To Entertain.* Review the words with children. Ask them to give examples of media written or produced for each purpose. Write children's suggestions in the chart.

Skill Points

- ✔ An author has a reason for writing. The author's reason is also called the **author's purpose**.
- ✔ An author can write to make you laugh, to explain something, to describe something, or to try to get you to think in a certain way.
- ✔ To figure out the author's purpose, ask yourself: *Is the story funny, serious, or sad? Why do I think so?*

Then distribute copies of Picture It! page 66.

- Have children look at the picture and tell what is happening.
- Read the story aloud. Ask: *What is the story about?* (a soccer game) *What is the author's purpose for writing this story?* (Possible answer: to describe an exciting game)
- Review the Skill Points with children.
- Have children look at the picture and words to identify the author's purpose.

Practice

Read aloud the directions on page 66. Reread or chorally read the story. Have children look at the picture and the story as they answer the questions.

Beginning Children can orally answer and mark and write their answers. Provide help with filling in circles and spelling.

Intermediate Children can first orally answer and then mark and write their answers on the page.

Advanced Children can mark and write their answers and check them by comparing their circles with a partner's and quietly reading aloud their writing.

Advanced High Children can mark and write their answers and check them by reviewing the story and making any necessary corrections.

Answers for page 66: 1. a soccer game; 2. Sample answers: They work together. They pass the ball to her. 3. Sample answers: to show how people work together, to show how people help each other

Multilingual Summaries

English

Abraham Lincoln

Abraham Lincoln was born February 12, 1809. He was born in Kentucky. Abe moved to Indiana when he was seven. He cut wood. He plowed fields. He read as much as he could.

Abe was honest. Abe was called "Honest Abe." He felt slavery was wrong. Abraham Lincoln was elected President of the United States.

President Lincoln wanted to end slavery. Abraham Lincoln signed a paper to set the slaves free. The Civil War began. He had to stop the fighting. He worked hard to put the country back together.

Spanish

Abraham Lincoln

Abraham Lincoln nació el 12 de febrero de 1809. Nació en Kentucky. Abe (así lo llamaban sus amigos) se mudó a Indiana cuando cumplió siete años de edad. Él cortó madera y labró los campos. También leyó tanto como pudo.

Abe era honesto, tanto que lo llamaban "El honesto Abe". Él siempre pensó que la esclavitud no era correcta. Abraham Lincoln fue electo el Presidente de Estados Unidos.

El Presidente Lincoln quería eliminar la esclavitud. Por eso firmó un documento para que se liberaran a los esclavos. La Guerra Civil inició. Y él tuvo que dejar su lucha. Trabajó muy duro para volver a encaminar al país.

Multilingual Summaries

Chinese

亞伯拉翰　林肯

亞伯拉翰　林肯於 1809 年 2 月 12 日出生在肯塔基州。 他在七歲時搬到了印地安那州。 他砍過柴、 耕過田， 一有時間就讀書。

亞伯很誠實。 大家都叫他「誠實的亞伯」。 他認為蓄奴是不對的。亞伯拉翰　林肯後來當選了美國總統。

林肯總統想要結束奴隸制度。 他簽署了一份解放奴隸的文件， 南北戰爭因而爆發。 為了停止戰爭， 他努力工作，以實現國家統一。

Vietnamese

Abraham Lincoln

Abraham Lincoln sanh ngày 12 tháng Hai, 1809. Ông sanh tại Kentucky. Abe dời đến ở tại Indiana khi được bảy tuổi. Ông chẻ củi. Ông cày bừa. Ông đọc rất nhiều khi nào được.

Abe là người thật thà. Abe được gọi là "Abe Thật Thà." Ông nghĩ vấn đề nô lệ là một việc sai. Abraham Lincoln được đắc cử tổng thống Hoa Kỳ.

Tổng thống Lincoln muốn chấm dứt vấn đề nô lệ. Abraham Lincoln ký giấy cho nô lệ được tự do. Cuộc nội chiến bắt đầu. Ông phải chấm dứt cuộc chiến tranh. Ông đã làm việc khó nhọc để thu gôm lại quốc gia.

Multilingual Summaries

Korean

에이브라함 링컨

에이브라함 링컨은 1809년 2월 12일에 켄터키 주에서 태어났다. 그는 7살 때 인디아나 주로 이사했다. 그는 나무를 자르고 밭을 갈았으며 가능한 한 독서를 많이 했다.

에이브라함은 정직해서 "정직한 에이브" 라고 불렸다. 그는 노예제도가 잘못된 것이라고 느꼈다. 에이브라함 링컨은 미국의 대통령으로 선출되었다.

링컨 대통령은 노예제도를 없애고 싶었다. 에이브라함 링컨이 노예 해방 문서에 서명했고 남북전쟁이 시작되었다. 그는 전쟁을 끝내야만 했다. 그는 나라를 다시 통합하기 위해 열심히 일했다.

Hmong

Abraham Lincoln

Abraham Lincoln yug thaum lub 2 Hli, hnub 12, xyoo1809. Nws yug nyob rau lub lav Kentucky. Abe tsiv mus nyob rau lub lav Indiana thaum nws muaj hnub nyoog 7 xyoo. Nws txiav taw. Nws laij av teb. Nws ntawv ntau npaum li nws nyeem tau.

Abe yog neeg ncaj. Abe rau hu ua "Honest Abe." Nws xav hais tias muab neeg coj los ua qhev tsis yog lawm. Abraham Lincoln rau xaiv los tuam thawj txwj rau lub teb chaw United States.

Tuam thawj tswj Lincoln txwv tsis pub muab neeg yuav ua qhev. Abraham Lincoln kos npe kom tso cov neeg raug yuav ua qhev tawm mus ua neej ywj pheej. Tso rog qab teb qaum teb sib tua thiaj pib. Rog loj pib tuaj. Nws yuav tsum cheem kev sib ntaus sib tua. Nws ua hauj lwm nyav kawg los rub lub teb chaw los ua ib ke dua.

Name ____________________

- **Read** *Trains Across the Country* again.
- In Box 1, **draw** a picture that shows one way people traveled before trains. **Write** a sentence that goes with your picture.
- In Box 2, **draw** a picture that shows how people travel today. **Write** a sentence that goes with your picture.

1.

____

____

____

2.

____

____

____

Family Link

Ask family members to tell you about how they have traveled. Ask if they have traveled by train.

Weekly Resources Guide for English Language Learner Support

For this week's content and language objectives, see p. 71e.

Instructional Strand	Day 1	Day 2
Concept Development	TEACHER'S EDITION • Concept Development, p. DI•54 • Anchored Talk, pp. 248j—248–249 • *Sing With Me* Big Book, p. 250a • Concept Talk Video ELL HANDBOOK • ELL Poster Talk, Concept Talk, p. 71c ELL POSTER 8 • Day 1 Activities	TEACHER'S EDITION • Concept Development, p. DI•54 • Anchored Talk, p. 254b • *Sing With Me* Big Book, p. 254a • Concept Talk Video ELL HANDBOOK • ELL Poster Talk, Concept Talk, p. 71c • Concept Talk Video Routine, p. 464 ELL POSTER 8 • Day 2 Activities
Phonics/Phonemic Awareness	TEACHER'S EDITION • Preteach Phonemic Awareness, p. DI•55 • Preteach Phonics, p. DI•55 • Decodable Reader 8A, pp. 252b–252c	TEACHER'S EDITION • Practice Phonemic Awareness, p. DI•55 • Listen and Write Phonics, p. DI•55
Listening Comprehension	TEACHER'S EDITION • Modified Read Aloud, p. DI•57 • *Sing With Me* Big Book, p. 250a • Read Aloud, p. 253b • Concept Talk Video ELL HANDBOOK • Concept Talk Video Routine, p. 464	TEACHER'S EDITION • Modified Read Aloud, p. DI•57 • *Sing With Me* Big Book, p. 254a • AudioText of *Scarcity* • Concept Talk Video ELL HANDBOOK • AudioText CD Routine, p. 464 • Steps in a Process, p. 479
Reading Comprehension	TEACHER'S EDITION • Teach Facts and Details, p. DI•59	TEACHER'S EDITION • Teach Facts and Details, p. DI•59 • Frontloading Reading, p. DI•60 ELL HANDBOOK • Picture It! Skill Instruction, pp. 72–72a • Multilingual Summaries, pp. 73–75
Vocabulary **High-Frequency Words** **Time and Order Words**	TEACHER'S EDITION • High-Frequency Words, p. DI•58 • Time and Order Words, p. DI•56 ELL HANDBOOK • Word Cards, p. 71 • ELL Vocabulary Routine, p. 456 ELL POSTER 8 • Day 1 Activities	TEACHER'S EDITION • High-Frequency Words, p. DI•58 • Time and Order Words, p. DI•56 ELL HANDBOOK • Word Cards, p. 71 • Multilingual Vocabulary List, pp. 429–440 ELL POSTER 8 • Day 2 Activities
Grammar and Conventions	TEACHER'S EDITION • Preteach Verbs That Add -*s*, p. DI•62	TEACHER'S EDITION • Reteach Verbs That Add -*s*, p. DI•62
Writing	TEACHER'S EDITION • Expository Nonfiction, p. DI•63 • Introduce Expository Nonfiction, pp. 253d–253e	TEACHER'S EDITION • Expository Nonfiction, pp. 267d–267e

This symbol indicates leveled instruction to address language proficiency levels.

Day 3	Day 4	Day 5
TEACHER'S EDITION • Concept Development, p. DI•54 • Anchored Talk, p. 268b • *Sing With Me* Big Book, p. 268a • Concept Talk Video ELL HANDBOOK • ELL Poster Talk, Concept Talk, p. 71c ELL POSTER 8 • Day 3 Activities	TEACHER'S EDITION • Concept Development, p. DI•54 • Anchored Talk, p. 272b • *Sing With Me* Big Book, p. 272a • Concept Talk Video ELL HANDBOOK • ELL Poster Talk, Concept Talk, p. 71c ELL POSTER 8 • Day 4 Activities	TEACHER'S EDITION • Concept Development, p. DI•54 • Concept Talk Video ELL HANDBOOK • ELL Poster Talk, Concept Talk, p. 71c ELL POSTER 8 • Day 5 Activities
ELL HANDBOOK • Phonics Transition Lesson, pp. 271, 273	TEACHER'S EDITION • Decodable Reader 8C, pp. 272e–272f ELL HANDBOOK • Phonics Transition Lesson, pp. 271, 273	TEACHER'S EDITION • Reteach Phonics, p. DI•56
TEACHER'S EDITION • *Sing With Me* Big Book, p. 268a • AudioText of *Scarcity* • Concept Talk Video ELL HANDBOOK • AudioText CD Routine, p. 464	TEACHER'S EDITION • *Sing With Me* Big Book, p. 272a • Concept Talk Video	TEACHER'S EDITION • Concept Talk Video
TEACHER'S EDITION • Sheltered Reading, p. DI•60 ELL HANDBOOK • Multilingual Summaries, pp. 73–75	TEACHER'S EDITION • ELL/ELD Reader Guided Reading, p. DI•61 ELL HANDBOOK • ELL Study Guide, p. 76	TEACHER'S EDITION • ELL/ELD Reader Guided Reading, p. DI•61 ELL HANDBOOK • ELL Study Guide, p. 76
ELL HANDBOOK • High-Frequency Words Activity Bank, p. 491 ELL POSTER 8 • Day 3 Activities	ELL HANDBOOK • High-Frequency Words Activity Bank, p. 491	TEACHER'S EDITION • Time and Order Words for Sequence, p. 276–277 ELL HANDBOOK • High-Frequency Words Activity Bank, p. 491
TEACHER'S EDITION • Grammar Jammer ELL HANDBOOK • Grammar Transition Lesson, pp. 327, 334 • Grammar Jammer Routine, p. 465	TEACHER'S EDITION • Grammar Jammer ELL HANDBOOK • Grammar Transition Lesson, pp. 327, 334	TEACHER'S EDITION • Grammar Jammer ELL HANDBOOK • Grammar Transition Lesson, pp. 327, 334
TEACHER'S EDITION • Let's Write It!, p. 270–271 • Writing Trait: Word Choice, p. 271a	TEACHER'S EDITION • Writer's Craft: Choosing Details, pp. 275c–275d	TEACHER'S EDITION • Writing for Tests, pp. 277h–277i

Poster Talk, Concept Talk

Question of the Week

How can we work together to meet people's needs?

Poster 8

Throughout the week, use the ELL Poster to help children produce and comprehend language, understand the concept, and build English vocabulary. Use the Question of the Week and other questions to help children share ideas in pairs, small groups, or the large group. Sample questions are shown, with examples of possible responses by children.

Weekly Concept and Language Goals

- Understand the concept of working together to meet people's needs
- Name some items needed to make a community garden

By the end of the lesson, children should be able to talk about and write one or more sentences about people working together to give one another what they need.

Daily Team Talk

Day 1	Day 2	Day 3	Day 4	Day 5
After Day 1 activities on Poster, ask questions such as *In the poster picture, how do the people by the doors work together to help others?*	After Day 2 activity on Poster, ask questions such as *How does the woman at the fruit stand help people get what they need?*	After Day 3 activity on Poster, ask questions such as *How can people work together when there isn't much water?*	After Day 4 activity on Poster, ask questions such as *How does a garden help the people in a community?*	After Day 5 activity on Poster, ask questions such as *What do people need to start a community garden?*
Beginning Open doors. **Intermediate** They hold the doors open. **Advanced** The people hold the doors open for the men with the sofa. **Advanced High** The people help the men carrying the sofa by holding open the doors for them.	**Beginning** Sells fruit. **Intermediate** She sells food. **Advanced** The woman sells food. People need food. **Advanced High** People need food, and the woman is selling food to them.	**Beginning** Share water. **Intermediate** They share the water. **Advanced** People can share the water. They can use less water. **Advanced High** People can make the water last longer by using less.	**Beginning** Grows food. **Intermediate** They grow food in a garden. **Advanced** The people can get food to eat from a garden. **Advanced High** The people in the community can grow the food they need in a garden.	**Beginning** Seeds. **Intermediate** Seeds and a shovel. **Advanced** People need ground, seeds, and water. **Advanced High** People will need ground, seeds, and tools to start a community garden.

This Week's Materials

Teacher's Edition pages 248j–277k

See the support for English language learners throughout the lesson, including ELL strategies and scaffold activities at points of use.

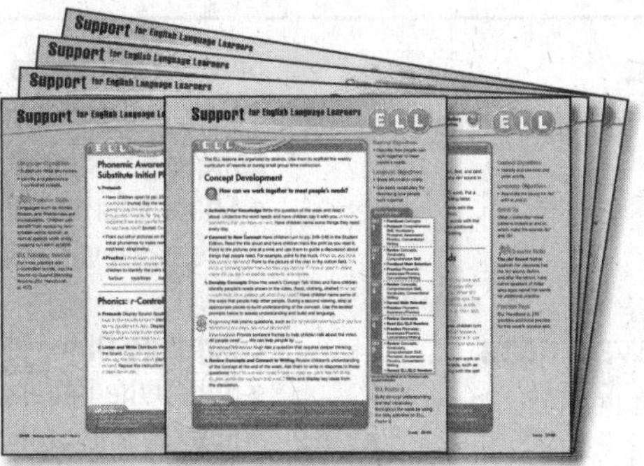

Teacher's Edition pages DI•54–DI•63

Differentiated Instruction for English language learners provides daily group activities that "frontload," or preteach, core instruction.

ELL Handbook pp. 71a–76

Find additional lesson materials that support the core lesson and the ELL instructional pages.

ELL Poster 8

ELD Reader 2.2.3

ELL Reader 2.2.3

Concept Literacy Reader

ELD, ELL Reader Teaching Guide

Concept Literacy Reader Teaching Guide

Technology

Online Teacher's Edition Use the digital version of the core teacher's edition for planning and instruction.

eReaders
This Week's ELL and ELD Readers and Concept Literacy Reader are also available in digital format.

This Week's Content and Language Objectives by Strand

Concept Development How can we work together to meet people's needs?	**Content Objective** • Describe how people can work together to meet people's needs. **Language Objectives** • Share information orally. • Use basic vocabulary for describing how people work together.
Phonics/Phonemic Awareness r-Controlled Vowels; Substitute Initial Phonemes	**Language Objectives** • Substitute initial phonemes. • Identify and pronounce *r*-controlled vowels.
Listening Comprehension Modified Read Aloud: "The Most Important Meal of the Day"	**Content Objective** • Monitor and adjust oral comprehension. **Language Objectives** • Discuss oral passages. • Use a graphic organizer to take notes.
Reading Comprehension Facts and Details	**Content Objectives** • Identify facts and details. • Monitor and adjust comprehension. **Language Objectives** • Discuss the difference between facts and details. • Understand important details of spoken language. • Summarize text using visual support.
Vocabulary High-Frequency Words	**Language Objectives** • Understand and use high-frequency vocabulary. • Learn new basic vocabulary.
Vocabulary Time and Order Words	**Content Objective** • Identify and use time and order words. **Language Objective** • Associate the sound for /er/ with *er* and *ir*.
Grammar and Conventions Verbs That Add *-s*	**Content Objective** • Identify verbs that end in *–s*. **Language Objectives** • Use verbs that end in *–s* in sentences. • Employ English spelling rules.
Writing Expository Nonfiction	**Content Objective** • Identify sentences that give information. **Language Objectives** • Write sentences that give information. • Explain with increasing detail. • Share feedback for editing and revising.

Word Cards for Vocabulary Activities

above	**ago**
enough	**toward**
whole	**word**

Leveled Support LS

Teacher Note: Beginning Teach two to three words. **Intermediate** Teach three to four words. **Advanced** Teach five to six words. **Advanced High** Teach all words.

Name ______________________________

Picture It!
Facts and Details

Look at the picture. **Read** the story.

Lunch with Friends

Three friends played on the swings. They had a good time.

Soon it was time for lunch. Oh, no! Kari forgot to bring her lunch to school. She was very hungry.

Kari's friends helped her. Tomás gave her an apple. Gabby gave Kari half of her sandwich. What nice friends!

Answer the questions.

1. How many friends played on the swings?

____

2. What did Tomás give Kari?

____

3. What did Gabby give Kari?

____

Facts and Details

Use this lesson to supplement or replace the skill lesson on page 253a of the Teacher's Edition. Display the Skill Points (at right) and share them with children.

Use the Skill Points to preteach facts and details.

Teach/Model

Beginning Say: *Some apples are red. Apples grow in the ocean.* Ask children which sentence is true. Say: *The first sentence is true. It tells a fact.* Show a photograph of an apple tree. Ask: *What details do you see in the photograph?*

Intermediate Write on the board: *Apples can be many colors. Apples can be green, red, pink, or yellow.* Read the sentences and have children identify details they heard. Ask: *Are these details facts? How can we prove that apples can be green, red, pink, or yellow?*

Advanced Write on the board and read aloud: *It is fun to pick apples. Apples grow on trees.* Ask children to copy the fact. Have them explain why the other sentence does not tell a fact. Have children illustrate the fact. Ask: *What details did you include in your drawing?*

Advanced High Read a short entry about apples from a children's encyclopedia. Ask children to recall details and facts they heard.

Then distribute copies of Picture It! page 72.

- Have children look at the pictures and tell what is happening in each one.
- Read the story aloud. Ask: *What is the story about? How do Kari's friends help her?*
- Review the Skill Points with children.
- Have children look at the pictures and words to identify the facts and details of the story.

Practice

Read aloud the directions on page 72. Reread or chorally read the story. Have children look at the picture and the story as they answer the questions.

Beginning Children can orally answer and, with help, write their answers.

Intermediate Children can first orally answer and then write their answers on the page.

Advanced Children can write their answers and check them by quietly reading them aloud or comparing them with a partner's.

Advanced High Children can write their answers and check them by reviewing the story and making any necessary corrections.

Answers for page 72: 1. three; 2. an apple; 3. half of her sandwich

Skill Points

- ✔ A **fact** is a piece of information that can be proven to be true.
- ✔ A **detail** is a small piece of information.
- ✔ Identifying facts and details can help you understand a selection.

Multilingual Summaries

English

Scarcity

People need resources. Resources can be scarce.

Cold weather can harm oranges. Oranges can become scarce. Not everyone can have oranges if they are scarce. Stores raise the prices. People could pay a higher price or they could buy another fruit.

Toys can be scarce. Stores charge a high price. Ben has to make a choice.

Gas was scarce in the 1970s. Not everyone could buy it. Some people walked. Some people took the train.

Spanish

La escasez

Las personas necesitan los recursos naturales. Estos recursos pueden escasear.

El clima muy frío puede dañar las naranjas. Y entonces las naranjas estarían escasas. No todos pueden conseguir naranjas si hay escasez. Las tiendas alzan los precios. Por eso, las personas comparan. Pueden pagar un precio más alto, o pueden comprar otra fruta.

Puede haber escasez de juguetes. Las tiendas piden un precio muy alto. Ben tiene que tomar una decisión.

Hubo escasez de combustible en los años setentas. No todos podían comprarlo. Algunas personas caminaban. Otras tomaban el tren.

Multilingual Summaries

Chinese

短缺

人們想要得到並使用資源， 而資源可能會短缺。

寒冷的天氣會使柳橙長得不好， 柳橙的供應量可能會因此而短缺。 如果柳橙少了，有人就會沒有柳橙吃。 假如人們還是想要買柳橙， 商店就會提高柳橙的價錢。 此時，人們就要做出選擇： 要麼以較高的價錢買柳橙， 要麼買別的水果。

玩具也可能短缺。 商店將提高玩具的價錢。 班必須做出選擇。

1970 年代汽油短缺時，不是人人都買得起汽油。 有些人走路、有些人騎腳踏車、 有些人則是搭火車。

Vietnamese

Sự Khan Hiếm

Người ta muốn và dùng nhiều tài nguyên. Tài nguyên có thể bị khan hiếm.

Thời tiết lạnh có thể làm hại cam. Cam trở nên khan hiếm. Không phải mọi người đều có cam để dùng khi nó bị khan hiếm. Người ta vẫn muốn mua chúng. Các cửa tiệm tăng giá lên. Người ta phải chọn lựa. Họ có thể mua với giá cao hơn. Hoặc họ có thể mua trái cây khác.

Đồ chơi cũng có thể khan hiếm. Các cửa tiệm tính giá cao hơn. Ben phải chọn lựa.

Xăng bị khan hiếm trong thập niên 1970. Không phải tất cả mọi người đều có thể mua nó. Một số người đi bộ. Một số đi xe đạp. Một số đi xe lửa.

Multilingual Summaries

Korean

부족함

사람들은 자원을 사용한다. 자원은 부족해질 수 있다.

날씨가 추우면 오렌지가 상할 수 있습니다. 그러면 오렌지가 부족해질 것이다. 오렌지가 부족해지면 모든 사람들이 오렌지를 먹을 수는 없다. 그래도 사람들이 오렌지를 사고 싶어하면 가게에서는 값을 올린다. 사람들은 선택을 한다. 더 비싼 값을 내거나, 다른 종류의 과일을 산다.

장난감도 부족해질 수 있다. 가게에서는 높은 값을 매긴다. 벤은 선택을 해야 한다.

1970년대에는 휘발유가 부족해서 모든 사람이 휘발유를 살 수는 없었다. 어떤 사람들은 걸어 다니고 어떤 사람들은 자전거를 탔다. 어떤 사람들은 기차를 탔다.

Hmong

Muaj Tsis Txaus

Neeg xav tau thiab xav siv qhov qho. Qhov qho ces tsis muaj tsis txaus.

Ntuj no ua rau txiv kab ntxwv tsis zoo. Txiv kab ntxwv muaj tsis txaus. Txhua tus neeg yuav tsis taut xiv kab ntxwv yog hais tias nws muaj tsis txaus. Neeg tseem xav yuav ntxiv. Kiab khw nce nqi rau. Neeg xaiv tau lwm yam. Lawv puas tuaj yeem them tus nqi siab zog. Lawv yuav tau lwm yam txiv ntoo.

Khoom ua si los txawj muaj tsis txaus. Kiab khw nce tus nqi rau. Ben kuj xav tau lwm yam.

Rog kuj txawj muaj tsis txaus nyob rau thaum 1970s. Tsis yog txhua tus yuav tau nws li. Muaj ib co neeg mus ko taw. Muaj ib cov neeg caij tsheb kauj vab. Muaj ib cov neeg caij tsheb nqaj.

Name ______________________________

- **Read** *A Home for Everybody* again.
- **Draw** an example of working together from the story.
- **Write** a sentence that goes with your picture.

____

____

____

Family Link

Ask family members to describe a time when they helped a neighbor.

Weekly Resources Guide for English Language Learner Support

For this week's content and language objectives, see p. 77e.

Instructional Strand	Day 1	Day 2
Concept Development	TEACHER'S EDITION • Concept Development, p. DI•75 • Anchored Talk, pp. 278j—278–279 • *Sing With Me* Big Book, p. 280a • Concept Talk Video ELL HANDBOOK • ELL Poster Talk, Concept Talk, p. 77c ELL POSTER 9 • Day 1 Activities	TEACHER'S EDITION • Concept Development, p. DI•75 • Anchored Talk, p. 284b • *Sing With Me* Big Book, p. 284a • Concept Talk Video ELL HANDBOOK • ELL Poster Talk, Concept Talk, p. 77c • Concept Talk Video Routine, p. 464 ELL POSTER 9 • Day 2 Activities
Phonics/Phonemic Awareness	TEACHER'S EDITION • Preteach Phonemic Awareness, p. DI•76 • Preteach Phonics, p. DI•76 • Decodable Reader 9A, pp. 282b–282c	TEACHER'S EDITION • Practice Phonemic Awareness, p. DI•76 • Listen and Write Phonics, p. DI•76
Listening Comprehension	TEACHER'S EDITION • Modified Read Aloud, p. DI•78 • *Sing With Me* Big Book, p. 280a • Read Aloud, p. 283b • Concept Talk Video ELL HANDBOOK • Concept Talk Video Routine, p. 464	TEACHER'S EDITION • Modified Read Aloud, p. DI•78 • *Sing With Me* Big Book, p. 284a • AudioText of *The Bremen Town Musicians* • Concept Talk Video ELL HANDBOOK • AudioText CD Routine, p. 464 • Problem and Solution, p. 477
Reading Comprehension	TEACHER'S EDITION • Teach Cause and Effect, p. DI•80	TEACHER'S EDITION • Teach Cause and Effect, p. DI•80 • Frontloading Reading, p. DI•81 ELL HANDBOOK • Picture It! Skill Instruction, pp. 78–78a • Multilingual Summaries, pp. 79–81
Vocabulary **High-Frequency Words** **Homophones**	TEACHER'S EDITION • High-Frequency Words, p. DI•79 • Homophones, p. DI•77 ELL HANDBOOK • Word Cards, p. 77 • ELL Vocabulary Routine, p. 456 ELL POSTER 9 • Day 1 Activities	TEACHER'S EDITION • High-Frequency Words, p. DI•79 • Homophones, p. DI•77 ELL HANDBOOK • Word Cards, p. 77 • Multilingual Vocabulary List, pp. 429–440 ELL POSTER 9 • Day 2 Activities
Grammar and Conventions	TEACHER'S EDITION • Preteach Plural Nouns That Change Spelling, p. DI•83	TEACHER'S EDITION • Reteach Plural Nouns That Change Spelling, p. DI•83
Writing	TEACHER'S EDITION • Write a Fairy Tale, p. DI•84 • Introduce Fairy Tale, pp. 283d–283e	TEACHER'S EDITION • Writing Trait: Organization, pp. 301d–301e

Unit 2 Week 4 The Bremen Town Musicians

This symbol indicates leveled instruction to address language proficiency levels.

Day 3	Day 4	Day 5
TEACHER'S EDITION • Concept Development, p. DI•75 • Anchored Talk, p. 302b • *Sing With Me* Big Book, p. 302a • Concept Talk Video ELL HANDBOOK • ELL Poster Talk, Concept Talk, p. 77c ELL POSTER 9 • Day 3 Activities	TEACHER'S EDITION • Concept Development, p. DI•75 • Anchored Talk, p. 306b • *Sing With Me* Big Book, p. 306a • Concept Talk Video ELL HANDBOOK • ELL Poster Talk, Concept Talk, p. 77c ELL POSTER 9 • Day 4 Activities	TEACHER'S EDITION • Concept Development, p. DI•75 • Concept Talk Video ELL HANDBOOK • ELL Poster Talk, Concept Talk, p. 77c ELL POSTER 9 • Day 5 Activities
ELL HANDBOOK • Phonics Transition Lesson, pp. 274, 278	TEACHER'S EDITION • Decodable Reader 9C, pp. 306e–306f ELL HANDBOOK • Phonics Transition Lesson, pp. 274, 278	TEACHER'S EDITION • Reteach Phonics, p. DI•77
TEACHER'S EDITION • *Sing With Me* Big Book, p. 302a • AudioText of *The Bremen Town Musicians* • Concept Talk Video ELL HANDBOOK • AudioText CD Routine, p. 464	TEACHER'S EDITION • *Sing With Me* Big Book, p. 306a • Concept Talk Video	TEACHER'S EDITION • Concept Talk Video
TEACHER'S EDITION • Sheltered Reading, p. DI•81 ELL HANDBOOK • Multilingual Summaries, pp. 79–81	TEACHER'S EDITION • ELL/ELD Reader Guided Reading, p. DI•82 ELL HANDBOOK • ELL Study Guide, p. 82	TEACHER'S EDITION • ELL/ELD Reader Guided Reading, p. DI•82 ELL HANDBOOK • ELL Study Guide, p. 82
ELL HANDBOOK • High-Frequency Words Activity Bank, p. 491 ELL POSTER 9 • Day 3 Activities	ELL HANDBOOK • High-Frequency Words Activity Bank, p. 491	TEACHER'S EDITION • Homophones, p. 312–313 ELL HANDBOOK • High-Frequency Words Activity Bank, p. 491
TEACHER'S EDITION • Grammar Jammer ELL HANDBOOK • Grammar Transition Lesson, pp. 315, 324 • Grammar Jammer Routine, p. 465	TEACHER'S EDITION • Grammar Jammer ELL HANDBOOK • Grammar Transition Lesson, pp. 315, 324	TEACHER'S EDITION • Grammar Jammer ELL HANDBOOK • Grammar Transition Lesson, pp. 315, 324
TEACHER'S EDITION • Let's Write It!, p. 304–305 • Writer's Craft: Beginning, Middle, and End, p. 305a	TEACHER'S EDITION • Revising Strategy, pp. 311d–311e	TEACHER'S EDITION • Writer's Craft: Plural Nouns, pp. 313h–313i

Poster Talk, Concept Talk

Question of the Week

Why is it a good idea to work together?

Poster 9

Throughout the week, use the ELL Poster to help children produce and comprehend language, understand the concept, and build English vocabulary. Use the Question of the Week and other questions to help children share ideas in pairs, small groups, or the large group. Sample questions are shown, with examples of possible responses by children.

Weekly Concept and Language Goals

- Know why it is good for people to work together
- Tell about how people work together

By the end of the lesson, children should be able to talk about and write one or more sentences about the benefits of working together.

Daily Team Talk

Day 1	Day 2	Day 3	Day 4	Day 5
After Day 1 activities on Poster, ask questions such as *In the poster picture, three children work together to build a snowman. How does working together make building the snowman easier?*	After Day 2 activity on Poster, ask questions such as *How are the children on the swings and the woman in the pink coat working together?*	After Day 3 activity on Poster, ask questions such as *How can you and your friends work together to make a local park better?*	After Day 4 activity on Poster, ask questions such as *How do you and your family work together to get a job done at home?*	After Day 5 activity on Poster, ask questions such as *How can working together make your homework easier?*
Beginning Not so much work. **Intermediate** They finish quickly. **Advanced** Working with more people made the job fast. **Advanced High** Working together, the children finished making the snowman more quickly.	**Beginning** She helps. **Intermediate** She gives them a push. **Advanced** The woman pushes the kids in the swings. **Advanced High** The woman is helping the children swing by giving them a push.	**Beginning** Clean up. **Intermediate** We could all pick up trash. **Advanced** We could work together to pick up garbage. **Advanced High** We could work as a team to throw all the litter in a garbage can.	**Beginning** Make dinner. **Intermediate** I set the table. **Advanced** We all work together to make dinner. **Advanced High** At dinnertime, I set the table, my dad cooks, and my mom cleans up.	**Beginning** Others help. **Intermediate** It takes less time. **Advanced** We can answer the questions quickly. **Advanced High** We can ask each other questions if we don't understand something.

This Week's Materials

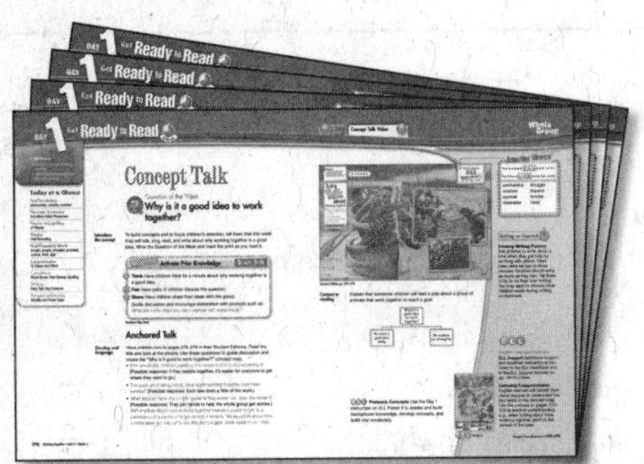

Teacher's Edition pages 278j–313k

See the support for English language learners throughout the lesson, including ELL strategies and scaffold activities at points of use.

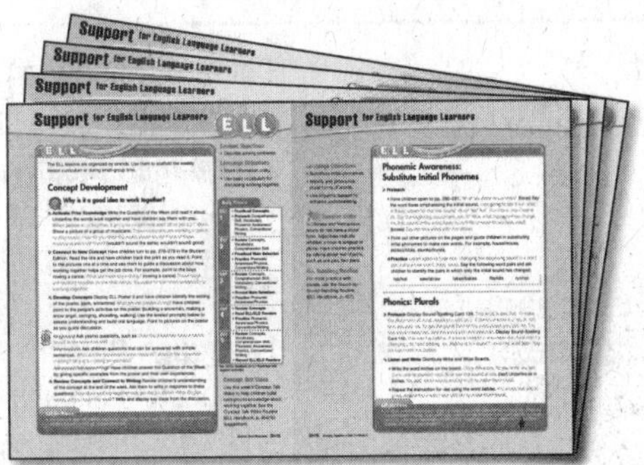

Teacher's Edition pages DI•75–DI•84

Differentiated Instruction for English language learners provides daily group activities that "frontload," or preteach, core instruction.

ELL Handbook pp. 77a–82

Find additional lesson materials that support the core lesson and the ELL instructional pages.

ELL Poster 9

ELD Reader 2.2.4

ELL Reader 2.2.4

Concept Literacy Reader

ELD, ELL Reader Teaching Guide

Concept Literacy Reader Teaching Guide

Technology

Online Teacher's Edition Use the digital version of the core teacher's edition for planning and instruction.

eReaders
This Week's ELL and ELD Readers and Concept Literacy Reader are also available in digital format.

This Week's Content and Language Objectives by Strand

Concept Development Why is it a good idea to work together?	**Content Objective** • Describe solving problems. **Language Objectives** • Share information orally. • Use basic vocabulary for discussing working together.
Phonics/Phonemic Awareness Plurals; Substitute Initial Phonemes	**Language Objectives** • Substitute initial phonemes. • Identify and pronounce plural forms of words. • Use linguistic support to enhance understanding.
Listening Comprehension Modified Read Aloud: "The Big Orange Cat"	**Content Objective** • Monitor and adjust oral comprehension. **Language Objectives** • Discuss oral passages. • Understand general meaning of spoken language. • Use a graphic organizer to take notes.
Reading Comprehension Cause and Effect	**Content Objectives** • Identify cause and effect. • Use cause and effect to aid comprehension. • Monitor and adjust comprehension. **Language Objectives** • Discuss evidence of cause and effect. • Retell causes and effects from reading. • Write causes and effects. • Summarize text using visual support.
Vocabulary High-Frequency Words	**Language Objectives** • Understand and use high-frequency vocabulary. • Expand initial vocabulary by learning routine classroom language.
Vocabulary Homophones	**Content Objective** • Identify and define homophones. **Language Objective** • Associate endings *–s, -es,* and *–ies* with the plural forms of words.
Grammar and Conventions Plural Nouns That Change Spelling	**Content Objective** • Identify and correctly use plural nouns that change spelling. **Language Objectives** • Speak using plural nouns that change spellings. • Write phrases and sentences with plurals that change spellings.
Writing Fairy Tale	**Content Objectives** • Identify words that indicate parts of a story. • Identify the characteristics of a fairy tale. **Language Objectives** • Write sentences showing the beginning, middle, and end of a story. • Explain with increasing detail. • Share feedback for editing and revising.

bought	**people**
pleasant	**probably**
scared	**shall**
sign	

Teacher Note: Beginning Teach two to three words. **Intermediate** Teach three to four words. **Advanced** Teach five to six words. **Advanced High** Teach all words.

Name ______________________________

Look at the picture. **Read** the story.

Going to the Fair

Cat and Pig were on the way to the fair. Cat was tired. "You can ride on my back," said Pig. "That's silly," said Cat. "Cats don't ride pigs. I will meet you there."

"I told you cats don't ride pigs," Cat said. "They ride bikes!"

Answer the questions.

1. Why did Pig ask Cat to ride on his back?
a. He wanted to trick Cat.
b. Cat was tired.

2. Why did Cat leave Pig?
a. He took a shorter way.
b. He got a bike to ride.

Cause and Effect

Use this lesson to supplement or replace the skill lesson on page 283a of the Teacher's Edition. Display the Skill Points (at right) and share them with children.

Use the Skill Points to preteach cause and effect.

Teach/Model

Beginning Pantomime riding a bike. Say: *I push the pedals on my bike. Will my bike move or stay still?* (move) Write on the board: *I push the pedals. The bike moves.* Help children identify the cause and the effect.

Intermediate Display the following and read aloud: *You ride your bike for a long time. You get tired.* Guide children to circle the cause and draw a box around the effect.

Advanced Give an example of cause and effect: *Ana cannot find her helmet. She cannot ride her bike.* Have children suggest another example of cause and effect.

Advanced High Give an example of an action that may cause an effect: *Sam's bike has a flat tire.* Ask children to suggest possible effects. (Sam cannot ride his bike. Sam fixes the tire.)

Then distribute copies of Picture It! page 78.

- Have children look at the pictures and tell what they see.
- Read the story aloud. Ask: *Why does Cat ride a bike?*
- Review the Skill Points with children.
- Have children look at the pictures and words to identify the cause and effect of the story.

Practice

Read aloud the directions on page 78. Reread or chorally read the story. Have children look at the pictures and the story as they answer the questions.

Beginning Children can orally answer and, with help, mark their answers.

Intermediate Children can first orally answer and then mark their answers on the page.

Advanced Children can mark their answers and check them by comparing them with a partner's answers.

Advanced High Children can mark their answers and check them by reviewing the story and making any necessary corrections.

Answers for page 78: 1. b; 2. b

Skill Points

- ✔ As you read, think about what is happening and why it is happening.
- ✔ Why something happens is the **cause**. What happens is the **effect**.

Multilingual Summaries

English

Read Together

The Bremen Town Musicians

An old donkey could not work hard anymore. He ran away to Bremen to be a musician. On the way he met a dog, a cat, and a rooster. They went with the donkey.

The animals came to a house. They saw three robbers inside. The robbers had food. The animals were hungry. They sang. The robbers ran away. The animals ate the food and went to sleep.

The robbers returned. One robber woke the cat, who scratched him. He woke the dog, who bit him. He tripped over the donkey, who kicked him. The rooster began to crow. The robbers ran away. The animals stayed. They sang together every night.

Spanish

Los músicos del pueblo de Bremen

Un burro viejo ya no podía trabajar más. Se escapó a Bremen a hacerse músico. En el camino conoció a un perro, a un gato y a un gallo. Ellos decidieron irse a acompañar al burro.

Los animales llegaron a una casa. Dentro de la casa había tres ladrones. Los ladrones tenían comida. Los animales estaban hambrientos. Comenzaron a cantar y los ladrones se fueron. Los animales comieron la comida y se fueron a dormir.

Los ladrones regresaron. Un ladrón despertó al gato y éste lo arañó. Despertó al perro y éste lo mordió. Tropezó con el burrito y éste lo pateó. El gallo comenzó a cantar. Todos los ladrones se fueron y los animales se quedaron. Ellos cantaban juntos todas las noches.

Multilingual Summaries

Chinese

不來梅鎮的音樂家

老驢子無法再賣命工作，所以主人不想養牠了。驢子決定逃走，到不來梅鎮當音樂家。途中牠遇到了一隻狗、一隻貓和一隻公雞，他們也很老了，跟隨驢子一起走。

動物們到了不來梅鎮，看到一棟房子，裡面有三個強盜，正在吃豐富的晚餐。動物們已很餓，牠們也想吃，於是靈機一動，開始唱歌，強盜以為有人來了，所以嚇得逃跑。動物們進了屋子，享用晚餐，吃完後便舒服地睡覺。

夜裡強盜們偷偷溜回來，其中一個進了屋子。他嚇到貓了，貓抓了他一把；他嚇到狗了，狗咬了他一口；他被驢子絆倒，驢子踢了他一腳。公雞開始大聲啼叫。那個強盜跌跌撞撞地逃出屋外，說房子裡有妖怪。所有強盜都嚇跑了，動物們於是就安心住了下來，每天晚上都一起快樂地唱歌。

Vietnamese

Các Nhạc Sĩ Phố Bremen

Một chú lừa già không thể làm việc nặng nhọc được nữa. Chủ không muốn giữ chú. Chú bỏ đi. Chú đi đến Bremen để làm nhạc sĩ. Trên đường đi chú gặp chó, mèo, và gà trống. Chúng cũng già nữa. Chúng cùng đi với lừa.

Các con thú này đến Bremen. Chúng thấy một căn nhà. Chúng thấy có ba tên trộm trong nhà. Ba tên trộm đang ăn một bữa ăn tối thịnh soạn. Các con thú đang đói bụng. Chúng ca hát, và các tên trộm bỏ đi. Các con thú vào nhà và ăn uống. Kế đến chúng đi ngủ.

Ba tên trộm quay trở lại. Một tên vào nhà. Nó làm mèo giật mình, mèo cào nó. Nó làm chó giật mình, chó cắn nó. Nó giẫm lên lừa, lừa đá nó. Gà trống bắt đầu gáy. Tên trộm nói là có ba yêu quái ở trong nhà. Tất cả mấy tên trộm bỏ chạy, nhưng các con thú ở lại. Chúng cùng nhau ca hát mỗi đêm.

Multilingual Summaries

Korean

브레멘의 음악대

당나귀가 늙어 더 이상 일을 못하자 주인은 당나귀가 필요 없어진다. 당나귀는 도망쳐서 음악가가 되려고 브레멘으로 가는 도중 개와 고양이, 수탉을 만나게 된다. 이들도 당나귀와 같이 모두 늙었고 같이 떠나기로 한다.

브레멘에 온 동물들은 집을 하나 발견하는데 그 안에는 저녁을 배불리 먹고 있는 도둑 세 명이 있다. 배가 고픈 동물들은 노래를 해서 도둑들을 쫓아내고 집안에 들어가 음식을 먹고 잠이 든다.

도둑들이 돌아온다. 그 중 한 명이 집 안으로 들어와서 고양이를 놀래 키자 고양이가 그를 할퀸다. 또 개를 놀래 켜 개에게 물리고 당나귀에 발이 걸려 넘어지자 이번엔 당나귀가 그를 차버린다. 수탉은 울기 시작하고… 도둑은 집에 괴물이 있다고 말하고 모두 도망을 가지만 남아 있는 동물들은 매일 밤 함께 노래를 부른다.

Hmong

Lub Zos Bremen Tus Tub Txawj Suab Nkauj

Ib tug zag laus laus ua tsis taus haujlwm hnyav ntxiv lawm. Nws tus tswv los tsis yuav nws lawm thiab. Nws thiaj khiav mus rau lub zos Bremen mus ua ib tug tub txawj suab nkauj. Thaum nws tabtom mus nws ntsib ib tug dev, ib tug miv, thiab ib tug lau qaib. Lawv kuj laus laus lawm thiab. Lawv thiaj nrog zag mus.

Cov tsiaj tuaj mus txog lub zos Bremen. Lawv pom ib lub tsev. Lawv pom peb tug tub sab nyob rau hauv lub tsev. Cov tub sab noj ib pluag hmo loj kawg nkaus. Cov tsiaj no kuj tshaib plab. Lawv hu nkauj ces cov tub sab thiaj li tawm mus lawm. Cov tsiaj mus sab hauv mus noj mov. Ces lawv thiaj li mus pw.

Cov tub sab rov qab los. Ib tug tub sab xub nkag mus hauv tsev ua ntej. Nws ua rau tus miv ceeb tus miv thiaj li khawb nws. Nws ua rau tus dev ceeb tus dev thiaj li tom nws. Nws dawm ko taw ntawm tus zag, tus zag thiaj li ncaws nws. Tus lau qaib thiaj li qua. Cov tub sab hais tias muaj dab nyob rau hauv lub tsev. Tagnrho cov tub sab thiaj li khiav tas lawm, tiamsis cov tsiaj nyob. Lawv hu nkauj txhua txhua hmo.

Name ____________________ **Big News in the Barn**

- **Read** *Big News in the Barn* again.
- **Draw** a picture of the barn before it was cleaned.
- Next **draw** a picture of the animals cleaning the barn.
- Then **draw** a picture of the barn after the animals cleaned it.

Barn (Before)

Barn (During)

Barn (After)

Family Link

Have family members tell you about a time when they worked with other people to get something done.

Weekly Resources Guide for English Language Learner Support

For this week's content and language objectives, see p. 83e.

Instructional Strand	Day 1	Day 2
Concept Development	TEACHER'S EDITION • Concept Development, p. DI•96 • Anchored Talk, pp. 314j—314–315 • *Sing With Me* Big Book, p. 316a • Concept Talk Video ELL HANDBOOK • ELL Poster Talk, Concept Talk, p. 83c ELL POSTER 10 • Day 1 Activities	TEACHER'S EDITION • Concept Development, p. DI•96 • Anchored Talk, p. 320b • *Sing With Me* Big Book, p. 320a • Concept Talk Video ELL HANDBOOK • ELL Poster Talk, Concept Talk, p. 83c • Concept Talk Video Routine, p. 464 ELL POSTER 10 • Day 2 Activities
Phonics/Phonemic Awareness	TEACHER'S EDITION • Preteach Phonemic Awareness, p. DI•97 • Preteach Phonics, p. DI•97 • Decodable Reader 10A, pp. 318b–318c	TEACHER'S EDITION • Practice Phonemic Awareness, p. DI•97 • Listen and Write Phonics, p. DI•97
Listening Comprehension	TEACHER'S EDITION • Modified Read Aloud, p. DI•99 • *Sing With Me* Big Book, p. 316a • Read Aloud, p. 319b • Concept Talk Video ELL HANDBOOK • Concept Talk Video Routine, p. 464	TEACHER'S EDITION • Modified Read Aloud, p. DI•99 • *Sing With Me* Big Book, p. 320a • AudioText of *One Good Turn* • Concept Talk Video ELL HANDBOOK • AudioText CD Routine, p. 464 • Story Comparison, p. 472
Reading Comprehension	TEACHER'S EDITION • Teach Compare and Contrast, p. DI•101	TEACHER'S EDITION • Teach Compare and Contrast, p. DI•101 • Frontloading Reading, p. DI•102 ELL HANDBOOK • Picture It! Skill Instruction, pp. 84–84a • Multilingual Summaries, pp. 85–87
Vocabulary **High-Frequency Words** **Unfamiliar Words**	TEACHER'S EDITION • High-Frequency Words, p. DI•100 • Unfamiliar Words, p. DI•98 ELL HANDBOOK • Word Cards, p. 83 • ELL Vocabulary Routine, p. 456 ELL POSTER 10 • Day 1 Activities	TEACHER'S EDITION • High-Frequency Words, p. DI•100 • Unfamiliar Words, p. DI•98 ELL HANDBOOK • Word Cards, p. 83 • Multilingual Vocabulary List, pp. 429–440 ELL POSTER 10 • Day 2 Activities
Grammar and Conventions	TEACHER'S EDITION • Preteach Possessive Nouns, p. DI•104	TEACHER'S EDITION • Reteach Possessive Nouns, p. DI•104
Writing	TEACHER'S EDITION • Write a Folk Tale, p. DI•105 • Introduce Folk Tale, pp. 319d–319e	TEACHER'S EDITION • Writer's Craft: Know Your Purpose, pp. 335c–335d

Unit 2 Week 5 *One Good Turn Deserves Another*

This symbol indicates leveled instruction to address language proficiency levels.

Day 3	Day 4	Day 5
TEACHER'S EDITION • Concept Development, p. DI•96 • Anchored Talk, p. 336b • *Sing With Me* Big Book, p. 336a • Concept Talk Video ELL HANDBOOK • ELL Poster Talk, Concept Talk, p. 83c ELL POSTER 10 • Day 3 Activities	TEACHER'S EDITION • Concept Development, p. DI•96 • Anchored Talk, p. 340b • *Sing With Me* Big Book, p. 340a • Concept Talk Video ELL HANDBOOK • ELL Poster Talk, Concept Talk, p. 83c ELL POSTER 10 • Day 4 Activities	TEACHER'S EDITION • Concept Development, p. DI•96 • Concept Talk Video ELL HANDBOOK • ELL Poster Talk, Concept Talk, p. 83c ELL POSTER 10 • Day 5 Activities
ELL HANDBOOK • Phonics Transition Lesson, pp. 253, 256	TEACHER'S EDITION • Decodable Reader 10C, pp. 340e–340f ELL HANDBOOK • Phonics Transition Lesson, pp. 253, 256	TEACHER'S EDITION • Reteach Phonics, p. DI•98
TEACHER'S EDITION • *Sing With Me* Big Book, p. 336a • AudioText of *One Good Turn* • Concept Talk Video ELL HANDBOOK • AudioText CD Routine, p. 464	TEACHER'S EDITION • *Sing With Me* Big Book, p. 340a • Concept Talk Video	TEACHER'S EDITION • Concept Talk Video
TEACHER'S EDITION • Sheltered Reading, p. DI•102 ELL HANDBOOK • Multilingual Summaries, pp. 85–87	TEACHER'S EDITION • ELL/ELD Reader Guided Reading, p. DI•103 ELL HANDBOOK • ELL Study Guide, p. 88	TEACHER'S EDITION • ELL/ELD Reader Guided Reading, p. DI•103 ELL HANDBOOK • ELL Study Guide, p. 88
ELL HANDBOOK • High-Frequency Words Activity Bank, p. 491 ELL POSTER 10 • Day 3 Activities	ELL HANDBOOK • High-Frequency Words Activity Bank, p. 491	TEACHER'S EDITION • Unfamiliar Words, p. 344–345 ELL HANDBOOK • High-Frequency Words Activity Bank, p. 491
TEACHER'S EDITION • Grammar Jammer ELL HANDBOOK • Grammar Transition Lesson, pp. 315, 325 • Grammar Jammer Routine, p. 465	TEACHER'S EDITION • Grammar Jammer ELL HANDBOOK • Grammar Transition Lesson, pp. 315, 325	TEACHER'S EDITION • Grammar Jammer ELL HANDBOOK • Grammar Transition Lesson, pp. 315, 325
TEACHER'S EDITION • Let's Write It!, p. 338–339 • Writing Trait: Sentences, p. 339a	TEACHER'S EDITION • Revising Strategy, pp. 343c–343d	TEACHER'S EDITION • Writer's Craft: Possessive Nouns, pp. 345h–345i

Poster Talk, Concept Talk

Question of the Week

How can we work together to solve problems?

ELL Poster 10

Throughout the week, use the ELL Poster to help children produce and comprehend language, understand the concept, and build English vocabulary. Use the Question of the Week and other questions to help children share ideas in pairs, small groups, or the large group. Sample questions are shown, with examples of possible responses by children.

Weekly Concept and Language Goals

- Understand that working together can help solve problems
- Name different ways of solving problems
- Describe ways to help someone with a problem

By the end of the lesson, children should be able to talk about and write one or more sentences about working together to solve problems.

Daily Team Talk

Day 1	Day 2	Day 3	Day 4	Day 5
After Day 1 activities on Poster, ask questions such as *In the poster picture, two girls on the bus are arguing. How can they solve their problem?*	After Day 2 activity on Poster, ask questions such as *How can you and your classmates work together to find a missing book?*	After Day 3 activity on Poster, ask questions such as *How can your friends help you if you have a problem?*	After Day 4 activity on Poster, ask questions such as *In the poster picture, a boy on the bus sees a woman running toward the bus. What can he do to help her?*	After Day 5 activity on Poster, ask questions such as *It is too noisy on the bus in the poster picture. What can the children do to solve this problem?*
Beginning Stop it. **Intermediate** Talk about something else. **Advanced** The girls can ask someone else to help them. **Advanced High** The girls can take turns talking and listening to each other.	**Beginning** Look for it. **Intermediate** We look in different places. **Advanced** We can make a plan. Each of us looks in one place. **Advanced High** Together we can plan how to split up and search different areas.	**Beginning** Listen and talk. **Intermediate** They listen and talk to you. **Advanced** Friends can listen and make you feel better. **Advanced High** Your friends can give you advice about how to solve the problem.	**Beginning** Tell the driver. **Intermediate** He can tell the bus driver about the woman. **Advanced** The boy can ask the bus driver to wait. **Advanced High** The boy can go to the bus driver and ask her to wait for the woman.	**Beginning** Be quiet. **Intermediate** They can stop shouting. **Advanced** The children can talk in quiet voices. **Advanced High** The children can talk more quietly.

This Week's Materials

Teacher's Edition pages 314j–345k

See the support for English language learners throughout the lesson, including ELL strategies and scaffold activities at points of use.

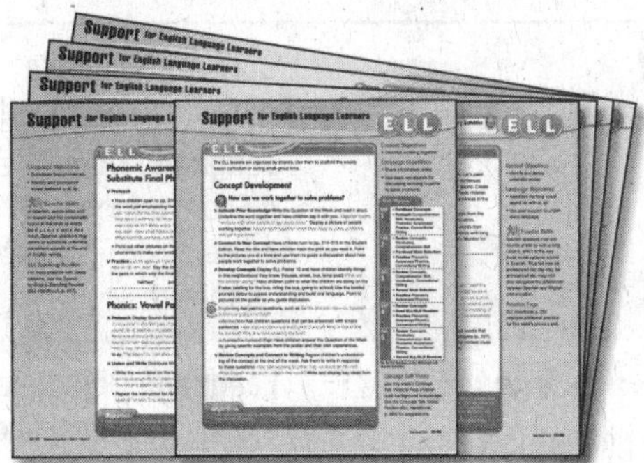

Teacher's Edition pages DI•96–DI•105

Differentiated Instruction for English language learners provides daily group activities that "frontload," or preteach, core instruction.

ELL Handbook pp. 83a–88

Find additional lesson materials that support the core lesson and the ELL instructional pages.

ELL Poster 10

ELD Reader 2.2.5

ELL Reader 2.2.5

Concept Literacy Reader

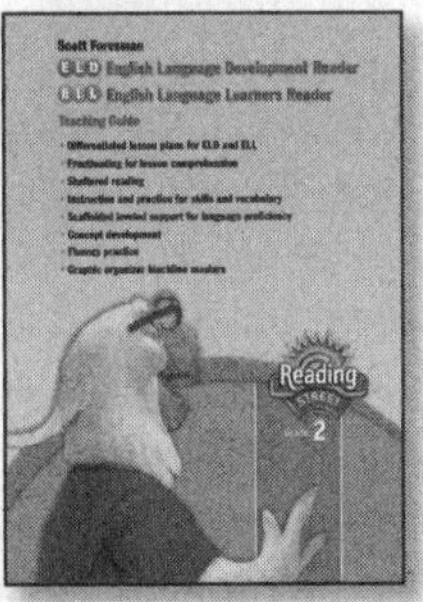

ELD, ELL Reader Teaching Guide

Concept Literacy Reader Teaching Guide

Technology

Online Teacher's Edition Use the digital version of the core teacher's edition for planning and instruction.

eReaders
This Week's ELL and ELD Readers and Concept Literacy Reader are also available in digital format.

This Week's Content and Language Objectives by Strand

Concept Development How can we work together to solve problems?	**Content Objective** • Describe working together. **Language Objectives** • Share information orally. • Use basic vocabulary for discussing working together to solve problems.
Phonics/Phonemic Awareness Vowel Patterns *a, ai, ay*; Substitute Final Phonemes	**Language Objectives** • Substitute final phonemes. • Identify and pronounce vowel patterns *a, ai, ay*.
Listening Comprehension Modified Read Aloud: "Two Folktales"	**Content Objective** • Monitor and adjust oral comprehension. **Language Objectives** • Discuss oral passages. • Share information and seek clarification. • Use a graphic organizer to take notes.
Reading Comprehension Compare and Contrast	**Content Objectives** • Identify compare and contrast. • Compare and contrast to aid comprehension. • Monitor and adjust comprehension. **Language Objectives** • Discuss differences and similarities between two things in a reading. • Use compare and contrast to retell a reading. • Internalize new academic language. • Write about compare and contrast. • Summarize text using visual support.
Vocabulary High-Frequency Words	**Language Objectives** • Understand high-frequency vocabulary. • Describe people using basic vocabulary.
Vocabulary Unfamiliar Words	**Content Objective** • Identify and define unfamiliar words. **Language Objectives** • Associate the long vowel sound /a/ with *ai, ay*. • Use peer support to understand language.
Grammar and Conventions Possessive Nouns	**Content Objectives** • Identify and use possessive nouns. • Correctly use possessive nouns in sentences. **Language Objective** • Speak and write using possessive nouns.
Writing Folk Tale	**Content Objectives** • Identify different ways to begin sentences. • Identify the characteristics of a folk tale. **Language Objectives** • Write story sentences with varied beginnings. • Share feedback for editing and revising.

Word Cards for Vocabulary Activities

behind	**brought**
door	**everybody**
minute	**promise**
sorry	

Teacher Note: Beginning Teach two to three words. **Intermediate** Teach three to four words. **Advanced** Teach five to six words. **Advanced High** Teach all words.

Name ___________________________

Picture It!
Compare and Contrast

Look at the pictures. **Read** the paragraph.

- In the *Snakes* circle, **write** things that are true only about snakes. In the *Crows* circle, **write** things that are true about crows. In the middle section, **write** how the two animals are alike.

How Animals Help Farmers

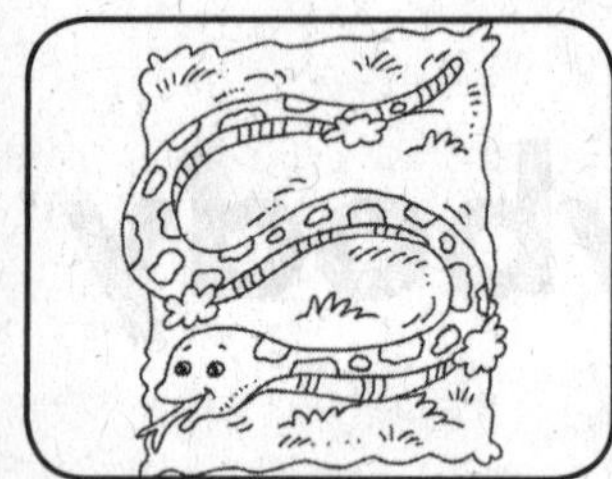

Snakes and crows both help farmers. Snakes eat mice that destroy farmers' plants. Crows eat bugs that also destroy farmers' plants. But these animals get food in different ways. Snakes first smell things with their tongues. They hunt at night. Crows first see things with their eyes. They hunt during the day.

Snakes	**Both**	**Crows**
______		______
______	______	______
______	______	______
______	______	______

Compare and Contrast

Use this lesson to supplement or replace the skill lesson on page 319a of the Teacher's Edition. Display the Skill Points (at right) and share them with children.

Use the Skill Points to preteach compare and contrast.

Teach/Model

Beginning Ask children to think about cats and dogs. Draw a simple picture of a cat and a dog on the board. Say: *Let's compare cats and dogs. Tell one way they are alike. Now let's contrast cats and dogs. Tell one way they are different.*

Intermediate Display the following and read aloud: *Snakes and worms have no legs. Snakes feel dry, but worms feel slimy.* Have children identify which sentence compares snakes and worms and which sentence contrasts them.

Advanced Compare two animals: *Cows and goats walk on four legs.* Have children suggest other ways cows and goats are alike. Then have children contrast the animals.

Advanced High Compare three animals. Say: *Frogs, turtles, and fish live in or near ponds.* Have children compare and contrast combinations of these animals. Write their suggestions in a Venn diagram on the board.

Then distribute copies of Picture It! page 84.

- Have children look at the pictures and tell what is happening in each.
- Read the story aloud. Ask: *Do snakes and crows help farmers in the same way?*
- Review the Skill Points with children.
- Have children look at the pictures and words to compare and contrast the two kinds of animals.

Practice

Read aloud the directions on page 84. Reread or chorally read the story. Have children look at the pictures and the paragraph as they answer the questions.

Beginning Children can orally answer and fill in the diagram. Provide help with writing and spelling words in the diagram.

Intermediate Children can first orally answer and then fill in the diagram.

Advanced Children can fill in the diagram and check their answers by quietly reading them aloud or comparing them with a partner's answers.

Advanced High Children can fill in the diagram and check their answers by silently rereading the story and making any necessary corrections.

Answers for page 84: *Both:* help farmers, eat things that destroy plants; *Snakes:* eat mice, smell things with tongues, hunt at night; *Crows:* eat bugs, see things with eyes, hunt during the day

Skill Points

- ✔ When you **compare** things, you tell how they are alike.
- ✔ When you **contrast** things, you tell how they are different.
- ✔ Words such as *like* and *also* are clues that things are being compared.
- ✔ Words such as *but* and *unlike* are clues that things are being contrasted.

Multilingual Summaries

English

One Good Turn Deserves Another

A mouse is going across the desert. A snake is trapped under a rock. The mouse moves the rock. The mouse does not think the snake will eat him. He says, "One good turn deserves another."

The mouse has to find a creature to agree with him. The mouse asks the crow. The crow agrees with the snake. The mouse asks the armadillo. The armadillo agrees with the snake. A coyote comes by. The coyote traps the snake under the rock. The mouse runs away. The coyote says, "One good turn deserves another."

Spanish

Una buena acción merece otra

Un ratón cruzaba el desierto. Una serpiente se encontraba atrapada debajo de una roca. El ratón movió la roca. Él no cree que la serpiente se lo comerá. Porque él cree que "Una buena acción merece otra".

El ratón debe encontrar a otra criatura que esté de acuerdo con él. Él le pregunta al cuervo. El cuervo está de acuerdo con la serpiente. Entonces le pregunta al armadillo. El armadillo también está de acuerdo con la serpiente. Un coyote se acerca. El coyote atrapa a la serpiente bajo la roca. El ratón se va corriendo. Entonces dice el coyote "Una buena acción merece otra".

Multilingual Summaries

Chinese

善有善報

一隻老鼠經過沙漠的時候， 發現有一隻蛇被困在石頭下。 老鼠搬開了石頭。 老鼠覺得蛇不會吃他。 他說：「善有善報。」

老鼠必須找到同意他看法的動物。 老鼠去問烏鴉。 烏鴉同意蛇的看法。 老鼠去問犰狳。 犰狳也同意蛇的看法。 一隻土狼走了過來。 土狼把蛇困在石頭下。 老鼠逃跑了。 土狼說：「善有善報。」

Vietnamese

Làm Lành thì Đáng Gặp Lành

Có một con chuột đi xuyên sa mạc. Một con rắn bị kẹt dưới cục đá. Con chuột dời cục đá đi. Con chuột không nghĩ rằng con rắn sẽ ăn thịt nó. Nó nói, "Làm lành thì đáng gặp lành."

Con chuột phải tìm một con vật khác đồng ý với với nó. Con chuột hỏi con quạ. Con quạ đồng ý với con rắn. Con chuột hỏi con armadillo (con tatu). Con armadillo đồng ý với con rắn. Rồi một con chó sói đi ngang qua. Con chó sói dùng cục đá đè con rắn xuống. Con chuột chạy thoát được. Chó sói nói, "Làm lành thì đáng gặp lành."

Multilingual Summaries

Korean

가는 말이 고와야 오는 말도 곱다

생쥐 한 마리가 사막을 지나가고 있었다. 뱀이 바위 밑에 깔려있다. 생쥐가 바위를 치워준다. 생쥐는 뱀이 자신을 먹을 거라고는 생각하지 않았다. 생쥐가 말한다. "가는 말이 고우면 오는 말도 고운 법이지."

생쥐는 자기와 같은 생각을 하는 동물을 찾아내야 했다. 생쥐가 까마귀에게 묻는다. 까마귀는 뱀과 생각이 같았다. 생쥐가 아르마딜로에게 물어본다. 아르마딜로도 뱀과 생각이 같았다. 코요테가 지나간다. 코요테가 뱀을 바위 밑에 깔아버린다. 생쥐는 달아났다. 코요테가 말한다. "가는 말이 고와야 오는 말도 고운 법이지."

Hmong

Ua Ib Qho Zoo Tau Ib Yam Zoo Rau

Muaj ib tug nas tsuag khiav hla lub tiaj suab puam. Muaj ib tug nab daig hauv lub qab pob zeb. Tus nas tsuag txav lub pob zeb. Tus nas tsuag tsis tau xav hais tias tus nab yuav noj nws. Nws hais tias, "Ua ib qho zoo tau ib yam zoo rau."

Tus nas tsuag yuav tsum nriav kom tau ib yam tsiaj dab tsi uas pom zoo li nws hais ntawd. Tus nas tsuag nug tus uab lag. Tus uab lag pom zoo nrog tus nab. Tus nas tsuag nug tus kum zaug. Tus kum zaub pom zoo nrog tus nab. Tus hma los txog ntawd. Tus hma muab tus nab cuab rau hauv lub qab pob zeb. Tus nas tsuag thiaj khiav lawm. Tus hma hais tias, "Ua ib qho zoo tau ib yam zoo rau."

Name ______________________________

- **Read** *Kids Can Do It!* again.
- **Draw** two pictures that show how kids can help. Use examples you read about.
- **Write** words or sentences that tell what the kid is doing to help in each picture.

______________________ ______________________

______________________ ______________________

Family Link

Show and explain your drawings to your family. Ask an adult to show you how you can help.

Weekly Resources Guide for English Language Learner Support

For this week's content and language objectives, see p. 89e.

Instructional Strand	Day 1	Day 2
Concept Development	TEACHER'S EDITION • Concept Development, p. DI•12 • Anchored Talk, pp. 348j—348–349 • *Sing With Me* Big Book, p. 350a • Concept Talk Video ELL HANDBOOK • ELL Poster Talk, Concept Talk, p. 89c ELL POSTER 11 • Day 1 Activities	TEACHER'S EDITION • Concept Development, p. DI•12 • Anchored Talk, p. 354b • *Sing With Me* Big Book, p. 354a • Concept Talk Video ELL HANDBOOK • ELL Poster Talk, Concept Talk, p. 89c • Concept Talk Video Routine, p. 464 ELL POSTER 11 • Day 2 Activities
Phonics/Phonemic Awareness	TEACHER'S EDITION • Preteach Phonemic Awareness, p. DI•13 • Preteach Phonics, p. DI•13 • Decodable Reader 11A, pp. 352b–352c	TEACHER'S EDITION • Practice Phonemic Awareness, p. DI•13 • Listen and Write Phonics, p. DI•13
Listening Comprehension	TEACHER'S EDITION • Modified Read Aloud, p. DI•15 • *Sing With Me* Big Book, p. 350a • Read Aloud, p. 353b • Concept Talk Video ELL HANDBOOK • Concept Talk Video Routine, p. 464	TEACHER'S EDITION • Modified Read Aloud, p. DI•15 • *Sing With Me* Big Book, p. 354a • AudioText of *Pearl and Wagner* • Concept Talk Video ELL HANDBOOK • AudioText CD Routine, p. 464 • Story Map B, p. 471
Reading Comprehension	TEACHER'S EDITION • Teach Author's Purpose, p. DI•17	TEACHER'S EDITION • Teach Author's Purpose, p. DI•17 • Frontloading Reading, p. DI•18 ELL HANDBOOK • Picture It! Skill Instruction, pp. 90–90a • Multilingual Summaries, pp. 91–93
Vocabulary **High-Frequency Words** **Antonyms**	TEACHER'S EDITION • High-Frequency Words, p. DI•16 • Antonyms, p. DI•14 ELL HANDBOOK • Word Cards, p. 89 • ELL Vocabulary Routine, p. 456 ELL POSTER 11 • Day 1 Activities	TEACHER'S EDITION • High-Frequency Words, p. DI•16 • Antonyms, p. DI•14 ELL HANDBOOK • Word Cards, p. 89 • Multilingual Vocabulary List, pp. 429–440 ELL POSTER 11 • Day 2 Activities
Grammar and Conventions	TEACHER'S EDITION • Preteach Verbs, p. DI•20	TEACHER'S EDITION • Reteach Verbs, p. DI•20
Writing	TEACHER'S EDITION • Write an Animal Fantasy, p. DI•21 • Introduce Animal Fantasy, pp. 353d–353e	TEACHER'S EDITION • Writing Trait: Voice, pp. 371d–371e

Unit 3 Week 1 Pearl and Wagner

Leveled Support (LS) This symbol indicates leveled instruction to address language proficiency levels.

Day 3	Day 4	Day 5
TEACHER'S EDITION • Concept Development, p. DI•12 • Anchored Talk, p. 372b • *Sing With Me* Big Book, p. 372a • Concept Talk Video ELL HANDBOOK • ELL Poster Talk, Concept Talk, p. 89c ELL POSTER 11 • Day 3 Activities	TEACHER'S EDITION • Concept Development, p. DI•12 • Anchored Talk, p. 376b • *Sing With Me* Big Book, p. 376a • Concept Talk Video ELL HANDBOOK • ELL Poster Talk, Concept Talk, p. 89c ELL POSTER 11 • Day 4 Activities	TEACHER'S EDITION • Concept Development, p. DI•12 • Concept Talk Video ELL HANDBOOK • ELL Poster Talk, Concept Talk, p. 89c ELL POSTER 11 • Day 5 Activities
ELL HANDBOOK • Phonics Transition Lesson, pp. 254, 257	TEACHER'S EDITION • Decodable Reader 11C, pp. 376e–376f ELL HANDBOOK • Phonics Transition Lesson, pp. 254, 257	TEACHER'S EDITION • Reteach Phonics, p. DI•14
TEACHER'S EDITION • *Sing With Me* Big Book, p. 372a • AudioText of *Pearl and Wagner* • Concept Talk Video ELL HANDBOOK • AudioText CD Routine, p. 464	TEACHER'S EDITION • *Sing With Me* Big Book, p. 376a • Concept Talk Video	TEACHER'S EDITION • Concept Talk Video
TEACHER'S EDITION • Sheltered Reading, p. DI•18 ELL HANDBOOK • Multilingual Summaries, pp. 91–93	TEACHER'S EDITION • ELL/ELD Reader Guided Reading, p. DI•19 ELL HANDBOOK • ELL Study Guide, p. 94	TEACHER'S EDITION • ELL/ELD Reader Guided Reading, p. DI•19 ELL HANDBOOK • ELL Study Guide, p. 94
ELL HANDBOOK • High-Frequency Words Activity Bank, p. 491 ELL POSTER 11 • Day 3 Activities	ELL HANDBOOK • High-Frequency Words Activity Bank, p. 491	TEACHER'S EDITION • Antonyms, p. 380–381 ELL HANDBOOK • High-Frequency Words Activity Bank, p. 491
TEACHER'S EDITION • Grammar Jammer ELL HANDBOOK • Grammar Transition Lesson, pp. 326, 332–333, 339 • Grammar Jammer Routine, p. 465	TEACHER'S EDITION • Grammar Jammer ELL HANDBOOK • Grammar Transition Lesson, pp. 326, 332–333, 339	TEACHER'S EDITION • Grammar Jammer ELL HANDBOOK • Grammar Transition Lesson, pp. 326, 332–333, 339
TEACHER'S EDITION • Let's Write It!, p. 374–375 • Writer's Craft: Personal Expression, p. 375a	TEACHER'S EDITION • Revising Strategy, pp. 379c–379d	TEACHER'S EDITION • Writer's Craft: Articles *a, an, the*, pp. 381h–381i

Poster Talk, Concept Talk

Question of the Week

When does support from others help with a creative idea?

ELL Poster 11

Throughout the week, use the ELL Poster to help children produce and comprehend language, understand the concept, and build English vocabulary. Use the Question of the Week and other questions to help children share ideas in pairs, small groups, or the large group. Sample questions are shown, with examples of possible responses by children.

Weekly Concept and Language Goals

- Understand that people need help with creative ideas
- Describe a creative idea for an invention made from boxes

By the end of the lesson, children should be able to talk about and write one or more sentences about helping others with their creative ideas.

Daily Team Talk

Day 1	Day 2	Day 3	Day 4	Day 5
After Day 1 activities on Poster, ask questions such as *In the poster picture, Harry designed a new tractor. What does his tractor look like?*	After Day 2 activity on Poster, ask questions such as *How did his uncle help Harry get an idea for a new kind of tractor?*	After Day 3 activity on Poster, ask questions such as *Harry's idea was a new kind of tractor. What was Pearl's idea in* Pearl and Wagner?	After Day 4 activity on Poster, ask questions such as *What idea do you have for something you can make from boxes?*	After Day 5 activity on Poster, ask questions such as *When has someone helped you with an idea you had?*
Beginning It's red. **Intermediate** The tractor is big and red. **Advanced** His tractor is red with big wheels. **Advanced High** Harry's tractor is red with big metal wheels. The back wheels have big spikes on them.	**Beginning** He had a car. **Intermediate** He gave Harry a ride in his new car. **Advanced** His uncle's new car made Harry want to build machines. **Advanced High** His uncle's new car inspired Harry. He became an engineer. Later, he designed a new kind of tractor.	**Beginning** Her robot. **Intermediate** She made a robot that eats trash. **Advanced** Pearl made a trash-eating robot. This was her idea. **Advanced High** Pearl's idea was to build a trash-eating robot out of boxes and string.	**Beginning** A new chair. **Intermediate** I can make a desk. I can study there. **Advanced** I can make places to store things in my closet. **Advanced High** I can build a house. It will be easy to put up and take down.	**Beginning** Mom and lemonade. **Intermediate** Mom made lemonade for me. **Advanced** My mom made lemonade. I sold it to people. **Advanced High** When I wanted to sell lemonade, my mom helped me make it.

This Week's Materials

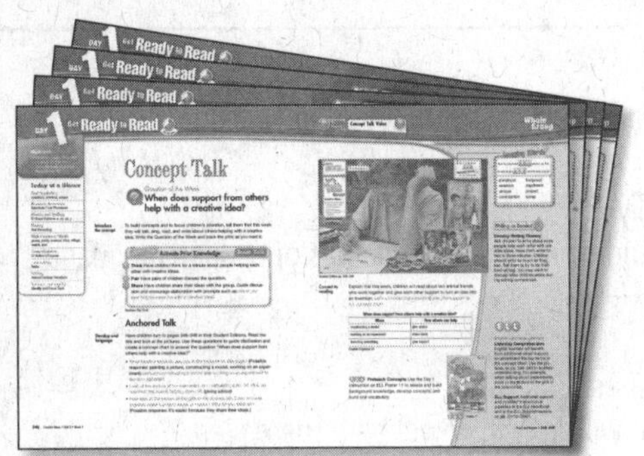
Teacher's Edition pages 348j–381k

See the support for English language learners throughout the lesson, including ELL strategies and scaffold activities at points of use.

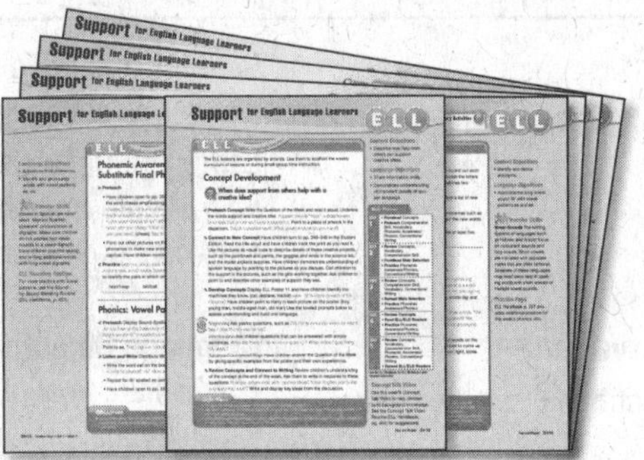
Teacher's Edition pages DI•12–DI•21

Differentiated Instruction for English language learners provides daily group activities that "frontload," or preteach, core instruction.

ELL Handbook pp. 89a–94

Find additional lesson materials that support the core lesson and the ELL instructional pages.

ELL Poster 11

ELD Reader 2.3.1

ELL Reader 2.3.1

Concept Literacy Reader

ELD, ELL Reader Teaching Guide

Concept Literacy Reader Teaching Guide

Technology

Online Teacher's Edition Use the digital version of the core teacher's edition for planning and instruction.

eReaders
This Week's ELL and ELD Readers and Concept Literacy Reader are also available in digital format.

This Week's Content and Language Objectives by Strand

Concept Development When does support from others help with a creative idea?	**Content Objective** • Describe how help from others can support creative ideas. **Language Objectives** • Share information orally. • Demonstrate understanding of important details of spoken language.
Phonics/Phonemic Awareness Vowel Patterns *ee, ea*; Substitute Final Phonemes	**Language Objectives** • Substitute final phonemes. • Identify and pronounce words with vowel patterns *ee, ea.*
Listening Comprehension Modified Read Aloud: "Kona's New Bat"	**Content Objective** • Monitor and adjust oral comprehension. **Language Objectives** • Discuss oral passages. • Use a graphic organizer to take notes.
Reading Comprehension Author's Purpose	**Content Objectives** • Recognize different purposes that authors have for writing. • Identify an author's purpose to aid comprehension. • Monitor and adjust comprehension. **Language Objectives** • Discuss an author's purpose for writing a text. • Describe an author's purpose. • Write about an author's purpose. • Summarize text using visual support.
Vocabulary High-Frequency Words	**Language Objectives** • Use accessible language to learn new and essential language. • Use high-frequency English words.
Vocabulary Antonyms	**Content Objective** • Identify and define antonyms. **Language Objective** • Associate the long vowel sound /ē/ with vowel patterns *ea* and *ee.*
Grammar and Conventions Verbs	**Content Objective** • Identify and correctly use verbs in sentences. **Language Objectives** • Speak using verbs in sentences. • Write phrases and sentences using verbs.
Writing Animal Fantasy	**Content Objectives** • Identify words that express the writer's ideas and feelings. • Identify the characteristics of an animal fantasy. **Language Objectives** • Write story sentences that show feelings and express ideas. • Share feedback for editing and revising.

Word Cards for Vocabulary Activities

guess	**pretty**
science	**shoe**
village	**watch**
won	

Teacher Note: Beginning Teach two to three words. **Intermediate** Teach three to four words. **Advanced** Teach five to six words. **Advanced High** Teach all words.

Name ______________________________

Look at the pictures. **Read** the story.

A Creative Idea

It was raining hard outside. Amy and Amir stayed inside. They drew pictures of their last soccer game. "I don't like to play soccer in the rain," said Amy. "My glasses get all wet, and I can't see."

That gave Amir a great idea. What if Amy's glasses had wipers like a car? She would never have to worry about the rain again!

Amy's mom is an inventor. She made Amy a pair of glasses with wipers, and they worked. Amir's idea was very good. Maybe he will be an inventor too!

Answer the questions.

1. What does the story tell about?
- **a.** the new glasses that Amir invented
- **b.** why you should not play soccer in the rain
- **c.** a silly soccer game
- **d.** how to draw great soccer pictures

2. Which best describes the purpose of the story?
- **a.** to persuade you to buy the glasses
- **b.** to tell you about Amir's invention
- **c.** to entertain you with a funny soccer story
- **d.** to describe Amy's mom's job

Author's Purpose

Use this lesson to supplement or replace the skill lesson on page 353a of the Teacher's Edition. Display the Skill Points (at right) and share them with children.

Use the Skill Points to preteach author's purpose.

Teach/Model

Beginning Read aloud part of the entry about inventions in a children's encyclopedia. Ask: *What is the author's purpose for writing this? Does the author want to make you laugh?* (no) *Does the author want to tell you about inventions?* (yes)

Intermediate Ask each child to point out his or her favorite selection in the Student Edition. After briefly reviewing each selection, ask: *What is the author's purpose? Why did the author write this?*

Advanced Display nonfiction and fiction books about inventions. Read aloud from the nonfiction book and ask: *What is this book about? What is the author's purpose in writing this book?* Repeat the process with the fiction book.

Advanced High Tell children that an author is writing a selection about a new invention, such as a time machine. Have children tell what the selection would be like if the author's purpose was to inform, to entertain, or to persuade readers.

Then distribute copies of Picture It! page 90.

- Have children look at the pictures and tell what is happening in each one.
- Read the story aloud. Ask: *Is this story funny, serious, or sad? Why do you think so?*
- Review the Skill Points with children.
- Have children look at the pictures and sentences to find clues about the author's purpose.

Practice

Read aloud the directions on page 90. Reread or chorally read the story. Have children look at the pictures and the story as they answer the questions.

Beginning Children can orally answer and, with help, mark their answers.

Intermediate Children can first orally answer and then mark the answers on the page.

Advanced Children can mark their answers and check them by comparing them with a partner's answers.

Advanced High Children can mark their answers and check them by silently rereading the story and making any necessary corrections.

Answers for page 90: 1. a; 2. b

Skill Points

- ✔ Keep in mind that the author has a reason or **purpose** for writing.
- ✔ An author can write to explain something.
- ✔ An author can write to tell a funny story.
- ✔ An author can write to try to get the reader to think or act in a certain way.

Multilingual Summaries

English

Pearl and Wagner: Two Good Friends

Pearl wants to make a robot for the Science Fair. Wagner says that he will win a prize.

Pearl makes a robot. Its mouth opens when Pearl pulls a string.

Wagner did not make anything. Pearl shows the robot to their teacher. Its head falls off. Pearl and Wagner fix it.

The judge comes to see the robot. It breaks again. Wagner climbs inside the robot. He speaks to the judge. She thinks that the robot talks! Then she finds Wagner inside.

The friends do not win a prize. Pearl knows that Wagner wanted to help. She is happy that she and Wagner are friends.

Spanish

Pearl y Wagner: Dos buenos amigos

Pearl quiere hacer un robot para la Feria de ciencias. Wagner dice que él ganará un premio.

Pearl hace un robot. Cuando Pearl tira de una cuerda, al robot se le abre la boca.

Wagner no hizo nada. Pearl le muestra el robot a la maestra. Al robot se le cae la cabeza. Pearl y Wagner se la arreglan.

La jueza llega a ver el robot. Éste se vuelve a romper. Wagner se mete dentro del robot y le habla a la jueza. ¡Ella piensa que el robot habla! Luego encuentra a Wagner adentro.

Los amigos no ganan el premio. Pearl sabe que Wagner quería ayudar. Ella está feliz porque Wagner y ella son amigos.

Multilingual Summaries

Chinese

珮兒和華格納是好朋友

珮兒想做個機械人參加科學比賽，華格納說他一定會贏。

珮兒的機械人做好了，只要繩子一拉，機械人的嘴巴就會張開。

華格納沒有做出任何東西來。珮兒把機械人拿給老師看，但是機械人的頭掉了下來。珮兒和華格納一起把它修好。

的時候，評判走過來看珮兒的機械人，可是機械人又壞了。華格納趕緊爬到機械人裡面去，躲在裡面跟評審說話。評審以為機械人會說話！不過後來她發現了躲在裡面的華格納。

比賽輸了，不過珮兒知道華格納只是想幫忙。珮兒很開心，因為她知道華格納是她的好朋友。

Vietnamese

Pearl và Wagner
Hai Người Bạn Thân

Cô bé Pearl muốn làm một người máy cho buổi Triển Lãm Khoa Học. Wagner nói là cậu sẽ đoạt giải thưởng.

Pearl làm một người máy. Khi Pearl kéo một sợi dây thì miệng của người máy mở ra.

Wagner không làm vật gì hết. Pearl đưa người máy cho thầy giáo xem. Đầu của người máy bị rớt. Pearl và Wagner sửa lại.

Vị giám khảo đến xem người máy. Người máy bị hư lần nữa. Wagner leo vào bên trong người máy. Cậu nói chuyện với vị giám khảo. Bà giám khảo nghĩ là người máy biết nói! Sau đó bà tìm ra là Wagner ở bên trong.

Đôi bạn không được giải thưởng. Pearl biết là Wagner muốn giúp mình. Cô bé vui mừng rằng mình và Wagner là bạn.

Multilingual Summaries

Korean

펄과 와그너는 좋은 친구

펄은 과학박람회에 낼 로봇을 만들고 싶어한다. 친구 와그너는 펄이 상을 탈 것이라고 얘기해준다.

펄은 줄을 잡아당기면 입이 벌어지는 로봇을 만든다.

와그너는 아무것도 만들지 않는다. 펄이 선생님께 로봇을 보여드리다가 그만 로봇의 머리가 떨어지자 와그너는 펄과 함께 로봇을 고친다.

박람회에서 심사위원이 로봇을 보러 왔지만 로봇이 또 고장 난다. 그러자 와그너는 로봇 안으로 기어올라가 심사위원에게 말을 한다. 펄은 로봇이 말을 하는 줄 알고 놀라지만 곧 그 안에 들어있는 와그너를 발견한다.

두 친구는 상을 타지는 못했지만 펄은 와그너가 자신을 도와주려 했다는 걸 알고는 그와 친구라는 사실에 기뻐한다.

Hmong

Pearl thiab Wagner Ob Tug Phoojywg Zoo

Pearl xav txua ib tug hlau uas txawj mus kev rau lub Science Fair. Wagner hais tias nws yuav yeej ib qho nqi zog.

Pearl txua tau ib tug hlau mus kev. Tus hlau no rua nws lub qhov ncauj thaum Pearl rub txoj hlua.

Wagner tsis ua ib yam dabtsi li. Pearl muab tus hlau no rau nws tus nais khus saib. Nws lub taubhau cia li hle los. Pearl thiab Wagner nkawd thiaj li kho rau.

Tus txiavtxim thiaj los saib tus hlau no. Lub taubhau rov qab hle dua thiab. Wagner thiaj li nce mus nyob sab hauv tus hlau no. Nws hais lus rau tus txiavtxim. Tus txiavtxim xav tias tus hlau no txawj hais lus. Ces nws txawm pom Wagner nyob sab hauv.

Ob tug phoojywg tsis yeej nqi zog. Pearl paub tias Wagner yeej txaus siab pab nws. Nws zoo siab tias nws thiab Wagner nkawd yog phoojywg.

Name ______________________________

- **Read** *Ada's Castle* again.
- **Label** everything that is needed to build a swing set.
- **Draw** a picture of a swing set at your school.
- **Label** everything that you think would be needed to build this swing set.

Family Link

Has anyone in your family ever built something for fun? Ask family members to describe what they built.

Weekly Resources Guide for English Language Learner Support

For this week's content and language objectives, see p. 95e.

Instructional Strand	Day 1	Day 2
Concept Development	TEACHER'S EDITION • Concept Development, p. DI•33 • Anchored Talk, pp. 382j—382–383 • *Sing With Me* Big Book, p. 384a • Concept Talk Video ELL HANDBOOK • ELL Poster Talk, Concept Talk, p. 95c ELL POSTER 12 • Day 1 Activities	TEACHER'S EDITION • Concept Development, p. DI•33 • Anchored Talk, p. 388b • *Sing With Me* Big Book, p. 388a • Concept Talk Video ELL HANDBOOK • ELL Poster Talk, Concept Talk, p. 95c • Concept Talk Video Routine, p. 464 ELL POSTER 12 • Day 2 Activities
Phonics/Phonemic Awareness	TEACHER'S EDITION • Preteach Phonemic Awareness, p. DI•34 • Preteach Phonics, p. DI•34 • Decodable Reader 12A, pp. 386b–386c	TEACHER'S EDITION • Practice Phonemic Awareness, p. DI•34 • Listen and Write Phonics, p. DI•34
Listening Comprehension	TEACHER'S EDITION • Modified Read Aloud, p. DI•36 • *Sing With Me* Big Book, p. 384a • Read Aloud, p. 387b • Concept Talk Video ELL HANDBOOK • Concept Talk Video Routine, p. 464	TEACHER'S EDITION • Modified Read Aloud, p. DI•36 • *Sing With Me* Big Book, p. 388a • AudioText of *Dear Juno* • Concept Talk Video ELL HANDBOOK • AudioText CD Routine, p. 464 • Story Map A, p. 470
Reading Comprehension	TEACHER'S EDITION • Teach Draw Conclusions/Make Inferences, p. DI•38	TEACHER'S EDITION • Teach Draw Conclusions/Make Inferences, p. DI•38 • Frontloading Reading, p. DI•39 ELL HANDBOOK • Picture It! Skill Instruction, pp. 96–96a • Multilingual Summaries, pp. 97–99
Vocabulary **High-Frequency Words** **Prefixes**	TEACHER'S EDITION • High-Frequency Words, p. DI•37 • Prefixes, p. DI•35 ELL HANDBOOK • Word Cards, p. 95 • ELL Vocabulary Routine, p. 456 ELL POSTER 12 • Day 1 Activities	TEACHER'S EDITION • High-Frequency Words, p. DI•37 • Prefixes, p. DI•35 ELL HANDBOOK • Word Cards, p. 95 • Multilingual Vocabulary List, pp. 429–440 ELL POSTER 12 • Day 2 Activities
Grammar and Conventions	TEACHER'S EDITION • Preteach Verbs with Singular and Plural Nouns, p. DI•41	TEACHER'S EDITION • Reteach Verbs with Singular and Plural Nouns, p. DI•41
Writing	TEACHER'S EDITION • Write a Friendly Letter, p. DI•42 • Introduce Friendly Letter, pp. 387d–387e	TEACHER'S EDITION • Writing Trait: Focus/Ideas, pp. 405d–405e

This symbol indicates leveled instruction to address language proficiency levels.

Day 3	Day 4	Day 5
TEACHER'S EDITION • Concept Development, p. DI•33 • Anchored Talk, p. 406b • *Sing with Me* Big Book, p. 406a • Concept Talk Video ELL HANDBOOK • ELL Poster Talk, Concept Talk, p. 95c ELL POSTER 12 • Day 3 Activities	TEACHER'S EDITION • Concept Development, p. DI•33 • Anchored Talk, p. 410b • *Sing with Me* Big Book, p. 410a • Concept Talk Video ELL HANDBOOK • ELL Poster Talk, Concept Talk, p. 95c ELL POSTER 12 • Day 4 Activities	TEACHER'S EDITION • Concept Development, p. DI•33 • Concept Talk Video ELL HANDBOOK • ELL Poster Talk, Concept Talk, p. 95c ELL POSTER 12 • Day 5 Activities
ELL HANDBOOK • Phonics Transition Lesson, pp. 254, 259	TEACHER'S EDITION • Decodable Reader 12C, pp. 410e–410f ELL HANDBOOK • Phonics Transition Lesson, pp. 254, 259	TEACHER'S EDITION • Reteach Phonics, p. DI•35
TEACHER'S EDITION • *Sing with Me* Big Book, p. 406a • AudioText of *Dear Juno* • Concept Talk Video ELL HANDBOOK • AudioText CD Routine, p. 464	TEACHER'S EDITION • *Sing with Me* Big Book, p. 410a • Concept Talk Video	TEACHER'S EDITION • Concept Talk Video
TEACHER'S EDITION • Sheltered Reading, p. DI•39 ELL HANDBOOK • Multilingual Summaries, pp. 97–99	TEACHER'S EDITION • ELL/ELD Reader Guided Reading, p. DI•40 ELL HANDBOOK • ELL Study Guide, p. 100	TEACHER'S EDITION • ELL/ELD Reader Guided Reading, p. DI•40 ELL HANDBOOK • ELL Study Guide, p. 100
ELL HANDBOOK • High-Frequency Words Activity Bank, p. 491 ELL POSTER 12 • Day 3 Activities	ELL HANDBOOK • High-Frequency Words Activity Bank, p. 491	TEACHER'S EDITION • Prefixes, p. 416–417 ELL HANDBOOK • High-Frequency Words Activity Bank, p. 491
TEACHER'S EDITION • Grammar Jammer ELL HANDBOOK • Grammar Transition Lesson, pp. 327, 334–336 • Grammar Jammer Routine, p. 465	TEACHER'S EDITION • Grammar Jammer ELL HANDBOOK • Grammar Transition Lesson, pp. 327, 334–336	TEACHER'S EDITION • Grammar Jammer ELL HANDBOOK • Grammar Transition Lesson, pp. 327, 334–336
TEACHER'S EDITION • Let's Write It!, p. 408–409 • Writer's Craft: Sequence, p. 409a	TEACHER'S EDITION • Revising Strategy, pp. 415d–415e	TEACHER'S EDITION • Writer's Craft: Verbs, pp. 417h–417i

Poster Talk, Concept Talk

Question of the Week

In what creative ways do we communicate?

Poster 12

Throughout the week, use the ELL Poster to help children produce and comprehend language, understand the concept, and build English vocabulary. Use the Question of the Week and other questions to help children share ideas in pairs, small groups, or the large group. Sample questions are shown, with examples of possible responses by children.

Weekly Concept and Language Goals

- Know that people communicate in creative ways
- Tell about different ways to communicate creatively
- Communicate creatively

By the end of the lesson, children should be able to talk about and write one or more sentences about communicating creatively.

Daily Team Talk

Day 1	Day 2	Day 3	Day 4	Day 5
After Day 1 activities on Poster, ask questions such as *In the poster pictures, children communicate with each other using letters and e-mails. What is another way people communicate?*	After Day 2 activity on Poster, ask questions such as *How can people use pictures to communicate in a creative way?*	After Day 3 activity on Poster, ask questions such as *How can you communicate with a child in China?*	After Day 4 activity on Poster, ask questions such as *Imagine you want to teach a friend a new dance. What can you do to communicate this information?*	After Day 5 activity on Poster, ask questions such as *What is another way the American and Chinese children in the poster pictures can communicate with each other?*
Beginning The phone. **Intermediate** They call each other on the phone. **Advanced** People use telephones to communicate. **Advanced High** Another way people communicate is by using telephones.	**Beginning** Show things. **Intermediate** Pictures show what things look like. **Advanced** People can draw pictures to show what things look like. **Advanced High** People can use pictures to show what something looks like or to tell a story.	**Beginning** Letters and e-mails. **Intermediate** I can send letters and e-mails to China. **Advanced** I can write letters and e-mails to the child. **Advanced High** I can write letters and e-mails and send them to the child in China. Then the child can send me letters and e-mails.	**Beginning** Show it. **Intermediate** I can do the dance. **Advanced** I can show my friend the dance. **Advanced High** First I show my friend the dance. Then we do the dance together.	**Beginning** Talk. **Intermediate** They can talk to each other. **Advanced** The children can get together and talk. **Advanced High** The American and Chinese children can meet and talk in person.

This Week's Materials

Teacher's Edition pages 382j–417k

See the support for English language learners throughout the lesson, including ELL strategies and scaffold activities at points of use.

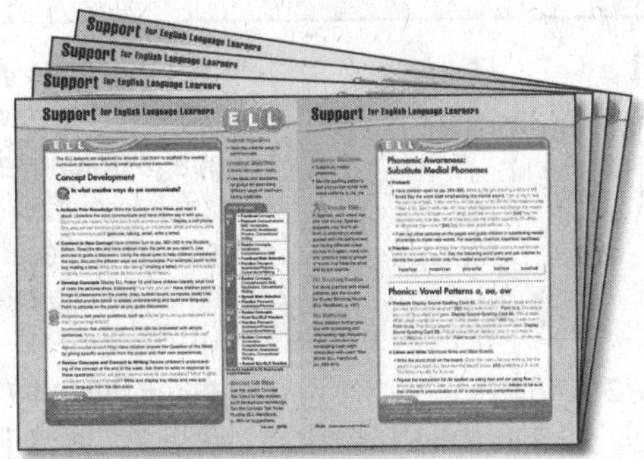
Teacher's Edition pages DI•33–DI•42

Differentiated Instruction for English language learners provides daily group activities that "frontload," or preteach, core instruction.

ELL Handbook pp. 95a–100

Find additional lesson materials that support the core lesson and the ELL instructional pages.

ELL Poster 12

ELD Reader 2.3.2

ELL Reader 2.3.2

Concept Literacy Reader

ELD, ELL Reader Teaching Guide

Concept Literacy Reader Teaching Guide

Technology

Online Teacher's Edition Use the digital version of the core teacher's edition for planning and instruction.

eReaders
This Week's ELL and ELD Readers and Concept Literacy Reader are also available in digital format.

This Week's Content and Language Objectives by Strand

Concept Development In what creative ways do we communicate?	**Content Objective** • Describe creative ways to communicate. **Language Objectives** • Share information orally. • Use basic and academic language for describing different ways of communicating creatively.
Phonics/Phonemic Awareness Phonics: Vowel Patterns *o, oa, ow*; Substitute Medial Phonemes	**Language Objectives** • Substitute medial phonemes. • Identify spelling patterns and pronounce words with vowel patterns *o, oa, ow*.
Listening Comprehension Modified Read Aloud: "Different Ways to Communicate"	**Content Objective** • Monitor and adjust oral comprehension. **Language Objectives** • Discuss oral passages. • Use a graphic organizer to take notes.
Reading Comprehension Draw Conclusions/Make Inferences	**Content Objectives** • Draw conclusions to aid comprehension. • Monitor and adjust comprehension. **Language Objectives** • Discuss evidence for drawing conclusions. • Retell a reading in order to draw conclusions. • Write conclusions drawn from a reading. • Summarize text using visual support.
Vocabulary High-Frequency Words	**Language Objectives** • Use accessible language to learn new and essential language. • Use high-frequency English words.
Vocabulary Prefixes	**Content Objective** • Identify and define prefixes in words. **Language Objective** • Comprehend language structures such as vowel patterns *o, oa,* and *ow*.
Grammar and Conventions Verbs with Singular and Plural Nouns	**Content Objective** • Identify and correctly use verbs with singular and plural nouns. **Language Objectives** • Speak using verbs with singular and plural nouns. • Correctly use verbs with singular and plural nouns.
Writing Friendly Letter	**Content Objectives** • Identify the characteristics of a friendly letter. • Use an outline to take notes during prewriting. **Language Objectives** • Write sentences that stick to a topic. • Share feedback for editing and revising.

Word Cards for Vocabulary Activities

answer	**company**
faraway	**parents**
picture	**school**
wash	

Teacher Note: Beginning Teach two to three words. **Intermediate** Teach three to four words. **Advanced** Teach five to six words. **Advanced High** Teach all words.

Name ______________________________

Picture It!
Draw Conclusions

Look at the pictures. **Read** the sentences.

Pen Pals

Ignacio is from Mexico City. He is drawing a picture of his pets to send to his pen pal in the United States.

Karen is from California. She is drawing a picture of her family to send to her pen pal in Mexico.

Karen and Ignacio are mailing their letters. They can't wait to learn more about each other!

Answer the questions below.

1. What does Ignacio's drawing tell you about him?

____

2. What does Karen's drawing tell you about her?

____

3. Do you think Karen and Ignacio like being pen pals? Why?

____

Draw Conclusions

Use this lesson to supplement or replace the skill lesson on page 387a of the Teacher's Edition. Display the Skill Points (at right) and share them with children.

Use the Skill Points to preteach draw conclusions.

Teach/Model

Beginning Pantomime opening a letter: *I got a letter.* Smile and act excited. Ask: *Am I happy I got a letter? How do you know?* Guide children to draw the conclusion that you are happy because you are smiling and acting excited as you open the letter.

Intermediate Say: *I have a new pen pal. I buy paper, envelopes, and stamps. What conclusion can you make?* (You will write a letter to your pen pal.) *What helped you make that conclusion?* (Paper, envelopes, and stamps are used to write letters.)

Advanced Say and pantomime: *I make a card. I take the card to the post office.* Have children suggest conclusions they can draw and explain how they drew their conclusions. (You will mail the card. Cards can be mailed at the post office.)

Advanced High Tell children this story: *I send a card to Aunt Emma. Then I send a letter to my cousin. Later, I send a photo to my grandmother. What conclusions can you draw about me?* Have children record and illustrate their conclusions.

Skill Points

- ✔ When you **draw a conclusion**, you figure out more about the characters and what happens in the story.
- ✔ Use what you read and what you know from real life to draw conclusions.
- ✔ When you draw a conclusion, ask yourself: *Does that make sense?*

Then distribute copies of Picture It! page 96.

- Have children look at the pictures and tell what is happening in each one.
- Read the sentences aloud. If necessary, explain what a pen pal is. Ask: *What can you tell about the children in the story?*
- Review the Skill Points with children.
- Have children look at the pictures to draw a conclusion about the characters in the story.

Practice

Read aloud the directions on page 96. Reread or chorally read the story. Have children look at the pictures and the story as they answer the questions.

Beginning Children can orally answer and, with help, write their answers. Provide help with writing and spelling.

Intermediate Children can first orally answer and then write their answers on the page.

Advanced Children can write their answers and check them by quietly reading them aloud or comparing them with a partner's answers.

Advanced High Children can write their answers and check them by reviewing the story and making any necessary corrections.

Answers for page 96: 1. Possible answer: He has a dog and two cats. 2. Possible answer: She has a big family. 3. Possible answer: Yes, they like being pen pals. They are friends even though they live far apart. They are excited to send and receive letters.

Multilingual Summaries

English

Dear Juno

Juno's grandmother lives in Korea. One day, Juno gets a letter from her. He cannot read Korean. He looks at the photograph and the flower that come in the letter. He knows what the letter is about.

Juno writes back to his grandmother. He draws pictures of his family and his dog. He puts in a leaf from his swinging tree. Juno's grandmother writes back. She sends colored pencils, a photograph, and a toy airplane. Juno knows that his grandmother is coming to visit. He is very happy.

Spanish

Querido Juno

La abuela de Juno vive en Corea. Un día, Juno recibe una carta de su abuela. Él no sabe leer coreano. Mira la fotografía y la flor que vienen en la carta. Él sabe de qué se trata la carta.

Juno le contesta la carta a su abuela. Dibuja a su familia y a su perro. Le pone una hoja del árbol donde él se columpia. La abuela de Juno le vuelve a escribir. Le manda lápices de colores, una fotografía y un avión de juguete. Juno sabe que la abuela va a venir a visitarlos. Él está muy feliz.

Multilingual Summaries

Chinese

親愛的朱諾

朱諾的祖母住在韓國。有一天，朱諾收到祖母寄給他的信。他看不懂韓文，不過看到和信一起寄過來的照片和小花，朱諾就明白信的內容了。

朱諾回了一封信給祖母，他畫了一張全家福，連狗狗也畫進去了，還從鞦韆樹上摘了片葉子，一起寄給祖母。不久之後，祖母回信了，她寄了顏色筆、一張照片和一架玩具飛機給朱諾。朱諾知道，祖母要來看他了，他很高興。

Vietnamese

Juno Yêu Quy

Bà của Juno sống ở Hàn Quốc. Một ngày nọ, Juno nhận được một lá thư của bà. Cậu bé không đọc được Hàn ngữ. Cậu nhìn vào tấm ảnh và cành hoa gởi trong thư. Cậu bé hiểu lá thư viết gì.

Juno viết thư lại cho bà. Cậu vẽ hình của gia đình và con chó của cậu. Cậu để vào thư một chiếc lá từ cây treo xích đu của mình. Bà của Juno viết thư lại. Bà gởi bút chì màu, một tấm ảnh, và một chiếc máy bay đồ chơi. Juno hiểu là bà của mình sắp đến thăm. Cậu rất vui mừng.

Multilingual Summaries

Korean

준오에게

어느 날 준오는 한국에 계신 할머니가 보낸 편지를 받지만 한국어를 몰라 편지와 같이 온 사진과 꽃을 보고 편지의 내용을 이해하게 된다.

준오는 할머니에게 답장으로 가족과 개를 그린 그림과 그네가 매달려 있는 나무의 잎을 하나 넣어 보낸다. 할머니는 다시 답장으로 색연필과 사진, 장난감 비행기를 보내준다. 준오는 할머니가 자신을 보러 올 것이라는 것을 알고 매우 행복해한다.

Hmong

Hmov Tshua Txog Juno

Juno pog nyob rau Kauslim tebchaws. Muaj ib hnub Juno txais ib tsab ntawv tuaj ntawm nws. Nws nyeem tsis tau lus Kauslim. Nws tsuas ntsia cov duab thiab cov paj uas nyob rau hauv daim ntawv. Nws paub hais tias daim ntawv ntawd hais txog dabtsi lawm.

Juno sau ntawv teb nws pog daim ntawv. Nws teeb duab txog nws tsevneeg thiab nws tus dev. Nws ntsaws ib daim nplooj uas nyob rau ntawm tsob ntoo nws ua si. Juno pog rov qab sau ntawv tuaj dua. Nws xa tau ib cov xaum thas xim, ib daim duab, thiab ib lub dav hlau ua si tuaj rau nws. Juno paub tias nws pog yuav tuaj xyuas nws. Ua rau nws zoo siab heev.

Name ______________________________

- **Read** *Express Yourself* again.
- **Draw** a picture to show how you express yourself.
  Write words or sentences to go with your picture.

Family Link

Do people in your family have special ways of expressing their ideas or interests? Find out! Ask family members why they enjoy those ways to express their ideas or interests.

Weekly Resources Guide for English Language Learner Support

For this week's content and language objectives, see p. 101e.

Instructional Strand	Day 1	Day 2
Concept Development	TEACHER'S EDITION • Concept Development, p. DI•54 • Anchored Talk, pp. 418j—418–419 • *Sing With Me* Big Book, p. 420a • Concept Talk Video ELL HANDBOOK • ELL Poster Talk, Concept Talk, p. 101c ELL POSTER 13 • Day 1 Activities	TEACHER'S EDITION • Concept Development, p. DI•54 • Anchored Talk, p. 424b • *Sing With Me* Big Book, p. 424a • Concept Talk Video ELL HANDBOOK • ELL Poster Talk, Concept Talk, p. 101c • Concept Talk Video Routine, p. 464 ELL POSTER 13 • Day 2 Activities
Phonics/Phonemic Awareness	TEACHER'S EDITION • Preteach Phonemic Awareness, p. DI•55 • Preteach Phonics, p. DI•55 • Decodable Reader 13A, pp. 422b–422c	TEACHER'S EDITION • Practice Phonemic Awareness, p. DI•55 • Listen and Write Phonics, p. DI•55
Listening Comprehension	TEACHER'S EDITION • Modified Read Aloud, p. DI•57 • *Sing With Me* Big Book, p. 420a • Read Aloud, p. 423b • Concept Talk Video ELL HANDBOOK • Concept Talk Video Routine, p. 464	TEACHER'S EDITION • Modified Read Aloud, p. DI•57 • *Sing With Me* Big Book, p. 424a • AudioText of *Anansi Goes Fishing* • Concept Talk Video ELL HANDBOOK • AudioText CD Routine, p. 464 • Story Map B, p. 471
Reading Comprehension	TEACHER'S EDITION • Teach Compare and Contrast, p. DI•59	TEACHER'S EDITION • Teach Compare and Contrast, p. DI•59 • Frontloading Reading, p. DI•60 ELL HANDBOOK • Picture It! Skill Instruction, pp. 102–102a • Multilingual Summaries, pp. 103–105
Vocabulary **High-Frequency Words** **Antonyms**	TEACHER'S EDITION • High-Frequency Words, p. DI•58 • Antonyms, p. DI•56 ELL HANDBOOK • Word Cards, p. 101 • ELL Vocabulary Routine, p. 456 ELL POSTER 13 • Day 1 Activities	TEACHER'S EDITION • High-Frequency Words, p. DI•58 • Antonyms, p. DI•56 ELL HANDBOOK • Word Cards, p. 101 • Multilingual Vocabulary List, pp. 429–440 ELL POSTER 13 • Day 2 Activities
Grammar and Conventions	TEACHER'S EDITION • Preteach Verbs for Past, Present, and Future, p. DI•62	TEACHER'S EDITION • Reteach Verbs for Past, Present, and Future, p. DI•62
Writing	TEACHER'S EDITION • Write a Narrative Poem, p. DI•63 • Introduce Narrative Poem, pp. 423d–423e	TEACHER'S EDITION • Writing Trait: Conventions, pp. 443c–443d

This symbol indicates leveled instruction to address language proficiency levels.

Day 3	Day 4	Day 5
TEACHER'S EDITION • Concept Development, p. DI•54 • Anchored Talk, p. 444b • *Sing With Me* Big Book, p. 444a • Concept Talk Video ELL HANDBOOK • ELL Poster Talk, Concept Talk, p. 101c ELL POSTER 13 • Day 3 Activities	TEACHER'S EDITION • Concept Development, p. DI•54 • Anchored Talk, p. 448b • *Sing With Me* Big Book, p. 448a • Concept Talk Video ELL HANDBOOK • ELL Poster Talk, Concept Talk, p. 101c ELL POSTER 13 • Day 4 Activities	TEACHER'S EDITION • Concept Development, p. DI•54 • Concept Talk Video ELL HANDBOOK • ELL Poster Talk, Concept Talk, p. 101c ELL POSTER 13 • Day 5 Activities
ELL HANDBOOK • Phonics Transition Lesson, pp. 282, 285	TEACHER'S EDITION • Decodable Reader 13C, pp. 448e–448f ELL HANDBOOK • Phonics Transition Lesson, pp. 282, 285	TEACHER'S EDITION • Reteach Phonics, p. DI•56
TEACHER'S EDITION • *Sing With Me* Big Book, p. 444a • AudioText of *Anansi Goes Fishing* • Concept Talk Video ELL HANDBOOK • AudioText CD Routine, p. 464	TEACHER'S EDITION • *Sing With Me* Big Book, p. 448a • Concept Talk Video	TEACHER'S EDITION • Concept Talk Video
TEACHER'S EDITION • Sheltered Reading, p. DI•60 ELL HANDBOOK • Multilingual Summaries, pp. 103–105	TEACHER'S EDITION • ELL/ELD Reader Guided Reading, p. DI•61 ELL HANDBOOK • ELL Study Guide, p. 106	TEACHER'S EDITION • ELL/ELD Reader Guided Reading, p. DI•61 ELL HANDBOOK • ELL Study Guide, p. 106
ELL HANDBOOK • High-Frequency Words Activity Bank, p. 491 ELL POSTER 13 • Day 3 Activities	ELL HANDBOOK • High-Frequency Words Activity Bank, p. 491	TEACHER'S EDITION • Antonyms, p. 450–451 ELL HANDBOOK • High-Frequency Words Activity Bank, p. 491
TEACHER'S EDITION • Grammar Jammer ELL HANDBOOK • Grammar Transition Lesson, pp.326, 328–330, 337–338, 340–341 • Grammar Jammer Routine, p. 465	TEACHER'S EDITION • Grammar Jammer ELL HANDBOOK • Grammar Transition Lesson, pp. 326, 328–330, 337–338, 340–341	TEACHER'S EDITION • Grammar Jammer ELL HANDBOOK • Grammar Transition Lesson, pp. 326, 328–330, 337–338, 340–341
TEACHER'S EDITION • Let's Write It!, p. 446–447 • Writer's Craft: Description, p. 447a	TEACHER'S EDITION • Revising Strategy, pp. 449d–449e	TEACHER'S EDITION • Writing Trait: Conventions, pp. 451h–451i

Question of the Week

How can creative thinking solve a problem?

Poster 13

Throughout the week, use the ELL Poster to help children produce and comprehend language, understand the concept, and build English vocabulary. Use the Question of the Week and other questions to help children share ideas in pairs, small groups, or the large group. Sample questions are shown, with examples of possible responses by children.

Weekly Concept and Language Goals

- Know how creative thinking solves a problem
- Tell about ways that creative thinking solved an everyday problem
- Tell about how they solved a problem with creative thinking

By the end of the lesson, children should be able to talk about and write one or more sentences about solving problems with creative thinking.

Daily Team Talk

Day 1	Day 2	Day 3	Day 4	Day 5
After Day 1 activities on Poster, ask questions such as *What creative idea do you think the rabbit has for getting out of the net?*	After Day 2 activity on Poster, ask questions such as *The fox uses a net to catch the rabbit. How does Turtle use a net to solve a problem in* Anansi Goes Fishing?	After Day 3 activity on Poster, ask questions such as *How can you and your friends use creative thinking to decide what to do on the playground each day?*	After Day 4 activity on Poster, ask questions such as *How do you use creative thinking to help you when you read?*	After Day 5 activity on Poster, ask questions such as *How can you use creative thinking to help you get something you want?*
Beginning Bite it. **Intermediate** He can bite the net. **Advanced** The rabbit can chew a hole in the net. **Advanced High** The rabbit can chew through the net and then jump to the ground.	**Beginning** It gets fish. **Intermediate** He catches fish in it. **Advanced** Turtle uses a net to catch fish in the river. **Advanced High** Turtle tricks Anansi into weaving a net to catch fish for Turtle to eat.	**Beginning** Take turns. **Intermediate** We take turns each day. **Advanced** We can take turns deciding. **Advanced High** We can take turns deciding what we will do on the playground.	**Beginning** Sound out words. **Intermediate** I sound out words I don't know. **Advanced** I look for clues to help me understand. **Advanced High** I ask myself questions and look for the answers as I read.	**Beginning** Say please. **Intermediate** Ask for it nicely. **Advanced** I can give good reasons. **Advanced High** I can explain what I will do in return if I get it.

This Week's Materials

Teacher's Edition pages 418j–451k

See the support for English language learners throughout the lesson, including ELL strategies and scaffold activities at points of use.

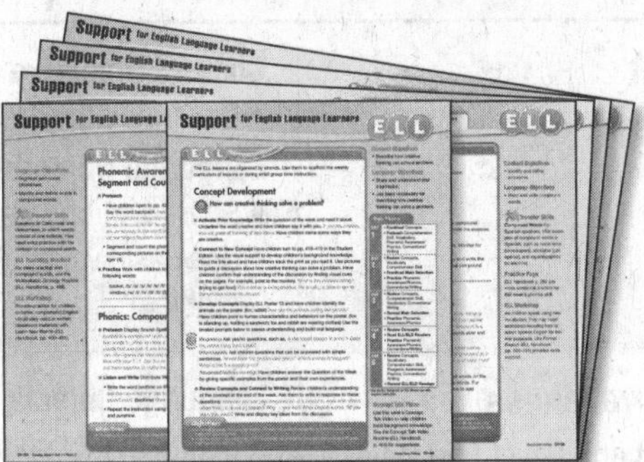

Teacher's Edition pages DI•54–DI•63

Differentiated Instruction for English language learners provides daily group activities that "frontload," or preteach, core instruction.

ELL Handbook pp. 101a–106

Find additional lesson materials that support the core lesson and the ELL instructional pages.

ELL Poster 13

ELD Reader 2.3.3

ELL Reader 2.3.3

Concept Literacy Reader

ELD, ELL Reader Teaching Guide

Concept Literacy Reader Teaching Guide

Technology

Online Teacher's Edition Use the digital version of the core teacher's edition for planning and instruction.

eReaders
This Week's ELL and ELD Readers and Concept Literacy Reader are also available in digital format.

This Week's Content and Language Objectives by Strand

Concept Development How can creative thinking solve a problem?	**Content Objective** • Describe how creative thinking can solve a problem. **Language Objectives** • Share and understand oral information. • Use basic vocabulary for describing how creative thinking can solve a problem.
Phonics/Phonemic Awareness Compound Words; Segment and Count Phonemes	**Language Objectives** • Segment and count phonemes. • Identify and define words in compound words.
Listening Comprehension Modified Read Aloud: "The Clever Monkey"	**Content Objective** • Monitor and adjust oral comprehension. **Language Objectives** • Discuss oral passages. • Use a graphic organizer to take notes.
Reading Comprehension Compare and Contrast	**Content Objectives** • Identify the difference between compare and contrast. • Identify details that are alike and different. • Monitor and adjust comprehension. **Language Objectives** • Discuss, retell, and write details that compare and contrast. • Summarize text using visual support.
Vocabulary High-Frequency Words	**Language Objectives** • Use accessible language to learn new and essential language. • Use high-frequency English words.
Vocabulary Antonyms	**Content Objective** • Identify and define antonyms. **Language Objective** • Read and write compound words.
Grammar and Conventions Verbs for Past, Present, and Future	**Content Objective** • Identify verbs for past, present, and future. **Language Objective** • Use verbs for past, present, and future in sentences.
Writing Narrative Poem	**Content Objectives** • Identify narrative poetry. • Identify words that rhyme. **Language Objectives** • Demonstrate comprehension by taking notes. • Narrate with increasing specificity.

Word Cards for Vocabulary Activities

been	**believe**
caught	**finally**
today	**tomorrow**
whatever	

Teacher Note: Beginning Teach two to three words. **Intermediate** Teach three to four words. **Advanced** Teach five to six words. **Advanced High** Teach all words.

Name ______________________________

Picture It!
Compare and Contrast

Look at the pictures. **Read** the story.

Champ's Snack

Abbey loved ice cream. She sat down to eat, but her hair kept getting in the way!

Abbey got a clip to hold her hair up. She wanted to taste her ice cream, not her hair. When she left the table, Champ came in. He liked ice cream too! His fur didn't get in the way of him eating.

Abbey sent Champ outside. Now she can have some ice cream. She will need a clean bowl first.

Answer the questions.

1. How are Abbey and Champ alike?

____

____

2. How are Abbey and Champ different?

____

____

Compare and Contrast

Use this lesson to supplement or replace the skill lesson on page 423a of the Teacher's Edition. Display the Skill Points (at right) and share them with children.

Use the Skill Points to preteach compare and contrast.

Teach/Model

Beginning Show children pictures of fruit. Say: *I eat these. A bird eats these.* Show a picture of cheese. Say: *I eat this. A bird does not eat this.* Guide children in comparing and contrasting you and the bird. (You both eat fruit. You eat cheese, but the bird does not.)

Intermediate Show pictures of a boy and a girl. Place pictures of food next to the boy and girl as you say: *He likes grapes best. She likes carrots best. They both like apples.* Guide children in comparing and contrasting the boy and girl.

Advanced Have children suggest snacks they enjoy. Write their suggestions on the board. Pointing to two snacks at a time and ask children to compare and contrast them. (For example: These are both sweet. This one is healthy, but that one is not.)

Advanced High Ask children to compare and contrast two objects in the classroom. Encourage them to use clue words such as *like, both, but,* and *different* to show comparisons and contrasts.

Then distribute copies of Picture It! page 102.

- Have children look at the pictures and tell what is happening in each one.
- Read the sentences aloud. Ask: *Are Abbey and Champ alike?*
- Review the Skill Points with children.
- Have children look at the pictures and sentences to compare and contrast Abbey and Champ.

Practice

Read aloud the directions on page 102. Reread or chorally read the story. Have children look at the pictures and the story as they answer the questions.

Beginning Children can orally answer and, with help, write their answers.

Intermediate Children can first orally answer and then write their answers on the page.

Advanced Children can write their answers and check them by quietly reading them aloud or comparing them with a partner's answers.

Advanced High Children can write their answers and check them by silently rereading the story and making any necessary corrections.

Answers for page 102: 1. They both like ice cream. 2. Abbey does not like hair in her ice cream. Champ does not mind fur in his ice cream.

Skill Points

- ✔ When you **compare** things, you tell how they are alike. When you **contrast** things, you tell how they are different.
- ✔ Clue words such as *like* and *both* show comparisons.
- ✔ Clue words such as *but* and *different* show contrasts.

Multilingual Summaries

English

Anansi Goes Fishing

Turtle will teach Anansi to fish. Anansi is lazy. He plans to make Turtle do all the work.

Turtle says that when he works, he becomes tired. Turtle says that now he can work, and Anansi can become tired. Because lazy Anansi doesn't want to be tired, he decides to work.

Anansi makes a net, catches a fish, and cooks the fish. While Anansi works, Turtle sleeps.

Turtle says that when he eats, he becomes full. Turtle says that now he will eat, and Anansi will become full. Because greedy Anansi wants to be full, he lets Turtle eat the fish. Turtle is full. Anansi is not.

Spanish

Anansi va a pescar

Tortuga le va a enseñar a Anansi a pescar. Anansi es perezoso. Planea dejar que Tortuga haga todo el trabajo.

Tortuga dice que cuando trabaja, se siente cansado. Tortuga le dice que ahora él va a trabajar y Anansi va a sentirse cansado. Como Anansi no quiere sentirse cansado, decide trabajar.

Anansi hace una red, atrapa un pescado y lo cocina. Mientras Anansi trabaja, Tortuga duerme.

Tortuga dice que cuando come, se siente lleno. Tortuga le dice que ahora él va a comer y Anansi va a sentirse lleno. Como el glotón Anansi quiere estar lleno, deja que Tortuga se coma el pescado. Tortuga está lleno, pero Anansi no.

Multilingual Summaries

Chinese

蜘蛛捕魚

烏龜要教蜘蛛捕魚，可是蜘蛛很懶惰，他想叫烏龜做所有的工作。

烏龜說只要他一工作，蜘蛛就會很累，現在他可以工作，不過累的是蜘蛛。因為懶惰的蜘蛛不想很累，所以他決定自己去工作。

蜘蛛結了一張網，捕到了魚，還把魚煮好。蜘蛛在工作的時候，烏龜卻在睡覺。

烏龜說只要他一吃東西，蜘蛛就會覺得飽，現在他要吃東西，不過會覺得飽的是蜘蛛。因為貪心的蜘蛛想吃得很飽，所以就讓烏龜吃魚。結果是烏龜飽了，蜘蛛卻還是很餓。

Vietnamese

Anansi Đi Câu Ca

Rùa sẽ dạy cho Anansi câu cá. Anansi lười biếng. Nó dự định là sẽ để cho Rùa làm hết mọi việc.

Rùa nói là khi nào Rùa làm việc, nó bị mệt. Rùa nói rằng bây giờ nó có thể làm việc và Anansi có thể bị mệt mỏi. Vì Anansi lười biếng không muốn bị mệt, nó quyết định đi làm việc.

Anansi làm một cái lưới, bắt được một con cá, và nấu con cá này. Trong khi Anansi làm việc thì Rùa ta ngủ.

Rùa nói khi nào nó ăn, nó bị no. Rùa nói bây giờ nó sẽ ăn và Anansi sẽ được no. Vì Anansi tham lam muốn được no, nó để Rùa ăn con cá. Rùa no bụng. Anansi bị đói.

Multilingual Summaries

Korean

낚시하러 간 아난시

거북이는 아난시에게 낚시하는 법을 가르쳐주려 하지만 게으른 아난시는 거북이가 모든 일을 다 하게 만들 계획이다.

거북이는 일을 하면 피곤해진다면서, 이제는 자기가 일을 하고 아난시가 피곤해질 차례라고 말한다. 게으른 아난시는 피곤해지고 싶지 않아 일을 하기로 하는데.

그물을 만들어 물고기를 잡고 요리를 하는 아난시. 아난시가 일하는 동안 거북이는 잠을 잔다.

거북이는 음식을 먹으면 배가 불러진다면서, 이제는 자기가 음식을 먹고 아난시의 배가 불러질 차례라고 말한다. 욕심 많은 아난시는 배불러지고 싶어 거북이가 생선을 먹도록 해 준다. 결국 거북이는 배가 부르지만 아난시는 그렇지 않다.

Hmong

Anansi Mus Nuv Ntses

Vaubkib yuav qhia Anansi nuv ntses. Anansi tub nkeeg. Nws xav kom Vaubkib ua tagnrho cov haujlwm rau nws.

Vaubkib hais tais thaum nws ua haujlwm ces ua rau nws nkees nkees. Vaubkib hais tias cia nws mam li ua haujlwm es cia Anansi mam li ua tus nkees nkees. Vim rau qhov Anansi tsis xav ua tus nkees nkees nws thiaj txiavtxim mus ua haujlwm.

Anansi mus ua ib lub zes, mus nuv ntses, thiab muab ntses coj los ua noj. Thaum Anansi ua haujlwm, Vaubkib pw.

Vaubkib hais tias nws tsau plam heev thaum nws noj mov tag. Vaubkis hais tias ziag no nws yuav noj xwb es Anansi mam ua tus tsau plab. Vim rau qhov Anansi yog ib tug neeg cuaj khaum nws mam li cia Vaubkib noj tus ntses. Vaubkib thiaj tsau plab. Anansi thiaj li tsis tsau plab.

Name ______________________

- **Read** *Chimps Use Tools!* again.
- **Write** to fill in the *What and Why* chart.

What and Why

What happens?	Why does it happen?
1. Termites are safe in their mounds.	**1.** ______________
2. The chimp finds a good tool.	**2.** ______________
3. The termites bite the stick and hold on.	**3.** ______________
4. ______________	**4.** The chimp can use a tool.

Family Link

Has any family member seen chimps at a zoo? Ask him or her to describe how the chimps acted.

Weekly Resources Guide for English Language Learner Support

For this week's content and language objectives, see p. 107e.

Instructional Strand	Day 1	Day 2
Concept Development	TEACHER'S EDITION • Concept Development, p. DI•75 • Anchored Talk, pp. 452j—452–453 • *Sing With Me* Big Book, p. 454a • Concept Talk Video ELL HANDBOOK • ELL Poster Talk, Concept Talk, p. 107c ELL POSTER 14 • Day 1 Activities	TEACHER'S EDITION • Concept Development, p. DI•75 • Anchored Talk, p. 458b • *Sing With Me* Big Book, p. 458a • Concept Talk Video ELL HANDBOOK • ELL Poster Talk, Concept Talk, p. 107c • Concept Talk Video Routine, p. 464 ELL POSTER 14 • Day 2 Activities
Phonics/Phonemic Awareness	TEACHER'S EDITION • Preteach Phonemic Awareness, p. DI•76 • Preteach Phonics, p. DI•76 • Decodable Reader 14A, pp. 456b–456c	TEACHER'S EDITION • Practice Phonemic Awareness, p. DI•76 • Listen and Write Phonics, p. DI•76
Listening Comprehension	TEACHER'S EDITION • Modified Read Aloud, p. DI•78 • *Sing With Me* Big Book, p. 454a • Read Aloud, p. 457b • Concept Talk Video ELL HANDBOOK • Concept Talk Video Routine, p. 464	TEACHER'S EDITION • Modified Read Aloud, p. DI•78 • *Sing With Me* Big Book, p. 458a • AudioText of *Rosa and Blanca* • Concept Talk Video ELL HANDBOOK • AudioText CD Routine, p. 464 • Cause and Effect, p. 476
Reading Comprehension	TEACHER'S EDITION • Teach Sequence, p. DI•80	TEACHER'S EDITION • Teach Sequence, p. DI•80 • Frontloading Reading, p. DI•81 ELL HANDBOOK • Picture It! Skill Instruction, pp. 108–108a • Multilingual Summaries, pp. 109–111
Vocabulary **High-Frequency Words** **Synonyms**	TEACHER'S EDITION • High-Frequency Words, p. DI•79 • Synonyms, p. DI•77 ELL HANDBOOK • Word Cards, p. 107 • ELL Vocabulary Routine, p. 456 ELL POSTER 14 • Day 1 Activities	TEACHER'S EDITION • High-Frequency Words, p. DI•79 • Synonyms, p. DI•77 ELL HANDBOOK • Word Cards, p. 107 • Multilingual Vocabulary List, pp. 429–440 ELL POSTER 14 • Day 2 Activities
Grammar and Conventions	TEACHER'S EDITION • Preteach More About Verbs, p. DI•83	TEACHER'S EDITION • Reteach More About Verbs, p. DI•83
Writing	TEACHER'S EDITION • Write for Tests: Realistic Fiction, p. DI•84 • Introduce Realistic Fiction, pp. 457d–457e	TEACHER'S EDITION • Realistic Fiction, pp. 469c–469d

Unit 3 Week 4 Rosa and Blanca

Leveled Support (LS) This symbol indicates leveled instruction to address language proficiency levels.

Day 3	Day 4	Day 5
TEACHER'S EDITION • Concept Development, p. DI•75 • Anchored Talk, p. 470b • *Sing With Me* Big Book, p. 470a • Concept Talk Video ELL HANDBOOK • ELL Poster Talk, Concept Talk, p. 107c ELL POSTER 14 • Day 3 Activities	TEACHER'S EDITION • Concept Development, p. DI•75 • Anchored Talk, p. 474b • *Sing With Me* Big Book, p. 474a • Concept Talk Video ELL HANDBOOK • ELL Poster Talk, Concept Talk, p. 107c ELL POSTER 14 • Day 4 Activities	TEACHER'S EDITION • Concept Development, p. DI•75 • Concept Talk Video ELL HANDBOOK • ELL Poster Talk, Concept Talk, p. 107c ELL POSTER 14 • Day 5 Activities
ELL HANDBOOK • Phonics Transition Lesson, pp. 254, 258	TEACHER'S EDITION • Decodable Reader 14C, pp. 474e–474f ELL HANDBOOK • Phonics Transition Lesson, pp. 254, 258	TEACHER'S EDITION • Reteach Phonics, p. DI•77
TEACHER'S EDITION • *Sing With Me* Big Book, p. 470a • AudioText of *Rosa and Blanca* • Concept Talk Video ELL HANDBOOK • AudioText CD Routine, p. 464	TEACHER'S EDITION • *Sing With Me* Big Book, p. 474a • Concept Talk Video	TEACHER'S EDITION • Concept Talk Video
TEACHER'S EDITION • Sheltered Reading, p. DI•81 ELL HANDBOOK • Multilingual Summaries, pp. 109–111	TEACHER'S EDITION • ELL/ELD Reader Guided Reading, p. DI•82 ELL HANDBOOK • ELL Study Guide, p. 112	TEACHER'S EDITION • ELL/ELD Reader Guided Reading, p. DI•82 ELL HANDBOOK • ELL Study Guide, p. 112
ELL HANDBOOK • High-Frequency Words Activity Bank, p. 491 ELL POSTER 14 • Day 3 Activities	ELL HANDBOOK • High-Frequency Words Activity Bank, p. 491	TEACHER'S EDITION • Words from Another Language, p. 478–479 ELL HANDBOOK • High-Frequency Words Activity Bank, p. 491
TEACHER'S EDITION • Grammar Jammer ELL HANDBOOK • Grammar Transition Lesson, pp. 329–330, 338, 341 • Grammar Jammer Routine, p. 465	TEACHER'S EDITION • Grammar Jammer ELL HANDBOOK • Grammar Transition Lesson, pp. 329–330, 338, 341	TEACHER'S EDITION • Grammar Jammer ELL HANDBOOK • Grammar Transition Lesson, pp. 329–330, 338, 341
TEACHER'S EDITION • Let's Write It!, p. 472–473 • Writing Trait: Word Choice, p. 473a	TEACHER'S EDITION • Writer's Craft: Description, pp. 477c–477d	TEACHER'S EDITION • Writing for Tests, pp. 479h–479i

Poster Talk, Concept Talk

Question of the Week

When does a creative idea lead to a surprise?

ELL Poster 14

Throughout the week, use the ELL Poster to help children produce and comprehend language, understand the concept, and build English vocabulary. Use the Question of the Week and other questions to help children share ideas in pairs, small groups, or the large group. Sample questions are shown, with examples of possible responses by children.

Weekly Concept and Language Goals

- Know that creative ideas can lead to a surprise
- Tell about a creative idea they had that led to a surprise

By the end of the lesson, children should be able to talk about and write one or more sentences about creative ideas that lead to surprises.

Daily Team Talk

Day 1	Day 2	Day 3	Day 4	Day 5
After Day 1 activities on Poster, ask questions such as *In the poster picture, what is the youngest girl's creative idea?*	After Day 2 activity on Poster, ask questions such as *The girls and their dad are buying a lot of fruit. What surprise can the girls make for their mom with the fruit?*	After Day 3 activity on Poster, ask questions such as *What creative idea did the sisters in* Rosa and Blanca *have that led to a surprise?*	After Day 4 activity on Poster, ask questions such as *When have you shared with someone and gotten a surprise in return?*	After Day 5 activity on Poster, ask questions such as *How have you surprised someone else with a creative idea?*
Beginning Holding apples. **Intermediate** Using her shawl. **Advanced** She uses her shawl to hold apples. **Advanced High** The girl doesn't have a bag to carry apples, so she uses her shawl.	**Beginning** A pie. **Intermediate** They can make her a pie. **Advanced** They can bake an apple pie for their mom. **Advanced High** The girls can surprise their mom with a pie made from the apples.	**Beginning** Gave food. **Intermediate** They shared their food. **Advanced** The sisters shared their vegetables with each other. **Advanced High** Each sister gave the other sister half of her tomatoes, corn, and chiles.	**Beginning** At lunch. **Intermediate** I gave some of my lunch and got bread. **Advanced** I shared my lunch with a friend and she gave me bread. **Advanced High** When my friend forgot her lunch, I shared mine. She surprised me with banana bread the next day.	**Beginning** Made a fort. **Intermediate** I used the sofa cushions to make a fort. **Advanced** Mom was surprised when I built a fort out of sofa cushions. **Advanced High** I surprised my mom when I built a great fort with the sofa cushions.

This Week's Materials

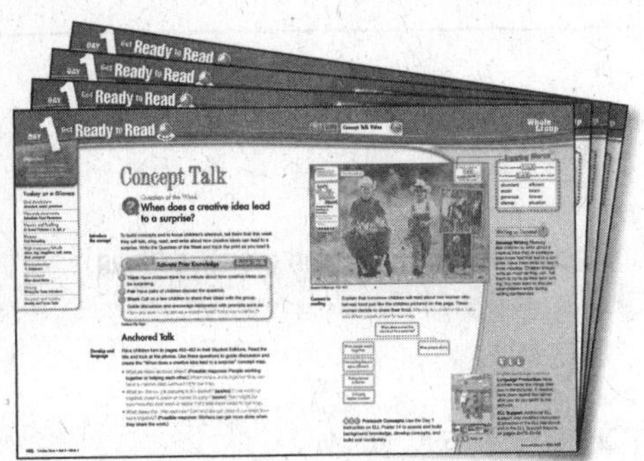

Teacher's Edition pages 452j–479k

See the support for English language learners throughout the lesson, including ELL strategies and scaffold activities at points of use.

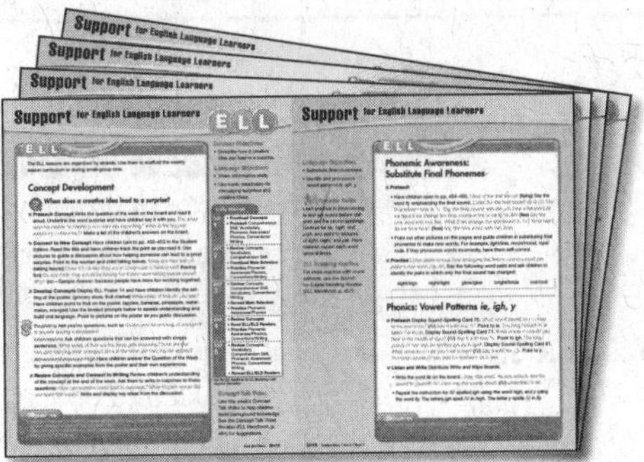

Teacher's Edition pages DI•75–DI•84

Differentiated Instruction for English language learners provides daily group activities that "frontload," or preteach, core instruction.

ELL Handbook pp. 107a–112

Find additional lesson materials that support the core lesson and the ELL instructional pages.

ELL Poster 14

ELD Reader 2.3.4

ELL Reader 2.3.4

Good Ideas!

By Leslie A. Rotsky

Concept Literacy Reader

ELD, ELL Reader Teaching Guide

Concept Literacy Reader Teaching Guide

Technology

Online Teacher's Edition Use the digital version of the core teacher's edition for planning and instruction.

eReaders
This Week's ELL and ELD Readers and Concept Literacy Reader are also available in digital format.

This Week's Content and Language Objectives by Strand

Concept Development When does a creative idea lead to a surprise?	**Content Objective** • Describe how a creative idea can lead to a surprise. **Language Objectives** • Share information orally. • Use basic vocabulary for discussing surprises and creative ideas.
Phonics/Phonemic Awareness Vowel Patterns *ie, igh, y;* Substitute Final Phonemes	**Language Objectives** • Substitute final phonemes. • Identify and pronounce vowel patterns *ie, igh, y.*
Listening Comprehension Modified Read Aloud: "Partners"	**Content Objective** • Monitor and adjust oral comprehension. **Language Objectives** • Discuss oral passages. • Use a graphic organizer to take notes. • Use visual support to enhance understanding.
Reading Comprehension Sequence	**Content Objectives** • Identify sequence. • Monitor and adjust comprehension. **Language Objectives** • Discuss sequence in stories. • Write using correct sequences. • Summarize text using visual support.
Vocabulary High-Frequency Words	**Language Objectives** • Use accessible language to learn new and essential language. • Use high-frequency English words.
Vocabulary Synonyms	**Content Objective** • Identify and define synonyms. **Language Objective** • Associate the long vowel sound /i/ with vowel patterns *ie, igh,* and *y.*
Grammar and Conventions More About Verbs	**Content Objective** • Identify future tense verbs. **Language Objective** • Speak and write using future tense verbs.
Writing Realistic Fiction	**Content Objectives** • Identify lively, interesting words. • Understand the definition of realistic fiction. **Language Objectives** • Create an example of realistic fiction. • Edit to add more lively, interesting words.

Word Cards for Vocabulary Activities

alone	**buy**
daughters	**half**
many	**their**
youngest	

Teacher Note: Beginning Teach two to three words. **Intermediate** Teach three to four words. **Advanced** Teach five to six words. **Advanced High** Teach all words.

Name ___________________________

Look at the pictures. **Read** the story.

- **Fill** in the boxes below. **Write** what happens first, next, and last in the story.

Damon's Wagon

Damon's dad bought plant food to help the grass grow. The bag was very heavy! Damon offered his wagon to help his dad, but his dad said no.

The bag was too heavy. Damon's dad dropped it, and it broke. Plant food spilled all over the driveway.

Damon's dad decided to use the wagon, after all. Damon was very happy to help.

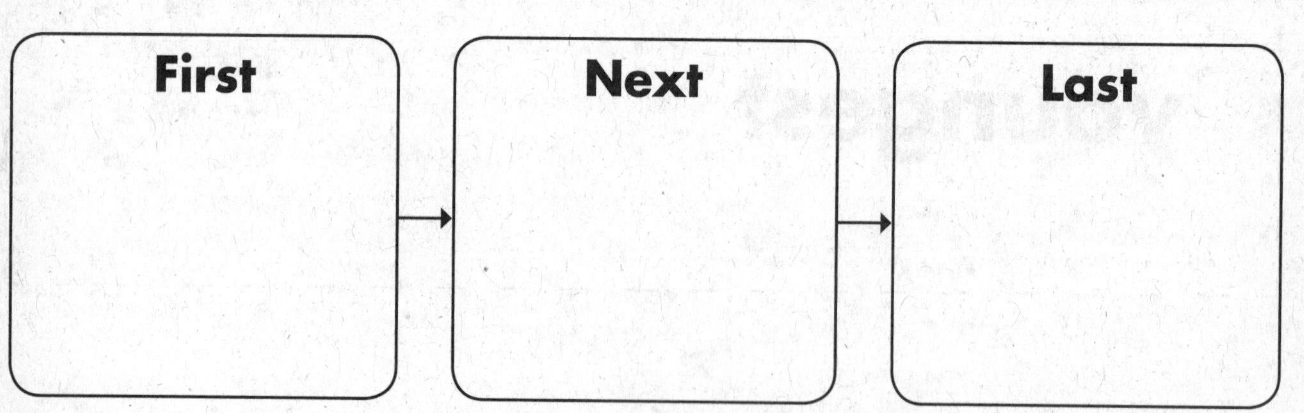

Sequence

Use this lesson to supplement or replace the skill lesson on page 457a of the Teacher's Edition. Display the Skill Points (at right) and share them with children.

Skill Points

- ✔ **Sequence** is the order in which things happen.
- ✔ Think about what happens first, next, and last in a story.
- ✔ Look for words such as *then* and *next* to figure out sequence.
- ✔ As you read, think about the order of events so you can keep track of what happens.

Use the Skill Points to preteach sequence.

Teach/Model

Beginning Draw three boxes on the board and label them *First, Next,* and *Last.* Review the events in a familiar story. Say: *Let's tell about the sequence of the story.* Guide children in identifying which events belong in each box.

Intermediate Give each child a piece of paper folded in three sections labeled *First, Next,* and *Last.* Tell a simple story with three events using the words *first, next,* and *last.* Have children choose one event and illustrate it in the appropriate section.

Advanced Review the story of *Jack and the Beanstalk.* Ask: *What is the sequence of events in this story? Tell the story's sequence. Use the words* first, next, *and* last.

Advanced High In a craft, gardening, or cooking magazine, find a sequence of photographs. Display the photographs out of order. Ask: *What is the correct sequence? Describe the sequence using the words* first, next, then, *and* last.

Then distribute copies of Picture It! page 108.

- Have children look at the pictures and tell what is happening in each one.
- Read the sentences aloud. Ask: *What happens first in the story? What happens next?*
- Review the Skill Points with children.
- Have children look at the pictures and words to find clues about the sequence of the story.

Practice

Read aloud the directions on page 108. Reread or chorally read the story. Have children look at the pictures and the story as they answer the questions.

Beginning Children can orally answer and fill in the diagram. Provide help with writing and spelling words in the diagram.

Intermediate Children can first orally answer and then fill in the diagram.

Advanced Children can fill in the diagram and check their answers by quietly reading them aloud or comparing them with a partner's answers.

Advanced High Children can fill in the diagram and check their answers by reviewing the story and making any necessary corrections.

Answers for page 108: *First:* Damon's dad told Damon he did not need help. *Next:* Damon's dad dropped the heavy bag. *Last:* Damon helped his dad pull the bag.

Multilingual Summaries

English

Rosa and Blanca

Rosa and Blanca are sisters. The sisters help each other. This makes their mother happy.

The sisters grow up. The sisters still help each other. Each wants to give half of her vegetables from her garden to the other. At night, each sister leaves vegetables in the other sister's kitchen. The sisters pass each other in the dark. In the morning, each sister is surprised. There are so many vegetables!

One day, Rosa is home when Blanca brings vegetables to her kitchen. Now the sisters understand. They tell their mother. Their mother is very happy. She says that she is the luckiest mother in the world.

Spanish

Rosa y Blanca

Rosa y Blanca son hermanas. Las hermanas se ayudan la una a la otra. Esto hace a su mamá muy feliz.

Las hermanas crecen. Ellas todavía se ayudan. Cada una quiere darle a la otra la mitad de los vegetales de su jardín. Por la noche, cada una le deja a la otra vegetales en la cocina. Las hermanas se cruzan en la oscuridad. En la mañana, cada hermana se sorprende. ¡Hay tantos vegetales!

Un día, Rosa está en la casa cuando Blanca lleva los vegetales a su cocina. Ahora las hermanas comprenden lo que pasa. Le cuentan a su mamá. Su mamá está muy feliz. Dice que es la mamá más afortunada del mundo.

Multilingual Summaries

Chinese

羅莎與布蘭卡

羅莎和布蘭卡是姊妹，兩人相親相愛，彼此幫忙，這讓媽媽覺得很高興。

兩姊妹長大後，還是一樣互相幫忙。兩個人都想把自己園子裡的蔬菜分一半給對方，於是就利用晚上，偷偷地把菜放到對方家裡的廚房。兩人在黑暗中擦身而過，彼此都沒有發覺。第二天一早醒來，兩姊妹都嚇了一跳，因為家裡竟然有很多蔬菜！

有一天，羅莎在家，剛巧看見布蘭卡把蔬菜放在她家廚房裡，這時兩姐妹才明白到底是怎麼一回事。她們把事情告訴媽媽，媽媽非常開心，並說自己是全世界最幸運的媽媽。

Vietnamese

Rosa và Blanca

Rosa và Blanca là hai chị em gái. Hai chị em này giúp đỡ nhau. Điều này làm cho mẹ của hai người rất vui lòng.

Hai chị em lớn lên. Họ vẫn còn giúp đỡ nhau. Mỗi người đều muốn cho phân nửa rau quả trồng ở vườn của mình cho người kia. Ban đêm, mỗi người mang rau quả đến để trong bếp của người kia. Hai chị em đi ngang nhau trong đêm tối. Đến sáng, mỗi chị đều ngạc nhiên. Có nhiều rau quả quá!

Một ngày nọ, Rosa đang ở nhà khi Blanca mang rau quả vào bếp của mình. Bấy giờ, hai chị em chợt hiểu. Họ nói cho mẹ nghe. Mẹ rất vui. Mẹ nói rằng bà là người mẹ may mắn nhất đời.

Multilingual Summaries

Korean

로사와 블랑카

로사와 블랑카 자매는 서로를 도와줘 엄마를 기쁘게 해드린다.

자매는 자라서도 여전히 서로를 도와준다. 각자의 정원에서 키운 야채의 반을 서로에게 주고 싶어 밤이 되면 서로의 부엌으로 가 야채를 놓고 온다. 어두운 밤이라 두 사람은 서로 알아보지 못하고 스쳐 지난다. 아침이 되면 부엌에 야채가 많이 쌓여있는 것을 보고 놀란다.

어느 날 로사가 집에 있는 동안 블랑카가 부엌에 야채를 몰래 가져다 놓는 것을 본다. 자매는 이제 모든 것을 이해하게 되고 엄마에게 이 이야기를 한다. 엄마는 이런 딸들을 두어 세상에서 가장 행복한 엄마라며 기뻐한다.

Hmong

Rosa thiab Blanca

Rosa thiab Blanca nkawd yog viv ncaus. Ob tug viv ncaus no ib leeg pab ib leeg. Qhov no ua rau nkawd niam zoo siab.

Ob tug viv ncaus tau loj los. Nkawd yeej tseem ib leeg pab ib leeg. Nkawd ib leeg xav faib ib leeg ib nrab zaub uas nyob hauv nkawd lub vaj. Thaum tsaus ntuj, nkawd ib leeg zais ib leeg ib cov zaum nqa tuaj tso rau hauv chav ua noj haus. Hmo ntuj nkawd ua li no los nkawd tsis sib pom li. Thaum sawv ntxov, ob tug viv ncaus ceeb. Ua cas yuav muaj cov zaub ntau ua luaj li.

Muaj ib hnub, Rosa nyob hauv tsev thaum nws pom Blanca nqa cov zaub tuaj tso rau nws chav ua noj haus. Ziag no ob tug viv ncaus no mam li totaub. Nkawd mus qhia rau nkawd niam. Nkawd niam zoo siab heev. Nws hais tias nws yog ib leej niam uas muaj hmoo tshaj plaws nyob rau hauv lub ntiajteb no.

Name ______________________ **American Hero Day**

- **Read** *American Hero Day* again.
- **Write** the answers to the questions.

Pages	Question	Answer
2–3	**1.** What did the cat do?	
4–5	**2.** What good idea does Carlos have?	
4–5	**3.** Who lends some hero masks to the class?	
6–7	**4.** Why do parents come to the classroom?	
7–8	**5.** Name two American heroes the children talked about.	

Family Link

Ask family members to tell you about their favorite American heroes.

Weekly Resources Guide for English Language Learner Support

For this week's content and language objectives, see p. 113e.

Instructional Strand	Day 1	Day 2
Concept Development	TEACHER'S EDITION • Concept Development, p. DI•96 • Anchored Talk, pp. 480j—480–481 • *Sing With Me* Big Book, p. 482a • Concept Talk Video ELL HANDBOOK • ELL Poster Talk, Concept Talk, p. 113c ELL POSTER 15 • Day 1 Activities	TEACHER'S EDITION • Concept Development, p. DI•96 • Anchored Talk, p. 486b • *Sing With Me* Big Book, p. 486a • Concept Talk Video ELL HANDBOOK • ELL Poster Talk, Concept Talk, p. 113c • Concept Talk Video Routine, p. 464 ELL POSTER 15 • Day 2 Activities
Phonics/Phonemic Awareness	TEACHER'S EDITION • Preteach Phonemic Awareness, p. DI•97 • Preteach Phonics, p. DI•97 • Decodable Reader 15A, pp. 484b–484c	TEACHER'S EDITION • Practice Phonemic Awareness, p. DI•97 • Listen and Write Phonics, p. DI•97
Listening Comprehension	TEACHER'S EDITION • Modified Read Aloud, p. DI•99 • *Sing With Me* Big Book, p. 482a • Read Aloud, p. 485b • Concept Talk Video ELL HANDBOOK • Concept Talk Video Routine, p. 464	TEACHER'S EDITION • Modified Read Aloud, p. DI•99 • *Sing With Me* Big Book, p. 486a • AudioText of *A Weed Is a Flower* • Concept Talk Video ELL HANDBOOK • AudioText CD Routine, p. 464 • K-W-L Chart, p. 467
Reading Comprehension	TEACHER'S EDITION • Teach Fact and Opinion, p. DI•101	TEACHER'S EDITION • Teach Fact and Opinion, p. DI•101 • Frontloading Reading, p. DI•102 ELL HANDBOOK • Picture It! Skill Instruction, pp. 114–114a • Multilingual Summaries, pp. 115–117
Vocabulary **High-Frequency Words** **Synonyms**	TEACHER'S EDITION • High-Frequency Words, p. DI•100 • Synonyms, p. DI•98 ELL HANDBOOK • Word Cards, p. 113 • ELL Vocabulary Routine, p. 456 ELL POSTER 15 • Day 1 Activities	TEACHER'S EDITION • High-Frequency Words, p. DI•100 • Synonyms, p. DI•98 ELL HANDBOOK • Word Cards, p. 113 • Multilingual Vocabulary List, pp. 429–440 ELL POSTER 15 • Day 2 Activities
Grammar and Conventions	TEACHER'S EDITION • Preteach Verbs *am, is, are, was, were,* p. DI•104	TEACHER'S EDITION • Reteach Verbs *am, is, are, was, were,* p. DI•104
Writing	TEACHER'S EDITION • Write a Review, p. DI•105 • Introduce Review, pp. 485d–485e	TEACHER'S EDITION • Writing Trait: Organization, pp. 507d–507e

Unit 3 Week 5 A Weed Is a Flower

This symbol indicates leveled instruction to address language proficiency levels.

Day 3	Day 4	Day 5
TEACHER'S EDITION • Concept Development, p. DI•96 • Anchored Talk, p. 508b • *Sing With Me* Big Book, p. 508a • Concept Talk Video ELL HANDBOOK • ELL Poster Talk, Concept Talk, p. 113c ELL POSTER 15 • Day 3 Activities	TEACHER'S EDITION • Concept Development, p. DI•96 • Anchored Talk, p. 512b • *Sing With Me* Big Book, p. 512a • Concept Talk Video ELL HANDBOOK • ELL Poster Talk, Concept Talk, p. 113c ELL POSTER 15 • Day 4 Activities	TEACHER'S EDITION • Concept Development, p. DI•96 • Concept Talk Video ELL HANDBOOK • ELL Poster Talk, Concept Talk, p. 113c ELL POSTER 15 • Day 5 Activities
	TEACHER'S EDITION • Decodable Reader 15C, pp. 512e–512f	TEACHER'S EDITION • Reteach Phonics, p. DI•98
TEACHER'S EDITION • *Sing With Me* Big Book, p. 508a • AudioText of *A Weed Is a Flower* • Concept Talk Video ELL HANDBOOK • AudioText CD Routine, p. 464	TEACHER'S EDITION • *Sing With Me* Big Book, p. 512a • Concept Talk Video	TEACHER'S EDITION • Concept Talk Video
TEACHER'S EDITION • Sheltered Reading, p. DI•102 ELL HANDBOOK • Multilingual Summaries, pp. 115–117	TEACHER'S EDITION • ELL/ELD Reader Guided Reading, p. DI•103 ELL HANDBOOK • ELL Study Guide, p. 118	TEACHER'S EDITION • ELL/ELD Reader Guided Reading, p. DI•103 ELL HANDBOOK • ELL Study Guide, p. 118
ELL HANDBOOK • High-Frequency Words Activity Bank, p. 491 ELL POSTER 15 • Day 3 Activities	ELL HANDBOOK • High-Frequency Words Activity Bank, p. 491	TEACHER'S EDITION • Synonyms, p. 516–517 ELL HANDBOOK • High-Frequency Words Activity Bank, p. 491
TEACHER'S EDITION • Grammar Jammer ELL HANDBOOK • Grammar Transition Lesson, pp. 329, 339 • Grammar Jammer Routine, p. 465	TEACHER'S EDITION • Grammar Jammer ELL HANDBOOK • Grammar Transition Lesson, pp. 329, 339	TEACHER'S EDITION • Grammar Jammer ELL HANDBOOK • Grammar Transition Lesson, pp. 329, 339
TEACHER'S EDITION • Let's Write It!, p. 510–511 • Writer's Craft: Commenting, p. 511a	TEACHER'S EDITION • Revising Strategy, pp. 515c–515d	TEACHER'S EDITION • Writer's Craft: Verbs, pp. 517h–517i

Poster Talk, Concept Talk

Question of the Week

Where do creative ideas come from?

Poster 15

Throughout the week, use the ELL Poster to help children produce and comprehend language, understand the concept, and build English vocabulary. Use the Question of the Week and other questions to help children share ideas in pairs, small groups, or the large group. Sample questions are shown, with examples of possible responses by children.

Weekly Concept and Language Goals

- Know where creative ideas come from
- Name a creative idea used every day
- Tell about where a creative idea came from

By the end of the lesson, children should be able to talk about and write one or more sentences about the origin of creative ideas.

Daily Team Talk

Day 1	Day 2	Day 3	Day 4	Day 5
After Day 1 activities on Poster, ask questions such as *In the poster picture, you can see many cookbooks. What creative ideas can the woman get from her cookbooks?*	After Day 2 activity on Poster, ask questions such as *George Washington Carver had creative ideas about food too. Where did his earliest ideas about plants come from?*	After Day 3 activity on Poster, ask questions such as *Have you ever made anything creative with food? Tell about what you made.*	After Day 4 activity on Poster, ask questions such as *What is a creative idea you use every day at school?*	After Day 5 activity on Poster, ask questions such as *Think of a creative idea you had at school. Where did the idea come from?*
Beginning Food to make. **Intermediate** She can get ideas of things to cook. **Advanced** The woman can find recipes for new foods. **Advanced High** In the cookbooks, the woman can read recipes for new foods to cook.	**Beginning** A garden. **Intermediate** He had a garden. **Advanced** When he was a child, he planted seeds in his own garden. **Advanced High** As a child, he planted a garden. His neighbors called him the Plant Doctor.	**Beginning** Fruit cup. **Intermediate** I made yogurt and fruit. **Advanced** I put fruit and granola on yogurt. **Advanced High** I made a yogurt sundae by stirring granola and fruit into my yogurt.	**Beginning** A pencil. **Intermediate** Someone thought of a pencil. **Advanced** Someone was creative and thought about how to make a pencil. **Advanced High** A creative idea I use every day at school is a mechanical pencil that doesn't need to be sharpened.	**Beginning** From my head. **Intermediate** I got the idea for my picture from noodles. **Advanced** I had the idea for my picture when I saw noodles and glitter. **Advanced High** The long noodles made me think of a giraffe's neck, so I made a sparkly giraffe from noodles and glitter.

This Week's Materials

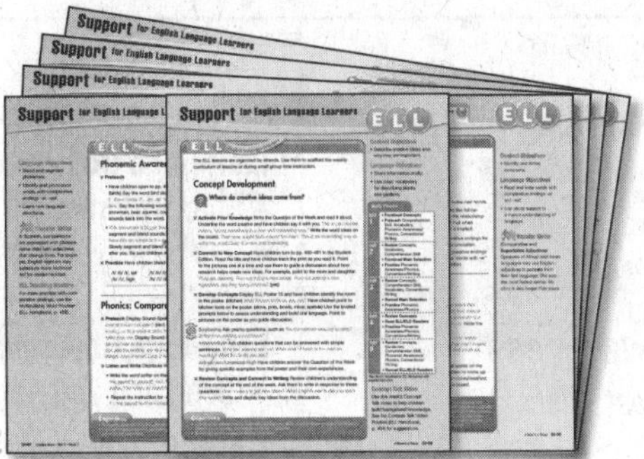

Teacher's Edition pages 480j–517k

See the support for English language learners throughout the lesson, including ELL strategies and scaffold activities at points of use.

Teacher's Edition pages DI•96–DI•105

Differentiated Instruction for English language learners provides daily group activities that "frontload," or preteach, core instruction.

ELL Handbook pp. 113a–118

Find additional lesson materials that support the core lesson and the ELL instructional pages.

ELL Poster 15

ELD Reader 2.3.5

ELL Reader 2.3.5

Concept Literacy Reader

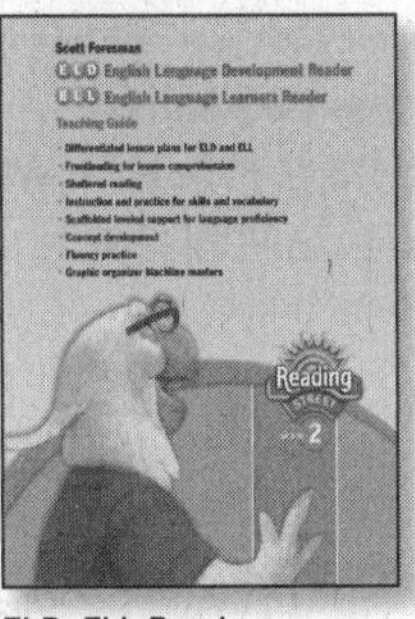

ELD, ELL Reader Teaching Guide

Concept Literacy Reader Teaching Guide

Technology

Online Teacher's Edition Use the digital version of the core teacher's edition for planning and instruction.

eReaders
This Week's ELL and ELD Readers and Concept Literacy Reader are also available in digital format.

This Week's Content and Language Objectives by Strand

Concept Development Where do creative ideas come from?	**Content Objective** • Describe creative ideas and why they are important. **Language Objectives** • Share information orally. • Use basic vocabulary for describing plants and gardens.
Phonics/Phonemic Awareness Comparative Endings *-er, -est*; Blend and Segment	**Language Objectives** • Blend and segment phonemes. • Identify and pronounce words with comparative endings *–er, -est.* • Learn new language structures.
Listening Comprehension Modified Read Aloud: "The Inventor"	**Content Objective** • Monitor and adjust oral comprehension. **Language Objectives** • Discuss oral passages. • Use a graphic organizer to take notes.
Reading Comprehension Fact and Opinion	**Content Objectives** • Identify facts and opinions to aid comprehension. • Monitor and adjust comprehension. **Language Objectives** • Discuss and write facts and opinions. • Retell facts and opinions from the reading. • Summarize text using visual support.
Vocabulary High-Frequency Words	**Language Objectives** • Use accessible language to learn new and essential language. • Use high-frequency English words.
Vocabulary Synonyms	**Content Objective** • Identify and define synonyms. **Language Objectives** • Read and write words with comparative endings *–er, -est.* • Use visual support to enhance understanding of language.
Grammar and Conventions Verbs *am, is, are, was, were*	**Content Objective** • Identify and use verbs *am, is, are, was, were.* **Language Objective** • Speak and write using future tense verbs.
Writing Review	**Content Objectives** • Identify a review. • Identify main ideas and details. **Language Objectives** • Write a review with a main idea and details. • Share feedback for editing and revising.

Word Cards for Vocabulary Activities

clothes	**hours**
money	**neighbor**
only	**question**
taught	

Teacher Note: Beginning Teach two to three words. **Intermediate** Teach three to four words. **Advanced** Teach five to six words. **Advanced High** Teach all words.

Name ______________________________

Look at the pictures. **Read** the story.

- **Write** two facts and two opinions on the chart below.

A Bright Idea

Thomas Edison was an inventor. He was one of the most creative people of his time.

He worked very hard to make electricity safe and cheap to use.

Electricity and light bulbs were in many homes because of his work. The bulbs lasted longer than candles. Electric light made it much easier to see at night. Everyone liked the electric light better than the candles.

Fact	Opinion

Fact and Opinion

Use this lesson to supplement or replace the skill lesson on page 485a of the Teacher's Edition. Display the Skill Points (at right) and share them with children.

Use the Skill Points to preteach fact and opinion.

Teach/Model

Beginning Show children a photo of the Wright brothers and their airplane. Say: *These men made the first airplane. Is this a fact or an opinion?* (fact) *Airplanes are fun to ride.* Ask: *Is this a fact or an opinion?* (opinion)

Intermediate Show children a picture of an ancient wheel. Display the following and read aloud: *The wheel is the best invention. Cars and bikes have wheels.* Guide children in identifying the fact. Say: *Tell me an opinion you have about cars or bikes.*

Advanced Write simple statements of fact and opinion on strips of paper. Give one fact and one opinion to pairs of children. Have the partners read the statements. Then have the group identify who read the fact and who read the opinion.

Advanced High Say: *Madam C.J. Walker invented hair care products. How can you prove that this is a fact?* (I can check in a book. I can ask someone who knows.) *We should buy her products.* Have children explain how they can tell that this is an opinion.

Then distribute copies of Picture It! page 114.

- Have children look at the pictures and tell what is happening in each one.
- Read the sentences aloud. Ask: *Can you find a fact in this story?*
- Review the Skill Points with children.
- Have children look at the sentences and pictures to find facts and opinions.

Practice

Read aloud the directions on page 114. Reread or chorally read the story. Have children look at the pictures and the story as they answer the questions.

Beginning Children can orally answer and fill in the chart. Provide help with writing and spelling words in the chart.

Intermediate Children can first orally answer and then fill in the chart.

Advanced Children can fill in the chart and check their answers by quietly reading them aloud or comparing them with a partner's answers.

Advanced High Children can fill in the chart and check their answers by rereading the story and making any necessary corrections.

Answers for page 114: Possible facts: Thomas Edison was an inventor. The bulbs lasted longer than candles. Possible opinions: He was one of the most creative people of his time. Everyone liked the electric light better than the candles.

Skill Points

- ✔ A **fact** can be proven true or false. You can check in a book, ask someone who knows, or see for yourself.
- ✔ An **opinion** tells someone's ideas or feelings. Clue words such as *best* and *should* show statements of opinion.
- ✔ As you read, ask yourself: *Can this sentence be proven true or false?*

Multilingual Summaries

English

A Weed Is a Flower

George Washington Carver was born a slave. As a boy, George asked questions about everything. He grew plants. He wanted to go to school. When he was ten, slavery ended. When he was older, George left home.

He worked hard. He saved money for college. At college, he studied plants. George learned so much that he later taught agriculture.

George taught farmers to plant new crops. Farmers did not believe that the new crops would sell. George discovered how to make many things with the new crops. The crops became important to the state of Alabama. George had become a great scientist.

Spanish

La mala hierba es una flor

George Washington Carver nació esclavo. De niño, hacía muchas preguntas sobre todo. Cultivaba plantas. Quería ir a la escuela. Cuando George tenía diez años se terminó la esclavitud. Cuando se hizo mayor, George se fue de su casa.

Trabajó duro. Ahorró dinero para ir a la universidad. En la universidad, estudió las plantas. Aprendió tanto que después enseñó agricultura.

George les enseñó a los granjeros a sembrar nuevos cultivos. Los granjeros no creían que estos cultivos se podían vender. George descubrió cómo hacer muchas cosas con los nuevos cultivos. Los cultivos se volvieron muy importantes en Alabama. George se había convertido en un gran científico.

Chinese

植物教授

喬治˙華盛頓˙卡佛的一生

喬治˙華盛頓˙卡佛出身於奴隸家庭。小時候，他對每一樣東西都充滿了好奇，他喜歡栽種植物，而且一直渴望能夠上學唸書。喬治十歲時，美國的奴隸制度被廢除了。稍微年長之後，喬治就離家出外工作。

他辛勤地工作，打算儲錢上大學。上了大學之後，他選擇研究植物。喬治讀了非常多的書，變得很有學問，後來他開始教授農業。

喬治教導農夫種植新作物，可是農夫不相信那可以賣錢。喬治於是想出了很多方法，利用新作物製造出其他東西。結果新作物變成了阿拉巴馬州的重要作物，喬治也成為了偉大的科學家。

Vietnamese

Ngọn Cỏ Dại là một Cành Hoa

Cuộc Đời của George Washington Carver

George Washington Carver sanh ra bị làm nô lệ. Từ khi còn là một cậu bé, George thắc mắc về mọi điều. Cậu bé trồng cây. Cậu bé muốn được đi học. Khi cậu được mười tuổi, chế độ nô lệ chấm dứt. Khi lớn lên, George rời nhà.

George cần cù làm việc. Ông để dành tiền đi học đại học. Ở trường đại học, ông học về thực vật. Ông học hỏi được nhiều đến nỗi sau này ông dạy môn nông nghiệp.

George dạy các nông phu trồng một loại cây nông nghiệp mới. Các nông phu đã không tin là loại cây nông nghiệp mới sẽ bán chạy. George khám phá cách chế biến ra nhiều thứ từ loại cây nông nghiệp mới. Loại cây này trở nên quan trọng ở Alabama. George trở thành một nhà bác học vĩ đại.

Multilingual Summaries

Korean

잡초도 꽃이다

조지 워싱턴 카버의 삶

노예로 태어난 조지 워싱턴 카버는 소년 시절 궁금한 것이 많았다. 그는 식물을 키웠으며 학교에 다니고 싶어했다. 조지가 열 살이 되던 해 노예 제도가 없어졌고, 성장한 조지는 집을 떠났다.

그는 열심히 일해 대학에 갈 돈을 모았다. 대학에서 식물을 공부한 조지는 많은 것을 배워 나중에 농업을 가르쳤다.

조지는 농부들에게 새 품종을 재배하는 법을 가르쳤지만 농부들은 새 품종이 잘 팔리지 않을 것이라고 생각했다. 조지는 새 품종으로 많은 것을 만드는 법을 알아냈고 이 품종은 앨라배마에서 중요한 작물이 되었다. 조지는 훌륭한 과학자가 된 것이다.

Hmong

Nroj Yog Paj
George Washington Carver Lub Neej

George Washington Carver yug los ua ib tug tub qhe. Thaum nws yog ib tug menyuam tub, George muaj lus nug txog txhua yam. Nws cog qoob cog loo. Nws xav mus kawm ntawv. Thaum nws muaj kaum xyoo ces kev ua qhev thiaj li tu. Thaum nws hlob tiav neeg, George thiaj li tawm hauv tsev mus lawm.

Nws ua haujlwm hnyav heev. Nws khaws nyiaj tseg yuav mus kawm ntawv qib siab. Nws mus kawm txog kev cog qoob cog loo thaum nws mus kawm ntawv qib siab. George kawm tau ntau yam nws thiaj li tau mus qhia ntawv txog kev ua liaj ua teb.

George qhia cov tub ua liaj ua teb kom lawv txawj cog cov qoob loo tshiab. Cov tub ua liaj ua teb tsis ntseeg tias lawv yuav muag tau nyiaj rau cov qoob loo tshiab no. George tau kawm ntxiv txog ntau yam ua nws tsim tau thaum nws siv cov qoob loo tshiab no. Cov qoob loo no tseem ceeb heev nyob rau Alabama. George los mus ua ib tug tibneeg kawm txujci zoo kawg.

Name ____________________

- **Read** *Inventions Help People* again.
- **Write** to fill in the *What and Why* chart.

What and Why

What was invented?	Why was it invented?
1. the washing machine	**1.** ____________________ ____________________
2. ____________________ ____________________	**2.** Writing would be easier.
3. cars	**3.** ____________________ ____________________
4. ____________________ ____________________	**4.** People could play a sport in the winter.

Family Link

Ask family members to describe inventions that they would like to create.

Weekly Resources Guide for English Language Learner Support

For this week's content and language objectives, see p. 119e.

Instructional Strand	Day 1	Day 2
Concept Development/Academic Language	TEACHER'S EDITION • Academic Language, p. DI•12 • Concept Development, p. DI•12 • Anchored Talk, pp. 20j—20–21 • *Sing With Me* Big Book, p. 21a • Concept Talk Video ELL HANDBOOK • ELL Poster Talk, Concept Talk, p. 119c ELL POSTER 16 • Day 1 Activities	TEACHER'S EDITION • Academic Language, p. DI•12 • Concept Development, p. DI•12 • Anchored Talk, p. 26b • *Sing With Me* Big Book, p. 26a • Concept Talk Video ELL HANDBOOK • ELL Poster Talk, Concept Talk, p. 119c • Concept Talk Video Routine, p. 464 ELL POSTER 16 • Day 2 Activities
Phonics and Spelling	TEACHER'S EDITION • Phonics and Spelling, p. DI•16 • Decodable Reader 16A, pp. 23c–23d	TEACHER'S EDITION • Phonics and Spelling, p. DI•16
Listening Comprehension	TEACHER'S EDITION • Modified Read Aloud, p. DI•15 • *Sing With Me* Big Book, p. 21a • Concept Talk Video ELL HANDBOOK • Concept Talk Video Routine, p. 464	TEACHER'S EDITION • Modified Read Aloud, p. DI•15 • *Sing With Me* Big Book, p. 26a • AudioText of *A Froggy Fable* • Concept Talk Video ELL HANDBOOK • AudioText CD Routine, p. 464 • Problem and Solution, p. 477
Reading Comprehension	TEACHER'S EDITION • Teach Draw Conclusions, p. DI•17	TEACHER'S EDITION • Teach Draw Conclusions, p. DI•17 • Frontloading Reading, p. DI•18 ELL HANDBOOK • Picture It! Skill Instruction, pp. 120–120a • Multilingual Summaries, pp. 121–123
Vocabulary **Basic and Lesson Vocabulary** **Vocabulary Skill: Multiple-Meaning Words**	TEACHER'S EDITION • Basic Vocabulary, p. DI•13 • Preteach Lesson Vocabulary, p. DI•13 • Multiple-Meaning Words, p. DI•16 ELL HANDBOOK • Word Cards, p. 119 • ELL Vocabulary Routine, p. 456 ELL POSTER 16 • Day 1 Activities	TEACHER'S EDITION • Basic Vocabulary, p. DI•13 • Reteach Lesson Vocabulary, p. DI•14 • Multiple-Meaning Words, p. DI•16 ELL HANDBOOK • Word Cards, p. 119 • Multilingual Vocabulary List, pp. 429–440 ELL POSTER 16 • Day 2 Activities
Grammar and Conventions	TEACHER'S EDITION • Preteach Adjectives and Our Senses, p. DI•20	TEACHER'S EDITION • Reteach Adjectives and Our Senses, p. DI•20
Writing	TEACHER'S EDITION • Main Idea and Supporting Details, p. DI•21 • Introduce Friendly Letter, pp. 25c–25d	TEACHER'S EDITION • Writer's Craft: Supporting Details, pp. 41d–41e

This symbol indicates leveled instruction to address language proficiency levels.

Day 3	Day 4	Day 5
TEACHER'S EDITION • Academic Language, p. DI•12 • Concept Development, p. DI•12 • Anchored Talk, p. 42b • *Sing With Me* Big Book, p. 42a • Concept Talk Video ELL HANDBOOK • ELL Poster Talk, Concept Talk. p. 119c ELL POSTER 16 • Day 3 Activities	TEACHER'S EDITION • Academic Language, p. DI•12 • Concept Development, p. DI•12 • Anchored Talk, p. 46b • *Sing With Me* Big Book, p. 46a • Concept Talk Video ELL HANDBOOK • ELL Poster Talk, Concept Talk, p. 119c ELL POSTER 16 • Day 4 Activities	TEACHER'S EDITION • Academic Language, p. DI•12 • Concept Development, p. DI•12 • Concept Talk Video ELL HANDBOOK • ELL Poster Talk, Concept Talk, p. 119c ELL POSTER 16 • Day 5 Activities
	TEACHER'S EDITION • Decodable Reader 16C, pp. 46e–46f	TEACHER'S EDITION • Phonics and Spelling, p. DI•16
TEACHER'S EDITION • *Sing With Me* Big Book, p. 42a • AudioText of *A Froggy Fable* • Concept Talk Video ELL HANDBOOK • AudioText CD Routine, p. 464	TEACHER'S EDITION • *Sing With Me* Big Book, p. 46a • Concept Talk Video	TEACHER'S EDITION • Concept Talk Video
TEACHER'S EDITION • Sheltered Reading, p. DI•18 ELL HANDBOOK • Multilingual Summaries, pp. 121–123	TEACHER'S EDITION • ELL/ELD Reader Guided Reading, p. DI•19 ELL HANDBOOK • ELL Study Guide, p. 124	TEACHER'S EDITION • ELL/ELD Reader Guided Reading, p. DI•19 ELL HANDBOOK • ELL Study Guide, p. 124
ELL HANDBOOK • High-Frequency Words Activity Bank, p. 491 ELL POSTER 16 • Day 3 Activities	ELL HANDBOOK • High-Frequency Words Activity Bank, p. 491	TEACHER'S EDITION • Multiple-Meaning Words, p. 52–53 ELL HANDBOOK • High-Frequency Words Activity Bank, p. 491
TEACHER'S EDITION • Grammar Jammer ELL HANDBOOK • Grammar Transition Lesson, pp. 366–368, 370–375 • Grammar Jammer Routine, p. 465	TEACHER'S EDITION • Grammar Jammer ELL HANDBOOK • Grammar Transition Lesson, pp. 366–368, 370–375	TEACHER'S EDITION • Grammar Jammer ELL HANDBOOK • Grammar Transition Lesson, pp. 366–368, 370–375
TEACHER'S EDITION • Let's Write It!, p. 44–45 • Writing Trait: Organization, p. 45a	TEACHER'S EDITION • Revising Strategy, pp. 51d–51e	TEACHER'S EDITION • Writer's Craft: Adjectives, pp. 53h–53i

Poster Talk, Concept Talk

Question of the Week

How can familiar things help us with changes?

Poster 16

Throughout the week, use the ELL Poster to help children produce and comprehend language, understand the concept, and build English vocabulary. Use the Question of the Week and other questions to help children share ideas in pairs, small groups, or the large group. Sample questions are shown, with examples of possible responses by children.

Weekly Concept and Language Goals

- Understand that familiar things help us with changes
- Name some familiar things
- Describe how familiar things would help you if you moved

By the end of the lesson, children should be able to talk about and write one or more sentences about how familiar things help us deal with changes.

Daily Team Talk

Day 1	Day 2	Day 3	Day 4	Day 5
After Day 1 activities on Poster, ask questions such as *In the poster picture, what familiar things does the woman have around her?*	After Day 2 activity on Poster, ask questions such as *How has the woman changed from the way she was in the photographs?*	After Day 3 activity on Poster, ask questions such as *How does looking at photographs make the woman feel?*	After Day 4 activity on Poster, ask questions such as *Imagine you move to a new place. What are some familiar things that can help you get used to the new place?*	After Day 5 activity on Poster, ask questions such as *What familiar things can help you when you change grades at school?*
Beginning Pictures. **Intermediate** There are pictures and a teddy bear. **Advanced** The woman has a teddy bear and a blanket. **Advanced High** The woman's familiar things are a photo album, a teddy bear, and a blanket.	**Beginning** She's old. **Intermediate** She was young then. She is old now. **Advanced** The woman is older now than she was in the photographs. **Advanced High** In the photographs, she is a younger woman doing things with her family. Now she is older and alone.	**Beginning** Happy. **Intermediate** The photographs make her happy. **Advanced** The woman looks at the photographs and she feels happy. **Advanced High** When the woman looks at the photographs, she feels happy.	**Beginning** My toys. **Intermediate** My bed, the family pictures, my pets. **Advanced** My books, my furniture, and my stuffed animals can help me. **Advanced High** The familiar things that I need in a new place are my desk, my pillow, and my rock collection.	**Beginning** My friends. **Intermediate** I know the school, the bus, and the teachers. **Advanced** The school is familiar. I know where everything is. **Advanced High** The grade is different, but the school is the same.

This Week's Materials

Teacher's Edition pages 20j–53k

See the support for English language learners throughout the lesson, including ELL strategies and scaffold activities at points of use.

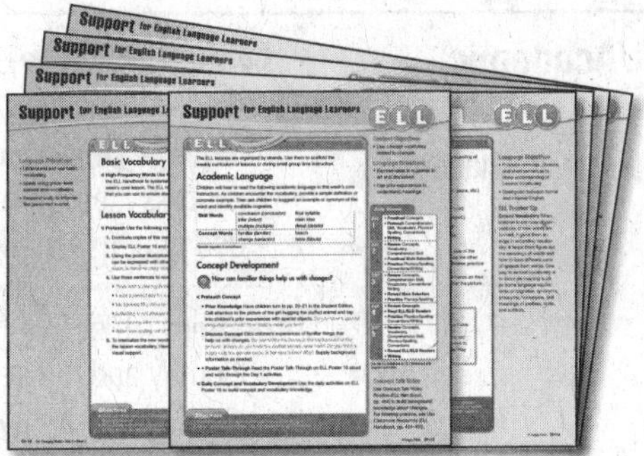

Teacher's Edition pages DI•12–DI•21

Differentiated Instruction for English language learners provides daily group activities that "frontload," or preteach, core instruction.

ELL Handbook pp. 119a–124

Find additional lesson materials that support the core lesson and the ELL instructional pages.

ELL Poster 16

ELD Reader 2.4.1

ELL Reader 2.4.1

Concept Literacy Reader

ELD, ELL Reader Teaching Guide

Concept Literacy Reader Teaching Guide

Technology

Online Teacher's Edition Use the digital version of the core teacher's edition for planning and instruction.

eReaders
This Week's ELL and ELD Readers and Concept Literacy Reader are also available in digital format.

This Week's Content and Language Objectives by Strand

Concept Development/Academic Language How can familiar things help us with changes?	**Content Objective** • Use concept vocabulary related to changes. **Language Objectives** • Express ideas in response to art and discussion. • Use prior experiences to understand meanings.
Phonics and Spelling Consonant + *-le*	**Content Objective** • Identify and define words with final syllable *–le.* **Language Objective** • Apply phonics and decoding skills to vocabulary.
Listening Comprehension Modified Read Aloud: "The Bathtub Beach Party"	**Content Objective** • Monitor understanding of spoken language. **Language Objectives** • Discuss oral passages. • Use a graphic organizer to take notes.
Reading Comprehension Draw Conclusions	**Content Objectives** • Use selection details and personal knowledge to draw conclusions. • Draw conclusions to aid comprehension. • Monitor and adjust comprehension. **Language Objectives** • Use visual support to read. • Retell facts that support a conclusion. • Draw and write a conclusion.
Vocabulary Basic and Lesson Vocabulary	**Language Objectives** • Understand and use basic vocabulary. • Speak using grade-level content area vocabulary. • Respond orally to information presented in print. • Produce drawings, phrases, and short sentences to show understanding of Lesson Vocabulary.
Vocabulary Multiple-Meaning Words	**Content Objective** • Distinguish sounds of English. **Language Objective** • Learn and use multiple-meaning words.
Grammar and Conventions Adjectives and Our Senses	**Content Objectives** • Identify and decode adjectives. • Use adjectives correctly. **Language Objectives** • Express ideas using adjectives. • Say adjectives and phrases with adjectives.
Writing Main Idea and Supporting Details	**Content Objective** • Identify main idea and details in a text. **Language Objectives** • Explain with increasing detail. • Write to explain using a main idea and details. • Share feedback for editing and revising.

Word Cards for Vocabulary Activities

clearing	**crashed**
perfect	**pond**
spilling	**splashing**
traveled	

Teacher Note: Beginning Teach two to three words. **Intermediate** Teach three to four words. **Advanced** Teach five to six words. **Advanced High** Teach all words.

Name ______________________________

Picture It!
Draw Conclusions

Look at the picture. **Read** the story.

Pancakes

Every Saturday, Niki's dad makes pancakes. He makes big pancakes shaped like animals. Niki loves her dad's pancakes.

One Saturday, Niki's dad is not home to make breakfast. Niki's sister sees she is sad. Her sister makes some pancakes. Niki frowns. Her sister tries hard to make her happy, but these pancakes are round. They are not in fun animal shapes. Niki does not want to hurt her sister's feelings, though. She tries the pancakes. They taste great!

Answer the questions below.

1. How does Niki feel about her sister's pancakes?
a. She is excited to try something new.
b. She wishes they looked like her dad's pancakes.
c. She thinks they are burnt.

2. How does Niki feel about her sister?
a. She is mad at her sister.
b. She is worried about her sister.
c. She is thankful for her sister.

Draw Conclusions

Use this lesson to supplement or replace the skill lesson on page 24a of the Teacher's Edition. Display the Skill Points (at right) and share them with children.

Use the Skill Points to preteach draw conclusions.

Teach/Model

Beginning Say and pantomime: *I am eating breakfast.* Smile and say *Yum!* Ask: *Is it morning or night?* (morning) *How do you know?* (We eat breakfast in the morning.) *Do I like breakfast? How do you know?* Guide children to draw the conclusion that you like breakfast because you smile and say *Yum!*

Intermediate Say and pantomime with a smile as you pat your stomach: *I just finished eating my breakfast. What conclusion can you make?* (You like what you ate for breakfast.) *How does my smile help you draw that conclusion?* (A smile shows that someone likes something.)

Advanced Say and pantomime: *I am eating breakfast. What time of day is it?* (morning) *I can draw the conclusion that it must be the morning. How do I know that?* (Breakfast is a meal that we eat in the morning.) Have children suggest other conclusions they can draw about you eating breakfast. (You are hungry. You like breakfast.)

Advanced High Say: *I always eat pancakes on Sundays. Today I am eating pancakes. What conclusion can you draw?* Encourage children to suggest as many conclusions as possible. (Today is Sunday. You like pancakes. You like to do certain things on certain days.)

Then distribute copies of Picture It! page 120.

- Have children look at the picture. Help them tell what the girl is doing.
- Read the story aloud. Ask: *What is Niki's dad doing?* Provide English words as needed to answer.
- Review the Skill Points with children.
- Have children look at the picture and story to draw conclusions about the characters and what happens in the story.

Practice

Read aloud the directions on page 120. Reread or chorally read the story. Have children look at the picture and the story as they answer the questions.

Beginning Children can orally answer and, with help, mark their answers.

Intermediate Children can first orally answer and then mark the answers on the page.

Advanced Children can mark their answers and check them by quietly reading them aloud or comparing them with a partner's.

Advanced High Children can mark their answers and check them by silently reading them and making any necessary corrections.

Answers for page 120: 1. b; 2. c

Skill Points

- ✔ When you **draw a conclusion**, you figure out more about the characters and what happens in the story.
- ✔ You can put together what you know about real life and what you have read to draw conclusions.

Multilingual Summaries

English

A Froggy Fable

A frog lived in a pond. He liked his life because it was always the same. Then his life changed. Otters splashed in the pond. Blue jays squawked near the pond. A tree crashed into the water. The frog was sad because his life had changed. He hid in a hole.

One morning, the frog was taken away from the pond. He was lost. He could not find his home for many weeks. Then he found his pond. He was happy to see the otters, the blue jays, and the fallen tree. He did not mind the changes, after all! He was happy to be home.

Spanish

Una fábula de ranas

Una rana vivía en un estanque. A él le gustaba su vida porque siempre era igual. Luego, su vida cambió. Unas nutrias se bañaron en el estanque. Unos azulejos cantaban cerca del estanque. Un árbol cayó sobre el agua. La rana estaba triste porque su vida había cambiado. Se escondió en un hoyo.

Una mañana, sacaron a la rana del estanque. Estaba perdida. No pudo encontrar su casa durante muchas semanas. Al fin, encontró su estanque. Estaba feliz de ver a las nutrias, a los azulejos y al árbol caído. Después de todo, ¡no le importaban los cambios! Estaba feliz de estar en casa.

Multilingual Summaries

Chinese

青蛙寓言

有一只青蛙住在一个池塘里，他很喜欢他的生活，因为每一天都一样。可是他的生活突然改变了，水獭在池塘里戏水，蓝槛鸟在池塘附近嘎嘎地叫，大树倒塌到水里。青蛙很不高兴，因为他的生活改变了；他躲在一个洞里。

一天早上，青蛙被带离池塘，迷路了，几个星期里他都找不到自己的家，最后他找到池塘了，看见水獭、蓝槛鸟、倒树令他很高兴。现在他不介意所有的改变，他很高兴可以回家。

Vietnamese

Bài Ngụ Ngôn Con Ếch

Một con ếch sống dưới ao. Nó thích đời sống của nó, vì xưa nay vẫn thế. Rồi thì cuộc đời đổi thay. Bọn rái cá lội bì bõm dưới ao. Chim Xanh kêu quác quác gần bên ao. Một cái cây đổ sầm xuống nước. Ếch buồn vì cuộc đời nó đã đổi thay. Nó ẩn mình trong hang.

Một buổi sáng nọ, nó phải rời xa ao. Nó bị lạc đường. Trong nhiều tuần lễ, nó không tìm được đường về. Thế rồi nó tìm thấy cái ao của nó. Nó sung sướng thấy lại bọn rái cá, chim xanh và cái cây đổ. Nó không phiền hà gì về các đổi thay. Nó sung sướng được ở nhà.

Multilingual Summaries

Korean

개구리 우화

개구리 한 마리가 연못에 살았습니다. 개구리는 자기 생활을 좋아했습니다. 왜냐하면 그것은 늘 똑같았기 때문이죠. 그런데 변화가 생겼습니다. 수달이 연못 물을 막 튀어댔습니다. 청어치는 연못 근처에서 까악까악 울어댔습니다. 나무는 연못 속으로 와르르 무너졌습니다. 개구리는 너무 슬펐습니다. 왜나하면 자기 삶이 변했기 때문이죠. 그래서 구멍 속으로 숨어버렸습니다.

어느 날 아침, 개구리는 연못 밖으로 떠밀려났습니다. 그만 길을 잃어버렸습니다. 집으로 가는 길을 몇 주동안 찾을 수가 없었습니다. 그러던 중 개구리는 다시 연못을 발견했습니다. 수달과, 청어치와, 쓰러진 나무를 발견하고 기뻤습니다. 변화따윈 아무렇지도 않았지요! 집으로 돌아온 것이 마냥 기쁘기만 했습니다.

Hmong

Qav Zaj Dabneeg

Ib tus qav nyob hauv ib lub pag dej. Nws nyiam nws lub neej, rau qhov nws zoo li qub txhua txhia nub. Tes nws lub neej txawm hloov. Ntshuab nthia rau hauv pag dej. Noog Xiav quaj qw ze lub pag dej. Tsob ntoo qhau los poob rau hauv cov dej. Tus qav tu siab, rau qhov nws lub neej ciali hloov. Nwg mus nkaum hauv ib lub qhov.

Muaj ib tagkig sawv ntxov, tus qav mag coj mus deb deb ntawm lub pag dej. Nws poob zoo. Nws nrhiav tsi tau nws lub tsev tau tsheej asthiv. Ces nws nrhiav tau nws lub pag dej. Nws zoo siab heev uas nws pom tus ntshuab, tus noog xiav, thiab tsob ntoo uas qaug. Nws tsi xav li cas rau qhov hloov lawm lua! Nwg zoo siab mus txog tsev.

Name ______________________

- **Read** *For Good Luck!* again.
- In the first box, **draw** the mother giving Lyn her treasure.
- In the second box, **draw** the mother giving David his treasure.
- On the line below each box, **write** a sentence to describe each picture.

____

____

Family Link

Does anyone in your family have a special treasure that brings good luck? Ask family members to tell you about a favorite treasure.

Weekly Resources Guide for English Language Learner Support

For this week's content and language objectives, see p. 125e.

Instructional Strand	Day 1	Day 2
Concept Development/Academic Language	TEACHER'S EDITION • Academic Language, p. DI•33 • Concept Development, p. DI•33 • Anchored Talk, pp. 54j—54–55 • *Sing With Me* Big Book, p. 55a • Concept Talk Video ELL HANDBOOK • ELL Poster Talk, Concept Talk, p. 125c ELL POSTER 17 • Day 1 Activities	TEACHER'S EDITION • Academic Language, p. DI•33 • Concept Development, p. DI•33 • Anchored Talk, p. 60b • *Sing With Me* Big Book, p. 60a • Concept Talk Video ELL HANDBOOK • ELL Poster Talk, Concept Talk, p. 125c • Concept Talk Video Routine, p. 464 ELL POSTER 17 • Day 2 Activities
Phonics and Spelling	TEACHER'S EDITION • Phonics and Spelling, p. DI•37 • Decodable Reader 17A, pp. 57c–57d	TEACHER'S EDITION • Phonics and Spelling, p. DI•37
Listening Comprehension	TEACHER'S EDITION • Modified Read Aloud, p. DI•36 • *Sing With Me* Big Book, p. 55a • Concept Talk Video ELL HANDBOOK • Concept Talk Video Routine, p. 464	TEACHER'S EDITION • Modified Read Aloud, p. DI•36 • *Sing With Me* Big Book, p. 60a • AudioText of *Life Cycle of a Pumpkin* • Concept Talk Video ELL HANDBOOK • AudioText CD Routine, p. 464 • Steps in a Process, p. 479
Reading Comprehension	TEACHER'S EDITION • Teach Sequence, p. DI•38	TEACHER'S EDITION • Teach Sequence, p. DI•38 • Frontloading Reading, p. DI•39 ELL HANDBOOK • Picture It! Skill Instruction, pp. 126–126a • Multilingual Summaries, pp. 127–129
Vocabulary **Basic and Lesson Vocabulary** **Vocabulary Skill: Antonyms**	TEACHER'S EDITION • Basic Vocabulary, p. DI•34 • Preteach Lesson Vocabulary, p. DI•34 • Antonyms, p. DI•37 ELL HANDBOOK • Word Cards, p. 125 • ELL Vocabulary Routine, p. 456 ELL POSTER 17 • Day 1 Activities	TEACHER'S EDITION • Basic Vocabulary, p. DI•34 • Reteach Lesson Vocabulary, p. DI•35 • Antonyms, p. DI•37 ELL HANDBOOK • Word Cards, p. 125 • Multilingual Vocabulary List, pp. 429–440 ELL POSTER 17 • Day 2 Activities
Grammar and Conventions	TEACHER'S EDITION • Preteach Adjectives for Number, Size, and Shape, p. DI•41	TEACHER'S EDITION • Reteach Adjectives for Number, Size, and Shape, p. DI•41
Writing	TEACHER'S EDITION • Descriptive Words, p. DI•42 • Introduce Expository Nonfiction, pp. 59c–59d	TEACHER'S EDITION • Expository Nonfiction, pp. 75d–75e

This symbol indicates leveled instruction to address language proficiency levels.

Day 3	Day 4	Day 5
TEACHER'S EDITION • Academic Language, p. DI•33 • Concept Development, p. DI•33 • Anchored Talk, p. 76b • *Sing with Me* Big Book, p. 76a • Concept Talk Video ELL HANDBOOK • ELL Poster Talk, Concept Talk, p. 125c ELL POSTER 17 • Day 3 Activities	TEACHER'S EDITION • Academic Language, p. DI•33 • Concept Development, p. DI•33 • Anchored Talk, p. 80b • *Sing with Me* Big Book, p. 80a • Concept Talk Video ELL HANDBOOK • ELL Poster Talk, Concept Talk, p. 125c ELL POSTER 17 • Day 4 Activities	TEACHER'S EDITION • Academic Language, p. DI•33 • Concept Development, p. DI•33 • Concept Talk Video ELL HANDBOOK • ELL Poster Talk, Concept Talk, p. 125c ELL POSTER 17 • Day 5 Activities
ELL HANDBOOK • Phonics Transition Lesson, pp. 263, 265	TEACHER'S EDITION • Decodable Reader 17C, pp. 80e–80f ELL HANDBOOK • Phonics Transition Lesson, pp. 263, 265	TEACHER'S EDITION • Phonics and Spelling, p. DI•37
TEACHER'S EDITION • *Sing with Me* Big Book, p. 76a • AudioText of *Life Cycle of a Pumpkin* • Concept Talk Video ELL HANDBOOK • AudioText CD Routine, p. 464	TEACHER'S EDITION • *Sing with Me* Big Book, p. 80a • Concept Talk Video	TEACHER'S EDITION • Concept Talk Video
TEACHER'S EDITION • Sheltered Reading, p. DI•39 ELL HANDBOOK • Multilingual Summaries, pp. 127–129	TEACHER'S EDITION • ELL/ELD Reader Guided Reading, p. DI•40 ELL HANDBOOK • ELL Study Guide, p. 130	TEACHER'S EDITION • ELL/ELD Reader Guided Reading, p. DI•40 ELL HANDBOOK • ELL Study Guide, p. 130
ELL HANDBOOK • High-Frequency Words Activity Bank, p. 491 ELL POSTER 17 • Day 3 Activities	ELL HANDBOOK • High-Frequency Words Activity Bank, p. 491	TEACHER'S EDITION • Antonyms, pp. 82–83—83a ELL HANDBOOK • High-Frequency Words Activity Bank, p. 491
TEACHER'S EDITION • Grammar Jammer ELL HANDBOOK • Grammar Transition Lesson, pp. 366–368, 371–372, 374 • Grammar Jammer Routine, p. 465	TEACHER'S EDITION • Grammar Jammer ELL HANDBOOK • Grammar Transition Lesson, pp. 366–368, 371–372, 374	TEACHER'S EDITION • Grammar Jammer ELL HANDBOOK • Grammar Transition Lesson, pp. 366–368, 371–372, 374
TEACHER'S EDITION • Let's Write It!, p. 78–79 • Writing Trait: Word Choice, p. 79a	TEACHER'S EDITION • Writer's Craft: Descriptive Words, pp. 81d–81e	TEACHER'S EDITION • Revising Strategy, pp. 83h–83i

Poster Talk, Concept Talk

Question of the Week

How do plants change over time?

Poster 17

Throughout the week, use the ELL Poster to help children produce and comprehend language, understand the concept, and build English vocabulary. Use the Question of the Week and other questions to help children share ideas in pairs, small groups, or the large group. Sample questions are shown, with examples of possible responses by children.

Weekly Concept and Language Goals

- Understand that plants change over time
- Name the parts of some plants
- Describe the changes that plants go through

By the end of the lesson, children should be able to talk about and write one or more sentences about changes that happen to plants.

Daily Team Talk

Day 1	Day 2	Day 3	Day 4	Day 5
After Day 1 activities on Poster, ask questions such as *Why do people plant watermelon seeds?*	After Day 2 activity on Poster, ask questions such as *In the poster pictures, what parts do the watermelon plants have ?*	After Day 3 activity on Poster, ask questions such as *Watermelons grow on a vine. What is another fruit that grows on a vine?*	After Day 4 activity on Poster, ask questions such as *How does a tree change over time?*	After Day 5 activity on Poster, ask questions such as *What do plants need to grow and change?*
Beginning To get watermelons. **Intermediate** The seeds grow into watermelons. **Advanced** People plant the seeds to grow watermelons. **Advanced High** People plant the seeds so they can grow and eat watermelons.	**Beginning** Seeds, leaves. **Intermediate** They have roots and leaves. **Advanced** The watermelon seeds grow roots and leaves. **Advanced High** First the watermelon seeds grow roots. Then they grow leaves. Finally, they grow flowers and watermelons.	**Beginning** A pumpkin. **Intermediate** Pumpkins grow on a vine. **Advanced** Grapes and pumpkins grow on vines. **Advanced High** Grapes and pumpkins are both fruits that grow on a vine.	**Beginning** It gets big. **Intermediate** A tree will grow tall. **Advanced** A tree grows taller. It gets more branches. **Advanced High** A tree starts as a seed. Then it is a small plant. The tree grows taller every year.	**Beginning** Water. **Intermediate** A plant needs sunlight. **Advanced** Plants need sunlight and water. **Advanced High** Plants need soil, sunlight, and water to grow.

This Week's Materials

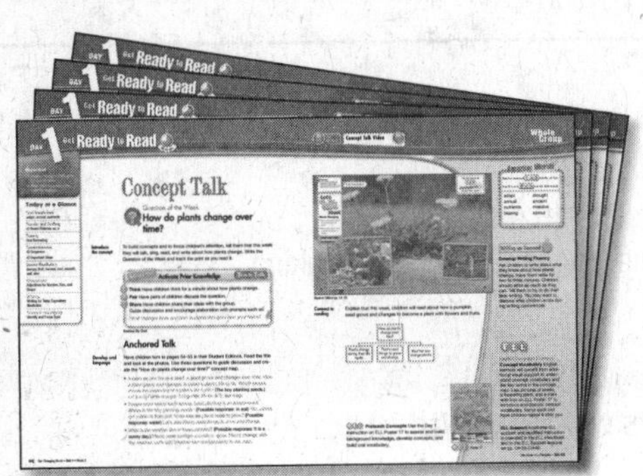

Teacher's Edition pages 54j–83k

See the support for English language learners throughout the lesson, including ELL strategies and scaffold activities at points of use.

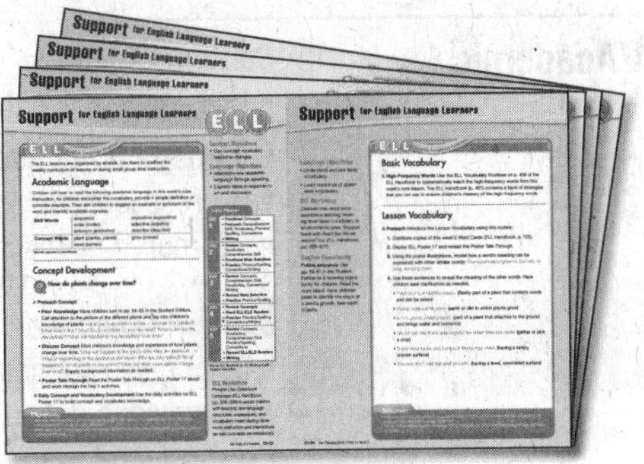

Teacher's Edition pages DI•33–DI•42

Differentiated Instruction for English language learners provides daily group activities that "frontload," or preteach, core instruction.

ELL Handbook pp. 125a–130

Find additional lesson materials that support the core lesson and the ELL instructional pages.

ELL Poster 17

ELD Reader 2.4.2

ELL Reader 2.4.2

Concept Literacy Reader

ELD, ELL Reader Teaching Guide

Concept Literacy Reader Teaching Guide

Technology

Online Teacher's Edition Use the digital version of the core teacher's edition for planning and instruction.

eReaders
This Week's ELL and ELD Readers and Concept Literacy Reader are also available in digital format.

This Week's Content and Language Objectives by Strand

Concept Development/Academic Language How do plants change over time?	**Content Objective** • Use concept vocabulary related to changes. **Language Objectives** • Express ideas in response to art and discussion. • Internalize new academic language through speaking.
Phonics and Spelling /ů/ Spelled *oo, u*	**Content Objectives** • Distinguish sounds of English. • Identify and define words with /ů/ spelled *oo, u.* **Language Objective** • Apply phonics and decoding skills to vocabulary.
Listening Comprehension Modified Read Aloud: "How the Tree Grew"	**Content Objective** • Monitor and adjust oral comprehension. **Language Objectives** • Discuss oral passages. • Use a graphic organizer to take notes. • Use contextual support to develop background knowledge.
Reading Comprehension Sequence	**Content Objectives** • Use signal words and order of events to identify correct sequence. • Use sequence to aid comprehension. • Monitor and adjust comprehension. **Language Objectives** • Discuss sequence of events. • Expand initial English vocabulary by describing people. • Draw and write a sequence of events.
Vocabulary Basic and Lesson Vocabulary	**Language Objectives** • Understand and use basic vocabulary. • Learn meanings of grade-level vocabulary. • Produce drawings, phrases, and short sentences to understand vocabulary.
Vocabulary Antonyms	**Content Objective** • Identify and use antonyms. **Language Objective** • Learn and use antonyms.
Grammar and Conventions Adjectives for Number, Size, and Shape	**Content Objectives** • Identify and decode adjectives. • Use adjectives correctly. **Language Objectives** • Learn new language structure. • Speak using adjectives. • Write phrases and sentences with adjectives.
Writing Descriptive Words	**Content Objective** • Identify descriptive words in a text. **Language Objectives** • Write using descriptive words to express ideas clearly. • Write using grammar structures. • Share feedback for editing and revising.

Word Cards for Vocabulary Activities

bumpy	**fruit**
harvest	**root**
smooth	**soil**
vine	

Teacher Note: Beginning Teach two to three words. **Intermediate** Teach three to four words. **Advanced** Teach five to six words. **Advanced High** Teach all words.

Name ____________________

Read Together

Look at the picture. **Read** the paragraph.

Pumpkins

Ben and Kate chose two pumpkins. The family used Ben's pumpkin to make treats. They cut a hole in the top of Ben's pumpkin. Then they scooped out the seeds. Mom baked the seeds to make a snack. Then Mom used pieces of the pumpkin to make a pie.

The family carved Kate's pumpkin. Kate drew eyes, a nose, and a smile. Mom cut out the face. They put the pumpkin on the front porch.

Answer the questions below.

1. What did the family make first?
  a. a pumpkin pie
  b. pumpkin seeds
  c. a jack-o'-lantern

2. What happened before they scooped out the seeds?
  a. They made a pie.
  b. They baked the seeds.
  c. They cut a hole in the top.

3. What happened after Mom cut out the face on the pumpkin?

____

Sequence

Use this lesson to supplement or replace the skill lesson on page 58a of the Teacher's Edition. Display the Skill Points (at right) and share them with children.

Skill Points

- ✔ **Sequence** is the order of events in a story.
- ✔ Think about what happens first, next, and last. Look for words such as *first, next, then, now,* and *finally* to help you figure out the order of events.

Use the Skill Points to preteach sequence.

Teach/Model

Beginning Say and pantomime this sequence: *I dig a hole. I plant a seed. I water the plant. I watch the plant grow.* Ask: *What did I do first?* (dig) Have children perform the actions with you as you repeat the sequence.

Intermediate Display the following and read aloud: *Water the seed. Plant a seed. Pick the pumpkin. Watch the seed grow.* Ask children to help you put the sentences in order, using the words *first, next, then,* and *last.*

Advanced Read aloud a recipe for roasting pumpkin seeds using short, simple sentences that begin with *first, next, then,* or *last.* Write the verb from each step in random order on the board. Ask children to put the verbs in order using sequence words.

Advanced High Start a sequence for children. Say: *First, the family drives to the pumpkin patch.* Ask children to think of things that can happen next. Encourage them to use sequence words such as *next, then, now,* and *finally.*

Then distribute copies of Picture It! page 126.

- Have children look at the picture. Help them tell what each person is doing in the picture. If necessary, briefly discuss the verb *to carve.*
- Read the story aloud. Ask: *What happens first in the story?* Provide English words as needed to answer.
- Review the Skill Points with children.
- Have children look at the pictures and words to find clues about the sequence of the story.

Practice

Read aloud the directions on page 126. Reread or chorally read the story. Have children look at the picture and the story as they answer the questions.

Beginning Children can orally answer and mark and write their answers. Provide help with writing and spelling.

Intermediate Children can first orally answer and then mark and write the answers on the page.

Advanced Children can mark and write their answers and check them by comparing their circles with a partner's and quietly reading aloud their writing.

Advanced High Children can mark and write their answers and check them by silently rereading the story and making any necessary corrections.

Answers for page 126: 1. b; 2. c; 3. They put the pumpkin on the front porch.

Multilingual Summaries

English

Life Cycle of a Pumpkin

A seed is planted in soil. A root grows out of the seed and into the soil. Leaves grow, and the plant becomes a vine. It grows longer and longer. The vine grows flowers. Bees bring pollen to the flowers. Parts of the flowers grow into pumpkins.

Pumpkins need water and sun. Insects can hurt pumpkins, so farmers protect the plants. The pumpkins grow bigger. Seeds and pulp grow inside. The outsides turn from green to orange. The vines turn brown in the fall. Then it is time to pick the pumpkins.

The farmers sell the pumpkins. People cook them.

Spanish

El ciclo de vida de una calabaza

Una semilla se siembra en la tierra. Una raíz crece fuera de la semilla y debajo de la tierra. Las hojas crecen y la planta se hace una enredadera. La planta crece más y más. De la enredadera, salen flores. Las abejas le traen polen a las flores. Algunas de las flores se convierten en calabazas.

Las calabazas necesitan agua y sol. Los insectos pueden dañar las calabazas, por eso los granjeros protegen las plantas. Las calabazas crecen mucho. Las semillas y la pulpa crecen dentro de ellas. La parte de afuera cambia de verde a color naranja. Las enredaderas se vuelven marrones en el otoño. Entonces, ya es tiempo de cosechar las calabazas.

Los granjeros venden las calabazas. Las personas las cocinan.

Multilingual Summaries

Chinese

南瓜的一生

南瓜從小種子開始發芽成長。種子種在泥土裡，根從種子長出來，然後慢慢伸進泥土裡。不久之後，葉子也長出來，變成了一種藤蔓植物。藤蔓越長越長，然後開出花朵來。蜜蜂把花粉帶到花朵裡，有些花朵就結出南瓜來。

南瓜需要澆水和曬太陽。昆蟲會吃南瓜，所以農夫要保護南瓜。南瓜越長越大，種子和果肉都長在南瓜裡面，南瓜的外面會從綠色變成橘色。藤蔓到了秋天會變成棕色，這便是收割南瓜的時候。

農夫把南瓜賣出去，人們把南瓜煮來吃。

所有南瓜都收割以後，農夫開始耕地。他會在春天的時候種下更多南瓜種子。

Vietnamese

Chu Kỳ Đời Sống của Quả Bí Đỏ

Quả bí đỏ bắt đầu từ hạt. Một hạt được trồng trong đất. Rễ mọc ra từ hạt và đâm vào đất. Lá mọc ra, và cái cây nhỏ trở thành dây leo. Dây mọc càng dài ra. Dây trổ nhiều hoa. Ong mang phấn đến cho các cánh hoa. Những phần của hoa trở thành những quả bí.

Bí đỏ cần có nước và ánh nắng mặt trời. Các côn trùng có thể làm hại những quả bí, vì vậy các bác nông phu bảo vệ những dây bí. Những quả bí to lớn thêm. Hạt và phần cơm của bí phát triển ở bên trong quả bí. Phần vỏ ngoài chuyển từ màu xanh sang màu cam. Dây bí ngả sang màu nâu vào mùa thu. Rồi đến lúc để hái những quả bí đó.

Các bác nông phu bán những quả bí đỏ. Người ta nấu những quả bí này.

Sau khi tất cả những quả bí đã được hái đi, bác nông phu cày bừa cánh đồng. Ông ấy sẽ gieo trồng thêm những hạt bí đỏ vào mùa xuân.

Multilingual Summaries

Korean

호박의 생명 주기

호박은 씨앗부터 출발한다. 씨앗이 땅에 뿌려지고 뿌리가 씨앗에서 나와 땅 속으로 자라며 잎사귀들이 자라고 묘목이 줄기로 바뀐다. 줄기는 무럭무럭 자라나서 꽃을 피우고 벌들이 꽃에 꽃가루를 옮긴다. 그리고 나서 꽃의 일부가 자라 호박이 된다.

호박은 물과 태양을 필요로 한다. 벌레들이 호박을 상하게 할 수 있기 때문에 농부들은 묘목을 보호한다. 호박은 무럭무럭 자라 씨앗과 과육이 호박 안쪽에서 자라며 호박 바깥쪽이 녹색에서 오렌지색으로 변한다. 가을이 되면 줄기가 갈색으로 변하고 그러면 호박을 딸 때가 된 것이다.

농부들은 호박을 팔고 사람들은 그 호박으로 요리를 한다.

호박을 다 수확하게 되면 농부는 밭을 일구고 봄이 되면 더 많은 호박씨를 뿌린다.

Hmong

Lub Neej Ntawm Ib Lub Taub

Cov taub pib los ntawm cov noob. Ib lub noob raug muab cog rau hauv av. Ib tug cag tawg kaus mus rau hauv av. Cov nplooj hlav, thiab tsob taub pib muaj hmab. Nws pib hlav ntev zuj zus. Tsob hmab pib tawg paj. Cov ntseeb nqa tej paj ntoos los rau cov paj. Tej txhia paj hlob los ua taub.

Cov taub yuav tsum muaj dej thiab lub hnub. Tej kab yeej ua kom cov taub hlob tsis tau, ces cov neeg ua teb thiaj li tiv thaiv cov taub. Cov taub loj hlob zuj zus. Tej noob pib muaj nyob hauv lub taub thiab daim tawv tuab zuj zus. Daim tawv xim ntshiab rais mus ua daim tawv xim xob. Cov hmab pauv mus ua xim ka-fas hauv lub caij nplooj ntoos zeeg. Ces txog lub sij hawm de cov taub.

Cov neeg ua teb muab cov taub muag. Cov neeg muab cov taub ua noj.

Tom qab cov taub raug muab de, tus neeg ua teb rov muab daim teb ncaws. Nws yuav rov cog dua lwm cov noob taub hauv lub caij nplooj ntoos hlav.

Name ____________________

- **Read** *Tomato Time!* again.
- Fill in the first web. **Write** two facts from the book.
- Fill in the second web. **Write** two details about tomatoes.

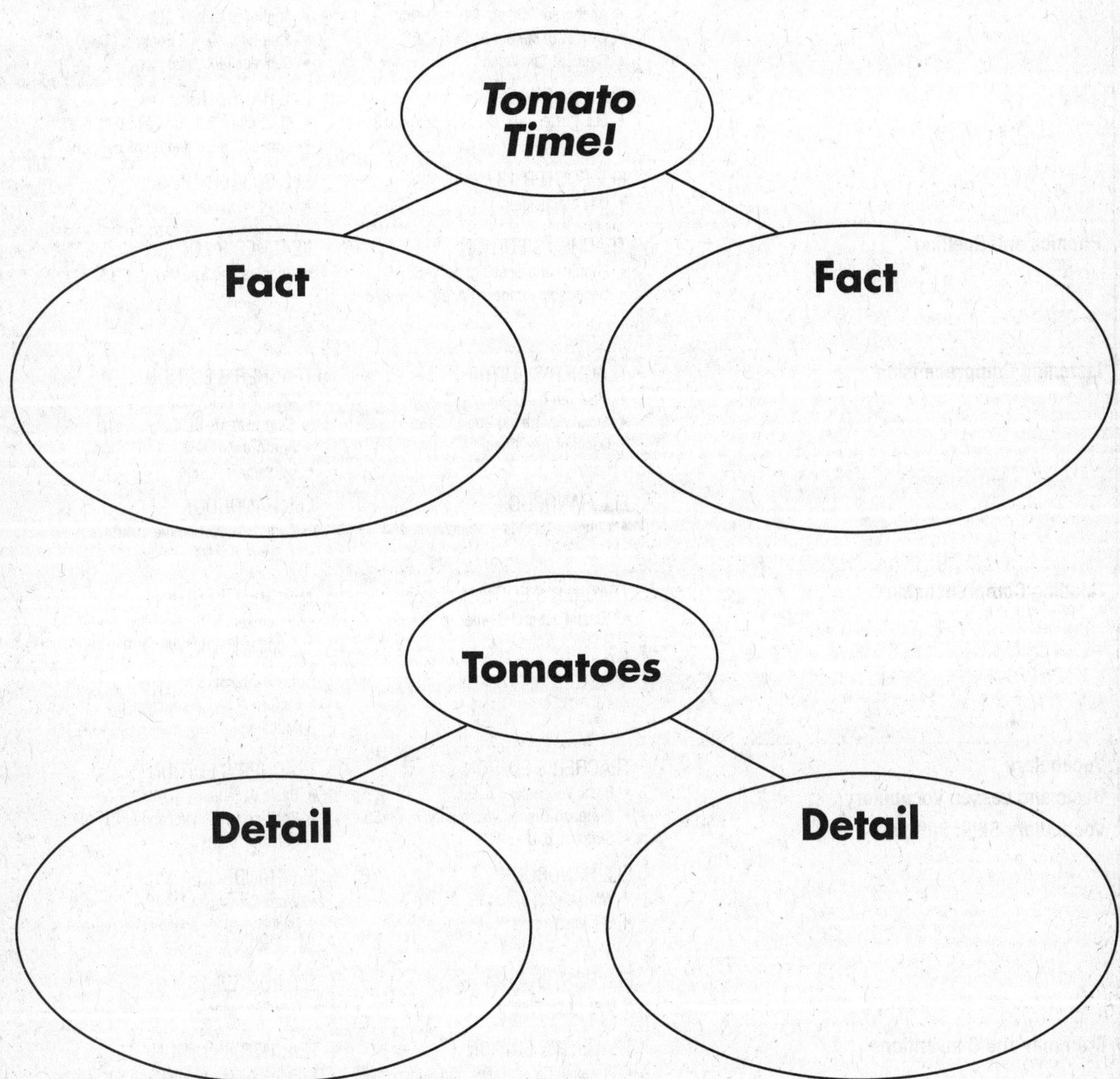

Family Link

Ask family members whether they like tomatoes. If they do, how do they like to eat them? If they do not, why not?

Weekly Resources Guide for English Language Learner Support

For this week's content and language objectives, see p. 131e.

Instructional Strand	Day 1	Day 2
Concept Development/Academic Language	TEACHER'S EDITION • Academic Language, p. DI•54 • Concept Development, p. DI•54 • Anchored Talk, pp. 84j—84–85 • *Sing with Me* Big Book, p. 85a • Concept Talk Video ELL HANDBOOK • ELL Poster Talk, Concept Talk, p. 131c ELL POSTER 18 • Day 1 Activities	TEACHER'S EDITION • Academic Language, p. DI•54 • Concept Development, p. DI•54 • Anchored Talk, p. 90b • *Sing with Me* Big Book, p. 90a • Concept Talk Video ELL HANDBOOK • ELL Poster Talk, Concept Talk, p. 131c • Concept Talk Video Routine, p. 464 ELL POSTER 18 • Day 2 Activities
Phonics and Spelling	TEACHER'S EDITION • Phonics and Spelling, p. DI•58 • Decodable Reader 18A, pp. 87c–87d	TEACHER'S EDITION • Phonics and Spelling, p. DI•58
Listening Comprehension	TEACHER'S EDITION • Modified Read Aloud, p. DI•57 • *Sing with Me* Big Book, p. 85a • Concept Talk Video ELL HANDBOOK • Concept Talk Video Routine, p. 464	TEACHER'S EDITION • Modified Read Aloud, p. DI•57 • *Sing with Me* Big Book, p. 90a • AudioText of *Soil* • Concept Talk Video ELL HANDBOOK • AudioText CD Routine, p. 464 • T-Chart, p. 480
Reading Comprehension	TEACHER'S EDITION • Teach Fact and Opinion, p. DI•59	TEACHER'S EDITION • Teach Fact and Opinion, p. DI•59 • Frontloading Reading, p. DI•60 ELL HANDBOOK • Picture It! Skill Instruction, pp. 132–132a • Multilingual Summaries, pp. 133–135
Vocabulary **Basic and Lesson Vocabulary** **Vocabulary Skill: Suffixes**	TEACHER'S EDITION • Basic Vocabulary, p. DI•55 • Preteach Lesson Vocabulary, p. DI•55 • Suffixes, p. DI•58 ELL HANDBOOK • Word Cards, p. 131 • ELL Vocabulary Routine, p. 456 ELL POSTER 18 • Day 1 Activities	TEACHER'S EDITION • Basic Vocabulary, p. DI•55 • Reteach Lesson Vocabulary, p. DI•56 • Suffixes, p. DI•58 ELL HANDBOOK • Word Cards, p. 131 • Multilingual Vocabulary List, pp. 429–440 ELL POSTER 18 • Day 2 Activities
Grammar and Conventions	TEACHER'S EDITION • Preteach Comparative and Superlative Adjectives, p. DI•62	TEACHER'S EDITION • Reteach Comparative and Superlative Adjectives, p. DI•62
Writing	TEACHER'S EDITION • Combining Sentences, p. DI•63 • Introduce Short Expository Report, pp. 89c–89d	TEACHER'S EDITION • Writer's Craft: Describing, pp.109d–109e

This symbol indicates leveled instruction to address language proficiency levels.

Day 3	Day 4	Day 5
TEACHER'S EDITION • Academic Language, p. DI•54 • Concept Development, p. DI•54 • Anchored Talk, p. 110b • *Sing with Me* Big Book, p. 110a • Concept Talk Video ELL HANDBOOK • ELL Poster Talk, Concept Talk, p. 131c ELL POSTER 18 • Day 3 Activities	TEACHER'S EDITION • Academic Language, p. DI•54 • Concept Development, p. DI•54 • Anchored Talk, p. 114b • *Sing with Me* Big Book, p. 114a • Concept Talk Video ELL HANDBOOK • ELL Poster Talk, Concept Talk, p. 131c ELL POSTER 18 • Day 4 Activities	TEACHER'S EDITION • Academic Language, p. DI•54 • Concept Development, p. DI•54 • Concept Talk Video ELL HANDBOOK • ELL Poster Talk, Concept Talk, p. 131c ELL POSTER 18 • Day 5 Activities
ELL HANDBOOK • Phonics Transition Lesson, pp. 266, 268	TEACHER'S EDITION • Decodable Reader 18C, pp. 114e–114f ELL HANDBOOK • Phonics Transition Lesson, pp. 266, 268	TEACHER'S EDITION • Phonics and Spelling, p. DI•58
TEACHER'S EDITION • *Sing with Me* Big Book, p. 110a • AudioText of *Soil* • Concept Talk Video ELL HANDBOOK • AudioText CD Routine, p. 464	TEACHER'S EDITION • *Sing with Me* Big Book, p. 114a • Concept Talk Video	TEACHER'S EDITION • Concept Talk Video
TEACHER'S EDITION • Sheltered Reading, p. DI•60 ELL HANDBOOK • Multilingual Summaries, pp. 133–135	TEACHER'S EDITION • ELL/ELD Reader Guided Reading, p. DI•61 ELL HANDBOOK • ELL Study Guide, p. 136	TEACHER'S EDITION • ELL/ELD Reader Guided Reading, p. DI•61 ELL HANDBOOK • ELL Study Guide, p. 136
ELL HANDBOOK • High-Frequency Words Activity Bank, p. 491 ELL POSTER 18 • Day 3 Activities	ELL HANDBOOK • High-Frequency Words Activity Bank, p. 491	TEACHER'S EDITION • Suffixes, pp. 118–119—119a ELL HANDBOOK • High-Frequency Words Activity Bank, p. 491
TEACHER'S EDITION • Grammar Jammer ELL HANDBOOK • Grammar Transition Lesson, pp. 368, 375 • Grammar Jammer Routine, p. 465	TEACHER'S EDITION • Grammar Jammer ELL HANDBOOK • Grammar Transition Lesson, pp. 368, 375	TEACHER'S EDITION • Grammar Jammer ELL HANDBOOK • Grammar Transition Lesson, pp. 368, 375
TEACHER'S EDITION • Let's Write It!, p. 112–113 • Writing Trait: Sentences, p. 113a	TEACHER'S EDITION • Revising Strategy, pp. 117c–117d	TEACHER'S EDITION • Writer's Craft: Adjectives, pp. 119h–119i

Poster Talk, Concept Talk

Question of the Week

What changes occur under the ground?

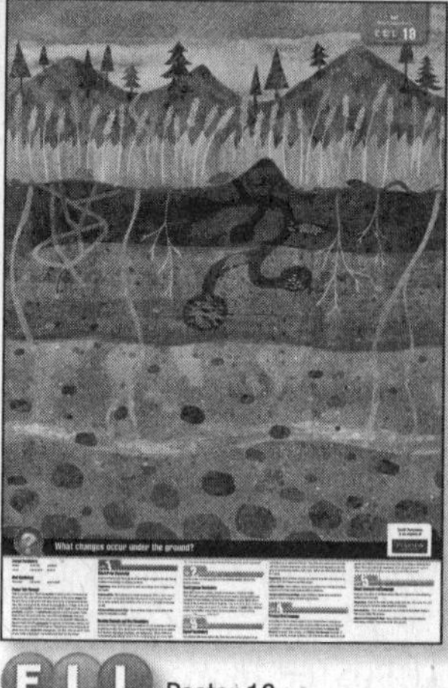
Poster 18

Throughout the week, use the ELL Poster to help children produce and comprehend language, understand the concept, and build English vocabulary. Use the Question of the Week and other questions to help children share ideas in pairs, small groups, or the large group. Sample questions are shown, with examples of possible responses by children.

Weekly Concept and Language Goals

- Understand that changes occur underground
- Name animals that live underground
- Describe how animals' actions can change the earth

By the end of the lesson, children should be able to talk about and write one or more sentences about changes that occur under the ground.

Daily Team Talk

Day 1	Day 2	Day 3	Day 4	Day 5
After Day 1 activities on Poster, ask questions such as *What things do you see underground in the poster picture?*	After Day 2 activity on Poster, ask questions such as *What are some animals that live under the ground?*	After Day 3 activity on Poster, ask questions such as *What are the animals in the poster picture building underground?*	After Day 4 activity on Poster, ask questions such as *How do animals that live underground change the earth?*	After Day 5 activity on Poster, ask questions such as *How does water get into the underground stream?*
Beginning Dirt and water. **Intermediate** There are rocks, dirt, and water. **Advanced** I see animal holes, roots, water, and rocks underground. **Advanced High** I see rocks, dirt, water, plant roots, and tunnels made by animals.	**Beginning** Bugs and worms. **Intermediate** Worms and moles live there. **Advanced** Snakes, worms, and mice live under the ground. **Advanced High** Moles, worms, snakes, and mice are animals that live underground.	**Beginning** Places for food. **Intermediate** They are making places to keep food. **Advanced** The animals are digging their homes. They store food and hide in them. **Advanced High** The animals are building underground homes where they can store food and stay safe and warm.	**Beginning** Dig in the dirt. **Intermediate** They dig in the dirt and move it around. **Advanced** The animals dig holes in the ground. **Advanced High** The animals dig holes and tunnels in the ground. The holes and tunnels change the earth.	**Beginning** Goes down. **Intermediate** Water goes from above down to the stream. **Advanced** Rain falls on the ground. The water runs down to the stream. **Advanced High** Rain falls on the top of the ground. It seeps through the soil into the underground stream.

This Week's Materials

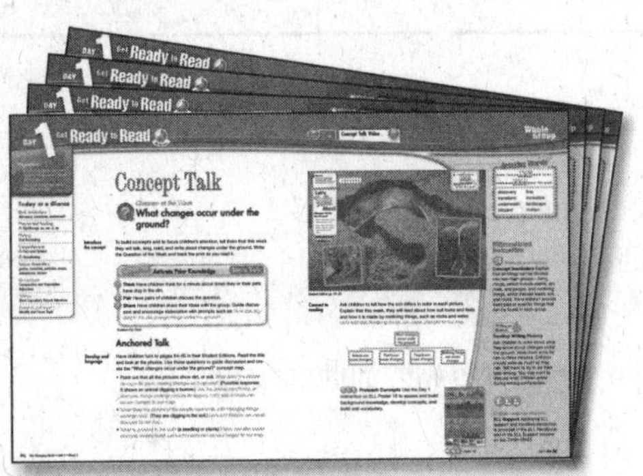
Teacher's Edition pages 84j–119k

See the support for English language learners throughout the lesson, including ELL strategies and scaffold activities at points of use.

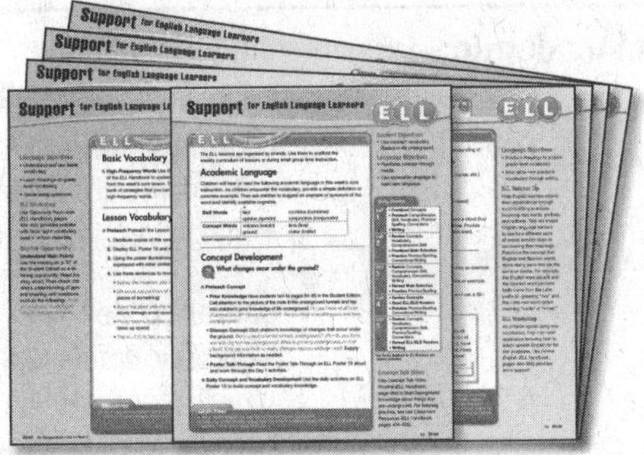
Teacher's Edition pages DI•54–DI•63

Differentiated Instruction for English language learners provides daily group activities that "frontload," or preteach, core instruction.

ELL Handbook pp. 131a–136

Find additional lesson materials that support the core lesson and the ELL instructional pages.

ELL Poster 18

ELD Reader 2.4.3

ELL Reader 2.4.3

Concept Literacy Reader

ELD, ELL Reader Teaching Guide

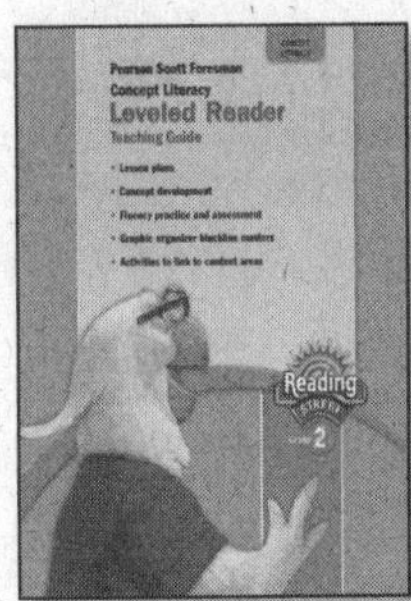
Concept Literacy Reader Teaching Guide

Technology

Online Teacher's Edition Use the digital version of the core teacher's edition for planning and instruction.

eReaders
This Week's ELL and ELD Readers and Concept Literacy Reader are also available in digital format.

This Week's Content and Language Objectives by Strand

Concept Development/Academic Language What changes occur under the ground?	**Content Objective** • Use concept vocabulary related to life underground. **Language Objectives** • Reinforce concepts through media. • Use accessible language to learn new language.
Phonics and Spelling /ou/ Spelled *ou, ow*	**Content Objective** • Identify, define, spell, and read words with diphthongs *ou, ow, oi,* and *oy*. **Language Objective** • Apply phonics and decoding skills to vocabulary.
Listening Comprehension Modified Read Aloud: "Visiting the Volcano"	**Content Objective** • Monitor and adjust oral comprehension. **Language Objectives** • Discuss oral passages. • Use a graphic organizer to take notes. • Ask and give information.
Reading Comprehension Fact and Opinion	**Content Objectives** • Identify facts and opinions in text. • Use facts and opinions to aid comprehension. • Monitor and adjust comprehension. **Language Objectives** • Adapt spoken language. • Discuss and retell facts and opinions. • Draw and write facts and opinions. • Summarize using visual support.
Vocabulary Basic and Lesson Vocabulary	**Language Objectives** • Understand and use basic vocabulary. • Learn meanings of grade-level vocabulary. • Speak using synonyms. • Produce drawings, phrases, and short sentences to acquire grade-level vocabulary.
Vocabulary Suffixes	**Content Objective** • Identify suffixes. **Language Objective** • Learn and use suffixes.
Grammar and Conventions Comparative and Superlative Adjectives	**Content Objectives** • Identify and decode adjectives. • Use superlative and comparative adjectives correctly. **Language Objective** • Speak and write phrases and sentences using superlative and comparative adjectives.
Writing Combining Sentences	**Content Objective** • Identify descriptive words in a text. **Language Objectives** • Write using descriptive words to express ideas clearly. • Share feedback for editing and revising.

grains	**material**
particles	**seep**
substances	**texture**

Leveled Support LS

Teacher Note: Beginning Teach two to three words. **Intermediate** Teach three to four words. **Advanced** Teach five to six words. **Advanced High** Teach all words.

Name ______________________________

Look at the picture. **Read** the paragraph.

Life Underground

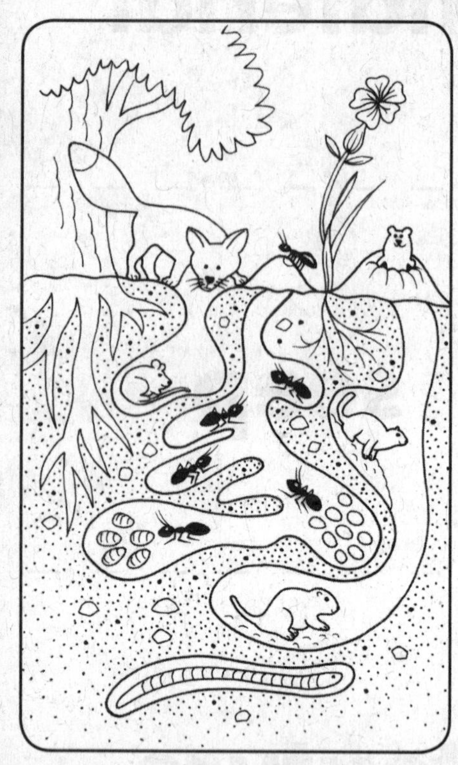

Living underground would not be fun. It is dark and dirty down there. Yet, many animals live in the ground. The ground can keep them safe from other animals. Animals can also find bugs or plant roots to eat in the ground. I think the fox must be the smartest animal. It only sleeps underground. It spends most of its time above ground. Some other animals spend their whole lives underground.

Circle to tell if the sentence is a fact or opinion.

1. Living underground would not be fun.
fact opinion

2. The ground can keep them safe from other animals.
fact opinion

3. They can also find bugs or plant roots to eat.
fact opinion

4. I think the fox must be the smartest animal.
fact opinion

Fact and Opinion

Use this lesson to supplement or replace the skill lesson on page 88a of the Teacher's Edition. Display the Skill Points (at right) and share them with children.

Use the Skill Points to preteach fact and opinion.

Teach/Model

Beginning Show children a picture of ants. Tell children one fact and one opinion about ants: *Ants are small. I think ants are interesting.* Guide children in deciding which statement tells a fact and which tells an opinion.

Intermediate Tell children to stand if you say a fact and to raise their arms if you say an opinion. Say a fact or an opinion about underground animals. Ask children to explain how they decided whether your statement gave a fact or an opinion.

Advanced Say: *Some worms live in soil. Is this a fact or an opinion?* (fact) Ask children to share their opinions about worms. Then discuss with them how they can find facts about worms.

Advanced High Read information about ants from a children's encyclopedia. Have children identify facts in the entry. Ask children to share their opinions about ants.

Then distribute copies of Picture It! page 132.

- Have children look at the picture. Help them tell what kinds of animals they see. If necessary, briefly discuss how the picture shows above ground and under ground.
- Read the paragraph aloud. Ask: *Can you find a fact in the paragraph?* Provide English words as needed to answer.
- Review the Skill Points with children.
- Have children look at the picture and paragraph to find facts and opinions.

Practice

Read aloud the directions on page 132. Reread or chorally read the paragraph. Have children look at the picture and the paragraph as they answer the questions.

Beginning Children can orally answer and, with help, circle their answers on the page.

Intermediate Children can first orally answer and then circle their answers on the page.

Advanced Children can circle their answers and check them by comparing their circles with a partner's.

Advanced High Children can circle their answers and check them by silently rereading the paragraphs to find clue words.

Answers for page 132: 1. opinion; 2. fact; 3. fact; 4. opinion

Skill Points

- ✔ A **fact** can be proven true or false. You can check in a book, ask someone who knows, or see for yourself.
- ✔ An **opinion** tells someone's beliefs or feelings. Clue words such as *I think* and *best* show statements of opinion.

Multilingual Summaries

English

Soil

Soil is in lots of places. Soil contains many things. It is a natural resource. Where does soil come from?

One material in soil is rock. Rocks are hard and made of minerals. They add nutrients to the soil. Another material is humus, tiny bits of dead plants and animals.

Air and water are also in soil. Soil forms where materials can pile up. Soil cannot form in some places.

Soil is different colors. It is made of many minerals and other materials. The materials give soil different colors and textures.

Spanish

La tierra

Hay tierra en todas partes. La tierra contiene muchas cosas. Es un recurso natural. ¿De dónde viene la tierra?

La tierra está formada por diferentes materiales. Uno de esos materiales es trocitos de piedra. Las piedras son duras y están formadas por minerales. Los minerales añaden nutrientes a la tierra. Otro material es el humus que consiste de trocitos de plantas y animales.

La tierra también contiene aire y agua. La tierra se forma sólo dónde se acumulan estos materiales.

Cada tipo de tierra tiene un color y una consistencia particular. El color y la consistencia de la tierra dependen de los materiales que la forman.

Multilingual Summaries

Chinese

土壤

到處都有土壤。 土壤裡含有許多物質。 它是一種自然資源。 土壤是打哪兒來的呢?

土壤是由多種不同的物質構成的。 其中一種物質是岩石。 岩石很硬，由礦物質構成。 這些礦物質增加了土壤的養份。

空氣是土壤中的第三種物質。 土壤中還含有水份。 平地就是由土壤構成的。 有些地方沒有辦法產生土壤。

土壤有各種顏色。 這是因為，土壤是由許多不同的礦物質構成的， 而礦物質的顏色各不相同。 土壤也會有不同的質地。

Vietnamese

Đất

Đất có ở rất nhiều nơi. Đất chứa nhiều thứ. Nó là nguồn tài nguyên thiên nhiên. Đất từ đâu đến?

Đất là từ nhiều loại vật liệu khác nhau. Một loại vật liệu là đá. Đá thì cứng. Đá là từ nhiều khoáng chất. Chúng cho thêm dinh dưỡng vào đất.

Không khí là loại vật liệu thứ ba trong đất. Nước cũng có trong đất. Đất thành hình trên vùng đất bằng. Đất không thể có ở vài nơi.

Đất có nhiều màu sắc. Nó được làm từ nhiều khoáng chất khác nhau. Khoáng chất có thể có nhiều màu khác nhau. Đất cũng có cấu trúc khác nhau.

Multilingual Summaries

Korean

흙

흙은 여기저기에 있다. 흙은 많은 것이 들어 있는 천연 자원이다. 흙은 어디서 생겨나는 걸까?

흙은 다양한 물질로 구성되어 있다. 그 중 하나는 바위다. 바위는 단단하다. 바위는 광물로 구성된다. 광물은 흙에 양분을 더해준다.

공기는 흙에 포함된 세 번째 물질이다. 흙에는 수분도 들어있다. 흙은 평평한 땅을 형성한다. 흙이 형성할 수 없는 장소도 있다.

흙의 색은 다양하다. 흙은 매우 다양한 광물로 이루어져 있다. 광물의 색은 다양하다. 또한 흙의 조직도 다양하다.

Hmong

Av

Av muaj nyob ntau qhov chaw. Av muaj ntau yam khoom nyob hauv. Nws yog cov khoom yug sia. Av txawm qhov twg los?

Av mas muaj ntau yam khoom los sib puab. Muaj ib yam khoom mas yog pob zeb. Pob zeb mas tawv heev. Pob zeb los yog cov khoom los yug sia ua. Tej no ntxiv kom av rog xwb.

Cua yog yam thib peb nyob hauv av. Dej los muaj nyob hauv av. Av los ua tej tiaj nrag. Av txawm tsis muaj nyob rau tej qhov chaw.

Av muaj txawv xim. Nws yog ntau yam khoom los sib puab ua av. Tej khoom los sib puab ua av no ntxawv xim. Av kuj muaj daim plaub sib ntxawv ib yam.

Name ____________________ **Prairie Dog Picnic**

- **Read** *Prairie Dog Picnic* again.
- **Draw** a picture of a prairie dog's underground home.
- **Write** three sentences that go with your picture.

1. ____________________

2. ____________________

3. ____________________

Family Link

Ask family members to tell you about their favorite wild animals.

Weekly Resources Guide for English Language Learner Support

For this week's content and language objectives, see p. 137e.

Instructional Strand	Day 1	Day 2
Concept Development/Academic Language	TEACHER'S EDITION • Academic Language, p. DI•75 • Concept Development, p. DI•75 • Anchored Talk, pp. 120j—120–121 • *Sing With Me* Big Book, p. 121a • Concept Talk Video ELL HANDBOOK • ELL Poster Talk, Concept Talk, p. 137c ELL POSTER 19 • Day 1 Activities	TEACHER'S EDITION • Academic Language, p. DI•75 • Concept Development, p. DI•75 • Anchored Talk, p. 126b • *Sing With Me* Big Book, p. 126a • Concept Talk Video ELL HANDBOOK • ELL Poster Talk, Concept Talk, p. 137c • Concept Talk Video Routine, p. 464 ELL POSTER 19 • Day 2 Activities
Phonics and Spelling	TEACHER'S EDITION • Phonics and Spelling, p. DI•79 • Decodable Reader 19A, pp. 123c–123d	TEACHER'S EDITION • Phonics and Spelling, p. DI•79
Listening Comprehension	TEACHER'S EDITION • Modified Read Aloud, p. DI•78 • *Sing With Me* Big Book, p. 121a • Concept Talk Video ELL HANDBOOK • Concept Talk Video Routine, p. 464	TEACHER'S EDITION • Modified Read Aloud, p. DI•78 • *Sing With Me* Big Book, p. 126a • AudioText of *The Night the Moon Fell* • Concept Talk Video ELL HANDBOOK • AudioText CD Routine, p. 464 • Story Map B, p. 471
Reading Comprehension	TEACHER'S EDITION • Teach Plot and Theme, p. DI•80	TEACHER'S EDITION • Teach Plot and Theme, p. DI•80 • Frontloading Reading, p. DI•81 ELL HANDBOOK • Picture It! Skill Instruction, pp. 138–138a • Multilingual Summaries, pp. 139–141
Vocabulary **Basic and Lesson Vocabulary** **Vocabulary Skill: Multiple-Meaning Words**	TEACHER'S EDITION • Basic Vocabulary, p. DI•76 • Preteach Lesson Vocabulary, p. DI•76 • Multiple-Meaning Words, p. DI•79 ELL HANDBOOK • Word Cards, p. 137 • ELL Vocabulary Routine, p. 456 ELL POSTER 19 • Day 1 Activities	TEACHER'S EDITION • Basic Vocabulary, p. DI•76 • Reteach Lesson Vocabulary, p. DI•77 • Multiple-Meaning Words, p. DI•79 ELL HANDBOOK • Word Cards, p. 137 • Multilingual Vocabulary List, pp. 429–440 ELL POSTER 19 • Day 2 Activities
Grammar and Conventions	TEACHER'S EDITION • Preteach Adverbs That Tell When or Where, p. DI•83	TEACHER'S EDITION • Reteach Adverbs That Tell When or Where, p. DI•83
Writing	TEACHER'S EDITION • Combining Sentences, p. DI•84 • Introduce Narrative Poem, pp. 125c–125d	TEACHER'S EDITION • Writer's Craft: Selecting a Story to Tell, pp. 143c–143d

Unit 4 Week 4 The Night the Moon Fell

LS Leveled Support This symbol indicates leveled instruction to address language proficiency levels.

Day 3	Day 4	Day 5
TEACHER'S EDITION • Academic Language, p. DI•75 • Concept Development, p. DI•75 • Anchored Talk, p. 144b • *Sing With Me* Big Book, p. 144a • Concept Talk Video ELL HANDBOOK • ELL Poster Talk, Concept Talk, p. 137c ELL POSTER 19 • Day 3 Activities	TEACHER'S EDITION • Academic Language, p. DI•75 • Concept Development, p. DI•75 • Anchored Talk, p. 148b • *Sing With Me* Big Book, p. 148a • Concept Talk Video ELL HANDBOOK • ELL Poster Talk, Concept Talk, p. 137c ELL POSTER 19 • Day 4 Activities	TEACHER'S EDITION • Academic Language, p. DI•75 • Concept Development, p. DI•75 • Concept Talk Video ELL HANDBOOK • ELL Poster Talk, Concept Talk, p. 137c ELL POSTER 19 • Day 5 Activities
ELL HANDBOOK • Phonics Transition Lesson, pp. 302, 304	TEACHER'S EDITION • Decodable Reader 19C, pp. 148e–148f ELL HANDBOOK • Phonics Transition Lesson, pp. 302, 304	TEACHER'S EDITION • Phonics and Spelling, p. DI•79
TEACHER'S EDITION • *Sing With Me* Big Book, p. 144a • AudioText of *The Night the Moon Fell* • Concept Talk Video ELL HANDBOOK • AudioText CD Routine, p. 464	TEACHER'S EDITION • *Sing With Me* Big Book, p. 148a • Concept Talk Video	TEACHER'S EDITION • Concept Talk Video
TEACHER'S EDITION • Sheltered Reading, p. DI•81 ELL HANDBOOK • Multilingual Summaries, pp. 139–141	TEACHER'S EDITION • ELL/ELD Reader Guided Reading, p. DI•82 ELL HANDBOOK • ELL Study Guide, p. 142	TEACHER'S EDITION • ELL/ELD Reader Guided Reading, p. DI•82 ELL HANDBOOK • ELL Study Guide, p. 142
ELL HANDBOOK • High-Frequency Words Activity Bank, p. 491 ELL POSTER 19 • Day 3 Activities	ELL HANDBOOK • High-Frequency Words Activity Bank, p. 491	TEACHER'S EDITION • Multiple-Meaning Words, p. 153a ELL HANDBOOK • High-Frequency Words Activity Bank, p. 491
TEACHER'S EDITION • Grammar Jammer ELL HANDBOOK • Grammar Transition Lesson, pp. 369, 376 • Grammar Jammer Routine, p. 465	TEACHER'S EDITION • Grammar Jammer ELL HANDBOOK • Grammar Transition Lesson, pp. 369, 376	TEACHER'S EDITION • Grammar Jammer ELL HANDBOOK • Grammar Transition Lesson, pp. 369, 376
TEACHER'S EDITION • Let's Write It!, p. 146–147 • Writing Trait: Voice, p. 147a	TEACHER'S EDITION • Revising Strategy, pp. 151c–151d	TEACHER'S EDITION • Writer's Craft: Rhyming Words, pp. 153h–153i

Poster Talk, Concept Talk

Question of the Week

Why are some changes difficult?

ELL Poster 19

Throughout the week, use the ELL Poster to help children produce and comprehend language, understand the concept, and build English vocabulary. Use the Question of the Week and other questions to help children share ideas in pairs, small groups, or the large group. Sample questions are shown, with examples of possible responses by children.

Weekly Concept and Language Goals

- Understand that some changes are difficult
- Name some difficult changes that people have to face
- Describe how we feel when these changes happen

By the end of the lesson, children should be able to talk about and write one or more sentences about changes that are difficult.

Daily Team Talk

Day 1	Day 2	Day 3	Day 4	Day 5
After Day 1 activities on Poster, ask questions such as *The family in the poster picture is moving into a new house. How can you tell?*	After Day 2 activity on Poster, ask questions such as *A window was broken during the family's move. What are some other things that can get broken during a move?*	After Day 3 activity on Poster, ask questions such as *The family has a new baby. What changes should people make when they are around a new baby?*	After Day 4 activity on Poster, ask questions such as *Imagine you move to a new neighborhood. How do you feel?*	After Day 5 activity on Poster, ask questions such as *What difficult changes do you face at the beginning of a new school year?*
Beginning I see boxes. **Intermediate** People put things in boxes when they move. **Advanced** The family has boxes to unpack. **Advanced High** The family is unpacking boxes. Their furniture hasn't arrived yet.	**Beginning** Glasses. **Intermediate** Things made of glass can break. **Advanced** Glasses and dishes can get broken. **Advanced High** Glasses, dishes, and furniture can get broken during a move.	**Beginning** No noise. **Intermediate** They should be quiet. **Advanced** People should talk and move in a quiet way. **Advanced High** People need to speak and move quietly so they don't wake the baby.	**Beginning** Not happy. **Intermediate** I feel sad. I miss my friends. **Advanced** I feel sad because I miss my friends and my old school. **Advanced High** I worry about making new friends and going to a new school.	**Beginning** Getting up early. **Intermediate** I get more homework. **Advanced** I have new classes without my friends. **Advanced High** I have new teachers and new subjects to learn.

This Week's Materials

Teacher's Edition pages 120j–153k

See the support for English language learners throughout the lesson, including ELL strategies and scaffold activities at points of use.

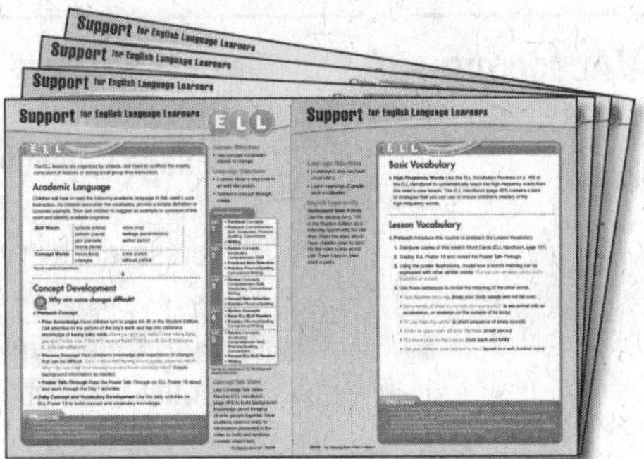

Teacher's Edition pages DI•75–DI•84

Differentiated Instruction for English language learners provides daily group activities that "frontload," or preteach, core instruction.

ELL Handbook pp. 137a–142

Find additional lesson materials that support the core lesson and the ELL instructional pages.

ELL Poster 19

ELD Reader 2.4.4

ELL Reader 2.4.4

Concept Literacy Reader

ELD, ELL Reader Teaching Guide

Concept Literacy Reader Teaching Guide

Technology

Online Teacher's Edition Use the digital version of the core teacher's edition for planning and instruction.

eReaders

This Week's ELL and ELD Readers and Concept Literacy Reader are also available in digital format.

This Week's Content and Language Objectives by Strand

Concept Development/Academic Language Why are some changes difficult?	**Content Objective** • Use concept vocabulary related to change. **Language Objectives** • Reinforce concepts through media. • Express ideas in response to art and discussion.
Phonics and Spelling Syllable Patterns	**Content Objective** • Identify and distinguish syllable patterns in words. **Language Objective** • Apply phonics and decoding skills to vocabulary.
Listening Comprehension Modified Read Aloud: "Someone New"	**Content Objective** • Monitor and adjust oral comprehension. **Language Objectives** • Discuss oral passages. • Use a graphic organizer to take notes. • Use contextual support to confirm understanding.
Reading Comprehension Plot and Theme	**Content Objectives** • Identify the plot and theme of a text. • Monitor and adjust comprehension. **Language Objectives** • Write the plot and theme of a text as you identify them. • Summarize using visual support.
Vocabulary Basic and Lesson Vocabulary	**Language Objectives** • Understand and use basic vocabulary. • Learn meanings of grade-level vocabulary. • Produce drawings, phrases, and short sentences to acquire grade-level vocabulary.
Vocabulary Multiple-Meaning Words	**Content Objective** • Identify and define multiple-meaning words. **Language Objective** • Discuss the meanings of multiple-meaning words.
Grammar and Conventions Adverbs That Tell When or Where	**Content Objective** • Decode and use adverbs that tell *when* or *where*. **Language Objectives** • Speak using adverbs that tell *when* or *where*. • Ask and give information. • Write phrases or sentences using adverbs that tell *when* or *where*.
Writing Combining Sentences	**Content Objective** • Identify words that show what an author is feeling. **Language Objectives** • Write a paragraph, showing the feelings that you (as the author) have toward the subject. • Share feedback for editing and revising.

Word Cards for Vocabulary Activities

balance	**canyons**
coral	**rattle**
slivers	**sway**
whisper	

Teacher Note: Beginning Teach two to three words. **Intermediate** Teach three to four words. **Advanced** Teach five to six words. **Advanced High** Teach all words.

Name ______________________________

Look at the pictures. **Read** the story.

A New School

Today is Miguel's first day at his new school. He feels sad. He does not know anyone here, and he misses his old school.

Miguel's new teacher seems nice. But Miguel is still a little shy and scared. Then his teacher smiles at him. He smiles too.

At recess, a boy in Miguel's class asks him to play. Miguel is having fun. Maybe this new school will be just as good as the old one!

Answer the questions below.

1. Tell what happens at the beginning of the story. How does Miguel feel?

____

____

2. What happens to change how Miguel feels?

____

3. Talk about what you think is the theme of this story.

Plot and Theme

Use this lesson to supplement or replace the skill lesson on page 124a of the Teacher's Edition. Display the Skill Points (at right) and share them with children.

Use the Skill Points to preteach plot and theme.

Teach/Model

Beginning Act out a story about your first day of school. Describe your actions with simple sentences, such as *We play ball.* Guide children in identifying the plot of your story. Provide the theme of the story. Ask: *Is this the big idea of the story? Why?*

Intermediate Ask children to think about their first day of school. Have them draw pictures to show the beginning, the middle, and the end of their day. Pair children and have them tell the plot of a story using their pictures. Guide them in explaining the theme of their story.

Advanced Pair children. Have one partner tell a story about his or her first day of school. Have the other partner draw pictures to show the plot of the story. Then partners trade roles. Ask them to work together to decide the big idea, or theme, of each story.

Advanced High Ask volunteers to share stories about their first day of school. Have the rest of the group identify the beginning, middle, and end of each story. Ask: *What is the big idea, or theme, of this story?*

Then distribute copies of Picture It! page 138.

- Have children look at the pictures. Help them tell what happens in each one.
- Read the sentences aloud. Ask: *What happens first in the story?* Provide English words as needed to answer.
- Review the Skill Points with children.
- Have children look at the pictures and sentences to determine what the theme of the story is.

Practice

Read aloud the directions on page 138. Reread or chorally read the story. Have children look at the pictures and the story as they answer the questions.

Beginning Children can orally respond and then write and say their answers. Provide help with writing and spelling.

Intermediate Children can first orally respond and then write and say their answers.

Advanced Children can write and say their answers and then check them by quietly reading aloud their writing or comparing their ideas with a partner's.

Advanced High Children can write and say their answers and check them by silently rereading the story and making any needed revisions.

Answers for page 138: 1. Miguel starts his first day at a new school. He feels sad. 2. Miguel's teacher and a boy in his class are nice to him. 3. Sample answer: The big idea of this story is that a change can be a good thing even if it is not easy.

Skill Points

- ✔ The **plot** is what happens in the beginning, middle, and end of a story.
- ✔ Every story has one big idea, or **theme.**
- ✔ Pay attention to what happens and the order in which it happens. What happens in the story can help you figure out the big idea.

Multilingual Summaries

English

The Night the Moon Fell

Luna the moon fell from the sky. She fell into the deep ocean. She broke into pieces at the bottom of the sea. The stars, birds, and flowers looked for her and asked Luna to return. But she was at the bottom of the sea.

Luna was sad. The fish in the sea became Luna's friends. They began to sweep together Luna's pieces. They patched and smoothed the pieces together. The fish used their scales and fins to glue Luna's pieces together. Luna floated back into the sky. The fish swam in the sky with her. That is why the moon shines in the sky. The stars float around the moon.

Spanish

La noche que se cayó la luna

Luna se cayó del cielo. Ella cayó en el océano profundo. Se hizo pedazos en el fondo del mar. Las estrellas, los pájaros y las flores la buscaban y le pedían a Luna que regresara. Pero ella estaba en el fondo del mar.

Luna estaba triste. Los peces del mar se volvieron sus amigos. Ellos comenzaron a juntar las piezas de Luna. Limpiaron y unieron las piezas. Los peces usaron sus escamas y sus aletas para pegar las piezas de Luna. Luna flotó de regreso al cielo. Los peces nadaron en el cielo con ella. Es por eso que la luna brilla en el cielo. Las estrellas flotan alrededor de la luna.

Multilingual Summaries

Chinese

夜空

月亮卢娜从天上掉下来，她跌到深海里，在海底里碎成千百片。星星、小鸟和鲜花到处寻找她，想请她回来，可是她在海底里。

卢娜很伤心，海里的鱼成为她的朋友。他们开始把卢娜的碎片收集、拼奏、整合起来，用他们的鳞和鳍把卢娜的碎片黏在一起。卢娜浮回天空，鱼伴着她在天空里游泳，这就是所以月亮在夜空里发亮，而星星在月亮旁边游走。

Vietnamese

Đêm

Mặt trăng Luna từ trên trời rơi xuống. Trăng rơi xuống biển sâu. Trăng vỡ ra từng mảnh dưới đáy biển. Sao, chim, và hoa tìm trăng Luna và yêu cầu Luna trở về. Nhưng trăng đã nằm dưới đáy biển.

Luna buồn. Cá dưới biển trở thành bạn của Luna. Chúng bắt đầu ráp các mảnh vỡ của Luna lại với nhau. Chúng dán và trau chuốc các mảnh vỡ lại với nhau. Cá dùng vảy và vi để gắn các mảnh của Luna lại với nhau. Luna lại nổi trở lại trên bầu trời. Cá cũng lội trên bầu trời với trăng. Đó là lý do tại sao mặt trăng chiếu sáng trên trời. Các vì sao trôi nổi quanh mặt trăng.

Multilingual Summaries

Korean

밤

달님 루나는 하늘에서 떨어졌습니다. 달님은 깊은 바다 속으로 빠졌습니다. 바다 깊은 속에서 산산조각이 났지요. 별들과, 새들과 꽃들이 달님을 찾아헤맸고, 루나에게 돌아오라고 말했습니다. 그러나 달님은 바다 깊숙히 있었습니다.

루나는 슬펐습니다. 바다 속의 물고기들이 루나의 친구가 되었습니다. 물고기들은 루나의 조각들을 쓸어 담기 시작했습니다. 부서진 조각들을 붙이고 매만졌습니다. 물고기들은 비늘과 지느러미를 이용해서 루나의 조각들을 모았습니다. 루나는 하늘로 다시 떠올랐습니다. 물고기들은 루나와 함께 하늘에서 헤엄쳤습니다. 그래서 달님이 하늘에서 환하게 비추는 거랍니다. 별들은 달님 주변을 떠돕니다.

Hmong

Mo Ntuj

Luna yog lub hlis poob saum ntuj. Nws poob tub tub rau hauv dej thables. Nws tawg ua ob peb thooj ntau ntau nyob hauv qab dej. Cov nub qub, noog, thiab paaj nrhiav nws thiab hais kom Luna rov los. Tiam sis nws nyob hauv qab dej thables lawm.

Luna tu siab kawg. Cov ntses hauv dej ciali ua Luna li phoojywg. Lawv pib muab Luna cheb los ua ib pawg. Lawv muab nws sis dhos thiab kho kom du du. Cov ntses siv lawv cov nplaim ntses thiab nplaim tis los muab Luna sis lo uake. Luna ntab rov qab rau sau lub ntuj. Cov ntses luam dej mus txog sau ntuj nrog nws. Vim li ntawd lub hlis thiaj li cig saum ntuj. Cov nub qub ya ib ncig lub hlis.

Name ______________________

- **Read** *Adam's New Soccer Team* again.
- **Write** answers to the questions.

Pages	Question	Answer
2	**1.** At the beginning of the story, what does Adam want?	
3–4	**2.** What does Adam do at practice?	
5	**3.** What does Adam think when he sees Sonny and Liam?	
6–7	**4.** What does Adam have to think about during the game?	
8	**5.** How does Adam feel at the end of the story?	

Family Link

Have family members tell you about a time when they had to make new friends.

Weekly Resources Guide for English Language Learner Support

For this week's content and language objectives, see p. 143e.

Instructional Strand	Day 1	Day 2
Concept Development/Academic Language	TEACHER'S EDITION • Academic Language, p. DI•96 • Concept Development, p. DI•96 • Anchored Talk, pp. 154j—154–155 • *Sing with Me* Big Book, p. 155a • Concept Talk Video ELL HANDBOOK • ELL Poster Talk, Concept Talk, p. 143c ELL POSTER 20 • Day 1 Activities	TEACHER'S EDITION • Academic Language, p. DI•96 • Concept Development, p. DI•96 • Anchored Talk, p. 160b • *Sing with Me* Big Book, p. 160a • Concept Talk Video ELL HANDBOOK • ELL Poster Talk, Concept Talk, p. 143c • Concept Talk Video Routine, p. 464 ELL POSTER 20 • Day 2 Activities
Phonics and Spelling	TEACHER'S EDITION • Phonics and Spelling, p. DI•100 • Decodable Reader 20A, pp. 157c–157d	TEACHER'S EDITION • Phonics and Spelling, p. DI•100
Listening Comprehension	TEACHER'S EDITION • Modified Read Aloud, p. DI•99 • *Sing with Me* Big Book, p. 155a • Concept Talk Video ELL HANDBOOK • Concept Talk Video Routine, p. 464	TEACHER'S EDITION • Modified Read Aloud, p. DI•99 • *Sing with Me* Big Book, p. 160a • AudioText of *The First Tortilla* • Concept Talk Video ELL HANDBOOK • AudioText CD Routine, p. 464 • Story Map B, p. 471
Reading Comprehension	TEACHER'S EDITION • Teach Plot and Theme, p. DI•101	TEACHER'S EDITION • Teach Plot and Theme, p. DI•101 • Frontloading Reading, p. DI•102 ELL HANDBOOK • Picture It! Skill Instruction, pp. 144–144a • Multilingual Summaries, pp. 145–147
Vocabulary **Basic and Lesson Vocabulary** **Vocabulary Skill: Prefixes**	TEACHER'S EDITION • Basic Vocabulary, p. DI•97 • Preteach Lesson Vocabulary, p. DI•97 • Prefixes, p. DI•100 ELL HANDBOOK • Word Cards, p. 143 • ELL Vocabulary Routine, p. 456 ELL POSTER 20 • Day 1 Activities	TEACHER'S EDITION • Basic Vocabulary, p. DI•97 • Reteach Lesson Vocabulary, p. DI•98 • Prefixes, p. DI•100 ELL HANDBOOK • Word Cards, p. 143 • Multilingual Vocabulary List, pp. 429–440 ELL POSTER 20 • Day 2 Activities
Grammar and Conventions	TEACHER'S EDITION • Preteach Adverbs That Tell How, p. DI•104	TEACHER'S EDITION • Reteach Adverbs That Tell How, p. DI•104
Writing	TEACHER'S EDITION • Writer's Purpose, p. DI•105 • Introduce Thank-You Note, pp. 159c–159d	TEACHER'S EDITION • Writing Trait: Focus/Ideas, pp. 177c–177d

Unit 4 Week 5 The First Tortilla

This symbol indicates leveled instruction to address language proficiency levels.

Day 3	Day 4	Day 5
TEACHER'S EDITION • Academic Language, p. DI•96 • Concept Development, p. DI•96 • Anchored Talk, p. 178b • *Sing with Me* Big Book, p. 178a • Concept Talk Video **ELL HANDBOOK** • ELL Poster Talk, Concept Talk, p. 143c **ELL POSTER 20** • Day 3 Activities	**TEACHER'S EDITION** • Academic Language, p. DI•96 • Concept Development, p. DI•96 • Anchored Talk, p. 182b • *Sing with Me* Big Book, p. 182a • Concept Talk Video **ELL HANDBOOK** • ELL Poster Talk, Concept Talk, p. 143c **ELL POSTER 20** • Day 4 Activities	**TEACHER'S EDITION** • Academic Language, p. DI•96 • Concept Development, p. DI•96 • Concept Talk Video **ELL HANDBOOK** • ELL Poster Talk, Concept Talk, p. 143c **ELL POSTER 20** • Day 5 Activities
ELL HANDBOOK • Phonics Transition Lesson, pp. 263, 265	**TEACHER'S EDITION** • Decodable Reader 20C, pp. 182e–182f **ELL HANDBOOK** • Phonics Transition Lesson, pp. 263, 265	**TEACHER'S EDITION** • Phonics and Spelling, p. DI•100
TEACHER'S EDITION • *Sing with Me* Big Book, p. 178a • AudioText of *The First Tortilla* • Concept Talk Video **ELL HANDBOOK** • AudioText CD Routine, p. 464	**TEACHER'S EDITION** • *Sing with Me* Big Book, p. 182a • Concept Talk Video	**TEACHER'S EDITION** • Concept Talk Video
TEACHER'S EDITION • Sheltered Reading, p. DI•102 **ELL HANDBOOK** • Multilingual Summaries, pp. 145–147	**TEACHER'S EDITION** • ELL/ELD Reader Guided Reading, p. DI•103 **ELL HANDBOOK** • ELL Study Guide, p. 148	**TEACHER'S EDITION** • ELL/ELD Reader Guided Reading, p. DI•103 **ELL HANDBOOK** • ELL Study Guide, p. 148
ELL HANDBOOK • High-Frequency Words Activity Bank, p. 491 **ELL POSTER 20** • Day 3 Activities	**ELL HANDBOOK** • High-Frequency Words Activity Bank, p. 491	**TEACHER'S EDITION** • Prefixes, p. 186–187 **ELL HANDBOOK** • High-Frequency Words Activity Bank, p. 491
TEACHER'S EDITION • Grammar Jammer **ELL HANDBOOK** • Grammar Transition Lesson, pp. 369, 377 • Grammar Jammer Routine, p. 465	**TEACHER'S EDITION** • Grammar Jammer **ELL HANDBOOK** • Grammar Transition Lesson, pp. 369, 377	**TEACHER'S EDITION** • Grammar Jammer **ELL HANDBOOK** • Grammar Transition Lesson, pp. 369, 377
TEACHER'S EDITION • Let's Write It!, p. 180–181 • Writer's Craft: Sequence, p. 181a	**TEACHER'S EDITION** • Revising Strategy, pp. 185c–185d	**TEACHER'S EDITION** • Writer's Craft: Adverbs, pp. 187h–187i

Poster Talk, Concept Talk

Question of the Week

How do changes in the weather affect us?

ELL Poster 20

Throughout the week, use the ELL Poster to help children produce and comprehend language, understand the concept, and build English vocabulary. Use the Question of the Week and other questions to help children share ideas in pairs, small groups, or the large group. Sample questions are shown, with examples of possible responses by children.

Weekly Concept and Language Goals

- Know that changes in the weather can affect people
- Name different kinds of changes in the weather
- Tell about how changes in the weather affect us

By the end of the lesson, children should be able to talk about and write one or more sentences about how changes in the weather affect people.

Daily Team Talk

Day 1	Day 2	Day 3	Day 4	Day 5
After Day 1 activities on Poster, ask questions such as *In the poster picture, the sun is shining, but rain is coming. How will it affect the family if it starts to rain?*	After Day 2 activity on Poster, ask questions such as *How does seeing the rain clouds affect how the dad feels?*	After Day 3 activity on Poster, ask questions such as *What kind of weather makes you want to stay inside?*	After Day 4 activity on Poster, ask questions such as *How did the weather change from yesterday to today?*	After Day 5 activity on Poster, ask questions such as *How do you feel when the sun is shining and it is warm outside?*
Beginning Get wet. **Intermediate** They will go inside. **Advanced** The family will stay inside the tent. **Advanced High** The family will go hiking while it is sunny and stay inside when it rains.	**Beginning** He's sad. **Intermediate** He looks worried. **Advanced** The dad is worried about the rain coming. **Advanced High** The dad is thinking about how the rain will change the family's day.	**Beginning** Rain. **Intermediate** In a storm. **Advanced** I want to be inside when it is raining. **Advanced High** I like to stay inside when it is stormy or snowy.	**Beginning** Sunny. **Intermediate** It is hot and sunny. **Advanced** Yesterday it was cold and wet. Today it is warm and the sun is shining. **Advanced High** The weather today is warmer and drier than it was yesterday.	**Beginning** Good. **Intermediate** I feel good. **Advanced** I am happy and want to be outside. **Advanced High** When it is warm and sunny, I feel happy and want to go outside to play.

This Week's Materials

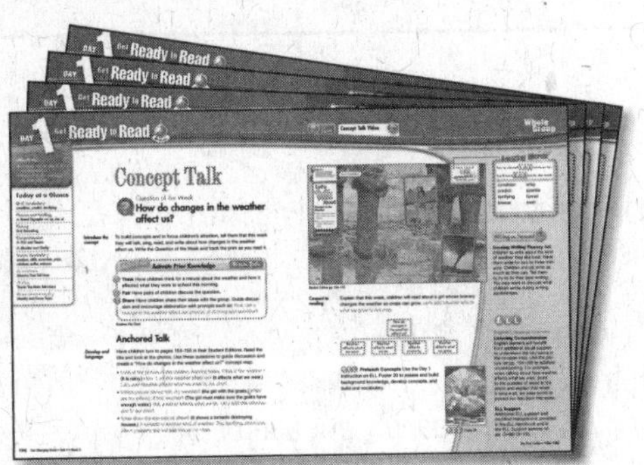
Teacher's Edition pages 154j–187k

See the support for English language learners throughout the lesson, including ELL strategies and scaffold activities at points of use.

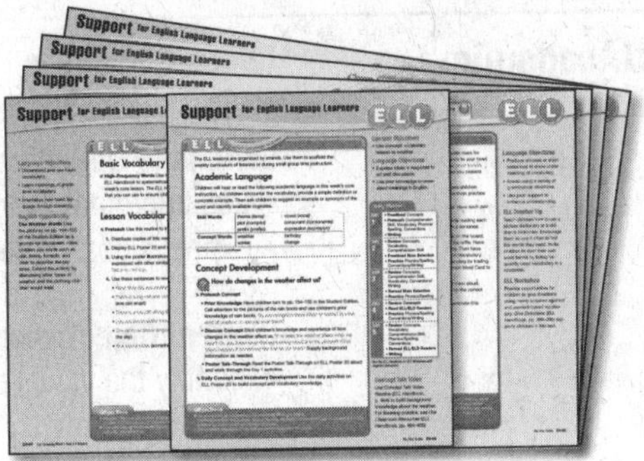
Teacher's Edition pages DI•96–DI•105

Differentiated Instruction for English language learners provides daily group activities that "frontload," or preteach, core instruction.

ELL Handbook pp. 143a–148

Find additional lesson materials that support the core lesson and the ELL instructional pages.

ELL Poster 20

ELD Reader 2.4.5

ELL Reader 2.4.5

Concept Literacy Reader

ELD, ELL Reader Teaching Guide

Concept Literacy Reader Teaching Guide

Technology

Online Teacher's Edition Use the digital version of the core teacher's edition for planning and instruction.

eReaders
This Week's ELL and ELD Readers and Concept Literacy Reader are also available in digital format.

This Week's Content and Language Objectives by Strand

Concept Development/Academic Language How do changes in the weather affect us?	**Content Objective** • Use concept vocabulary related to weather. **Language Objectives** • Use prior knowledge to understand meanings in English. • Express ideas in response to art and discussion.
Phonics and Spelling Vowel Digraphs *oo, ue, ew, ui*	**Content Objectives** • Identify the vowel digraph /ü/ in words. • Review the vowel digraph /ü/ spelled *oo, ue, ew,* and *ui.* **Language Objective** • Apply phonics and decoding skills to vocabulary.
Listening Comprehension Modified Read Aloud: "Old Man Winter"	**Content Objective** • Monitor and adjust oral comprehension. **Language Objectives** • Discuss oral passages. • Use a graphic organizer to take notes. • Speak using grade-level vocabulary.
Reading Comprehension Plot and Theme	**Content Objectives** • Identify the plot and theme of a text. • Monitor and adjust comprehension. **Language Objectives** • Write the plot and theme of a text as you identify them. • Summarize using visual support.
Vocabulary Basic and Lesson Vocabulary	**Language Objectives** • Understand and use basic vocabulary. • Learn meanings of grade-level vocabulary. • Internalize new basic language through speaking. • Produce drawings, phrases, and short sentences to acquire grade-level vocabulary. • Speak using a variety of grammatical structures.
Vocabulary Prefixes	**Content Objective** • Identify and define the prefix *re-*. **Language Objective** • Discuss the meanings of the prefix *re-*.
Grammar and Conventions Adverbs That Tell How	**Content Objective** • Decode and use adverbs that tell *how.* **Language Objectives** • Speak using adverbs that tell *how.* • Write phrases or sentences using adverbs that tell *how.*
Writing Expressing the Writer's Purpose	**Content Objective** • Identify words that show the author's purpose. **Language Objectives** • Write a paragraph, showing the feelings that you (as the author) have for writing. • Share feedback for editing and revising.

Word Cards for Vocabulary Activities

awaken	**cliffs**
mountain	**prize**
rainbow	**suffer**
volcano	

Teacher Note: Beginning Teach two to three words. **Intermediate** Teach three to four words. **Advanced** Teach five to six words. **Advanced High** Teach all words.

Name ____________________

Look at the picture. **Read** the paragraph.

The Great Fiesta

Maria's grandma was coming tomorrow. "The harvest this year was poor," her parents told her. "We do not have enough food for a big fiesta. We cannot invite everyone to a party for Grandma." Maria had an idea. She went to the family next door. She told them tomorrow there would be a fiesta with plenty of food. "Please bring a bowl of beans," she said. The neighbors agreed. Then she went to the next family and asked them to come. "But you must bring a bowl of squash," she told them. They agreed. Maria went from house to house. Some were bringing tortillas. Some were bringing chiles. The next day, the whole village came for the fiesta. They enjoyed plenty of food!

Answer the questions.

1. What was Maria's problem in the story?

____

2. What did Maria do to solve this problem?

____

3. Circle the theme of the story.
People can cooperate to make something big.
There is always plenty of food at a fiesta.

Plot and Theme

Use this lesson to supplement or replace the skill lesson on page 158a of the Teacher's Edition. Display the Skill Points (at right) and share them with children.

Use the Skill Points to preteach plot and theme.

Teach/Model

Review the story *The Three Little Pigs*. Prepare picture cards that show the main events of the story.

Beginning Show children the picture cards. Say: *The wolf blows down the straw house and the wood house. How do the pigs solve their problem?* (They go to the third house, which is made of bricks.) Guide children in identifying the theme of the story.

Intermediate Say: *The plot of the story has a problem and a solution. What is the pigs' problem?* (The wolf blows down two of their houses.) *How do they solve their problem?* (They hide in a house he can't blow down.) Help children discuss the theme of the story.

Advanced Ask children to tell a story that has a problem and a solution to the problem. Ask: *What lesson, or theme, can we learn from this story?*

Advanced High Pair children. Provide a problem for a story: *The Wilsons are on a camping trip. They want to make dinner, but they don't have cooking tools. What can they do?* Ask children to tell a story that offers a solution to this problem. Ask: *What is the theme, or big idea, of your story?*

Then distribute copies of Picture It! page 144.

- Have children look at the picture. Help them tell what kinds of food they see. If necessary, briefly discuss the word *fiesta*.
- Read the story aloud. Ask: *What does Maria do?* Provide English words as needed to answer.
- Review the Skill Points with children.
- Have children look at the picture and sentences and think about the theme of the story.

Practice

Read aloud the directions on page 144. Reread or chorally read the story. Have children look at the picture and the story as they answer the questions.

Beginning Children can orally answer and then, with help, write and circle their answers on the page. Provide help with writing and spelling.

Intermediate Children can first orally answer and then write and circle their answers on the page.

Advanced Children can write and circle their answers and check them by quietly reading aloud their writing and comparing their choice with a partner's.

Advanced High Children can write and circle their answers and check them by reviewing the story and making any necessary corrections.

Answers for page 144: 1. Her parents did not have enough food for a fiesta for Grandma. 2. Maria asked other families to bring food for the fiesta. 3. People can cooperate to make something big.

Skill Points

- ✔ The **plot** is what happens in a story. It can include a problem and the solution.
- ✔ The **theme** is the big idea of a story.
- ✔ Look at the title and the pictures. Ask yourself: *What do I think the story will be about? Do I know anything about this?*

Multilingual Summaries

English

The First Tortilla

Jade is a girl who lives in a village. The village is below a huge volcano. The village does not have good harvests, because there is no rain. The Mountain Spirit is angry. That is why there is so little rain. Jade brings a gift to the Mountain Spirit. Maybe the gift will help the village!

The Mountain Spirit says he will send rain. He gives Jade a gift: corn. She brings the corn to the village. The people of the village learn how to grow corn. They also learn how to use corn to make a special bread. The bread is the first tortilla.

Spanish

La primera tortilla

Jade es una niña que vive en un pueblo. El pueblo está debajo de un enorme volcán. El pueblo no tiene buenas cosechas porque no llueve. El Espíritu de la Montaña está enojado. Por eso hay tan poca lluvia. Jade le lleva un regalo al Espíritu de la Montaña. ¡Quizá el regalo ayudará al pueblo!

El Espíritu de la Montaña dice que mandará lluvia. Le da a Jade un regalo: maíz. Ella lleva el maíz al pueblo. Las personas del pueblo aprenden a cosechar maíz. También aprenden a usar el maíz para hacer un pan especial. El pan es la primera tortilla.

Multilingual Summaries

Chinese

墨西哥薄饼的起源

杰德是一个乡村姑娘，她住的村在一个大火山的下面，因为雨水不足，村的每年收成都不好；雨水不足是因为山灵不高兴。一天，杰德把一份礼物带给山灵，她想这份礼物可能可以帮助她的村。

山灵说他会降雨，并给杰德一份礼物：玉米。杰德把礼物带回村里，村里的人都学会了种玉米，也学会了怎样用玉米做出一种很特别的面包，这就是墨西哥薄饼。

Vietnamese

Cái Bánh Mì Bột Bắp Đầu Tiên

Jade là cô gái ở trong một ngôi làng. Làng ở bên dưới một ngọn núi lửa khổng lồ. Làng không thu hoạch được nhiều, vì không có mưa. Thần Núi tức giận. Vì vậy mà ít mưa quá. Jade mang biếu Thần Núi một món quà. Có thể món quà sẽ giúp ích cho làng!

Thần Núi nói sẽ gởi mưa đến. Ông ta cho Jade một món quà: đó là bắp. Jade mang bắp về làng. Dân làng học cách trồng bắp. Họ cũng học cách dùng bắp để làm một thứ bánh mì đặc biệt. Bánh mì đó là cái bánh mì bột bắp đầu tiên.

Korean

첫번째 토티야

제이드는 어느 마을에 사는 소녀입니다. 그 마을은 큰 화산 아래 있습니다. 그 마을엔 비가 내리지 않기 때문에 좋은 수확을 하지 못합니다. 산신령님이 화가 났습니다. 그래서 비가 거의 오지 않는 것이지요. 제이드는 산신령님에게 선물을 가져왔습니다. 아마 선물이 마을을 구할 수 있을런지 모르죠!

산신령님은 비를 내려주겠다고 말했습니다. 산신령님은 제이드에게 옥수수를 선물로 주었습니다. 제이드는 옥수수를 마을로 가져왔습니다. 마을 사람들은 어떻게 옥수수를 재배하는지 배웠습니다. 또 옥수수로 특별한 빵을 만드는 것을 배웠습니다. 이 빵이 바로 첫번째 토티야랍니다.

Hmong

Thawj Daim Nplem Pliab

Jade yog ib tus ntxhais nyob hauv ib lub zos. Lub zos nyob hauv qab ib lub roob hluav taws. Lub zog qoob loo tuaj tsi zoo, rau qhov nws tsi muaj nag los. Tus Dab Roob npau tawg. Vim li ntawd thiaj tsi tshuam muaj nag los. Jade nqa ib pob khoomplig tuaj rau tus Dab Roob. Tej zaum qhov khoomplig no yuav pab lub zos!

Tus Dab Roob hais tias nws mam xa nag los. Nwg muab Jade ib qho khoomplig: pobkws. Nws coj lub pobkws rau tom zos. Cov tibneeg hauv lub zos xyaum cog pobkws. Lawv xyaum muab pobkws ua ib daim qhaub chij tshwjxeeb. Daim qhaub chij no yog thawj daim nplem pliab.

Name ______________________________ **How Is the Weather?**

- **Read** *How Is the Weather?* again.
- **Draw** a picture that shows your favorite weather. **Draw** yourself enjoying the weather.
- **Label** as many things in your picture as you can. Look at the book if you need help.

My Favorite Weather

Family Link

Have family members tell you about their favorite weather. Then have them describe their least favorite weather.

Weekly Resources Guide for English Language Learner Support

For this week's content and language objectives, see p. 149e.

Instructional Strand	Day 1	Day 2
Concept Development/Academic Language	TEACHER'S EDITION • Academic Language, p. DI•12 • Concept Development, p. DI•12 • Anchored Talk, pp. 190j—190–191 • *Sing with Me* Big Book, p. 191a ELL HANDBOOK • ELL Poster Talk, Concept Talk, p. 149c ELL POSTER 21 • Day 1 Activities	TEACHER'S EDITION • Academic Language, p. DI•12 • Concept Development, p. DI•12 • Anchored Talk, p. 196b • *Sing with Me* Big Book, p. 196a ELL HANDBOOK • ELL Poster Talk, Concept Talk, p. 149c • Concept Talk Video Routine, p. 464 ELL POSTER 21 • Day 2 Activities
Phonics and Spelling	TEACHER'S EDITION • Phonics and Spelling, p. DI•16 • Decodable Reader 21A, pp. 193c–193d	TEACHER'S EDITION • Phonics and Spelling, p. DI•16
Listening Comprehension	TEACHER'S EDITION • Modified Read Aloud, p. DI•15 • *Sing with Me* Big Book, p. 191a • Concept Talk Video ELL HANDBOOK • Concept Talk Video Routine, p. 464	TEACHER'S EDITION • Modified Read Aloud, p. DI•15 • *Sing with Me* Big Book, p. 196a • AudioText of *Fire Fighter!* • Concept Talk Video ELL HANDBOOK • AudioText CD Routine, p. 464 • Story Map B, p. 471
Reading Comprehension	TEACHER'S EDITION • Teach Fact and Opinion, p. DI•17	TEACHER'S EDITION • Teach Fact and Opinion, p. DI•17 • Frontloading Reading, p. DI•18 ELL HANDBOOK • Picture It! Skill Instruction, pp. 150–150a • Multilingual Summaries, pp. 151–153
Vocabulary **Basic and Lesson Vocabulary** **Vocabulary Skill: Suffix *-ly***	TEACHER'S EDITION • Basic Vocabulary, p. DI•13 • Preteach Lesson Vocabulary, p. DI•13 • Suffix *-ly*, p. DI•16 • Concept Talk Video ELL HANDBOOK • Word Cards, p. 149 • ELL Vocabulary Routine, p. 456 ELL POSTER 21 • Day 1 Activities	TEACHER'S EDITION • Basic Vocabulary, p. DI•13 • Reteach Lesson Vocabulary, p. DI•14 • Suffix *-ly*, p. DI•16 • Concept Talk Video ELL HANDBOOK • Word Cards, p. 149 • Multilingual Vocabulary List, pp. 429–440 ELL POSTER 21 • Day 2 Activities
Grammar and Conventions	TEACHER'S EDITION • Preteach Pronouns, p. DI•20	TEACHER'S EDITION • Reteach Pronouns, p. DI•20
Writing	TEACHER'S EDITION • Using Exact Words to Express Meaning, p. DI•21 • Introduce Narrative Nonfiction, pp. 195c–195d	TEACHER'S EDITION • Writing Craft: Sequence, pp. 211d–211e

This symbol indicates leveled instruction to address language proficiency levels.

Day 3	Day 4	Day 5
TEACHER'S EDITION • Academic Language, p. DI•12 • Concept Development, p. DI•12 • Anchored Talk, p. 212b • *Sing with Me* Big Book, p. 212a • Concept Talk Video ELL HANDBOOK • ELL Poster Talk, Concept Talk, p. 149c ELL POSTER 21 • Day 3 Activities	TEACHER'S EDITION • Academic Language, p. DI•12 • Concept Development, p. DI•12 • Anchored Talk, p. 216b • *Sing with Me* Big Book, p. 216a • Concept Talk Video ELL HANDBOOK • ELL Poster Talk, Concept Talk, p. 149c ELL POSTER 21 • Day 4 Activities	TEACHER'S EDITION • Academic Language, p. DI•12 • Concept Development, p. DI•12 • Concept Talk Video ELL HANDBOOK • ELL Poster Talk, Concept Talk, p. 149c ELL POSTER 21 • Day 5 Activities
ELL HANDBOOK • Phonics Transition Lesson, pp. 291, 294, 298, 301	TEACHER'S EDITION • Decodable Reader 21C, pp. 216e–216f ELL HANDBOOK • Phonics Transition Lesson, pp. 291, 294, 298, 301	TEACHER'S EDITION • Phonics and Spelling, p. DI•16
TEACHER'S EDITION • *Sing with Me* Big Book, p. 212a • AudioText of *Fire Fighter!* • Concept Talk Video ELL HANDBOOK • AudioText CD Routine, p. 464	TEACHER'S EDITION • *Sing with Me* Big Book, p. 216a • Concept Talk Video	TEACHER'S EDITION • Concept Talk Video
TEACHER'S EDITION • Sheltered Reading, p. DI•18 ELL HANDBOOK • Multilingual Summaries, pp. 151–153	TEACHER'S EDITION • ELL/ELD Reader Guided Reading, p. DI•19 ELL HANDBOOK • ELL Study Guide, p. 154	TEACHER'S EDITION • ELL/ELD Reader Guided Reading, p. DI•19 ELL HANDBOOK • High-Frequency Words Activity Bank, p. 491
ELL HANDBOOK • High-Frequency Words Activity Bank, p. 491 ELL POSTER 21 • Day 3 Activities	ELL HANDBOOK • High-Frequency Words Activity Bank, p. 491	TEACHER'S EDITION • Suffixes, pp. 220–221–221a ELL HANDBOOK • High-Frequency Words Activity Bank, p. 491
TEACHER'S EDITION • Grammar Jammer ELL HANDBOOK • Grammar Transition Lesson, pp. 378, 380 • Grammar Jammer Routine, p. 465	TEACHER'S EDITION • Grammar Jammer ELL HANDBOOK • Grammar Transition Lesson, pp. 378, 380	TEACHER'S EDITION • Grammar Jammer ELL HANDBOOK • Grammar Transition Lesson, pp. 378, 380
TEACHER'S EDITION • Let's Write It!, p. 214–215 • Writing Trait: Word Choice, p. 215a	TEACHER'S EDITION • Revising Strategy, pp. 219c–219d	TEACHER'S EDITION • Writer's Craft: Pronouns, pp. 221h–221i

Poster Talk, Concept Talk

Question of the Week

Why should we be responsible for doing a good job?

Poster 21

Throughout the week, use the ELL Poster to help children produce and comprehend language, understand the concept, and build English vocabulary. Use the Question of the Week and other questions to help children share ideas in pairs, small groups, or the large group. Sample questions are shown, with examples of possible responses by children.

Weekly Concept and Language Goals

- Know about being responsible in a job
- Tell how people can be responsible in their jobs

By the end of the lesson, children should be able to talk about and write one or more sentences about why it is important to do a good job.

Daily Team Talk

Day 1	Day 2	Day 3	Day 4	Day 5
After Day 1 activities on Poster, ask questions such as *In the poster picture, who is responsible for cleaning the floors?*	After Day 2 activity on Poster, ask questions such as *Why is it important that the painters do a good job painting the new community center?*	After Day 3 activity on Poster, ask questions such as *What job are you responsible for at home?*	After Day 4 activity on Poster, ask questions such as *In* Fire Fighter! *Liz checks the hoses to make sure they screw tightly to the truck. How is this being responsible?*	After Day 5 activity on Poster, ask questions such as *How can you be responsible in your job as a student?*
Beginning The boy. **Intermediate** The boy with the broom. **Advanced** The boy with the broom is cleaning the floors. **Advanced High** The boy with the broom and the girl with the dustpan are responsible for cleaning the floors.	**Beginning** So it looks nice. **Intermediate** Painting the community center will make it look good. **Advanced** People will want to come to a clean, neat community center. **Advanced High** A community center should be a place where people want to spend time. So it is important that the building look clean and fresh.	**Beginning** My room. **Intermediate** I clean my room. **Advanced** I keep my room clean at home. **Advanced High** I am responsible for making my bed and keeping my room clean.	**Beginning** Getting ready. **Intermediate** She is being safe. **Advanced** She wants to make sure the truck is ready for a fire. **Advanced High** Liz makes sure that the fire truck and hoses are ready the next time the fire alarm rings.	**Beginning** Listen. **Intermediate** I can listen to my teacher. **Advanced** I can listen carefully to what my teacher tells me. **Advanced High** I can pay attention when my teacher talks and do my homework.

This Week's Materials

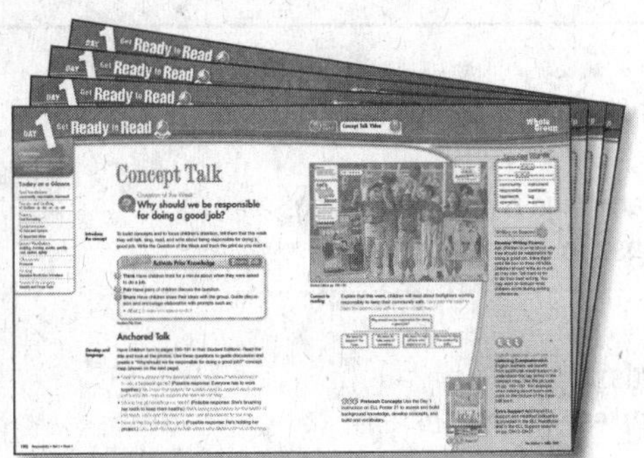
Teacher's Edition pages 190j–221k

See the support for English language learners throughout the lesson, including ELL strategies and scaffold activities at points of use.

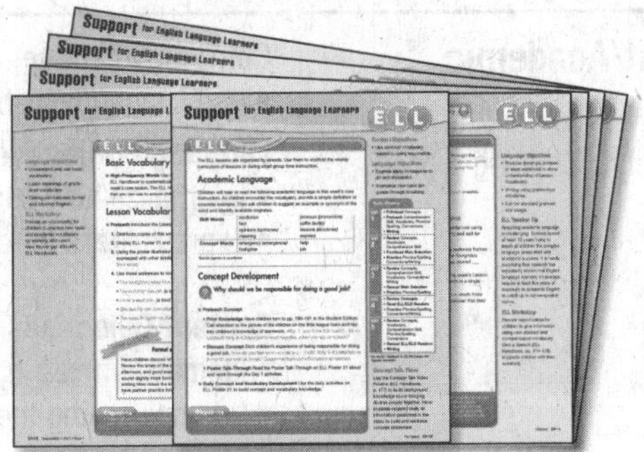
Teacher's Edition pages DI•12–DI•21

Differentiated Instruction for English language learners provides daily group activities that "frontload," or preteach, core instruction.

ELL Handbook pp. 149a–154

Find additional lesson materials that support the core lesson and the ELL instructional pages.

Poster 21

ELD Reader 2.5.1

ELL Reader 2.5.1

Concept Literacy Reader

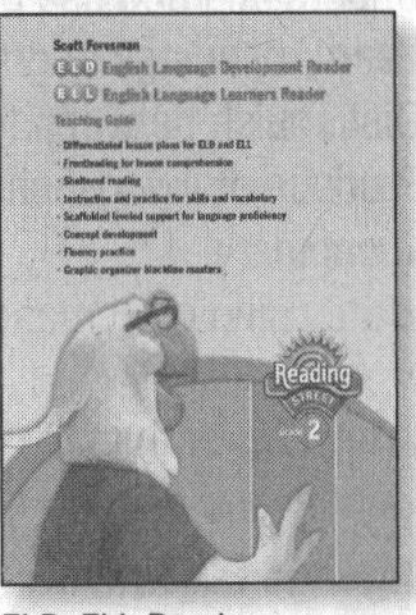
ELD, ELL Reader Teaching Guide

Concept Literacy Reader Teaching Guide

Technology

Online Teacher's Edition Use the digital version of the core teacher's edition for planning and instruction.

eReaders
This Week's ELL and ELD Readers and Concept Literacy Reader are also available in digital format.

This Week's Content and Language Objectives by Strand

Concept Development/Academic Language Why should we be responsible for doing a good job?	**Content Objective** • Use concept vocabulary related to being responsible. **Language Objectives** • Internalize new basic language through speaking. • Express ideas in response to art and discussion.
Phonics and Spelling Suffixes *–ly, -ful, -er, -or*	**Content Objectives** • Identify suffixes in words. • Practice saying the suffixes *–ly, -ful, -er, -or.* **Language Objective** • Apply phonics and decoding skills to vocabulary.
Listening Comprehension Modified Read Aloud: "Ahmed, the Helper"	**Content Objective** • Monitor and adjust oral comprehension. **Language Objectives** • Discuss oral passages. • Use a graphic organizer to take notes.
Reading Comprehension Fact and Opinion	**Content Objectives** • Distinguish between facts and opinions. • Identify facts and opinions to aid comprehension. • Monitor and adjust comprehension. **Language Objectives** • Discuss and retell evidence for facts and opinions. • Write facts and opinions from a text as you identify them. • Summarize using visual support.
Vocabulary Basic and Lesson Vocabulary	**Language Objectives** • Understand and use basic vocabulary. • Learn meanings of grade-level vocabulary. • Distinguish between formal and informal English. • Produce drawings, phrases, and short sentences to acquire grade-level vocabulary. • Write using grammatical structures.
Vocabulary Suffix *-ly*	**Content Objective** • Identify and define *–ly* words. **Language Objective** • Discuss how the suffix *–ly* changes the meaning of a word.
Grammar and Conventions Pronouns	**Content Objective** • Decode and use pronouns. **Language Objectives** • Speak and write phrases or sentences using pronouns. • Edit for pronoun agreement.
Writing Using Exact Words to Express Meaning	**Content Objective** • Identify words that express an author's meaning. **Language Objectives** • Write a paragraph using words that express meaning. • Share feedback for editing and revising.

building	**burning**
masks	**quickly**
roar	**station**
tightly	

Teacher Note: Beginning Teach two to three words. **Intermediate** Teach three to four words. **Advanced** Teach five to six words. **Advanced High** Teach all words.

Name ______________________________

Picture It!
Fact and Opinion

Look at the picture. **Read** the paragraph.

Fire Drill

Today we had a fire drill at school. The teacher explained our plan. Then, a loud bell rang. The bell sounded scary. We lined up at the door. We followed the teacher outside. Our teacher checked to make sure everyone was outside safely. We stood outside until it was time to go back in. When the bell rang, we went back inside. It was good to practice what to do if there is a real fire.

Write one fact and one opinion from the story.

Fact	**Opinion**

Fact and Opinion

Use this lesson to supplement or replace the skill lesson on page 194a of the Teacher's Edition. Display the Skill Points (at right) and share them with children.

Use the Skill Points to preteach fact and opinion.

Teach/Model

Beginning Act out smiling, putting on a helmet, and riding a bike. Say: *It is fun to ride a bike. I wear my helmet when I ride my bike.* Then ask: *Which sentence tells an opinion? Which sentence tells a fact?*

Intermediate Say: *I ride my bike every day after school. How do you know this sentence tells a fact?* (The action can be proven true.) *I think my bike is the best one. How do you know this sentence tells an opinion?* (It tells a belief.)

Advanced Show a picture of a child riding a bike and wearing a helmet. Tell one fact about the picture, such as *This bike is blue.* Ask children to tell other facts about the picture. Then ask volunteers to share their opinions about bikes.

Advanced High Make a two-column chart labeled *Facts* and *Opinions.* Ask each child to say a fact or an opinion about bicycle safety. Have the rest of the group decide whether the statement is a fact or opinion. Write it in the appropriate column. Ask children how they decided.

Then distribute copies of Picture It! page 150.

- Have children look at the picture. Help them describe what they see. If necessary, briefly discuss what a *fire drill* is.
- Read the paragraph aloud. Ask: *Can you find a fact in the paragraph?* Provide English words as needed to answer.
- Review the Skill Points with children.
- Have them look at the picture and paragraph to find facts and opinions.

Practice

Read aloud the directions on page 150. Reread or chorally read the story. Have children look at the picture and the story as they answer the questions.

Beginning Children can orally answer and write words in the chart. Provide help with writing and filling in a chart correctly.

Intermediate Children can first orally answer and then write their answers in the chart.

Advanced Children can write their answers in the chart and check them by quietly reading aloud their writing.

Advanced High Children can write their answers in the chart and check them by looking for clue words in the story and making any necessary corrections.

Answers for page 150: Possible facts: The teacher explained our plan. A loud bell rang. We followed the teacher outside. Our teacher checked to make sure everyone was outside safely. We stood outside until it was time to go back in. When the bell rang, we went back inside. Possible opinions: The bell sounded scary. It was good to practice what to do if there is a real fire.

Skill Points

- ✔ A **fact** can be proven true or false. You can check in a book, ask someone who knows, or see for yourself.
- ✔ An **opinion** tells someone's beliefs or feelings. Clue words such as *I think* and *best* show statements of opinion.
- ✔ If you are not sure if you are reading facts or opinions, go back and reread.

Multilingual Summaries

English

Fire Fighter!

Firefighters work in the fire station. The alarm rings! Liz, Dan, and Anthony slide down the pole. They put on fireproof clothes. They ride to the fire in a fire truck.

An old house is on fire. No one lives there now. But someone saw a boy playing there this morning. Liz hooks up the hose to a fire hydrant. She helps to spray the fire. Dan and Anthony search for the boy. They can't find him. They run out before the roof falls. Someone tells them that the boy is safe.

Later, the fire is out. Anthony sprays water on the coals. Liz winds up the hoses. They go back to the station. They are tired and hungry. They sit down to eat, but the alarm rings again!

Spanish

¡Bomberos!

Los bomberos trabajan en la estación. ¡Suena la alarma! Liz, Dan y Anthony bajan por el poste. Se visten con ropas a prueba de fuego. Van rumbo al incendio en el camión de bomberos.

Una casa vieja está ardiendo. Ahora nadie vive allí. Pero alguien vio a un niño jugando allí en la mañana. Liz enrosca la manguera a una boca de incendios. Ella ayuda a echarle agua al fuego. Dan y Anthony buscan al niño. No lo pueden encontrar. Salen corriendo antes de que el techo se derrumbe. Alguien les dice que el niño está a salvo.

Después, se apaga el incendio. Anthony riega con agua los maderos quemados. Liz enrolla las mangueras. Regresan a la estación. Están cansados y hambrientos. Se sientan a comer, pero ¡la alarma suena otra vez!

Multilingual Summaries

Chinese

勇敢的消防員！

消防員在消防站工作。警報響了！麗茲、丹和安東尼沿著消防滑竿滑下去，然後穿上防火衣，跳上消防車趕到失火的地方去。

原來是一棟舊房子著火了，幸好現在已沒有人住在裡面，但有人說今天早上看到一個男孩在那裡玩耍。麗茲把消防水管接到消防栓上，幫忙噴水滅火。丹和安東尼衝進失火的房子裡找小男孩，但是找不到。屋頂要塌下來了，他們才不得已趕緊離開。後來有人告訴他們，小男孩沒事。

不久之後，火滅了。安東尼在焦炭上灑水，麗茲把消防水管收好，然後返回消防站。他們又累又餓，正坐下來吃飯的時候，警報又響了！

Vietnamese

Lính Cứu Hỏa!

Các người lính cứu hỏa làm việc ở trạm cứu hỏa. Chuông báo động reo vang! Liz, Dan, và Anthony tuột xuống cây cột. Họ mặc quần áo chống cháy vào. Họ lên xe cứu hỏa để đi đến nơi có hỏa hoạn.

Một căn nhà cũ đang bốc cháy. Không có ai đang sống ở đó. Nhưng có người thấy một đứa bé trai chơi ở đó hồi sáng này. Liz gắn vòi nước chữa lửa vào ống nước. Cô giúp phun nước vào lửa. Dan và Anthony đi tìm đứa bé. Họ không tìm thấy nó. Họ chạy ra trước khi mái nhà đổ sập xuống. Có người nói là đứa bé được bình an.

Lát sau, lửa được dập tắt. Anthony phun nước vào các đống than. Liz cuộn các vòi nước lại. Họ trở về trạm. Họ đều mệt và đói. Họ ngồi xuống để ăn, nhưng chuông báo động lại reo vang lần nữa!

Multilingual Summaries

Korean

소방관

소방관들은 소방서에서 일한다. 경보음이 울리고 리즈와 댄 그리고 안소니가 기둥을 타고 내려가 방화복을 입는다. 이들은 소방차를 타고 화재 현장으로 달려간다.

오래된 집 한 채가 불에 타고 있다. 지금은 그 집에 아무도 살고 있지 않지만 오늘 아침 한 소년이 그 집에서 놀고 있는 것을 누군가가 보았다. 리즈가 소화전에 호스를 연결시켜 물 뿌리는 것을 돕는다. 댄과 앤소니는 그 소년을 찾아보지만 찾지 못하고 지붕이 무너지기 전에 밖으로 나온다. 누군가가 그 소년은 무사하다고 말해준다.

나중에 화재가 정리되자 앤소니는 타고 남은 재에 물을 뿌린다. 리즈가 호스를 감은 후 모두 소방서로 돌아간다. 지치고 배고픈 이들은 허기를 채우려고 앉았지만 다시 경보음이 울린다.

Hmong

Cov Neeg Tua Hluav Taws

Cov neeg tua hluav taws ua hauj lwm hauv lub tsev tua hluav taws. Lub tswb quaj. Liz, Dan, thiab Anthony nqis mus sab hauv qab siv ib tug pas. Lawv hnav cov khaub ncaws tiv tau hluav taws. Lawv caij lub tsheb tua hluav taws mus rau qhov chaw muaj hluav taws.

Ib lub tsev qub qub tau kub hnyiab. Tsis muaj leej twg nyob hauv. Tiam sis muaj ib tug neeg uas tau pom ib tug me nyuam tub ua siv nyob hauv tag kis ntawd. Liz tau muab txoj hlua dej mus tauj tus kais dej tua hluav taws. Nws pab tsuag dej mus rau cov hluav taws. Dan thiab Anthony nrhiav tus me nyuam tub. Nkawd nrhiav tsis tau nws. Nkawd tau tawm hauv lub tsev ua ntev lub tsev tau vau. Ib tug neeg tau hais tias tus me nyuam tub yeej nyob zoo.

Tom qab ntawd, cov hluav taws tau tuag. Anthony tau tsuag dej rau cov ncaig. Liz muab txoj hlua dej kauv. Lawv rov qab mus tom lub tsev tua hluav taws. Lawv tau nkees thiab tshaib plab. Lawv zaum noj mov, tiam sis lub tswb tau quaj dua.

Name ______________________________

- **Read** *At the Fire Station* again.
- **Draw** a picture that shows what the book is about.
- **Write** a sentence that goes with your picture.

____

____

Family Link

Ask family members to share what they know about firefighters and fire safety.

Weekly Resources Guide for English Language Learner Support

For this week's content and language objectives, see p. 155e.

Instructional Strand	Day 1	Day 2
Concept Development/Academic Language	TEACHER'S EDITION • Academic Language, p. DI•33 • Concept Development, p. DI•33 • Anchored Talk, pp. 222j—222–223 • *Sing with Me* Big Book, p. 223a • Concept Talk Video ELL HANDBOOK • ELL Poster Talk, Concept Talk, p. 155c ELL POSTER 22 • Day 1 Activities	TEACHER'S EDITION • Academic Language, p. DI•33 • Concept Development, p. DI•33 • Anchored Talk, p. 228b • *Sing with Me* Big Book, p. 228a • Concept Talk Video ELL HANDBOOK • ELL Poster Talk, Concept Talk, p. 155c • Concept Talk Video Routine, p. 464 ELL POSTER 22 • Day 2 Activities
Phonics and Spelling	TEACHER'S EDITION • Phonics and Spelling, p. DI•37 • Decodable Reader 22A, pp. 225c–225d	TEACHER'S EDITION • Phonics and Spelling, p. DI•37
Listening Comprehension	TEACHER'S EDITION • Modified Read Aloud, p. DI•36 • *Sing with Me* Big Book, p. 223a • Concept Talk Video ELL HANDBOOK • Concept Talk Video Routine, p. 464	TEACHER'S EDITION • Modified Read Aloud, p. DI•36 • *Sing with Me* Big Book, p. 228a • AudioText of *Carl the Complainer* • Concept Talk Video ELL HANDBOOK • AudioText CD Routine, p. 464 • Story Map A, p. 470
Reading Comprehension	TEACHER'S EDITION • Teach Cause and Effect, p. DI•38	TEACHER'S EDITION • Teach Cause and Effect, p. DI•38 • Frontloading Reading, p. DI•39 ELL HANDBOOK • Picture It! Skill Instruction, pp. 156–156a • Multilingual Summaries, pp. 157–159
Vocabulary **Basic and Lesson Vocabulary** **Vocabulary Skill: Dictionary Skill**	TEACHER'S EDITION • Basic Vocabulary, p. DI•34 • Preteach Lesson Vocabulary, p. DI•34 • Dictionary Skill, p. DI•37 ELL HANDBOOK • Word Cards, p. 155 • ELL Vocabulary Routine, p. 456 ELL POSTER 22 • Day 1 Activities	TEACHER'S EDITION • Basic Vocabulary, p. DI•34 • Reteach Lesson Vocabulary, p. DI•35 • Dictionary Skill, p. DI•37 ELL HANDBOOK • Word Cards, p. 155 • Multilingual Vocabulary List, pp. 429–440 ELL POSTER 22 • Day 2 Activities
Grammar and Convention	TEACHER'S EDITION • Preteach Singular and Plural Pronouns, p. DI•41	TEACHER'S EDITION • Reteach Singular and Plural Pronouns, p. DI•41
Writing	TEACHER'S EDITION • Sequence of Events and Time-Order Transition Words, p. DI•42 • Introduce Realistic Fiction, pp. 227c–227d	TEACHER'S EDITION • Writer's Craft: Sequence, pp. 247d–247e

Unit 5 Week 2 Carl the Complainer

This symbol indicates leveled instruction to address language proficiency levels.

Day 3	Day 4	Day 5
TEACHER'S EDITION • Academic Language, p. DI•33 • Concept Development, p. DI•33 • Anchored Talk, p. 248b • *Sing with Me* Big Book, p. 248a • Concept Talk Video ELL HANDBOOK • ELL Poster Talk, Concept Talk, p. 155c ELL POSTER 22 • Day 3 Activities	TEACHER'S EDITION • Academic Language, p. DI•33 • Concept Development, p. DI•33 • Anchored Talk, p. 252b • *Sing with Me* Big Book, p. 252a • Concept Talk Video ELL HANDBOOK • ELL Poster Talk, Concept Talk, p. 155c ELL POSTER 22 • Day 4 Activities	TEACHER'S EDITION • Academic Language, p. DI•33 • Concept Development, p. DI•33 • Concept Talk Video ELL HANDBOOK • ELL Poster Talk, Concept Talk, p. 155c ELL POSTER 22 • Day 5 Activities
ELL HANDBOOK • Phonics Transition Lesson, pp. 288–289, 295–296	TEACHER'S EDITION • Decodable Reader 22C, pp. 252e–252f ELL HANDBOOK • Phonics Transition Lesson, pp. 288–289, 295–296	TEACHER'S EDITION • Phonics and Spelling, p. DI•37
TEACHER'S EDITION • *Sing with Me* Big Book, p. 248a • AudioText of *Carl the Complainer* • Concept Talk Video ELL HANDBOOK • AudioText CD Routine, p. 464	TEACHER'S EDITION • *Sing with Me* Big Book, p. 252a • Concept Talk Video	TEACHER'S EDITION • Concept Talk Video
TEACHER'S EDITION • Sheltered Reading, p. DI•39 ELL HANDBOOK • Multilingual Summaries, pp. 157–159	TEACHER'S EDITION • ELL/ELD Reader Guided Reading, p. DI•40 ELL HANDBOOK • ELL Study Guide, p. 160	TEACHER'S EDITION • ELL/ELD Reader Guided Reading, p. DI•40 ELL HANDBOOK • ELL Study Guide, p. 160
ELL HANDBOOK • High-Frequency Words Activity Bank, p. 491 ELL POSTER 22 • Day 3 Activities	ELL HANDBOOK • High-Frequency Words Activity Bank, p. 491	TEACHER'S EDITION • Dictionary Skills, p. 254–255 ELL HANDBOOK • High-Frequency Words Activity Bank, p. 491
TEACHER'S EDITION • Grammar Jammer ELL HANDBOOK • Grammar Transition Lesson, pp. 378, 380 • Grammar Jammer Routine, p. 465	TEACHER'S EDITION • Grammar Jammer ELL HANDBOOK • Grammar Transition Lesson, pp. 378, 380	TEACHER'S EDITION • Grammar Jammer ELL HANDBOOK • Grammar Transition Lesson, pp. 378, 380
TEACHER'S EDITION • Let's Write It!, p. 250–251 • Writing Trait: Organization, p. 251a	TEACHER'S EDITION • Revising Strategy, pp. 253d–253e	TEACHER'S EDITION • Writer's Craft: Pronouns, pp. 255h–255i

Poster Talk, Concept Talk

Question of the Week

How can we be responsible community members?

Poster 22

Throughout the week, use the ELL Poster to help children produce and comprehend language, understand the concept, and build English vocabulary. Use the Question of the Week and other questions to help children share ideas in pairs, small groups, or the large group. Sample questions are shown, with examples of possible responses by children.

Weekly Concept and Language Goals

- Know how to be a responsible member of a community
- Tell about ways that people help each other
- Name things that can be done in the community

By the end of the lesson, children should be able to talk about and write one or more sentences about being responsible community members.

Daily Team Talk

Day 1	Day 2	Day 3	Day 4	Day 5
After Day 1 activities on Poster, ask questions such as *In the poster picture, there is litter on the ground. Does a responsible member of the community leave litter on the ground? Why or why not?*	After Day 2 activity on Poster, ask questions such as *What can people in the poster picture do to make their community better?*	After Day 3 activity on Poster, ask questions such as *Why is having a cookout with neighbors good for the community?*	After Day 4 activity on Poster, ask questions such as *Imagine you want to write a petition to change something in your school. What will your petition be about?*	After Day 5 activity on Poster, ask questions such as *What are some ways that you can help people in your community?*
Beginning No. **Intermediate** No. It looks bad. **Advanced** No, because litter is ugly and dirty. **Advanced High** A responsible person does not leave litter because litter makes the community ugly and dirty.	**Beginning** Stop noise. **Intermediate** They can help each other. **Advanced** They can work together to stop the construction noise. **Advanced High** The neighbors can pick up trash, sign the petition, and share their cookout.	**Beginning** Friends. **Intermediate** They will become friends. **Advanced** The neighbors will spend time together. **Advanced High** A cookout is a good way for neighbors to get to know each other.	**Beginning** Lunch. **Intermediate** How long we have for lunch. **Advanced** I want to make our time for lunch longer. **Advanced High** I will write a petition about more time for lunch.	**Beginning** Be friends. **Intermediate** I can be quiet. **Advanced** I can pick up trash when I see it. **Advanced High** I can ride my bike on the sidewalk and help my neighbors carry their groceries.

This Week's Materials

Teacher's Edition pages 222j–255k

See the support for English language learners throughout the lesson, including ELL strategies and scaffold activities at points of use.

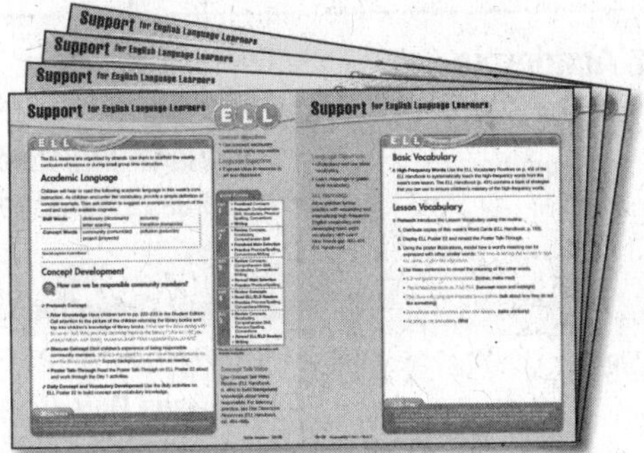
Teacher's Edition pages DI•33–DI•42

Differentiated Instruction for English language learners provides daily group activities that "frontload," or preteach, core instruction.

ELL Handbook pp. 155a–160

Find additional lesson materials that support the core lesson and the ELL instructional pages.

ELL Poster 22

ELD Reader 2.5.2

ELL Reader 2.5.2

Concept Literacy Reader

ELD, ELL Reader Teaching Guide

Concept Literacy Reader Teaching Guide

Technology

Online Teacher's Edition Use the digital version of the core teacher's edition for planning and instruction.

eReaders
This Week's ELL and ELD Readers and Concept Literacy Reader are also available in digital format.

This Week's Content and Language Objectives by Strand

Concept Development/Academic Language How can we be responsible community members?	**Content Objective** • Use concept vocabulary related to being responsible. **Language Objective** • Express ideas in response to art and discussion.
Phonics and Spelling Prefixes *un-*, *re-*, *pre-*, and *dis-*	**Content Objective** • Review prefixes *un-*, *re-*, *pre-*, and *dis-*. **Language Objective** • Apply phonics and decoding skills to vocabulary.
Listening Comprehension Modified Read Aloud: "Salmon in the River"	**Content Objective** • Monitor and adjust oral comprehension. **Language Objectives** • Discuss oral passages. • Use a graphic organizer to take notes.
Reading Comprehension Cause and Effect	**Content Objectives** • Identify causes and effects in reading. • Monitor and adjust comprehension. **Language Objectives** • Discuss causes and effects from the story. • Explain the cause of an effect in the story. • Summarize using visual support.
Vocabulary Basic and Lesson Vocabulary	**Language Objectives** • Understand and use basic vocabulary. • Learn meanings of grade-level vocabulary. • Distinguish between formal and informal English. • Produce drawings, phrases, and short sentences to acquire grade-level vocabulary.
Vocabulary Dictionary Skill	**Content Objective** • Use a dictionary to define multiple-meaning words. **Language Objective** • Discuss the dictionary entries of multiple-meaning words.
Grammar and Conventions Singular and Plural Pronouns	**Content Objective** • Correctly use singular and plural pronouns. **Language Objectives** • Speak using singular and plural pronouns. • Write sentences with singular and plural pronouns.
Writing Sequence of Events and Time-Order Transition Words	**Content Objectives** • Identify sequence of events. • Identify time-order transition words. **Language Objectives** • Write a paragraph using time-order words that indicate sequence of events. • Share feedback for editing and revising.

Word Cards for Vocabulary Activities

annoy	**complain**
mumbles	**P.M.**
shrugs	**signature**

Teacher Note: Beginning Teach two to three words. **Intermediate** Teach three to four words. **Advanced** Teach five to six words. **Advanced High** Teach all words.

Name ______________________________

Picture It!
Cause and Effect

Look at the pictures. **Read** the paragraph.

Recycling

Max and Linda saw a lot of paper in the trash can. They wanted to recycle it. They knew they could not do the project by themselves. They asked their friends for help. The class wrote a letter to the principal. They asked her about recycling. Everyone in the class signed the letter. The principal talked to Max and Linda. She was happy about their plan. The whole school started recycling paper!

Write a cause and an effect on the chart.

Cause		Effect
Max and Linda see a lot of paper in the trash can.	→	1. ______________________________
2. ______________________________	→	The principal says the whole school can recycle paper.

Cause and Effect

Use this lesson to supplement or replace the skill lesson on page 226a of the Teacher's Edition. Display the Skill Points (at right) and share them with children.

Use the Skill Points to preteach cause and effect.

Teach/Model

Beginning Crumple a sheet of paper, smooth it out, and show it to children. Say: *The paper is wrinkled. I crumpled the paper.* Help children identify the cause (you crumpled the paper) and the effect (the paper is wrinkled).

Intermediate Display the following and read aloud: *I drink all the water. The bottle is empty.* Guide children in labeling the cause (I drink all the water) and the effect (the bottle is empty) with the appropriate words.

Advanced Give an example of cause and effect: *Because the recycle bin is full, I take the bin to the recycling center.* Have children suggest other examples of *cause* and *effect.*

Advanced High Give an example of an event that is caused by something else: *Julia wants to recycle cans at home.* Have children suggest possible causes of this effect. (Julia learns about recycling in school. Julia has a new recycle bin. Julia wants to help the environment.)

Then distribute copies of Picture It! page 156.

- Have children look at the pictures. Help them tell what is happening in each one. If necessary, briefly discuss the verb *to recycle.*
- Read the paragraph aloud. Ask: *What happens in the story? Why does it happen?* Provide English words as needed to answer.
- Review the Skill Points with children.
- Have children look at the pictures and words to explain cause and effect in the story.

Practice

Read aloud the directions on page 156. Reread or chorally read the story. Have children look at the pictures and the story as they answer the questions.

Beginning Children can orally answer and write words on the lines in chart. Provide help as needed.

Intermediate Children can first orally answer and then write their answers on the lines in the chart.

Advanced Children can write their answers on the lines in the chart and check them by comparing their charts to the paragraph.

Advanced High Children can write their answers in the chart and check them by silently reviewing the story and making any necessary corrections.

Answers for page 156: 1. They ask their friends to help recycle the paper. 2. The class writes a letter to the principal asking for paper recycling.

Skill Points

- ✔ Look for what happens in a story. Think about why it happens.
- ✔ An **effect** is what happens. A **cause** is why it happens.
- ✔ Clue words such as *because, so,* and *since* help you figure out what happens and why.

Multilingual Summaries

English

Carl the Complainer

Carl complains a lot. His friends call him Carl the Complainer. Carl complains about the park. He wants it to stay open later.

Carl and Dale start a petition to keep the park open later. They tell their friends about the petition. They try to get people to sign the petition. No one will listen to them.

Carl and his friends go to the park. They get 108 signatures. Carl and his friends go to the town council meeting. Carl makes a speech. The council members vote. Carl's petition works. The park will stay open later.

Spanish

El quejoso Carl

Carl se queja mucho. Sus amigos lo llaman el quejoso Carl. Carl se queja por el parque. Él quiere que permanezca abierto hasta tarde.

Carl y Dale hacen una solicitud para que el parque se quede abierto hasta tarde. Les comentan a sus amigos sobre esta solicitud. Tratan de hacer que la gente firme la nota. Pero nadie los escucha.

Carl y sus amigos van al parque. Consiguen 108 firmas. Carl y sus amigos van hasta el consejo de la ciudad. Carl se dirige a las personas. Los miembros del consejo votan. La solicitud de Carl funcionó. El parque estará abierto hasta tarde.

Multilingual Summaries

Chinese

愛抱怨的卡爾

卡爾很愛抱怨。 他的朋友都叫他「愛抱怨的卡爾」。 卡爾抱怨公園。他希望公園的開放時間能夠更長一些。

卡爾和戴爾發起了延長公園開放時間的請願活動。 他們跟朋友們說有關請願活動的事。 他們試著去說服人們簽署請願書。 但沒有人理他們。

卡爾和他的朋友們來到了公園。 有 108 個人簽署了請願書。 卡爾和他的朋友們又來參加鎮公所代表會議， 卡爾在會議中發表了演說。 鎮公所代表投票表決。 卡爾的請願活動成功了。 公園的開放時間將會延長。

Vietnamese

Carl là Người Thích Phàn Nàn

Carl hay phàn nàn lắm. Các bạn gọi nó là Carl Phàn Nàn. Carl phàn nàn về công viên. Nó muốn công viên đóng cửa trễ.

Carl và Dale bắt đầu làm thỉnh nguyện thư để xin công viên đóng cửa trễ. Chúng nói cho các bạn nghe về thỉnh nguyện thư. Chúng cố gắng tìm người ký tên vào thỉnh nguyện thư. Không ai muốn nghe chúng.

Carl và các bạn của nó đến công viên. Chúng kiếm được 108 chữ ký. Carl và các bạn của nó đi đến buổi họp hội đồng thành phố. Carl đọc bài tường trình. Các ủy viên hội đồng bỏ phiếu. Thỉnh nguyện thư của Carl được chấp nhận. Công viên sẽ đóng cửa trễ.

Multilingual Summaries

Korean

투덜이 칼

칼은 자주 투덜거린다. 친구들은 그를 '투덜이 칼' 이라고 부른다. 칼은 공원에 대해 투덜거린다. 그는 공원이 더 늦게까지 열기를 바란다.

칼과 데일이 공원을 더 늦게까지 열어달라고 청원하기 시작한다. 그들은 친구들에게 청원에 대해 얘기한다. 또, 청원서에 서명할 사람들을 찾는다. 아무도 그들의 말에 귀 기울이지 않았다.

칼과 친구들이 공원에 간다. 그들은 108명의 서명을 받았다. 칼과 친구들은 지방 의회에 간다. 칼이 연설을 한다. 의원들이 투표를 한다. 칼의 청원이 받아들여진다. 공원은 더 늦게까지 열려있게 될 것이다.

Hmong

Carl Tus Neeg Ntau Ncauj

Carl mas ntau ncauj heev. Nws cov phooj ywg hu nws hu ua Carl tu neeg ntau ncauj. Carl ntau ncauj txog lub chaw ua si. Nws xav kom qhib kom lig lig.

Carl thiab Dale nkawd pib ib daim ntawv rau npe kom qhib lub chaw ua si kom lig lig. Nkawd qhia rau nkawd cov phooj ywg cov daim ntawv ntawd. Lawv nriav kom neeg pab sau npe rau daim ntawv ntawd. Tsis muaj neeg kam ntseeg lawv.

Carl thiab nws cov phooj ywg mus lawm tim chaw ua si. Lawv thov tau li 108 tus neeg sau npe. Carl thiab nws cov phooj ywg mus rau nram cov nom lub rooj sib tham. Carl hais lus. Cov nom hauv nroog pov npav xaiv. Carl daim ntawv sau npe us hauj lwm. Lub chaw ua si yuav qhib mus txog lig lig.

Name ______________________

- **Read** *Save the Ducks!* again.
- **Draw** pictures to show how the ducks are saved in the story. **Write** words or sentences to go with your pictures.

First (pages 2–3)

Second (pages 4–7)

Third (page 8)

Family Link

Ask family members to describe how they have helped or cared for an animal.

Weekly Resources Guide for English Language Learner Support

For this week's content and language objectives, see p. 161e.

Instructional Strand	Day 1	Day 2
Concept Development/Academic Language	TEACHER'S EDITION • Academic Language, p. DI•54 • Concept Development, p. DI•54 • Anchored Talk, pp. 256j—256–257 • *Sing with Me* Big Book, p. 257a • Concept Talk Video ELL HANDBOOK • ELL Poster Talk, Concept Talk, p. 161c ELL POSTER 23 • Day 1 Activities	TEACHER'S EDITION • Academic Language, p. DI•54 • Concept Development, p. DI•54 • Anchored Talk, p. 262b • *Sing with Me* Big Book, p. 262a • Concept Talk Video ELL HANDBOOK • ELL Poster Talk, Concept Talk, p. 161c • Concept Talk Video Routine, p. 464 ELL POSTER 23 • Day 2 Activities
Phonics and Spelling	TEACHER'S EDITION • Phonics and Spelling, p. DI•58 • Decodable Reader 23A, pp. 259c–259d	TEACHER'S EDITION • Phonics and Spelling, p. DI•58
Listening Comprehension	TEACHER'S EDITION • Modified Read Aloud, p. DI•57 • *Sing with Me* Big Book, p. 257a • Concept Talk Video ELL HANDBOOK • Concept Talk Video Routine, p. 464	TEACHER'S EDITION • Modified Read Aloud, p. DI•57 • *Sing with Me* Big Book, p. 262a • AudioText of *Bad Dog, Dodger!* • Concept Talk Video ELL HANDBOOK • AudioText CD Routine, p. 464 • Cause and Effect, p. 476
Reading Comprehension	TEACHER'S EDITION • Teach Plot and Theme, p. DI•59	TEACHER'S EDITION • Teach Plot and Theme, p. DI•59 • Frontloading Reading, p. DI•60 ELL HANDBOOK • Picture It! Skill Instruction, pp. 162–162a • Multilingual Summaries, pp. 163–165
Vocabulary **Basic and Lesson Vocabulary** **Vocabulary Skill: Classify and Categorize**	TEACHER'S EDITION • Basic Vocabulary, p. DI•55 • Preteach Lesson Vocabulary, p. DI•55 • Classify and Categorize, p. DI•58 ELL HANDBOOK • Word Cards, p. 161 • ELL Vocabulary Routine, p. 456 ELL POSTER 23 • Day 1 Activities	TEACHER'S EDITION • Basic Vocabulary, p. DI•55 • Reteach Lesson Vocabulary, p. DI•56 • Classify and Categorize, p. DI•58 ELL HANDBOOK • Word Cards, p. 161 • Multilingual Vocabulary List, pp. 429–440 ELL POSTER 23 • Day 2 Activities
Grammar and Conventions	TEACHER'S EDITION • Preteach Using *I* and *Me*, p. DI•62	TEACHER'S EDITION • Reteach Using *I* and *Me*, p. DI•62
Writing	TEACHER'S EDITION • Journal Entry, p. DI•63 • Introduce Journal Entry, pp. 261c–261d	TEACHER'S EDITION • Writer's Craft: Sequence, pp. 277d–277e

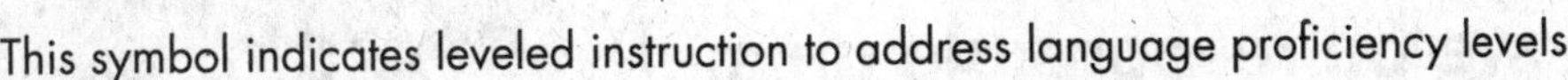

Unit 5 Week 3 Bad Dog, Dodger!

This symbol indicates leveled instruction to address language proficiency levels.

Day 3	Day 4	Day 5
TEACHER'S EDITION • Academic Language, p. DI•54 • Concept Development, p. DI•54 • Anchored Talk, p. 278b • *Sing with Me* Big Book, p. 278a • Concept Talk Video ELL HANDBOOK • ELL Poster Talk, Concept Talk, p. 161c ELL POSTER 23 • Day 3 Activities	TEACHER'S EDITION • Academic Language, p. DI•54 • Concept Development, p. DI•54 • Anchored Talk, p. 282b • *Sing with Me* Big Book, p. 282a • Concept Talk Video ELL HANDBOOK • ELL Poster Talk, Concept Talk, p. 161c ELL POSTER 23 • Day 4 Activities	TEACHER'S EDITION • Academic Language, p. DI•54 • Concept Development, p. DI•54 • Concept Talk Video ELL HANDBOOK • ELL Poster Talk, Concept Talk, p. 161c ELL POSTER 23 • Day 5 Activities
ELL HANDBOOK • Phonics Transition Lesson, p. 239, 245	TEACHER'S EDITION • Decodable Reader 23C, pp. 282e–282f ELL HANDBOOK • Phonics Transition Lesson, pp. 239, 245	TEACHER'S EDITION • Phonics and Spelling, p. DI•58
TEACHER'S EDITION • *Sing with Me* Big Book, p. 278a • AudioText of *Bad Dog, Dodger!* • Concept Talk Video ELL HANDBOOK • AudioText CD Routine, p. 464	TEACHER'S EDITION • *Sing with Me* Big Book, p. 282a • Concept Talk Video	TEACHER'S EDITION • Concept Talk Video
TEACHER'S EDITION • Sheltered Reading, p. DI•60 ELL HANDBOOK • Multilingual Summaries, pp. 163–165	TEACHER'S EDITION • ELL/ELD Reader Guided Reading, p. DI•61 ELL HANDBOOK • ELL Study Guide, p. 166	TEACHER'S EDITION • ELL/ELD Reader Guided Reading, p. DI•61 ELL HANDBOOK • ELL Study Guide, p. 166
ELL HANDBOOK • High-Frequency Words Activity Bank, p. 491 ELL POSTER 23 • Day 3 Activities	ELL HANDBOOK • High-Frequency Words Activity Bank, p. 491	TEACHER'S EDITION • Classify/Categorize, p. 286–287 ELL HANDBOOK • High-Frequency Words Activity Bank, p. 491
TEACHER'S EDITION • Grammar Jammer ELL HANDBOOK • Grammar Transition Lesson, pp. 378, 380 • Grammar Jammer Routine, p. 465	TEACHER'S EDITION • Grammar Jammer ELL HANDBOOK • Grammar Transition Lesson, pp. 378, 380	TEACHER'S EDITION • Grammar Jammer ELL HANDBOOK • Grammar Transition Lesson, pp. 378, 380
TEACHER'S EDITION • Let's Write It!, p. 280–281 • Writing Trait: Voice, p. 281a	TEACHER'S EDITION • Revising Strategy, pp. 285c–285d	TEACHER'S EDITION • Writer's Craft: Pronouns, pp. 287h–287i

Poster Talk, Concept Talk

Question of the Week

How can we be responsible animal owners?

ELL Poster 23

Throughout the week, use the ELL Poster to help children produce and comprehend language, understand the concept, and build English vocabulary. Use the Question of the Week and other questions to help children share ideas in pairs, small groups, or the large group. Sample questions are shown, with examples of possible responses by children.

Weekly Concept and Language Goals

- Know about being a responsible pet owner
- Tell about the needs of different pets
- Tell what people do to care for their pets

By the end of the lesson, children should be able to talk about and write one or more sentences about how to be a good pet owner.

Daily Team Talk

Day 1	Day 2	Day 3	Day 4	Day 5
After Day 1 activities on Poster, ask questions such as *In the poster picture, the boy is giving his dog a bath. Why is it important to keep pets clean?*	After Day 2 activity on Poster, ask questions such as *Why is the boy washing his dog outside instead of in the house?*	After Day 3 activity on Poster, ask questions such as *What does a pet bird need that cats and dogs do not need?*	After Day 4 activity on Poster, ask questions such as *What should pet owners do every day for their pets?*	After Day 5 activity on Poster, ask questions such as *Imagine you are taking a dog for a walk. What will you bring with you?*
Beginning Smell good. **Intermediate** So the pets smell good. **Advanced** It isn't healthy for pets to be dirty. **Advanced High** Keeping pets clean is important for their health.	**Beginning** It's better. **Intermediate** Water can get on the floor. **Advanced** The dog would get the floor wet and dirty. **Advanced High** Washing a big dog is too messy to do inside the house.	**Beginning** A cage. **Intermediate** It needs a cage and seeds. **Advanced** A pet bird needs a cage to live in. Cats and dogs do not. **Advanced High** A pet bird needs a cage with a perch and a cover.	**Beginning** Feed them. **Intermediate** Give them water and food. **Advanced** They have to make sure their pets have food and water. **Advanced High** Pet owners should feed their pets, give them water, and play with them.	**Beginning** A leash. **Intermediate** I will bring a leash. **Advanced** I will bring a leash and a bag with me on the walk. **Advanced High** I will put the dog on a leash and bring a bag to clean up after the dog.

This Week's Materials

Teacher's Edition pages 256j–287k

See the support for English language learners throughout the lesson, including ELL strategies and scaffold activities at points of use.

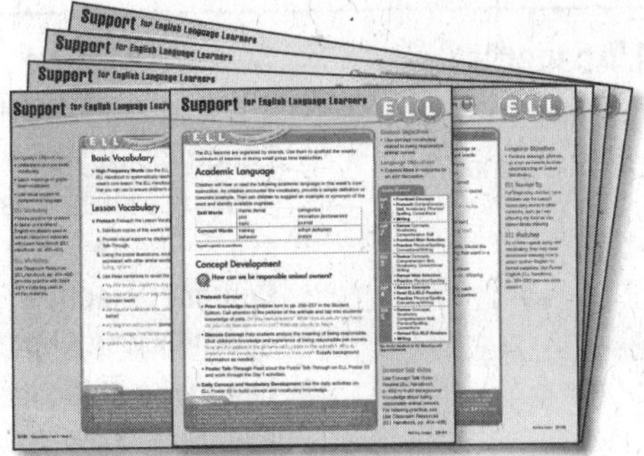

Teacher's Edition pages DI•54–DI•63

Differentiated Instruction for English language learners provides daily group activities that "frontload," or preteach, core instruction.

ELL Handbook pp. 161a–166

Find additional lesson materials that support the core lesson and the ELL instructional pages.

ELL Poster 23

ELD Reader 2.5.3

ELL Reader 2.5.3

Concept Literacy Reader

ELD, ELL Reader Teaching Guide

Concept Literacy Reader Teaching Guide

Technology

Online Teacher's Edition Use the digital version of the core teacher's edition for planning and instruction.

eReaders
This Week's ELL and ELD Readers and Concept Literacy Reader are also available in digital format.

This Week's Content and Language Objectives by Strand

Concept Development/Academic Language How can we be responsible animal owners?	**Content Objective** • Use concept vocabulary related to being responsible animal owners. **Language Objective** • Express ideas in response to art and discussion.
Phonics and Spelling Consonant Patterns *kn, wr, gn*	**Content Objective** • Identify words with consonant patterns *kn, wr,* and *gn*. **Language Objective** • Apply phonics and decoding skills to vocabulary.
Listening Comprehension Modified Read Aloud: "Manuel's New Puppy"	**Content Objective** • Monitor and adjust oral comprehension. **Language Objectives** • Discuss oral passages. • Use a graphic organizer to take notes.
Reading Comprehension Plot and Theme	**Content Objectives** • Identify the plot and theme of a story. • Monitor and adjust comprehension. **Language Objectives** • Discuss the plot and theme of a story. • Give examples to explain the plot and theme. • Summarize using visual support.
Vocabulary Basic and Lesson Vocabulary	**Language Objectives** • Understand and use basic vocabulary. • Learn meanings of grade-level vocabulary. • Use visual support to comprehend language. • Produce drawings, phrases, and short sentences to show understanding of Lesson Vocabulary.
Vocabulary Classify and Categorize	**Content Objective** • Classify and categorize information. **Language Objectives** • Discuss how to classify and categorize words. • Learn relationship between sounds and letters.
Grammar and Conventions Using *I* and *Me*	**Content Objective** • Use *I* and *me* correctly in sentences. **Language Objectives** • Speak in complete sentences. • Write sentences using *I* and *me* correctly.
Writing Writers Reveal What They Know About A Topic	**Content Objectives** • Identify sequence of events in a story. • Share information about a topic. • Monitor written language production. **Language Objectives** • Write paragraphs using words that indicate knowledge of a topic. • Share feedback for editing and revising.

Word Cards for Vocabulary Activities

chased	**chewing**
dripping	**grabbed**
practice	**treat**
wagged	

Teacher Note: Beginning Teach two to three words. **Intermediate** Teach three to four words. **Advanced** Teach five to six words. **Advanced High** Teach all words.

Name ________________________

Picture It!
Plot and Theme

Look at the pictures. **Read** the story.

Oh Brother!

Mom and Dad went out to dinner. Nana stayed with Jack and me. We tried to play a game, but Jack took the pieces.

Then Nana and I painted pictures. Jack painted his face!

Finally, Nana sent Jack to bed early. She and I ate ice cream. Jack loves ice cream. I know next time he will behave!

Answer the questions below.

1. Explain what happens at the beginning of the story.

____

____

2. What happens to Jack at the end of the story? Why does this happen?

____

____

3. Talk about what you think is the big idea of this story.

Plot and Theme

Use this lesson to supplement or replace the skill lesson on page 260a of the Teacher's Edition. Display the Skill Points (at right) and share them with children.

Use the Skill Points to preteach plot and theme.

Teach/Model

Beginning Tell a simple story that has an easily identifiable theme. Ask children to draw three pictures to show the beginning, middle, and end of the story's plot. Guide them in identifying the theme.

Intermediate Give each child a sheet of paper divided into three sections. Have children draw three pictures to show the plot, or beginning, middle, and end, of a story. Pair children to tell their stories. Ask: *What is the theme, or big idea, of your story?*

Advanced Begin a story about a mischievous cat. Ask children to share ideas for the plot. After the story is complete, have children draw pictures of what happens in the beginning, middle, and end. Then discuss the theme of the story with children.

Advanced High Give children a story theme, such as *When we work together, we get more done.* Have pairs of children create a story that shows the theme. Then have partners summarize the plot of their stories.

Then distribute copies of Picture It! page 162.

- Have children look at the pictures. Help them tell what happens in each one.
- Read the story aloud. Ask: *What does Jack do?* Provide English words as needed to answer.
- Review the Skill Points with children.
- Have children look at the pictures and sentences and think about the theme of the story.

Practice

Read aloud the directions on page 162. Reread or chorally read the story. Have children look at the pictures and the story as they answer the questions.

Beginning Children can orally answer and then write and say their answers. Provide help with writing and spelling.

Intermediate Children can first orally answer and then write and say their answers.

Advanced Children can write and say their answers and check them by quietly reading aloud their writing and comparing their ideas to a partner's.

Advanced High Children can write and say their answers and check them by silently rereading the story and making any necessary corrections.

Answers for page 162: 1. Nana baby-sits. She and the girl try to play a game. Jack takes the pieces. 2. Jack has to go to bed early. He did not get ice cream because he did not behave. 3. Sample answer: The big idea of this story is that if you do not behave, you may not get the things you want.

Skill Points

- ✔ The **plot** is what happens in the beginning, the middle, and the end of a story.
- ✔ The **theme** is the big idea of a story.
- ✔ Look at the title and the pictures. Ask yourself: *What do I think the story will be about? Do I know anything about this?*

Multilingual Summaries

English

Bad Dog, Dodger!

Sam gets a puppy for his birthday. He names the dog Dodger. Dodger does many bad things. Dodger knocks over the trash. Dodger jumps in the bathtub with Molly. Dodger chews Sam's baseball cap. Dodger pulls down the curtains.

Sam's mom puts Dodger outside. Dodger jumps over the fence. He follows Sam to school. Dodger makes a mess in the classroom. Dodger runs onto the field at Sam's baseball game. He grabs a bat and runs away with it.

Now, Sam gets up early. He trains Dodger. Sam teaches Dodger to fetch. Sam teaches Dodger how to stay. Sam brings Dodger to a baseball game. Dodger catches a foul ball. Dodger is a good dog.

Spanish

¡Dodger, perro malcriado!

A Sam le regalan un perrito el día de su cumpleaños. Le pone el nombre de Dodger. Dodger hace muchísimas picardías. Dodger voltea la basura. Dodger salta en la bañera con Molly. Dodger mastica la gorra de béisbol de Sam. Dodger arranca las cortinas.

La mamá de Sam saca a Dodger fuera de la casa. Dodger salta la cerca. Sigue a Sam a la escuela. Dodger hace daños en la clase. Dodger corre por el campo de juego cuando Sam juega béisbol. Agarra un bate y sale corriendo con él.

Ahora Sam se levanta temprano. Entrena a Dodger. Sam le enseña a buscar y traer cosas. Sam le enseña cómo quedarse quieto. Sam lleva a Dodger al juego de béisbol. Dodger agarra una pelota que se iba al *foul*. Dodger es un buen perro.

Multilingual Summaries

Chinese

壞狗狗，道奇！

山姆生日那天收到一隻小狗狗當生日禮物，山姆幫牠取了一個名字，叫道奇。道奇不乖，做了很多壞事：牠打翻垃圾桶，和莫利一起跳進澡盆裡，亂咬山姆的棒球帽，還把窗簾扯下來。

山姆的媽媽把道奇關在屋外，可是道奇卻跳過籬笆，跟著山姆到學校去，把教室弄得亂七八糟。道奇跑到山姆比賽棒球的運動場上，牠接到別人打出來的球，然後一溜煙地跑掉了。

終於，山姆決定要好好訓練道奇，他起了個大早，教道奇接東西，還教牠坐下。 山姆帶道奇一起去參加棒球比賽，比賽時道奇接到一個界外球。道奇真是好狗狗。

Vietnamese

Dodger, Chó Hư!

Sam được một chú chó con vào sinh nhật của mình. Nó đặt tên cho con chó là Dodger. Dodger làm nhiều điều hư xấu. Dodger làm ngả thùng rác. Dodger nhảy vào bồn tắm với Molly. Dodger cắn nón chơi bóng chày của Sam. Dodger kéo màn cửa xuống.

Mẹ của Sam đem Dodger ra ngoài. Dodger nhảy qua hàng rào. Nó theo Sam đi học. Dodger tiêu tiểu bừa bãi trong lớp học. Ở trận đấu bóng chày của Sam, Dodger chạy ra ngoài sân đấu. Nó gặm lấy cây gậy đánh bóng rồi bỏ chạy.

Bây giờ, Sam thức dậy sớm. Cậu quyết định phải huấn luyện Dodger. Sam dạy Dodger chạy đi lấy đồ. Sam dạy Dodger ngồi tại chỗ. Sam dẫn Dodger đến một trận đấu bóng chày. Dodger chụp được một quả bóng đánh trái luật. Dodger là một con chó ngoan.

Multilingual Summaries

Korean

도저는 나쁜 개!

샘은 생일 선물로 강아지 한 마리를 받아 도저라고 이름짓는다. 도저는 나쁜 일을 많이 저지른다. 쓰레기통을 뒤집어 놓고 몰리와 함께 목욕통으로 뛰어들며 샘의 야구 모자를 물어뜯고 또 커튼을 끌어내리도 한다.

샘의 어머니는 도저를 밖에 내보낸다. 도저는 울타리를 뛰어넘어 샘을 따라 학교에 가서 교실을 난장판으로 만들어버린다. 또한 샘의 야구 경기장으로 달려가 야구 방망이를 물고 도망친다.

이제 샘은 일찍 일어난다. 도저를 교육 좀 시켜야겠다고 결심한 것이다. 샘은 도저에게 물건을 가져오는 것과 가만히 있는 법을 가르친 후 도저를 데리고 야구장에 간다. 도저가 파울볼을 가지고 온다. 도저는 말을 잘 듣는다.

Hmong

Aub Phem, Dodger!

Thaum Sam hnub yug nws tau ib tug me nyuam aub. Nws hu tus aub hu ua Dodger. Dodger ua ntau yam phem. Dodger ncaws lub thoob khib nyiab vau. Dodger dhia mus rau hauv lub dab da dej nrog Molly. Dodger muab Sam lub kaus mom noj. Dodger rub tej ntaub thaiv qhov rais.

Sam niam cab Dodger mus nraum zoov. Dodger dhia mus saum daim laj kab. Nws raws Sam mus kawm ntawv. Dodger ua hoob kawm ntawv ntxhov tas. Dodger dhia mus nraum zoov mus nraum chav ua si. Nws cab tus pas ntaus npas thiab dhia khiav mus.

Nim no, Sam sawv ntxov ntxov. Nws txiav txim siab qhuab qhia Dodger. Sam qhia Dodger mus khawv khoom. Sam qhia Dodger nyob twb ywm. Sam coj Dodger mus saib lawv ntau npas. Dodger txhom tau lub npas uas lawv ntaus tawm qhov chaw ntau npas. Dodger yog ib tug aub zoo.

Name ______________________

- **Read** *Puppy Show* again.
- **Complete** the *What and Why* chart.

What and Why

What happened in the story?	Why did this happen?
1. Abby and Caleb plan to train their puppies. (pages 2–3)	**1.** ______________________
2. ______________________	**2.** because the puppies tried to run away (page 4)
3. The puppies wagged their tails. (page 7)	**3.** ______________________
4. ______________________	**4.** because the puppies heeled, sat, stayed, and came when they were called (page 8)

Family Link

Has anyone in your family ever trained a pet? Have family members describe what they did to train the pet.

Weekly Resources Guide for English Language Learner Support

For this week's content and language objectives, see p. 167e.

Instructional Strand	Day 1	Day 2
Concept Development/Academic Language	TEACHER'S EDITION • Academic Language, p. DI•75 • Concept Development, p. DI•75 • Anchored Talk, pp. 288j—288–289 • *Sing with Me* Big Book, p. 289a • Concept Talk Video ELL HANDBOOK • ELL Poster Talk, Concept Talk, p. 167c ELL POSTER 24 • Day 1 Activities	TEACHER'S EDITION • Academic Language, p. DI•75 • Concept Development, p. DI•75 • Anchored Talk, p. 294b • *Sing with Me* Big Book, p. 294a • Concept Talk Video ELL HANDBOOK • ELL Poster Talk, Concept Talk, p. 167c • Concept Talk Video Routine, p. 464 ELL POSTER 24 • Day 2 Activities
Phonics and Spelling	TEACHER'S EDITION • Phonics and Spelling, p. DI•79 • Decodable Reader 24A, pp. 291c–291d	TEACHER'S EDITION • Phonics and Spelling, p. DI•79
Listening Comprehension	TEACHER'S EDITION • Modified Read Aloud, p. DI•78 • *Sing with Me* Big Book, p. 289a • Concept Talk Video ELL HANDBOOK • Concept Talk Video Routine, p. 464	TEACHER'S EDITION • Modified Read Aloud, p. DI•78 • *Sing with Me* Big Book, p. 294a • AudioText of *Horace and Morris but mostly Dolores* • Concept Talk Video ELL HANDBOOK • AudioText CD Routine, p. 464 • Problem and Solution, p. 477
Reading Comprehension	TEACHER'S EDITION • Teach Character and Setting, p. DI•80	TEACHER'S EDITION • Teach Character and Setting, p. DI•80 • Frontloading Reading, p. DI•81 ELL HANDBOOK • Picture It! Skill Instruction, pp. 168–168a • Multilingual Summaries, pp. 169–171
Vocabulary **Basic and Lesson Vocabulary** **Vocabulary Skill: Compound Words**	TEACHER'S EDITION • Basic Vocabulary, p. DI•76 • Preteach Lesson Vocabulary, p. DI•76 • Compound Words, p. DI•79 ELL HANDBOOK • Word Cards, p. 167 • ELL Vocabulary Routine, p. 456 ELL POSTER 24 • Day 1 Activities	TEACHER'S EDITION • Basic Vocabulary, p. DI•76 • Reteach Lesson Vocabulary, p. DI•77 • Compound Words, p. DI•79 ELL HANDBOOK • Word Cards, p. 167 • Multilingual Vocabulary List, pp. 429–440 ELL POSTER 24 • Day 2 Activities
Grammar and Conventions	TEACHER'S EDITION • Preteach Different Kinds of Pronouns, p. DI•83	TEACHER'S EDITION • Reteach Different Kinds of Pronouns, p. DI•83
Writing	TEACHER'S EDITION • Pronouns and Quotation Marks, p. DI•84 • Introduce Animal Fantasy, pp. 293c–293d	TEACHER'S EDITION • Writer's Craft: Sequence, pp. 313d–313e

Unit 5 Week 4 Horace and Morris but mostly Dolores

This symbol indicates leveled instruction to address language proficiency levels.

Day 3	Day 4	Day 5
TEACHER'S EDITION • Academic Language, p. DI•75 • Concept Development, p. DI•75 • Anchored Talk, p. 314b • *Sing with Me* Big Book, p. 314a • Concept Talk Video ELL HANDBOOK • ELL Poster Talk, Concept Talk, p. 167c ELL POSTER 24 • Day 3 Activities	TEACHER'S EDITION • Academic Language, p. DI•75 • Concept Development, p. DI•75 • Anchored Talk, p. 318b • *Sing with Me* Big Book, p. 318a • Concept Talk Video ELL HANDBOOK • ELL Poster Talk, Concept Talk, p. 167c ELL POSTER 24 • Day 4 Activities	TEACHER'S EDITION • Academic Language, p. DI•75 • Concept Development, p. DI•75 • Concept Talk Video ELL HANDBOOK • ELL Poster Talk, Concept Talk, p. 167c ELL POSTER 24 • Day 5 Activities
ELL HANDBOOK • Phonics Transition Lesson, p. 238, 244	TEACHER'S EDITION • Decodable Reader 24C, pp. 318e–318f ELL HANDBOOK • Phonics Transition Lesson, p. 238, 244	TEACHER'S EDITION • Phonics and Spelling, p. DI•79
TEACHER'S EDITION • *Sing with Me* Big Book, p. 314a • AudioText of *Horace and Morris but mostly Dolores* • Concept Talk Video ELL HANDBOOK • AudioText CD Routine, p. 464	TEACHER'S EDITION • *Sing with Me* Big Book, p. 318a • Concept Talk Video	TEACHER'S EDITION • Concept Talk Video
TEACHER'S EDITION • Sheltered Reading, p. DI•81 ELL HANDBOOK • Multilingual Summaries, pp. 169–171	TEACHER'S EDITION • ELL/ELD Reader Guided Reading, p. DI•82 ELL HANDBOOK • ELL Study Guide, p. 172	TEACHER'S EDITION • ELL/ELD Reader Guided Reading, p. DI•82 ELL HANDBOOK • ELL Study Guide, p. 172
ELL HANDBOOK • High-Frequency Words Activity Bank, p. 491 ELL POSTER 24 • Day 3 Activities	ELL HANDBOOK • High-Frequency Words Activity Bank, p. 491	TEACHER'S EDITION • Compound Words, p. 322–323 ELL HANDBOOK • High-Frequency Words Activity Bank, p. 491
TEACHER'S EDITION • Grammar Jammer ELL HANDBOOK • Grammar Transition Lesson, pp. 378, 380 • Grammar Jammer Routine, p. 465	TEACHER'S EDITION • Grammar Jammer ELL HANDBOOK • Grammar Transition Lesson, pp. 378, 380	TEACHER'S EDITION • Grammar Jammer ELL HANDBOOK • Grammar Transition Lesson, pp. 378, 380
TEACHER'S EDITION • Let's Write It!, p. 316–317 • Writer's Craft: Dialogue, p. 317a	TEACHER'S EDITION • Revising Strategy, pp. 321c–321d	TEACHER'S EDITION • Writing Trait: Conventions, pp. 323h–323i

Question of the Week

How can we be responsible friends and neighbors?

ELL Poster 24

Throughout the week, use the ELL Poster to help children produce and comprehend language, understand the concept, and build English vocabulary. Use the Question of the Week and other questions to help children share ideas in pairs, small groups, or the large group. Sample questions are shown, with examples of possible responses by children.

Weekly Concept and Language Goals

- Know how to be a responsible friend and neighbor
- Name ways that people can help in their neighborhoods
- Name traits of a good neighbor

By the end of the lesson, children should be able to talk about and write one or more sentences about how to be responsible friends and neighbors.

Daily Team Talk

Day 1	Day 2	Day 3	Day 4	Day 5
After Day 1 activities on Poster, ask questions such as *In the poster picture, how are the people on the street being good neighbors?*	After Day 2 activity on Poster, ask questions such as *Look at the boys with the clubhouse. How can they be good neighbors to the girl standing behind them?*	After Day 3 activity on Poster, ask questions such as *Imagine you have a neighborhood clubhouse. What will you have in your clubhouse?*	After Day 4 activity on Poster, ask questions such as *How should you treat your neighbors?*	After Day 5 activity on Poster, ask questions such as *How can you help a neighbor who hurts her arm and can't carry heavy things?*
Beginning They wave. **Intermediate** They wave to each other. **Advanced** The man is helping by carrying a box. **Advanced High** The man carries a box up to his neighbor's door while the woman waves.	**Beginning** Say hi. **Intermediate** Let her in. **Advanced** They could invite her into the club. **Advanced High** The boys could invite the girl into their clubhouse.	**Beginning** Games. **Intermediate** I will have games. **Advanced** I will have different games to play. **Advanced High** I would keep board games and sports equipment in my clubhouse.	**Beginning** Be nice. **Intermediate** I should be kind. **Advanced** I should be polite and friendly. **Advanced High** It is important to act polite and friendly to my neighbors.	**Beginning** Carry her things. **Intermediate** I can carry bags. **Advanced** I can help her carry her groceries. **Advanced High** I can offer to carry her groceries and water her plants until her arm feels better.

This Week's Materials

Teacher's Edition pages 288j–323k

See the support for English language learners throughout the lesson, including ELL strategies and scaffold activities at points of use.

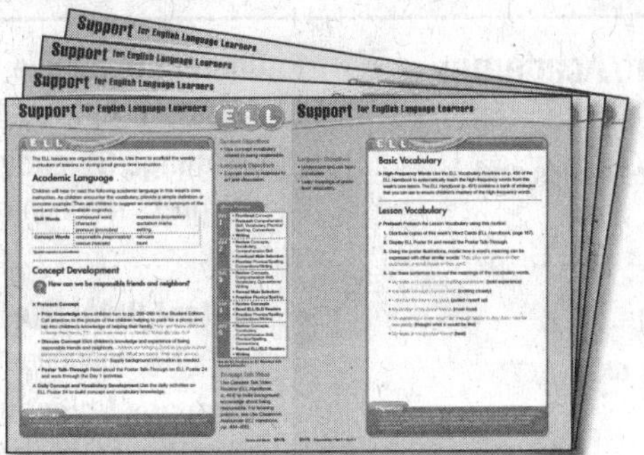

Teacher's Edition pages DI•75–DI•84

Differentiated Instruction for English language learners provides daily group activities that "frontload," or preteach, core instruction.

ELL Handbook pp. 167a–172

Find additional lesson materials that support the core lesson and the ELL instructional pages.

ELL Poster 24

ELD Reader 2.5.4

ELL Reader 2.5.4

Concept Literacy Reader

ELD, ELL Reader Teaching Guide

Concept Literacy Reader Teaching Guide

Technology

Online Teacher's Edition Use the digital version of the core teacher's edition for planning and instruction.

eReaders
This Week's ELL and ELD Readers and Concept Literacy Reader are also available in digital format.

This Week's Content and Language Objectives by Strand

Concept Development/Academic Language How can we be responsible friends and neighbors?	**Content Objective** • Use concept vocabulary related to being responsible. **Language Objective** • Express ideas in response to art and discussion.
Phonics and Spelling Consonant Patterns *ph, gh, ck*	**Content Objective** • Identify consonant patterns *ph, gh, ck.* **Language Objective** • Apply phonics and decoding skills to vocabulary.
Listening Comprehension Modified Read Aloud: "Friends to the Rescue"	**Content Objective** • Monitor and adjust oral comprehension. **Language Objectives** • Discuss oral passages. • Use a graphic organizer to take notes.
Reading Comprehension Plot and Theme	**Content Objectives** • Identify the characters of a story. • Tell the setting of a story. • Monitor and adjust comprehension. **Language Objectives** • Discuss the characters and setting from the story. • Give examples to identify the characters and setting. • Summarize using visual support.
Vocabulary Basic and Lesson Vocabulary	**Language Objectives** • Understand and use basic vocabulary. • Learn meanings of grade-level vocabulary. • Produce drawings, phrases, and short sentences to show understanding of Lesson Vocabulary.
Vocabulary Compound Words	**Content Objective** • Identify and define words in compound words. **Language Objective** • Discuss the meaning of compound words.
Grammar and Conventions Different Kinds of Pronouns	**Content Objective** • Use different kinds of pronouns correctly. **Language Objectives** • Speak with correct pronouns. • Write sentences using different kinds of pronouns correctly.
Writing Pronouns and Quotation Marks	**Content Objectives** • Identify and use pronouns correctly. • Use quotation marks correctly in writing. **Language Objectives** • Write paragraphs using pronouns and quotation marks. • Share feedback for editing and revising.

Word Cards for Vocabulary Activities

adventure	**climbed**
clubhouse	**exploring**
greatest	**truest**
wondered	

Teacher Note: Beginning Teach two to three words. **Intermediate** Teach three to four words. **Advanced** Teach five to six words. **Advanced High** Teach all words.

Name ______________________________

Picture It!
Character and Setting

Look at the pictures. **Read** the story.

Can I Go to the Zoo?

Marc's class went to the zoo, but Marc was in bed with a broken leg. He asked his mom if he could go to the zoo. His mom said, "No, Dr. White told you to stay in bed for two days." All day Marc thought about the fun his friends were having on the trip.

After school, Marc heard the doorbell ring. Marc heard voices, but he just rolled over on his bed. Suddenly, Mai and Devon walked in. "Surprise!" they yelled. They gave him pictures of the animals they had seen. It was like going to the zoo. Marc was happy to have such good friends.

Answer the questions below.

1. Who is this story mostly about?

____

2. How does Marc feel in the first paragraph?

a. sleepy **b.** sad **c.** excited

3. Where does the story take place?

a. the zoo **b.** the hospital **c.** Marc's house

Character and Setting

Use this lesson to supplement or replace the skill lesson on page 292a of the Teacher's Edition. Display the Skill Points (at right) and share them with children.

Use the Skill Points to preteach character and setting.

Teach/Model

Review the fable *The Lion and the Mouse.*

Beginning Say: *The lion is one character in the story. Who is the other character?* (the mouse) *What is the setting of the story?* (the jungle)

Intermediate Have children draw a picture of the two main characters in the setting of *The Lion and the Mouse.* Help them label the parts of their picture with the words *Character* and *Setting.*

Advanced Tell children the fable *The Tortoise and the Hare.* Ask them to identify the characters and setting of the story. Say: *We can tell more about characters. Which character thinks he is clever?* (the hare) *Which character is slow?* (tortoise)

Advanced High Ask children to identify the characters and setting of *The Tortoise and the Hare.* Say: *We can tell more about characters by what they do. What are some words that tell more about the tortoise and the hare?* Write children's suggestions on the board.

Then distribute copies of Picture It! page 168.

- Have children look at the pictures. Help them tell what happens in each one.
- Read the story aloud. Ask: *What character is the story about? What happens in the story?* Provide English words as needed to answer.
- Review the Skill Points with children.
- Have children give you examples from the picture that helped them determine the characters and setting of the story.

Practice

Read aloud the directions on page 168. Reread or chorally read the story. Have children look at the pictures and the story as they answer the questions.

Beginning Children can orally answer and write and mark their answers. Provide help with writing and marking if necessary.

Intermediate Children can first orally answer and then write and mark their answers on the page.

Advanced Children can write and mark their answers and check them by quietly reading aloud their writing and comparing their circles with a partner's.

Advanced High Children can write and mark their answers and check them by silently rereading their writing and checking their circles. Then they can make any necessary corrections.

Answers for page 168: 1. Marc; 2. b; 3. c

Skill Points

✔ A **character** is a person or animal in a story.

✔ Authors tell the reader what the characters look like and what they say and do.

✔ The **setting** is where and when a story takes place.

Multilingual Summaries

English

Horace and Morris but mostly Dolores

Dolores, Horace, and Morris are friends. They like to explore. Then Horace and Morris join a club. Girls cannot join this club. Horace and Morris won't play with Dolores. Dolores is sad. She joins a club for girls. She soon becomes bored.

The girls in the club don't like to explore. Dolores quits the club. Chloris quits too. They find Horace and Morris and Boris. They all like to explore. Horace, Morris, Dolores, Chloris, and Boris build their own clubhouse.

Spanish

Horacio y Morris pero sobre todo Dolores

Dolores, Horacio y Morris son amigos. Les gusta explorar. Horacio y Morris se hacen miembros de un club. Las niñas no pueden pertenecer al club. Horacio y Morris no jugarán con Dolores. Dolores está triste. Ella se afilia al club de las niñas. Se aburre enseguida.

A las niñas del club no les gusta explorar. Dolores deja el club. Chloris también lo deja. Después se encuentran con Horacio, Morris y Boris. A todos les gusta explorar. Horacio, Morris, Dolores, Chloris y Boris forman su propio club.

Multilingual Summaries

Chinese

多洛蕾斯是大功臣

多洛蕾斯、哈瑞斯和莫利斯是朋友，他們都喜歡探險。哈瑞斯和莫利斯參加了一個社團，因為女生不能參加這個社團，所以哈瑞斯和莫利斯以後就不跟多洛蕾斯玩了。多洛蕾斯好難過。她去參加一個女生的社團，可是過沒多久，就開始覺得無聊。

社團裡的女生不喜歡探險，所以多洛蕾斯就不去那個社團了，有一隻叫做克蘿莉斯的老鼠也不去了，她們找到哈瑞斯、莫利斯和伯里斯。因為大家都喜歡探險，所以哈瑞斯、莫利斯、多洛蕾斯、克蘿莉斯和伯里斯就合力建了一個專屬他們的社團小屋。

Vietnamese

Horace và Morris nhưng phần nhiều là Dolores

Dolores, Horace, và Morris là bạn. Chúng thích thám hiểm. Rồi Horace và Morris gia nhập một câu lạc bộ. Con gái không được vào câu lạc bộ này. Horace và Morris không chơi với Dolores. Dolores buồn. Cô bé gia nhập một câu lạc bộ dành cho con gái. Chẳng bao lâu cô bé thấy chán.

Các cô gái trong câu lạc bộ không thích thám hiểm. Dolores bỏ câu lạc bộ. Chloris cũng bỏ nữa. Họ đi tìm Horace, Morris, và Boris. Ai trong chúng nó cũng thích thám hiểm. Horace, Morris, Dolores, Chloris, và Boris lập ra một câu lạc bộ riêng.

Multilingual Summaries

Korean

호레이스와 모리스 그리고 돌로레스

돌로레스와 호레이스, 그리고 모리스는 친구 사이로 모두 탐험을 좋아한다. 호레이스와 모리스가 한 클럽에 가입하는데 여자들은 이 클럽에 가입할 수 없어 돌로레스와는 어울리지 않는다. 돌로레스는 슬퍼하며 여자애들만을 위한 클럽에 가입을 하지만 곧 싫증이 난다.

클럽의 여자애들이 탐험을 싫어하기에 돌로레스는 클럽을 그만 두었고 클로리스라는 이름의 한 귀여운 여자 아이도 클럽을 그만둔다. 그들은 호레이스와 모리스 그리고 보리스를 찾는다. 모두들 탐험을 좋아한다. 호레이스, 모리스, 돌로레스, 클로리스, 그리고 보리스는 그들만의 클럽 회관을 만든다.

Hmong

Horace thiab Morris Tiam sis Feem Ntau Yog Dolores

Dolores, Horace, and Morris yog phooj ywg. Lawv nyiam mus saib xyuas ntau yam kawm. Ces Horace thiab Morris koom nrog ib lub koom haum. Cov me nyuam ntxhais koom nrog lub koom haum no tsis tau. Horace thiab Morris tsis kam ua si nrog Dolores. Dolores tu siab. Nws koom nrog ib lub koom haum rau cov me nyuam ntxhais. Tsis ntev nws laj laj koom nrog lub koom haum no.

Cov me nyuam ntxhais tsis nyiam mus saib xyuas ntau yam kawm. Dolores tau tso lub koom haum no tseg. Ib tug nas hu ua Chloris kuj tau tso lub koom haum no tseg thiab. Nkawd nrhiav tau Horace thiab Morris thiab Boris. Lawv sawv daws nyiam mus siab xyuas ntau yam kawm. Horace, Morris, Dolores, Chloris, and Boris tau tsim tsa ib lub koom haum rau lawv tus kheej.

Name ______________________________

- **Read** *Hello, Friend!* again.
- In Box 1, **draw** a picture that shows one way to make a new friend. **Write** a sentence that goes with your picture.
- In Box 2, **draw** a picture that shows one way to be a good friend. **Write** a sentence that goes with your picture.

1.

2.

______________________________ ______________________________

______________________________ ______________________________

______________________________ ______________________________

Family Link

Have family members tell you how they are good friends to other people.

Weekly Resources Guide for English Language Learner Support

For this week's content and language objectives, see p. 173e.

Instructional Strand	Day 1	Day 2
Concept Development/Academic Language	TEACHER'S EDITION • Academic Language, p. DI•96 • Concept Development, p. DI•96 • Anchored Talk, pp. 324j—324–325 • *Sing with Me* Big Book, p. 325a • Concept Talk Video ELL HANDBOOK • ELL Poster Talk, Concept Talk, p. 173c ELL POSTER 25 • Day 1 Activities	TEACHER'S EDITION • Academic Language, p. DI•96 • Concept Development, p. DI•96 • Anchored Talk, p. 330b • *Sing with Me* Big Book, p. 330a • Concept Talk Video ELL HANDBOOK • ELL Poster Talk, Concept Talk, p. 173c • Concept Talk Video Routine, p. 464 ELL POSTER 25 • Day 2 Activities
Phonics and Spelling	TEACHER'S EDITION • Phonics and Spelling, p. DI•100 • Decodable Reader 25A, pp. 327c–327d	TEACHER'S EDITION • Phonics and Spelling, p. DI•100
Listening Comprehension	TEACHER'S EDITION • Modified Read Aloud, p. DI•99 • *Sing with Me* Big Book, p. 325a • Concept Talk Video ELL HANDBOOK • Concept Talk Video Routine, p. 464	TEACHER'S EDITION • Modified Read Aloud, p. DI•99 • *Sing with Me* Big Book, p. 330a • AudioText of *The Signmaker's Assistant* • Concept Talk Video ELL HANDBOOK • AudioText CD Routine, p. 464 • Story Map A, p. 470
Reading Comprehension	TEACHER'S EDITION • Teach Main Idea, p. DI•101	TEACHER'S EDITION • Teach Main Idea, p. DI•101 • Frontloading Reading, p. DI•102 ELL HANDBOOK • Picture It! Skill Instruction, pp. 174–174a • Multilingual Summaries, pp. 175–177
Vocabulary **Basic and Lesson Vocabulary** **Vocabulary Skill: Suffixes**	TEACHER'S EDITION • Basic Vocabulary, p. DI•97 • Preteach Lesson Vocabulary, p. DI•97 • Suffixes, p. DI•100 ELL HANDBOOK • Word Cards, p. 173 • ELL Vocabulary Routine, p. 456 ELL POSTER 25 • Day 1 Activities	TEACHER'S EDITION • Basic Vocabulary, p. DI•97 • Reteach Lesson Vocabulary, p. DI•98 • Suffixes, p. DI•100 ELL HANDBOOK • Word Cards, p. 173 • Multilingual Vocabulary List, pp. 429–440 ELL POSTER 25 • Day 2 Activities
Grammar and Conventions	TEACHER'S EDITION • Preteach Contractions, p. DI•104	TEACHER'S EDITION • Reteach Contractions, p. DI•104
Writing	TEACHER'S EDITION • Writing Sentences, p. DI•105 • Introduce Humorous Fiction, pp. 329c–329d	TEACHER'S EDITION • Humorous Fiction, pp. 347c–347d

Unit 5 Week 5 The Signmaker's Assistant

This symbol indicates leveled instruction to address language proficiency levels.

Day 3	Day 4	Day 5
TEACHER'S EDITION • Academic Language, p. DI•96 • Concept Development, p. DI•96 • Anchored Talk, p. 348b • *Sing with Me* Big Book, p. 348a • Concept Talk Video ELL HANDBOOK • ELL Poster Talk, Concept Talk, p. 173c ELL POSTER 25 • Day 3 Activities	TEACHER'S EDITION • Academic Language, p. DI•96 • Concept Development, p. DI•96 • Anchored Talk, p. 352b • *Sing with Me* Big Book, p. 352a • Concept Talk Video ELL HANDBOOK • ELL Poster Talk, Concept Talk, p. 173c ELL POSTER 25 • Day 4 Activities	TEACHER'S EDITION • Academic Language, p. DI•96 • Concept Development, p. DI•96 • Concept Talk Video ELL HANDBOOK • ELL Poster Talk, Concept Talk, p. 173c ELL POSTER 25 • Day 5 Activities
ELL HANDBOOK • Phonics Transition Lesson, pp. 262, 264	TEACHER'S EDITION • Decodable Reader 25C, pp. 352e–352f ELL HANDBOOK • Phonics Transition Lesson, pp. 262, 264	TEACHER'S EDITION • Phonics and Spelling, p. DI•100
TEACHER'S EDITION • *Sing with Me* Big Book, p. 348a • AudioText of *The Signmaker's Assistant* • Concept Talk Video ELL HANDBOOK • AudioText CD Routine, p. 464	TEACHER'S EDITION • *Sing with Me* Big Book, p. 352a • Concept Talk Video	TEACHER'S EDITION • Concept Talk Video
TEACHER'S EDITION • Sheltered Reading, p. DI•102 ELL HANDBOOK • Multilingual Summaries, pp. 175–177	TEACHER'S EDITION • ELL/ELD Reader Guided Reading, p. DI•103 ELL HANDBOOK • ELL Study Guide, p. 178	TEACHER'S EDITION • ELL/ELD Reader Guided Reading, p. DI•103 ELL HANDBOOK • ELL Study Guide, p. 178
ELL HANDBOOK • High-Frequency Words Activity Bank, p. 491 ELL POSTER 25 • Day 3 Activities	ELL HANDBOOK • High-Frequency Words Activity Bank, p. 491	TEACHER'S EDITION • Suffixes, p. 356–357 ELL HANDBOOK • High-Frequency Words Activity Bank, p. 491
TEACHER'S EDITION • Grammar Jammer ELL HANDBOOK • Grammar Transition Lesson, pp. 283, 286 • Grammar Jammer Routine, p. 465	TEACHER'S EDITION • Grammar Jammer ELL HANDBOOK • Grammar Transition Lesson, pp. 283, 286	TEACHER'S EDITION • Grammar Jammer ELL HANDBOOK • Grammar Transition Lesson, pp. 283, 286
TEACHER'S EDITION • Let's Write It!, p. 350–351 • Writing Trait: Sentences, p. 351a	TEACHER'S EDITION • Writer's Craft: Sentence Length and Sentence Beginnings, pp. 355c–355d	TEACHER'S EDITION • Revising Strategy, pp. 357h–357i

Poster Talk, Concept Talk

Question of the Week

How can we be responsible when we make a mistake?

ELL Poster 25

Throughout the week, use the ELL Poster to help children produce and comprehend language, understand the concept, and build English vocabulary. Use the Question of the Week and other questions to help children share ideas in pairs, small groups, or the large group. Sample questions are shown, with examples of possible responses by children.

Weekly Concept and Language Goals

- Know the concept of "taking responsibility"
- Name ways to fix mistakes when they are made
- Tell what to do when we cannot fix a mistake

By the end of the lesson, children should be able to talk about and write one or more sentences about things we should do when we make a mistake.

Daily Team Talk

Day 1	Day 2	Day 3	Day 4	Day 5
After Day 1 activities on Poster, ask questions such as *How do you think the girls in the poster picture feel about their mistake?*	After Day 2 activity on Poster, ask questions such as *How are the girls taking responsibility for their mistake?*	After Day 3 activity on Poster, ask questions such as *Imagine you accidentally break a window at school. What should you do?*	After Day 4 activity on Poster, ask questions such as *What would you do if you forgot to do your chores?*	After Day 5 activity on Poster, ask questions such as *What is the first thing you should do when you make a mistake?*
Beginning Bad. **Intermediate** They feel very bad. **Advanced** The girls wish they hadn't drawn on the sign. **Advanced High** The girls are upset that they made a mistake.	**Beginning** Cleaning. **Intermediate** They are cleaning the sign. **Advanced** The girls are washing off their drawings. **Advanced High** The girls are washing the sign with soap and water to remove their drawings.	**Beginning** Say sorry. **Intermediate** Tell an adult. **Advanced** I should tell an adult about the broken window. **Advanced High** I should explain to a teacher what I did and apologize for my mistake.	**Beginning** Do them now. **Intermediate** Start doing them right away. **Advanced** I would do my chores as soon as I could. **Advanced High** I would apologize and do the chores as soon as I remembered.	**Beginning** Say I'm sorry. **Intermediate** Tell someone that I am sorry. **Advanced** I should apologize for what I did wrong. **Advanced High** I should apologize for my mistake and offer to fix it if I can.

This Week's Materials

Teacher's Edition pages 324j–357k

See the support for English language learners throughout the lesson, including ELL strategies and scaffold activities at points of use.

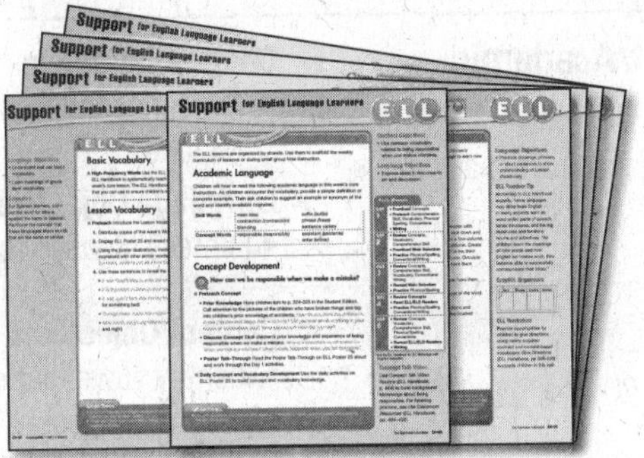

Teacher's Edition pages DI•96–DI•105

Differentiated Instruction for English language learners provides daily group activities that "frontload," or preteach, core instruction.

ELL Handbook pp. 173a–178

Find additional lesson materials that support the core lesson and the ELL instructional pages.

ELL Poster 25

ELD Reader 2.5.5

ELL Reader 2.5.5

Concept Literacy Reader

ELD, ELL Reader Teaching Guide

Concept Literacy Reader Teaching Guide

Technology

Online Teacher's Edition Use the digital version of the core teacher's edition for planning and instruction.

eReaders
This Week's ELL and ELD Readers and Concept Literacy Reader are also available in digital format.

This Week's Content and Language Objectives by Strand

Concept Development/Academic Language How can we be responsible when we make a mistake?	**Content Objective** • Use concept vocabulary related to being responsible when one makes mistakes. **Language Objective** • Express ideas in response to art and discussion.
Phonics and Spelling Vowel Patterns *aw, au,* and *al*	**Content Objectives** • Identify vowel patterns *aw, au,* and *al.* • Review consonant patterns *ph, gh, ck,* and *ng.* **Language Objective** • Apply phonics and decoding skills to vocabulary.
Listening Comprehension Modified Read Aloud: "Hat Dance"	**Content Objective** • Monitor and adjust oral comprehension. **Language Objectives** • Discuss oral passages. • Use a graphic organizer to take notes.
Reading Comprehension Main Idea	**Content Objectives** • Distinguish between main ideas and details. • Identify the main idea of a story. • Monitor and adjust comprehension. **Language Objectives** • Discuss the main idea of a story. • Understand the main points of spoken language. • Write the main idea of an original story. • Summarize using visual support.
Vocabulary Basic and Lesson Vocabulary	**Language Objectives** • Understand and use basic vocabulary. • Learn meanings of grade-level vocabulary. • Produce drawings, phrases, and short sentences to show understanding of Lesson Vocabulary.
Vocabulary Suffixes	**Content Objective** • Identify and define suffixes. **Language Objective** • Discuss the meaning suffixes.
Grammar and Conventions Contractions	**Content Objective** • Decode, correctly form, and use contractions. **Language Objectives** • Write sentences with contractions. • Distinguish if contractions are formal or informal.
Writing Sentences	**Content Objectives** • Identify variety in sentence beginnings. • Identify when to combine sentences. **Language Objectives** • Write paragraphs, using variety in sentences. • Share feedback for editing and revising.

Word Cards for Vocabulary Activities

afternoon	**blame**
ideas	**important**
signmaker	**townspeople**

Teacher Note: Beginning Teach two to three words. **Intermediate** Teach three to four words. **Advanced** Teach five to six words. **Advanced High** Teach all words.

Name ______________________________

Look at the pictures. **Read** the paragraphs.

Puppy Problems

Puppies are cute. They can also cause problems. They like to chew on things. They may chew shoes, tables, or your homework. You cannot always watch puppies, though.

You can train your puppy to stop chewing. When you see it chew something it should not chew, tell the puppy, "NO chew." Take the object away. Then, give your puppy a chew toy. Tell the puppy, "Good chew." Pet your puppy. Your puppy will learn that it should chew only on its toys.

Answer the questions below.

1. What is the first paragraph mostly about?
 a. Puppies eat your homework.
 b. Puppies are awake at night.
 c. Puppies chew on things.

2. What is the second paragraph mostly about?

____

____

Main Idea and Details

Use this lesson to supplement or replace the skill lesson on page 328a of the Teacher's Edition. Display the Skill Points (at right) and share them with children.

Use the Skill Points to preteach main idea and details.

Teach/Model

Beginning Show children a photo from a nonfiction book about pets. Ask: *What is the main idea of the photo? What are details in the photo?*

Intermediate Display the following and read aloud: *A dog can be a child's best friend. A child can play catch with a dog. A child can walk a dog.* Guide children in identifying the main idea and the details that tell more about the main idea.

Advanced Give an example of a main idea and details: *A parakeet can be a good pet. It does not need much room. A parakeet needs a cage, water, and seeds.* Have children suggest other examples of main ideas and details about pets.

Advanced High Read information about puppies in a children's encyclopedia. Focus on one aspect such as growth or food. Ask children to identify the main idea and the details that support the main idea.

Then distribute copies of Picture It! page 174.

- Have children look at the pictures. Help them tell what happens in each one. If necessary, briefly discuss the verb *to train.*
- Read the story aloud. Ask: *What is the story mostly about?* Provide English words as needed to answer.
- Review the Skill Points with children.
- Have children tell you which sentence contains the main idea. Ask them to find details that tell more about it.

Skill Points

✔ The **main idea** is the most important idea in a selection. You can often find the main idea near the beginning of a selection. Look for the sentence that answers the question: *What is this paragraph mostly about?*

✔ **Details** tell more about the main idea.

Practice

Read aloud the directions on page 174. Reread or chorally read the story. Have children look at the pictures and the paragraphs as they answer the questions.

Beginning Children can orally answer and mark and write their answers. Provide help with writing and spelling.

Intermediate Children can first orally answer and then mark and write their answers on the page.

Advanced Children can mark and write their answers and check them by comparing their circle to a partner's and quietly reading aloud their writing.

Advanced High Children can mark and write their answers and check them by silently reviewing the paragraphs and making any necessary corrections.

Answers for page 174: 1. c; 2. You can train your puppy not to chew things.

Multilingual Summaries

English

Read Together

The Signmaker's Assistant

Norman works for the town signmaker. People love the beautiful signs they make. Norman wants to grow up to be a signmaker too.

One day Norman makes a new sign. He puts a sign on the school door that says "No School Today." Teachers and students see the sign and go home. Then Norman puts silly new signs all over town.

People get angry about the new signs. They tear down all the signs. Norman is sorry. He stays up all night to make new signs. In the morning, he apologizes to everyone.

Spanish

El asistente del rotulista

Norman trabaja para el rotulista del pueblo. La gente adora los letreros que ellos hacen. Norman quiere hacerse rotulista cuando sea mayor también.

Un día, Norman hace un nuevo letrero. Pone el letrero que dice "Hoy no hay clases" en la puerta de la escuela. Los maestros y los estudiantes ven el letrero y se van a sus casas. Luego, Norman pone nuevos letreros tontos por todo el pueblo.

La gente se enoja con los nuevos letreros y los quitan todos. Norman está arrepentido. Se queda despierto toda la noche para hacer nuevos letreros. En la mañana se disculpa con todo el mundo.

Multilingual Summaries

Chinese

招牌師父的助手

諾曼在鎮上的招牌師父那兒工作。大家都喜歡他們做的漂亮招牌。諾曼長大以後也想當招牌師父。

有一天，諾曼做了一個新招牌。他把招牌掛在學校門口，上面寫著「今天停課」。老師和學生看見招牌後就回家了。然後，諾曼在整個鎮上都放滿了他新做的蠢招牌。

大家對這些新招牌很生氣，他們把招牌全部拆掉了。諾曼覺得很對不起大家，於是整夜不睡趕工做新招牌。第二天早上，他向大家道歉了。

Vietnamese

Phụ Tá của Ông Thợ Làm Bảng Hiệu

Norman làm việc cho ông thợ làm bảng hiệu của thành phố. Người ta yêu thích những bảng hiệu đẹp của họ làm. Norman muốn khi lớn lên sẽ trở thành thợ làm bảng hiệu.

Ngày nọ Norman làm một bảng mới. Cậu bé để một cái bảng trên cửa trường có ghi: "Hôm Nay Trường Đóng Cửa." Thầy cô và học sinh thấy bảng này và quay về nhà. Sau đó Norman để những bảng vớ vẩn khắp nơi trong thành phố.

Người ta tức giận vì những tấm bảng mới này. Họ phá hủy tất cả các bảng. Norman ân hận. Cậu thức suốt đêm để làm những tấm bảng mới. Đến sáng, cậu ta xin lỗi mọi người.

Korean

간판 제작자의 조수

노먼은 마을에 있는 간판 제작소에서 일하는데 사람들은 여기서 만드는 예쁜 간판을 좋아한다. 노먼도 커서 간판 제작자가 되고 싶어한다.

어느 날 노먼은 새로운 간판을 만드는데 "금일 휴교" 라고 써 있는 간판을 학교 문에 단다. 선생님과 학생들이 간판을 보고 집으로 돌아간다. 그 후 노먼은 마을 전체에 장난기 있는 새 간판을 단다.

사람들은 새로운 간판 때문에 화가 단단히 나서 모든 간판을 떼 버린다. 노먼은 미안하게 생각하며 새 간판을 만들면서 밤을 샌다. 아침이 되자 노먼은 모든 사람들에게 사과를 한다.

Hmong

Tus Neeg Tsim Tej Pib Tus Pab Cuam

Norman ua hauj lwm rau lub zos tus uas tsim tej pib. Tib neeg nyiam cov pib zoo nkauj uas nws ua. Norman xav hlob los ua ib tug neeg tsim tej pib thiab.

Muaj ib hnub Norman tau ua ib daim pib tshiab. Nws muab daim pib dai rau saum lub tsev kawm ntawv lub qhov rooj uas hais tias "Tsis Kawm Ntawv Hnub No." Cov nais khus thiab cov tub ntxhias kawm ntawv pom daim pib thiab mus tsev. Ces Norman muab tej pib tsis tseem ceeb tso thoob plaws lub zos.

Tib neeg npaw taws txog tej pib tshiab. Lawv dua tag nrho cov pib. Norman tau tu siab. Nws nyob ib hmo ua ib cov pib tshiab. Yav sawv ntxov, nws tau hais thov txim rau sawv daws.

Name ______________________

Three Little Kittens Learn a Lesson

- **Read** *Three Little Kittens Learn a Lesson* again.
- In Box 1, **draw** a picture of the kittens doing the wrong thing.
- In Box 2, **draw** a picture of the kittens doing the right thing.
- **Answer** the question below.

1.

2.

Why do you think the author wrote the story?

o to teach something

o to share feelings

o to be funny

Family Link

Have family members tell you about a time when they learned a lesson.

Weekly Resources Guide for English Language Learner Support

For this week's content and language objectives, see p. 179e.

Instructional Strand	Day 1	Day 2
Concept Development/Academic Language	TEACHER'S EDITION • Academic Language, p. DI•12 • Concept Development, p. DI•12 • Anchored Talk, pp. 360j—360–361 • *Sing with Me* Big Book, p. 361a • Concept Talk Video ELL HANDBOOK • ELL Poster Talk, Concept Talk, p. 179c ELL POSTER 26 • Day 1 Activities	TEACHER'S EDITION • Academic Language, p. DI•12 • Concept Development, p. DI•12 • Anchored Talk, p. 366b • *Sing with Me* Big Book, p. 366a • Concept Talk Video ELL HANDBOOK • ELL Poster Talk, Concept Talk, p. 179c • Concept Talk Video Routine, p. 464 ELL POSTER 26 • Day 2 Activities
Phonics and Spelling	TEACHER'S EDITION • Phonics and Spelling, p. DI•16 • Decodable Reader 26A, pp. 363c–363d	TEACHER'S EDITION • Phonics and Spelling, p. DI•16
Listening Comprehension	TEACHER'S EDITION • Modified Read Aloud, p. DI•15 • *Sing with Me* Big Book, p. 361a • Concept Talk Video ELL HANDBOOK • Concept Talk Video Routine, p. 464	TEACHER'S EDITION • Modified Read Aloud, p. DI•15 • *Sing with Me* Big Book, p. 366a • AudioText of *Just Like Josh Gibson* • Concept Talk Video ELL HANDBOOK • AudioText CD Routine, p. 464 • Story Map A, p. 470
Reading Comprehension	TEACHER'S EDITION • Teach Compare and Contrast, p. DI•17	TEACHER'S EDITION • Teach Compare and Contrast, p. DI•17 • Frontloading Reading, p. DI•18 ELL HANDBOOK • Picture It! Skill Instruction, pp. 180–180a • Multilingual Summaries, pp. 181–183
Vocabulary **Basic and Lesson Vocabulary** **Vocabulary Skill: Homophones**	TEACHER'S EDITION • Basic Vocabulary, p. DI•13 • Preteach Lesson Vocabulary, p. DI•13 • Homophones, p. DI•16 ELL HANDBOOK • Word Cards, p. 179 • ELL Vocabulary Routine, p. 456 ELL POSTER 26 • Day 1 Activities	TEACHER'S EDITION • Basic Vocabulary, p. DI•13 • Reteach Lesson Vocabulary, p. DI•14 • Homophones, p. DI•16 ELL HANDBOOK • Word Cards, p. 179 • Multilingual Vocabulary List, pp. 429–440 ELL POSTER 26 • Day 2 Activities
Grammar and Conventions	TEACHER'S EDITION • Preteach Capital Letters, p. DI•20	TEACHER'S EDITION • Reteach Capital Letters, p. DI•20
Writing	TEACHER'S EDITION • Story Organization, p. DI•21 • Introduce Realistic Fiction, pp. 365c–365d	TEACHER'S EDITION • Writing Trait: Organization, pp. 381d–381e

Unit 6 Week 1 Just Like Josh Gibson

This symbol indicates leveled instruction to address language proficiency levels.

Day 3	Day 4	Day 5
TEACHER'S EDITION • Academic Language, p. DI•12 • Concept Development, p. DI•12 • Anchored Talk, p. 382b • *Sing with Me* Big Book, p. 382a • Concept Talk Video **ELL HANDBOOK** • ELL Poster Talk, Concept Talk, p. 179c **ELL POSTER 26** • Day 3 Activities	**TEACHER'S EDITION** • Academic Language, p. DI•12 • Concept Development, p. DI•12 • Anchored Talk, p. 386b • *Sing with Me* Big Book, p. 386a • Concept Talk Video **ELL HANDBOOK** • ELL Poster Talk, Concept Talk, p. 179c **ELL POSTER 26** • Day 4 Activities	**TEACHER'S EDITION** • Academic Language, p. DI•12 • Concept Development, p. DI•12 • Concept Talk Video **ELL HANDBOOK** • ELL Poster Talk, Concept Talk, p. 179c **ELL POSTER 26** • Day 5 Activities
ELL HANDBOOK • Phonics Transition Lesson, pp. 276–277, 280–281	**TEACHER'S EDITION** • Decodable Reader 26C, pp. 386e–386f **ELL HANDBOOK** • Phonics Transition Lesson, pp. 274, 276–278, 280–281	**TEACHER'S EDITION** • Phonics and Spelling, p. DI•16
TEACHER'S EDITION • *Sing with Me* Big Book, p. 382a • AudioText of *Just Like Josh Gibson* • Concept Talk Video **ELL HANDBOOK** • AudioText CD Routine, p. 464	**TEACHER'S EDITION** • *Sing with Me* Big Book, p. 386a • Concept Talk Video	**TEACHER'S EDITION** • Concept Talk Video
TEACHER'S EDITION • Sheltered Reading, p. DI•18 **ELL HANDBOOK** • Multilingual Summaries, pp. 181–183	**TEACHER'S EDITION** • ELL/ELD Reader Guided Reading, p. DI•19 **ELL HANDBOOK** • ELL Study Guide, p. 184	**TEACHER'S EDITION** • ELL/ELD Reader Guided Reading, p. DI•19 **ELL HANDBOOK** • ELL Study Guide, p. 184
ELL HANDBOOK • High-Frequency Words Activity Bank, p. 491 **ELL POSTER 26** • Day 3 Activities	**ELL HANDBOOK** • High-Frequency Words Activity Bank, p. 491	**TEACHER'S EDITION** • Homophones, p. 390–391 **ELL HANDBOOK** • High-Frequency Words Activity Bank, p. 491
TEACHER'S EDITION • Grammar Jammer **ELL HANDBOOK** • Grammar Transition Lesson, pp. 312–313, 319–321 • Grammar Jammer Routine, p. 465	**TEACHER'S EDITION** • Grammar Jammer **ELL HANDBOOK** • Grammar Transition Lesson, pp. 312–313, 319–321	**TEACHER'S EDITION** • Grammar Jammer **ELL HANDBOOK** • Grammar Transition Lesson, pp. 312–313, 319–321
TEACHER'S EDITION • Let's Write It!, p. 384–385 • Writer's Craft: Sequence, p. 385a	**TEACHER'S EDITION** • Revising Strategy, pp. 389c–389d	**TEACHER'S EDITION** • Writer's Craft: Transition Words, pp. 391h–391i

Poster Talk, Concept Talk

Question of the Week

Why are sports traditions important in our country?

Poster 26

Throughout the week, use the ELL Poster to help children produce and comprehend language, understand the concept, and build English vocabulary. Use the Question of the Week and other questions to help children share ideas in pairs, small groups, or the large group. Sample questions are shown, with examples of possible responses by children.

Weekly Concept and Language Goals

- Know the importance of sports traditions
- Name objects related to baseball
- Tell about what people do at sports events

By the end of the lesson, children should be able to talk about and write one or more sentences about sports traditions.

Daily Team Talk

Day 1	Day 2	Day 3	Day 4	Day 5
After Day 1 activities on Poster, ask questions such as *In the poster picture, what is the job of the woman on the kickball field?*	After Day 2 activity on Poster, ask questions such as *In the poster picture, children are playing kickball on a field. What other sports are played on a field?*	After Day 3 activity on Poster, ask questions such as *What sports equipment do you need to play baseball?*	After Day 4 activity on Poster, ask questions such as *What do you like to do at sports events?*	After Day 5 activity on Poster, ask questions such as *Major sports events, such as the Super Bowl or the World Cup, are sports traditions. What is your favorite sports tradition?*
Beginning For rules. **Intermediate** Making sure they follow the rules. **Advanced** She is the umpire and is in charge of the rules. **Advanced High** The umpire's job is to make sure the players follow the rules of the game.	**Beginning** Baseball. **Intermediate** Baseball is played on a field. **Advanced** People play baseball and softball on fields. **Advanced High** Teams play football and baseball on fields.	**Beginning** A bat and ball. **Intermediate** You need a bat and a ball. **Advanced** A player needs a glove, a bat, and a ball. **Advanced High** Everyone needs a bat, a glove, and a ball to play baseball. The catcher also needs a mask and pads.	**Beginning** Cheer. **Intermediate** I like to cheer. **Advanced** I love to cheer for my team. **Advanced High** I love to eat popcorn and cheer for my favorite players.	**Beginning** The *World Cup.* **Intermediate** I like the World Series. **Advanced** My family watches World Cup soccer matches together. **Advanced High** I always look forward to watching the Summer and Winter Olympics.

This Week's Materials

Teacher's Edition pages 360j–391k

See the support for English language learners throughout the lesson, including ELL strategies and scaffold activities at points of use.

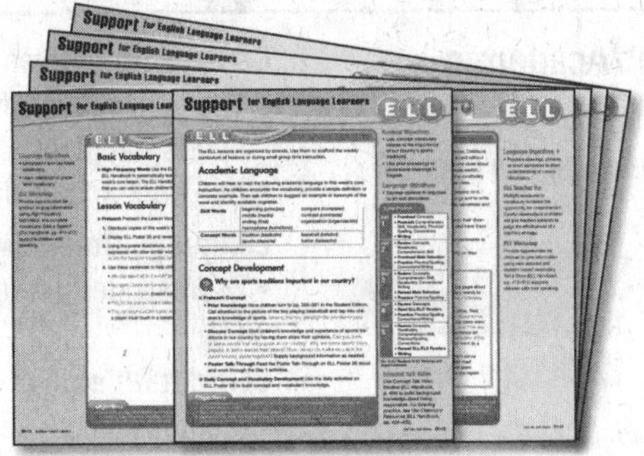
Teacher's Edition pages DI•12–DI•21

Differentiated Instruction for English language learners provides daily group activities that "frontload," or preteach, core instruction.

ELL Handbook pp. 179a–184

Find additional lesson materials that support the core lesson and the ELL instructional pages.

ELL Poster 26

ELD Reader 2.6.1

ELL Reader 2.6.1

Concept Literacy Reader

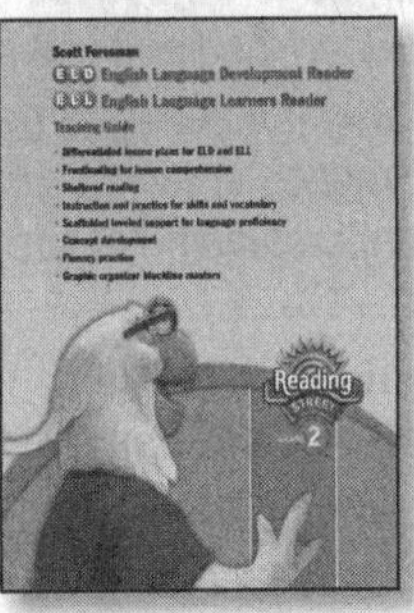

ELD, ELL Reader Teaching Guide

Concept Literacy Reader Teaching Guide

Technology

Online Teacher's Edition Use the digital version of the core teacher's edition for planning and instruction.

eReaders
This Week's ELL and ELD Readers and Concept Literacy Reader are also available in digital format.

This Week's Content and Language Objectives by Strand

Concept Development/Academic Language What sports traditions are important in our country?	**Content Objectives** • Use concept vocabulary related to the importance of our country's sports traditions. • Use prior knowledge to understand meanings in English. **Language Objective** • Express ideas in response to art and discussion.
Phonics and Spelling Inflected Endings *–s* and *-ed*	**Content Objective** • Identify inflected endings *-s* and *-ed.* **Language Objective** • Apply phonics and decoding skills to vocabulary.
Listening Comprehension Modified Read Aloud: "A New Kind of Ball"	**Content Objective** • Monitor and adjust oral comprehension. **Language Objectives** • Discuss oral passages. • Use a graphic organizer to take notes.
Reading Comprehension Compare and Contrast	**Content Objectives** • Distinguish between comparing and contrasting. • Compare and contrast elements of a story to aid in comprehension. • Monitor and adjust comprehension. **Language Objectives** • Discuss comparisons and contrasts. • Write about comparisons and contrasts from personal experience. • Summarize using visual support.
Vocabulary Basic and Lesson Vocabulary	**Language Objectives** • Understand and use basic vocabulary. • Learn meanings of grade-level vocabulary. • Produce drawings, phrases, and short sentences to show understanding of Lesson Vocabulary.
Vocabulary Homophones	**Content Objective** • Identify and define homophones. **Language Objective** • Discuss the different meanings of homophones.
Grammar and Conventions Capital Letters	**Content Objective** • Identify capitalization rules. **Language Objective** • Write sentences using capitalization correctly.
Writing Story Organization	**Content Objective** • Identify the beginning, middle, and ending of a story. **Language Objectives** • Write a story with a beginning, middle, and strong ending. • Share feedback for editing and revising.

Word Cards for Vocabulary Activities

bases	**cheers**
field	**plate**
sailed	**threw**

Teacher Note: Beginning Teach two to three words. **Intermediate** Teach three to four words. **Advanced** Teach five to six words. **Advanced High** Teach all words.

Name ______________________________

Picture It!
Compare and Contrast

Look at the pictures. **Read** the two paragraphs.

- **Fill in** the chart. **Write** how the two sports are alike. **Write** how the two sports are different.

The Best Sport

My friend Maya and I play different sports. I think baseball is more fun. I can throw the ball, hit the ball, and run fast. We use bats and gloves. Also, the games are always outside!

Maya thinks that basketball is better. She likes to run fast and shoot the ball. She is glad she doesn't need any extra gear to play. She also likes to play inside. Which do you like better?

Baseball and Basketball

How They Are Alike	How They Are Different

Compare and Contrast

Use this lesson to supplement or replace the skill lesson on page 364a of the Teacher's Edition. Display the Skill Points (at right) and share them with children.

Use the Skill Points to preteach compare and contrast.

Teach/Model

Beginning Display a tennis ball and a basketball. Say: *Let's compare these things. Are they the same shape?* (yes) *Let's contrast the balls. Are they different colors?* (yes)

Intermediate Display a baseball. Have children describe it. Say: *Find something you can compare to the baseball.* Have each child share how his or her object compares to the baseball. Then have the child contrast the object to the baseball.

Advanced Review the game of baseball. Ask children to draw a picture of their favorite sport. Remind them to use as many details as possible. Then have children show their pictures and compare and contrast their sport with baseball.

Advanced High Ask children to tell about their favorite sports. After each child has a chance to share, pair children. Ask: *How do your favorite sports compare? How do they contrast?*

Then distribute copies of Picture It! page 180.

- Have children look at the pictures and describe what the children are doing in each.
- Read the paragraphs aloud. Ask: *How are baseball and basketball alike?* Provide English words as needed to answer.
- Review the Skill Points with children.
- Have children look at the pictures and sentences to find clues about comparing and contrasting.

Practice

Read aloud the directions on page 180. Reread or chorally read the story. Have children look at the pictures and the story as they answer the questions.

Beginning Children can orally answer and write their answers in the chart. Provide help with writing and spelling.

Intermediate Children can first orally answer and then fill in the chart.

Advanced Children can write their answers in the chart and check them by comparing their chart with a partner's or quietly reading their completed chart aloud.

Advanced High Children can write their answers in the chart and check them by silently rereading each column and making any necessary corrections.

Answers for page 180: Sample answers: *Alike:* Both sports use a ball. Players run and throw the ball. Players wear uniforms. *Different:* Baseball players use bats and gloves. They hit the ball with the bat. Baseball is played on a field. Basketball is played on a court.

Skill Points

- ✔ When you **compare** two things, you tell how they are alike.
- ✔ When you **contrast** two things, you tell how they are different.
- ✔ You can compare and contrast things you read about with things you already know.

Multilingual Summaries

English

Read Together

Just Like Josh Gibson

Grandmama's favorite baseball player was Josh Gibson. He was an excellent hitter. Grandmama's father saw Gibson play on the day that she was born. He wanted his daughter to be a great baseball player too.

In Grandmama's childhood, girls did not play in baseball games. She watched her cousin Danny play. Danny's team let Grandmama play while they practiced. She was a very good player. They were sorry that she could not be on the team.

Danny hurt his arm. The team needed another player. They let Grandmama play. She played as well as Josh Gibson. Grandmama still has the ball.

Spanish

Igual que Josh Gibson

El jugador de béisbol favorito de mi abuela era Josh Gibson. Era un excelente bateador. El papá de mi abuela vio a Gibson jugar el día que ella nació. Él quería que su hija también fuera una gran jugadora de béisbol.

Cuando mi abuela era pequeña, las niñas no jugaban al béisbol. Ella siempre veía jugar a su primo Danny. El equipo de Danny dejaba jugar a mi abuela cuando ellos practicaban. Era muy buena jugadora. Ellos sentían mucho que ella no pudiera formar parte del equipo.

Un día Danny se lastimó el brazo. El equipo necesitaba otro jugador y por eso dejaron jugar a mi abuela. Ella jugó tan bien como Josh Gibson. Mi abuela todavía guarda la pelota.

Multilingual Summaries

Chinese

跟喬許˙吉布森一樣出色

祖母最喜愛的棒球選手是喬許˙吉布森，他是一個很出色的擊球手。祖母出生那天，她爸爸剛好看了吉布森的棒球比賽。他希望女兒也是一個偉大的棒球選手。

祖母的小時候，女孩子不能打棒球，她只能看她表哥丹尼玩。當丹尼的球隊練習時，也讓祖母跟他們一起打棒球。祖母的棒球打得很好，可是他們還是不能讓她加入球隊。

有一次，丹尼的手臂受了傷，他們棒球隊需要另一個選手來代替他。他們讓祖母參加比賽，結果她打得跟喬許˙吉布森一樣好。直到現在，祖母仍保留著當時比賽用的球。

Vietnamese

Giống Như Josh Gibson

Cầu thủ chơi bóng chày mà Bà thích nhất là Josh Gibson. Ông ấy là một người đánh xuất sắc. Ba của Bà xem Gibson chơi bóng đúng vào ngày bà chào đời. Ông cũng muốn con gái của mình được trở thành một cầu thủ chơi bóng chày tuyệt hảo.

Thời niên thiếu của Bà, con gái không ai chơi đấu bóng chày. Bà xem anh họ của mình là Danny chơi. Đội của Danny để cho Bà chơi khi họ đang tập dợt. Bà là một người chơi giỏi. Họ tiếc là bà không được vào trong đội.

Danny bị đau cánh tay. Đội cần một người vào thay. Họ để cho Bà vào chơi. Bà chơi giỏi như Josh Gibson. Bà vẫn còn giữ quả bóng.

Multilingual Summaries

Korean

조쉬 깁슨처럼

할머니가 제일 좋아하는 야구 선수는 조쉬 깁슨으로 그는 훌륭한 타자였다. 할머니의 아버지는 할머니가 태어난 날에 깁슨의 야구 경기를 보았다. 아버지는 딸도 위대한 야구선수가 되길 원했다.

할머니가 어릴 적에 여자애들은 야구 경기를 하지 않았다. 할머니는 사촌인 대니가 경기하는 것을 지켜보았다. 대니의 팀은 연습 경기에선 할머니도 끼워 주었는데 할머니는 야구에 소질이 있었다. 대니의 팀원들은 할머니가 팀원이 될 수 없는 것을 아쉬워했다.

대니가 팔을 다치자 팀에서는 다른 선수가 필요했다. 그들은 할머니를 경기에서 뛰게 했고 할머니는 조쉬 깁슨처럼 훌륭히 경기를 했다. 할머니는 아직도 그 야구공을 갖고 있다.

Hmong

Zoo Ib Yam Li Josh Gibson

Tus neeg ntau pob uas pog nyiam tshaj yog Josh Gibson. Nws keeb ntau pob heev. Pog txiv tau pom Gibson ntau pob hnub uas pog tau yug. Nws xav kom nws tus ntxhais txhawj ntau pob thiab.

Thaum pog tseem yog me nyuam yaus, cov me nyuam ntxhais tsis ntau pob. Nws saib nws tus num Danny ntau pob. Danny pab ntau pob cia pog ntau pob thaum lawv xyaum. Nws yog ib tug txhawj ntau pob. Lawv tu siab nws nrog lawv ntau pob tsis tau.

Danny ua rau nws txhais caj npab mob. Nws pab ntau pob xav tau ib tug ntau pob ntxiv. Lawv cia pog ntau pob. Nws ntau pob keej ib yam li Josh Gibson. Pog tseem tau lub pob.

Name ______________________

- **Read** *Play Ball!* again.
- Pick a sport other than baseball. **Write** the name of that sport at the top of the circle on the right.
- Use the Venn diagram to show how the two sports are alike and how they are different. You can **write** things you need to play the sport and actions that happen when you play.

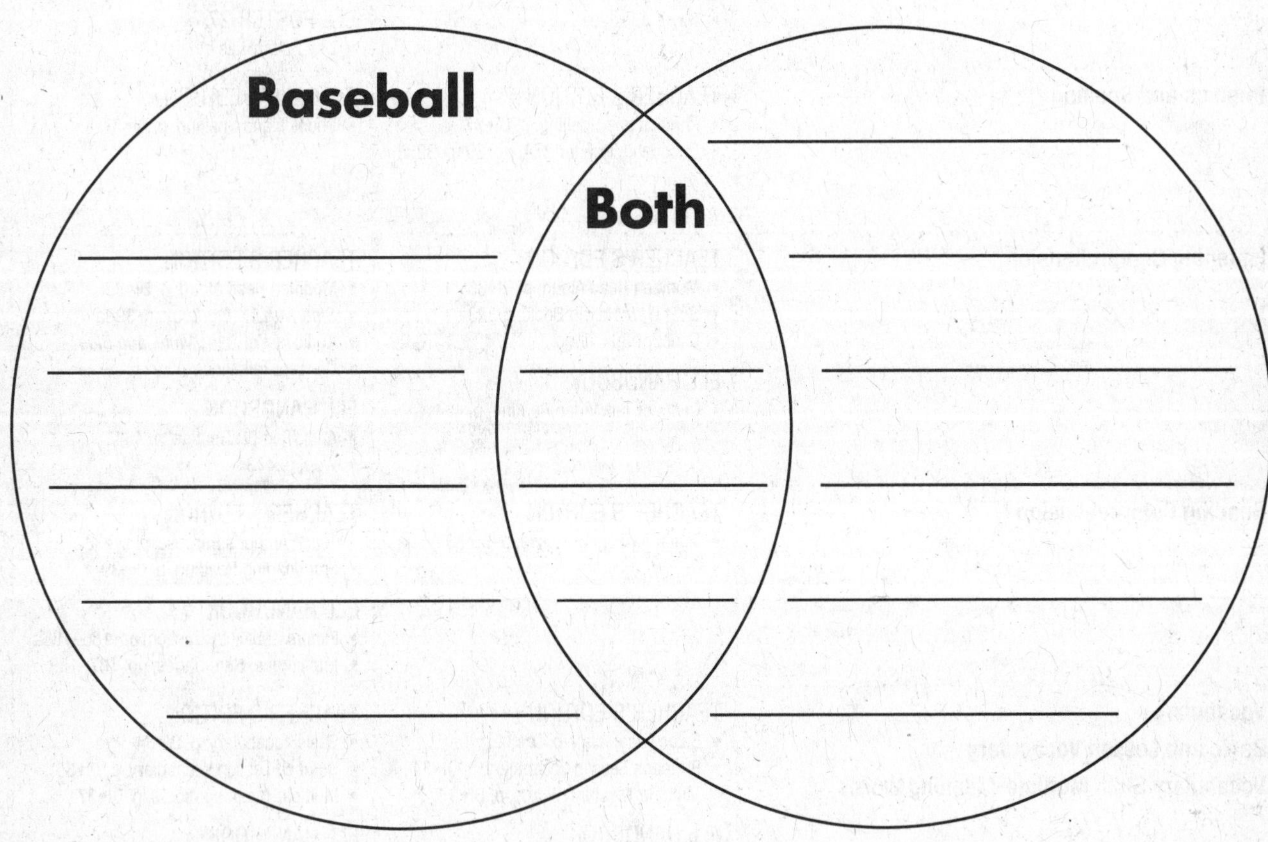

Family Link

Has anyone in your family ever played on a team? Ask family members to tell what they like about playing on a team.

Weekly Resources Guide for English Language Learner Support

For this week's content and language objectives, see p. 185e.

Instructional Strand	Day 1	Day 2
Concept Development/Academic Language	TEACHER'S EDITION • Academic Language, p. DI•33 • Concept Development, p. DI•33 • Anchored Talk, pp. 392j—392–393 • *Sing with Me* Big Book, p. 393a • Concept Talk Video ELL HANDBOOK • ELL Poster Talk, Concept Talk, p. 185c ELL POSTER 27 • Day 1 Activities	TEACHER'S EDITION • Academic Language, p. DI•33 • Concept Development, p. DI•33 • Anchored Talk, p. 398b • *Sing with Me* Big Book, p. 398a • Concept Talk Video ELL HANDBOOK • ELL Poster Talk, Concept Talk, p. 185c • Concept Talk Video Routine, p. 464 ELL POSTER 27 • Day 2 Activities
Phonics and Spelling	TEACHER'S EDITION • Phonics and Spelling, p. DI•37 • Decodable Reader 27A, pp. 395c–395d	TEACHER'S EDITION • Phonics and Spelling, p. DI•37
Listening Comprehension	TEACHER'S EDITION • Modified Read Aloud, p. DI•36 • *Sing with Me* Big Book, p. 393a • Concept Talk Video ELL HANDBOOK • Concept Talk Video Routine, p. 464	TEACHER'S EDITION • Modified Read Aloud, p. DI•36 • *Sing with Me* Big Book, p. 398a • AudioText of *Red, White, and Blue* • Concept Talk Video ELL HANDBOOK • AudioText CD Routine, p. 464 • Web, p. 473
Reading Comprehension	TEACHER'S EDITION • Teach Author's Purpose, p. DI•38	TEACHER'S EDITION • Teach Author's Purpose, p. DI•38 • Frontloading Reading, p. DI•39 ELL HANDBOOK • Picture It! Skill Instruction, pp. 186–186a • Multilingual Summaries, pp. 187–189
Vocabulary **Basic and Lesson Vocabulary** **Vocabulary Skill: Multiple-Meaning Words**	TEACHER'S EDITION • Basic Vocabulary, p. DI•34 • Preteach Lesson Vocabulary, p. DI•34 • Multiple-Meaning Words, p. DI•37 ELL HANDBOOK • Word Cards, p. 185 • ELL Vocabulary Routine, p. 456 ELL POSTER 27 • Day 1 Activities	TEACHER'S EDITION • Basic Vocabulary, p. DI•34 • Reteach Lesson Vocabulary, p. DI•35 • Multiple-Meaning Words, p. DI•37 ELL HANDBOOK • Word Cards, p. 185 • Multilingual Vocabulary List, pp. 429–440 ELL POSTER 27 • Day 2 Activities
Grammar and Conventions	TEACHER'S EDITION • Preteach Quotation Marks, p. DI•41	TEACHER'S EDITION • Reteach Quotation Marks, p. DI•41
Writing	TEACHER'S EDITION • Expressing Feelings, p. DI•42 • Introduce Descriptive Poem, pp. 397c–397d	TEACHER 'S EDITION • Writing Trait: Voice, pp. 417d–417e

Unit 6 Week 2 Red, White, and Blue

This symbol indicates leveled instruction to address language proficiency levels.

Day 3	Day 4	Day 5
TEACHER'S EDITION • Academic Language, p. DI•33 • Concept Development, p. DI•33 • Anchored Talk, p. 418b • *Sing with Me* Big Book, p. 418a • Concept Talk Video ELL HANDBOOK • ELL Poster Talk, Concept Talk, p. 185c ELL POSTER 27 • Day 3 Activities	TEACHER'S EDITION • Academic Language, p. DI•33 • Concept Development, p. DI•33 • Anchored Talk, p. 422b • *Sing with Me* Big Book, p. 422a • Concept Talk Video ELL HANDBOOK • ELL Poster Talk, Concept Talk, p. 185c ELL POSTER 27 • Day 4 Activities	TEACHER'S EDITION • Academic Language, p. DI•33 • Concept Development, p. DI•33 • Concept Talk Video ELL HANDBOOK • ELL Poster Talk, Concept Talk, p. 185c ELL POSTER 27 • Day 5 Activities
	TEACHER'S EDITION • Decodable Reader 27C, pp. 422e–422f	TEACHER'S EDITION • Phonics and Spelling, p. DI•37
TEACHER'S EDITION • *Sing with Me* Big Book, p. 418a • AudioText of *Red, White, and Blue* • Concept Talk Video ELL HANDBOOK • AudioText CD Routine, p. 464	TEACHER'S EDITION • *Sing with Me* Big Book, p. 422a • Concept Talk Video	TEACHER'S EDITION • Concept Talk Video
TEACHER'S EDITION • Sheltered Reading, p. DI•39 ELL HANDBOOK • Multilingual Summaries, pp. 187–189	TEACHER'S EDITION • ELL/ELD Reader Guided Reading, p. DI•40 ELL HANDBOOK • ELL Study Guide, p. 190	TEACHER'S EDITION • ELL/ELD Reader Guided Reading, p. DI•40 ELL HANDBOOK • ELL Study Guide, p. 190
ELL HANDBOOK • High-Frequency Words Activity Bank, p. 491 ELL POSTER 27 • Day 3 Activities	ELL HANDBOOK • High-Frequency Words Activity Bank, p. 491	TEACHER'S EDITION • Multiple-Meaning Words, p. 424–425 ELL HANDBOOK • High-Frequency Words Activity Bank, p. 491
TEACHER'S EDITION • Grammar Jammer ELL HANDBOOK • Grammar Transition Lesson, pp. 350, 364 • Grammar Jammer Routine, p. 465	TEACHER'S EDITION • Grammar Jammer ELL HANDBOOK • Grammar Transition Lesson, pp. 350, 364	TEACHER'S EDITION • Grammar Jammer ELL HANDBOOK • Grammar Transition Lesson, pp. 350, 364
TEACHER'S EDITION • Let's Write It!, p. 420–421 • Writer's Craft: Express Feelings, p. 421a	TEACHER'S EDITION • Revising Strategy, pp. 423d–423e	TEACHER'S EDITION • Writer's Craft: Quotation Marks, pp. 425h–425i

Question of the Week

What traditions and celebrations involve our country's flag?

Poster 27

Throughout the week, use the ELL Poster to help children produce and comprehend language, understand the concept, and build English vocabulary. Use the Question of the Week and other questions to help children share ideas in pairs, small groups, or the large group. Sample questions are shown, with examples of possible responses by children.

Weekly Concept and Language Goals

- Know that the flag is important to our country's traditions
- Tell why the flag is important to America
- Name holidays when the flag is important

By the end of the lesson, children should be able to talk about and write one or more sentences about flag celebrations.

Daily Team Talk

Day 1	Day 2	Day 3	Day 4	Day 5
After Day 1 activities on Poster, ask questions such as *The poster picture shows some symbols of the United States. What is another symbol of our country?*	After Day 2 activity on Poster, ask questions such as *What happened to the number of stars on the flag?*	After Day 3 activity on Poster, ask questions such as *When do people fly the American flag?*	After Day 4 activity on Poster, ask questions such as *How do you honor the flag every day?*	After Day 5 activity on Poster, ask questions such as *What songs do we sing to honor the flag?*
Beginning The White House. **Intermediate** The White House is a symbol. **Advanced** Uncle Sam is a symbol of our country. **Advanced High** Uncle Sam and the White House are important symbols of the United States of America.	**Beginning** Lots of stars. **Intermediate** There are many stars now. **Advanced** The number of stars has grown. **Advanced High** There were thirteen stars for the thirteen colonies. Now there are fifty stars for the fifty states.	**Beginning** July 4. **Intermediate** On the Fourth of July. **Advanced** The flag is important on Independence Day. **Advanced High** Many people fly the flag on Independence Day, Veterans' Day, and Memorial Day.	**Beginning** The Pledge. **Intermediate** We say the Pledge. **Advanced** We put our hand on our heart and say the Pledge of Allegiance. **Advanced High** We recite the Pledge of Allegiance while facing the flag.	**Beginning** National anthem. **Intermediate** We sing our national anthem. **Advanced** People sing "The Star-Spangled Banner" before some events. **Advanced High** People sing "The Star-Spangled Banner" to honor the flag. It is our national anthem.

This Week's Materials

Teacher's Edition pages 392j–425k

See the support for English language learners throughout the lesson, including ELL strategies and scaffold activities at points of use.

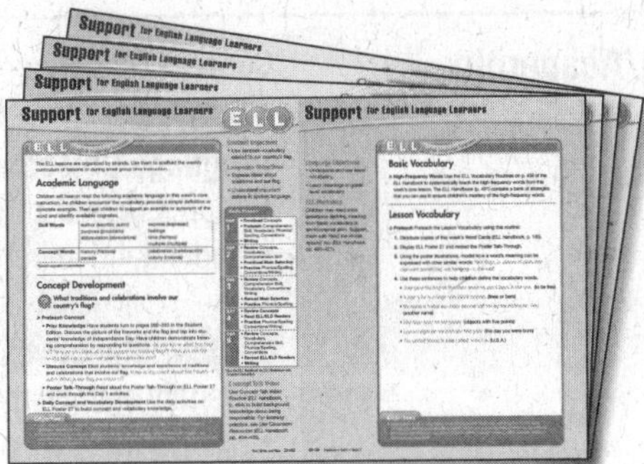

Teacher's Edition pages DI•33–DI•42

Differentiated Instruction for English language learners provides daily group activities that "frontload," or preteach, core instruction.

ELL Handbook pp. 185a–190

Find additional lesson materials that support the core lesson and the ELL instructional pages.

ELL Poster 27

ELD Reader 2.6.2

ELL Reader 2.6.2

Concept Literacy Reader

ELD, ELL Reader Teaching Guide

Concept Literacy Reader Teaching Guide

Technology

Online Teacher's Edition Use the digital version of the core teacher's edition for planning and instruction.

eReaders
This Week's ELL and ELD Readers and Concept Literacy Reader are also available in digital format.

This Week's Content and Language Objectives by Strand

Concept Development/Academic Language What traditions and celebrations involve our country's flag?	**Content Objective** • Use concept vocabulary related to our country's flag. **Language Objectives** • Express ideas in response to art and discussion. • Understand important details in spoken language.
Phonics and Spelling Abbreviations	**Content Objectives** • Identify abbreviations. • Review inflectional endings **Language Objective** • Apply phonics and decoding skills to vocabulary.
Listening Comprehension Modified Read Aloud: "The Secret"	**Content Objective** • Monitor and adjust oral comprehension. **Language Objectives** • Discuss main points and details in oral passages. • Use a graphic organizer to take notes.
Reading Comprehension Author's Purpose	**Content Objectives** • Identify different purposes authors have for writing. • Monitor and adjust comprehension. **Language Objectives** • Identify the author's purpose in writing. • Write a sentence for a specific purpose. • Summarize using visual support.
Vocabulary Basic and Lesson Vocabulary	**Language Objectives** • Understand and use basic vocabulary. • Learn meanings of grade-level vocabulary. • Produce drawings, phrases, or short sentences to show understanding of Lesson Vocabulary.
Vocabulary Multiple-Meaning Words	**Content Objective** • Identify and define multiple-meaning words. **Language Objective** • Discuss the different meanings of multiple-meaning words.
Grammar and Conventions Quotation Marks	**Content Objective** • Identify the correct use of quotation marks. **Language Objective** • Write sentences using quotation marks correctly.
Writing Expressing Feelings	**Content Objectives** • Identify the ways feelings are expressed in writing. • Explain with specificity and detail when writing. **Language Objectives** • Write a paragraph that expresses feelings. • Share feedback for editing and revising.

Word Cards for Vocabulary Activities

America	**birthday**
flag	**freedom**
nicknames	**stars**
stripes	

Teacher Note: Beginning Teach two to three words. **Intermediate** Teach three to four words. **Advanced** Teach five to six words. **Advanced High** Teach all words.

Name ______________________________

- **Look** at the picture. **Read** the paragraph.
- **Answer** the questions below.

What a Day!

The Fourth of July is a holiday. It is the best holiday of the year. We have a party with the other families on our street. We hang the United States flag. I think it is very pretty. The flag has thirteen stripes and fifty stars. There is a star for each state in the country. At the end of the night, we watch the fireworks. Fireworks are great! I love the Fourth of July.

1. What things can you see on the Fourth of July?

____

2. How do people have fun on the Fourth of July?
a. They go to work. **b.** They have a party.
c. They go to school.

3. Tell why you think the author wrote this paragraph.

____

____

Author's Purpose

Use this lesson to supplement or replace the skill lesson on page 396a of the Teacher's Edition. Display the Skill Points (at right) and share them with children.

Skill Points

- ✔ The **author's purpose** is his or her reason for writing.
- ✔ An author can write to share important information, to explain something, or to tell an interesting or funny story.
- ✔ Ask yourself questions before, during, or after you read to figure out the author's purpose.

Use the Skill Points to preteach author's purpose.

Teach/Model

Beginning Say: *An author writes facts about holidays. What is her purpose for writing?* (to explain) *An author writes a funny skit about a family party. What is his purpose for writing?* (to entertain; to tell a story)

Intermediate Read aloud part of an informational selection about celebrations. Ask: *What is the author's purpose? How can you tell?* Repeat the activity with a how-to book and a humorous children's book.

Advanced Write on the board: *To Entertain, To Inform, To Explain.* Ask: *How can you tell when an author writes to entertain?* Have children give examples. List them on the board. Repeat the process for the other purposes.

Advanced High On the board, write simple directions for drawing a United States flag. Ask children to explain how the purpose of this example is different from that of an encyclopedia article about the flag or a fictional story about the Fourth of July.

Then distribute copies of Picture It! page 186.

- Have children look at the picture and describe what is happening.
- Read the paragraph aloud. Ask: *What is the paragraph about?* (celebrating the Fourth of July) *What is the author trying to do?* (Answers will vary.)
- Review the Skill Points with children.
- Have children look at the picture and sentences to find clues about the author's purpose.

Practice

Read aloud the directions on page 186. Reread or chorally read the paragraph. Have children look at the picture and the paragraph as they answer the questions.

Beginning Children can orally respond and mark and write their answers. Provide help with writing and spelling.

Intermediate Children can first orally respond and then mark and write their answers on the page.

Advanced Children can mark and write their answers and check them by comparing their answers to a partner's and quietly reading aloud their writing.

Advanced High Children can mark and write their answers and check them by silently reviewing the paragraph and making any necessary corrections.

Answers for page 186: 1. flag, fireworks, other families; 2. b; 3. to tell why the Fourth of July is the best holiday

Multilingual Summaries

English

Red, White, and Blue

No one is sure who created the American flag. In the 1700s, America didn't have a flag. During the American Revolution, America needed a flag.

In 1777, Congress decided that the flag should have thirteen red and white stripes. It would have thirteen white stars on a blue background.

At first, another star and stripe were added whenever the United States added a new state. In 1818, Congress decided that the flag would have only thirteen stripes. A star would stand for each state.

Today our flag has fifty stars. We celebrate the flag every June 14, which is Flag Day.

Spanish

Rojo, blanco y azul

Nadie sabe quién creó la bandera norteamericana. En los años 1700, Estados Unidos no tenía una bandera. Durante la Guerra de Independencia, los norteamericanos necesitaban tener una bandera.

En 1777, el Congreso decidió que la bandera debería tener trece franjas rojas y trece franjas blancas. Tendría trece estrellas blanco en un fondo azul.

Al principio le añadían a la bandera una estrella y una franja por cada estado que se agregaba. En 1818, el Congreso decidió que la bandera tendría sólo trece franjas. Se le agregaría, sin embargo, una estrella por cada estado.

Hoy en día nuestra bandera tiene cincuenta estrellas. Cada 14 de junio se celebra el Día de la Bandera.

Multilingual Summaries

Chinese

紅、白、藍

沒有人可以確定美國國旗究竟是誰創的。十八世紀，美國還沒有國旗。獨立戰爭期間，美國人才覺得他們需要一面國旗。

1777 年，美國國會決定，國旗要有 13 條紅白相間的條紋，以及 13 顆白色襯著藍底的星星。

剛開始的時候，美國每增加一州，就會在國旗加上一顆星星和一條條紋。1818 年，美國國會決定，國旗以後都只有 13 條條紋，而每一顆星星則代表著一州。

如今，美國國旗上總共有 50 顆星星。每年 6 月 14 日是美國的國旗紀念日，美國人會為國旗慶祝一番。

Vietnamese

Đỏ, Trắng, và Xanh

Không ai biết rõ ai là người đã tạo ra lá cờ Hoa Kỳ. Trong những năm 1700, Hoa Kỳ không có cờ. Vào thời kỳ Cách Mạng Hoa Kỳ, nước này mới cần có một lá cờ.

Vào năm 1777, Quốc Hội quyết định lá cờ phải có mười ba sọc đỏ và trắng. Cờ sẽ có mười ba ngôi sao trên một nền xanh.

Thoạt đầu, một ngôi sao và một sọc được thêm vào mỗi khi Hiệp Chủng Quốc Hoa Kỳ có thêm một tiểu bang. Vào năm 1818, Quốc Hội quyết định rằng lá cờ sẽ chỉ có mười ba sọc. Một ngôi sao tiêu biểu cho mỗi tiểu bang.

Ngày nay lá cờ của chúng ta có năm mươi ngôi sao. Chúng ta mừng lễ kỷ niệm lá cờ vào ngày 14 Tháng Sáu mỗi năm, đó là Ngày Kỷ Niệm Lá Cờ.

Multilingual Summaries

Korean

빨강, 하양, 파랑

성조기를 만든 사람이 누구인지 아무도 정확히 알지 못한다. 1700년대에 미국은 국기가 없었다. 미국 독립 혁명 시기에 미국은 국기가 필요했다.

1777년 의회는 국기가 13 개의 빨간색과 흰색 줄로 구성되어야 한다고 결정했고 파란색 배경에 13개의 흰 별을 그려 넣었다.

처음에 미국은 새로운 주가 하나씩 생길 때마다 별과 줄을 추가했다. 1818년에 의회는 국기에 13개의 줄과 각 주를 상징하는 별이 포함되도록 결정했다.

오늘날 성조기에는 50개의 별이 있고 미국인들은 국기제정기념일인 6월 14일마다 이 날을 기념한다.

Hmong

Liab, Dawb, thiab Xiav

Tsis muaj leej twg paub tseeb tseeb leej twg yog tus tsim Mikas tus Chij. Hauv xyoo 1700, lub chaws Mikas tsis muaj ib tug chij. Thaum lub sij hawm Mikas Sawv Tua A-kis, Mikas yuav tsum muaj ib tug chij.

Hauv xyoo 1777, Tsoom Fwv txiav txim tias tus chij yuav tsum muaj kaum peb txoj kab liab thiab dawb. Nws muaj kawm peb lub hnub qub dawb nyob ntawm qhov chaw xiav.

Ua ntej, ib lub hnub qub thiab ib txoj kab raug muab ntxiv rau tus chij thaum muaj ib lub xeev tshiab. Hauv xyoo 1818, Tsoom Fwv txiav txim tias tus chij yuav tsum muaj kaum peb txoj kab xwb. Ib lub hnub qub yuav sawv cev rau ib lub xeev.

Hnub no peb tus chij muaj tsib caug lub hnub qub. Peb ua kev zoo siab rau tus chij hauv lub Rau Hlis Ntuj Hnub Tim 14, uas hu ua Hnub Chij.

Name ____________________ **The Stars and Stripes**

- **Read** *The Stars and Stripes* again.
- **Draw** a picture to show the American flag in 1776, 1777, and today.
- **Write** words or a sentence to go with your pictures.

Picture of the American Flag	Words or Sentence
1776	____________ ____________
1777	____________ ____________
Today	____________ ____________

Family Link
Ask family members to explain what the flag of the United States means to them.

Weekly Resources Guide for English Language Learner Support

For this week's content and language objectives, see p. 191e.

Instructional Strand	Day 1	Day 2
Concept Development/Academic Language	TEACHER'S EDITION • Academic Language, p. DI•54 • Concept Development, p. DI•54 • Anchored Talk, pp. 426j—426–427 • *Sing with Me* Big Book, p. 427a • Concept Talk Video ELL HANDBOOK • ELL Poster Talk, Concept Talk, p. 191c ELL POSTER 28 • Day 1 Activities	TEACHER'S EDITION • Academic Language, p. DI•54 • Concept Development, p. DI•54 • Anchored Talk, p. 432b • *Sing with Me* Big Book, p. 432a • Concept Talk Video ELL HANDBOOK • ELL Poster Talk, Concept Talk, p. 191c • Concept Talk Video Routine, p. 464 ELL POSTER 28 • Day 2 Activities
Phonics and Spelling	TEACHER'S EDITION • Phonics and Spelling, p. DI•58 • Decodable Reader 28A, pp. 429c–429d	TEACHER'S EDITION • Phonics and Spelling, p. DI•58
Listening Comprehension	TEACHER'S EDITION • Modified Read Aloud, p. DI•57 • *Sing with Me* Big Book, p. 427a • Concept Talk Video ELL HANDBOOK • Concept Talk Video Routine, p. 464	TEACHER'S EDITION • Modified Read Aloud, p. DI•57 • *Sing with Me* Big Book, p. 432a • AudioText of A *Birthday Basket for Tía* • Concept Talk Video ELL HANDBOOK • AudioText CD Routine, p. 464 • Three-Column Chart, p. 481
Reading Comprehension	TEACHER'S EDITION • Teach Draw Conclusions, p. DI•59	TEACHER'S EDITION • Teach Draw Conclusions, p. DI•59 • Frontloading Reading, p. DI•60 ELL HANDBOOK • Picture It! Skill Instruction, pp. 192–192a • Multilingual Summaries, pp. 193–195
Vocabulary **Basic and Lesson Vocabulary** **Vocabulary Skill: Words From Other Languages**	TEACHER'S EDITION • Basic Vocabulary, p. DI•55 • Preteach Lesson Vocabulary, p. DI•55 • Words From Other Languages ELL HANDBOOK • Word Cards, p. 191 • ELL Vocabulary Routine, p. 456 ELL POSTER 28 • Day 1 Activities	TEACHER'S EDITION • Basic Vocabulary, p. DI•55 • Reteach Lesson Vocabulary, p. DI•56 • Words From Other Languages ELL HANDBOOK • Word Cards, p. 191 • Multilingual Vocabulary List, pp. 429–440 ELL POSTER 28 • Day 2 Activities
Grammar and Conventions	TEACHER'S EDITION • Preteach Prepositions, p. DI•62	TEACHER'S EDITION • Reteach Prepositions, p. DI•62
Writing	TEACHER'S EDITION • Word Order Makes Sense, p. DI•63 • Introduce Invitation Letter, pp. 431c–431d	TEACHER'S EDITION • Writing Trait: Sentences, pp. 447d–447e

Unit 6 Week 3 A Birthday Basket for Tía

Leveled Support LS This symbol indicates leveled instruction to address language proficiency levels.

Day 3	Day 4	Day 5
TEACHER'S EDITION • Academic Language, p. DI•54 • Concept Development, p. DI•54 • Anchored Talk, p. 448b • *Sing with Me* Big Book, p. 448a • Concept Talk Video ELL HANDBOOK • ELL Poster Talk, Concept Talk, p. 191c ELL POSTER 28 • Day 3 Activities	TEACHER'S EDITION • Academic Language, p. DI•54 • Concept Development, p. DI•54 • Anchored Talk, p. 452b • *Sing with Me* Big Book, p. 452a • Concept Talk Video ELL HANDBOOK • ELL Poster Talk, Concept Talk, p. 191c ELL POSTER 28 • Day 4 Activities	TEACHER'S EDITION • Academic Language, p. DI•54 • Concept Development, p. DI•54 • Concept Talk Video ELL HANDBOOK • ELL Poster Talk, Concept Talk, p. 191c ELL POSTER 28 • Day 5 Activities
ELL HANDBOOK • Phonics Transition Lesson, pp. 303, 305	TEACHER'S EDITION • Decodable Reader 28C, pp. 452e–452f ELL HANDBOOK • Phonics Transition Lesson, pp. 303, 305	TEACHER'S EDITION • Phonics and Spelling, p. DI•58
TEACHER'S EDITION • *Sing with Me* Big Book, p. 448a • AudioText of *A Birthday Basket for Tía* • Concept Talk Video ELL HANDBOOK • AudioText CD Routine, p. 464	TEACHER'S EDITION • *Sing with Me* Big Book, p. 452a • Concept Talk Video	TEACHER'S EDITION • Concept Talk Video
TEACHER'S EDITION • Sheltered Reading, p. DI•60 ELL HANDBOOK • Multilingual Summaries, pp. 193–195	TEACHER'S EDITION • ELL/ELD Reader Guided Reading, p. DI•61 ELL HANDBOOK • ELL Study Guide, p. 196	TEACHER'S EDITION • ELL/ELD Reader Guided Reading, p. DI•61 ELL HANDBOOK • ELL Study Guide, p. 196
ELL HANDBOOK • High-Frequency Words Activity Bank, p. 491 ELL POSTER 28 • Day 3 Activities	ELL HANDBOOK • High-Frequency Words Activity Bank, p. 491	TEACHER'S EDITION • Words From Other Languages, p. 456–457 ELL HANDBOOK • High-Frequency Words Activity Bank, p. 491
TEACHER'S EDITION • Grammar Jammer ELL HANDBOOK • Grammar Jammer Routine, p. 465	TEACHER'S EDITION • Grammar Jammer	TEACHER'S EDITION • Grammar Jammer
TEACHER'S EDITION • Let's Write It!, p. 450–451 • Writer's Craft: Choosing Details, p. 451a	TEACHER'S EDITION • Revising Strategy, pp. 455c–455d	TEACHER'S EDITION • Writer's Craft: Capitalization in a Letter, pp. 457h–457i

Poster Talk, Concept Talk

Question of the Week

Why are family celebrations special?

ELL Poster 28

Throughout the week, use the ELL Poster to help children produce and comprehend language, understand the concept, and build English vocabulary. Use the Question of the Week and other questions to help children share ideas in pairs, small groups, or the large group. Sample questions are shown, with examples of possible responses by children.

Weekly Concept and Language Goals

- Know that family celebrations are important to people
- Name ways that families can celebrate
- Tell about a family celebration

By the end of the lesson, children should be able to talk about and write one or more sentences about family celebrations.

Daily Team Talk

Day 1	Day 2	Day 3	Day 4	Day 5
After Day 1 activities on Poster, ask questions such as *How did the family in the poster picture decorate for the party?*	After Day 2 activity on Poster, ask questions such as *In the poster picture, the boy's aunt brings a cake. What other celebrations have cake?*	After Day 3 activity on Poster, ask questions such as *In the poster picture, the family celebrates a graduation. What is the reason for the celebration in this week's story?*	After Day 3 activity on Poster, ask questions such as *In the poster picture, the family celebrates a graduation. What do families do at celebrations?*	After Day 5 activity on Poster, ask questions such as *Besides birthdays, what does your family get together to celebrate?*
Beginning Balloons. **Intermediate** They made a sign. **Advanced** People got balloons and made a banner. **Advanced High** The family bought bunches of balloons and hung a banner that says "Congratulations."	**Beginning** Birthdays. **Intermediate** At birthday parties. **Advanced** People have cake at birthday parties. **Advanced High** My family eats cake at birthdays, weddings, and other important events.	**Beginning** A birthday. **Intermediate** An aunt's birthday. **Advanced** They are having a surprise birthday party. **Advanced High** The family is having a surprise birthday party for their great-aunt.	**Beginning** Games. **Intermediate** Families play games. **Advanced** Some families sing and dance at parties. **Advanced High** My family plays music and games and tells stories during our celebrations.	**Beginning** Holidays. **Intermediate** We celebrate holidays. **Advanced** My whole family comes to our house on Thanksgiving. **Advanced High** My family and all of our relatives get together every summer for a family reunion.

This Week's Materials

Teacher's Edition pages 426j–457k

See the support for English language learners throughout the lesson, including ELL strategies and scaffold activities at points of use.

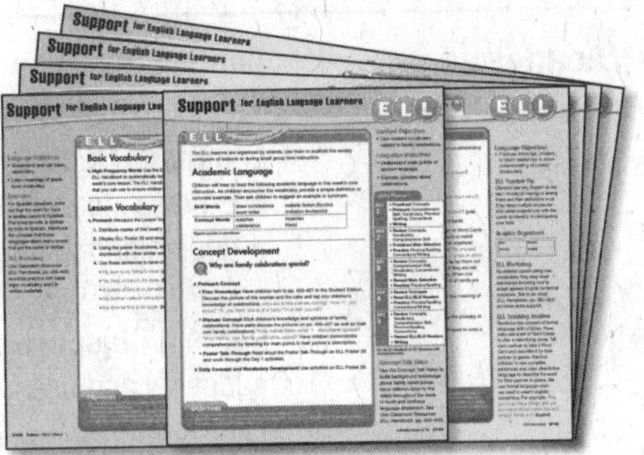

Teacher's Edition pages DI•54–DI•63

Differentiated Instruction for English language learners provides daily group activities that "frontload," or preteach, core instruction.

ELL Handbook pp. 191a–196

Find additional lesson materials that support the core lesson and the ELL instructional pages.

ELL Poster 28

ELD Reader 2.6.3

ELL Reader 2.6.3

Concept Literacy Reader

ELD, ELL Reader Teaching Guide

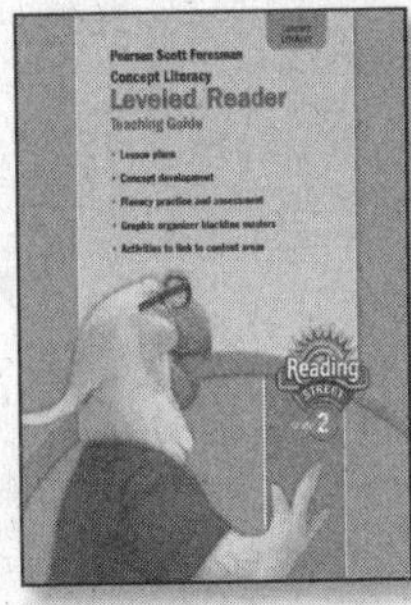

Concept Literacy Reader Teaching Guide

Technology

Online Teacher's Edition Use the digital version of the core teacher's edition for planning and instruction.

eReaders
This Week's ELL and ELD Readers and Concept Literacy Reader are also available in digital format.

This Week's Content and Language Objectives by Strand

Concept Development/Academic Language Why are family celebrations special?	**Content Objective** • Use concept vocabulary related to family celebrations. **Language Objectives** • Express ideas in response to art and discussion. • Understand main points of spoken language.
Phonics and Spelling Final syllables *–tion, -ture, -ion*	**Content Objective** • Identify and use final syllables *–tion, -ture, -ion.* **Language Objective** • Apply phonics and decoding skills to vocabulary.
Listening Comprehension Modified Read Aloud: "Three Poems Celebrating Families"	**Content Objective** • Monitor and adjust oral comprehension. **Language Objectives** • Discuss oral passages. • Use a graphic organizer to take notes.
Reading Comprehension Draw Conclusions	**Content Objectives** • Use illustrations and content to draw conclusions. • Comprehend vocabulary used in written materials. • Monitor and adjust comprehension. **Language Objectives** • Use personal knowledge and experience in drawing conclusions. • Discuss evidence for drawing conclusions. • State conclusions drawn from a reading. • Summarize using visual support.
Vocabulary Basic and Lesson Vocabulary	**Language Objectives** • Understand and use basic vocabulary. • Learn meanings of grade-level vocabulary. • Produce drawings, phrases, or short sentences to show understanding of Lesson Vocabulary.
Vocabulary Words From Other Languages	**Content Objective** • Identify and define words from other languages. **Language Objective** • Recognize directionality of English reading.
Grammar and Conventions Prepositions	**Content Objective** • Identify and use prepositions correctly. **Language Objective** • Speak and write using prepositions correctly.
Writing Word Order Makes Sense	**Content Objective** • Recognize importance of word order to meaning. **Language Objectives** • Write an informal letter of invitation. • Share feedback for editing and revising.

Word Cards for Vocabulary Activities

aunt	**bank**
basket	**collects**
favorite	**present**

Leveled LS Support

Teacher Note: Beginning Teach two to three words. **Intermediate** Teach three to four words. **Advanced** Teach five to six words. **Advanced High** Teach all words.

Name ______________________________

Look at the picture. **Read** the paragraph.

The Piñata

Clara asked Sam and Sarah to help fill the piñata for her party.
"This is a great piñata! Last year I had one that looked like a fish," Sarah said.
"Mine was a flower!" said Clara. "I loved all the pretty colors."
"I love breaking the piñata and getting prizes!" said Sam. They all agreed.

Answer the questions below.

1. What kind of party is Clara having? How do you know?

____

____

2. Is this the first time the children have seen a piñata? How do you know?

____

____

Draw Conclusions

Use this lesson to supplement or replace the skill lesson on page 430a of the Teacher's Edition. Display the Skill Points (at right) and share them with children.

Use the Skill Points to preteach draw conclusions.

Teach/Model

Beginning Act out opening a gift box and expressing surprise and joy. Ask: *I am opening a gift. Did I like the gift or not?* (You liked it.) *How do you know?* (You were surprised, excited, and happy when you saw it.)

Intermediate Say: *I buy a gift. I put a bow on it. I take the gift to my friend's house. What conclusions can you make?* (It is your friend's birthday. Your friend is having a party.) *How did the details help you draw that conclusion?* (We give gifts and have parties for people's birthdays.)

Advanced Show children a picture from a fiction book about parties or birthdays. Have them draw conclusions about the picture. Guide them in writing sentences that state their conclusions.

Advanced High Tell children a story about a birthday party or celebration you had as a child. Have them draw conclusions about events or characters in your story. Ask: *How did you draw this conclusion?* Encourage children to explain how they drew their conclusions.

Then distribute copies of Picture It! page 192.

- Read the paragraph aloud and have children look at the picture. Ask: *What are the children doing?* If necessary, explain what a piñata is in greater detail.
- Review the Skill Points with children.
- Have children look at the picture and paragraph to draw conclusions about the characters and what happens in the story.

Practice

Read aloud the directions on page 192. Reread or chorally read the story. Have children look at the picture and the story as they answer the questions.

Beginning Children can orally answer and write their answers on the lines. Provide help with writing and spelling.

Intermediate Children can first orally answer and then write their answers on the page.

Advanced Children can write their answers and check them by quietly reading them aloud or comparing them with a partner's.

Advanced High Children can write their answers and check them by silently reading them and making any necessary corrections.

Answers for page 192: 1. It is a birthday party. A banner says "Happy Birthday." 2. No, the girls both had a piñata last year. Sam says breaking it is his favorite part.

Skill Points

- ✔ When you **draw a conclusion**, you figure out more about the characters and what happens in a story.
- ✔ You can put together what you know about real life and what you have read to draw conclusions.

Multilingual Summaries

English

A Birthday Basket for Tía

It is Tía's ninetieth birthday. Tía is Cecilia's great-aunt. Cecilia's mother gets ready for the surprise party. Cecilia puts presents in a basket for Tía.

Cecilia puts in a book that Tía reads to her. Cecilia puts in a mixing bowl that they use to make cookies. Cecilia puts in a flowerpot. She puts in a teacup. She puts in the ball they play with. Cecilia decorates the basket with flowers.

Cecilia helps her mother get ready for the party. Family and friends and musicians come. Tía is surprised when she gets to the party. She likes her presents. Tía and Cecilia dance together.

Spanish

Una cesta de cumpleaños para Tía

Hoy se celebran los noventa años de Tía. Ella es la tía abuela de Cecilia. La mamá de Cecilia se prepara para hacerle la fiesta sorpresa. Cecilia pone en una cesta los regalos para Tía.

Cecilia pone un libro que Tía siempre le lee. Pone un tazón de mezclar que usan cuando hacen galletas. Pone un florero. Pone una taza para el té. Pone la pelota con la que ellas juegan. Cecilia decora la cesta con flores.

Cecilia ayuda a su mamá a prepararlo todo para la fiesta. Más tarde llegan la familia, los amigos y los músicos. Tía se sorprende cuando llega a la fiesta. A ella le gustan mucho los regalos. Tía y Cecilia bailan juntas.

Multilingual Summaries

Chinese

蒂亞的生日禮物籃

今天是蒂亞的 90 歲生日，蒂亞是賽西莉亞的姑婆。賽西莉亞的媽媽準備為蒂亞辦一個驚喜的生日會。賽西莉亞將禮物放進籃子裡送給蒂亞。

賽西莉亞把蒂亞讀給她聽的書放進去，把她們做餅乾用的攪拌碗放進去，把花盆放進去，把茶杯放進去，把她們玩的球放進去，最後，賽西莉亞還用鮮花裝飾籃子。

賽西莉亞幫媽媽準備生日會。家人、朋友和樂手都來了。蒂亞看到大家為她開的生日會時，非常驚訝。她喜歡她的禮物，而且還跟賽西莉亞一起跳舞。

Vietnamese

Một Giỏ Quà Sinh Nhật cho Tia

Đây là lễ Sinh Nhật lần thứ chín mươi của Tia. Tia là Bà Cô của Cecilia. Mẹ của Cecilia chuẩn bị một bữa tiệc bất ngờ. Cecilia đặt các món quà vào một cái giỏ cho Bà Cô Tia.

Cecilia đặt vào một quyển sách mà Bà Cô Tia đọc cho cô bé. Cecilia đặt vào một cái thau để pha trộn mà họ dùng để làm bánh. Cecilia đặt vào một chậu để trồng hoa. Cô bé đặt vào một tách để dùng trà. Cô bé đặt một quả bóng để họ cùng chơi. Cecilia trang trí cái giỏ với những cành hoa.

Cecilia giúp mẹ chuẩn bị bữa tiệc. Bạn bè, gia đình và các nhạc sĩ đến. Bà Cô Tia ngạc nhiên khi bà đến nơi. Bà thích những món quà. Cecilia và Bà Cô Tia cùng nhau nhảy múa.

Multilingual Summaries

Korean

티아 할머니의 생일 바구니

오늘은 세실리아의 대고모인 티아 할머니의 90번째 생일이다. 세실리아의 어머니는 깜짝 파티를 준비하고 있고 세실리아는 티아 할머니를 위해 바구니에 선물들을 넣는다.

세실리아는 티아 할머니가 그녀에게 읽어준 책 한 권과 과자를 구울 때 쓰던 대접, 화분, 찻잔과 함께 가지고 놀던 공을 넣고 꽃으로 바구니를 장식한다.

세실리아는 어머니가 파티 준비하는 것을 돕고 가족들과 친구들과 음악가들이 집에 도착한다. 티아 할머니는 파티장에 도착해서 깜짝 놀란다. 선물을 마음에 들어 하는 티아 할머니와 세실리아가 함께 춤을 춘다.

Hmong

Ib Lub Kawm Rau Tia Hnub Yug

Yog Tia lub kaum cuaj xyoo hnub yug. Tia yog Cecilia tus phauj koob. Cecilia niam npaj rau pluag mov noj zoo siab rau hnub yug. Cecilia tso tej khoom plig rau hauv lub kawm rau Tia.

Cecilia tso ib phau ntawv uas Tia nyeem rau nws. Cecilia tso ib lub tais uas lawv siv ci khaub noom. Cecilia tso ib tsob paj rau hauv. Nws tso ib lub khob hauv dej kub rau hauv. Nws tso ib lub npas uas nkawd tau ua siv nrog rau hauv. Cecilia muab tej paj ntoos los ua kom lub kawm zoo nkauj.

Cecilia pab nws niam npaj rau pluag mov noj zoo siab. Tsev neeg thiab cov phooj ywg thiab cov neeg ntau nkauj tau tuaj. Tia zoo siab kawg thaum nws tuaj txog. Nws nyiam nws cov khoom plig. Tia thiab Cecilia seev cev ua ke.

Name ______________________

- **Read** *Twelve Grapes for the New Year* again.
- **Draw** a picture that shows how Benito and his family celebrate the new year. **Label** the things in your picture.
- **Write** a sentence that tells what Benito is doing.
- **Write** a sentence that tells why he is doing it.

____

____

____

____

Family Link

Have family members describe their favorite family traditions. Ask why those traditions are their favorites.

Weekly Resources Guide for English Language Learner Support

For this week's content and language objectives, see p. 197e.

Instructional Strand	Day 1	Day 2
Concept Development/Academic Language	TEACHER'S EDITION • Academic Language, p. DI•75 • Concept Development, p. DI•75 • Anchored Talk, pp. 458j—458–459 • *Sing with Me* Big Book, p. 459a • Concept Talk Video ELL HANDBOOK • ELL Poster Talk, Concept Talk, p. 197c ELL POSTER 29 • Day 1 Activities	TEACHER'S EDITION • Academic Language, p. DI•75 • Concept Development, p. DI•75 • Anchored Talk, p. 464b • *Sing with Me* Big Book, p. 464a • Concept Talk Video ELL HANDBOOK • ELL Poster Talk, Concept Talk, p. 197c • Concept Talk Video Routine, p. 464 ELL POSTER 29 • Day 2 Activities
Phonics and Spelling	TEACHER'S EDITION • Phonics and Spelling, p. DI•79 • Decodable Reader 29A, pp. 461c–461d	TEACHER'S EDITION • Phonics and Spelling, p. DI•79
Listening Comprehension	TEACHER'S EDITION • Modified Read Aloud, p. DI•78 • *Sing with Me* Big Book, p. 459a • Concept Talk Video ELL HANDBOOK • Concept Talk Video Routine, p. 464	TEACHER'S EDITION • Modified Read Aloud, p. DI•78 • *Sing with Me* Big Book, p. 464a • AudioText of *Cowboys* • Concept Talk Video ELL HANDBOOK • AudioText CD Routine, p. 464 • T-Chart, p. 480
Reading Comprehension	TEACHER'S EDITION • Teach Sequence, p. DI•80	TEACHER'S EDITION • Teach Sequence, p. DI•80 • Frontloading Reading, p. DI•81 ELL HANDBOOK • Picture It! Skill Instruction, pp. 198–198a • Multilingual Summaries, pp. 199–201
Vocabulary **Basic and Lesson Vocabulary** **Vocabulary Skill: Unfamiliar Words**	TEACHER'S EDITION • Basic Vocabulary, p. DI•76 • Preteach Lesson Vocabulary, p. DI•76 • Unfamiliar Words, p. DI•79 ELL HANDBOOK • Word Cards, p. 197 • ELL Vocabulary Routine, p. 456 ELL POSTER 29 • Day 1 Activities	TEACHER'S EDITION • Basic Vocabulary, p. DI•76 • Reteach Lesson Vocabulary, p. DI•77 • Unfamiliar Words, p. DI•79 ELL HANDBOOK • Word Cards, p. 197 • Multilingual Vocabulary List, pp. 429–440 ELL POSTER 29 • Day 2 Activities
Grammar and Conventions	TEACHER'S EDITION • Preteach Commas, p. DI•83	TEACHER'S EDITION • Reteach Commas, p. DI•83
Writing	TEACHER'S EDITION • Comparing and Contrasting Two Things, p. DI•84 • Introduce Compare-and-Contrast Text, pp. 463c–463d	TEACHER'S EDITION • Writing Trait: Focus/Ideas, pp. 487d–487e

This symbol indicates leveled instruction to address language proficiency levels.

Day 3	Day 4	Day 5
TEACHER'S EDITION • Academic Language, p. DI•75 • Concept Development, p. DI•75 • Anchored Talk, p. 488b • *Sing with Me* Big Book, p. 488a • Concept Talk Video ELL HANDBOOK • ELL Poster Talk, Concept Talk, p. 197c ELL POSTER 29 • Day 3 Activities	TEACHER'S EDITION • Academic Language, p. DI•75 • Concept Development, p. DI•75 • Anchored Talk, p. 492b • *Sing with Me* Big Book, p. 492a • Concept Talk Video ELL HANDBOOK • ELL Poster Talk, Concept Talk, p. 197c ELL POSTER 29 • Day 4 Activities	TEACHER'S EDITION • Academic Language, p. DI•75 • Concept Development, p. DI•75 • Concept Talk Video ELL HANDBOOK • ELL Poster Talk, Concept Talk, p. 197c ELL POSTER 29 • Day 5 Activities
ELL HANDBOOK • Phonics Transition Lesson, pp. 292, 299	TEACHER'S EDITION • Decodable Reader 29C, pp. 492e–492f ELL HANDBOOK • Phonics Transition Lesson, pp. 292, 299	TEACHER'S EDITION • Phonics and Spelling, p. DI•79
TEACHER'S EDITION • *Sing with Me* Big Book, p. 488a • AudioText of *Cowboys* • Concept Talk Video ELL HANDBOOK • AudioText CD Routine, p. 464	TEACHER'S EDITION • *Sing with Me* Big Book, p. 492a • Concept Talk Video	TEACHER'S EDITION • Concept Talk Video
TEACHER'S EDITION • Sheltered Reading, p. DI•81 ELL HANDBOOK • Multilingual Summaries, pp. 199–201	TEACHER'S EDITION • ELL/ELD Reader Guided Reading, p. DI•82 ELL HANDBOOK • ELL Study Guide, p. 202	TEACHER'S EDITION • ELL/ELD Reader Guided Reading, p. DI•82 ELL HANDBOOK • ELL Study Guide, p. 202
ELL HANDBOOK • High-Frequency Words Activity Bank, p. 491 ELL POSTER 29 • Day 3 Activities	ELL HANDBOOK • High-Frequency Words Activity Bank, p. 491	TEACHER'S EDITION • Unfamiliar Words, p. 494–495 ELL HANDBOOK • High-Frequency Words Activity Bank, p. 491
TEACHER'S EDITION • Grammar Jammer ELL HANDBOOK • Grammar Transition Lesson, pp. 349, 362–363 • Grammar Jammer Routine, p. 465	TEACHER'S EDITION • Grammar Jammer ELL HANDBOOK • Grammar Transition Lesson, pp. 349, 362–363	TEACHER'S EDITION • Grammar Jammer ELL HANDBOOK • Grammar Transition Lesson, pp. 349, 362–363
TEACHER'S EDITION • Let's Write It!, p. 490–491 • Writer's Craft: Compare/Contrast Words, p. 491a	TEACHER'S EDITION • Revising Strategy, pp. 493d–493e	TEACHER'S EDITION • Writer's Craft: Clue Words and Commas, pp. 495h–495i

Poster Talk, Concept Talk

Question of the Week

What can we learn about cowboy traditions?

Poster 29

Throughout the week, use the ELL Poster to help children produce and comprehend language, understand the concept, and build English vocabulary. Use the Question of the Week and other questions to help children share ideas in pairs, small groups, or the large group. Sample questions are shown, with examples of possible responses by children.

Weekly Concept and Language Goals

- Know the importance of cowboys and their traditions
- Tell how cowboys do their jobs
- Tell how cowboys keep the tradition alive

By the end of the lesson, children should be able to talk about and write one or more sentences about the cowboy way of life.

Daily Team Talk

Day 1	Day 2	Day 3	Day 4	Day 5
After Day 1 activities on Poster, ask questions such as *Why is the cowboy in the poster picture throwing a rope around the cow?*	After Day 2 activities on Poster, ask questions such as *Where are the cowboys taking the herd?*	After Day 3 activity on Poster, ask questions such as *What things did cowboys need to do their job?*	After Day 4 activity on Poster, ask questions such as *What do you think cowboys did around the campfire at night?*	After Day 5 activity on Poster, ask questions such as *Where can you go to learn more about cowboy traditions?*
Beginning It's running. **Intermediate** The cow is running away. **Advanced** He wants to keep the cows together. **Advanced High** The cowboy wants to keep all the cows together in a herd.	**Beginning** To the town. **Intermediate** They are taking them to the town. **Advanced** They are taking the cows to the town near the hills. **Advanced High** The cowboys are taking the herd to the town to be sold.	**Beginning** Ropes and horses. **Intermediate** They needed rope and a horse. **Advanced** Cowboys needed rope to catch cows. **Advanced High** Cowboys needed a horse to ride and a rope to catch cows.	**Beginning** Talk. **Intermediate** They told stories. **Advanced** They ate dinner and told stories. **Advanced High** They probably ate dinner, told stories, and went to sleep around the campfire.	**Beginning** Books. **Intermediate** I can use a computer. **Advanced** I could look in an encyclopedia. **Advanced High** I can go to the library to look for books about cowboys. I can ask my grandfather to tell me stories about the Old West.

This Week's Materials

Teacher's Edition pages 458j–495k

See the support for English language learners throughout the lesson, including ELL strategies and scaffold activities at points of use.

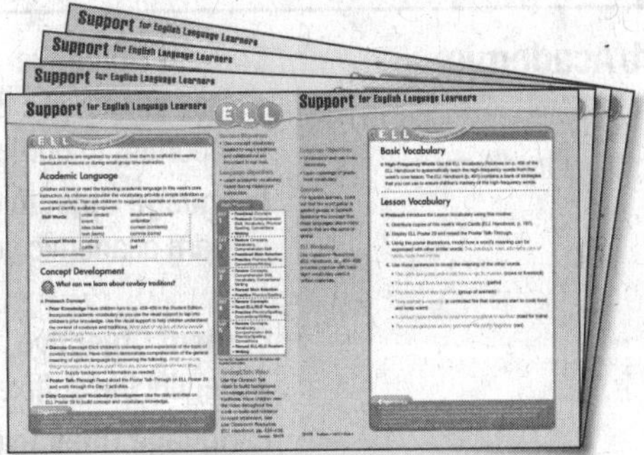

Teacher's Edition pages DI•75–DI•84

Differentiated Instruction for English language learners provides daily group activities that "frontload," or preteach, core instruction.

ELL Handbook pp. 197a–202

Find additional lesson materials that support the core lesson and the ELL instructional pages.

ELL Poster 29

ELD Reader 2.6.4

ELL Reader 2.6.4

Concept Literacy Reader

ELD, ELL Reader Teaching Guide

Concept Literacy Reader Teaching Guide

Technology

Online Teacher's Edition Use the digital version of the core teacher's edition for planning and instruction.

eReaders
This Week's ELL and ELD Readers and Concept Literacy Reader are also available in digital format.

This Week's Content and Language Objectives by Strand

Concept Development/Academic Language What can we learn about cowboy traditions?	**Content Objective** • Use concept vocabulary related to ways traditions and celebrations are important in our lives. **Language Objective** • Learn academic vocabulary heard during classroom instruction.
Phonics and Spelling Suffixes *-less* and *-ness*	**Content Objective** • Identify the suffixes *–less* and *–ness* in words. **Language Objective** • Apply phonics and decoding skills to vocabulary.
Listening Comprehension Modified Read Aloud: "The Modern Cowboy"	**Content Objective** • Monitor and adjust oral comprehension. **Language Objectives** • Discuss oral passages. • Use a graphic organizer to take notes.
Reading Comprehension Sequence	**Content Objectives** • Identify sequence to aid comprehension. • Identify cause and effect to aid comprehension. • Monitor and adjust comprehension. **Language Objectives** • Discuss evidence for sequence. • Retell cause and effect from a reading. • Summarize using visual support.
Vocabulary Basic and Lesson Vocabulary	**Language Objectives** • Understand and use basic vocabulary. • Learn meanings of grade-level vocabulary. • Produce drawings, phrases, or short sentences to show understanding of Lesson Vocabulary.
Vocabulary Unfamiliar Words	**Content Objective** • Identify and define unfamiliar words. **Language Objective** • Discuss the meanings of unfamiliar words.
Grammar and Conventions Commas	**Content Objective** • Identify and use commas. **Language Objectives** • Speak using a variety of sentence lengths and types, with increasing accuracy and ease, as more English is required. • Use proper inflection when reading aloud sentences that include commas.
Writing Comparing and Contrasting Two Things	**Content Objective** • Identify comparison and contrast in text. **Language Objectives** • Write paragraphs using comparison and contrast. • Share feedback for editing and revising.

Word Cards for Vocabulary Activities

campfire	**cattle**
cowboy	**galloped**
herd	**railroad**
trails	

Teacher Note: Beginning Teach two to three words. **Intermediate** Teach three to four words. **Advanced** Teach five to six words. **Advanced High** Teach all words.

Name ______________________________

Picture It!
Sequence

Look at the pictures. **Read** the paragraphs.

- **What** happens in the story? **Write** the events shown in the story.
- Be sure to write them in the order in which they happened.

The Storm

The cowboys are moving their cattle. First, the cowboys see the sky turn dark.

Then, rain falls. Next, thunder booms and scares the cattle. The cattle run. The cowboys know what to do.

The storm is over. The cattle are quiet again, so the cowboys eat their dinner.

First ______________________________

Then ______________________________

Next ______________________________

Last ______________________________

Sequence

Use this lesson to supplement or replace the skill lesson on page 462a of the Teacher's Edition. Display the Skill Points (at right) and share them with children.

Use the Skill Points to preteach sequence.

Teach/Model

Prepare four picture cards showing a farm story with a recognizable sequence. Include benchmarks such as the sun or familiar meals to mark the passage of time.

Beginning Tell children a simple story using the picture cards. Ask: *Which card shows what happens first?* Have children point to the correct card. Repeat the process, asking children what happens then, next, and last.

Intermediate Use the picture cards to tell a story. Show children the cards with two out of sequence. Ask: *How do you know this happens first/next/last in the story?*

Advanced Display the picture cards in order on the board ledge. Ask children to narrate the sequence of events using words such as *first, next, then, now,* and *finally*. Write their sentences on the board above the corresponding pictures.

Advanced High Pair children. Have partners draw pictures of events from stories they make up. Then have partners share their stories with the group, using words such as *first, next, then, now,* and *finally*.

Then distribute copies of Picture It! page 198.

- Have children look at the pictures and describe what is happening in each one.
- Read the sentences aloud. Ask: *What happens first in the story? What happens next?*
- Review the Skill Points with children.
- Have children look at the pictures and words to find clues about the order of events in the story.

Practice

Read aloud the directions on page 198. Reread or chorally read the story. Have children look at the pictures and the story as they answer the questions.

Beginning Children can orally answer and write their answers on the lines. Provide help with writing and spelling.

Intermediate Children can first orally answer and then write their answers on the page.

Advanced Children can write their answers and check them by comparing their sequence with a partner's or quietly reading aloud their writing.

Advanced High Children can write their answers and check them by silently rereading the story's sequence and making any necessary corrections.

Answers for page 198: First, the cowboys see the sky turn dark. Then, rain falls. Next, thunder scares the cattle. The cattle run. Last, the cowboys eat dinner.

Skill Points

- ✔ **Sequence** is the order of events in a story.
- ✔ Think about what happens first, next, and last.
- ✔ Look for words such as *first, next, then, now,* and *finally* to help you figure out the order of events.

Multilingual Summaries

English

Cowboys

In the 1800s, cowboys lived on cattle ranches in the western United States. Twice a year, cowboys rounded up the cattle. They herded cattle to a market town to be sold. The cows and cowboys walked on a long trail to get to a market town. This trail drive might take months.

At night, the cook made a meal for the cowboys. Cowboys went to sleep early. They slept on the ground.

Sometimes a cowboy's job was dangerous. Many dangerous things could happen. Frightened cattle could stampede. Rustlers could steal cattle. At the end of the trail, cowboys were paid. Then they took baths!

Spanish

Vaqueros

En los años 1800, los vaqueros vivían en ranchos ganaderos en el oeste de Estados Unidos. Dos veces al año, reunían el ganado. Llevaban la manada a un pueblo con un mercado para venderlo. Las vacas y los vaqueros recorrían largas sendas para llegar al mercado. A veces ese viaje duraba meses.

Por las noches, el cocinero preparaba la comida para los vaqueros. Los vaqueros se acostaban temprano. Ellos dormían en el piso.

Algunas veces, el trabajo de los vaqueros era difícil. Podían pasar cosas muy peligrosas. El ganado asustado podía salir en estampida. Los ladrones podían robarse al ganado. Al final de la jornada, los vaqueros recibían su paga. ¡Entonces se bañaban!

Multilingual Summaries

Chinese

牛仔

十九世紀時，美國西部的牛仔住在大牧場裡。牛仔每年都要把牛集合起來兩次，將整群牛趕到鎮上市場賣。牛仔和牛要沿著長長的小路走到鎮上去，這可能會花上好幾個月的時間。

晚上，廚師會煮飯給牛仔吃。牛仔吃完以後很早就睡了。他們沒有床，只能睡在地上。

牛仔的工作有時會很危險，什麼驚險的事情也可能發生，像是受驚嚇的牛會到處亂跑，偷牛賊會前來偷牛。到達目的地以後，牛仔就可以拿到薪金，然後他們會去洗個香噴噴的好澡。

Vietnamese

Những Người Chăn Bò

Vào những năm 1800 ở miền tây Hoa Kỳ, những người chăn bò sống ở những trang trại nuôi bò. Mỗi năm hai lần, những người chăn bò đi gom đàn bò về. Họ lùa đàn bò đi đến phố chợ để bán. Những con bò và người chăn đi trên một chặng đường dài để đi đến phố chợ. Chặng đường này có thể đi mất mấy tháng.

Đêm đến, đầu bếp nấu ăn cho những người chăn bò. Những người chăn bò đi ngủ sớm. Họ ngủ trên đất.

Thỉnh thoảng công việc của một người chăn bò trở nên nguy hiểm. Nhiều điều nguy hiểm có thể xảy ra. Đàn bò hoảng sợ có thể chạy tán loạn. Những tên trộm bò có thể ăn cắp đàn bò. Ở cuối chặng đường, những người chăn bò được trả tiền. Lúc đó họ đi tắm!

Multilingual Summaries

Korean

카우보이

1800년대 미국 서부에서는 카우보이들이 소 방목장에서 살았다. 일년에 두 번 카우보이들은 소 떼를 몰아들였다. 그들은 소를 몰아서 장에 내다 팔았는데 장에 도착하기 위해서는 소들도 카우보이들도 몇 달이 걸리는 기나긴 산길을 걸어야만 했다.

밤에는 요리사가 카우보이를 위해 음식을 만들었다. 카우보이들은 일찍 잠을 청했는데 땅바닥에서 잠을 잤다.

때때로 카우보이의 일은 위험했다. 놀란 소들이 일제히 우르르 달아나버리거나 가축 도둑들이 소를 훔쳐가는 그런 많은 위험한 일들이 벌어질 수도 있었다. 여정이 끝날 때 카우보이들은 돈을 받고는 목욕을 즐겼다.

Hmong

Cowboys

Thaum 1800 yuav kawg nyob hauv sab hnub poob ntawm lub Teb Chaws Mikas cov cowboys tau nyob hauv tej teb yug tsiaj txhua. Ob zaug ib xyoos, cov cowboys tau tav cov nyuj. Lawv tav cov nyuj mus rau qhov chaw muag nyuj thiab muab cov nyuj muag. Cov nyuj thiab cov cowboys mus kev ua ke kom mus txog qhov chaw muag nyuj. Tej zaum yuav siv li ntau lub hlis thiaj mus txog.

Thaum tsaus ntuj, tus uas mov noj ua mov rau cov cowboys noj. Cov cowboys mus pw ntxov ntxov. Lawv pw hauv pem teb.

Txhia zaus cov cowboy txoj hauj lwm txaus ntshai heev. Yeej muaj tau ntau yam txaus ntxhais uas tshwm sim. Cov nyuj uas ntshai yeej ceeb thiab dhia. Cov tub sab yeej nyiag tau cov nyuj. Thaum kawg, cov cowboy khwv tau nyiaj. Ces lawv da dej.

Name ___________________

- **Read** *What Does a Cowboy Do?* again.
- **Complete** the *What and Why* chart.

What and Why

Page	What happened?	Why?
3	**1.** Cowboys take cattle to market.	**1.** ___________
4	**2.** ___________	**2.** This is how ranchers got their cattle to market.
5	**3.** Cowboys wear hats, boots, leather chaps, and gloves.	**3.** ___________
6	**4.** ___________	**4.** A cowboy needs a saddle to ride his horse.

Family Link

Ask family members to tell what they think it would be like to be a cowboy or cowgirl.

Weekly Resources Guide for English Language Learner Support

For this week's content and language objectives, see p. 203e.

Instructional Strand	Day 1	Day 2
Concept Development/Academic Language	TEACHER'S EDITION • Academic Language, p. DI•96 • Concept Development, p. DI•96 • Anchored Talk, pp. 496j—496–497 • *Sing with Me* Big Book, p. 497a • Concept Talk Video ELL HANDBOOK • ELL Poster Talk, Concept Talk, p. 203c ELL POSTER 30 • Day 1 Activities	TEACHER'S EDITION • Academic Language, p. DI•96 • Concept Development, p. DI•96 • Anchored Talk, p. 502b • *Sing with Me* Big Book, p. 502a • Concept Talk Video ELL HANDBOOK • ELL Poster Talk, Concept Talk, p. 203c • Concept Talk Video Routine, p. 464 ELL POSTER 30 • Day 2 Activities
Phonics and Spelling	TEACHER'S EDITION • Phonics and Spelling, p. DI•100 • Decodable Reader 30A, pp. 499c–499d	TEACHER'S EDITION • Phonics and Spelling, p. DI•100
Listening Comprehension	TEACHER'S EDITION • Modified Read Aloud, p. DI•99 • *Sing with Me* Big Book, p. 497a • Concept Talk Video ELL HANDBOOK • Concept Talk Video Routine, p. 464	TEACHER'S EDITION • Modified Read Aloud, p. DI•99 • *Sing with Me* Big Book, p. 502a • AudioText of *Grace for President* • Concept Talk Video ELL HANDBOOK • AudioText CD Routine, p. 464 • Story Map B, p. 471
Reading Comprehension	TEACHER'S EDITION • Teach Facts and Details, p. DI•101	TEACHER'S EDITION • Teach Facts and Details, p. DI•101 • Frontloading Reading, p. DI•102 ELL HANDBOOK • Picture It! Skill Instruction, pp. 204–204a • Multilingual Summaries, pp. 205–207
Vocabulary **Basic and Lesson Vocabulary** **Vocabulary Skill: Multiple-Meaning Words**	TEACHER'S EDITION • Basic Vocabulary, p. DI•97 • Preteach Lesson Vocabulary, p. DI•97 • Multiple-Meaning Words, p. DI•100 ELL HANDBOOK • Word Cards, p. 203 • ELL Vocabulary Routine, p. 456 ELL POSTER 30 • Day 1 Activities	TEACHER'S EDITION • Basic Vocabulary, p. DI•97 • Reteach Lesson Vocabulary, p. DI•98 • Multiple-Meaning Words, p. DI•100 ELL HANDBOOK • Word Cards, p. 203 • Multilingual Vocabulary List, pp. 429–440 ELL POSTER 30 • Day 2 Activities
Grammar and Conventions	TEACHER'S EDITION • Preteach Commas in Compound Sentences, p. DI•104	TEACHER'S EDITION • Reteach Commas in Compound Sentences, p. DI•104
Writing	TEACHER'S EDITION • Using Vivid Words to Appeal to Readers, p. DI•105 • Writing for Tests: Persuasive Statements, pp. 501c–501d	TEACHER'S EDITION • Writing for Tests: Persuasive Statements, pp. 519c–519d

This symbol indicates leveled instruction to address language proficiency levels.

Day 3	Day 4	Day 5
TEACHER'S EDITION • Academic Language, p. DI•96 • Concept Development, p. DI•96 • Anchored Talk, p. 520b • *Sing with Me* Big Book, p. 520a • Concept Talk Video ELL HANDBOOK • ELL Poster Talk, Concept Talk, p. 203c ELL POSTER 30 • Day 3 Activities	TEACHER'S EDITION • Academic Language, p. DI•96 • Concept Development, p. DI•96 • Anchored Talk, p. 524b • *Sing with Me* Big Book, p. 524a • Concept Talk Video ELL HANDBOOK • ELL Poster Talk, Concept Talk, p. 203c ELL POSTER 30 • Day 4 Activities	TEACHER'S EDITION • Academic Language, p. DI•96 • Concept Development, p. DI•96 • Concept Talk Video ELL HANDBOOK • ELL Poster Talk, Concept Talk, p. 203c ELL POSTER 30 • Day 5 Activities
ELL HANDBOOK • Phonics Transition Lesson, pp. 290, 297	TEACHER'S EDITION • Decodable Reader 30C, pp. 524e–524f ELL HANDBOOK • Phonics Transition Lesson, pp. 290, 297	TEACHER'S EDITION • Phonics and Spelling, p. DI•100
TEACHER'S EDITION • *Sing with Me* Big Book, p. 520a • AudioText of *Grace for President* • Concept Talk Video ELL HANDBOOK • AudioText CD Routine, p. 464	TEACHER'S EDITION • *Sing with Me* Big Book, p. 524a • Concept Talk Video	TEACHER'S EDITION • Concept Talk Video
TEACHER'S EDITION • Sheltered Reading, p. DI•102 ELL HANDBOOK • Multilingual Summaries, pp. 205–207	TEACHER'S EDITION • ELL/ELD Reader Guided Reading, p. DI•103 ELL HANDBOOK • ELL Study Guide, p. 208	TEACHER'S EDITION • ELL/ELD Reader Guided Reading, p. DI•103 ELL HANDBOOK • ELL Study Guide, p. 208
ELL HANDBOOK • High-Frequency Words Activity Bank, p. 491 ELL POSTER 30 • Day 3 Activities	ELL HANDBOOK • High-Frequency Words Activity Bank, p. 491	TEACHER'S EDITION • Multiple-Meaning Words, p. 528–529 ELL HANDBOOK • High-Frequency Words Activity Bank, p. 491
TEACHER'S EDITION • Grammar Jammer ELL HANDBOOK • Grammar Transition Lesson, pp. 349, 362 • Grammar Jammer Routine, p. 465	TEACHER'S EDITION • Grammar Jammer ELL HANDBOOK • Grammar Transition Lesson, pp. 349, 362	TEACHER'S EDITION • Grammar Jammer ELL HANDBOOK • Grammar Transition Lesson, pp. 349, 362
TEACHER'S EDITION • Let's Write It!, p. 522–523 • Writing Trait: Word Choice, p. 523a	TEACHER'S EDITION • Writing Trait: Using Vivid Words, pp. 527c–527d	TEACHER'S EDITION • Revising Strategy, pp. 529h–529i

Poster Talk, Concept Talk

Question of the Week

How are different traditions celebrated and shared?

Poster 30

Throughout the week, use the ELL Poster to help children produce and comprehend language, understand the concept, and build English vocabulary. Use the Question of the Week and other questions to help children share ideas in pairs, small groups, or the large group. Sample questions are shown, with examples of possible responses by children.

Weekly Concept and Language Goals

- Know how traditions and celebrations are shared
- Name ways that people get ready for celebrations
- Tell about the importance of food at celebrations

By the end of the lesson, children should be able to talk about and write one or more sentences about celebrations.

Daily Team Talk

Day 1	Day 2	Day 3	Day 4	Day 5
After Day 1 activities on Poster, ask questions such as *How do you think the people in the poster picture feel?*	After Day 2 activity on Poster, ask questions such as *How did the people in the poster picture get ready for this celebration?*	After Day 3 activity on Poster, ask questions such as *The celebration in the poster picture happens outside. What is another celebration that happens outside?*	After Day 4 activity on Poster, ask questions such as *Food is an important part of many celebrations. What kind of food does your family have at a Thanksgiving celebration?*	After Day 5 activity on Poster, ask questions such as *How does your family celebrate New Year's Eve?*
Beginning Happy. **Intermediate** They are excited. **Advanced** People are excited that the woman won the election. **Advanced High** People are thrilled that their candidate won the election. They are going to celebrate.	**Beginning** Got food. **Intermediate** People made signs. **Advanced** They set up tables with food and made signs. **Advanced High** The people in charge had to prepare food, paint signs, and set up chairs.	**Beginning** The Fourth of July. **Intermediate** People celebrate the Fourth of July outside. **Advanced** Many people have a party outside on Independence Day. **Advanced High** My family has a barbecue and watches fireworks outside on Independence Day.	**Beginning** Turkey. **Intermediate** We have turkey and mashed potatoes. **Advanced** Our family likes to eat turkey, mashed potatoes, and green beans. **Advanced High** My mom always makes turkey and stuffing. My grandmother brings pumpkin pie.	**Beginning** Dancing. **Intermediate** We sing and dance. **Advanced** We play music and blow horns. **Advanced High** My family celebrates with fun songs and crazy dances.

This Week's Materials

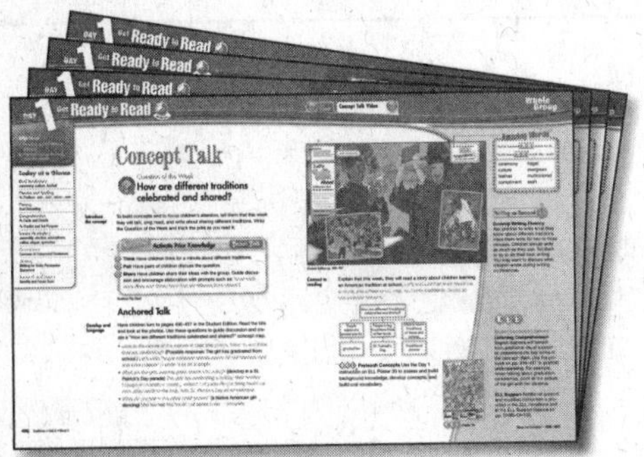

Teacher's Edition pages 496j–529k

See the support for English language learners throughout the lesson, including ELL strategies and scaffold activities at points of use.

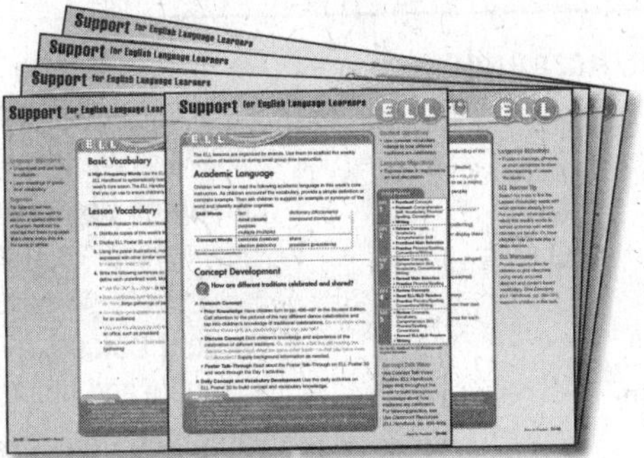

Teacher's Edition pages DI•96–DI•105

Differentiated Instruction for English language learners provides daily group activities that "frontload," or preteach, core instruction.

ELL Handbook pp. 203a–208

Find additional lesson materials that support the core lesson and the ELL instructional pages.

ELL Poster 30

ELD Reader 2.6.5

ELL Reader 2.6.5

Election Day

By Harriet Sigerman

Concept Literacy Reader

ELD, ELL Reader Teaching Guide

Concept Literacy Reader Teaching Guide

Technology

Online Teacher's Edition Use the digital version of the core teacher's edition for planning and instruction.

eReaders
This Week's ELL and ELD Readers and Concept Literacy Reader are also available in digital format.

This Week's Content and Language Objectives by Strand

Concept Development/Academic Language How are different traditions celebrated and shared?	**Content Objective** • Use concept vocabulary related to how different traditions are celebrated. **Language Objective** • Express ideas in response to art and discussion.
Phonics and Spelling Prefixes *mis-*, *mid-*, and *non-*	**Content Objective** • Identify and define words with prefixes. **Language Objective** • Apply phonics and decoding skills to vocabulary.
Listening Comprehension Modified Read Aloud: "Karin Remembers Saint Lucia Day"	**Content Objective** • Monitor and adjust oral comprehension. **Language Objectives** • Discuss oral passages. • Use a graphic organizer to take notes.
Reading Comprehension Facts and Details	**Content Objectives** • Distinguish facts from details. • Identify facts and details to aid comprehension. • Monitor and adjust comprehension. **Language Objectives** • Discuss evidence for facts and details. • Retell facts and details from a reading. • Summarize using visual support.
Vocabulary Basic and Lesson Vocabulary	**Language Objectives** • Understand and use basic vocabulary. • Learn meanings of grade-level vocabulary. • Produce drawings, phrases, or short sentences to show understanding of Lesson Vocabulary.
Vocabulary Unfamiliar Words	**Content Objective** • Identify unfamiliar words. **Language Objectives** • Spell familiar English words. • Learn and write the meanings of multiple-meaning words.
Grammar and Conventions Commas in Compound Sentences	**Content Objective** • Correctly form compound sentences using commas. **Language Objectives** • Speak using compound sentences with connecting words. • Write using commas in compound sentences.
Writing Using Vivid Words to Appeal to Readers	**Content Objective** • Use vivid words to appeal to readers. **Language Objectives** • Write paragraphs using vivid words to appeal to readers. • Share feedback for editing and revising.

Word Cards for Vocabulary Activities

microphone	**slogan**
rallies	**speeches**
election	**assembly**

Leveled Support

Teacher Note: Beginning Teach two to three words. **Intermediate** Teach three to four words. **Advanced** Teach five to six words. **Advanced High** Teach all words.

Name ______________________________

Picture It!
Facts and Details

Look at the picture. **Read** the story.

Sweet Fifteen

Today is Carmen's birthday. She turns fifteen. It is a very important birthday. It means Carmen is not a little girl. Now, she is a young lady.

Carmen's family is having a big party. She has a pretty dress. She dances with her friends and her family. Everyone is having a good time. Her mom brings out cake. Everyone sings to Carmen. The party is over. Carmen thinks it was the best party ever!

Answer the questions below.

1. How old is Carmen today?
○ 10 ○ 15 ○ 20

2. Who has a party for Carmen?
○ Carmen's family ○ Carmen's friends
○ Carmen's classmates

3. Write a detail about Carmen's party.

____

____

Facts and Details

Use this lesson to supplement or replace the skill lesson on page 500a of the Teacher's Edition. Display the Skill Points (at right) and share them with children.

Skill Points

✔ **Facts** can be proven true. You can check in a book, ask someone who knows, or see for yourself.

✔ **Details** are pieces of information.

Use the Skill Points to preteach facts and details.

Teach/Model

Beginning Say: *I am ___ years old.* Guide children in identifying the statement as a fact. Then have them draw details they remember from their birthdays.

Intermediate Display the following and read aloud: *My birthday is on ___. My dad will give me a gift.* Guide children in circling the fact (your date of birth) and underlining the detail.

Advanced Show children the current month on a calendar. Ask them to state facts about the month or week, such as *My birthday is on a Friday. This is the month of May.* Guide children in identifying which facts may also be considered details.

Advanced High Tell children a fact about a celebration. Ask: *How can you prove this is a fact?* (I can check a book. I can see for myself. I can ask someone who knows.) Then help children write details about their favorite celebrations.

Then distribute copies of Picture It! page 204.

- Have children look at the picture and describe what they see.
- Read the paragraphs aloud. Ask: *Can you find a fact in the story?*
- Review the Skill Points with children.
- Have children look at the picture and paragraphs to find facts and details.

Practice

Read aloud the directions on page 204. Reread or chorally read the story. Have children look at the picture and the story as they answer the questions.

Beginning Children can orally answer and mark and write their answers. Provide help with writing and spelling.

Intermediate Children can first orally answer and then mark and write their answers on the page.

Advanced Children can mark and write their answers and check them by comparing their marks with a partner's and quietly reading aloud their writing.

Advanced High Children can mark and write their answers and check them by silently rereading the story and making any necessary corrections.

Answers for page 204: 1. 15; 2. Carmen's family; 3. Sample answers: Carmen has a pretty dress. She dances with her friends. Carmen's mom brings out a cake. Everyone sings to Carmen.

Multilingual Summaries

English

Grace for President

Grace cannot believe it when her teacher says that our country has never had a woman President. Grace decides that she will be the first woman to be President of the United States. Some students laugh, but Grace believes that she can be President.

The class decides to have an election for school President. Grace is one candidate. Thomas Cobb is another candidate.

The candidates have campaigns to win votes. They make slogans, signs, and speeches. Thomas is not worried about the election. The class has more boys than girls. He thinks the boys will all vote for him. The election is very close. Grace wins!

Spanish

Grace para presidente

Grace no puede creer cuando su maestra dice que nuestro país nunca ha tenido una mujer presidente. Decide que ella será la primera en los Estados Unidos. Algunos se ríen.

La clase decide elegir al presidente de la escuela. Grace es una de los candidatos. Thomas Cobb tambien es un candidato.

Ellos hacen campaña con carteles y discursos. Thomas no se preocupa. Hay más niños que niñas. Él piensa que los niños votarán por él. La elección es cerrada. ¡Grace gana!

Multilingual Summaries

Chinese

格蕾思竞选班主席

当老师告诉格蕾思这个国家从来没有一个女总统的时候，格蕾思简直不能相信；她决定成为第一位美国女总统。有些同学取笑她，但格蕾思相信她可以成为总统。

班同学决定选出一位班主席，格蕾思是其中一个候选人，托马斯・科布是另一个候选人。

两个候选人都进行竞选活动，他们都有标语、横额，也发表演说。格蕾思致力于竞选活动，但托马斯一点也不担心会落选，因为班里的男生比女生多，他以为所有的男生都会选他，结果票数很接近，但格蕾思赢了！

Vietnamese

Grace vào chức Chủ Tịch !

Grace không thể tin được khi cô giáo nói nước ta có một phụ nữ làm Tổng Thống. Thế rồi Jade quyết định mình sẽ là phụ nữ đầu tiên làm Tổng Thống Hoa Kỳ. Một vài học sinh cười, nhưng Grace tin rằng mình sẽ trở thành Tổng Thống.

Cả lớp quyết định bầu cử một Chủ Tịch trường Grace là một ứng viên. Thomas Cobb là một ứng viên khác trong cuộc bầu cử.

Các ứng viên vận động để được thắng cử. Họ làm những khẩu hiệu, biểu ngữ và diễn thuyết. Grace vận động ráo riết. Thomas thì không lo lắng gì về cuộc bầu cử. Lớp học có nhiều nam sinh hơn nữ sinh. Thomas nghĩ rằng mọi nam sinh sẽ bỏ phiếu cho mình. Cuộc bầu cử rất sát nút. Grace thắng cử!

Multilingual Summaries

Korean

그레이스를 대통령으로!

그레이스는 선생님이 우리 나라에서는 한 번도 여자 대통령이 없었다고 말씀 하셨을 때 믿을 수가 없었다. 그레이스는 미국 첫 번째 여자 대통령이 되기로 마음먹었다. 어떤 학생들은 비웃지만, 그레이스는 자기가 대통령이 될 수 있을 거라 믿는다.

우리 학년에서 학교 회장 선거를 하기로 결정했다. 그레이스는 후보 중 한 명이다. 토마스 코브는 또 다른 후보이다.

후보자들은 선거에 이기기 위해 유세를 한다. 구호와, 표지와, 연설을 준비한다. 그레이스는 자신의 유세를 열심히 준비했다. 토마스는 선거에 대해 걱정하지 않았다. 우리 학년엔 여자보다 남자가 더 많다. 토마스는 모든 남학생이 자기를 뽑을 거라고 생각했다. 선거는 막상막하였다. 그레이스가 이겼다!

Hmong

Grace ua Thawj Tswj

Grace tsi ntseeg li thaus nws tug xibfwb qhia hais tias peb lub tebchaws tsi tau muaj pojniam ua tus Thawj Tswj li. Grace txiav txim siab tias nws mam ua thawj tus pojniam los ua tus Thawj Tswv lub tebchaws United States. Ib txhia menyuam kawm ntawv luag, tiamsis Grace ntseeg tias nwg ua tau tus Thawj Tswj.

Lub hoob txiav txim tias cia peb xaiv tus Thawj Tswj rau lub tsev kawm ntawv. Grace yog ib tus nrog tw dhia. Thomas Cobb yog ib tus nrog tw dhia rau txoj kev xaiv no thiab.

Cov sis tw tau mus sis tw kom pov npav rau lawv. Lawv ua ntawv qhauj, duab eb qhauj, thiab hais lus qhauj. Grace siv zog rau nws txojkev sis tw. Thomas tsi txhawj txog txoj kev sis xaiv no. Lub hoob muaj menyuam tub ntau dua menyuam ntxhais. Thomas xav tias cov tub yuav xaiv tagnrho rau nws. Txoj kev xaiv yeej sis npaug li thiab. Grace yeej!

Name ________________________________

- **Read** *A Wild Onion Dinner* again.
- Use the information in the book to **answer** the questions.

Pages	Question	Answer
2–3	**1.** What happens at the beginning of the story?	
4–5	**2.** Who are the Muscogee?	
4–5	**3.** What is the Muscogee tradition in the story?	
6–7	**4.** Who goes to the dinner with David and his mom?	
8	**5.** Why does Marco think that the food at the dinner must be especially good?	

Family Link

Have family members describe their favorite holiday foods. Ask them to explain on which holiday they eat those foods.

page 30, Picture It!
1. Lin
2. friendly
3. Possible answers: It takes place in front of Lin's new home. It takes place on the street where Lin lives.

page 34, ELL Reader Study Guide
Responses will vary. Labels could include *field, tree, bush, house, road, snow, stop sign, building, store, car, street, red light, people.*

page 36, Picture It!
Main Idea: Astronauts are people who go into space.
Details: wear special clothes; use special tools; live in space for months; travel on a space shuttle

page 40, ELL Reader Study Guide
Pictures should show astronauts flying to or walking on the Moon. Pictures should include a spacecraft and three astronauts inside or a spacecraft with two astronauts on the surface of the Moon. Possible sentence: *My picture shows the first trip to the Moon.*

page 42, Picture It!
1. by a lake
2. summer
3. Guide children to talk about how Ana and Pedro feel about camping. Sample response: *They like to camp. I can tell because they are smiling, Ana says it was a great day, and Pedro agrees with her.*

page 46, ELL Reader Study Guide
Children draw pictures of the characters in the woods and label the characters in the scene.

page 48, Picture It!
1. planning a trip to the beach
2. b

page 52, ELL Reader Study Guide
1. A saguaro is a cactus.
2. It looks fat after it rains.
3. Some seeds make new cactus.
4. Spines have sharp tips.
5. They help animals have places to live. They help the soil.

page 60, Picture It!
1. Marie let him out.
2. Marie called him.

page 64, ELL Reader Study Guide
Answers may vary, but the pictures should coincide with what children write about the sequence of the story.
Beginning: The boy falls off his bike. His mother calls 9-1-1.
Middle: An ambulance comes to help the boy. He is taken to the hospital.
End: Alan broke his leg. He will be okay because he has a cast on his leg.

page 66, Picture It!
1. a soccer game
2. Possible answers: They work together. They pass the ball to her.
3. Possible answers: to show how people work together; to show how people help each other

page 70, ELL Reader Study Guide
1. Children should draw and write about one way people traveled before trains.
2. Children should draw and write about how people travel today.

page 72, Picture It!
1. three
2. an apple
3. half of her sandwich

page 76, ELL Reader Study Guide
Children should draw and write about one way people work together in the story.

page 78, Picture It!
1. b
2. b

page 82, ELL Reader Study Guide
Children should draw and write about the barn before, during, and after the cleaning. Possible written responses: The barn is messy and needs to be cleaned for the new piglet. The animals run round, trying to clean the barn, but it is still messy. The animals work together to clean the barn.

page 84, Picture It!
Both: help farmers, eat things that destroy plants;
Snakes: eat mice, smell things with tongues, hunt at night;
Crows: eat bugs, see things with eyes, hunt during the day

page 88, ELL Reader Study Guide
Children should use ideas from the reader to draw pictures of kids helping in two different ways.

page 90, Picture It!
1. a
2. b

page 94, ELL Reader Study Guide
Accept any reasonable responses such as wood, metal, rubber, workers, slide, swing.

page 96, Picture It!
1. Possible answer: He has a dog and two cats.
2. Possible answer: She has a big family.
3. Possible answer: Yes, they like being pen pals. They are friends even though they live far apart. They are excited to send and receive letters.

page 100, ELL Reader Study Guide
Answers will vary. Children should draw and write about ways in which they express themselves.

page 102, Picture It!
1. They both like ice cream.
2. Abbey does not like hair in her ice cream. Champ does not mind fur in his ice cream.

page 106, ELL Reader Study Guide
1. They feel safe.
2. The chimp needs to catch termites.
3. Termites can't see the chimps.
4. Termites bite the stick.

page 108, Picture It!
First, Damon's dad told Damon he did not need help. Next, Damon's dad dropped the heavy bag. Last, Damon helped his dad pull the bag.

page 112, ELL Reader Study Guide
1. The cat spilled paint on the masks.
2. Carlos suggested they borrow masks from a school that also celebrates American Hero Day.
3. Mrs. Clay, the teacher from the other school, lends the masks to the children.
4. The parents come to see the children celebrate Hero Day at their school.
5. The children talk about Ben Franklin and Sally Ride.

page 114, Picture It!
Possible facts: Thomas Edison was an inventor. The bulbs lasted longer than candles.
Possible opinions: He was one of the most creative people of his time. Everyone liked the electric light better than the candles.

page 118, ELL Reader Study Guide
1. Washing clothes would be easier.
2. the typewriter
3. Getting from one place to another would be easier.
4. the game of basketball

page 120, Picture It!
1. b
2. c

page 124, ELL Reader Study Guide
Children should draw pictures reflecting story events and write about them.

page 126, Picture It!
1. b
2. c
3. They put the pumpkin on the porch.

page 130, ELL Reader Study Guide
Facts: Tomatoes are fruits. Tomatoes have vitamins.
Details: Tomatoes can be big or small. Tomatoes grow on vines.

page 132, Picture It!
1. opinion
2. fact
3. fact
4. opinion

page 136, ELL Reader Study Guide
Children should show a prairie dog's underground home. Check that children write three complete sentences to accompany their drawings.

page 138, Picture It!
1. Miguel starts his first day at a new school. He is sad.
2. Miguel's teacher and a boy in his class are nice to him.
3. Possible answer: The big idea of this story is that a change can be a good thing even if it is not easy.

page 142, ELL Reader Study Guide
1. He wants to be with his old team in his old neighborhood.
2. He wishes he were with his other friends.
3. He thinks about his old team.
4. He has to remember to pass the ball to his teammates.
5. He feels like a part of the team.

page 144, Picture It!
1. Her parents did not have enough food for a fiesta for Grandma.
2. Maria asked other families to bring food for the fiesta.
3. People can cooperate to make something big.

page 148, ELL Reader Study Guide
Children should draw pictures of themselves enjoying the weather and label as many items in the pictures as they can.

page 150, Picture It!
Possible facts: The teacher explained our plan. A loud bell rang. We followed the teacher outside. Our teacher checked to make sure everyone was outside safely. We stood outside until it was time to go back in. When the ball rang, we went back inside.
Possible opinion: The bell sounded scary. It was good to practice what to do if there is a real fire.

page 154, ELL Reader Study Guide
Pictures and content will vary but should reflect the contents of the book.

page 156, Picture It!
Effect: They ask their friends to help recycle the paper.
Cause: The class writes a letter to the principal asking for paper recycling.

page 160, ELL Reader Study Guide
Children should draw pictures that demonstrate how the ducks are saved. Possible responses: First, the volunteers take the ducks to the vet. Second, the vets clean off the oil and give the ducks medicine. Third, the volunteers return the ducks to clean water.

page 162, Picture It!
1. Nana baby-sits. She and the girl try to play a game. Jack takes the pieces.
2. Jack has to go to bed early. He did not get ice cream because he did not behave.
3. Sample response: The big idea of this story is that if you do not behave, you may not get the things you want.

page 166, ELL Reader Study Guide
1. because puppy training is part of their 4-H project
2. The children called *Come!* and pulled their leashes.
3. because they liked learning
4. Every puppy won a prize at the puppy show.

page 168, Picture It!
1. Marc
2. b
3. c

page 172, ELL Reader Study Guide
Illustrations will vary but should demonstrate ways to make a friend and be a friend, such as shaking hands and sharing.

page 174, Picture It!
1. c
2. You can train your puppy not to chew things.

page 178, ELL Reader Study Guide
to teach something

page 180, Picture It!
Possible responses: Alike: Both sports use a ball. Players run and throw the ball. Players wear uniforms. *Different:* Baseball players use bats and gloves. They hit the ball with the bat. Baseball is played on a field. Basketball is played on a court.

page 184, ELL Reader Study Guide
Accept reasonable responses. Possible responses: *Baseball:* mitt, base, bat, small ball; *Both:* run, field, ball; *Soccer:* net, kick, large ball

page 186, Picture It!
1. flag, fireworks, other families
2. b
3. to tell why the Fourth of July is the best holiday

page 190, ELL Reader Study Guide
Illustrations should demonstrate how the flags looked in 1776 and 1777 and how they look today. Possible sentences:
1776 It has stripes instead of stars. It has a snake.
1777 It has a circle of stars. It has thirteen stars.
Today it has fifty stars.

page 192, Picture It!
1. It is a birthday party. A banner says "Happy birthday."
2. No, the girls both had a piñata last year. Sam says breaking it is his favorite part.

page 196, ELL Reader Study Guide
Illustrations should show Benito and his family members eating grapes. Sentences should explain that the family eats twelve grapes as a tradition to celebrate the coming of the New Year.

page 198, Picture It!
First, the cowboys see the sky turn dark.
Then, rain falls.
Next, thunder scares the cattle. The cattle run.
Last, the cowboys eat dinner.

page 202, ELL Reader Study Guide
1. At the market, the owner sells the cattle.
2. Long ago, cowboys rode horses and herded cattle to the market.
3. A cowboy's clothes help protect him from the weather.
4. A cowboy needs a saddle.

page 204, Picture It!
1. 15
2. Carmen's family
3. Sample responses: Carmen has a pretty dress. She dances with her friends. Carmen's mom brings out a cake. Everyone sings to Carmen.

page 208, ELL Reader Study Guide
1. David invites Marco and his mom to pick wild onions with him and his mom.
2. The Muscogee are a group of Native Americans.
3. The Muscogee tradition is picking wild onions in the spring and then having a Wild Onion dinner.
4. Marco and his mom go to the dinner with David and his mom.
5. Marco thinks the food must be good because so many people come to the dinner.

Part 3
Phonics Instruction for English Language Learners

Contents

Introduction to the Phonics Transition Lessons

Phonological and phonemic awareness, phonics, and word study are critical components of literacy instruction for English learners. The core lessons in *Reading Street* provide the explicit, systematic instruction that all children need to become fluent readers and writers. The following Phonics Transition Lessons and Practice Pages will supplement the core instruction with customized lessons that meet the particular needs of English learners. Lessons and Practice Pages are divided into three sections:

- **Phonological Awareness and Concepts of Print** English learners may not have learned to distinguish word boundaries, syllables, rhymes, or phonemes within words in English, or even in their home languages. Some children also may be unfamiliar with English print conventions such as the alphabet and left-to-right directionality. This section provides activities that can be used at any time to develop phonological awareness and concepts of print.
- **Problem Sounds in English** These lessons cover the phonemes that are typically the most challenging for English learners, such as easily confused consonants and short vowel sounds. In some cases, a Model Lesson is provided along with notes for using the same lesson format with related phonics skills. Lessons in this section include Pronunciation Tips that teachers can use to help children produce the target phonemes. A Practice Page for every lesson provides strong visual support for instruction and offers additional practice.
- **Word Study** An understanding of word parts and word origins is a powerful tool for English learners. The Word Study Lessons reinforce the core instruction and include suggestions for making connections with the home language. The Practice Pages provide visual support and context for the target skills.

Throughout the Phonics Transition Lessons, a **Transfer Skills** feature identifies specific challenges faced by English language learners as they acquire the target skills.

In addition to the Phonics Transition Lessons and Practice Pages, you can supplement core phonics instruction with routines such as the following:

- **Strengthen oral language skills.** Allow beginning speakers to work with partners when completing phonics activities. Encourage children to talk about their work with English, and provide other oral language opportunities with the target words.
- **Teach word meanings.** Before teaching the phonics skills, introduce the target words orally to children by using them in activities such as riddle games, songs, chants, or asking and answering questions that use the words.
- **Provide alternate instruction.** If children have limited literacy skills, use resources such as the *Reading Street Intervention Kit* or *Early Reading Intervention (ERI)* to provide literacy instruction at the level where children can participate and learn.
- **Relate to the home language.** Whenever possible, help children build on what they already know by making connections between each target phonics skill and the home language. Use available resources such as bilingual staff members, bilingual dictionaries, and language Web sites to gather information about the home language.
- **Engage children as active learners.** Children who are acquiring English may have a stronger awareness of language than monolingual speakers. Build their knowledge with engaging activities that explicitly show the patterns and structures of language. Consider using games such as **Phonics Four** and **Word Hunt** on the next page.

Phonics Four

Use with page 217.

Make and distribute copies of page 217. Work with children to generate a class list of twenty or more words that reflect the target phonics skills that children have recently studied—for example, short vowel words. Write each word on a card. Have children choose sixteen words from the list and write them in random order in the squares on page 217. Help children cut out the star markers at the bottom of the page (or use other markers). Shuffle the cards, and read aloud one card at a time. Children should look for each word on their paper and cover it with a star marker. The first child to have four marked words in a row (horizontally, vertically, or diagonally) calls out "Phonics Four!" Note: For children in early stages of literacy, write consonants in the squares, and have children listen for words that begin with the consonants.

Word Hunt

Use with page 218.

Choose a target phonics skill, such as "Words with long *a*" or "Words with the *-ing* ending," and write it at the top of a copy of page 218. Make and distribute copies to individuals, partners, or small groups. Have children look around the classroom and school, in books and magazines, and perhaps at home for words that have the particular phonics feature. They can list the words in the chart on page 218, and either draw or attach (with a glue stick or tape) pictures that illustrate the words. Conclude by having children share the words they find.

Name ___________________________

Phonics Four

- **Write** the words that your teacher gives you. Write one word in each square.
- **Listen** to the words. When you hear a word that is in a square, **cover** it with a star marker.
- When you have four covered words in a row, **say** "Phonics Four!"

- **Cut out** the star markers. **Use** them in the game.

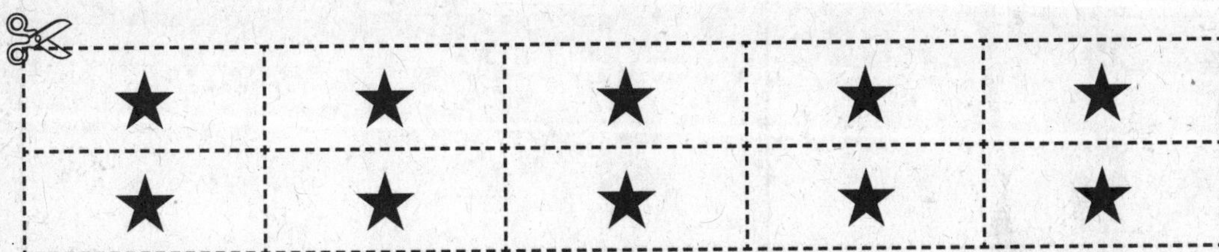

Name ___________________________

Word Hunt: Words with ___________

- **Find** words that share a sound or a spelling pattern.
- **Write** the words. **Add** pictures that go with the words.
- **Tell** your words to a friend.

Word	Picture

English learners may have difficulty noticing certain sounds of spoken English—recognizing syllable boundaries, hearing rhymes, or distinguishing phonemes. *Reading Street* provides the explicit instruction in phonological and phonemic awareness that English language learners need to develop strong literacy skills. These activities will build phonemic awareness.

Phonemic Awareness Activities

Rhyme Recognition and Production Show children words that rhyme, such as *cat, hat; hill, fill;* and *sky, pie.* Talk about the rhyming sounds. Then share a short rhyming text with children, such as a nursery rhyme. Ask children to listen for words that end with the same sounds. Say the rhyme again, pausing before each rhyming word so that children can supply the word. Then say word pairs, and have children raise their hands if the words rhyme: *bat, cat; cat, car; like, bike; cold, coat.* Provide a word that is easily rhymed (such as *stop* or *bake*), and invite children to name words that rhyme with it.

Syllable Segmentation and Blending Gather pictures or objects that represent a meaningful category of words, such as animal names, fruits, or classroom items. Have children name one of the items. Repeat the word, and clap for each syllable. Invite children to do the same for the remaining items. Have children tell how many syllables each word has. Then say aloud the separate syllables of a word *(wa-ter-mel-on),* and invite children to say the whole word.

Phoneme Isolation Gather picture cards that include some items that begin with a target sound, such as /b/. Say the sound, and have children repeat it several times. Then show the cards, name the items, and ask children whether or not each item begins with the target sound. After children are comfortable identifying initial sounds, adapt the game for identifying the final sound and then the middle sound in words.

Phoneme Blending and Segmentation Gather picture cards of one-syllable words with three or four phonemes. Tell children you will say the sounds in one of the words so that they can guess the word. For example: /p/ /e/ /n/ *(pen).* Then show a card, name the item, and invite children to separate the word into individual sounds: *hat,* /h/ /a/ /t/.

Transfer Skills

Many factors can influence children's understanding of print conventions. Children may be emergent readers of non-alphabetic languages or languages with alphabets quite different from the English alphabet. Some English learners may be familiar with reading left to right and top to bottom, as in English. Others may be accustomed to reading text from right to left or from the bottom to the top of the page. Some have little experience with printed text. For children who are unfamiliar with English print conventions, activities such as these will help develop print awareness and strengthen literacy skills.

Print Awareness Activities

Parts of a Book Show children how to hold a book, with the spine on the left and the front cover showing. Point out and explain the title, author byline, and illustrator's name. Turn to the selection pages and read a sentence or two. Discuss how the illustrations go with the text. Page through the book, and show how the narrative continues. Point to the text on each page. Then have children practice holding the book correctly, finding the title and author, turning the pages, and pointing to the text on each page.

Letters and Words Display text in a large format, such as a Big Book page. Read aloud a sentence, pointing to each word as you read. Then frame one word with your fingers and read it aloud. Explain that it is a word, and point out the spacing before and after the word. Point out the letters within the word, and count the letters. Then invite children to point to other words on the page and to count the letters within the words.

Tracking Print As you read a book aloud, put your finger on the starting point in the text on each page. Show that you read from left to right by moving your finger along lines of text. Use your finger to show how to sweep back from the end of a line to the beginning of another, and how to find the beginning of the text on the next page. Then have children use their fingers to show the correct movement as you read the text aloud again.

Writing the Alphabet Children should be introduced systematically to all the letters of the English alphabet. Children can practice writing letters, punctuation marks, and numbers, using page 221 or 222 as a handwriting guide.

Name ______________________________

The Alphabet

- **Practice** writing the letters of the alphabet.
- **Write** more of the letters on other paper.

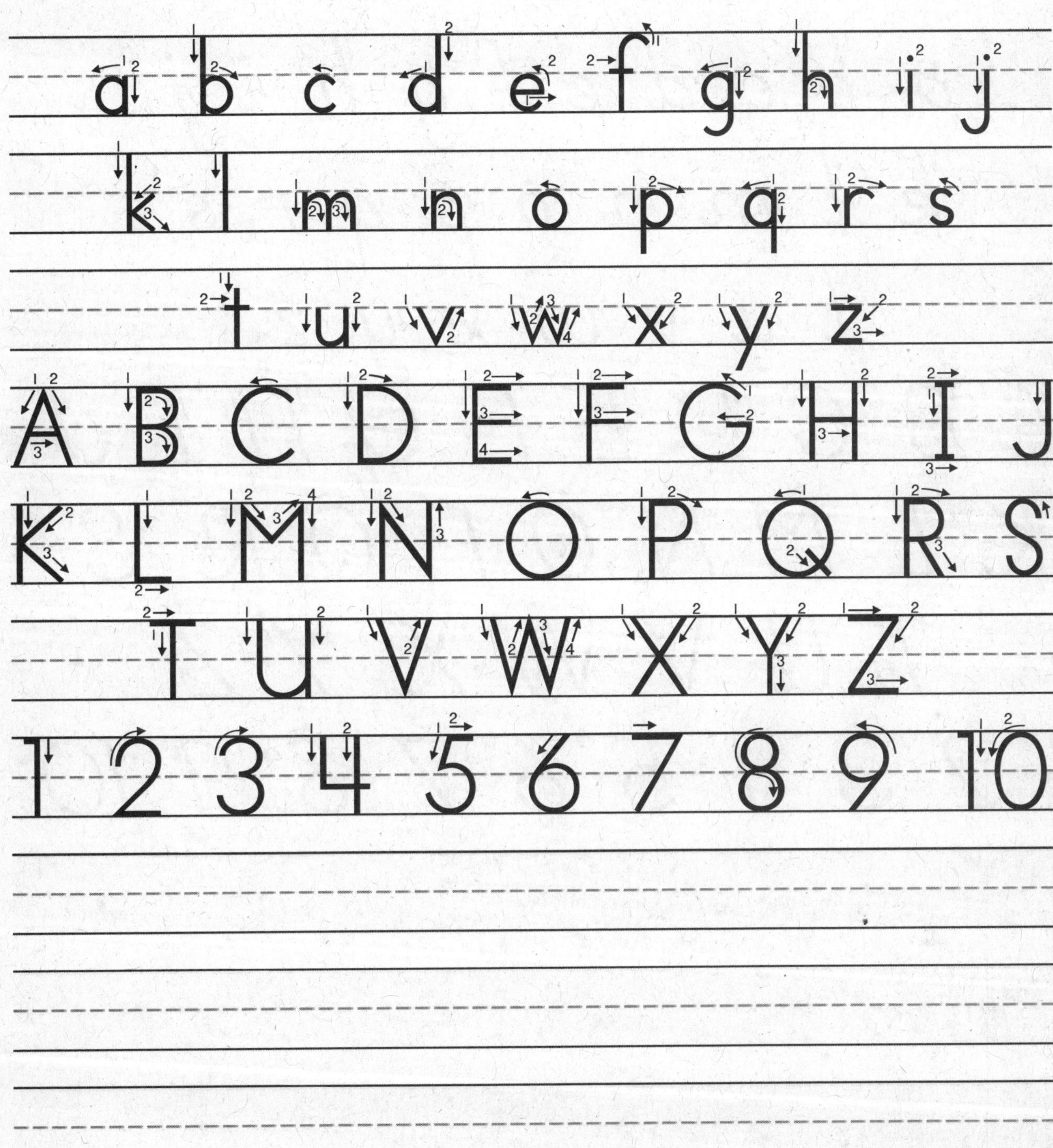

The D'Nealian™ Alphabet

- **Practice** writing the letters of the alphabet.
- **Write** more of the letters on other paper.

Transfer Skills

The phonemes of certain English consonants may be unfamiliar to English language learners or easily confused with other phonemes. For example, the /sh/ sound does not exist in Spanish, Chinese, and some other languages. Speakers of some Asian languages may find it hard to hear and pronounce /r/ and /l/ as separate phonemes. The following lessons provide practice with certain consonant pairs that English language learners may find troublesome. You can develop similar lessons for other consonant sounds that are difficult for your students. This model lesson gives you a pattern for teaching.

☆ Model Lesson: Words with *b* and *p*

Use with page 226.

Preteach Copy and distribute page 226. Have children point to the two items at the top of the page. Say: *I will say the names of these things. Listen to the beginning sound in each word:* bat, pin. Have students repeat the words after you. Say: *What sound do you hear at the beginning of each word?* bat, */b/, /b/;* pin, */p/, /p/. Are they the same sound?* (no)

Teach/Model Write *bat* and *pin* on the board. Underline the *b* and the *p*. Tell children: *Let's practice saying the sounds of these letters.* Share the Pronunciation Tip.

Read the directions above Row 1 on page 226. Then say the name of each picture, clearly pronouncing the /b/ or /p/. Have children circle the correct letter for each picture. Row 1 words: *bee, pig, box, park.*

Repeat the process for Row 2, pointing out that this time they should listen for the ending sound of each word. Row 2 words: *cup, tub, web, top.*

Practice Have children look at the pictures in Row 3, say the names of the pictures, and write the words. Row 3 words: *pin, bat.*

Assess Make another copy of page 226, and cut out the pictures in each row. Group the pictures from Row 1 in one pile, and the pictures from Row 2 in another. Prepare a sheet of paper with two columns headed with the words bat and pin. Give each child the first pile of cards. Have the child say the name of the picture and place each card under the word that begins with the same sound. Then prepare a two-column chart with the headings *cub* and *cap*. Give each child the second pile of cards to sort by the ending sound.

Pronunciation Tip /b/ and /p/
When you say /b/, your lips start out together. Then they open, and a tiny puff of air comes out of your mouth. If you touch your throat, you can feel it move because your voice box is on. Try it: /b/, /b/. Now, when you say /p/, your lips start out together again. Then they open, and a puff of air comes out. But put your hand on your throat. When you say /p/, your throat doesn't move. Your voice box is off. Try it: /p/, /p/. Try both sounds: /b/ and /p/.

Adapting the ☆ Model Lesson

Use the lesson format above to teach other difficult consonants. The following information will help you customize each lesson. Note that Row 2 of each of the additional worksheets keeps the focus on beginning sounds rather than shifting to ending sounds, which is the focus of Row 2 of this model lesson.

Notes for Additional Lessons

Words with *b* and *v*

Use with page 227.

Teach/Model Row 1 of page 227: *vest, bag, ball, vase* (Children will circle the correct initial letter below each picture.); Row 2: *box, vet, bus, vine* (Children will write the correct initial letter to complete the word below each picture.)

Practice Row 3: *bed, van*

Assess Create just one pile of cards for children to sort, using all the pictures in Rows 1 and 2. Use these words as column headings: bed, van.

Pronunciation Tip
/b/ and /v/ *When you say /b/, your lips start out together. Then they open and a tiny puff of air comes out of your mouth. If you touch your throat, you can feel it move because your voice box is on. Can you hold a /b/ sound? Try it: /b/, /b/, /b/. No, you can't hold it. When you say /v/, you can hold it: /vvvv/. Your voice box is still on. Your top teeth touch your bottom lip.*

Words with *c* /k/ and *g*

Use with page 228.

Teach/Model Row 1 of page 228: *cage, game, car, goat* (Children will circle the correct initial letter below each picture.); Row 2: *cat, gull, gate, cup* (Children will write the correct initial letter to complete the word below each picture.)

Practice Row 3: *can, gas*

Assess Create just one pile of cards for children to sort, using all the pictures in Rows 1 and 2. Use these words as column headings: can, gas.

Pronunciation Tip
***c* /k/ and /g/** *When you say /k/, the back of your tongue is humped in the back of your mouth. Your voice box is off. Try it: /k/, /k/. When you say /g/, your tongue is in the same place. The back of your tongue is humped in the back of your mouth. But when you say /g/, your voice box is on. Feel your throat move: /g/, /g/. Try both sounds: /k/, /g/.*

Words with *ch* and *sh*

Use with page 229.

Teach/Model Row 1 of page 229: *chain, chair, shop, shoe;* Row 2: *chick, shell, chin, sheep* (Children will circle the correct initial digraph below each picture in Rows 1 and 2.)

Practice Row 3: *chin, ship*

Assess Create just one pile of cards for children to sort, using all the pictures in Rows 1 and 2. Use these words as column headings: chin, ship.

Pronunciation Tip
/ch/ and /sh/ *When you say /ch/, your lips are open and your teeth are close together. Your tongue moves as you make the sound. Can you hold a /ch/ sound? Try it: /ch/, /ch/. No, you can't hold it. When you say /sh/, your lips are also open and your teeth are close together. But your tongue doesn't move, and you can hold the sound: /shhh/. Try it: /shhh/, /shhh/.*

Words with *d* and *th*

Use with page 230.

Teach/Model Row 1 of page 230: *dad, duck, thirteen;* Row 2: *day, thumb, dig* (Children will circle the correct letter(s) for each initial sound below each picture in Rows 1 and 2.)

Pronunciation Tip
/d/, /ŦH/ *(this),* and /th/ *(thin)* *When you say /d/, the tip of your tongue touches above your top teeth. Your voice box is on*

Notes for Additional Lessons

(continued from page 224)

Practice Row 3: *dog, thirty*

Assess Create just one pile of cards for children to sort, using all the pictures in Rows 1 and 2. Use these words as column headings: dog, thirty.

when you say /d/. Can you hold a /d/ sound? Try it: /d/, /d/. No, you can't hold it. When you say /ŦH/ in a word like this, your voice box is also on: /ŦH/. But your tongue is between your teeth, and you can hold the sound. Try it: /ŦHHHHH/. When you say /th/ in a word like thin, your voice box is off, and you can hold the sound: /thhhhh/.

Words with *j* and *y*

Use with page 231.

Teach/Model Row 1 of page 231: *yak, yell, jar, jump;* Row 2: *jam, yard, juggle, yo-yo* (Children will circle the correct initial letter below each picture.)

Practice Row 3: *jet, yarn*

Assess Create just one pile of cards for children to sort, using all the pictures in Rows 1 and 2. Use these words as column headings: *jet, yarn.*

Pronunciation Tip
/j/ and /y/ *When you say /j/, your tongue is up and your lips are open. Your teeth are close together. Try it: /j/, /j/. When you say /y/, your teeth are farther apart. Your tongue is behind your lower teeth. Say /y/ and feel your tongue behind your lower teeth: /y/, /y/. Try both sounds: /j/, /y/.*

Words with *l* and *r*

Use with page 232.

Teach/Model Row 1 of page 232: *rain, lake, rope, lock* (Children will circle the correct initial letter below each picture.); Row 2: *rod, leg, rake, lid* (Children will write the correct initial letter to complete the word below each picture.)

Practice Row 3: *log, rug*

Assess Create just one pile of cards for children to sort, using all the pictures in Rows 1 and 2. Use these words as column headings: *log, rug.*

Pronunciation Tip
/l/ and /r/ *When you say /l/, the tip of your tongue touches above your top teeth and stays there. Say /l/ and feel your throat move. Your voice box is on when you say /l/. Try it: /l/, /l/. When you say /r/, your voice box is on again. The tip of your tongue goes toward the roof of your mouth, but doesn't touch it. Try it: /r/, /r/. Try both sounds: /l/, /r/.*

Words with *t* and *th*

Use with page 233.

Teach/Model Row 1 of page 233: *tie, thirty, thumb;* Row 2: *thigh, tent, toe* (Children will circle the correct letter(s) for each beginning sound below each picture in Rows 1 and 2.)

Practice Row 3: *ten, thorn*

Assess Create just one pile of cards for children to sort, using all the pictures in Rows 1 and 2. Use these words as column headings: *ten, thorn.*

Pronunciation Tip
/t/ and /th/ (*thick*) *When you say /t/, the tip of your tongue touches above your top teeth. Say /t/ and feel the tip of your tongue. Can you hold the /t/ sound? Try it: /t/, /t/. No, you can't hold the sound. When you say /th/ in a word like thick, you can hold the sound: /thhhhh/. The tip of your tongue comes out between your teeth. Try it: /thhhhh/, /thhhhh/. Try both sounds: /t/, /thhhhh/.*

Name ______________________

Words with *b* and *p*

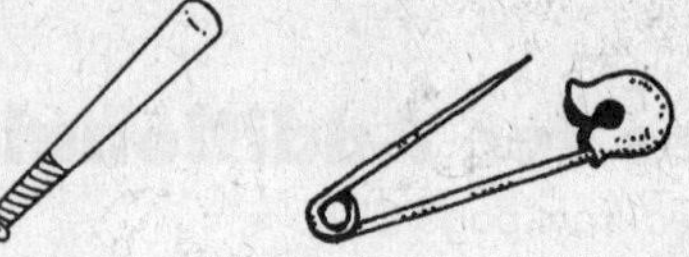

- If the word begins with the sound of *b* in *bat*, **circle** the *b*.
- If the word begins with the sound of *p* in *pin*, **circle** the *p*.

ROW 1

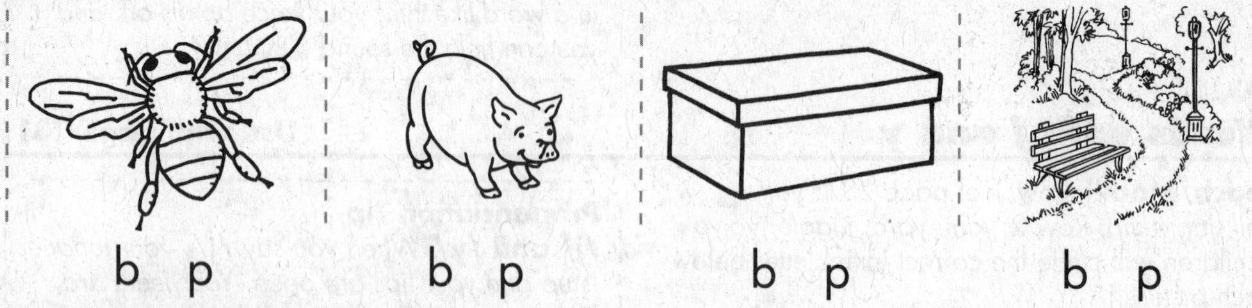

b p   b p   b p   b p

- If the word ends with the sound of *b* in *cub*, **circle** the *b*.
- If the word ends with the sound of *p* in *cap*, **circle** the *p*.

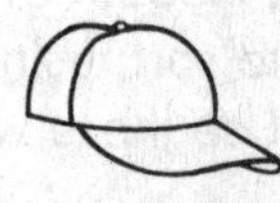

ROW 2

b p   b p   b p   b p

- **Look** at each picture. **Say** its name. **Write** the word.

ROW 3

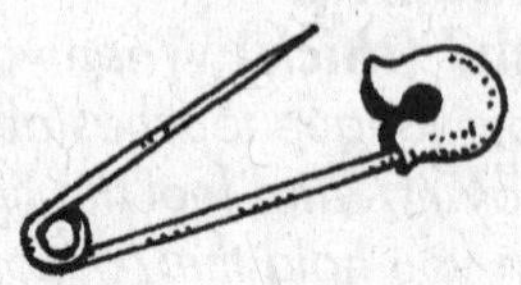

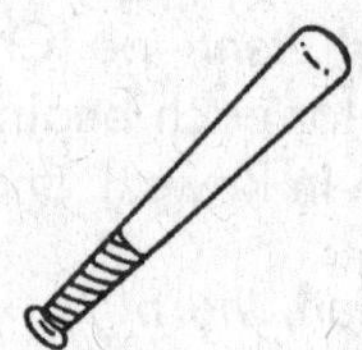

Name ______________________

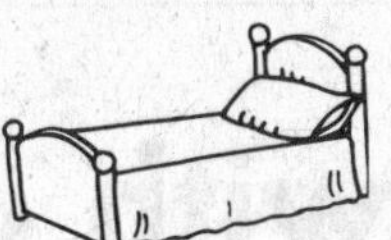

Words with *b* and *v*

- If the word begins with the sound of *b* in *bed,* **circle** the *b.*
- If the word begins with the sound of *v* in *van,* **circle** the *v.*

ROW 1

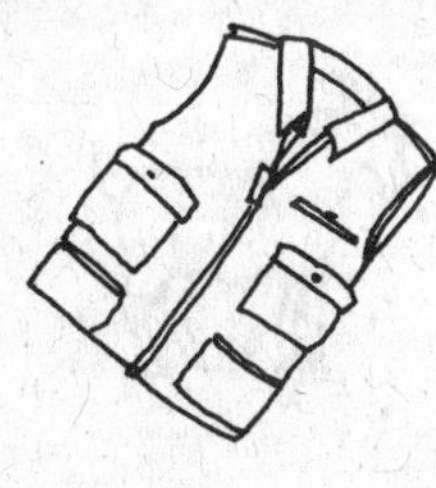

b v

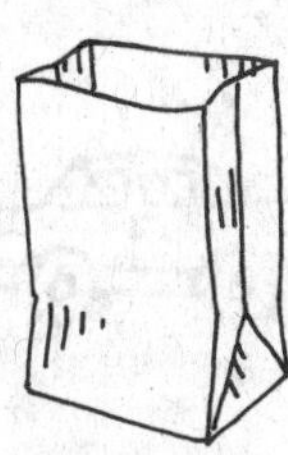

b v

b v

b v

- If the word begins with the sound of *b* in *bed,* **write** *b.*
- If the word begins with the sound of *v* in *van,* **write** *v.*

ROW 2

______ ox

______ et

______ us

______ ine

- **Look** at each picture. **Say** its name. **Write** the word.

ROW 3

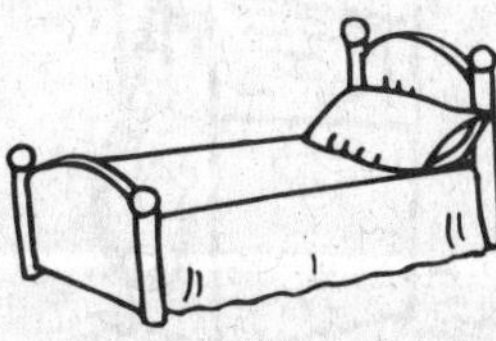

____

____

Name ______________________________

Words with *c* /k/ and *g*

- If the word begins with the sound of *c* in *can,* **circle** the *c*.
- If the word begins with the sound of *g* in *gas,* **circle** the *g*.

ROW 1

c g

c g

c g

c g

- If the word begins with the sound of *c* in *can,* **write** *c*.
- If the word begins with the sound of *g* in *gas,* **write** *g*.

ROW 2

_____ at

_____ ull

_____ ate

_____ up

- **Look** at each picture. **Say** its name. **Write** the word.

ROW 3

____

____

Name ______________________________

Words with *ch* and *sh*

- If the word begins with the sound of *ch* in *chin*, **circle** the *ch*.
- If the word begins with the sound of *sh* in *ship*, **circle** the *sh*.

ROW 1

ch sh

ch sh

ch sh

ch sh

ROW 2

ch sh

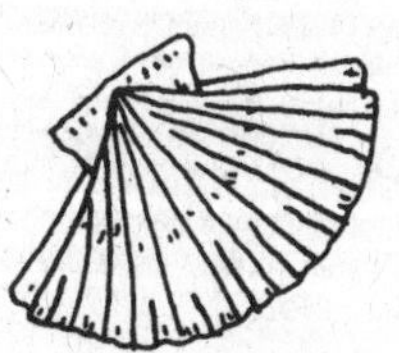
ch sh

ch sh

ch sh

- **Look** at each picture. **Say** its name. **Write** the word.

ROW 3

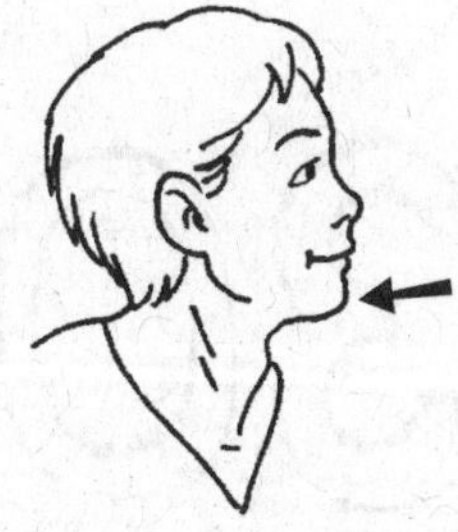
____

____

Name ______________________________

Words with *d* and *th*

- If the word begins with the sound of *d* in *dog*, **circle** the *d*.
- If the word begins with the sound of *th* in *thirty*, **circle** the *th*.

ROW 1

d th

d th

d th

ROW 2

d th

d th

d th

- **Look** at each picture. **Say** its name. **Write** the beginning of the word.

ROW 3

_____og

30
_____irty

Name ______________________________

Words with *j* and *y*

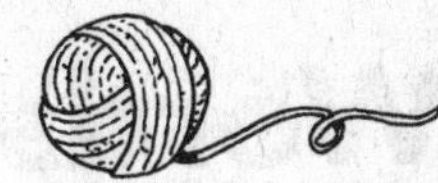

- If the word begins with the sound of *j* in *jet*, **circle** the *j*.
- If the word begins with the sound of *y* in *yarn*, **circle** the *y*.

ROW 1

j y

j y

j y

j y

ROW 2

j y

j y

j y

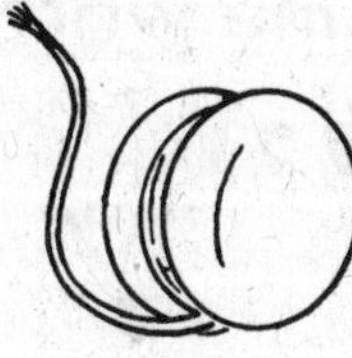

j y

- **Look** at each picture. **Say** its name. **Write** the first letter.

ROW 3

______et

______arn

Name ______________________

Words with *l* and *r*

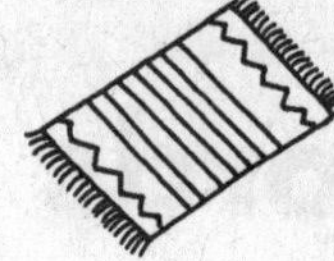

- If the word begins with the sound of *l* in *log,* **circle** the *l.*
- If the word begins with the sound of *r* in *rug,* **circle** the *r.*

ROW 1

l r

l r

l r

l r

- If the word begins with the sound of *l* in *log,* **write** *l.*
- If the word begins with the sound of *r* in *rug,* **write** *r.*

ROW 2

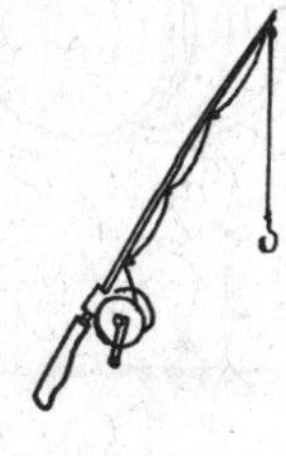
_____od

_____eg

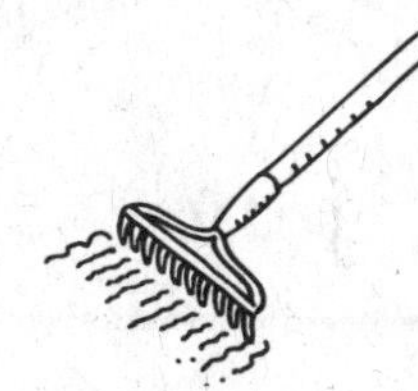
_____ake

_____id

- **Look** at each picture. **Say** its name. **Write** the word.

ROW 3

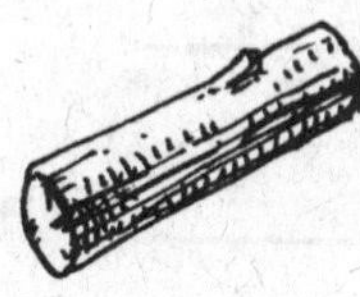
____

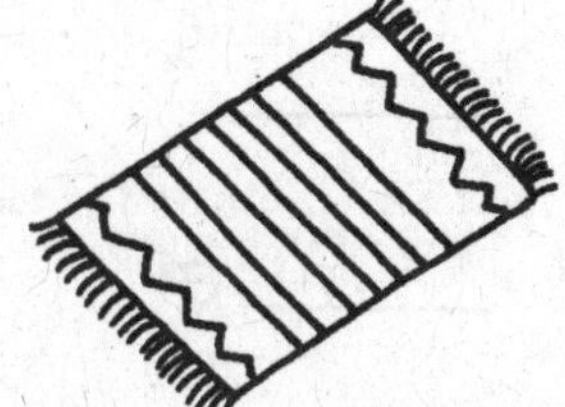
____

Name ______________________

Words with *t* and *th*

- If the word begins with the sound of *t* in *ten*, **circle** the *t*.
- If the word begins with the sound of *th* in *thorn*, **circle** the *th*.

ROW 1

t th

t th

t th

ROW 2

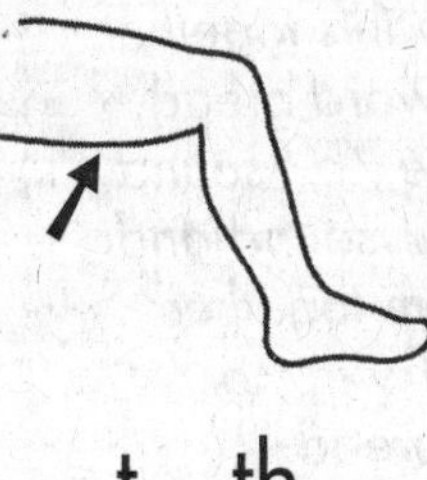

t th

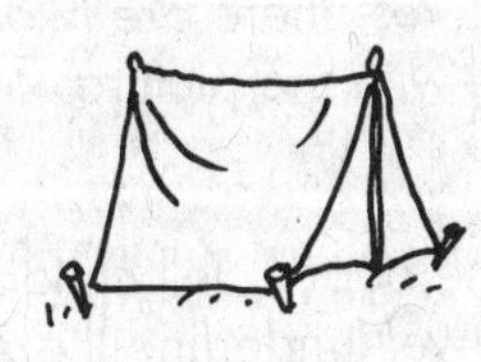

t th

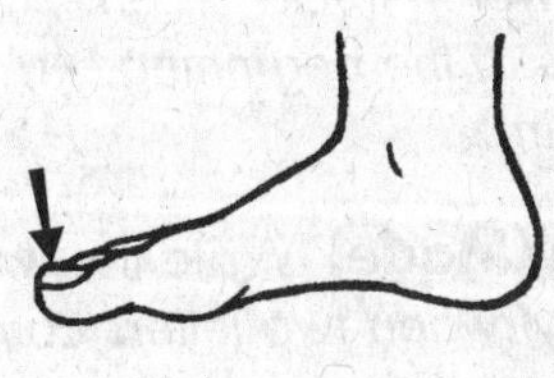

t th

- **Look** at each picture. **Say** its name. **Write** the word.

ROW 3

Consonant Blends

Transfer Skills

Consonant blends in English words often are challenging for English learners because their home languages may not combine consonant phonemes in similar ways at the beginnings and ends of words. For example, Spanish speakers may add the sound /e/ at the beginning of words with *s*-blends, saying *estop, esleep,* etc. Speakers of Greek, Italian, Spanish, and other languages may not hear the distinct phonemes in final consonant blends and may omit letters when writing the words. The following lessons provide practice with consonant blends. If your children are struggling with particular blends, you can develop similar lessons targeted to those blends.

Initial Consonant Blends Use with page 240.

Preteach Copy and distribute page 240. Have children point to clapping hands at the top of the page. Say: *This picture shows a clap, /k/ /l/ /a/ /p/. What vowel sound do you hear in* clap*? That's right, short a, /a/. In the word* clap*, how many sounds do you hear before the /a/ sound? Say it with me:* clap, */k/ /l/ /a/ /p/. That's right, this word has two sounds before the vowel: /k/ /l/. Now point to the truck. What two sounds do you hear before the vowel in* truck*? Listen: /t/ /r/ /u/ /k/. Yes, there are two sounds at the beginning: /t/ /r/.* Continue with the picture for *swim*.

Teach/Model Write the word *swim* on the board. Tell children: *Usually, when two letters come before a vowel* (underline the *sw*), *we blend the sounds of the letters: /s/ /w/.../s/ /w/ /i/ /m/. Say it with me:* swim, */s/ /w/ /i/ /m/.* Repeat for *clap*.

Help children name the items in Row 1 on page 240 *(bread, flute, skirt, smile)*. Repeat each name, stretching the sound of every letter so children can hear the initial blend. Then say: *I'll say each word again. Circle the letters that you blend together at the beginning of the word:* bread, flute, skirt, smile.

Practice Have children look at the pictures in Row 2 on page 240. Help them name each picture *(block, step, frog, spot)*. Have children write the initial blend to complete each name, choosing from the blends listed in the box. Then have children look at the pictures in Row 3. Help them name each picture *(clap, crib, flag, swim)*. Finally, ask them to write the names.

Assess Prepare numbered word cards, with a blend written on each side: (1) *cr/cl;* (2) *gr/gl;* (3) *tr/dr;* (4) *sk/sp;* (5) *sl/sm*. Give each child the cards. Have the child find the correctly numbered card, listen to the word you say, and display the correct initial blend. Words to use for each card are: (1) *crab;* (2) *glue;* (3) *drip;* (4) *skip;* (5) *smell*.

Pronunciation Tip
Initial consonant blends *When a word begins with two consonants like* b *and* r, *blend the sounds of the two consonants together. In the word* bread, *take the /b/ sound and /r/ sound and put them together: /br/. Try it: /br/,* /br/, bread.

Final Consonant Blends Use with page 241.

Preteach Copy and distribute page 241. Have children point to the picture of the hand at the top of the page. Say: *This picture shows a hand, /h/ /a/ /n/ /d/. What vowel sound do you hear in* hand*? That's right, short a, /a/. In the word* hand, *how many sounds do you hear after the /a/ sound? Say it with me:* hand, */h/ /a/ /n/ /d/. That's right, this word has two sounds after the vowel: /n/ /d/.* Repeat for *lamp.*

Teach/Model Write the word *hand* on the board. Tell children: *Usually, when two letters come after a vowel* (underline the *nd*), *we blend the sounds of the letters: /n/ /d/.../h/ /a/ /n/ /d/. Say it with me:* hand, */h/ /a/ /n/ /d/.* Repeat for *lamp.*

Help children name the items in Row 1 on page 241 *(milk, sand, mask, nest).* Repeat each name, stretching the sound of every letter so children can hear the final blend. Then say: *I'll say each word again. Circle the letters that you blend together at the end of the word:* milk, sand, mask, nest.

Practice Have children look at the pictures in Row 2 on page 241. Help them name each picture *(vest, desk, jump, tent).* Have children write the final blend to complete each name, choosing from the blends listed in the box. Then have children look at the pictures in Row 3. Help them name each picture *(cast, belt, lamp, hand).* Finally, ask them to write the names.

Assess Prepare numbered word cards, with a blend written on each side: (1) *mp/nd;* (2) *nd/nk;* (3) *nd/st;* (4) *st/ft;* (5) *lt/lk.* Give each child the cards. Have the child find the correctly numbered card, listen to the word you say, and display the correct final blend. Words to use for each card are: (1) *lump;* (2) *bank;* (3) *pond;* (4) *rest;* (5) *silk.*

Pronunciation Tip Final consonant blends *When a word ends with two consonants like* l *and* k, *you blend the sounds of the two consonants together. In the word* milk, *take the /l/ sound and /k/ sound and put them together: /lk/. Try it: /lk/, /lk/,* milk.

3-Letter Consonant Blends Use with page 242.

Preteach Copy and distribute page 242. Have children point to the picture of the splash at the top of the page. Say: *This picture shows a splash, /s/ /p/ /l/ /a/ /sh/. What vowel sound is in* splash? *That's right, short a, /a/. In the word* splash, *how many sounds do you hear before the /a/ sound? Say it with me:* splash, */s/ /p/ /l/ /a/ /sh/. That's right, this word has three sounds before the vowel: /s/ /p/ /l/.*

Teach/Model Write the word *splash* on the board. Tell children: *Usually, when two or three letters come before a vowel* (underline the *spl*), *we blend the sounds of the letters: /s/ /p/ /l/.../s/ /p/ /l/ /a/ /sh/. Say it with me:* splash, */s/ /p/ /l/ /a/ /sh/.* Now write *stress* on the board. Ask children: *What letter sounds do we blend in this word?* Underline the *str* and elicit from children the blended word: /s/ /t/ /r/ /e/ /s/.

Help children name the items in Row 1 on page 242 *(screen, strap, string)*. Repeat each name, stretching the sound of every letter so children can hear the initial blend. Then say: *I'll say each word again. Circle the letters that you blend together at the beginning of the word:* screen, strap, string.

Practice Have children look at the pictures in Rows 2 and 3 on page 242. Help them name each picture *(splint, spring, stripe, strong, strum, splash)*. Have children circle the word below each picture that names it. Then ask them to underline the three letters at the beginning of the word that are blended.

Assess Make another copy of page 242, and cut out the pictures for *splash, splint, strap, string, stripe,* and *strong*. Prepare a sheet of paper with two columns headed with the blends *spl* and *str*. Give each child the pile of picture cards. Have the child say the name of the pictures and place each card under the blend that begins the word.

Pronunciation Tip
3-letter blends
When a word begins with three consonants like s, c, *and* r, *you blend the sounds of the three consonants together. In the word* screen, *take the /s/ sound, the /k/ sound, and the /r/ sound and put them together: /skr/. Try it: /skr/, /skr/,* screen.

Speakers of languages such as Japanese, Korean, or Spanish may need assistance distinguishing between the /sh/ and /ch/ sounds. The following lesson provides practice for hearing and producing words with the /ch/ sound. Offer examples of /sh/ words such as *ship*, *show*, and *wish* as a contrast to words with the /ch/ sound.

Words with *wh* /hw/; *ch, tch* /ch/

Use with page 243.

Preteach Copy and distribute page 243. Have children point to the picture of a wheel at the top of the page. Say: *This is a wheel, /hw/ /ē/ /l/. How many sounds do you hear before the /ē/ sound? That's right, one sound: /hw/. Say it with me: /hw/, /hw/, wheel.* Now point to the *chick*. Ask: *How many sounds do you hear before the /i/ sound? Listen: /ch/ /i/ /k/. Yes, there is one sound before the vowel: /ch/.* Repeat this drill for the word *itch*.

Teach/Model Write the word *wheel* on the board. Underline the *wh* in the word. Say: *The sound /hw/ in* wheel *is spelled* wh. *Say it with me: wheel, /hw/ /ē/ /l/.* Now write *chick* on the board. Underline the *ch* in the word and say: *The sound /ch/ is at the beginning of the word* chick. *Say it with me: chick, /ch/ /i/ /k/.* Explain that the letters *ch* can come at the beginning or end of a word. Then write *itch* on the board. Underline the *tch* in the word and say: *The sound /ch/ is at the end of the word* itch. *Say it with me: itch, /i/ /ch/.* Explain that the letters *tch* are not found at the beginning of English words.

Help children name the items in Row 1 on page 243 *(whale, chin, whistle, patch)*. Repeat each name, stretching out the sound of each letter so children can hear the /hw/ or /ch/ sound in each word. Say: *I am going to read the words again. This time, circle which letters are found in the words:* whale, chin, whistle, patch. Review the answers as a class. *(wh, ch, wh, tch)*

Practice Have children look at the pictures in Row 2 on page 243. Help them name each picture (*sandwich, whisper, check, watch*). Have them write the consonant digraph to complete each name, choosing from the digraphs listed in the box. Then have children look at the pictures in Row 3, say the name of each picture, and write the names *(whale, catcher, chimp, chin)*.

Assess Make another copy of page 243 and cut out the pictures for *whale, chin, patch, sandwich, whisper,* and *watch*. Give each child the pile of picture cards. Read the words aloud to the class and pause after each word so children can find and hold up the corresponding picture card.

Pronunciation Tip Words with *wh* /hw/; *ch, tch* /ch/ Remind children that in English, sometimes two or three letters produce one sound. Review previously learned consonant digraphs *sh* and *th*.

Transfer Skills

French, Hmong, and Spanish do not have the hard /j/ sound that is heard in words like *judge* and *lodge*. Provide additional practice saying and writing words with *-dge*.

Words with *ph, gh* /f/; dge /j/

Use with page 244.

Preteach Copy and distribute page 244. Have children point to the picture of a graph at the top of the page. Say: *This is a graph, /g/ /r/ /a/ /f/. How many sounds do you hear after the /a/ sound? Say it with me: /f/, /f/, graph. That's right, there is one sound after the vowel: /f/.* Now point to the *laugh*. Ask: *How many sounds do you hear after the /a/ sound? Listen: /l/ /a/ /f/. Yes, there is one sound after the vowel: /f/.* Repeat this drill for the word *bridge*.

Teach/Model Write the word *graph* on the board. Underline the *ph* in the word and tell children: *The sound /f/ in* graph *is spelled* ph. *Say it with me: graph, /g/ /r/ /a/ /f/.* Explain that the letters *ph* can come at the beginning, middle, or end of a word. Now write *laugh* on the board. Underline the *gh* in the word and say: *The sound /f/ is at the end of the word* laugh. *Say it with me: laugh, /l/ /a/ /f/.* Then write *bridge* on the board. Underline the *dge* in the word and say: *The sound /j/ is at the end of the word* bridge. *Say it with me: bridge, /b/ /r/ /i/ /j/.* Explain that the letters *gh* and *dge* are not commonly found at the beginning of English words.

Help children name the items in Row 1 on page 244 *(phone, laugh, dolphin, judge)*. Repeat each name, stretching out the sound of each letter so children can hear the /f/ or /j/ sound in each word. Say: *I am going to read the words again. This time, circle the letters that can be found in the words:* phone, laugh, dolphin, judge. Review the answers as a class *(ph, gh, ph, dge)*.

Practice Have children look at the pictures in Row 2 on page 244. Help them name each picture *(elephant, badge, photo, gopher)*. Have them write the consonant sound to complete each name, choosing from the letters listed in the box. Then have children look at the pictures in Row 3, say the name of each picture, and write the names *(phone, trophy, cough, dolphin)*.

Assess Make another copy of page 244 and cut out the pictures for *phone, laugh, dolphin, bridge, judge,* and *cough*. Prepare a sheet of paper with three columns that are labeled with the consonant letter patterns *ph, gh,* and *dge*. Give each child the pile of picture cards. Have children say the names of the pictures and place each card under the letters that each word contains.

Pronunciation Tip
Words with *ph, gh* /f/; *dge* /j/
Demonstrate to children that when you produce the sound /f/, your upper teeth rest gently on your bottom lip. To generate the sound /j/, your upper and bottom teeth come almost completely together and your lips move outwards

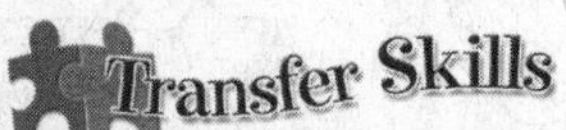

Children who are literate in their home languages may be familiar with the concept of silent letters. In Spanish, the letter *h* is always silent, and the letter *u* is silent when it follows a *q*. In French, the letter *s* at the end of a word is often silent. Discuss children's awareness of silent letters in their home languages before introducing *kn, wr, gn,* and *mb.*

Words with *kn, wr, gn, mb*

Use with page 245.

Preteach Copy and distribute page 245. Have children point to the picture of a doorknob at the top of the page. Say: *This is a knob, /n/ /o/ /b/, knob. What sound do you hear at the beginning of the word* knob*? Say it with me: /n/, /n/, knob. That's right, the sound is /n/.* Now point to the *wrist.* Ask: *What sound do you hear at the beginning of the word* wrist*? Listen: /r/ /i/ /s/ /t/. Yes, the sound is /r/.* Repeat this drill for the word *comb.*

Teach/Model Write the word *knob* on the board. Underline the *kn* in the word and tell children: *The sound /n/ in* knob *is spelled* kn. *Say it with me: knob, /n/ /o/ /b/. Can you tell me which letter in the word* knob *is silent? That's right, the* k *is silent.* Now write *wrist* on the board. Underline the *wr* in the word and say: *The sound /r/ is at the beginning of the word* wrist. *Say it with me:* wrist, */r/ /i/ /s/ /t/. Can you tell me which letter in the word* wrist *is silent? That's right, the* w *is silent.* Repeat this drill for the word *comb.*

Help children name the items in Row 1 on page 245 *(wreath, knife, gnat, comb).* Repeat each name, stretching out the sound of each letter so children can hear the consonant sounds in each word. Say: *I am going to read the words again:* wreath, knife, gnat, comb. *This time, circle the letters that can be found in the words.* Review the answers as a class *(wr, kn, gn, mb).*

Practice Have children look at the pictures in Row 2 on page 245. Help them name each picture *(knob, wrist, sign, limb).* Have them write the letter patterns to complete each name, choosing from the letters listed in the box. Then have children look at the pictures in Row 3, say the name of each picture, and write the names *(knee, write, sign, climb).*

Assess Create word cards that contain the silent consonant letter patterns *kn, wr, gn,* and *mb.* Give each child the pile of word cards. Read the following words aloud to the class: *knob, knock, knit, write, wrist, wreath, sign, gnat, design, lamb, comb,* and *numb.* Pause after each word so children can find and hold up the card that contains the letter pattern that corresponds to the word.

Pronunciation Tip Words with *kn, wr, gn, mb* Offer several examples of words containing letter patterns with silent consonants *(knob, wrist, sign, lamb).* See if children can point out the silent letter as they look at and hear each word.

Name ________________________________

Initial Consonant Blends

- **Listen** for the first two sounds.
- **Circle** the correct letters.

ROW 1

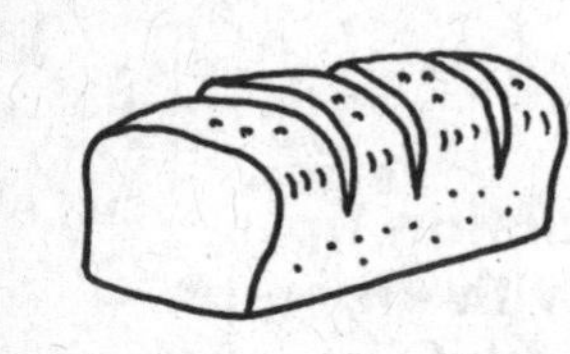

br bl

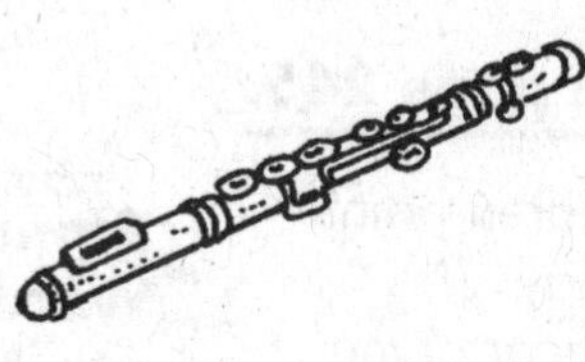

fl gl

sm sk

sm fl

- **Look** at each picture. **Say** its name. **Write** the letters.

bl	fr	sp	st

ROW 2

____ock

____ep

____og

____ot

- **Look** at each picture. **Say** its name.
- **Write** the name of the picture.

ROW 3

Name ______________________________

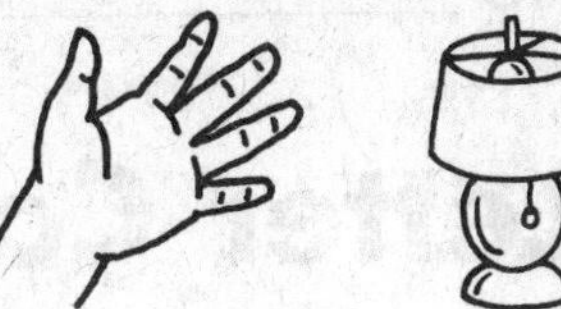

Final Consonant Blends

- **Listen** for the last two sounds.
- **Circle** the correct letters.

ROW 1

lk lt	mp nd	sk nd	lp st

- **Look** at each picture. **Say** its name. **Write** the letters.

mp nt sk st

ROW 2

	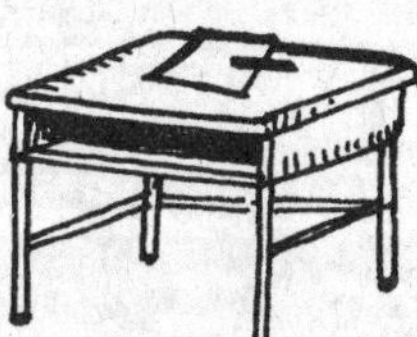		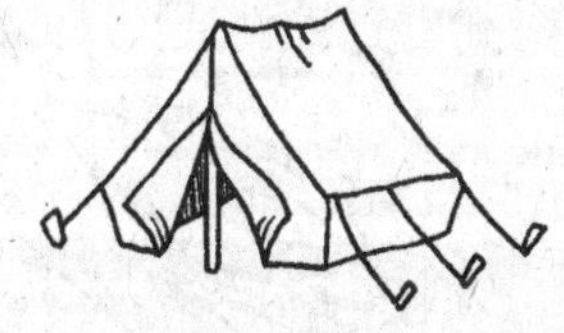
ve____	de____	ju____	te____

- **Look** at each picture. **Say** its name.
- **Write** the name of the picture.

ROW 3

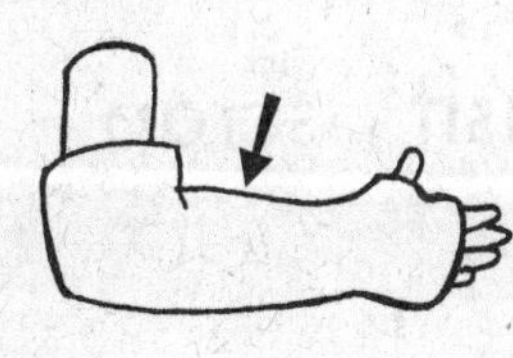			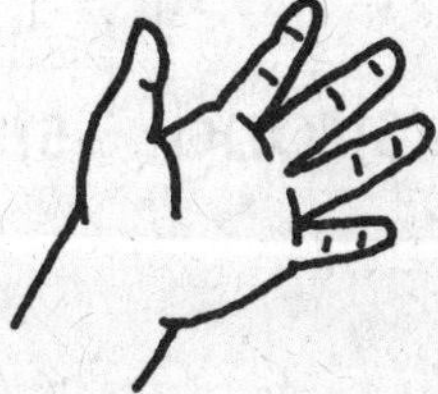
________	________	________	________

Name ______________________________

3-Letter Consonant Blends

- **Listen** for the first three sounds.
- **Circle** the correct letters.

ROW 1

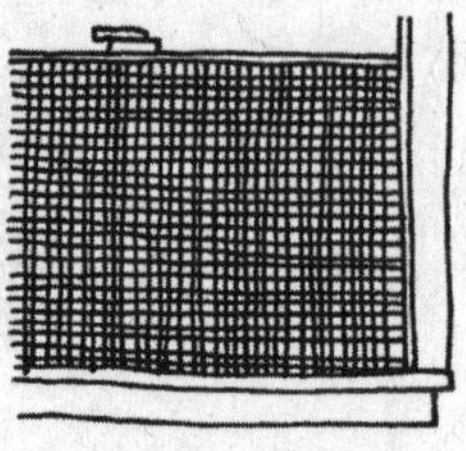

scr spl

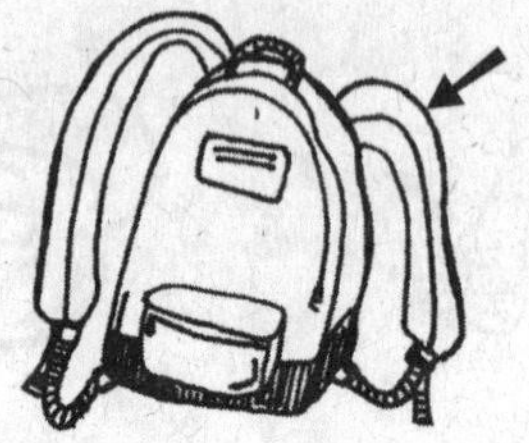

spl str

str spr

- **Look** at each picture. **Say** its name.
- **Circle** the word that names each picture. **Underline** the blended letters.

ROW 2

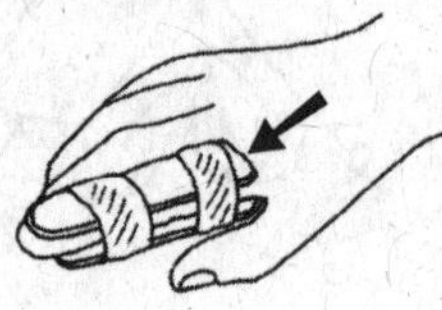

splint strip

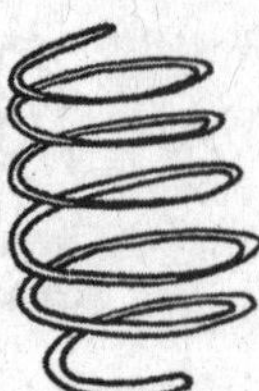

scrap spring

stripe sports

ROW 3

strong strand

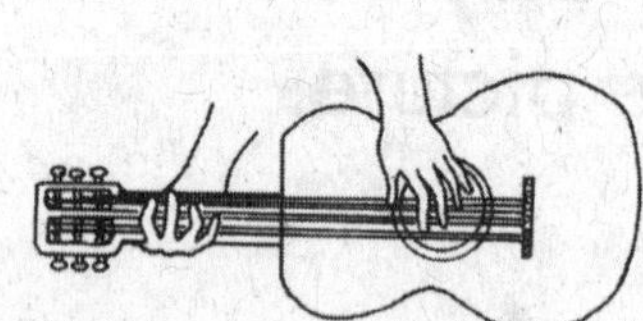

splat strum

splash scrap

Name ______________________________

Words with *wh* /hw/; *ch, tch* /ch/

- **Listen** for the beginning and ending sounds.
- **Circle** the correct letters.

ROW 1

wh wr

sh ch

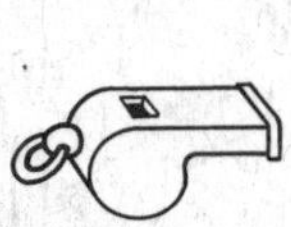

tr wh

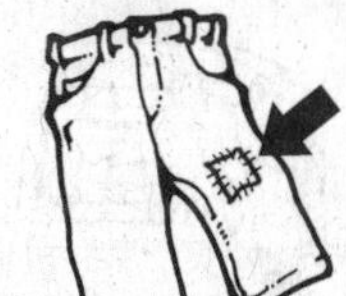

ck tch

- **Look** at each picture. **Say** its name. **Write** the letters.

wh	ch	tch

ROW 2

sandwi____

____isper

____eck

wa____

- **Look** at each picture. **Say** its name.
- **Write** the name of the picture.

ROW 3

____

____

____

____

Name ________________________________

Words with *ph, gh* /f/; *dge* /j/

- **Listen** for the sounds /f/ or /j/ in each word.
- **Circle** the correct letters.

ROW 1

ph mp   gr gh   fr ph   tg dge

- **Look** at each picture. **Say** its name. **Write** the letters.

ph gh dge

ROW 2

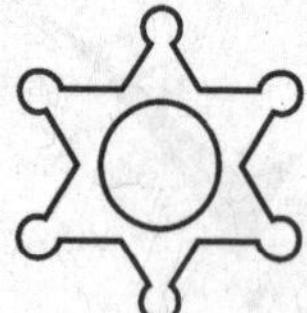

ele____ant   ba____   ____oto   go____er

- **Look** at each picture. **Say** its name.
- **Write** the name of the picture.

ROW 3

____________ ____________ ____________ ____________

Name ______________________________

Words with *kn, wr, gn, mb*

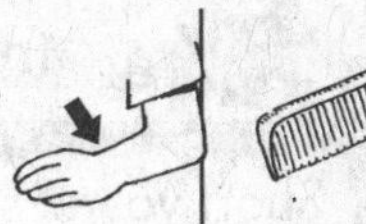

- **Listen** for the sound at the beginning or end of each word.
- **Circle** the correct letters.

ROW 1

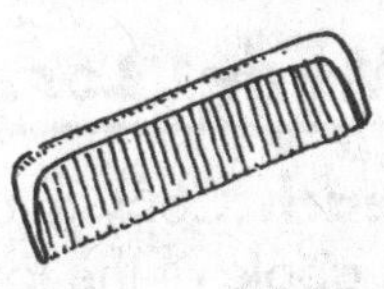

wh wr | kr kn | gn gr | mn mb

- **Look** at each picture. **Say** its name. **Write** the letters.

kn wr gn mb

ROW 2

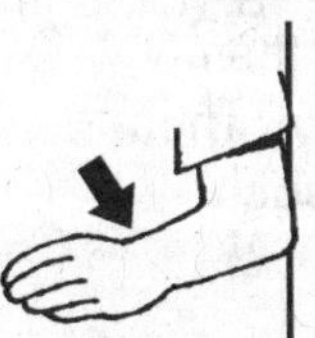

____ob | ____ist | si____ | li____

- **Look** at each picture. **Say** its name.
- **Write** the name of the picture.

ROW 3

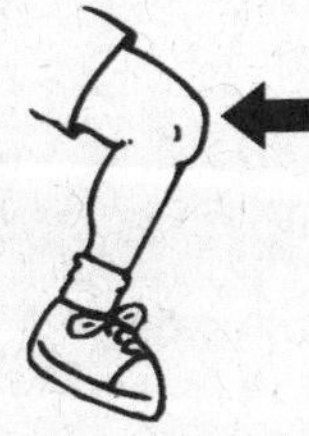
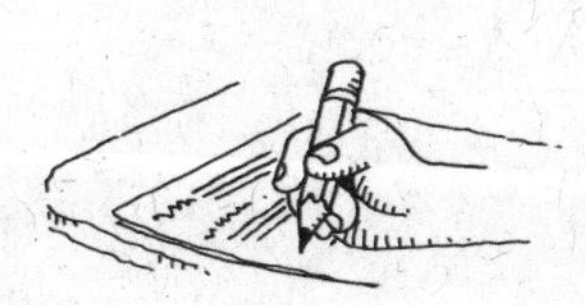

Transfer Skills

Short vowel sounds may be challenging for many English learners because they are unfamiliar sounds. They do not have exact equivalents in languages such as Spanish, Chinese, Hmong, and others. Children may confuse short vowel sounds such as /e/ and /i/ when reading, speaking, and writing in English. The following lessons provide practice for hearing and producing short vowel sounds. The Model Lesson gives you a pattern for teaching.

☆ Model Lesson: Short *a* Use with page 248.

Preteach Copy and distribute page 248. Have children point to the apple at the top of the page. Say: *This is an apple. Apple begins with /a/. Say it with me: /a/, /a/, /a/, apple.*

Teach/Model Tell children: *The /a/ sound is one sound of the letter* a. *We call this sound short* a. *Repeat these /a/ words after me:* cap, am, mat, pan.

Help children name the items in Row 1 on page 248 *(fan, mop, hat, ant)*. Repeat each name, clearly pronouncing the vowel in each word. Then say: *I'll say these words again. If you hear the /a/ sound, circle the picture:* fan, mop, hat, ant. Children should circle the *fan, hat,* and *ant* pictures—but not the *mop.*

Practice Have children look at the pictures in Row 2 on page 248. Help them read the words below each picture. Have them circle the word that names each picture *(pan, rag, cat, cap)*. Then have them look at the pictures in Row 3, say the name of each picture, and write the names *(fan, can, bat, ant)*.

Assess Tell children: *I will say some word pairs. Raise your hand when you hear the /a/ sound:* pat, pet; hot, hat; bad, bed; man, main; rug, rag. Then have children repeat the word pairs after you, striving for the correct pronunciation of /a/. Keep in mind that children who have difficulty pronouncing /a/ may still be able to comprehend short /a/ words that they hear or read.

Pronunciation Tip
short *a* *When you say /a/, your jaw and tongue are down. Say /a/ and feel your jaw and tongue go down.*

Adapting the ☆ Model Lesson

Use the same lesson format above to teach the vowel sounds /e/, /i/, /o/, and /u/. The following information will help you customize each lesson.

Notes for Additional Lessons

Short *e*

Use with page 249.

Teach Use these /e/ words: *fed, hen, leg, set.* Row 1 of page 249: *egg, pen, bed, gnat* (Children will circle *egg, pen, bed.*)

Practice Row 2: *ten, step, men, vest;* Row 3: *pen, net, leg, bed*

Assess Use these word pairs: *set, sat; tin, ten; net, not; sell, sale.*

Pronunciation Tip
short *e* *When you say /e/, your mouth is open. Your tongue is behind your bottom teeth. Say /e/. Did your mouth open? Say /e/ again.*

Short *i*

Use with page 250.

Teach Use these /i/ words: *rib, itch, fig, kit.* Row 1 of page 250: *bib, bat, fish, leg* (Children will circle *bib* and *fish.*)

Practice Row 2: *dig, lid, wig, sick;* Row 3: *pig, six, bib, zip*

Assess Use these word pairs: *pan, pin; sit, sat; left, lift; did, dad.*

Pronunciation Tip
short *i* *When you say /i/, your mouth is open, and your tongue is slightly lowered. Say /i/. Is your mouth open, and is your tongue slightly lowered? Practice: /i/.*
In Spanish, the letter *i* is pronounced /ē/. Point out that this letter has different sounds in English.

Short *o*

Use with page 251.

Teach Use these /o/ words: *ox, cot, jog, pop.* Row 1 of page 251: *rock, box, cat, frog* (Children will circle *rock, box,* and *frog.*)

Practice Row 2: *pot, lock, fox, dog;* Row 3: *box, mop, top, mom*

Assess Use these word pairs: *top, tap; get, got; hat, hot; net, not.*

Pronunciation Tip
short *o* *When you say /o/, your mouth is open and your jaw drops. Put your hand under your chin and say /o/. See, your mouth opened and your jaw dropped.*
In Spanish, the sound of letter *a* is similar to /o/ in English. Examples: *Mami/Mom; Papá/Poppa.*

Short *u*

Use with page 252.

Teach Use these /u/ words: *up, bun, hug, jump.* Row 1 of page 252: *tub, truck, mop, drum* (Children will circle *tub, truck,* and *drum.*)

Practice Row 2: *bug, cup, duck, sub;* Row 3: *bus, sun, tub, rug*

Assess Use these word pairs: *fun, fin; bed, bud; hut, hot; dug, dig.*

Pronunciation Tip
short *u* *When you say /u/, your mouth is open, and your tongue is down. Say /u/ again. Is your mouth open? Is your tongue down?*

Name ______________________________

Words with Short *a*

- **Listen** for the sound of *a* in *apple*.
- **Circle** the pictures of words that have this sound.

ROW 1

- **Look** at each picture. **Say** its name.
- **Circle** the word that names each picture.

ROW 2

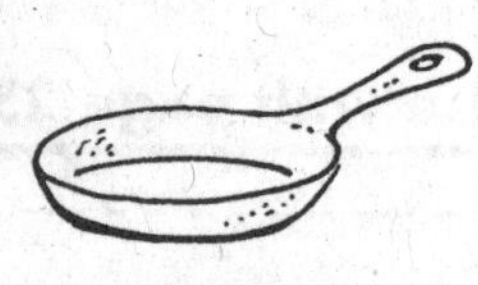 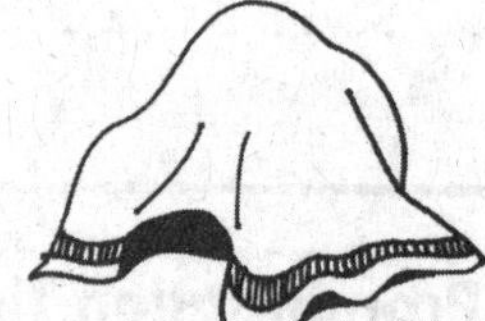  

pen	rag	cat	cape
pan	rug	cot	cap

- **Look** at each picture. **Say** its name.
- **Write** the name of the picture.

ROW 3

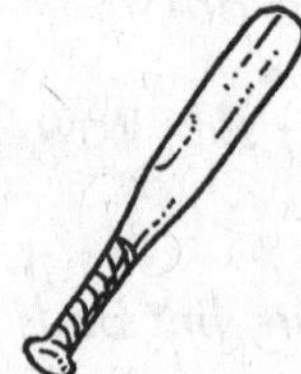 

Name ______________________________

Words with Short *e* 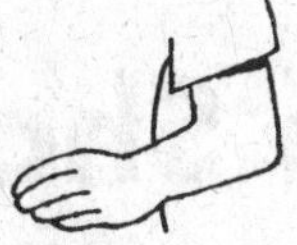

- **Listen** for the sound of *e* in *elbow*.
- **Circle** the pictures of words that have this sound.

ROW 1

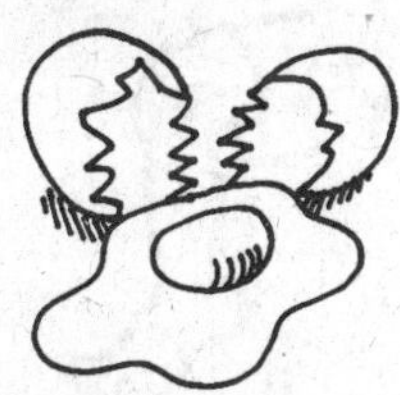  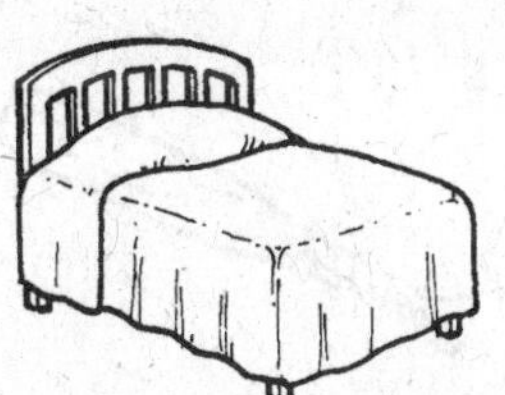 

- **Look** at each picture. **Say** its name.
- **Circle** the word that names each picture.

ROW 2

	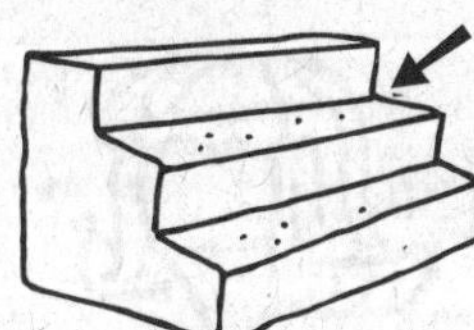		
tin	step	main	vast
ten	stop	men	vest

- **Look** at each picture. **Say** its name.
- **Write** the name of the picture.

ROW 3

 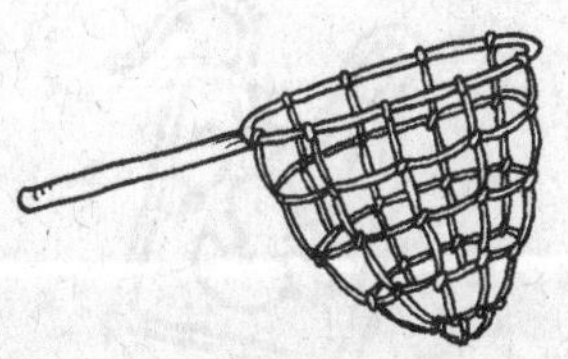  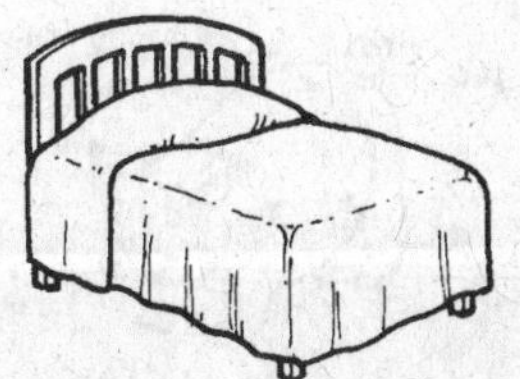

______ ______ ______ ______

Name ______________________________

Words with Short *i*

- **Listen** for the sound of *i* in *inch.*
- **Circle** the pictures of words that have this sound.

ROW 1

 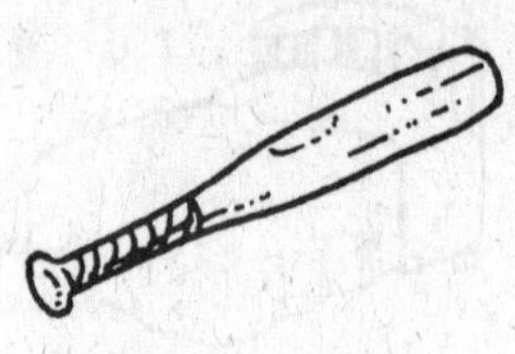  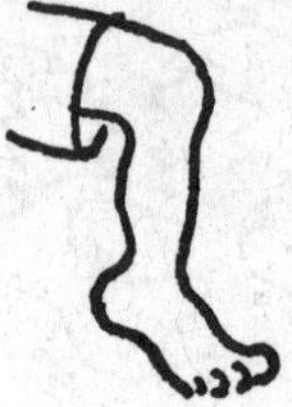

- **Look** at each picture. **Say** its name.
- **Circle** the word that names each picture.

ROW 2

dog dig

lid lad

wig wag

sock sick

- **Look** at each picture. **Say** its name.
- **Write** the name of the picture.

ROW 3

Name ______________________________

Words with Short o

- **Listen** for the sound of *o* in *ox.*
- **Circle** the pictures of words that have this sound.

ROW 1

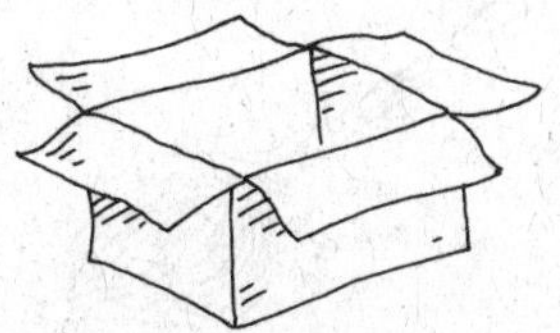

- **Look** at each picture. **Say** its name.
- **Circle** the word that names each picture.

ROW 2

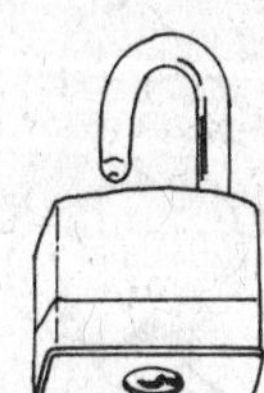

pot	lock	fox	dig
pat	luck	fix	dog

- **Look** at each picture. **Say** its name.
- **Write** the name of the picture.

ROW 3

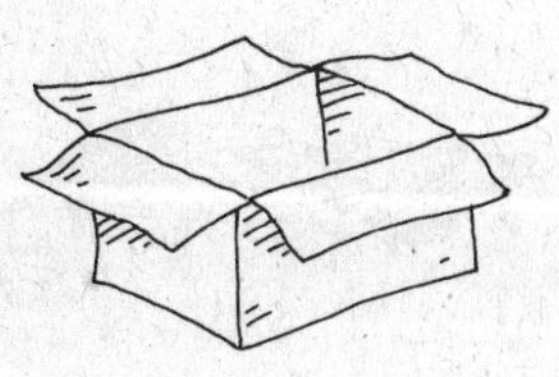

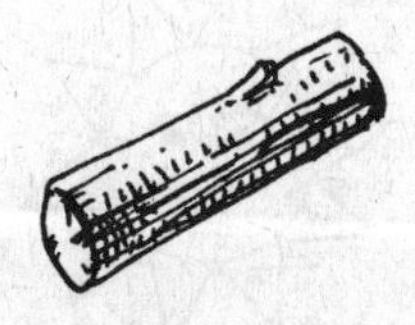

Name ______________________________

Words with Short *u*

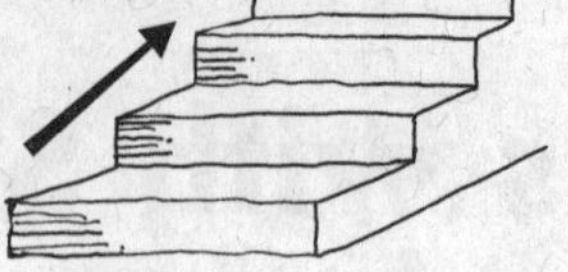

- **Listen** for the sound of *u* in *up*.
- **Circle** the pictures of words that have this sound.

ROW 1

   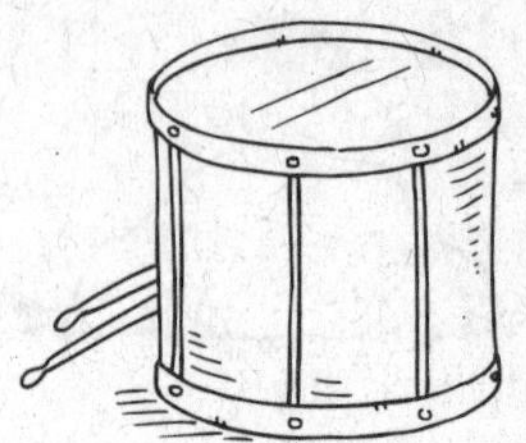

- **Look** at each picture. **Say** its name.
- **Circle** the word that names each picture.

ROW 2

bug bag   cap cup   dock duck   sub sob

- **Look** at each picture. **Say** its name.
- **Write** the name of the picture.

ROW 3

______________ ______________ ______________ ______________

Transfer Skills

Long vowels and the vowel digraphs that produce long vowel sounds can be confusing for English learners. For example, in Spanish and other languages, silent vowels are rare. Children may want to pronounce the silent *e* at the end of words with spelling patterns *a_e, e_e, i_e, o_e,* and *u_e* words, or both vowels in digraphs such as *ai* and *oa*. The following lessons provide practice for hearing, producing, and spelling long vowel sounds. This model lesson gives you a pattern for teaching.

☆ Model Lesson: Long *a* Use with page 256.

Preteach Copy and distribute page 256. Have children point to the picture of the ape at the top of the page. Say: *This is an ape.* Ape *begins with /ā/. Say it with me: /ā/, /ā/, ape.* Repeat for *train* and *hay.* Say: *Ape, train, hay. They all have the /ā/ sound.*

Teach/Model Tell children: *The sound /ā/ is called long* a. *Repeat these /ā/ words after me:* ape, train, hay, brave, main.

Help children name the items in Row 1 on page 256 *(braid, rake, apple, tray).* Repeat each name, clearly pronouncing the vowel in each word. Then say: *I'll say these words again. If you hear the /ā/ sound, circle the picture:* braid, rake, apple, tray. Children should circle the *braid, rake,* and *tray* pictures—but not the *apple.*

Point out that there are different ways of spelling long *a* words. Write a 3-column chart on the board with the headings *a_e, ai,* and *ay.* List the words *ape, train,* and *hay* in the columns where they belong. Add the long *a* words from Row 1 to the chart. Invite children to suggest other long *a* words they know that can be added to the chart.

Practice Have children look at the pictures in Row 2 on page 256. Help them read the words below each picture. Have them circle the word that names each picture. *(cane, day, rain, plane)* Then have them look at the pictures in Row 3. Explain: *Say the name of each picture. Then write the word. Remember that the /ā/ sound can be spelled in different ways.* (Children should write *plane, rain, hay, ape.*)

Assess Tell children: *I will say some word pairs. Raise your hand when you hear the /ā/ sound:* sail, sell; back, bake; late, let; gum, game; tap, tape. Then have children repeat the word pairs after you, striving for the correct pronunciation of /ā/. Remember that difficulties with pronunciation do not necessarily indicate difficulties in comprehension.

Pronunciation Tip
long *a* *When you start to say /ā/, your mouth is open. Your tongue is in the middle of your mouth. To finish the sound /ā/, your tongue and your jaw move up a little. Try it: /ā/, /ā/, ape.* The long *a* sound is similar to the Spanish digraph *ei.* Example: *rain/reina* (queen).

Adapting the ☆ Model Lesson

Use the same lesson format above to teach the long vowels /ē/, /ī/, /ō/, and /ū/ and the vowel sounds of *y.* The following information will help you customize each lesson.

Notes for Additional Lessons

Long *e*

Use with page 257.

Teach Use these /ē/ words: *eagle, feet, me, beat, we.* Row 1 of page 257: *leaf, egg, bee, pig.* (Children circle pictures for *leaf* and *bee.*) Make a 3-column chart with the headings *ea, ee,* and *e.* List the words *eagle, feet, me, leaf, bee,* and other long *e* words that children suggest.

Practice Row 2: *seal, sleep, meat, he;* Row 3: *meat, seal, feet, me.*

Assess Use these word pairs: *deep, dip; seat, sit; read, ride; mean, main; feel, fell.*

Pronunciation Tip
long *e* *When you say /ē/, your lips are stretched wide. Your mouth has a little smile when you say /ē/. Try it: /ē/, /ē/.* The long *e* sound is similar to the sound of *i* in Spanish. Examples: *need/nido* (nest); *see/sí* (yes).

Long *i*

Use with page 258.

Teach Use these /ī/ words: *ice, tie, night, sigh, pile.* Row 1 of page 258: *kite, fish, child, high.* (Children circle pictures for *kite, child,* and *high.*) Make a 4-column chart with the headings *i_e, ie, ild,* and *igh.* List the words *ice, tie, night, kite, child, high,* and other long *i* words that children suggest.

Practice Row 2: *bike, tie, light, nine;* Row 3: *child, light, tie, ice.*

Assess Use these word pairs: *mat, might; fine, fan; hid, hide; mild, made; mice, mouse.*

Pronunciation Tip
long *i* *When you start to say /ī/, your mouth is open and your jaw drops. Your tongue is down. To finish the sound /ī/, your tongue and your jaw move up. Try it: /ī/, /ī/.* The long *i* sound is similar to the Spanish digraphs *ai* and *ay.* Examples: *I/hay* (there is/are); *bike/baile* (dance).

Long *o*

Use with page 259.

Teach Use these /ō/ words: *rope, snow, boat, grow, sold.* Row 1 of page 259: *soap, mop, fold, bow* (Children circle pictures for *soap, fold,* and *bow.*) Make a 4-column chart with the headings *o_e, oa, old,* and *ow.* List the words *rope, snow, boat, soap, fold, blow,* and other long *o* words that children suggest.

Practice Row 2: *goat, cone, mow, gold;* Row 3: *gold, cone, snow, boat.*

Assess Use these word pairs: *coat, cot; hop, hope; crow, crew; ball, bowl; note, not.*

Pronunciation Tip
long *o* *When you say /ō/, your mouth is round. Try it: /ō/, /ō/.* The long *o* sound is similar to the sound of *o* in Spanish. Example: *no/no.*

Notes for Additional Lessons

Long *u*

Use with page 260.

Teach Use these /ū/ words: *flute, moon, juice, chew, blue, cute.* Row 1 of page 260: *sun, tube, fruit, boot* (Children circle pictures for *tube, fruit, boot.*) Make a 5-column chart with the headings *u_e, ue, ui, ew,* and *oo.* List the words *flute, moon, juice, chew, blue, tube, fruit, boot,* and other long *u* words that children suggest.

Practice Row 2: *suit, pool, cube, glue;* Row 3: *glue, cube, flute, moon.*

Assess Use these word pairs: *tune, tin; foam, fume; too, toe; shut, shoot; grew, grow.*

Pronunciation Tip
long *u* *When you say /ū/ in a word like* rule, *your mouth is round and the opening is small. Try it: /ū/, /ū/. When you say /ū/ in a word like* use, *your lips start out in a line. Then they move into a little round circle. Try it: /ū/, /ū/.* The long *u* sound in words like *tube* is similar to the sound of *u* in Spanish: *tube/tubo* (tube). The long *u* sound in words like *unit* is similar to the sound of *iu* or *yu* in Spanish: *unit/yugo* (yoke).

The Vowel Sounds of *y*

Use with page 261.

Teach Use these /ī/ words: *sky, my, try.* Use these /ē/ words: *bunny, sandy, pretty.* Note that both Rows 1 and 2 are part of the "Teach" section on page 261. Row 1: *fry, bee, cry, fly.* (Children circle pictures for *fry cry,* and *fly.*) Row 2: *puppy, tie, twenty, city.* (Children circle pictures for *puppy, twenty,* and *city.*) Make a 2-column chart with the headings *y in sky* and *y in bunny.* List the words *sky, fry, cry, fly, bunny, puppy, twenty, city,* and other appropriate words that children suggest.

Practice Row 3: *twenty, fly, bunny, sky.*

Assess Use these word pairs for /ī/: *shy, she; by, bay; fly, flee.* Use these word pairs for /ē/: *sandy, Sunday; silly, sigh; buddy, buy.*

Pronunciation Tip
vowel sounds of *y* *When you say a word like* funny, *the letter* y *sounds like a long* e. *To say it, your lips are stretched wide and your mouth has a little smile. Try it: /ē/, /ē/,* funny. *When you say a word like* by, *the letter* y *sounds like a long* i. *To say it, your mouth opens and your jaw drops. Then your jaw and tongue move up. Try it: /ī/, /ī/,* by.

Name ___________________________________

Words with Long *a*

- **Listen** for the sound of *a* in *ape.*
- **Circle** the pictures of words that have this sound.

ROW 1

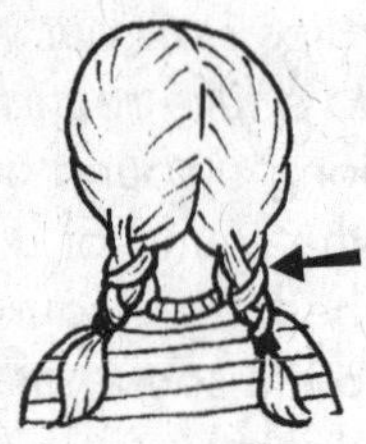
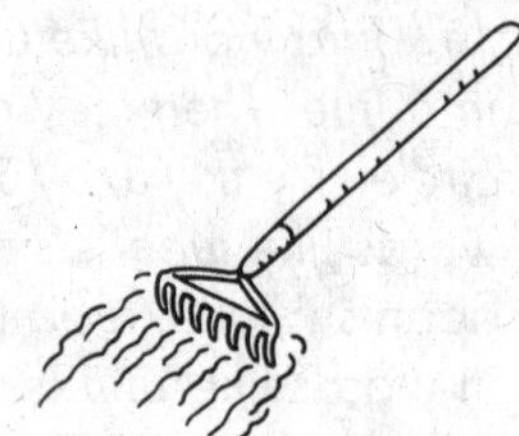

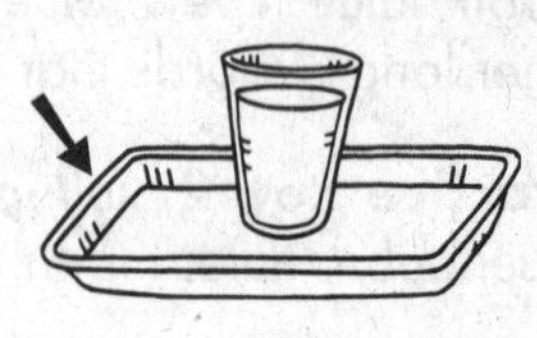

- **Look** at each picture. **Say** its name.
- **Circle** the word that names each picture.

ROW 2

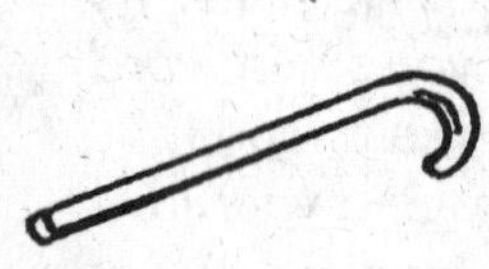

can	day	ran	plane
cane	dad	rain	plan

- **Look** at each picture. **Say** its name.
- **Write** the name of the picture.

ROW 3

Name ______________________________

Words with Long e

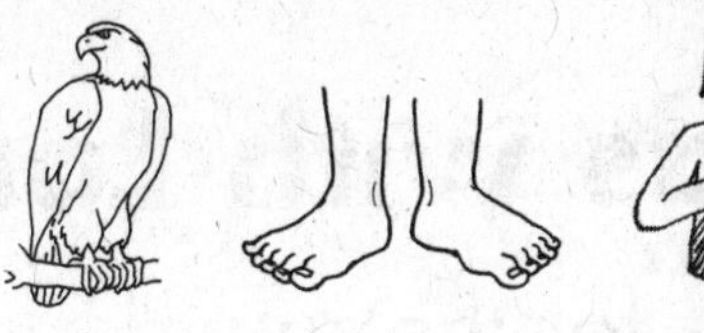

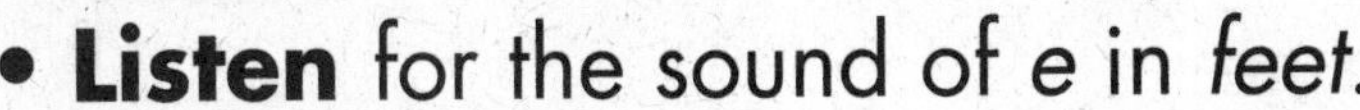

- **Listen** for the sound of *e* in *feet.*
- **Circle** the pictures of words that have this sound.

ROW 1

 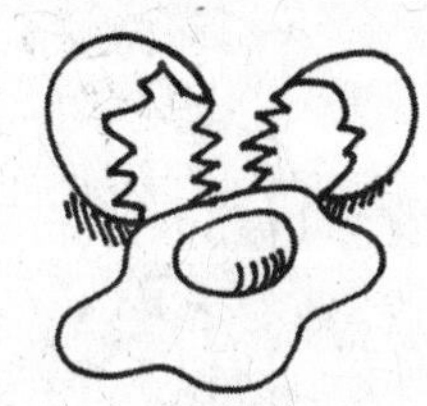  

- **Look** at each picture. **Say** its name.
- **Circle** the word that names each picture.

ROW 2

  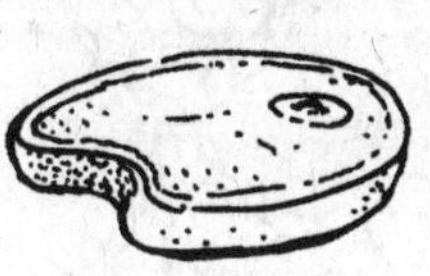 

seal sell	slip sleep	meat met	hay he

- **Look** at each picture. **Say** its name.
- **Write** the name of the picture.

ROW 3

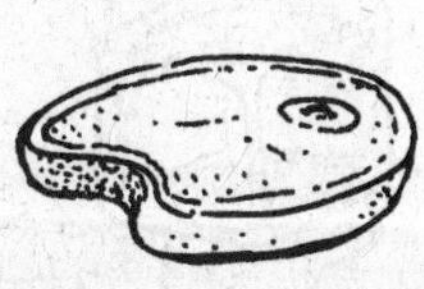  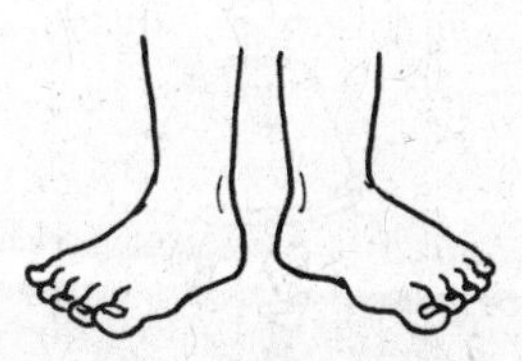 

__________ __________ __________ __________

Name ______________________________

Words with Long *i*

- **Listen** for the sound of *i* in *tie.*
- **Circle** the pictures of words that have this sound.

ROW 1

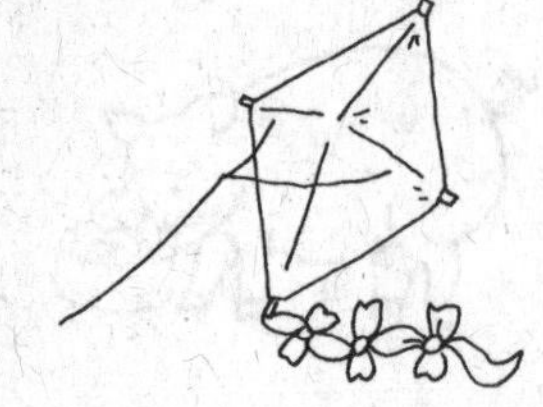

- **Look** at each picture. **Say** its name.
- **Circle** the word that names each picture.

ROW 2

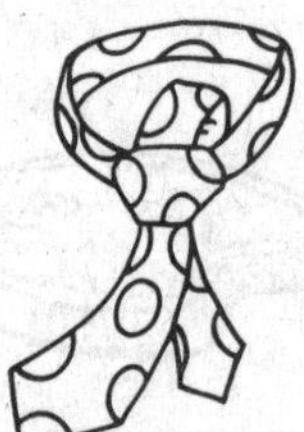
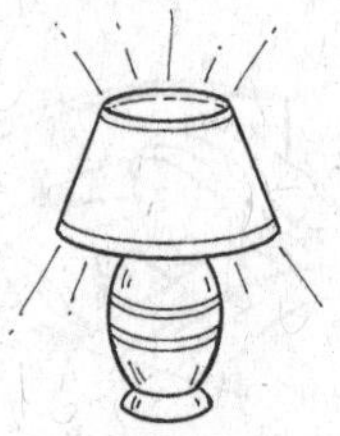

bake	tie	light	none
bike	tea	let	nine

- **Look** at each picture. **Say** its name.
- **Write** the name of the picture.

ROW 3

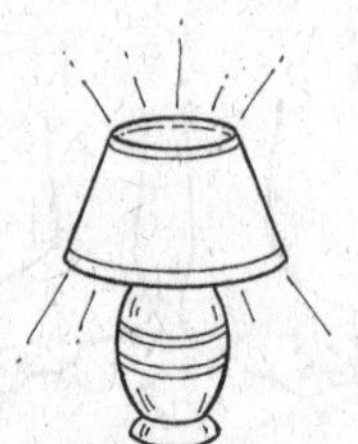

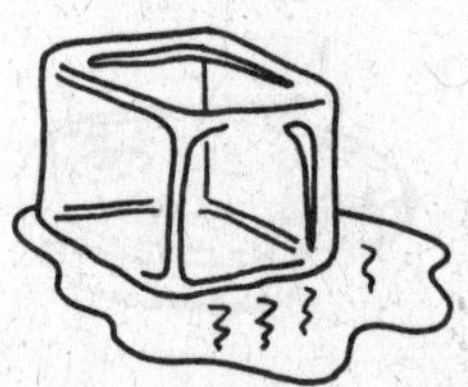

Name ______________________________

Words with Long *o*

- **Listen** for the sound of *o* in *rope.*
- **Circle** the pictures of words that have this sound.

ROW 1

  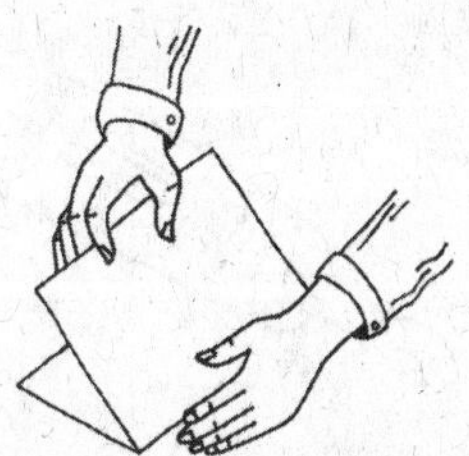 

- **Look** at each picture. **Say** its name.
- **Circle** the word that names each picture.

ROW 2

	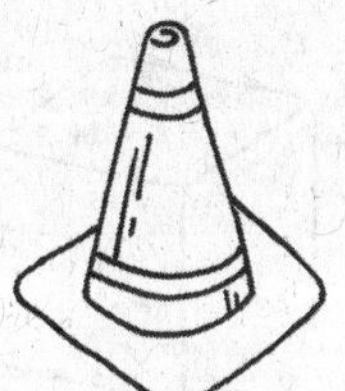		
got goat	cane cone	moo mow	gold good

- **Look** at each picture. **Say** its name.
- **Write** the name of the picture.

ROW 3

 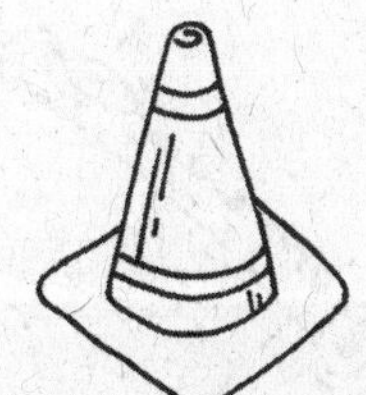  

Name ___________________________

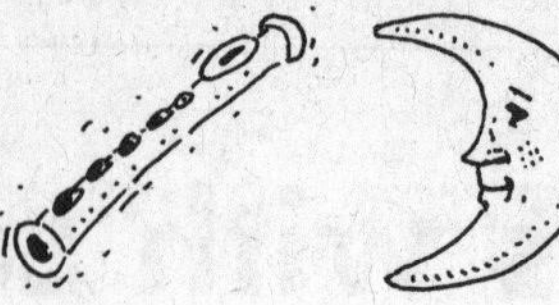

Words with Long *u*

- **Listen** for the sound of *u* in *flute.*
- **Circle** the pictures of words that have this sound.

ROW 1

- **Look** at each picture. **Say** its name.
- **Circle** the word that names each picture.

ROW 2

suit
sit

pool
pill

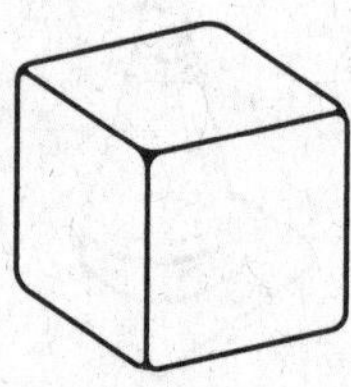

cub
cube

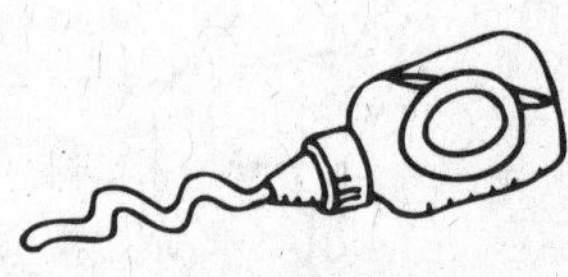

glee
glue

- **Look** at each picture. **Say** its name.
- **Write** the name of the picture.

ROW 3

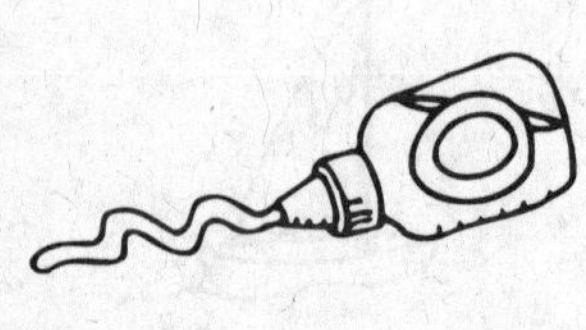

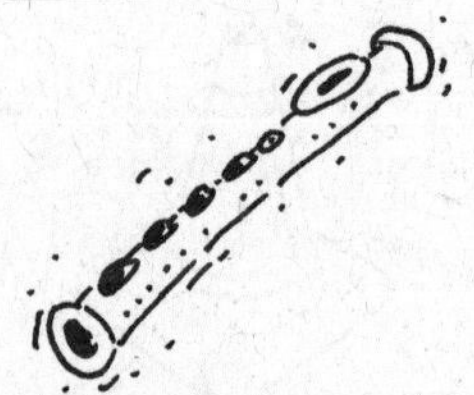

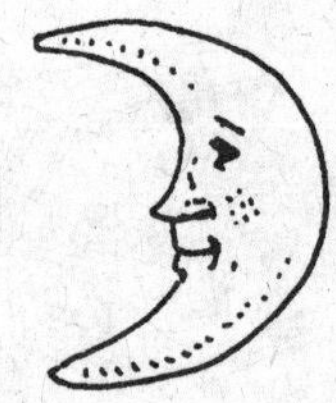

Name ______________________________

Vowel Sounds of *y*

- **Listen** for the sound of *y* in *sky*.
- **Circle** the pictures of words that have this sound.

ROW 1

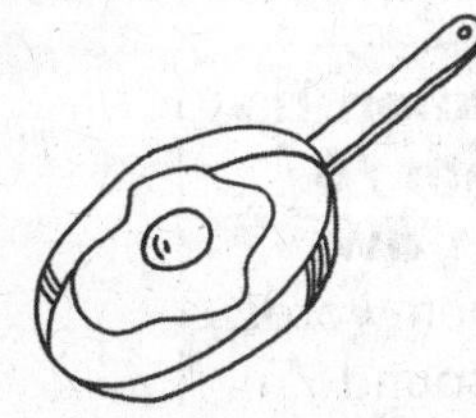

- **Listen** for the sound of *y* in *bunny*.
- **Circle** the pictures of words that end with this sound.

ROW 2

- **Look** at each picture. **Say** its name.
- **Write** the name of the picture.

ROW 3

Transfer Skills

Children may need assistance with *au(gh)* words such as *caught* and *taught*, in which the *gh* is silent. Practice the words along with words containing the vowel patterns *aw*, *au*, and *al* as in *paw*, *sauce*, and *salt*.

Words with /ȯ/ Spelled as *aw, au, al*

Use with page 264.

Preteach Copy and distribute page 264. Have children point to a wall in the room. Say: *This is a* wall. *What vowel sound do you hear in the word* wall*? Say it with me: /ȯ/, /ȯ/,* wall. Repeat this drill for the words *ball, claw, launch, yawn,* and *talk*, eliciting from children that all these words contain the same vowel sound.

Teach/Model Write the word *ball* on the board. Underline the *al* in the word and tell children: *When the letter* a *is followed by* l, *it often makes the /ȯ/ sound. Say it with me: ball /b/ /ȯ/ /l/.* Now write *claw* on the board. Underline the *aw* in the word and ask children: *What letters make the /ȯ/ sound in this word? That's right,* aw. *Say it with me: claw, /k/ /l/ /ȯ/.* Point out and underline the vowel spellings as you read the words. Ask children if they can identify one letter that both words contain (the vowel *a*).

Help children name the items in Row 1 on page 264 *(wall, fan, yawn, ant)*. Repeat each name, stretching out the sound of each letter so children can hear the vowel sound in each word. Say: *I am going to read the words again:* wall, fan, yawn, ant. *This time, circle the pictures for words that contain the /ȯ/ sound.* Review the answers as a class *(wall, yawn)*.

Practice Have children look at the pictures in Row 2 on page 264. Help them read the words below each picture. Have them circle the word that names each picture *(ball, paw, hawk, launch)*. Then have them look at the pictures in Row 3, say the name of each picture, and write the names *(salt, sauce, ball, straw)*.

Assess Make another copy of page 264 and cut out the pictures for *ball, paw, launch, salt,* and *straw*. Give each child the pile of picture cards. Read the words aloud to the class and pause after each word so children can find and hold up the corresponding picture card.

Pronunciation Tip Words with /ȯ/ Spelled as *aw, au, al* When words end in the sound /ȯ/, the /ȯ/ sound is usually spelled *aw*.

Transfer Skills

Speakers of Chinese, French, Italian, Korean, Spanish, and Urdu may have difficulty distinguishing /ů/ spelled *oo* and /ü/ spelled *oo*. Help them practice saying and writing word pairs like these: took/tool; shook/shoot; cook/cool.

Words with /ů/ Spelled *oo*

Use with page 265.

Preteach Copy and distribute page 265. Have children point to the picture of a book at the top of the page. Say: *This is a book, /b/ /ů/ /k/, book. What vowel sound do you hear in the word* book*? Say it with me: book, /b/ /ů/ /k/, /ů/, /ů/, book. That's right, the sound is /ů/.*

Teach/Model Write the word *book* on the board. Underline the oo in the word and tell children: *The sound /ů/ in* book *is spelled* oo. *Say it with me: book, /b/ /ů/ /k/.* Point to each spelling as you say its sounds. Then run your hand under the word *book* as you blend the whole word: /b/ /ů/ /k/.

Help children name the items in Row 1 on page 265 *(foot, boat, wood, hood)*. Repeat each name, clearly pronouncing the vowel sound in each word. Say: *I am going to say these words again. If you hear the /ů/ sound, circle the picture.* Children should circle *foot, wood*, and *hood*, but not *boat*.

Practice Have children look at the pictures in Row 2 on page 265. Help them name each picture *(cook, wood, look, hook)*. Have them circle the word that names each picture. Then have children look at the pictures in Row 3, say the name of each picture, and write the names *(book, foot, hoof)*.

Assess Tell children: *I will say some word pairs. Raise your hand when you hear the /ů/ sound:* nook, knock; took, tool; shook, shall; cook, cool. Then have children repeat the word pairs after you, striving for the correct pronunciation of /ů/.

Pronunciation Tip
Words with /ů/ spelled *oo*
Demonstrate how to pronounce the sound /ů/ for children having difficulty. Point out how your lips move slightly outwards when you make the sound.

Name ______________________

Words with /ȯ/ spelled *aw, au, al*

- **Listen** for the sound of *aw* in *claw.*
- **Circle** the pictures of words that have this sound.

ROW 1

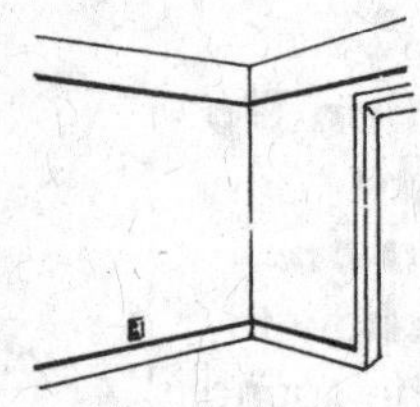

- **Look** at each picture. **Say** its name.
- **Circle** the word that names each picture.

ROW 2

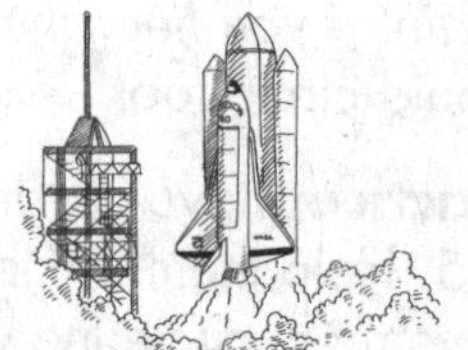

ball bell	pal paw	hawk hat	lunch launch

- **Look** at each picture. **Say** its name.
- **Write** the name of the picture.

ROW 3

Name ____________________

Words with /u̇/ spelled *oo*

- **Listen** for the sound of *oo* in *book.*
- **Circle** the pictures of words that have this sound.

ROW 1

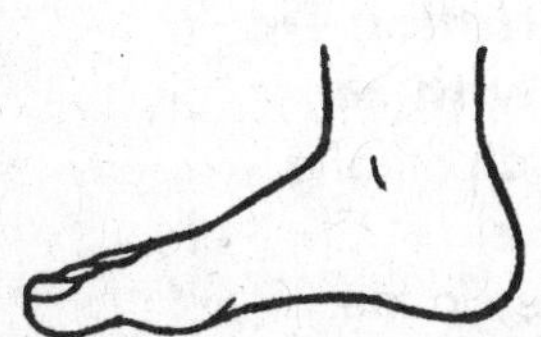

- **Look** at each picture. **Say** its name.
- **Circle** the word that names each picture.

ROW 2

cook
check

work
wood

lock
look

hook
hard

- **Look** at each picture. **Say** its name.
- **Write** the name of the picture.

ROW 3

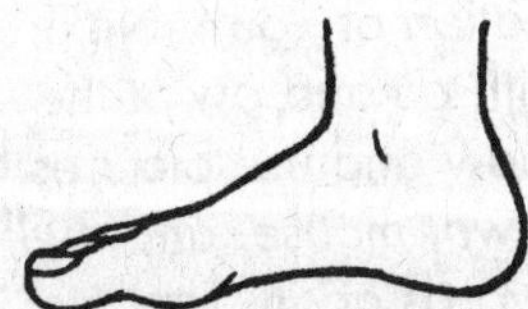

Transfer Skills

Explain to children who speak German or Spanish that the vowels *au* are similar in pronunciation to *ow* /ou/ in English. Use the examples *haus (house)* and *frau (wife)* in German, and *la jaula (birdcage)* and *la flauta (flute)* in Spanish.

Words with *ou, ow* — Use with page 268.

Preteach Copy and distribute page 268. Have children point to the picture of a crown at the top of the page. Say: *This is a crown, /k/ /r/ /ou/ /n/, crown. What vowel sound do you hear in the word* crown? *Say it with me: crown, /ou/, /ou/, crown. That's right, the sound is /ou/.* Now point to the *house*. Ask: *What vowel sound do you hear in the word* house? *Listen: /h/ /ou/ /s/. Yes, the sound is /ou/.*

Teach/Model Write the word *crown* on the board. Underline the *ow* in the word and tell children: *The sound /ou/ in* crown *is spelled* ow. *Say it with me: crown, /k/ /r/ /ou/ /n/.* Point to each spelling as you say its sounds. Then run your hand under *crown* as you blend the whole word: /k/ /r/ /ou/ /n/. Now write *house* on the board. Underline the *ou* in the word and say: *The sound /ou/ in* house *is spelled* ou. *Say it with me: house, /h/ /ou/ /s/.* Articulate the sounds in the word and blend the word with the class.

Help children name the items in Row 1 on page 268 *(couch, moon, owl, frown)*. Repeat each name, clearly pronouncing the vowel sound in each word. Say: *I am going to say these words again:* couch, moon, owl, frown. *If you hear the /ou/ sound, circle the picture.* Children should circle *couch, owl,* and *frown,* but not *moon.*

Practice Have children look at the pictures in Row 2 on page 268. Help them name each picture *(crown, couch, clown, mouse)*. Have them write the diphthongs to complete each name, choosing from the letters provided. Then have children look at the pictures in Row 3, say the name of each picture, and write the names *(cloud, cow, house, frown)*.

Assess Tell children: *I will say some word pairs. Raise your hand when you hear the /ou/ sound:* plow, blow; grow, how; owl, snow; goose, south. Then have children repeat the word pairs after you, striving for the correct pronunciation of /ou/. Next, make a two-column chart on the board with *ou* and *ow* at the top of the chart. Pronounce words they know and use pictures to reinforce meaning *(cloud, cow, house, frown, mouse, and owl)*. Have students tell you which column the words go in. Let them help you spell the words as you write them in the correct column.

Pronunciation Tip Words with *ou, ow* In a diphthong, each vowel contributes to the sound that is heard.

Transfer Skills

The pronunciation of the diphthong *oy* is very similar in Spanish and English. Point out the similarities in pronouncing the vowels in Spanish words such as *hoy, doy, soy* and English words such as *toy* and *boy*. Introduce *oi* words with the same pronunciation: *soil, noise, join.*

Words with *oi, oy*

Use with page 269.

Preteach Copy and distribute page 269. Have children point to the picture of a coin at the top of the page. Say: *This is a coin, /k/ /oi/ /n/, coin. What vowel sound do you hear in the word* coin? *Say it with me: coin, /oi/, /oi/, coin. That's right, the sound is /oi/.* Now point to the *toy*. Ask: *What vowel sound do you hear in the word toy? Listen: /t/ /oi/. Yes, the sound is /oi/.*

Teach/Model Write the word *coin* on the board. Underline the *oi* in the word and tell children: *The sound /oi/ in* coin *is spelled* oi. *Say it with me: coin, /k/ /oi/ /n/.* Point to each spelling as you say its sounds. Then run your hand under *coin* as you blend the whole word: k/ /oi/ /n/. Now write *toy* on the board. Underline the *oy* in the word and say: *The sound /oi/ in* toy *is spelled* oy. *Say it with me: toy, /t/ /oi/.* Articulate the sounds in the word and blend the word with the class.

Help children name the items in Row 1 on page 269 *(box, soil, boy, join)*. Repeat each name, clearly pronouncing the vowel sound in each word. Say: *I am going to say these words again. If you hear the /oi/ sound, circle the picture.* Children should circle *soil, boy,* and *join,* but not *box.*

Practice Have children look at the pictures in Row 2 on page 269. Help them name each picture *(joy, oil, point, toy)*. Have them write the diphthongs to complete each name, choosing from the letters provided. Then have children look at the pictures in Row 3, say the name of each picture, and write the names *(coin, boy)*.

Assess Tell children: *I will say some word pairs. Raise your hand when you hear the /oi/ sound:* soy, soon; enjoy, rock; choice, short; foil, coat; join, born. Then have children repeat the word pairs after you, striving for the correct pronunciation of /oi/.

Pronunciation Tip Words with *oi, oy* In a diphthong, each vowel contributes to the sound that is heard.

Name ________________________________

Words with *ou, ow*

- **Listen** for the sound of *ow* in *crown.*
- **Circle** the pictures of words that have this sound.

ROW 1

- **Look** at each picture. **Say** its name.
- **Circle** the correct letters.

ROW 2

cr____n	c____ch	cl____n	m____se
ou ow	ou ow	ou ow	ou ow

- **Look** at each picture. **Say** its name. **Write** the word.

ROW 3

Name ________________________________

Words with *oi, oy*

- **Listen** for the sound of *oy* in *toy.*
- **Circle** the pictures of words that have this sound.

ROW 1

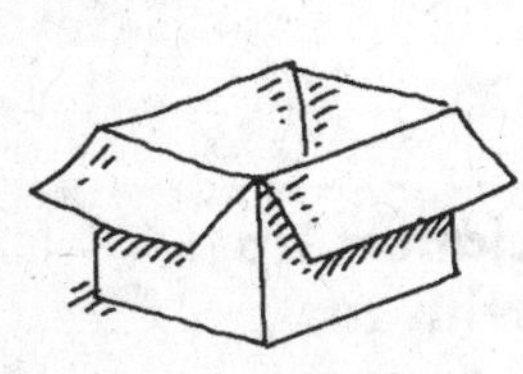

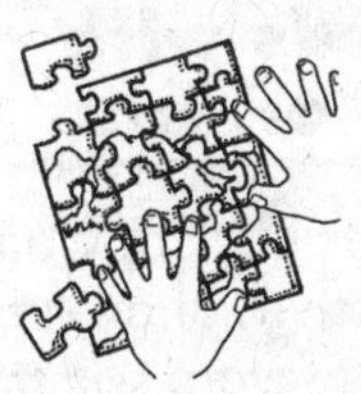

- **Look** at each picture. **Say** its name.
- **Circle** the correct letters.

ROW 2

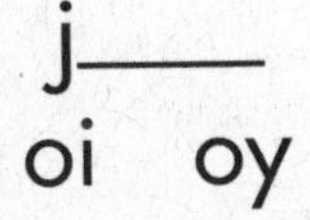

j____	____l	p____nt	t____
oi oy	oi oy	oi oy	oi oy

- **Look** at each picture. **Say** its name.
- **Write** the word.

ROW 3

____

____

r-Controlled Vowels

Transfer Skills

The /r/ sound is flapped or rolled in languages such as Spanish, Polish, Farsi, and Arabic, so speakers of these languages may have difficulty pronouncing words with *r*-controlled vowels, especially in words such as *part* and *turn,* when *r* is followed by a final consonant. The following lessons provide practice for hearing and pronouncing words with *r*-controlled vowels.

Words with *ar, are, air, or, ore*

Use with page 272.

Preteach Copy and distribute page 272. Have children point to the picture of an arm at the top of the page. Say: *This is an arm. Say the word with me:* arm. Arm *starts with the letter* a, *but the* a *doesn't make the sound /a/ or /ā/, does it?* Arm *has a different sound.* Repeat for the pictures of *fork* and *hair,* eliciting from the children that these words also have different sounds from the short or long vowel sounds.

Teach/Model Write the words *arm, fork,* and *hair* on the board. Challenge children to find the letter that all three words have. Underline the *r* in each word as they make the discovery. Say: A, o, *and* ai *sound different when the letter* r *comes right after them. We call these sounds* r-*controlled. Say the words with me and listen for how the vowels sound before* r: arm, fork, hair. Refer to the Pronunciation Tip to help children say the sounds correctly.

Then help children name the pictures in Rows 1 and 2 of page 272 (*car, barn, corn, store, horn, jar, yarn, score*). Lead them to conclude that every word has an *r* after the *a* or *o*. Then ask children to draw a line from each picture in Row 1 to the picture in Row 2 with a rhyming name. Have children say the rhyming pairs aloud when they have completed the matching (*car/jar, barn/yarn, corn/horn, store/score*).

Practice Have children look at the pictures in Row 3. Help them to name the pictures (*share, hair, square, chair*). Then ask them to circle the correct word below each picture. Finally, have them write the words. You might want to write the different spellings on the board, or point them out in the title of the worksheet.

Assess Slowly say a list of words. Have children raise their hands each time they hear an *r*-controlled vowel sound. Use these words: *star, stand, stop, snore, scarf, air, apple, aim, stair, stay, horse, hose.*

Pronunciation Tip
Words with *ar, are, air, or, ore*
When you say words like far, dare, *and* more, *you make the vowel sound first. Then you bring your lips together for the /r/ sound. Try it:* far, dare, more.

Spanish does not have a sound that is equivalent to /er/, so Spanish speakers may pronounce *heard* as *heerd* or *later* as *la-tair.* The following lessons provide practice for hearing and pronouncing words with *r*-controlled vowels.

Words with *er, ir, ur* and *eer, ear*

Use with page 273.

Preteach Copy and distribute page 273. Have children point to the picture of a fern at the top of the page. Say: *This kind of plant is called a* fern. *Say the word with me:* fern. *This word has an* e *in the middle, but it doesn't make the sound /e/ or /ē/, does it?* Fern *has a different sound, /er/. Say it with me: /er/, /er/,* fern. Repeat for *bird* and *ear*, eliciting from the children that these words also have different sounds from the short or long vowel sounds.

Teach/Model Tell children: *The /er/ sound is an* r-controlled *sound. Repeat these /er/ words after me:* fern, bird, word, hurt. Refer to the Pronunciation Tip to help children say the sounds correctly.

Help children name the pictures in Row 1 on page 273 *(purse, girl, stir, star)*. Repeat each name, clearly pronouncing the r-controlled vowel sound in each word. Then say: *I'll say these words again. If you hear the /er/ sound, circle the picture:* purse, girl, stir, star. Children should circle the *purse, girl,* and *stir* pictures—but not the *star.*

Point out that there are different ways of spelling /er/ words. Write a 3-column chart on the board with the headings *er, ir,* and *ur.* List *fern* and *bird* in the columns where they belong. Add the /er/ words from Row 1 to the chart. Invite children to suggest other /er/ words that can be added to the chart.

Tell children: *The sound of* ea *in* ear *is also an* r-controlled *sound. Repeat these words after me:* ear, near, cheer, steer. Point out that there are different ways of spelling words with this sound. Write the preceding words on the board to demonstrate.

Help children name the pictures in Row 2 on page 273 *(deer, shirt, hear, tear)*. Repeat each name, clearly pronouncing the *r*-controlled vowel sound in each word. Then say: *I'll say these words again. If you hear the sound of* ear, *circle the picture:* deer, shirt, hear, tear. Children should circle the *deer, hear* and *tear* pictures—but not the *shirt.*

Practice Have children look at the pictures in Row 3. Have them name the pictures. Then ask them to circle the correct word below each picture *(ear, deer, bird, fern)*. Have them write the words.

Assess Slowly say a list of words. Have children raise their hands each time they hear an *r*-controlled vowel sound. Use these words: *germ, gel, grab, swirl, switch, ride, hurt, fear, fry, first, spun, spear.*

Pronunciation Tip Words with /er/ and /ēr/ *When you say words like* sir *and* word, *you put your lips close together and hold them: /er/, /er/. When you say a word like* fear, *your lips start out in a line. Then you bring your lips together for the /r/ sound. Try it: /ēr/, /ēr/,* fear.

Name ______________________________

Words with *ar, are, air, or, ore*

- **Look** at each picture. **Say** its name.
- **Draw a line** between words that rhyme.

ROW 1

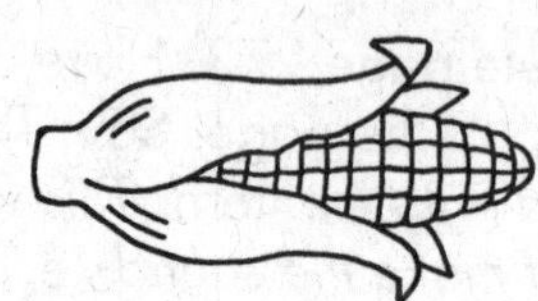

ROW 2

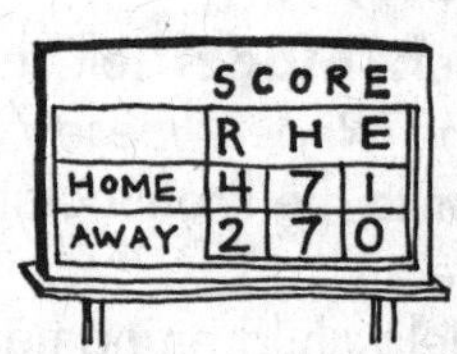

- **Look** at each picture. **Say** its name.
- **Circle** the correct word. **Write** the name of the picture.

ROW 3

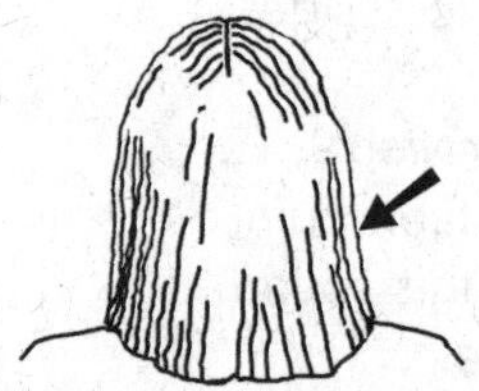

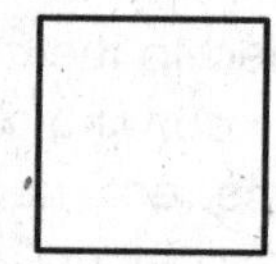

shape share	hair hail	squat square	chair chain
______	______	______	______

Name ______________________________

Words with *er, ir, ur* and *eer, ear*

- **Listen** for the sound of *er* in *fern*.
- **Circle** the pictures of words that have this sound.

ROW 1

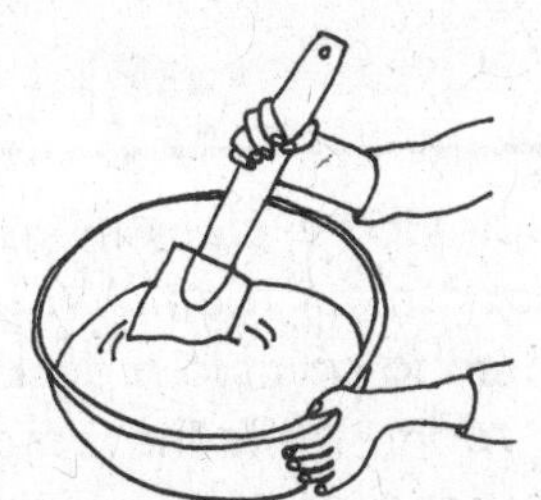

- **Listen** for the sound of *ear*.
- **Circle** the pictures of words that have this sound.

ROW 2

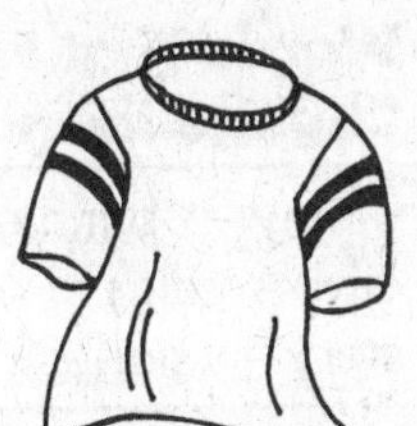

- **Look** at each picture. **Say** its name.
- **Circle** the correct word. **Write** the name of the picture.

ROW 3

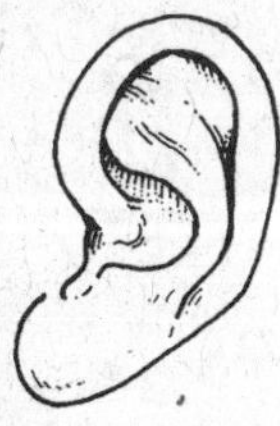
eat ear
____

deer deal
____

bird bat
____

fun fern
____

Inflected endings may be challenging for English learners. For example, in Chinese, Hmong, and Korean, nouns do not have a plural form. Children may need practice adding *-s* and *-es* to show plural nouns. In languages such as Polish and Spanish, adjectives, as well as verbs and nouns, have inflected endings. The following lessons provide practice with the inflected endings of nouns and verbs in English.

Plurals *-s, -es* — Use with page 278.

Preteach Ask children to point to the clock in your room. Say: *Good! We only have one clock in our room.* Write the word *clock* on the board. Then ask children to point to a desk. Say: *Yes! There are many desks in our room.* Write the word *desks* on the board. Then review the two words, pointing at them and saying: *Clock, desks. We have one clock. We have many desks. What is at the end of this word* (point to *desks) that tells you it means more than one? Yes, it is the letter* s. (Underline the *s.)*

Teach/Model Present the different ways to form plurals. Create a simple chart on the board with these headings and examples.

Most Words: Add *-s*	Words That End in *s, sh, ch, x,* or *z:* Add *-es*	Words That End in *y:* Change the *y* to *i;* Add *-es*
book → book<u>s</u> pencil → pencil<u>s</u> marker → marker<u>s</u>	fox → fox<u>es</u> class → class<u>es</u> wish → wish<u>es</u>	bunny → bunn<u>ies</u> city → cit<u>ies</u> story → stor<u>ies</u>

Point to the chart and talk about each column. Say: *Most of the time, we just add an* s, *like* book/books. *Sometimes, though, we have to look for certain letters at the end of a word. Say the letters with me.* (Point to *s, sh, ch, x,* and *z* in the heading of the second column.) *When we see these letters, we add* -es. *This word,* fox, *ends with* x. *So, we add* -es. *We also have to look for a* y *at the end of a word. When we see that, we make a change. We change the* y *to an* i, *then add* -es. *See,* bunny *becomes* bunnies.

Practice Copy and distribute page 278. Model how the first three items were completed, using a think-aloud strategy, such as: *Find number 1. The word is* dress. *How do I write the word that names more than one dress? First, I look at the ending.* Dress *ends in* s. *That's why the check mark is there. What do I do when a word ends in* s*? Yes, I add* -es. *That's why that check mark is there. Now I can write the word.* Have children complete the page by following the steps to figure out each plural form. (See answers on page 308.)

Assess Write these words on self-stick notes: *fox, puppy, brush, cap, sky, pin, bunch, girl.* Have each child place the words in the correct column of the chart on the board. Challenge them to then write or spell aloud the plural forms.

Possessives

Use with page 279.

Preteach Call one boy and one girl to stand next to you. Hand the boy a pen. Say: *This is the boy's pen.* Write *boy's* on the board. Hand the girl a pen, saying: *This is the girl's pen.* Write *girl's* on the board. Then divide the class into boys and girls, and have them stand on different sides of the room. Motion to the boys' side of the room and say: *This is the boys' side of the room.* Motion to the girls' side and say: *This is the girls' side of the room.* Write *boys'* and *girls'* on the board, under *boy's* and *girl's.* Circle all of the apostrophes in the words and say: *Today we will learn what these mean.* Invite the children to return to their seats.

Teach/Model You will be teaching children about singular and plural possessives. Use a simple T-chart on the board:

One Has or Owns It: 's	More Than One Has or Owns It: s'
boy's girl's	boys' girls'

Refer to the apostrophes you have circled in the words on the board. Say: *These are called apostrophes. They can tell you that someone has or owns something. When I gave the pen to [boy student's name], it was his pen. It was the boy's pen. He is only one boy, so I added 's to the word* boy. (Point to the word *boy's.*) *Boys, when you were standing over there, that part of the room was yours. It was the boys' side. You are many boys, so I just added an apostrophe to the word* boys. (Point to the word *boys'.*) Show the children the chart, and write the words in the correct columns. Repeat for *girls'/girl's.* Ask children to suggest additional examples.

Practice Copy and distribute page 279. Have children cut apart the word strips at the bottom of the page. Tell them that each strip matches one of the pictures. Children should match the possessive forms to pictures showing one or more than one animal, then paste or tape the strips in place. (See answers on page 308.)

Assess Make an extra copy of page 279 and cut out the pictures. Make word cards: *'s, s', cat, goat, dog.* Show the children a picture and have them select the two word cards that form the proper possessive.

Verb Endings
-s, -ed, -ing

Use with page 280.

Preteach Write the word *ask* on the board. Say: *I like it when you ask me questions. It means you want to learn. Remember yesterday when [name of student] asked me about [topic]?* Write the word *asked* above *ask* on the board. Say: *This class asks lots of good questions.* Write *asks* beside *ask. I'm surprised that you are not asking me about why I'm writing these words on the board.* Write *asking* beside *asks.*

Teach/Model Draw a simple table around the words you have written on the board, adding headings as shown below.

PAST	asked		
NOW	ask	asks	is/are asking

Point to *ask* and say: *We change this word by adding endings to it.* Underline the *-ed* in *asked. This ending says the action already happened.* Underline the *-s* in *asks. This ending says someone is doing the action now.* Underline the *-ing* in *asking. We use this ending with the word* is *or* are. *Let's add another word to the chart:* jump. Work with children to fill in the verb forms for *jump.* Ask children to suggest additional examples.

Practice Copy and distribute page 280. Read the words *Yesterday* and *Today* and talk about how the first item was completed. Help children identify the pictures and read the words, then have children finish the page on their own. (See answers on page 308.)

Assess Erase the words in the table on the board. Then write a base word and ask children to write in the other verb forms. Use any of these verbs: *call, rest, walk, lock, spell.*

More Verb Endings
-s, -ed, -ing

Use with page 281.

Preteach Write *I smile.* on the board. Read the sentence and smile. Find a child who is smiling back at you. Say and write *[Name of student] smiles.* Below that, write *We are smiling.* Read this sentence and then end by saying and writing, *We smiled.* Underline the *-s, -ing,* and *-ed* in the words. Remind children that they know these word endings. Today they will learn about using these endings when they need to make spelling changes.

Teach/Model You will teach the children about dropping the final *e* and doubling consonants before adding inflected endings. Create the chart below for display. Leave space for the example words (*smile* and *shop*), which you will fill in as you teach.

	Add *-s*	**Add *-ed***	**Add *-ing***
Word ends with *e* smile	✓ smiles	Drop the *e.* smiled	Drop the *e.* smiling
Short vowel, ends with consonant shop	✓ shops	Double the consonant. shopped	Double the consonant. shopping

Refer back to the sentences you wrote on the board. Circle the *e* in *smile.* Say: *This word ends in* e. *The* e *is dropped when you add* -ed *or* -ing. Write *smile* in all four places on the chart. Then talk about adding the endings. *I want to add* -s. *The check mark means I can just add it without changing anything. I want to add* -ed. *The rule is to drop the* e. Erase the *e* in *smile,* then add the ending. Repeat to record *smiling* on the chart. Follow the same teaching pattern for the word *shop.*

Practice Copy and distribute page 281. Read the words *Yesterday* and *Today* and talk about how the first item was completed. Help children identify the pictures and read the words. Leave the chart on display as children write the correct verb forms to complete the page. (See answers on page 308.)

Assess Erase the example words in the chart you used for teaching. Then write a base word and ask children to write in the other verb forms. Use any of these verbs: *sip, wag, hum, shine, name, use.*

Name ______________________________

Plurals *-s, -es*

STEP 1 **Look** at the word for one.	**STEP 2** **Look** at how the word ends.						**STEP 3** **Think** about what to add.			**STEP 4** **Write** the word for more than one.
	-s	-sh	-ch	-x	-z	-y	-s	-es	y to i, then -es	
dress	✓							✓		**dresses**
slide							✓			**slides**
baby						✓			✓	**babies**
box										______
fly										______
can										______

Name ______________________________

Possessives

- **Cut out** the words.
- **Match** the words and pictures.

dog's bone	**dogs' porch**	**goats' hill**
goat's can	**cat's toy**	**cats' plate**

Name ______________________________

Verb Endings *-s, -ed, -ing*

- **Look** at the pictures.
- **Read** the words.
- **Add** the correct endings. **Write** the new words.

	Yesterday	Today
play	He played.	Dan plays. He is playing.
help	She ______.	Sue ______. She is ______.
paint	He ______.	Brad ______. He is ______.
talk	They ______.	Maria ______. Sam ______. They are ______.

Name ______________________________

More Verb Endings *-s, -ed, -ing*

- **Look** at the pictures.
- **Read** the words.
- **Add** the correct endings. **Write** the new words.

	Yesterday	Today
nap	She napped.	Fran naps. She is napping.
grin	He ____________.	Chad ____________. He is ____________.
mope	They ____________.	Jack ____________. Ann ____________. They are ____________.
race	They ____________.	Barb ____________. Tia ____________. They are ____________.

Compound Words, Contractions, and Cognates

Transfer Skills

Compound words exist in many languages, including Spanish, Vietnamese, Haitian Creole, German, and Russian. Children may readily understand the concept of compound words but may need additional help with decoding to break English compound words into their parts. Some languages, such as the Romance languages, include **contractions**, but English language learners may need help recognizing them in English and using apostrophes correctly. **Cognates** are words that share origins and appear in similar forms in different languages. For example, the English word *lion* has Greek and Latin origins and has similar forms in other languages: *leon* (Spanish), *lion* (French), and *lew* (Polish). For speakers of languages that share word origins with English, the study of cognates can be a powerful vocabulary-building tool. The following lessons provide practice with compound words, contractions, and cognates.

Compound Words

Use with page 285.

Preteach Write the word *sun* on the board, and draw a picture of the Sun above it. Say: *The word* sun *is found in many longer words, like* sunshine. Write *shine* after *sun*. Then write *sun* again, and elicit from children other compound words that start with *sun* (examples: *sunrise, sunset, sunlight, sunburn, sundown, sunblock).* Write each word on the board. Underline *sun* in each one and read the words together.

Teach/Model Tell children that you have been writing compound words. Write information about compound words as simple equations:

Compound Word = 2 words

Compound Word = 1 small word + 1 small word

backpack = back + pack

Below the right side of the last equation, write the words of several common compounds and ask children to blend the words, saying a compound word for you to write. Some words you might use are: *sand + box, snow + ball, rain + drop.*

Some Spanish examples are *abre + latas = abrelatas; rasca + cielos = rascacielos; para + sol = parasol.*

Practice Copy and distribute page 285. Do the first example together, and then help children complete Row 1. For Row 2, help children read the words in the lists. Then tell them to choose a word from each list to write a compound word to name each picture *(bathtub, necktie, bedroom, teapot).* Help children name the pictures if necessary. (See answers on page 309.)

Assess Make two sets of word cards. Set 1: *cup, flash, team, out.* Set 2: *cake, light, work, side.* Keep them separate. Give each child the sets and ask him or her to form four compound words. *(cupcake, flashlight, teamwork, outside).*

Contractions *n't, 'll, 'm, 's* Use with page 286.

Preteach Say: *I'm so happy to be at school today! Aren't you? It's a great day. We'll have fun today!* Write *I'm, aren't, it's,* and *we'll* on the board. Say: *Some of the words I just used are called* contractions. *A contraction is one word that is made from two words put together and made shorter, such as when I say* I'm *instead of* I am.

Teach/Model Display this chart, which shows how a contraction is formed. Talk through each row so children can actually see how four common contractions are made.

Start with two words.	Drop one or more letters.	Add ' and close up the word.
it is	it ~~i~~s	it's
you will	you ~~wi~~ll	you'll
I am	I ~~a~~m	I'm
has not	has n~~o~~t	hasn't

Add a fifth row to the chart, working with the children to form *can't* from *can not.*

Spanish examples are: *a el al* and *de el del.* No apostrophes are used.

Practice Copy and distribute page 286. Have children draw lines to connect each contraction to the words from which it is formed. The first example has been done for them. Point out that the words in the third column will have more than one line drawn to them. At the bottom of the page, children will practice writing contractions. (See answers on page 309.)

Assess Make an extra copy of page 286. Cut off the left column, where the contractions are listed. Use this list. Point to a contraction, and have children say the two words from which it is formed.

Cognates

Use with page 287.

Preteach Ask children if anyone knows how to say the word for *animal* in another language. Write down the languages and the words they say on a chart like the one below. Point out that some of the words are a lot like *animal* in English. Tell children that when words look or sound similar and have a similar meaning in different languages, they are called *cognates.* Invite children to suggest other cognates they know in English and other languages, and, if possible, make lists of the words.

English	Spanish	Tagalog	Italian
animal	animal	hayop	animale

Use this lesson with fluent speakers of languages that have many cognates of English words, such as Spanish, Portuguese, French, and, to a lesser extent, Haitian Creole, Polish, Russian, and Tagalog (Filipino).

Teach/Model Tell children that they can look for cognates when they read. Cognates can help them understand more words in English. Explain that when they see an English word they don't know, children should think about whether the word looks or sounds like a word in their home language. If it does, they can use clues in the other words and in the pictures to decide if it has the same meaning as the home-language word.

Point out that sometimes words in different languages are "false friends"—they look almost the same, but they don't mean the same thing. For example, the English word *trap* looks like the Spanish word *trapo,* but *trap* is really *trampa* in Spanish, and *trapo* is the Spanish word for *rag.* Ask children if they know other examples of "false friends."

Practice Copy and distribute page 287. Ask children to look at the pictures and translate the English words into a language they know. Children can say or write the words. Then have them decide whether the word pairs are cognates. Tell them: *To find out if an English word is a cognate of a word you know in another language, ask yourself:* Does this word look like a word in my language? Does it seem to have the same meaning as that word in my language? *If you can say yes to both questions, the words are cognates.*

Assess Have children say or write five examples of cognate pairs in English and their home language, and one example of "false friends."

Name ______________________________

Compound Words

- **Read** the compound word.
- **Find** the two small words. **Draw a line** between them.

ROW 1

inside bedtime homework anyway

- **Look** at each picture.
- **Write** the compound word. Use a word from List A and a word from List B.

ROW 2

______________________________ ______________________________

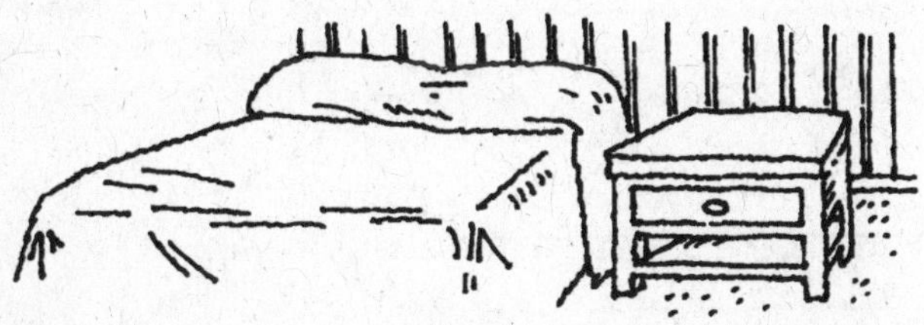

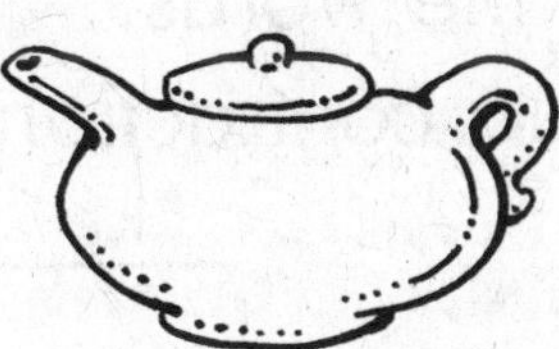

______________________________ ______________________________

List A	List B
neck	tub
bed	tie
bath	pot
tea	room

Name ____________________

Contractions *n't, 'll, 'm, 's*

- **Read** the contraction.
- **Draw a line** from it to the correct words.

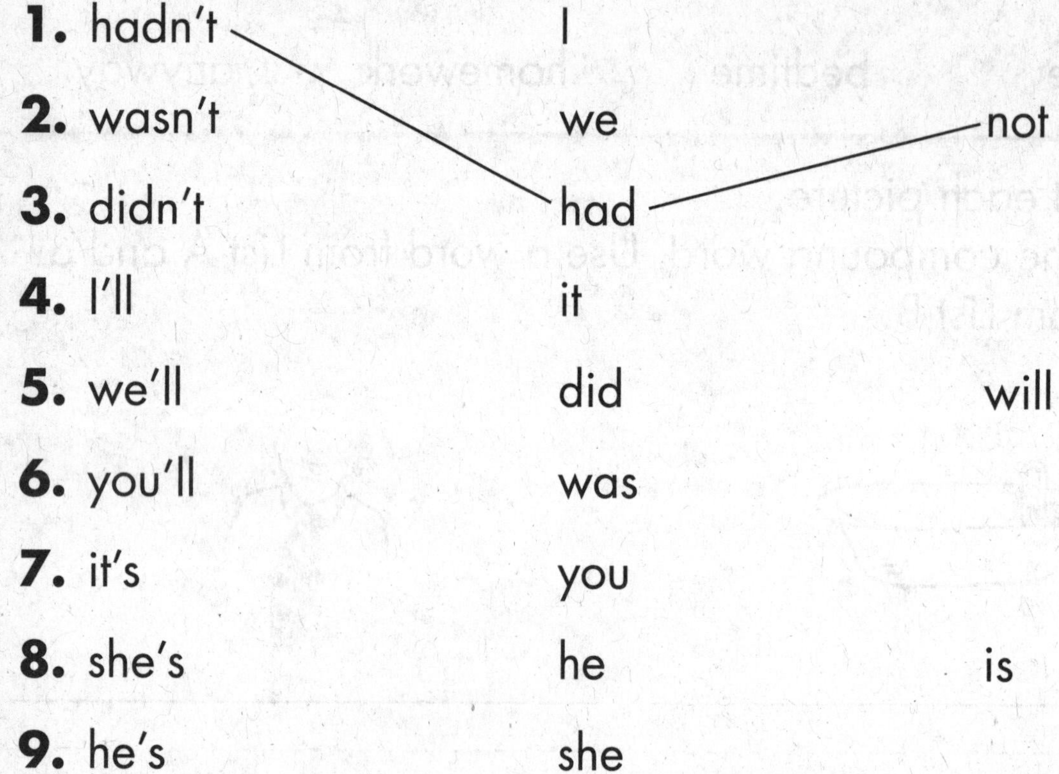

1. hadn't	I	
2. wasn't	we	not
3. didn't	had	
4. I'll	it	
5. we'll	did	will
6. you'll	was	
7. it's	you	
8. she's	he	is
9. he's	she	

- **Read** the words.
- **Write** a contraction.

10. I am ____________________

11. they will ____________________

12. is not ____________________

Name ______________________________

Cognates

- **Say** or **write** these English words in another language.
- Then tell if the two words are cognates.

English	______________ (name of language)	Are they cognates? (yes/no)
calendar		
doctor		
palace		
sandal		
train		

Prefixes and Suffixes

Transfer Skills

Some English prefixes and suffixes have equivalent forms in the Romance languages. For example, the prefix *im-* in English (*impossible*) corresponds to the French *im-* (*impossible*) and the Spanish *im-* (*imposible*). Students who are literate in these languages may be able to transfer their understanding of prefixes and suffixes by using parallel examples in the home language and in English. Some suggestions ore provided below for Spanish. The following lessons provide additional practice with prefixes and suffixes.

Prefixes *un-* and *re-*

Use with page 295.

Introduce Take a ribbon, string, or piece of yarn, and tie a bow. Say: *I tie a bow.* Then untie it, saying, *I untie the bow.* Tie the bow again and say: *Now I retie the bow.* Write *tie, untie,* and *retie* on the board. Underline *un-* and *re-*. Repeat the tying demonstration, and elicit from the students what *untie* and *retie* mean.

Teach Present the prefixes *un-* and *re-*. Explain how they change the meaning of a word, using the chart below.

Prefix	+ Base Word	= New Word
un- (not)	fold lock wind	unfold unlock unwind
re- (again)	fold read play	refold reread replay

Explain that *un-* also can be used in words that describe feelings or ways of being. Give the examples of *unhappy, unkind,* and *unsafe*. Spanish examples include *infeliz, incompleto, recontar,* and *rehacer.*

Practice Copy and distribute page 295. The children will choose a prefix to add to the base word, and write the new word that makes sense in the blank. If necessary, read aloud the verbs and sentences, or ask for volunteers to read them. (See answers on page 309.)

Assess Create word cards with these prefixes and base words: *un-, re-, like, heat, play, use, lucky.* Have children use the cards in different combinations to make words that have prefixes. Then have children show you a base word without a prefix, add a prefix, say the new word, and tell you what it means.

Prefixes *pre-* and *dis-*   Use with page 296.

Preteach Hold up a storybook and ask children: *What do we usually do before we read a new book? Yes, we talk about the title and the cover. We look at the pictures. We think about what the story might be like. This is called* prereading. *We do these things before we read.* Write *preread* on the board and underline *pre-*. Say: *The prefix* pre- *means "before." So, we preread before we read.*

Teach/Model Present this chart to review *pre-* and to introduce *dis-*.

Prefix	+ Base Word	= New Word
pre- (before)	read made	preread premade
dis- (not)	like agree	dislike disagree

Point out that if children know what the base word means, they should be able to figure out what the new word means. Spanish examples include *predecir, desorden,* and *desacuerdo.*

Practice Copy and distribute page 296. At the top of the page, children circle the correct meaning for a word with a prefix that is supported by an illustration. Then they write words with prefixes to match meanings and pictures. (See answers on page 309.)

Assess Create word cards with these prefixes and base words: *pre-, dis-, cook, made, like, trust.* Have children use the cards in different combinations to make words that have prefixes. Then have children show you a base word without a prefix, add a prefix, say the new word, and tell you what it means.

Transfer Skills

Point out to Spanish speakers that the prefix *mid-* is related to the Spanish word *medio*, which means *half* or *middle*. Use cognates such as *midnight/medianoche* and *midday/mediodifa* as examples.

Prefixes *mis-*, *mid-*, and *non*

Use with page 297.

Preteach Write the word *dog* on the board, but misspell it so that it reads *dag*. Point to the word and say: *Did I spell this word correctly? No, I did not spell the word correctly. I misspelled the* word. *What do you think the word* misspelled *means?* Repeat the misspelling demonstration until you are sure that children understand that *misspell* means to spell something wrong. Conduct further demonstrations with the words *midair* (throw an eraser or pen in the air) and *nonstop* (say: *without stopping*).

Teach/Model Present the prefixes *mis-*, *mid-*, and *non-*. Using the chart below, explain how they change the meaning of a word.

Prefix	+ Base Word	= New Word
mis- (not or wrong)	place	misplace
mid- (in the middle of)	day	midday
non- (not or without)	stick	nonstick

Practice Copy and distribute page 297. The children will choose a prefix to add to the base word and write the new word that makes sense in the blank. If necessary, read aloud the words and sentences. (See answers on page 309.)

Assess Create word cards with these prefixes and base words: *mis-, mid-, non-, stop, spell, point, day, fiction, place.* Have children use the cards in different combinations to make words that have prefixes. As an additional challenge, have children show you a base word without a prefix, add a prefix, say the new word, and tell you what it means.

Suffixes *-ly* and *-ful* — Use with page 298.

Preteach Write *cheerful* on the board. Say the word and ask if anyone feels cheerful today. Underline *-ful* and explain that it means "full of." Say: *So, if I feel full of hope, what word could I use to say how I feel?* Write *hopeful* on the board, underlining *-ful*. Explain that *-ful* is a suffix. A suffix is added to the end of a word to change the meaning.

Teach/Model Present this chart to review *-ful* and to introduce *-ly*.

Suffix	What It Means	Examples	Spanish
-ful	full of; tell what something is like	joyful, careful	-oso cuidadoso
-ly	tell how something is done	softly, neatly	-mente suavemente

Practice Copy and distribute page 298. Read the directions to the children, and model completing the first item. Use a think-aloud strategy, such as: *Find number 1. The picture shows a boy running. Let's read the first sentence beside the picture: "He is quick." The word* quick *is in dark type. That's the word we need to change by adding a suffix. Let's read the second sentence: "He runs ..." How can we change* quick *so that it will fit in the sentence? That's right; we need to add* -ly. *Write* quickly *in the blank.* Have children complete the page. If necessary, read aloud the sentences, or ask for volunteers to do so. (See answers on page 309.)

Assess Prepare word cards. On one side, write a base word. On the other side, write a phrase that will tell children which suffix to add. Have children read the two sides, then tell you the new word. Ideas for cards:

safe/tell how it is done (safely) peace/tell what it is like (peaceful)

kind/tell how it is done (kindly) play/tell what it is like (playful)

Suffixes *-less* and *-ness* Use with page 299.

Preteach Show children the trashcan. Say: *Everything in here is useless to me. I do not use it.* Write *useless* on the board and underline *-less*. Say: *This suffix changes the base word to mean "it does not have." So* useless *means "it does not have a use."*

Teach/Model Present this chart to review *-less* and to introduce *-ness*.

Suffix	What It Means	Examples
-less	does not have	fearless (does not have fear)
-ness	has	goodness (has good)

Practice Copy and distribute page 299. Read the directions to the children, and model completing the first item. Use a think-aloud strategy, such as: *Find number 1. The picture shows a woman awake in bed. Let's read the first sentence beside the picture: "She did not sleep last night." The word* sleep *is in dark type. That's the word we need to change by adding a suffix. Let's read the second sentence: "She was ..." How can we change* sleep *so that it will fit in the sentence? That's right; we need to add -less. Write* sleepless *in the blank.* Have children complete the page. If necessary, read aloud the sentences, or ask for volunteers to do so. (See answers on page 309.)

Assess Create word strips with meanings of words that have suffixes. Have children read the strips, or read the strips aloud. If you read the strips aloud, show the phrases so students can see the underlined target base words. Then have children say the word that is described. Suggested strips:

does not have <u>fear</u> (fearless)

has only <u>dark</u> (darkness)

does not make <u>sense</u> (senseless)

has <u>swift</u> speed (swiftness)

Suffixes *-able, -ible* **Use with page 300.**

Preteach Write *likeable* on the board. Say the word and ask children if they think puppies are likeable. Underline *-able* and explain it means "able to." Say: *So, if we are able to read something, what word could we use to describe it?* Write *readable* on the board, underlining *-able*. Explain that *-able* is a suffix. Remind children that a suffix is added to the end of a word to change the meaning.

Teach/Model Present this chart to review *-able* and to introduce *-ible*.

Suffix	What It Means	Examples
-able	"able to" or "can be"	enjoyable, useable, readable
-ible	has the quality of	collectible, reversible

Practice Copy and distribute page 300. Read the directions to the children, and model completing the first item. Use a think-aloud strategy, such as: *Find number 1. The picture shows two friends playing together. Let's read the first sentence beside the picture: "I like her." The word* like *is in dark type. That's the word we need to change by adding a suffix to the end. Let's read the second sentence: "She is. . ." How can we change* like *so that it will fit in the sentence? That's right, we need to add* -able. *Write* likeable *in the blank.* Have children complete the page, guiding practice as needed. If necessary, read aloud the sentences, or ask individuals to do so. (See answers on page 309.)

Assess Make word cards. On one side, write a base word. On the other side, write a phrase that will tell children which suffix to add. Have children read the two sides and then tell you the new word. Make sentences together using the words to check understanding or have children pantomime a word and have the others guess the *-able/-ible* word. Ideas for cards: *use/able to (useable); read/able to (readable); reverse/has the quality of (reversible); collect/has the quality of (collectible).*

Suffixes *-er, -or*

Use with page 301.

Preteach Write *ballplayer* on the board. Say the word and ask children if any of them play ball. Underline *-er* and explain that it means "a person or thing that ______." Then say: *If a man acts in a movie, what is he? Yes, an actor.* Write *actor* on the board, underlining *-or*. Tell children that *-or* also means "a person or thing that ______." Explain that *-er* and *-or* are *suffixes*. Remind children that a suffix is added to the end of a word to change the meaning.

Teach/Model Present this chart to review *-er* and *-or*.

Suffix	What it Means	Examples
-er, -or	a person or thing that ______	teacher, opener, sailor, collector

Practice Copy and distribute page 301. Read the directions to the children, and model completing the first item. Use a think-aloud strategy, such as: *Find number 1. The picture shows a person farming. Let's read the first sentence beside the picture: "This man grows food on his farm." The word* farm *is in dark type. That's the word we need to change by adding a suffix. Let's read the second sentence: "He is a. . ." How can we change* farm *so that it will fit in the sentence? That's right, we need to add* -er. *Write* farmer *in the blank.* Have children complete the page, guiding them as needed. If necessary, read the sentences aloud. (See answers on page 309.)

Assess Create word strips with meanings of words that have suffixes. Have children read the strips silently or read the strips aloud to children. If you read the strips aloud, show the phrases so children can see the underlined target base words. Then have children say the word that is described. Ideas for strips: *a person who <u>teaches</u> (teacher); a person who <u>paints</u> (painter); something that <u>opens</u> things (opener); a person who <u>sails</u> (sailor); something that <u>beeps</u> (beeper).*

Name ______________________________

Prefixes *un-* and *re-*

- **Look** at the pictures. **Read** the sentences.
- **Circle** a prefix. **Write** the new word.

re / un heat

____

We ______________ the bread.

re / un lock

____

We ______________ the door.

re / un cap

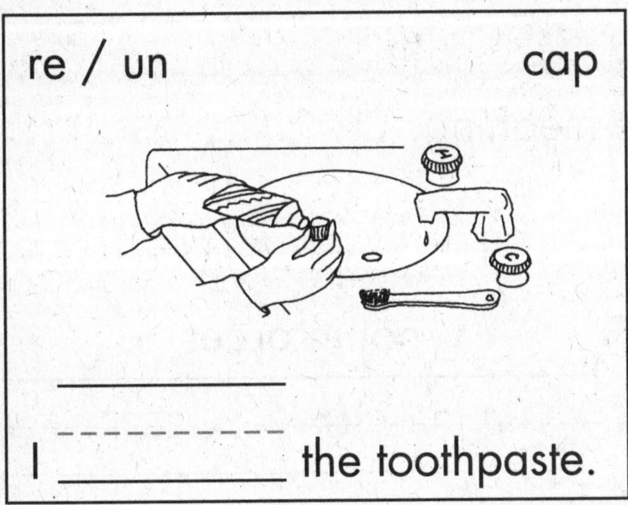

____

I ______________ the toothpaste.

re / un use

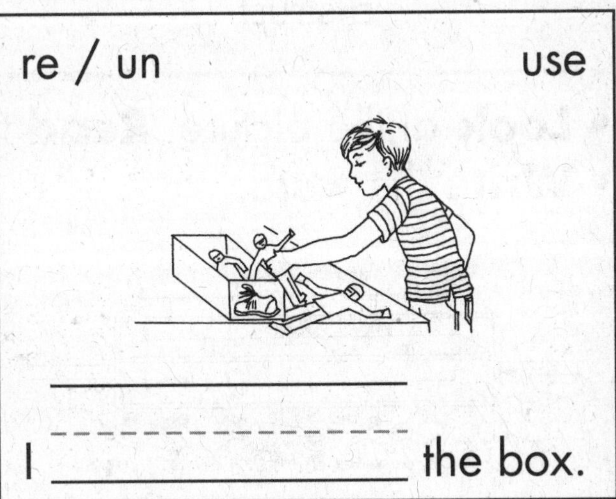

____

I ______________ the box.

re / un zip

____

I ______________ my jacket.

re / un read

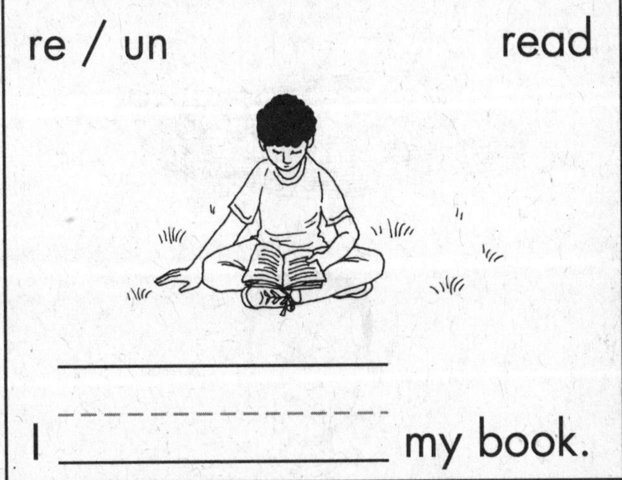

____

I ______________ my book.

Name ______________________________

Prefixes *pre-* and *dis-*

- **Look** at the picture. **Read** the word.
- **Circle** the correct meaning.

preheat

heat before
heat again
do not heat

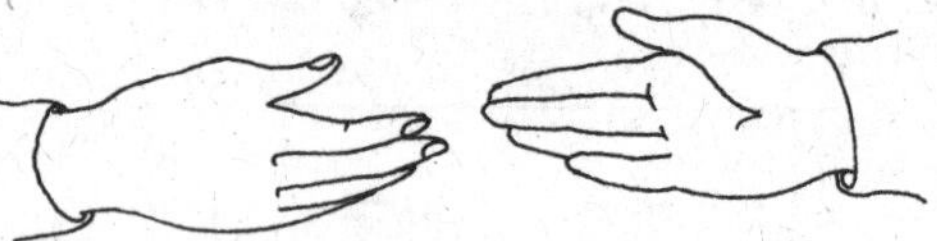

distrust

trust before
trust again
do not trust

- **Look** at the picture. **Read** the meaning.
- **Write** the word.

not in order

____

pay before

____

do not like

____

Name ______________________________

Prefixes *mis-*, *mid-*, and *non-*

- **Look** at the pictures. **Read** the sentences.
- **Circle** a prefix. **Write** the new word.

mis / mid / non fiction

She looks at the ____________________ book.

mis / mid / non read

She doesn't want to ____________________ any words.

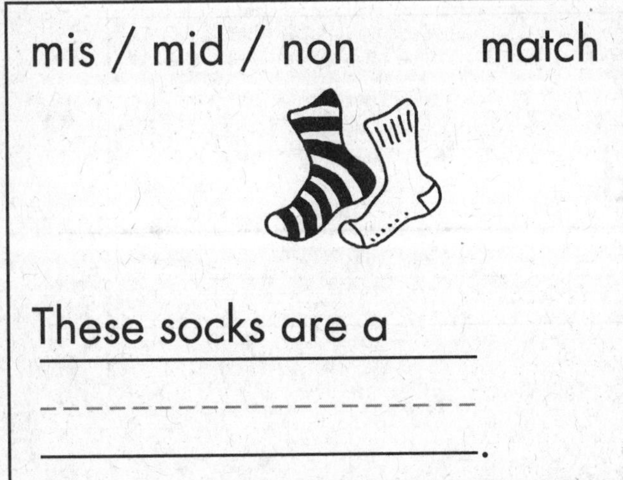

mis / mid / non match

These socks are a ____________________.

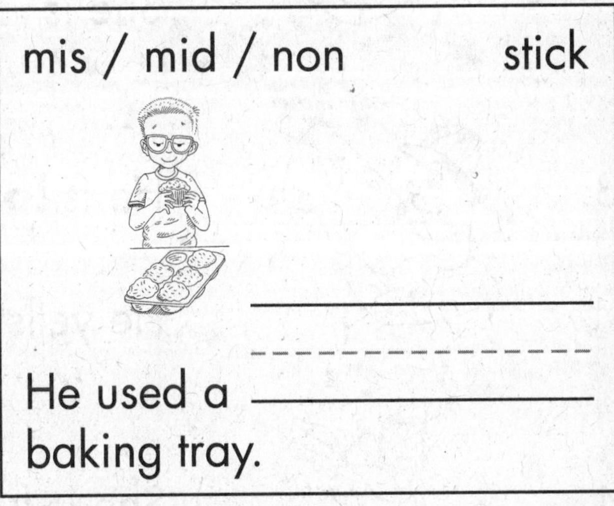

mis / mid / non stick

He used a ____________________ baking tray.

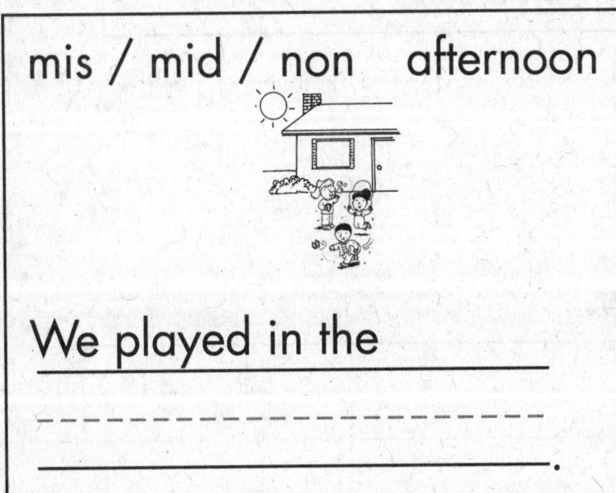

mis / mid / non afternoon

We played in the ____________________.

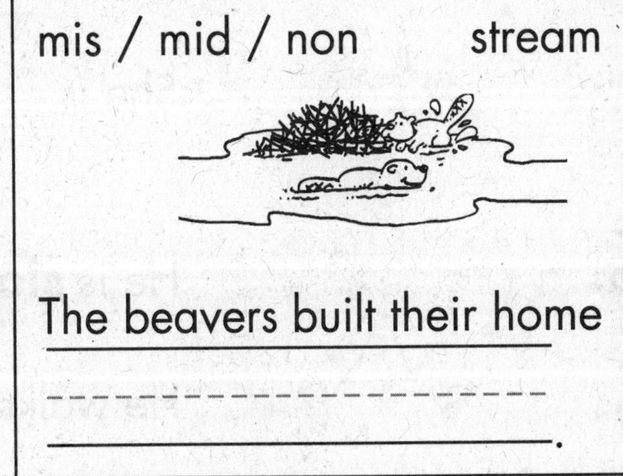

mis / mid / non stream

The beavers built their home ____________________.

Name ______________________________

Suffixes *-ly* and *-ful*

- **Read** the sentences. **Look** at the dark word.
- **Add** *-ly* or *-ful* to make a new word. **Write** the word.

1. 

He is **quick.**

He runs ______________________.

2. 

She is full of **cheer.**

She is ______________________.

3. 

He is **loud.**

He yells ______________________.

4. 

She is full of **grace.**

She is ______________________.

5. 

He is **slow.**

He walks ______________________.

Name ______________________

Suffixes *-less* and *-ness*

- **Read** the sentence. **Look** at the dark word.
- **Add** *-less* or *-ness* to make a new word. **Write** the word.

1. 
She did not **sleep** last night.
She was ______________.

2. 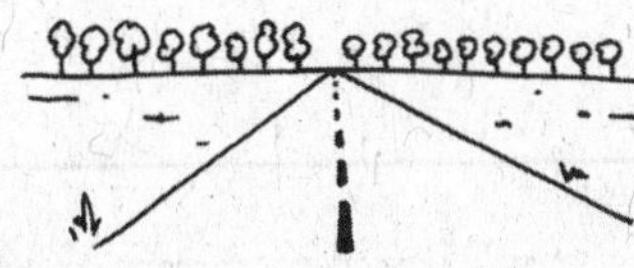
The road has no **end.**
It is ______________.

3. 
The fig is very **sweet.**
It has ______________.

4. 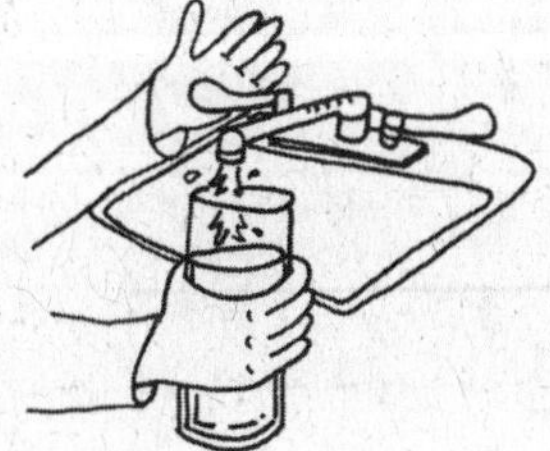
Water has no **taste.**
It is ______________.

5. 
I do not see a **cloud.**
The sky is ______________.

6. 
The man seems very **sad.**
His face shows ______________.

Name ______________________________

Suffixes *-able* and *-ible*

- **Read** the sentence. **Look** at the dark word.
- **Add** *-able* or *-ible* to make a new word. **Write** the word.

1. I **like** her.

She is ______________________.

2. 

I **collect** stamps.

They are ______________________.

3. 

I **adore** my cute puppy.

My puppy is ______________________.

4. 

He can **fix** the flat tire.

It is ______________________.

5. 

We can **do** this math.

It is ______________________.

Name ______________________________

Suffixes *-er* and *-or*

- **Read** the sentence. **Look** at the dark word.
- **Add** *-er* or *-or* to make a new word. **Write** the word.

1. 

This man grows food on his **farm.**

He is a ______________________.

2. 

These people **act** on a stage.

This man is an ______________________.

3. 

The man **bakes** food at his store.

He is a ______________________.

4. 

She works at a **bank.**

She is a ______________________.

5. 

The girl likes to **paint** pictures.

She is a ______________________.

6. 

I **sail** the boat on the ocean.

I am a ______________________.

Speakers of monosyllabic languages such as Cantonese, Hmong, Khmer, Korean, and Vietnamese may pronounce a two-syllable word as two separate words. Have children practice saying multisyllabic words.

Syllables VC/CV, VC/V, V/CV

Use with page 304.

Preteach Copy and distribute page 304. Point to the picture of a *basket* at the top of the page. Ask: *What is this? Yes, this is a basket.* Ask: *How many vowel sounds do you hear in the word* basket? *Say and clap it with me:* bas, ket, basket. *That's right, there are two vowel sounds /a/ and /i/.* Now point to the *tulip.* Ask: *How many vowel sounds do you hear in the word* tulip? *Let's clap together. Listen:* tu lip, tulip. *Yes, there are two vowel sounds, so there are two syllables.* Repeat this drill with the word *cabin.*

Teach/Model Write the word *basket* on the board. Draw a line between the two syllables and tell children: *When a word has more than one vowel sound, divide it into parts.* Explain that when there are two consonants between two vowels, you divide the word between the consonants. Now write *tulip* on the board. Draw a line between the *u* and the *l.* Say: *This word has one consonant between two vowels. In the word* tulip, *the consonant goes with the second vowel, making the first vowel long. Say it with me: tulip, tu/lip.* Then write *cabin* on the board. Draw a line between the *b* and the *i* and say: *This word also has one consonant between two vowels. But in the word* cabin, *the consonant goes with the first vowel, making the first vowel short. Say it with me: cabin, cab/in.*

Practice Help children read the words in Row 1 on page 304. Clap as you read each word to emphasize the syllable break in the word. Say: *I am going to read the words again. This time,clap along with me. Then draw a line between the first and second syllable of each word.* Review the answers as a class *(bet/ter, lad/der, shad/ow, win/dow).* For Row 2, help children read the words in the lists. Then tell them to choose from the words in the lists to name each picture *(wagon, zebra, robot, window).*

Assess Make word cards with the following word parts: *so, fa, ze, bra, ro, bot, wag,* and *on.* Give each pair of children a pile of word cards. Have them try putting the various word parts together to create complete words. If necessary, list the words *sofa, zebra, robot,* and *wagon* on the board.

Pronunciation Tip Syllables VC/CV, VC/V, V/CV
Explain to children that a word has as many syllables as it has vowel sounds.

Transfer Skills

The suffix *-tion* has similar forms in other languages such as French (*-tion*), Spanish (*-ción*, *-sión*), and Portuguese (*-ção*). Children can look for cognates for *-tion* words in other languages. For example, the English word *direction* is *direction* in French, *dirección* in Spanish, and *direção* in Portuguese.

Syllables *-tion*, *-ture*, *-ion*

Use with page 305.

Introduce Copy and distribute page 305. Have children point to the picture of an *onion*. Say: *This is an onion, /o/ /n/ /y/ /ə/ /n/. How many vowel sounds do you hear in the word* onion*? Say it with me, /o/ /n/ /y/ /ə/ /n/,* onion. *That's right, there are two vowel sounds.* Now point to the *lotion*. Ask: *How many vowel sounds do you hear in the word* lotion*? Listen: /l/ /o/ /sh/ /ə/ /n/, lotion. Yes, there are two vowel sounds so there are two syllables.* Repeat this drill with the word *picture*.

Teach Explain that the spelling patterns *-tion*, *-ture*, and *-ion* form their own syllables. Display the following chart:

-tion	*-ture*	*-ion*
mo/tion, motion	pic/ture, picture	on/ion, onion
ac/tion, action	na/ture, nature	stal/lion, stallion

Practice Help children read the words in Row 1 on page 305. Clap as you read each word to emphasize the syllable break in the word. Say: *I am going to read the words again. This time, draw a line between the first and second syllable of each word.* Review the answers as a class *(fic/tion, na/ture, on/ion, mix/ture)*. For Row 2, help children read the words in the box. Then tell them to choose from the words in the box to name each picture *(picture, onion, creature, station)*.

Assess Make word cards with the following word parts: *fic-*, *sta-*, *mix-*, *pic-*, *on-*, *-tion*, *-ture*, and *-ion*. Give pairs of children a pile of word cards. Have them try putting the various word parts together to create complete words. If necessary, list the words *fiction*, *station*, *mixture*, *picture*, and *onion*, on the board.

Pronunciation Tip
Syllables *-tion*, *-ture*, *-ion* Remind children that a word has as many syllables as it has vowel sounds.

Name ____________________________________

Syllables VCCV, VCV

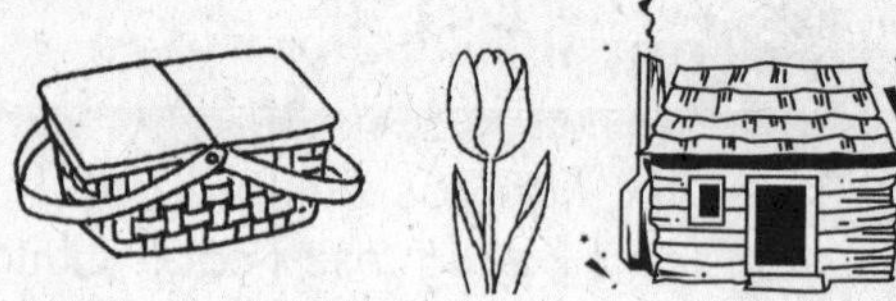

- **Read** the word.
- **Find** the two syllables. **Draw a line** between them.

ROW 1

better ladder shadow window

- **Look** at each picture.
- **Read** the words in the lists.
- **Write** the word. Choose from long-vowel words and short-vowel words.

ROW 2

Words with Long Vowels	Words with Short Vowels
robot	window
sofa	robin
pony	wagon
zebra	candle

Name ______________________________

Syllables *-tion, -ture, -ion*

- **Read** the word.
- **Find** the first and second syllables. **Draw a line** between them.

ROW 1

fiction nature onion mixture

- **Look** at each picture.
- **Read** the words in the box below.
- **Write** the word.

ROW 2

____

____

____

____

onion
picture
station
creature

Pages 223–225: Confusing Consonants

Assess
b and *p:* under *bat:* bee, box; under *pin:* pig, park; under *cub:* tub, web; under *cap:* cup, top
b and *v:* under *bed:* bag, ball, box, bus; under *van:* vest, vase, vet, vine
c /k/ and *g:* under *can:* cage, car, cat, cup; under *gas:* game, goat, gull, gate
ch and *sh:* under *chin:* chain, chair, chick, chin; under *ship:* shop, shoe, shell, sheep
d and *th:* under *dog:* dad, duck, day, dig; under *thirty:* thirteen, thumb
j and *y:* under *jet:* jar, jump, jam, juggle; under *yarn:* yak, yell, yard, yo-yo
l and *r:* under *log:* lake, lock, leg, lid; under *rug:* rain, rope, rod, rake
t and *th:* under *ten:* tie, tent, toe; under *thorn:* thirty, thumb, thigh

page 226: Words with *b* and p
Row 1: b, p, b, p
Row 2: p, b, b, p
Row 3: pin, bat

page 227: Words with *b* and *v*
Row 1: v, b, b, v
Row 2: b, v, b, v
Row 3: bed, van

page 228: Words with *c* /k/ and *g*
Row 1: c, g, c, g
Row 2: c, g, g, c
Row 3: can, gas

page 229: Words with *ch* and *sh*
Row 1: ch, ch, sh, sh
Row 2: ch, sh, ch, sh
Row 3: chin, ship

page 230: Words with *d* and *th*
Row 1: d, d, th
Row 2: d, th, d
Row 3: d, th

page 231: Words with *j* and *y*
Row 1: y, y, j, j
Row 2: j, y, j, y
Row 3: j, y

page 232: Words with *l* and *r*
Row 1: r, l, r, l
Row 2: r, l, r, l
Row 3: log, rug

page 233: Words with *t* and *th*
Row 1: t, th, th
Row 2: th, t, t
Row 3: ten, thorn

pages 234–236: Consonant Blends

Assess
Initial Consonant Blends: 1. cr; 2. gl; 3. dr; 4. sk; 5. sm
Final Consonant Blends: 1. mp; 2. nk; 3. nd; 4. st; 5. lk
3-Letter Consonant Blends: under *spl:* splash, splint; under *str:* strap, string, stripe, strong

pages 237–239: Consonant Digraphs, Consonant Sounds, and Silent Consonants

Assess
wh /hw/; *ch, tch* /ch/: whale, chin, patch sandwich, whisper, watch
ph: phone, dolphin; *gh:* laugh, cough; *dge:* bridge, judge
kn: knob, knock, knit; *wr:* write, wrist, wrench; *gn:* gnat, design; *mb:* lamb, comb, numb

page 240: Initial Consonant Blends
Row 1: br, fl, sk, sm
Row 2: bl, st, fr, sp
Row 3: clap, crib, flag, swim

page 241: Final Consonant Blends
Row 1: lk, nd, sk, st
Row 2: st, sk, mp, nt
Row 3: cast, belt, lamp, hand

page 242: 3-Letter Consonant Blends
Row 1: scr, str, str
Row 2: splint, spring, stripe
Row 3: strong, strum, splash

page 243: Words with *wh* /hw/; *ch, tch* /ch/
Row 1: wh, ch, wh, tch
Row 2: ch, wh, ch, tch
Row 3: whale, catcher, itch (or scratch), chin

page 244: Words with *ph, gh* /f/; *dge* /j/
Row 1: ph, gh, ph, dge
Row 2: ph, dge, ph, ph
Row 3: (tele)phone, trophy, cough, dolphin

page 245: Words with *kn, wr, gn, mb*
Row 1: wr, kn, gn, mb
Row 2: kn, wr, gn, mb
Row 3: knee, write, sign, climb

pages 246–247: Short Vowels
Assess
Short *a:* pat, hat, bad, man, rag
Short *e:* set, ten, net, sell
Short *i:* pin, sit, lift, did
Short *o:* top, got, hot, not
Short *u:* fun, bud, hut, dug

page 248: Words with Short *a*
Row 1: fan, hat, ant
Row 2: pan, rag, cat, cap
Row 3: fan, can, bat, ant

page 249: Words with Short *e*
Row 1: egg, pen, bed
Row 2: ten, step, men, vest
Row 3: pen, net, leg, bed

page 250: Words with Short *i*
Row 1: bib, fish
Row 2: dig, lid, wig, sick
Row 3: pig, six, bib, zip

page 251: Words with Short *o*
Row 1: rock, box, frog
Row 2: pot, lock, fox, dog
Row 3: box, mop, log, mom

page 252: Words with Short *u*
Row 1: tub, truck, drum
Row 2: bug, cup, duck, sub
Row 3: bus, sun, tub, rug

pages 253–255: Long Vowels
Assess
Long *a:* sail, bake, late, game, tape
Long *e:* deep, seat, read, mean, feel
Long *i:* might, fine, hide, mild, mice
Long *o:* coat, hope, crow, bowl, note
Long *u:* tune, fume, too, shoot, grew
Vowel Sounds of *y:* shy, by, fly, sandy, silly, buddy

page 256: Words with Long *a*
Row 1: braid, rake, tray
Row 2: cane, day, rain, plane
Row 3: plane, rain, hay, ape

page 257: Words with Long *e*
Row 1: leaf, bee
Row 2: seal, sleep, meat, he
Row 3: meat, seal, feet, me

page 258: Words with Long *i*
Row 1: kite, child, high
Row 2: bike, tie, light, nine
Row 3: child, light, tie, ice

page 259: Words with Long *o*
Row 1: soap, fold, bow
Row 2: goat, cone, mow, gold
Row 3: gold, cone, snow, boat

page 260: Words with Long *u*
Row 1: tube, fruit, boot
Row 2: suit, pool, cube, glue
Row 3: glue, cube, flute, moon

page 261: Vowel Sounds of *y*
Row 1: fry, cry, fly
Row 2: puppy, twenty, city
Row 3: twenty, fly, bunny, sky

pages 262-263: Vowel Patterns
Assess
aw, au, al: ball, paw, launch, salt, straw
oo: nook, took, shook, cook

page 264: Words with /ȯ/ spelled as *aw, au, al*
Row 1: wall, yawn
Row 2: ball, paw, hawk, launch
Row 3: salt sauce, ball, straw

page 265: Words with /u̇/ spelled *oo*
Row 1: foot, wood, hood
Row 2: cook, wood, look, hook
Row 3: book, foot, hoof

pages 266–267: Diphthongs
Assess
ow, ou: plow, how, owl, south
oi, oy: soy, enjoy, choice, foil, join

page 268: Words with *ou, ow*
Row 1: couch, owl, frown
Row 2: ow, ou, ow, ou
Row 3: cloud, cow, house, frown

page 269: Words with *oi, oy*
Row 1: soil, boy, join
Row 2: oy, oi, oi, oy
Row 3: coin, boy

pages 270–271: *r*-Controlled Vowels
Assess
ar, are, air, or, ore: star, snore, scarf, air, stair, horse
er, ir, ur, and *eer, ear:* germ, swirl, hurt, first, spear

page 272: Words with *ar, are, air, or, ore*
Rows 1 and 2: car, jar; barn, yarn; corn, horn; store, score
Row 3: share, hair, square, chair

page 273: Words with *er, ir, ur* and *eer, ear*
Row 1: purse, girl, stir
Row 2: deer, hear, tear
Row 3: ear, deer, bird, fern

pages 274–277: Inflected Endings
Assess
Plurals *-s, -es:* Add *-s:* cap, pin, girl; Add *-es:* fox, brush, bunch; Change *y* to *i* and add *-es:* puppy, sky
Possessives: one cat: cat's; two cats: cats'; one goat: goat's; two goats: goats'; one dog: dog's; two dogs: dogs'
Verb Endings *-s, -ed, -ing:* call: called, call, calls, is/are calling; rest: rested, rest, rests, is/are resting; walk: walked, walk, walks, is/are walking; lock: locked, lock, locks, is/are locking; spell: spelled, spell, spells, is/are spelling
More Verb Endings *-s, -ed, -ing:* sip: sips, sipped, sipping; wag: wags, wagged, wagging; hum: hums, hummed, humming; shine: shines, shined, shining; name: names, named, naming; use: uses, used, using

page 278: Plurals *-s, -es*
box: *-x, -es,* boxes; fly: *-y, y* to *i* then *-es,* flies; can: *-s,* cans

page 279: Possessives
Row 1: dog's bone; cat's toy; goat's can
Row 2: cats' plate; dogs' porch; goats' hill

page 280: Verb Endings *-s, -ed, -ing*
helped, helps, helping; painted, paints, painting; talked, talks, talks, talking

page 281: More Verb Endings *-s, -ed, -ing*
grinned, grins, grinning; moped, mopes, mopes, moping; raced, races, races, racing

pages 282–284: Compound Words, Contractions, and Cognates, Assess
Compound Words: cupcake, flashlight, teamwork, outside
Contractions *n't, 'll, 'm, 's:* hadn't, had not; wasn't, was not; didn't, did not; I'll, I will; we'll, we will; you'll, you will; it's, it is; she's, she is; he's, he is
Cognates: Answers will vary.

page 285: Compound Words
Row 1: in/side; bed/time; home/work; any/way
Row 2: bathtub, necktie, bedroom, teapot

page 286: Contractions *n't, 'll, 'm, 's*
2. wasn't, was, not; **3.** didn't, did, not; **4.** I'll, I, will; **5.** we'll, we, will; **6.** you'll, you, will; **7.** it's, it, is; **8.** she's, she, is; **9.** he's, he, is; **10.** I'm; **11.** they'll; **12.** isn't

page 287: Cognates
Answers will vary. Spanish answers are: calendario, yes; doctor, yes, or médico, no; palacio, yes; sandalia, yes, or huarache, no; tren, yes

pages 288–294: Prefixes and Suffixes
Assess
Prefixes *un-* and *re-*: unlike, not like; unlucky, not lucky; reheat, heat again; replay, play again; reuse, use again
Prefixes *pre-* and *dis-*: precook, cook before; premade, made before; dislike, do not like; distrust, do not trust
Prefixes *mis-*, *mid-*, and *non-*: misspell, misplace, midpoint, midday, nonfiction, nonstop
Suffixes *-ly* and *-ful*: safely, peaceful, kindly, playful
Suffixes *-less* and *-ness*: fearless, darkness, senseless, swiftness
Suffixes *-able, -ible*: useable, readable, reversible, collectible
Suffixes *-er, -or*: teacher, painter, opener, sailor, beeper

page 295: Prefixes *un-* and *re-*
reheat; unlock; uncap; reuse; unzip; reread

page 296: Prefixes *pre-* and *dis-*
heat before; do not trust
disorder; prepay; dislike

page 297: Prefixes *mis-*, *mid-*, and *non-*
nonfiction; misread; mismatch; nonstick; midafternoon; midstream

page 298: Suffixes *-ly* and *-ful*
1. quickly; **2.** cheerful; **3.** loudly; **4.** graceful; **5.** slowly

page 299: Suffixes *-less* and *-ness*
1. sleepless; **2.** endless; **3.** sweetness; **4.** tasteless; **5.** cloudless; **6.** sadness

page 300: Suffixes *-able, -ible*
1. likeable; **2.** collectible; **3.** adorable; **4.** fixable; **5.** doable

page 301: Suffixes *-er, -or*
1. farmer; **2.** actor; **3.** baker; **4.** banker; **5.** painter; **6.** sailor

pages 302–303: Syllable Patterns
Assess
VCCV, VCV: sofa, zebra, robot, wagon
-tion, -ture, -ion: fiction, station, mixture, picture, onion

page 304: Syllables VCCV, VCV
Row 1: bet/ter, lad/der, shad/ow, win/dow
Row 2: wagon, zebra, robot, window

page 305: Syllables *-tion, -ture, -ion*
Row 1: fic/tion, na/ture, on/ion, mix/ture
Row 2: picture, onion, creature, station

Part 4
Grammar Instruction for English Language Learners

Contents

Introduction to the Grammar Transition Lessons

English language learners may have experience mainly with their home languages, and the grammars of different languages vary widely. As these students encounter English, keep in mind that their home languages may differ in aspects such as the following:

- The languages may use different word order than English does.
- They may not use the same parts of speech as English does.
- Their tense structures may be simpler or more complex than English tense structure.
- Nouns and adjectives that are neutral in English may be masculine or feminine in a child's home language.

For teachers, it is vitally helpful to remember that grammar is much more than a set of rules for saying and writing sentences correctly. Grammar primarily consists of the ways that speakers and writers of a language communicate ideas, mainly in sentences. As students learn the meanings of new words and how English sentences work, they become able to successfully communicate their ideas. They will gradually learn rules, read and write punctuation, and eventually become proficient in standard English usage.

The core grammar and writing lessons in *Reading Street* provide the systematic instruction that students need to write. The following Grammar Transition Lessons and Practice Pages will supplement the core instruction with customized lessons that meet the particular needs of English learners.

Each group of grammar lessons covers a topic, such as Nouns, Verbs, or Sentences. Each lesson is supported by a reproducible Practice Page that provides strong context for the skill. Throughout the Grammar Transition Lessons, a **Transfer Skills** feature identifies challenges faced by English learners, based on the grammar of their home languages, as well as language knowledge that can transfer to English. Each lesson also includes a **Grammar in Action** feature to reinforce the skill through active learning.

In addition to the Grammar Transition Lessons and Practice Pages, you can further support grammar instruction with routines such as the following:

- **Emphasize sentence meaning.** Encourage children to try to understand and convey ideas rather than focusing only on separate words. Build their knowledge by presenting many examples that show how English sentences convey meaning. Include sentences that the children say or write.
- **Strengthen oral language skills.** Allow beginning English speakers to work with partners when completing grammar activities, talking about what English words and sentences mean. Encourage students to make up new phrases and sentences together.
- **Engage children as active learners.** Children who are acquiring English will make mistakes. They need encouragement rather than constant correction. Let children sing, chant, and play language games together. Allow them to communicate freely and have fun with English.
- **Relate to the home language.** Whenever possible, help children build on what they already know by making connections between a target grammar skill and the home language. Use available resources, such as bilingual staff members, language Web sites, and the children themselves, to gather information about the home language.

Nouns

Transfer Skills

Nouns

Children's home languages also have words for people, places, animals, and things. To help them learn English nouns, bring items—apples, hats, dolls, stuffed toys, dishes, and so forth—for vocabulary building.

Grammar *in Action*

Oral Language Have partners look through picture books and say the nouns for people or things in the pictures.

Nouns

Preteach Point to objects in the room, and have children name them. Tell children: *We have names for the things around us. A noun is a word that names something or somebody.*

Teach/Model Present the concept and provide examples:

- A noun names a person, a place, an animal, or a thing.

Person	Place	Animal	Thing
boy	school	bird	desk

Practice/Assess Copy and distribute pages 316 and 317. Before children complete either page, read the directions aloud and name the items in the picture. (See answers on page 382.)

Transfer Skills

Proper Nouns

- Children whose home languages are non-alphabetic, such as Chinese, Korean, and Japanese, may need extra practice writing names with letters.
- In some Asian languages, family names appear first in persons' names. Point out that, in English, the family name follows the person's first name.

Grammar *in Action*

Special People and Places On chart paper, have children draw pictures and write or dictate the names of people and places that are special to them. Help them use capital letters.

Proper Nouns

Special Names

Preteach Have children practice writing their names. Point out that each child's name begins with a capital letter. Tell children: *Each of us has our own special name. A proper noun is the special name of a person, place, animal, or thing.* Then show children how to write names with capital letters.

Teach/Model Present the concept and provide examples:

- A proper noun names a special person, place, animal, or thing.
- A proper noun begins with a capital letter.

Special Person	Special Place	Special Animal	Special Thing
Alex	Mexico	Fluffy	London Bridge

Practice/Assess Copy and distribute pages 318 and 319. Before children complete either page, read the directions aloud and name the items in the picture. (See answers on page 382.)

Special Titles

Preteach Write the names of various school staff members on the board, including titles such as *Mr., Mrs.,* and *Dr.* Read the names aloud with children, and underline the titles as you say them.

Teach/Model Present the concept and provide examples:

- A title can come before the name of a person.
- A title begins with a capital letter. Some titles end with a period.

Title	Example
Mr. (mister)	Mr. Lee
Mrs. (missus)	Mrs. Mills
Ms. (miz)	Ms. Lopez
Miss (miss)	Miss Witt
Dr. (doctor)	Dr. Po

Practice/Assess Copy and distribute page 320. Read the directions aloud before children complete the page. If appropriate, read the questions aloud. (See answers on page 382.) If appropriate, have children read their own answers aloud.

Transfer Skills

Titles

- Children may not realize that in English, the title *Doctor* is used for both men and women.
- For Spanish-speaking children, compare the titles *Mr., Mrs.,* and *Miss* to *Señor (Sr.), Señora (Sra.),* and *Señorita (Srta.)*. Point out that in English, *Mr.* and *Mrs.* are almost always used before the person's name, not alone.

Grammar *in Action*

Oral Language Have children practice introducing adult staff members to each other, using the correct titles.

Days, Months, and Holidays

Preteach Ask children to name today's day and date. Write them on the board, and point out that the names of the day and month begin with capital letters.

Teach/Model Present the concept and provide several examples:

- The names of the days of the week, months of the year, and holidays begin with capital letters.

Days of the Week	Months of the Year		Holidays (Examples)
Sunday Monday Tuesday Wednesday Thursday Friday Saturday	January February March April May June	July August September October November December	New Year's Day Valentine's Day Thanksgiving

Practice/Assess Copy and distribute page 321. Read the directions aloud. Go through the sample calendar with children before they complete the page. (See answers on page 382.)

Transfer Skills

Days and Months

In languages including Spanish, French, Polish, and Vietnamese, the names of days and months are not usually capitalized.

Grammar *in Action*

Capital Letters Sing this song to the tune of "Clementine": *Sunday, Monday, Tuesday, Wednesday, Thursday, Friday, Saturday.* Say: *The days of the week start with capital letters, just like months and holidays.* Have children point to the names of the days on a calendar as they are mentioned.

Transfer Skills

Plural Nouns
In some languages, including Chinese, Hmong, and Vietnamese, nouns do not have plural forms. Instead, the plural is indicated with an adjective.

Grammar *in Action*

Ten Fingers Pantomime this chant with children: *I have ten fingers. I have ten toes. / I have one mouth. I have one nose. / I have one chin. I have one head. / I have two eyes that close in bed.* List parts of the body under "one" and "more than one" (with *-s*).

One and More Than One

Preteach Point to one book and say: *a book*. Point to two books and say: *books*. Repeat with *a girl* and *girls*. Have children name other singular and plural nouns as you point to them. Say: *Some nouns name one thing. They are called* singular nouns. *Some nouns name more than one thing. They are called* plural nouns.

Teach/Model Present the concept and provide examples:
- Add -s to most nouns to form the plural, to tell about more than one.

One	More Than One
girl	girls
school	schools
dog	dogs

Practice/Assess Copy and distribute page 322. Help children name the singular and plural nouns in the picture. (See answers on page 382.)

Transfer Skills

Plural Noun Endings
Spanish-speaking children who have begun to read may be familiar with using *-s* and *-es* endings for plural nouns, as in the Spanish words for plants and flowers: *plantas* and *flores*.

Grammar *in Action*

Look Around the Classroom Sing to the tune of "Did You Ever See a Lassie?": *Please look around the classroom, the classroom, the classroom. Please look around the classroom, the classroom right now. Find boxes and lunches and glasses and brushes. Please look around the classroom, the classroom right now.* Have children find the items.

Plural Nouns That Add *-s* and *-es*

Preteach Point to two chairs and say: *chairs*. Repeat with (lunch)boxes or other items represented by a plural noun with an *-es* ending. Tell children: *We usually add* -s *to form the plural. But if the noun ends in* -ch, -sh, -s, -ss, *or* -x, *we add* -es.

Teach/Model Present the concept and provide examples:
- Most nouns add *-s: books, girls.*
- Some nouns add *-es: boxes, brushes, classes.*

Add *-s*	Add *-es*
girls schools dogs books teachers	lunches dishes buses classes boxes

Practice/Assess Copy and distribute page 323. Help children name the plural nouns in the picture. (See answers on page 382.)

Plural Nouns That Change Spelling

Preteach Say: *The children brush their teeth. The women tap their feet.* Tell children: *Most nouns add -s or -es to form the plural, but some change spelling to form the plural, like* children, teeth, women, *and* feet.

Teach/Model Present the concept and provide examples:

- Most nouns add *-s* or *-es: books, girls, boxes, brushes.*
- Some nouns change spelling to form the plural.

child/children	foot/feet	life/lives	man/men
mouse/mice	tooth/teeth	wolf/wolves	woman/women

Practice/Assess Copy and distribute page 324. Help children name the plural nouns in the picture. (See answers on page 382.)

Transfer Skills

Irregular Plural Nouns
English learners may add -s to irregular nouns as they speak or write: *gooses, childrens, wolfs, clothings.* Provide practice with nouns that have different plural forms.

Grammar *in Action*

Share this poem; have children use plush toys or drawings of mice to act it out: *Past my feet ran two little mice. Or was it one mouse passing twice?*

Possessive Nouns

Preteach Give a book to each of three children. Stand by one child and lead the class in saying: *This is (child's name).* Then point to the book and say: *This is (child's name)'s book.* Repeat with the other children. Then have all the children show their books. Say: *These are the students' books.* Write the four possessive nouns on the board. Explain: *To show that a person, place, or thing has or owns something, add an apostrophe* (point to one) *and the letter* s. *Just add an apostrophe* (point) *when the noun is plural and ends in* s.

Teach/Model Present the concept and provide examples:

- To form a possessive noun, add an apostrophe (') and -s when the noun is singular.
- Just add an apostrophe when the noun is plural and ends in *s*.

S. Nouns	Possessive	Pl. Nouns	Possessive
friend	friend's name	boys	boys' caps
girl	girl's book	cats	cats' bowls
school	school's library	puppies	puppies' toys

Practice/Assess Copy and distribute page 325. Help children read and understand the caption below each picture. (See answers on page 382.)

Transfer Skills

Possessive Nouns
In many languages, speakers show possession in phrases rather than noun endings. Show students how to change phrases such as *the tail of the bunny* to *the bunny's tail,* in order to show possession in English.

Grammar *in Action*

In Other Words Provide sentences such as these, and ask students to rephrase them using possessive nouns: *This book belongs to the girl. (This is the girl's book.) These chairs belong to the children. (These are the children's chairs.)*

Name ___________________________________

Picturing Nouns

Practice

- **Find** the people. **Circle** each person with a **blue** crayon.
- **Find** the animals. **Circle** each animal with a **red** crayon.
- **Find** the things. **Circle** each thing with a **brown** crayon.

Assess

- **Talk** about the picture. **Name** some of the people, animals, and things you see in the picture.

Name ____________________

Nouns

Practice

- **Look** at the picture.
- **Name** the people, places, animals, and things in the picture.

People	Places	Animals	Things
woman	zoo	zebra	tree

Assess

- **Look** around the room. What do you see?
- **Write** four nouns. **Name** things that you see.

____

Name ______________________________

Picturing Proper Nouns

Practice

- **Draw** a picture of yourself. **Write** your name on the line.

My name is ______________________________.

Assess

- **Say** the name of your friend: *My friend's name is....*

Name ________________________________

Special Names

Practice

- **Look** at the picture. **Find** the people, animals, and places that have special names.
- **Write** the names. Begin with capital letters.

Names of People	Names of Animals	Names of Places
Tom		

Assess

- **Write** or **say** the names of two people you know.

____

- **Write** or **say** the names of two special places you know.

____

Name ____________________

Special Titles

Practice

Title	Use with:
Mr.	a man
Ms.	a woman
Mrs.	a married woman
Miss	an unmarried girl or woman
Dr.	a doctor (male or female)

- **Look** at the pictures. **Read** the questions.
- **Write** the name of each person.
- **Include** a title before each person's name.

1. Who is cooking? ____________________

2. Who is singing? ____________________

3. Who is helping a cat? ____________________

4. Who is teaching? ____________________

Assess

- **Write** or **say** the names of two adults you know. Include their titles.

____

Name ______________________________

Days, Months, and Holidays

Practice

- Use this class calendar to **answer** the questions.
- Remember to **begin** the names of days, months, and holidays with capital letters.

May						
Sunday	Monday	Tuesday	Wednesday	Thursday	Friday	Saturday
1	2	3 LIBRARY VISIT	4	5	6	7
8 Mother's Day	9	10 LIBRARY VISIT	11	12	13	14
15	16	17 LIBRARY VISIT	18	19 FIELD TRIP	20	21
22	23	24 LIBRARY VISIT	25	26	27	28
29	30 Memorial Day	31 LIBRARY VISIT				

1. What holiday is on Monday, May 30? ______________

2. What holiday is on Sunday, May 8? ______________

3. When is the field trip? ______________

4. When does the class visit the library? ______________

Assess

- In the United States, Mother's Day always falls on the same day of the week. **Write** or **say** the name of that day.

____

Name ______________________________

One and More Than One

Practice

- **Look** at the picture.
- **Write** three singular nouns. **Write** four plural nouns.

Singular Nouns	Plural Nouns
tree	flowers

Assess

- **Look** around the room. What do you see?
- **Write** or **say** two singular nouns and three plural nouns.

____

Name ______________________________

Plural Nouns That Add *-s* and *-es*

Practice

- **Look** at the picture.
- **Write** three plural nouns with *-s*. **Write** three plural nouns with *-es*.

Add *-s*	Add *-es*
swings	benches

Assess

Write or **say** the plural of *box*. Use this word in a sentence.

____

Name ___________________________________

Plural Nouns That Change Spelling

Practice

- **Look** at the picture.
- **Circle** three nouns that change spelling in the plural form.

Assess

Write or **say** the plural forms of these words: *man, woman,* and *child.*

____

Name ______________________________

Possessive Nouns

Practice

- **Look** at the pictures. **Read** the words below.
- **Circle** the correct possessive nouns.

1. (Pals, Pal's) bowl

2. the (dogs', dog's) toys

3. the (cats, cat's) ball

4. the two (frogs', frog's) legs

Assess

- **Write** or **say** something that your classmate has.

____

Transfer Skills

Action Verbs
English verb endings are simpler than verb endings in languages such as Spanish and Polish, which use different endings for person and number of subjects. Provide examples of English verbs with no added endings, used in sentences such as *We eat* and *They can run.*

Grammar *in Action*

Oral Language Perform this cheer with children, acting out the verbs: *Action words tell what we do: swim, run, and talk to you! Sit, stand, and touch the sky! Jump, twist, and wave good-bye!* Brainstorm other actions for the cheer.

Action Verbs

Preteach Perform these actions as you narrate, and have children repeat your words and actions: *I clap. I walk. I sit. Which words tell what I do? (clap, walk, sit) A word that tells what we do is called a* verb.

Teach/Model Present the concept and provide examples:
- An action verb tells what we do.

I play. You sing. They jump. The dogs bark.

Practice/Assess Copy and distribute page 332 and/or 333. Help children understand each action verb. (See answers on page 382 and 383.)

Transfer Skills

Verb Endings
Children who speak highly inflected languages such as Russian and Spanish may need practice adding -*s* to verbs in present tense with third-person singular subjects. Help children see the difference between -*s* on plural nouns and -*s* on verbs: *He bakes a pie; She runs.*

Grammar *in Action*

Charades Provide picture cards or word cards of verbs such as *eat, sleep, jump, run, wave.* Have children choose a card and pantomime the action for others to guess: *Gina waves; Gina runs.*

Verbs for Now

Verbs That Add *-s*

Preteach Gesture as you narrate: *She sits here. He sits here. She sees me. He sees me. The word* sits *is a verb. The word* sees *is a verb. A verb can tell what one person, animal, or thing does now. Many verbs that tell about now end in -s: sits; sees.*

Teach/Model Present the concept and provide examples:
- Verbs in present tense tell what happens now.

She sees me. He sits. The girl runs. The ball rolls.

Practice/Assess Copy and distribute page 334. Help children describe the picture. (See answers on page 383.)

Verbs That Add *-s, -es*

Preteach Say these sentences as you act them out (using the pronouns *his* and *He* if appropriate): *The teacher touches the board. The teacher washes her hands. She passes the papers to us.* Ask: *Which words tell what the teacher is doing? (touches, washes, passes)* Display the verbs and explain: *You know that we add -s to a verb to tell what a person, animal, or thing does. But sometimes we add -es to a verb. Some verbs are easier to say that way.* Demonstrate to children by adding only /s/ to *pass* or *wash*. Then have them add *-es* so they can hear the extra syllable: *passes, washes.*

Teach/Model Present the concept and provide examples:

- Add -s to a verb to tell what a person, animal, or thing does.
- Add -es if the verb ends in *ch, sh, x,* or *ss*.

Add *-s*	jumps, plays, paints, runs, walks, eats
Add *-es*	teaches, washes, kisses, brushes, fixes

Practice/Assess Copy and distribute page 335. Remind children to add *-es* to some verbs. (See answers on page 383.)

Transfer Skills

Present Tense
Help children recognize that -s and -es verb endings, although they are spelled differently, are similar. Provide examples in context rather than in word lists: *Ana rides a bike; Tom talks quietly; Mia brushes her hair; Dad fixes a lamp.*

Grammar *in Action*

Oral Language Teach children this song (to the tune of "On Top of Old Smoky"). Have them mime the actions: *Some days in the morning, Mom tickles my feet. She brushes my hair, and she kisses my cheek.* Think of other verses with *washes, fixes, teaches.*

Verbs That Do Not Add *-s*

Preteach Say these sentences, gesturing as you speak: *The children play. Two boys jump rope. Three girls run.* Ask: *Which words tell what they do? (play, jump, run)* Write the verbs on the board. Explain: *You know that we add -s to a verb to tell what one person, animal, or thing does. To tell what two or more people, animals, or things do, we do* **not** *add -s to the verb. Also, after the word I or the word you we do not add -s to the verb: I walk home. You ride the bus.*

Teach/Model Present the concept and provide examples:

- Do **not** add -s to a verb that tells what two or more people, animals, or things do.
- Do **not** add -s to a verb that tells what I do or what you do.

The men plant trees. The birds sing. You play a game.

Practice/Assess Copy and distribute page 336. Review the meanings of the verbs. (See answers on page 383.)

Transfer Skills

Verbs with Plural Subjects
Guide children of various language backgrounds so they do not add -s to both the subjects and verbs, as in *The girls walks.* Help them practice saying and/or writing examples, such as *The girls walk, the boys smile,* and *we sing.*

Grammar *in Action*

-s or no -s? Write these words on cards: *The dogs, The girls, Max, My mom.* Write these verbs on another set: *sing, jump, run, play.* Have children draw a card from each set in order to create a sentence.

Transfer Skills

Past Tense
In Chinese, Hmong, and Vietnamese, verbs do not change to show the tense. Instead, adverbs or expressions of time indicate when an action has taken place. Help children use past tense verbs in conversations.

Grammar *in Action*

Make It Past Display a list of verbs: *walk, play, jump, call, move, push, listen, watch.* Begin to tell a story: *Yesterday I walked to the park with my friend.* Have children add to the story, using the verbs from the list in the past tense.

Transfer Skills

Past Tense Ending
Assure children that the *-ed* ending for past tense verbs is always spelled *-ed,* regardless of how it is pronounced.

Grammar *in Action*

Verb Cube Make a verb cube by covering a small empty box with paper. (The box should look as much like a cube as possible.) Write these verbs on the sides: *planted, waited, counted, melted, painted, visited.* Have children take turns tossing the cube. Invite them to say the verb, then use it in a sentence or act it out.

Verbs for the Past

-ed With the Sound of /t/ and /d/

Preteach Say these sentences, and display the verbs: *Yesterday I walked to the park. I played with my dog. He barked at a cat. I pulled at his leash.* Explain: *I did these things yesterday, in the past. Many verbs that tell about the past end with* -ed. *Sometimes the* -ed *sounds like /t/, as in* walked *and* barked. *Sometimes the* -ed *sounds like /d/, as in* played *and* pulled.

Teach/Model Present the concept and provide examples:
- Verbs in past tense tell what happened in the past.
- Many verbs in past tense end with *-ed.*

Sound of /t/	I asked her to play. We jumped rope. I helped her and she thanked me.
Sound of /d/	I opened the door and called your name. You cleaned your room.

Practice/Assess Copy and distribute page 337 after teaching the /əd/ sound of *-ed,* below.

-ed With the Sound of /əd/

Preteach Say, gesturing: *Yesterday, I visited my friend. We planted some flowers. I counted four flowers.* Display the verbs and explain: *I did these things in the past: visited, planted, counted. These verbs end with* -ed, *like the verbs we saw before. For these verbs, the* -ed *sounds like /əd/. Listen: visited, planted, counted.*

Teach/Model Present the concept and provide examples:
- Many verbs in past tense end with *-ed* that sounds like /əd/.

Sound of /əd/	I wanted my water to be cold. I needed some ice. I waited one hour. I lifted my glass. The ice had melted, so I added more ice.

Practice/Assess Copy and distribute page 337. Review the three sounds of *-ed.* (See answers on page 383.)

Verbs for the Future

Preteach Say: *What will I do after school today? I will go home. I will eat an orange. I will play with my sister.* Explain: *Verbs can tell about action in the future. The future may be later today, next week, or even next year.* Write one of the statements and point out the word *will.* Say: *To talk about the future, put the word* will *before the verb.*

Teach/Model Present the concept and provide examples:
- Verbs in future tense tell what will happen in the future.

I will visit Alicia.
We will see a movie.
Mom will drive me home.

Practice/Assess Copy and distribute page 338. Help children describe the picture. Review the meanings of the verbs. (See answers on page 383.)

Transfer Skills

Future Tense
Spanish, Haitian Creole, and Hmong speakers may use present tense in places where English calls for future tense. Help children practice verbs in statements such as *Tomorrow I will* ______ and *After school, we will* ______.

Grammar *in Action*

Oral Language Brainstorm weekend activities, such as *play, visit, sleep, plant, read.* Ask: *What will you do this weekend?* Have children answer, starting with *I will* or *We will.* Invite children to pantomime the actions.

Am, Is, Are, Was, and Were

Preteach Make statements such as these: *I am your teacher. Lorena is a good student. Priya and Chong are friends.* Explain: *In these sentences, the verbs* am, is, *and* are *do not tell what someone does. They tell what someone is.* Am, is, *and* are *tell about now. Listen to these sentences: Yesterday was Tuesday. Two children were sick on Tuesday.* Was *and* were *tell about the past.*

Teach/Model Present the concept and provide examples:
- Use *is* and *was* to tell about one person, place, animal, or thing.
- Use *are* and *were* to tell about more than one.
- Use *am* and *was* with *I.* Use *are* and *were* with *you.*

	am, is, are, was, were
Now	I am happy. You are happy. Celi is happy. The cat is happy. Celi and I are happy.
Past	Yesterday my lunch was good. My friends were hungry last night.

Practice/Assess Copy and distribute page 339. Help children describe the picture. (See answers on page 383.)

Transfer Skills

Forms of *to be*
- In Chinese, Hmong, and Haitian Creole, *to be* is not required in some sentences. If children say *I happy,* practice with sentences such as *I am happy* and *We are tired.*
- Tell Spanish speakers that English speakers say *We are hungry* rather than *We have hunger,* and *I am six years old* rather than *I have six years.*

Grammar *in Action*

Oral Language Give pairs an empty Now/Past Chart to fill in. Pairs can then share their sentences, while other students listen and tell if the sentences are correct.

Verbs for Present and for Past

Preteach Write and say the following expressions: *She walks. He talks.* Point out that these verbs tell us what happens now, or in the present. Write and say: *She walked. He talked.* Explain that these verbs tell what happened in the past.

Teach/Model Present the concept and provide examples:

- Some verbs that tell about the past end in *-ed*.
- Expressions of time, such as *last month, yesterday*, or *last year* can also help children recognize actions in the past.

Verbs in the Present	helps, plays, paints, walks, fixes, picks
Verbs in the Past	helped, played, painted, walked, fixed, picked

Practice/Assess Copy and distribute page 340. Before children complete the page, read the directions aloud and name the actions in the pictures. (See answers on page 383.)

Transfer Skills

Verb Tense
In Spanish, French, and Portuguese, verb endings indicate the tense of the verb. In Chinese, Hmong, and Vietnamese, verbs do not change to show the tense. Adverbs or expressions of time indicate when an action takes place.

Grammar *in Action*

Present or past? Write the following verbs: *picked, plants, dances, helped, jumped*, and *works*. Read each verb, pausing to allow children to respond with one clap for a verb in the present and two claps for a verb in the past.

Verbs for Past, Present, and Future

Introduce Write and say the following sentences: *Mary walked to school. (past) She walks everyday. (present) She will walk home later. (future)* Identify the action that took place in the past, the action that is happening in the present, and the action that will happen in the future.

Teach Present the concept and provide examples:

- Some verbs tell about the past. They may end in *-ed*.
- Some verbs tell about the present. They may end in *-s* or have no ending.
- Verbs in the future tense tell what will happen in the future. These verbs begin with *will*.

Verbs in the Past	waited, called, learned
Verbs in the Present	waits, wait, calls, call, learns, learn
Verbs in the Future	will wait, will call, will learn

Practice/Assess Copy and distribute page 341. Before children complete the page, read the directions aloud and name the actions in the picture. (See answers on page 383.)

Transfer Skills

Word Order
Word order in sentences varies across languages. In Spanish, the verb can appear before the subject. In Korean, the verb appears at the end of the sentence. Provide extra practice with word order in sentences.

Grammar *in Action*

Signal Words for Time Write the following signal words: *yesterday, now*, and *tomorrow*. In pairs, have children think of a sentence containing each signal word. Monitor for correct use of the past, present, and future tenses.

Contractions with *Not*

Preteach Say and display these sentences: *I do not know. I don't know. These two sentences mean the same thing. The word* don't *is the words* do *and* not *put together. It is called a* contraction. *We can make a contraction by putting a verb together with the word* not. *An apostrophe takes the place of the* o *in* not.

Teach/Model Present the concept and provide examples:

- A contraction is a short way to put two words together.
- An apostrophe takes the place of a letter or letters.

They do not see me.	They don't see me.
You are not walking.	You aren't walking.
I did not get a pen.	I didn't get a pen.
That is not my dog.	That isn't my dog.

Practice/Assess Copy and distribute page 342. Help children describe the picture. (See answers on page 383.)

Transfer Skills

Contractions

- Spanish-speaking children will know these contractions: *al* = *a* + *el*; *del* = *de* + *el*. Explain the apostrophe in English.
- In Spanish, Haitian Creole, and other languages, double negatives (comparable to *I did not do nothing)* are correct. Explain how *-n't* is used in English.

Grammar *in Action*

Oral Language Display *don't, isn't, didn't,* and *aren't.* Have children rephrase these sentences using contractions: *Cats do not bark. That is not true. I did not know. My dogs are not big.*

More Contractions

Preteach Say these sentences: *I am your teacher. I'm your teacher. I said the same thing twice. In the second sentence, I made a contraction from* I am. *We can make a contraction with a pronoun, such as* I, you, he, she, *or* they. *Put it with a verb such as* am, will, are, *or* is.

Teach/Model Present the concept and provide examples:

- Make a contraction with a pronoun plus *am, will, are,* or *is.*

If you are going, I am going too.	If you're going, I'm going too.
She is my sister.	She's my sister.
You are my friend.	You're my friend.
I will go now.	I'll go now.

Practice/Assess Copy and distribute page 343. Read the items with both answer choices. (See answers on page 383.)

Transfer Skills

More Contractions

Children may hear *I'm* and *it's* repeatedly but may not recognize them as contractions. Have children make these word cards: *I, am, I'm, it, is, it's.* Have them match the contraction to its words.

Grammar *in Action*

Oral Language Sing together, and motion toward the subjects mentioned: *Now we're all together, together, together. Now we're all together, together right now. I'm here, and you're here, and she's here, and he's here. Now we're all together, together right now.*

Name ______________________

Picturing Verbs

Practice

- **Draw** a picture of yourself playing.
- **Draw** a picture of yourself sitting.

play

sit

Assess

- **Think** of something else you can do. **Draw** a picture of yourself doing it.

Name ____________________

Action Verbs

Practice

- **Look** at the picture. **Read** the sentences.
- **Circle** the action verb in each sentence.

1. I sit in my yard.
2. The birds sing.
3. I look at the birds.

Assess

- **Write** or **say** a sentence about what you do. Use one of these action verbs: *eat, read, play, run.*

Name ______________________________

Verbs That Add *-s*

Practice

- **Look** at the picture. **Read** the sentences.
- **Circle** the correct verb to complete each sentence.

1. Ray (kick, kicks) the ball.

2. Lucy (runs, run) fast.

3. Max (stop, stops) the ball.

Assess

- **Look** at the picture. **Write** or **say** a sentence about the mom. Use *claps* or *sits*.

Name ______________________________

Verbs That Add *-s, -es*

Practice

- **Look** at the picture. **Read** the sentences.
- **Write** the correct verb to complete each sentence.

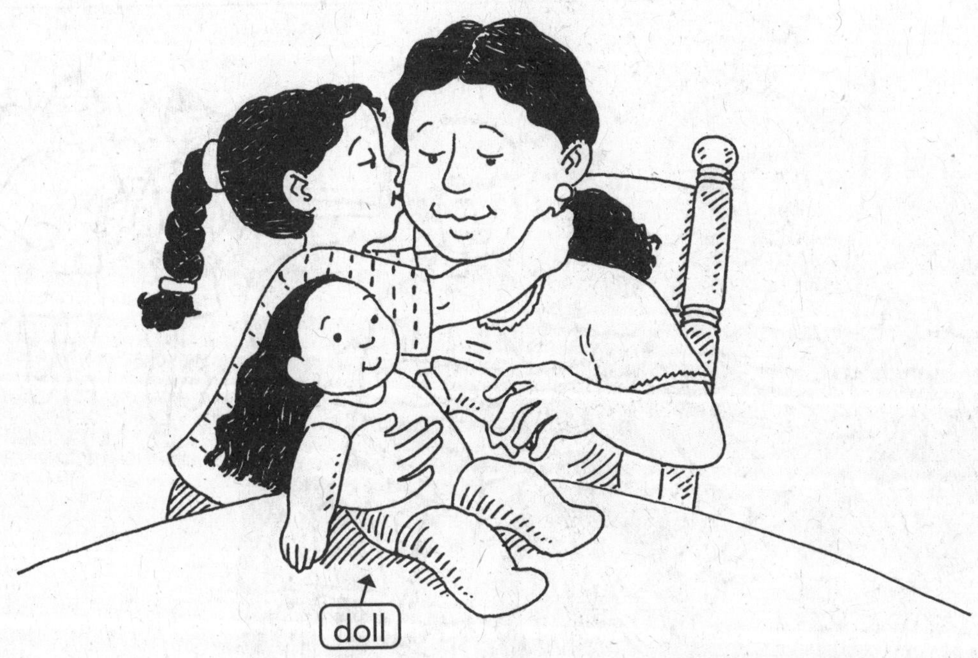

1. Mom ______________ Lili's doll. (fix, fixes)

2. Lili ______________ Mom. (huges, hugs)

3. Lili ______________ Mom. (kiss, kisses)

Assess

- **Look** at the picture. **Say** another sentence about the doll. Use the verb *washes.*

Name ______________________________

Verbs That Do Not Add *-s*

Practice

- **Look** at the picture. **Read** the sentences.
- **Circle** the correct verb to complete each sentence.

1. Tim and I (ride, rides) our bikes.

2. Mom and Dad (run, runs) on the path.

3. Tim (sing, sings) a silly song.

4. I (smile, smiles) at the song.

Assess

Write or **say** a sentence about Mom and Dad. Use the verb *sing*.

Name ___________________________

Verbs for the Past

Practice

- **Look** at the picture. **Read** the sentences.
- **Circle** the correct verb to complete each sentence.

1. Yesterday, I (visit, visited) my grandmother.

2. We (bakes, baked) bread.

3. I (cleaned, cleans) the bowl with my finger.

Assess

Have you ever helped in the kitchen? **Write** or **say** a sentence about it. Use *cooked* or *baked*.

____

Name ________________________________

Verbs for the Future

Practice

- **Look** at the picture. **Read** the sentences. **Read** the verbs in the box.
- **Write** the correct verb that tells about the future.

Mama Duck ____________________ all her babies to swim.

Soon, the baby ducks ____________________ big and strong.

They all ____________________ in the pond with no help.

will swim	will teach	will grow

Assess

- What do you think will happen when the baby ducks are grown? **Write** or **say** a sentence about it.

Name ______________________________

Am, Is, Are, Was, and *Were*

Practice

- **Look** at the picture. **Read** the sentences.
- **Circle** the correct verb in each sentence.

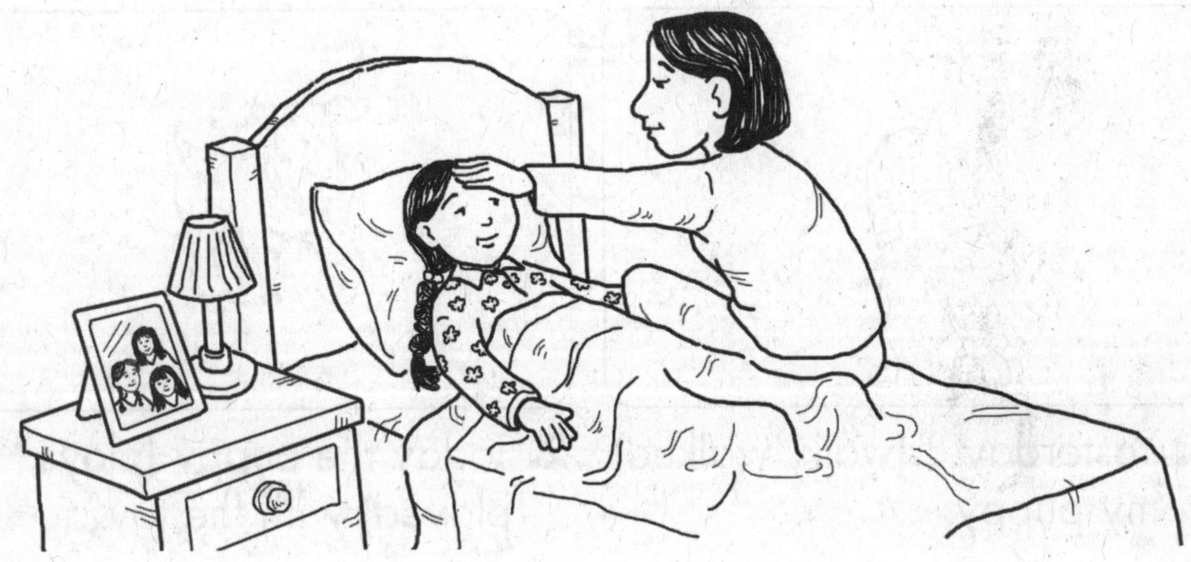

1. Yesterday, I (are, was) sick.

2. Today I (am, are) still sick.

3. Last week, my sisters (was, were) both sick.

4. Mom (is, are) very nice to me.

5. She and I (are, is) talking.

Assess

- **Write** or **say** a sentence about the sick girl. Use the verb *is*.

____

Name ______________________________

Verbs for Present and for Past

Practice

- **Look** at the pictures. **Read** the sentences.
- **Circle** the correct verb.

1. Yesterday, I (walk, walked) my puppy.

2. Today the puppy (plays, played) with the toy.

3. Now my puppy (smells, smelled) the flowers.

4. Last night, I (brush, brushed) my puppy.

Assess

- **Say and write** a sentence about the puppy. Use the verb *play* or *walk*.

Name ________________________________

Verbs for Past, Present, and Future

Practice

- **Look** at the picture. **Read** the sentences. **Read** the verbs in the box.
- **Write** the correct verb that tells about the present, past, or future.

1. My grandfather likes to ____________________ flowers.

2. Last year, we ____________________ a fruit tree in the garden.

3. Next year, we ____________________ vegetables.

plant	planted	will plant

Assess

- **Say** and **Write** a sentence about the picture.

____

Does your sentence describe the past, present, or future?

____

Name ______________________________

Contractions with *Not*

Practice

- **Look** at the picture. **Read** the sentences.
- **Write** the contraction for the underlined words.

1. Oh, no! I <u>did not</u> bring my umbrella. ____________________

2. It <u>was not</u> raining this morning. ____________________

3. I <u>do not</u> want to get wet! ____________________

Assess

- **Write** or **say** a sentence about getting wet. Use one of these contractions: *don't, didn't,* or *isn't.*

____

Name ______________________________

More Contractions

Practice

- **Look** at the picture. **Read** the sentences.
- **Circle** the correct contraction to complete each sentence.

1. (I'm, I'll) going out to play.

2. (She's, I'll) play with you!

3. Thanks! (You're, You'll) the best, Dad!

Assess

- **Write** or **say** a sentence about the boy. Use the contraction *he's.*

____

Putting Words Together Meaningful word groups in English may not always be self-evident to children whose home languages may use different patterns of word order. Restate children's sentences to help familiarize them with correct word order in English.

Puzzle Pieces Write phrases such as these on cardstock: *The yellow cat / My red car / runs fast.* Cut each phrase apart into large puzzle pieces. Mix them up. Read each piece randomly. Help children put the pieces together so they form meaningful word groups.

Transfer Skills

Meaningful Sentences Help children understand that sentences in English should make sense—and they will understand English sentences more and more as they learn more English words.

Grammar *in Action*

Word Cards Write these words on individual cards: *on the sat A cat bed.* Have children draw a card and hold the card up. Read each card, and make sure children know the meaning of each word. Help children arrange themselves to make the sentence *A cat sat on the bed.*

Meaningful Word Groups

Phrases

Preteach Say and write these words on the board: *dog, little,* and *the.* Ask: *What do these words mean? Let's look at them one at a time. The first word names a kind of animal. The second word tells a size. The word* the *by itself doesn't tell me anything. These words are like pieces of a puzzle. They don't mean very much when they are put together this way. Look what happens when I arrange the words differently:* the little dog. *These words really mean something when they are put together this way. They help me think of a little dog.*

Teach/Model Present the concept and provide examples:

- Meaningful word groups make sense when we say or read them together.

Meaningful:	a red cat	sat on a mat
Not meaningful:	cat my a	red a sat

Practice/Assess Copy and distribute page 351 after the second lesson on Meaningful Word Groups (below).

Sentences

Preteach Write these words on large cards: *dog, away, ran,* and *the.* Say them and post them on the board: Ask: *Do these words tell us anything? Can we arrange these words so that they do tell us something?* The dog ran away. *Now these words tell us something. They tell us that the dog ran away. We put these words together so they would tell us something. We made a sentence.* Write the sentence on the board. *When you write a sentence, it starts with a capital letter. It ends with a dot called a period.*

Teach/Model Present the concept and provide examples:

- A meaningful word group that tells something is called a *sentence.*

Meaningful:	A fat cat can run.	
Not meaningful:	cat run can	A fat

Practice/Assess Copy and distribute page 351. Read the words together. Remind children what a sentence looks like. (See answers on page 383.)

Naming Parts of Sentences (Subjects)

Preteach Say this sentence: *The girl walks to school.* Ask: *Who is this sentence about? (the girl)* Explain that "The girl" is the naming part of the sentence. It tells whom or what the sentence is about. The naming part is called the *subject* of the sentence. It can tell who or what does something.

Teach/Model Present the concept and provide examples:

- The naming part, or subject, tells who or what the sentence is about.

Mom bought mangoes. Lisa eats a mango. The mango is sweet.

Practice/Assess Copy and distribute page 352 and/or 353. Before children complete either page, read the directions aloud and help them name the items in the picture. (See answers on page 383.)

Subjects
In Spanish, subjects do not precede predicates as often as in English. Spanish verb endings allow subjects to follow verbs or to be understood. Provide many examples of English sentences, rather than abstract explanations, to help children learn what the subjects are.

Grammar *in Action*

Who Took a Mango?
Write children's names on cardstock mango cut-outs. Put them in a dish. Pick a name to start the game: *"Miguel took a mango from the mango dish."* Miguel: *"Who, me?"* Group: *"Yes, you!"* Miguel: *"Not me!"* Pick another name and repeat. Tell children that each name is a subject of a sentence.

Action Parts of Sentences (Predicates)

Preteach Say this sentence again: *The girl walks to school.* Ask: *What does the girl do? (walks to school)* Explain that this is the action part of the sentence. It tells what a person or thing does. The action part is called the *predicate* of the sentence.

Teach/Model Present the concept and provide examples:

- The action part, or predicate, of a sentence tells what the subject does.

We walk home. Mom drives the car. We go to the store.

Practice/Assess Copy and distribute page 354 and/or 355. Before children complete either page, read the sentences aloud and help them describe each picture. (See answers on page 384.)

Transfer Skills

Predicates
In English predicates, verbs often are followed by objects, as in *drank the water.* However, in Korean and Hindi, the verb often appears at the end of a sentence. Help students practice building English sentences with word strips or cards containing subjects, verbs, and objects.

Grammar *in Action*

Charades Have children mime actions for others to guess. Give this model: *Lu rides a bike; Lu eats an apple.* Explain that each action part is a new predicate.

Transfer Skills

Word Order
Help students see that word order strongly affects meaning in English. *The puppy barked at Kay* has a different meaning from *Kay barked at the puppy.* Have children practice changing the word order in sentences to express different meanings.

Grammar *in Action*

Correct Order Help partners make cards with parts of sentences: *My friend / rides a bike. Rides a bike / my friend. Plays / the dog. The dog / plays. The bird / sings. Sings / the bird.* Have partners say the parts and build sentences in correct word order.

Word Order

Preteach Display these sentences and read them aloud, gesturing: *The bird flies. Flies the bird.* Ask: *What is the naming part of the first sentence? (The bird) The second sentence does not sound right. The words are not in the right order to make a sentence. In an English sentence, the naming part usually comes first. The action part usually comes after the naming part.*

Teach/Model Present the concept and provide examples:

- Sentences need to have words in the right order.
- In a statement, the naming part usually comes first. The action part usually comes next.

In the right order:	The dog barks.
Not in the right order:	Barks the dog.

Practice/Assess Copy and distribute page 356. Help children describe the picture. (See answers on page 384.)

Transfer Skills

Complete Sentences
In Spanish and Chinese, speakers do not need to include some pronouns as sentence subjects because the context may make the pronoun unnecessary. Have students practice including such pronouns in English.

Grammar *in Action*

Time to Listen Read these groups of words. Have children raise their hands each time they hear a complete sentence. *My brother. We walk to school. We ride the bus. In the car. After school.* Invite children to say sentences.

Complete Sentences

Preteach Display and read these groups of words: *Tom went to the library. To the library.* Say: *The first group of words is a sentence. What is the naming part? (Tom) What is the action part? (went to the library) The second group of words, "to the library," is not a complete sentence. There is no naming part or action part. A complete sentence needs a naming part and an action part.*

Teach/Model Present the concept and provide examples:

- A complete sentence needs a naming part and an action part.

Complete	Rai eats lunch.
Incomplete	Her lunch in a bag.

Practice/Assess Copy and distribute page 357. As an extension, have children choose a fragment from the Practice and create a sentence from it. (See answers on page 384.)

Types of Sentences

Telling Sentences

Preteach Display and read these sentences: *We jump rope. My brother plays with toy cars.* Say: *Let's look at these sentences. Each one starts with a capital letter and ends with a period. Each one tells something, so it is a telling sentence. A telling sentence is called a* statement. It states, or tells, something.

Teach/Model Present the concept and provide examples:

- A sentence that tells something is called a *statement.*
- It begins with a capital letter and ends with a period.

Statements
That cat is black.
My mom likes cats.
We have two cats.

Practice/Assess Copy and distribute page 358. Remind children that a statement begins with a capital letter and ends with a period. (See answers on page 384.)

Transfer Skills

Statements
Children who read in Spanish may recognize that a sentence begins with a capital letter and ends with a period. The Spanish word for "capital letter" is *mayúscula,* and the period is called *punto* (which can mean "point," "dot," or "period").

Grammar *in Action*

Make a Statement Make sets of cards such as these: The cat / sees / the bird. / The bird / sees / the cat. Mix the cards, and have children form statements. Remind them to put the capital letter at the beginning and the period at the end.

Questions

Preteach Say: *Listen to these sentences: What is your name? Where do you live? How old are you? Do you have any cats?* Ask: *How are these sentences different from statements? They each ask something.* Write two of the sentences on the board. Ask: *How else are they different? Each one ends with a question mark. A sentence that asks something is called a* question.

Teach/Model Present the concept and provide examples:

- A sentence that asks something is called a *question.*
- It starts with a capital letter and ends with a question mark.

Questions
How are you?
What is your teacher's name?
Where is your school?

Practice/Assess Copy and distribute page 359. Help children describe the picture. (See answers on page 384.)

Transfer Skills

Questions

- Help children understand that questions in English often begin with words such as *who, what, when, where, how, do,* and *did.*
- Speakers of Asian languages often form questions by adding words to statements, comparable to *The water is cold, no?* Provide extra practice with English questions.

Grammar *in Action*

Oral Language Have children ask each other questions about what they did yesterday. For example, *What did you eat for lunch? Who played games with you?*

Transfer Skills

Exclamations
The exclamation mark at the end of an exclamation is the same in English and Spanish. Tell Spanish-speaking students that, in English, there is no exclamation mark at the beginning of the sentence.

Grammar *in Action*

Oral Language Say these sentences and have children repeat them as exclamations: *That dog is big. He is barking. I can't hear you.*

Exclamations

Preteach Write and say in an excited voice: *I am very happy!* Have children repeat, and then ask: *What feeling does that sentence tell about? (excitement; happiness) Whenever you say something with strong feeling, you are saying an exclamation. A written exclamation begins with a capital letter and ends with an exclamation mark.*

Teach/Model Present the concept and provide examples:

- An exclamation is a sentence that shows strong feeling.
- It begins with a capital letter and ends with an exclamation mark.

Exclamations

This is fun! This swing goes high! I can touch the sky!

Practice/Assess Copy and distribute page 360. Practice intonation of exclamations. (See answers on page 384.)

Transfer Skills

Commands
Help children recognize that, in English, a command usually does not state the person ("you") who is commanded to do something. English commands also may not state that the action should be done now. "Please take this to the office" means "(You) please take this to the office (now)."

Grammar *in Action*

Time to Listen Share this poem. Have children mime the actions mentioned in the commands: *1, 2: Tie your shoe. 3, 4: Touch the floor. 5, 6: Pick up sticks. 7, 8: Close the gate. 9, 10: Twist and bend.* Brainstorm other rhyming commands.

Commands

Preteach Give children various commands such as these: *Please stand up. Walk to the front of the class. Say hello. Sit down.* Ask: *How are these sentences the same? In each one, I am telling you to do something. A sentence that tells someone to do something is called a command. It begins with a capital letter and ends with a period.*

Teach/Model Present the concept and provide examples:

- A command is a sentence that tells someone to do something.
- It begins with a capital letter and ends with a period.

Commands

Come to my house. Play with me. Draw me a picture.

Practice/Assess Copy and distribute page 361. Read the sentences aloud. (See answers on page 384.)

Compound Sentences and Commas

Preteach Display and read these sentences: *I went to Mimi's house. We ate lunch.* Explain: *These two sentences have ideas that go together. We can join them to make a longer sentence:* I went to Mimi's house, and we ate lunch. *Here's what to do* (demonstrate as you talk): *Take out the period in the first sentence; put in a comma instead. Add* and. *Add the second sentence, starting with a lowercase letter. To join sentences that have opposite ideas, use* but: I went to the library, but it was closed.

Teach/Model Present the concept and provide examples:

- A compound sentence has two sentences joined by a comma and the word *and* or *but*.

Simple Sentences	I am 8 years old. I am in the second grade. Joe likes bikes. He does not have one yet.
Compound Sentences	I am 8 years old, and I am in the second grade. Joe likes bikes, but he does not have one yet.

Practice/Assess Copy and distribute page 362. In the first compound sentence, help children see the two simple sentences. (See answers on page 384.)

Transfer Skills

Compound Sentences
Children may have difficulty seeing the clauses in a compound sentence. Point out the conjunction *(and; but)* in the examples. Give additional practice finding the subject and verb within independent clauses.

Grammar *in Action*

Commas in Compounds Write these sentence pairs on sentence strips: *Juanita likes cats. She doesn't like dogs. / Ana loves animals. She has many pets.* On cards, write *and, but,* and two commas. Distribute cards and sentence strips, and have children join the sentences with a comma plus *and* or *but.*

More About Commas

Preteach Display these examples: *July 4, 1776; Thursday, July 4; Chicago, IL 60626; I like blue, red, and yellow.* Explain: *Commas tell us where to pause, or slow down. We use commas in many ways. We use commas in dates. We use commas in addresses. We use commas to separate three or more things in a list.*

Teach/Model Present the concept and provide examples:

- Use commas in dates: *February 14, 1963*
- Use commas in addresses: *Salinas, CA 93908*
- Use commas to separate three or more things: *Ben, Alma, and Cindy went home.*

Practice/Assess Copy and distribute page 363. Read the sentences, and pause where the commas belong. (See answers on pages 384 and 385.)

Transfer Skills

Commas in Dates
Children may be familiar with dates in which the day number comes first, as in *4 July 1776.* Show how the comma helps separate the day number from the year number in dates as written in the United States.

Grammar *in Action*

All About Me Have children write sentences about themselves using these models: *I was born on February 7, 2001. I was born in Houston, Texas.*

Transfer Skills

Quotation Marks
The punctuation for quotations varies across languages. For example, in Spanish double quotation marks ("") or angled quotation marks (« ») may be used.

Grammar *in Action*

Correct or Incorrect?
Display correct and incorrect examples of quotations marks in a sentence. Display the sentences *"She goes to school"* (incorrect) and *She said, "Go to school."* (correct). Offer several examples and ask children to identify correct and incorrect usage.

Quotation Marks

Preteach Explain to children that quotation marks are used in a dialogue to set apart the exact words a character speaks. Quotation marks are always used in pairs. Display and read examples: *My brother said, "I am tired." "You should go to bed," I said.* Point out clue words such as *I said* to determine who said the words.

Teach/Model Present the concept and provide examples:

- Quotation marks show the beginning and the end of words a person says.
- The speaker's name and words such as **asked** and **said** are not inside the quotation marks.

> "What is your favorite sport?" asked Lara. I said,
> "Soccer is my favorite sport."

Practice/Assess Copy and distribute page 364. Review the use of quotation marks with children and add quotation marks to sentence number 1 together. (See answers on page 385.)

Transfer Skills

Paragraph Indents
The writing systems of children's home languages may have different conventions for paragraphs. Have children practice finding paragraph indents in classroom texts.

Grammar *in Action*

What Sentence Does Not Belong? Read aloud a brief paragraph. In your paragraph, include one sentence that does not tell about the same idea. Ask children to identify the sentence that does not belong in the paragraph.

Paragraphs

Introduce Write and say this paragraph, making sure to include an indentation at the beginning of the paragraph: *Tomorrow is Marty's last day of first grade. His class is going to celebrate. All his friends are happy. They will play games together in the morning. It will be fun!* Ask: *What is this paragraph about?* Explain: *This is a group of sentences that describes Marty's last day of school.*

Teach Present the concept and provide examples:

- A paragraph is a group of sentences about the same idea.
- The first sentence tells the main (most important) idea and is usually indented.
- The sentences that follow give details about the main idea.

> I have a baby sister named Sara. (**Main Idea**) She is very cute and funny. Sara likes to make silly noises and play games. I have a lot of fun with my sister. (**Details**)

Practice/Assess Copy and distribute page 365. Discuss the picture and read the sentences. If necessary, work with children to put the sentences in a logical order. (See answers on page 385.)

Name ___________________________

Meaningful Word Groups

Practice

- **Read** each group of words.
- **Draw** what each group means.

a big cat	The big cat has a hat.

Assess

Which of the word groups is a sentence? **Point** to it, and **read** it aloud.

Name ______________________________

Picturing Sentences: Naming Parts

Practice

- **Read** the sentence.
- Who or what is the sentence about? **Color** that animal in the picture.

The dog likes to run.

Assess

- **Say** a new sentence using the same naming part.

Name ______________________________

Naming Parts of Sentences (Subjects)

Practice

- **Look** at the picture. **Read** the sentences.
- **Circle** the naming part of each sentence. It is the subject.

1. Mom opens a can.

2. Ted gets the pan.

3. The pan is on the top shelf.

Assess

- **Write** or **say** a new sentence. Use the naming part of one of the sentences above.

Name ______________________________

Picturing Sentences: Action Parts

Practice

- **Read** the sentence.
- What is the action part? **Circle** the picture that shows the action part.

Dad holds a book.

Assess

- **Say** a new sentence about yourself. Use the same action part.

Name ________________________________

Action Parts of Sentences (Predicates)

Practice

- **Look** at the picture. **Read** the sentences.
- **Circle** the action part of each sentence. It is the predicate.

1. I play with my cat.

2. A dog barks at him.

3. My cat runs away.

Assess

- **Write** or **say** a new sentence. Tell what happens next.

Name ___________________________

Word Order

Practice

- **Look** at the picture. **Read** the sentences.
- **Circle** the sentences with the words in the right order.

1. I drew a picture.
Drew a picture I.

2. This is my house.
My house this is.

3. Is green and white my house.
My house is green and white.

Assess

- **Look** at the picture again. **Say** another sentence about it.

Name ___________________________

Complete Sentences

Practice

- **Look** at the picture. **Read** the groups of words.
- **Circle** each group of words that is a complete sentence.

1. How the woman. The woman sells oranges.

2. She cuts the oranges. Lemons and oranges at the market.

3. Oranges and lemons. You can buy honey too.

Assess

- **Choose** one of the incomplete sentences. **Add** more words to make a complete sentence.

____

Name ______________________________

Telling Sentences

Practice

- **Look** at the picture. **Read** the sentences.
- **Write** each telling sentence correctly.

1. this is Lobo's party

____

2. we gave Lobo a new toy

____

3. we had fruit

____

4. Lobo had fun

____

Assess

- **Write** or **say** another statement about Lobo's party.

____

Name ___________________________

Questions

Practice

- **Look** at the picture. **Read** the sentences.
- **Circle** each question.

1. I do not see you. Where are you?

2. Are you here? I will find you.

3. I see you by the tree. Can you run fast now?

Assess

- Pretend you are looking for the boy. What would you ask? **Write** or **say** the question.

Name ___________________________

Exclamations

Practice

- **Look** at the picture.
- **Write** the exclamation that each person says.

Push me too!
I am going high!
My arms are tired!

Assess

- What would you say if you were going fast?

Name ______________________________

Commands

Practice

- **Look** at the pictures.
- **Circle** the sentences that are commands.

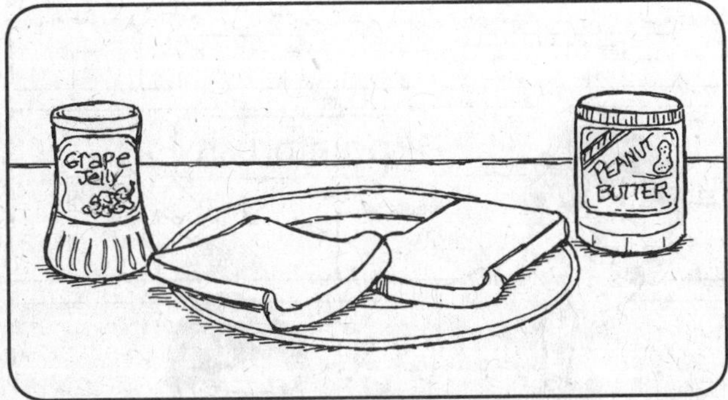

1. This is how to make a sandwich.

2. Put peanut butter on a slice of bread.

3. Put jelly on the other slice.

4. It's easy!

Assess

- **Write** or **tell** how to make a peanut butter and jelly sandwich. Use commands. Use these words: *get, put, cut, eat.*

____

____

Name ___________________________________

Compound Sentences and Commas

Practice

- **Look** at the pictures. **Read** each sentence.
- **Add** a comma where it is needed in each sentence.

1. Dad made a birdhouse and I will put it in the tree.

2. I got the hammer and nails but only Dad used them.

3. Dad made the birdhouse and now we can paint it.

4. We look all over but we do not see the paintbrush!

Assess

- **Read** the compound sentences aloud. Pause at each comma.

Name ______________________________

More About Commas

Practice

- **Look** at the picture. **Read** the sentences.
- **Add** commas to the sentences.

We took a trip on May 14 2005. We went to Santa Barbara California. We saw Rosa Gus Maria and Eva. We came home on Sunday May 22.

Assess

- **Write** or **say** a sentence about a place you visited. Name three things you saw there.

____

Name ______________________________

Quotation Marks

Practice

- **Look** at the picture. **Read** the sentences.
- **Add** quotation marks.

1. I am hungry! said Olivia.

2. John said, Good! It's time for lunch.

3. Let's make sandwiches. What kind do you like? asked Olivia

4. I like ham and cheese sandwiches, answered John.

5. Olivia said, I like ham and cheese too.

6. Let's make ham and cheese sandwiches, then! John said.

Assess

Write or **say** a sentence that needs quotation marks. **Check** that the quotes are correctly placed.

Name ______________________________

Paragraphs

Practice

- **Read** the sentences.
- **Write** the sentences in order.
- **Indent** the paragraph.

1. Soccer is a fun sport.

2. Everyone has to follow the rules.

3. Many people enjoy the game.

4. Coaches have a big job.

5. They make it fun and safe for everyone!

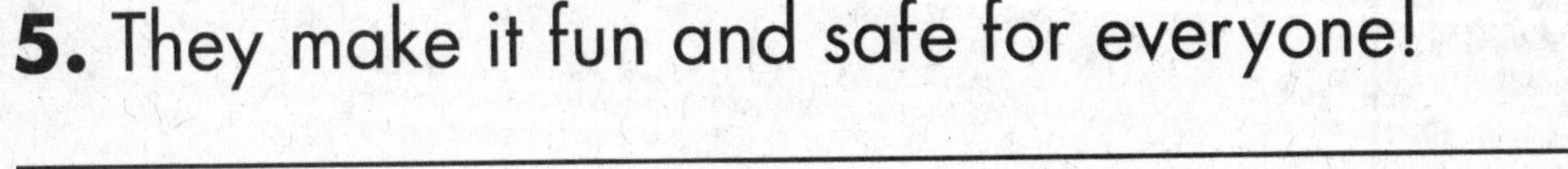

Assess

- Why do we use paragraphs in writing?
  Say or **write** your answer.

Transfer Skills

Color Names

- Help children learn the English words for colors through many encounters.
- Speakers of Polish and other languages may express choices among objects using adjectives without nouns: "I want the blue." Help children add the noun.

Grammar *in Action*

Time to Listen Sing to the tune of "Frère Jacques," having children call out different colored clothing each time: *Who is wearing a red sweater? Please stand up. Please stand up. Show us your red sweater. Show us your red sweater. Thank you very much. Thank you very much.*

Adjectives

Adjectives for Colors

Preteach Display a box of crayons. Pull out a crayon as you point out items in that color: *This is a red crayon. What else in this room is red? Ah, here is a red book.* Repeat with other colors. Explain: *The words* red, yellow, blue, green, orange, brown, purple, *and* black *tell more about things. They are adjectives. Adjectives tell more about a person, place, or thing. Some adjectives are the names of colors.*

Teach/Model Present the concept and provide examples:

- Some adjectives name colors.

yellow house, **red** apple, **blue** car, **green** grass, **orange** crayon, **brown** shoe, **purple** ball, **black** cat

Practice/Assess Copy and distribute page 370 and/or 371 after teaching *Adjectives for Shapes.*

Transfer Skills

Shapes

Help children understand that the word *square* can be used both as an adjective and as a shape name (noun). The word *round* is an adjective, but the shape name is *circle.*

Grammar *in Action*

Oral Language Have partners take turns describing a monster for the other to draw: *Draw two round heads. Draw a square body. Draw three oval eyes.* Afterward, have children show their monsters and describe them to the class.

Adjectives for Shapes

Preteach Point out items in the room as you draw their shapes in the air with your finger: *Here is a round rug (or clock). What else is round? Here is a square block. What else is square?* Explain: *The words* round *and* square *are adjectives. Some adjectives name shapes.*

Teach Model Present the concept and provide examples:

- Some adjectives name shapes.

round circle, **round** dot; **square** window, **square** paper; **oval** egg

Practice/Assess Copy and distribute page 370 and/or 371. Before children complete either page, review color words and shape words. (See answers on page 385.)

Adjectives for Size

Preteach Display pictures of animals of various sizes: *Here is a small mouse. Here is a big whale. A giraffe has a long neck. A turtle has short legs.* Explain: *Some adjectives describe size.* Big, small, long, *and* short *are just a few of the adjectives that describe the size of a person, place, animal, or thing.*

Teach/Model Present the concept and provide examples:

- Some adjectives describe size.

big man, **small** dog, **long** line, **short** tree

Practice/Assess Copy and distribute page 372. Discuss the characteristics of each animal. (See answers on page 385.)

Transfer Skills

Adjectives for Size
In Spanish and Vietnamese, adjectives may follow nouns, as in the name *Río Grande* ("big river"). Help children write adjectives before nouns in English.

Grammar *in Action*

Oral Language Review words for animal body parts, such as *tail, head, ears, eyes, legs.* Have children give animal clues for a partner to guess: *I am a small animal. I have long ears. I can hop.* (rabbit)

Adjectives for What Kind

Preteach Point out items in the room as you describe them: *This is an old table. What kind of table is this? (old) This is a new book. What kind of book is this? (new)* Continue with other items around the room. Explain: *The words* old *and* new *are just a few adjectives that tell what kind.*

Teach/Model Present the concept and provide examples:

- Some adjectives tell what kind.

dark socks, **cold** milk, **loud** noise, **wet** shoes, **happy** children

Practice/Assess Copy and distribute page 373. Help children describe the picture. Review the meanings of different adjectives for what kind. (See answers on page 385.)

Transfer Skills

Adjectives for What Kind
Spanish adjective endings match the gender and number of the nouns they modify. Help children see that English adjectives do not have gender or plural endings. The word *new* stays the same in *a new toy, new toys, a new teacher,* and *new teachers.* Help children practice with various adjectives and nouns.

Grammar *in Action*

Time to Listen Pose this riddle: *I went outside, and what did I find? I found a cat. Ask me what kind.* Sample answers: *Was it an old cat? Was it a sad cat?* Continue with other "found" items.

Transfer Skills

Number Words
Some English number words have cognates in other languages: the Spanish word for *three* is *tres;* the Russian word for *three* sounds similar to *tree;* and the Haitian Creole word for *six* is *sis* (pronounced like *cease*).

Grammar *in Action*

Time to Listen Teach children this rhyme. Have them point to the body parts mentioned: *I have two eyes. I have one nose. I have two arms. I have ten toes. I have five fingers on each hand. I have two legs so I can stand.* Say other parts of the body that fit the rhyme.

Adjectives for How Many

Preteach Present two groups of children, one with two boys and one with three girls. Say: *Here are two boys. Here are three girls. There are five children.* Explain: Two, three, *and* five *are number words. They can tell how many people, places, animals, or things.*

Teach/Model Present the concept and provide examples:
- Some adjectives tell how many.

three monkeys, **four** schools, **one** child, **two** feet, **five** fingers

Practice/Assess Copy and distribute page 374. Review numbers one through ten. (See answers on page 385.)

Transfer Skills

Adjectives That Compare
Many languages do not use comparative endings. Children may need extra practice with *-er* and *-est* endings. In Spanish, Korean, and Hmong, comparisons are made with phrases, similar to *more sad.* If children use *more happy* or *most old,* help them learn *happier, happiest, older,* and *oldest.*

Grammar *in Action*

Classroom Comparisons
Have pairs of children find pairs or sets of objects in the classroom to compare. For example, one eraser might be smaller than another, while one book might be the heaviest of three. Have children present their findings.

Adjectives That Compare

Preteach Draw two long lines of different lengths on the board. Point to the shorter line and say: *This line is long.* Point to the longer line and say: *This line is longer.* Write *long* and *longer.* Say: *You know that* long *is an adjective for size.* Longer *compares the two lines. Most adjectives that we can use to compare end in* -er: longer, shorter, happier. Draw a longer line. Say: *This line is the longest.* Write *longest.* Say: Longest *compares all three lines.*

Teach/Model Present the concept and provide examples:
- Add *-er* to most adjectives when you compare two persons, places, animals, or things.
- Add *-est* to most adjectives when you compare three or more persons, places, or things.

A dog is smaller than a cow.
If you see a cow, a dog, and a frog, the frog is the smallest of the three.

Practice/Assess Copy and distribute page 375. Have children read their answers aloud. (See answers on page 385.)

Adverbs

Adverbs That Tell *When* and *Where*

Preteach Say these sentences: *Yesterday we came to school.* Ask: *When did we come to school? (yesterday)* Continue: *We played outside.* Ask: *Where did we play? (outside) The word* yesterday *tells more about the verb* came. Outside *tells more about the verb* played. Yesterday *and* outside *are called* adverbs. *Adverbs tell more about verbs.*

Teach/Model Present the concept and provide examples:

- An adverb tells more about a verb.
- An adverb can tell *when* and *where* something happens.

When	I'm leaving now. I'll see you soon.
Where	I sleep here. I walk outside.

Practice/Assess Copy and distribute page 376. Encourage children to write other adverbs in the chart. (See answers on page 385.)

Adverbs That Tell *How*

Preteach Say and act out this chant: *Slowly I turn. Loudly I clap! Quietly I walk. Quickly I tap!* Explain: Slowly, loudly, quietly, *and* quickly *are adverbs. They tell* how *something happens.*

Teach/Model Present the concept and provide examples:

- An adverb can tell *how* something happens.
- Many adverbs that tell *how* end in *-ly,* like *happily* and *sadly.*

The children sit quietly and listen carefully.

Practice/Assess Copy and distribute page 377. Read the sentences aloud to children. (See answers on page 385.)

Transfer Skills

Adverb Placement and Use
If children place adverbs in unusual positions, as in *We today sang a song*, show many examples of adverbs in English sentences. If children use adverbs as nouns *(Here is good school)* provide extra practice.

Grammar *in Action*

Say When and Where
Say sentences such as *I want to play.* Have children rephrase by adding adverbs for when and where: *I want to play later. I want to play inside.*

Transfer Skills

Adverbs That Tell How
Many languages do not strongly distinguish adjectives from adverbs. Children may use adjectives as adverbs: for example, *run slow* and *talk glad.* Help children recognize adverbs with *-ly (slowly, gladly)*, but point out that not all *-ly* words are adverbs. (For example, *friendly* is an adjective.)

Grammar *in Action*

Time to Listen Write adverbs on slips of paper: *slowly, quickly, loudly, sleepily.* Display them. Have a volunteer choose one. Give a command, such as *Walk to the door.* The volunteer must walk in the manner of the adverb. The child who guesses the adverb takes the next turn.

Name ___________________________

Picturing Adjectives

Practice

- **Draw** a big tree. **Draw** red apples in it.

Assess

- **Tell** more about your tree. Use words for colors and shapes.

Name ______________________________

Adjectives for Colors and Shapes

Practice

- **Look** at the picture. **Read** the sentences.
- **Circle** each word that names a color or shape.

1. Give me some white paper, please.

2. I can draw that black dog.

3. The dog is on the round rug.

4. I will use a blue pencil.

5. I have a square eraser.

Assess

Which adjectives are the names of colors? Which adjectives tell about shapes? **Write** them here.

Colors	Shapes

Name ______________________________

Adjectives for Size

Practice

- **Look** at the pictures. **Read** the words.
- **Draw** a line from each animal to the words that tell about it.

elephant

short legs

giraffe

big ears

turtle

long neck

Assess

- **Write** or **say** a sentence about one of the animals. Use one of these words: *big, small, long,* or *short.*

____

Name ____________________________

Adjectives for What Kind

Practice

- **Look** at the picture. **Read** the sentences. **Read** the words in the box.
- **Write** the adjective from the box that completes each sentence.

1. Mom tells a ____________________ story.

2. Mom and I will drink ____________________ tea with lemon.

3. Today is a ____________________ day.

funny	cold	hot

Assess

- **Say** what kind of clothes you like to wear on a cold day.

Name ______________________________

Adjectives for How Many

Practice

- **Look** at the picture. **Read** the sentences.
- **Write** an adjective to complete each sentence. Use words from the box.

1. Hal has ____________________ basketball in his room.

2. On the wall, there are ____________________ pictures.

3. Hal has ____________________ books.

4. He has ____________________ cars.

one	two	three	four	five

Assess

- **Look** around your classroom. What do you see two of?

____

Name ___________________________

Adjectives That Compare

Practice

- **Look** at the picture. **Read** the sentences.
- **Circle** the correct adjective to complete each sentence.

1. Kuni is (taller, tallest) than Nelly.

2. Lucila is the (tallest, taller) of the three girls.

3. Kuni's dress is (long, longer) than Nelly's dress.

4. Nelly's dress is the (shorter, shortest) dress of all.

Assess

- Who wears the longest dress? Who is the shortest girl? **Write** or **say** your answers.

____

Name ______________________________

Adverbs That Tell *When* and *Where*

Practice

- **Look** at the picture. **Read** the sentences.
- **Circle** the adverb in each sentence that tells when or where.

1. Tonight my school has Open House.

2. Look, Dad. I sit here.

3. I made this picture yesterday.

4. We play outside for recess.

Assess

Which adverbs tell when? Which tell where? **Write** them here.

When	Where

Name ______________________________

Adverbs That Tell *How*

Practice

- **Look** at the picture. **Read** the sentences.
- **Write** the correct adverb in each sentence.

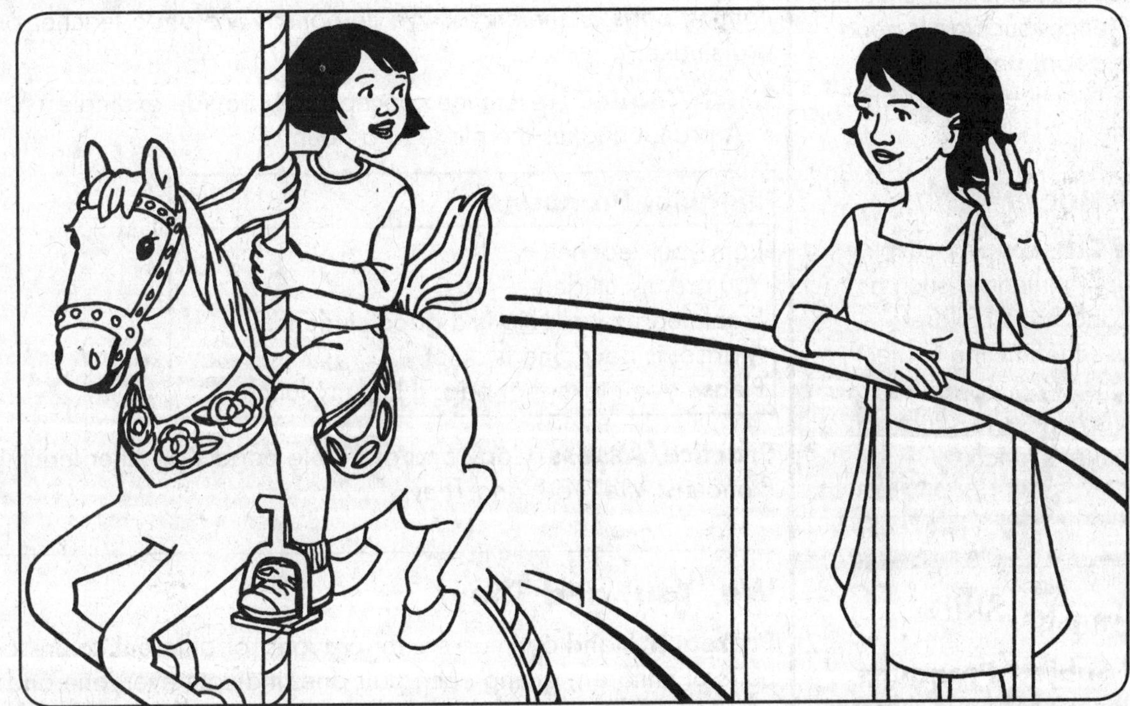

1. The music plays ______________. (loudly, carefully)

2. My horse goes around ______________. (loudly, slowly)

3. I ride my horse ______________. (happily, angrily)

4. Mom waves ______________ when she sees me. (sadly, quietly)

Assess

Write or **say** a sentence about something that is slow. Use the word *slowly*.

____

Transfer Skills

Subject Pronouns
In languages such as Spanish, Chinese, Vietnamese, Korean, and Hmong, some subject pronouns can be omitted from sentences because the context indicates the subject. If children say sentences such as *Is good* (for *It is good*) and *Am tired*, provide practice using subject pronouns.

Grammar *in Action*

In the Classroom Display and read sentences such as these, and have children rephrase them using subject pronouns: *Ana sits in this row. Max sits here. The sandwich is the teacher's lunch.*

Transfer Skills

Plural Subject Pronouns
Many languages have different words to indicate *you* singular and *you* plural. Reassure children that in English, *you* can refer to one person or more than one person.

Grammar *in Action*

Noun to Pronoun Write sentences such as these on strips: *Reina, Tran, and Cali play with cars. The dog and cat run fast. Peter and you will sit.* Cut them into subject and predicate. Create strips with *We, You,* and *They*. Have children replace the noun strips with pronoun strips. Help them read the new sentences.

Pronouns

I, You, He, She, and It

Preteach Point to yourself, and say *I am a teacher.* Point to and look at a child near you, and say *You are a student.* Point to a boy and say *He is a student.* Point to a girl and say *She is a student.* Explain: *Pronouns such as* I, you, he, *and* she *are used in place of nouns such as people's names. These pronouns are used in the naming parts of sentences. We do not say* Me am a teacher *or* Him is a student.

Teach/Model Present the concept and provide examples:
- A pronoun takes the place of a noun.

Singular Pronouns
I am your teacher. You are my student. Frank learns well. He is a good student. Marisol is new. She is quiet. Please don't take that bag. It has my lunch.

Practice/Assess Copy and distribute page 380 after teaching *Pronouns: We, You, and They.*

We, You, and They

Preteach Hand out markers (or crayons) of different colors to pairs of children, giving each pair one. Indicate everyone and say: *We all have markers.* Point to and look at a pair of children near you, and say, for example: *You have a blue marker.* Point to another pair and say: *They have a red marker.* Explain: *The words* we, you, *and* they *are pronouns. They tell about more than one.*

Teach/Model Present the concept and provide examples:
- *We, you,* and *they* tell about more than one.

Plural Pronouns
Pat and I play outside. We have fun. You and Ida take the rope. You can jump. Min and Ismael have a ball. They play soccer.

Practice/Assess Copy and distribute page 380. Review gender and number of subject pronouns. (See answers on page 385.)

Pronouns After Action Verbs

Me, You, Him, Her, and It

Preteach Display and read these sentences: *Give the book to me. She called you. That book belongs to her. I saw him yesterday.* Explain: *Pronouns such as* me, you, him, *and* her *are used after action verbs, or after words such as* for, at, with, *or* to. *They are used in the action parts of sentences. We do not say* Give the book to I *or* You saw he yesterday.

Teach/Model Present the concept and provide examples:

- Different pronouns are used in the action parts of sentences, after an action verb or preposition.
- *You* is used in either part of a sentence.

Singular Pronouns
Pedro called me. I sang "Happy Birthday" to him. I will sing her a song. She will love it.

Practice/Assess Copy and distribute page 381 after teaching *Us, You, and Them.*

Us, You, and Them

Preteach Display and read these sentences: *Li and Pam sang for us. We heard them. I will sing you a song.* Explain: *The pronouns* us, them, *and* you *tell about more than one. They are used after action verbs, or after words such as* for, at, with, *or* to.

Teach/Model Present the concept and provide examples:

- The pronouns *us, them,* and *you* are used in the action parts of sentences, after an action verb or preposition.

Plural Pronouns
Mari and I will have a race. Will you watch us? The chairs are in the way. Please move them. We will race you and Ben. We will run with you.

Practice/Assess Copy and distribute page 381. Help children describe the picture. (See answers on page 385.)

Transfer Skills

Object Pronouns
Spanish, Chinese, and Vietnamese speakers and other English learners may use subject pronouns as objects *(We like she; Yan saw they)* until they have enough practice in English to recognize and use pronoun forms well.

Grammar *in Action*

Finish the Sentence Pose open-ended sentences, cueing object pronoun endings by gesturing to different people in the room: *I will help...* [gesture toward a girl] Children should finish the sentence: *her.*

Transfer Skills

Plural Object Pronouns
Some languages distinguish the gender of *them* with two different words. Reassure children that in English, *them* is used for males, females, and things. Also, remind children that *them* does not need *-s.*

Grammar *in Action*

Time to Listen Display *us, them,* and *you.* Have children call out pronouns to finish the rhymes: *I bring these flowers for Gina and Clem. These pretty flowers are just for ______. / My friends and I ride on the bus. Come along, and ride with ______. / My very best friends are you and Sue. I'm glad that I am friends with ______!*

Name ________________________________

Pronouns

Practice

- **Look** at the picture. **Read** the sentences.
- **Circle** the correct pronoun to complete each sentence.

1. Serena and (I, me) are friends.

2. (Us, We) eat lunch together.

3. Today we had soup. (It, They) was very good.

4. Serena did not like the soup. (She, He) ate the sandwich.

Assess

- **Write** or **say** a sentence about the friends at lunch. Start with the pronoun *They*.

____

Name ________________________________

Pronouns After Action Verbs

Practice

- **Look** at the picture. **Read** the sentences.
- **Circle** the correct pronoun to complete each sentence.

1. My grandfather made a paper airplane. I am holding (them, it).
2. My sister wants an airplane. He will make one for (her, him).
3. We like the airplanes. We will fly (they, them) outside.
4. Grandpa will play with (us, we).

Assess

- **Write** or **say** a sentence about the paper airplanes. Use the pronoun *them*.

____

page 316: Picturing Nouns

Practice
People: adults, children;
Animals: bird, dogs;
Things: ball, park, kites, table, tree

Assess
Answers will vary. Children may name any of the nouns above.

page 317: Nouns

Practice
People: boy, girl, woman, man;
Places: zoo, Butterfly Garden park;
Animals: bird, butterfly, elephant, zebra;
Things: table, sign, tree, flower

Assess
Answers will vary. Children should write or say the names of items found in the classroom.

page 318: Picturing Proper Nouns

Practice
Answers will vary. Make sure children's names begin with capital letters.

Assess
Answers will vary. Explain that the friend's name is a special name that begins with a capital letter.

page 319: Special Names

Practice
Names of People: Tom, Ann, Kim, Mrs. Garza;
Names of Animals: Buddy, Daisy, Ruby;
Names of Places: Soto Town Park, Tigers Field

Assess
Answers will vary. Children should write or say the names of specific people and places, beginning each name with a capital letter if writing.

page 320: Special Titles

Practice
1. Mr. Ed Green; **2.** Miss Ann Cho;
3. Dr. Sara Mesa; **4.** Mr. Sam Myers.

Assess
Answers will vary. Verify that children include a title such as Mr., Ms., Dr., etc., when writing each name of adults they know.

page 321: Days, Months, and Holidays

Practice
1. Memorial Day; **2.** Mother's Day;
3. Thursday, May 19; **4.** on Tuesdays

Assess
Sunday

page 322: One and More Than One

Practice
Singular Nouns: tree, sun, nest;
Plural Nouns: girls, birds, flowers, blocks

Assess
Answers will vary, but should include two singular and three plural nouns. Children should write or say the names of items found in the classroom.

page 323: Plural Nouns That Add *-s* and *-es*

Practice
Nouns that add -s: swings, clouds, hats
Nouns that add -es: benches, bushes, dresses

Assess
Children should add *-es* to *box: boxes*. Sentences will vary, but should include the word *boxes*.

page 324: Plural Nouns That Change Spelling

Practice
women, children, mice

Assess
men, women, children

page 325: Possessive Nouns

Practice
1. Pal's; **2.** dogs'; **3.** cat's; **4.** frogs'

Assess
Answers will vary. Watch for correct use of the apostrophe in written responses.

page 332: Picturing Verbs

Practice
Children should draw themselves playing and sitting.

Assess
Answers will vary, but students may use any of the action verbs they have learned.

page 333: Action Verbs

Practice
1. sit; **2.** sing; **3.** look

Assess
Answers will vary, but children may write sentences

such as: *I eat grapes; I run; I play a game.*

page 334: Verbs That Add *-s*

Practice

1. kicks; **2.** runs; **3.** stops

Assess

Answers will vary, but children may write sentences such as *The mom claps* or *The mom sits.*

page 335: Verbs That Add *-s, -es*

Practice

1. fixes; **2.** hugs; **3.** kisses

Assess

Answers will vary, but children may say a sentence such as *Mom washes the doll.*

page 336: Verbs That Do Not Add *-s*

Practice

1. ride; **2.** run; **3.** sings; **4.** smile

Assess

Answers will vary, but children may write a sentence such as *Mom and Dad sing the song.*

page 337: Verbs for the Past

Practice

1. visited; **2.** baked; **3.** cleaned

Assess

Answers will vary, but children may write a sentence such as *I baked a cake.*

page 338: Verbs for the Future

Practice

Mama duck <u>will teach</u> her babies to swim. Soon, the baby ducks <u>will grow</u> big and strong. They <u>will swim</u> in the pond with no help.

Assess

Answers will vary, but children may write a sentence such as *The ducks will teach their babies to swim.*

page 339: *Am, Is, Are, Was,* and *Were*

Practice

1. was; **2.** am; **3.** were; **4.** is; **5.** are

Assess

Answers will vary, but children may write a sentence such as *The girl is sick.*

page 340: Verbs for Present and for Past

Practice

1. walked; **2.** plays; **3.** smells; **4.** brushed

Assess

Answers will vary, but children may write a sentence that includes a verb in the past, present, or future tense.

page 341: Verbs for Past, Present, and Future

Practice

1. plant; **2.** planted; **3.** will plant

Assess

Answers will vary, but children may write a sentence that includes the present or past tense of *plant.*

page 342: Contractions With *Not*

Practice

1. didn't; **2.** wasn't; **3.** don't

Assess

Answers will vary, but students may write a sentence such as *I don't like to get wet.*

page 343: More Contractions

Practice

1. I'm; **2.** I'll; **3.** You're

Assess

Answers will vary, but students may write a sentence such as *He's going to play with his dad.*

page 351: Meaningful Word Groups

Practice

Children should draw a cat for the first group of words and a cat wearing a hat or playing with a hat for the second.

Assess

The big cat has a hat is a sentence.

page 352: Picturing Sentences: Naming Parts

Practice

The sentence is about the dog.

Assess

Answers will vary; possible sentences: *The dog runs in the park; The dog can run fast.*

page 353: Naming Parts of Sentences (Subjects)

Practice
1. Mom; **2.** Ted; **3.** The pan

Assess
Answers will vary; possible sentences:
The pan is big; Ted will eat.

page 354: Picturing Sentences: Action Parts

Practice
The action part is *holds a book.*

Assess
Answers will vary; possible sentences:
I hold a book.

page 355: Action Parts of Sentences (Predicates)

Practice
1. play with my cat; **2.** barks at him;
3. runs away

Assess
Answers will vary; possible sentences:
I call my cat; I run after him.

page 356: Word Order

Practice
1. I drew a picture; **2.** This is my house;
3. My house is green and white.

Assess
Answers will vary, but make sure children start sentences with the subject or use another word order that makes sense.

page 357: Complete Sentences

Practice
1. The woman sells oranges. **2.** She cuts the oranges.
3. You can buy honey too.

Assess
Answers will vary; possible sentences:
She sells lemons and oranges at the market; Oranges and lemons are round.

page 358: Telling Sentences

Practice
1. This is Lobo's party. **2.** We gave Lobo a new toy.
3. We had fruit. **4.** Lobo had fun.

Assess
Answers will vary; possible statements:
We ate the fruit; Lobo liked the toy.

page 359: Questions

Practice
1. Where are you? **2.** Are you here?
3. Can you run fast now?

Assess
Answers will vary; possible questions:
Can you see me? Will I find you?

page 360: Exclamations

Practice
Girl swinging would say: "I am going high!"
Girl not swinging would say: "Push me too!"
The father would say: "My arms are tired!"

Assess
Answers will vary. Encourage children to imagine themselves on a roller coaster or other fast ride. Some suggestions: *This is fun! I want more rides!*

page 361: Commands

Practice
Sentences 2 and 3 are commands.

Assess
Answers will vary, but children may write *Get bread, peanut butter, and jelly. Put peanut butter on one slice. Put jelly on the other slice. Cut the sandwich. Eat the sandwich.*

page 362: Compound Sentences and Commas

Practice
1. Dad made a birdhouse, and I will put it in the tree.
2. I got the hammer and nails, but only Dad used them.
3. Dad made the birdhouse, and now we can paint it.
4. We look all over, but we do not see the paintbrush!

Assess
Make sure children pause at each comma.

page 363: More About Commas

Practice
We took a trip on May 14, 2005. We went to Santa Barbara, California. We saw Rosa, Gus, Maria, and Eva. We came home on Sunday, May 22.

Assess
Answers will vary, but children should use a comma after each item in the series.

page 364: Quotation Marks

Practice
1. "I am hungry!" said Olivia. **2.** John said, "Good! It's time for lunch." **3.** "Let's make sandwiches. What kind do you like?" asked Olivia. **4.** "I like ham and cheese sandwiches," answered John. **5.** Olivia said, "I like ham and cheese too." **6.** "Let's make ham and cheese sandwiches, then!" John said.

Assess
Answers will vary. Children should write a sentence that includes quotation marks.

page 365: Paragraphs

Practice
Soccer is a fun sport. Everyone has to follow the rules. Many people enjoy the game. Coaches have a big job. They make it fun and safe for everyone!

Assess
Answers will vary, but children may explain that a paragraph is a group of sentences that contain a main idea and details.

page 370: Picturing Adjectives

Practice
Drawings will vary, but children should draw a tree with red apples in it.

Assess
Answers will vary. Children may say their tree is tall and green. They may say the apples are round and red.

page 371: Adjectives for Colors and Shapes

Practice
1. white; **2.** black; **3.** round; **4.** blue; **5.** square

Assess
Colors: white, black, blue; Shapes: round, square

page 372: Adjectives for Size

Practice
elephant—big ears; giraffe—long neck;
turtle—short legs

Assess
Answers will vary. Children may write a sentence such as *The elephant has big ears.*

page 373: Adjectives for What Kind

Practice
1. funny; **2.** hot; **3.** cold

Assess
Answers will vary, but children may mention warm clothing.

page 374: Adjectives for How Many

Practice
1. one; **2.** three; **3.** five; **4.** four

Assess
Answers will vary. Verify that children use *two* as an adjective.

page 375: Adjectives That Compare

Practice
1. taller; **2.** tallest; **3.** longer; **4.** shortest

Assess
Lucila wears the longest dress; Nelly is the shortest girl.

page 376: Adverbs That Tell *When* and *Where*

Practice
1. Tonight; **2.** here; **3.** yesterday; **4.** outside

Assess
When: tonight, yesterday; Where: here, outside

page 377: Adverbs That Tell *How*

Practice
1. loudly; **2.** slowly; **3.** happily; **4.** quietly

Assess
Answers will vary, but children may write a sentence such as *A turtle walks slowly.*

page 380: Pronouns

Practice
1. I; **2.** We; **3.** It; **4.** She

Assess
Answers will vary, but children may write a sentence such as *They eat lunch.*

page 381: Pronouns After Action Verbs

Practice
1. it; **2.** her; **3.** them; **4.** us

Assess
Answers will vary, but children may write or say a sentence such as *The children fly them.*

Part 5
Workshops for English Language Learners

Contents

Introduction to English Language Learner Workshops

To develop their skills in English, English language learners need instruction that integrates speaking, listening, reading, and writing. While core lesson content encourages the development of these skills, English language learners need targeted instruction to navigate listening and speaking in situations that, for native speakers, come naturally. Children first using spoken English may have difficulty with:

- knowing appropriate times to use formal and informal English
- using the correct syntax patterns for sentences, including placement of nouns, verbs, adjectives, and prepositions
- expressing opinions and feelings
- using the transactional language of the classroom
- retelling or summarizing a message in English

In addition, children who are newcomers or who have not interacted with instructional materials in English may have difficulty with the following:

- interacting with environmental print and understanding what information they can get from reading the words around them
- using classroom resources, such as maps and dictionaries
- expanding their knowledge and use of academic vocabulary words
- using graphic organizers to record ideas and organize information

For teachers, it is vitally important to remember that learning English is about more than learning words and their meanings; it is also about comfortably speaking and comprehending spoken English. Speakers and listeners need to master a complex set of skills that includes producing sounds, stressing patterns, and using correct intonation. Speakers need to take turns, rephrase spoken language in their own words, and provide feedback.

Each one of these lessons covers a particular topic with both a lesson for the teacher and a reproducible blackline master for children. The lessons are designed to be fluid and needs-based. Some of the lessons will correspond to the core lessons. Others can be introduced when you notice that children need the instruction. The workshop on group discussion, for example, can be introduced when you notice that children are struggling to use the transactional give-and-take language in group discussions.

All workshops follow a format:

- A **Preteach** section provides simple scripted language that allows you to introduce the strategy or skill and explain why it is important for children to use.
- The **Teach/Model** section involves children while you carefully scaffold instruction in the skill or strategy.
- In the **Practice** section, children begin to take ownership of the skill.
- Each workshop includes an **Assess** section, with ideas for both assessment and corrective feedback.
- **Leveled Support** suggestions allow children to practice the skills at their individual levels of proficiency and progress from level to level.
- An accompanying **blackline master** allows for practice with the skill. The master often includes a rubric for self-assessment or a word bank to be used multiple times.

Many of the blackline masters can be used multiple times. When you see a rubric, for example, have children rate themselves on the first learning of a new skill. Gauge children's growth in that skill and reintroduce the master and the rubric, allowing children to measure their own progress. Based on children's needs, consider how to integrate the workshops into your instruction and use them multiple times to measure children's growth as users of classroom and conversational English. Graphic organizers such as webs and outline forms can be duplicated for use multiple times. Assess children's use of these visuals and use your informal assessment to plan for instruction.

Use Informal English

Preteach Model informal language for children and explain: *The words I use depend on who I am talking to and why I am speaking. I use some kinds of words when talking to certain adults, or people that I don't know well. I use different words when I am talking with my friends or family. When talking to friends or family, I might use words that are not serious, like okay, or hi. I might not always say whole sentences. I usually don't have to plan ahead what I am going to say. It's more like having a conversation.*

Teach/Model With a volunteer, act out the scene on the left side of the page. Model using informal language, such as sentence fragments. Then model rating your knowledge using the rubric.

Practice Direct children to look at the second picture. Explain that in the picture, two friends are talking at a party. Why would their language be informal? (*They are friends having fun at a party. They do not need to speak in a serious way.*) What phrases might the friend say? (*What fun! Hooray!*) For additional practice, children can draw another scenario that calls for informal English and use that drawing as the basis for roleplay. As children role-play, work with them to create a bank of words and phrases that they use when they are with their friends or family.

Assess Assess children's conversations to clear up any misconceptions about informal English. Review children's ratings. Revisit the workshop so that students can reevaluate their progress in recognizing speaking situations in which informal language is acceptable and using appropriate language.

Beginning Have children do a simple role-play activity in which one child acts as a child in class and the other acts as a new child who is trying to find a certain room in the building. The children may use informal English.

Intermediate Ask children to work with partners to role-play a conversation with a brother or sister. Remind children that this kind of talking is not usually as serious as when talking to some adults or people that we don't know well. But these words should not be rude.

Advanced/Advanced High Have children create new scenarios where they might use informal language and model appropriate language they might use and hear.

Name ______________________________

Act out what is happening in the picture. Say what the people would be saying.

Draw a situation in which you could use informal English.

Circle the picture for each sentence. Tell how you speak with friends and family.

I am polite when I speak to friends or family.

I know when I can use words like *okay* or *hi*.

I listen to others before I speak.

Use Formal English

Transfer Skills

Some languages, such as Spanish, French, and Arabic, feature formal language. The form of the word used depends on the audience and occasion. As you teach these children about formal language, compare these instances to children's experiences with their home languages.

Preteach Model formal language for children and explain: *The words I use depend on who I am talking to and why I am speaking. When I am talking with older people or to bigger groups, I use more serious language. When I say someone's name, I say* Mrs. *or* Mr. *I don't use words like,* hi *or* okay. *I might say* hello *or* very well. *My speech may be slower. I might take more time to think about what I am going to say.*

Teach/Model With a volunteer, act out the scene on the left side of the page. Model using formal language, such as titles. Then model rating your knowledge using the rubric. *When I speak to a teacher or other adult, I call them* Miss, Mr., *and* Mrs. *I ask questions using polite words, such as* please.

Practice Direct children to look at the second picture. Explain that in the picture, a girl is introducing a friend to her grandparents. Why would she use formal language? (*to show respect for her grandparents*) What phrases might the friend say? *(Pleased to meet you.)* For additional practice, children can draw another scenario that calls for formal English and use that drawing as the basis for role-play. As children role-play, work with them to create a bank of words and phrases used in formal English for their reference.

Assess Assess children's conversations to clear up any misconceptions about formal language. Review children's ratings. Revisit the workshop so that children can reevaluate their progress in recognizing formal speaking situations and using appropriate language.

Beginning Have children do a simple role-play activity in which one child acts as a child and the other as the principal. The child should use formal language in greeting the principal.

Intermediate Ask children to work with partners to role-play introducing themselves in a formal situation, like a club meeting. Write out the children's introductions and have them read them back to you. Identify phrases that make the speech formal, such as *It's nice to meet you.*

Advanced/Advanced High Have children create new scenarios where they might use formal language and model appropriate language they might use and hear.

Name ____

Act out what is happening in the picture. Say what the people would be saying.

Circle the picture for each sentence. Tell how you speak to adults.

When I talk to adults:

I use *Mr., Mrs., Ms.,* and *Miss* when saying names.

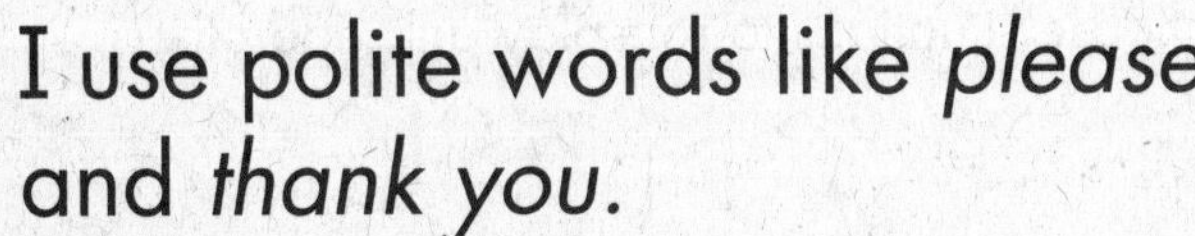

I use polite words like *please* and *thank you.*

When I talk to a group:

I think about what I am going to say.

I slow down my words.

Distinguish Between Formal and Informal English

Teaching Tip
The use of formal and informal language depends on social context. Help children understand that the type of language is dependent on who they are speaking to, their familiarity with the speaker, the purpose for speaking, and the larger audience. Give paired examples and ask children which example would require more formal English, such as: *You are playing a board game with your friend. His mom asks if you would like a snack.*

Preteach Explain: *Informal language is more casual or relaxed. You might talk this way with your friends. Formal language does not use casual language, like slang. You might use formal language more with adults, like your teachers.* Have children name differences between formal and informal language. Then write these examples of informal English on the board. Have children say the same phrases in more formal English. Examples: *Hi, teach, How are ya'? What's up?*

Teach/Model With a volunteer, act out the first scene of the child shaking hands with an adult. Ask children to identify if they would use formal or informal English. Why would they use that type of English? What words or phrases would they use? *When I speak to a teacher or other adult, I use titles such as* Miss, Mr., *and* Mrs. *If I am meeting them for the first time, I might say things like* How do you do? *or* It is nice to meet you.

Practice Direct children to look at the second picture. Have them identify if this is a formal or informal speaking situation. With partners, have them take turns telling what the children might say to each other when skating. Model using informal language or slang, such as referring to a friend as *dude* or talking about *grinding* on their skateboards.

Assess Have children use the T-chart to record situations in which they would use formal or informal English in the correct columns. Assess their placements of the situations to see if they need more support in distinguishing between when to use formal and informal English. Have them choose situations to role-play and add other situations to the chart.

Beginning Show children magazine pictures of various settings (e.g., a business meeting, family watching television). Ask the children to indicate whether the people in the situation would use formal or informal English.

Intermediate Write an informal conversation on the board. (Sample: *Hey John. Wanna play a game?*) Have the children work with partners to repeat the conversation. Then, have them role-play the conversation again, this time substituting formal language for the informal.

Advanced/Advanced High Have children work with partners to talk about a soccer game. The first conversation should be telling a friend about a game. The second conversation should be a recap of the game for the school announcements.

Name ______________________________

Act out what is happening in the picture. Say what the people would be saying.

Decide if the language you used was formal or informal.

Read each situation. Write each situation in the chart under *Formal English* or *Informal English.*

Write and share your own situations. Have others decide if they are formal or informal.

playing a game with friends
meeting a new teacher
asking for help at the store
helping a younger brother

Formal English	Informal English

Give Directions

Teaching Tip
Have children collect examples of directions, such as recipes, or directions for putting something together. Discuss how they are the same, such as clear steps and sequence words to keep steps in order. Display examples for children to use as models.

Preteach *I am going to give you directions for making a cheese sandwich: Last, eat the sandwich. Next, put the bread slices together. Second, put the cheese on the bread. First, take out two pieces of bread and some cheese. Did those directions make sense? What was wrong? They did not make sense because they are out of order! When we give directions, we need to be sure the steps are clear. The steps need to be in order.*

Teach/Model Provide a simple scenario for children, such as *I want to give directions for getting from our classroom to the lunchroom.* Ask children to provide steps as you write them on the board. Help them to use sequence (*order*) words, such as *first, next,* and *last.* Guide them to use clear directions: *How can we make that direction easier to understand? Can we break that up into more than one step? Are those steps in the right order? Can you describe that step with more details?* Read the directions back. Can children use the directions to find the lunchroom? As children form the directions with you, write sequence words on the board for children's reference.

Practice Place children in groups and ask them to give directions orally for a simple task, like sharpening a pencil, folding a sheet of paper, or drawing a triangle. One child can give directions while the others complete the task. Do the directions make sense? Guide practice as needed. Have volunteers share the best examples with the class.

Assess Listen in as children give directions. Assess their ability to provide clear steps and use sequence words.

Beginning On index cards, write steps or draw simple pictures for a simple process. Put one step per card. Give the cards to groups of children and have them work together to place the cards in order. Then children can say or read the directions aloud.

Intermediate/Advanced Provide out-of-order directions without order words. Have children place the directions in order and say them aloud, inserting sequence words to add organization.

Advanced High Have children work with partners to create a list of sequence words they can use in giving directions. Then have them give directions for a simple task, using words from their list.

Name ____

Write order words in the box. Look at the examples.

Sequence Words	
first	**next**
second	**last**

Use the sentence starters to give directions.

First, you should . . .
Second, . . .
Next, . . .
After that, . . .
Finally, . . .

Ask a friend to follow your directions.Can your friend follow them? How can you make them better?

Circle the picture for each sentence. Tell how you give directions.

I can give directions with more than one or two steps.

I use order words (*first, second, next, last*).

My directions are clear. People can follow them.

Teaching Tip
As children are able, make directions more complex. Start with simple one- or two-step directions for children to follow, both oral and written. Then gradually increase the complexity of the directions you give and have children restate the directions to clarify meaning.

Preteach *I have to follow directions every day. This morning, I followed directions for making breakfast in the microwave. I follow directions when I drive to school. I had to read the directions for using the DVD player when I showed you a video. And my teacher books have directions for teaching lessons. It is important to look at the steps in directions and read them (or listen) carefully to follow them.*

Teach/Model *Listen as I give you directions.* Give children directions for gestures, such as *First, raise your hand. Next, stand up. Then jump up and down twice.* Point out important features of directions: time order words that organize directions and steps that need to be completed in order.

Practice Have children work in pairs to complete the worksheet. In the first part, they should cut out the pictures and place them in the correct order. Then they can use the pictures to say the steps of the directions. In the second part, they should draw steps. They can trade drawings with partners to give directions.

Assess Assess children's oral and written work to check their ability to follow directions. Be sure that children understand they need to look for important details in directions and follow steps in order. Help them to understand that restating directions helps to clarify understanding.

Beginning Give simple, one- or two-step directions for children to follow. Ask them to restate the most important details of each step before they follow it.

Intermediate Gather directions for children, such as recipes or directions for making or building simple things at home. Have them look for sequence words or other clues to order as well as the important details in the steps. Discuss in small groups, then practice giving each other directions.

Advanced/Advanced High Provide directions for making or doing something. Have children work in small groups to discuss the directions and complete the tasks.

Name ______________________________

Look at the pictures.

Cut them out and place them in order.

Talk about the directions. Can you follow them?

Draw three pictures. Show three steps in brushing your teeth.

Cut out the pictures. Mix them up.

Give them to a classmate. Put them in the right order.

Use Classroom Language

Teaching Tip
While some classroom language is straightforward transactional language that children need to practice in order to learn, other classroom language is idiomatic and may be confusing for children. When you tell children to "line up," for example, they may think of drawing a line or putting up a line like a clothesline. Tell children the meanings of the idiomatic phrases used in the classroom in language they can understand.

Preteach *Everyday in class, we communicate with each other. We ask questions and give directions. We work in groups. Children listen and ask for help from classmates and from the teacher. We have some words and sentences that we use often in the classroom. It's important for us to know how to use classroom language to get help, work with others, and understand what is happening around us in class.*

Teach/Model Ask several children to assist you in a role-play. *Please take out your books. Open your books to page 15.* Assist children as needed to open their books to the correct page. *I used classroom language. You hear your teacher ask all the time to open your books to a certain page. That means that you can see that page in front of you.* Pairs can role-play, taking turns saying the classroom language and opening their books to the correct page.

Practice Help children gather examples of classroom language to record on a chart in the classroom. Use the worksheet to get started. Have children role-play using the language. As children think of more examples of classroom language, add the examples to the wall chart.

Assess As children role-play and use classroom language, listen to the conversations and clear up any misconceptions. Continue to have children add examples to the worksheet and the chart in the classroom.

Beginning Give simple examples of classroom language for children to use, role-playing a scenario such as a student asking another student or the teacher to repeat what he or she said.

Intermediate/Advanced Have children role-play a scenario in which they are trying to understand a new word. They can use classroom language such as *What does ______ mean? How do you say ______ in English?*

Advanced High Have children create reference sheets or posters to use in the classroom that capture various examples of classroom language. Children can illustrate the posters to show the situations in which they use the classroom language and teach those words and phrases to others.

Name ____

Look at the pictures.

Act out the pictures with a partner.

Say the words that you would use. Some ideas are on the page.

Circle the rating for each sentence. Tell how you use classroom language.

I ask for help in English.			
I can help a classmate in English			
I understand the teacher's directions.			

Learn New Words

Teaching Tip
Make multiple copies of p. 401. As you introduce words tied to the reading selections, as well as words from content areas, children can add to their own dictionaries of new words. Challenge children to refer to their dictionaries and use the new words four times in their writing and speaking to internalize meaning.

Preteach Copy p. 401 or display it. Explain: *Sometimes, when we read or hear a word we think we don't know, there may be a little bit that we do know about it. Is there a part of the word that I know? I also try to remember where I've seen or heard this word before. Then I try to describe the word in a way that is easy for me to understand. Sometimes I even draw a picture to help me remember what the word means. Then I use the word many times so I don't forget the meaning.*

Teach/Model Model how to use the chart with a word from a reading selection or from content-area studies, such as *reptile.* Write the word on the line. Then model rating your knowledge: *A* 1 *means that I don't know anything about this word. A* 4 *means I know it so well that I can tell someone else what it means. I understand what a reptile is, but I'm not sure I could tell someone else what it means. I'll give it a* 3. Then explain or describe a reptile and write a description. Be sure that your description uses simple language that all children understand.

Practice Write a word for children to copy on the chart. Pronounce the word, then have children say it three times. Ask children to rate their knowledge of the word. Then guide children to describe the word to build understanding. Give an example of how the word relates to a class experience, tell a story that includes the word, or show a picture that defines the word. After you have defined the word, children should create their own descriptions of the word on their charts. Children can work in pairs or small groups.

Assess Assess children's word descriptions to clear up any misconceptions about the words. Look over word understanding ratings and periodically have children reevaluate their understandings of the words. Give children multiple opportunities to listen, speak, read, and write with the new words, to internalize meaning.

Beginning Rather than write word meanings, children can draw and label pictures of the words.

Intermediate Have children use the words in simple spoken sentences that they share with partners. Listen in for correct word use.

Advanced/Advanced High Children can use a dictionary or glossary to reinforce their understandings of the words.

Name ________________________________

Write the word on the line.

Rate how well you understand the word.

1 I don't know the word.

2 I think I know what the word means.

3 I know the word. I can use it in a sentence.

4 I can teach this word to someone else.

Describe the word in a way that helps you understand it.

Word: ____________ My Understanding 1 2 3 4

Describe the word: ______________________________

____

Word: ____________ My Understanding 1 2 3 4

Describe the word: ______________________________

____

Word: ____________ My Understanding 1 2 3 4

Describe the word: ______________________________

____

Ask Clarifying Questions

Teaching Tip
Write the list of the question starters on chart paper for children to use as a reference for speaking and writing. Be sure to pause often during teaching or giving directions. Children need wait time to process the language. Give multiple opportunities to ask questions if children need clarification.

Preteach *If I don't understand something, I need to ask the person speaking to repeat what they said. Then I can understand it. That is called* clarifying. *I ask questions to be sure I understand. I also ask questions when I am reading. I ask questions before I read, while I read, and after I read. That helps me understand what I am reading.*

Teach/Model Work with a child to role-play a situation in which you would ask a clarifying question. Have the child give you simple directions for doing something. As the student speaks, find an opportunity to ask a question such as *What does that mean? Can you repeat that, please?* or *How do you do that?*

Practice Share the worksheet with children and talk about situations in which children would use each of the clarifying questions. Then point out the question-starters. Have children use the question-starters to ask questions about a selection you have recently read.

Assess As children role-play asking clarifying questions, assess their ability to ask the questions in appropriate situations. Provide multiple opportunities to practice using question starters. Assess children's ability to use those question words to form questions that make sense.

Beginning Have children role-play situations with you in which they ask for assistance for completing a math problem or other classroom task.

Intermediate/Advanced Have children work in small groups to identify questions they would ask the teacher, their parents, or other children in a group to clarify their understanding.

Advanced High Have student use the "5Ws and an H" to ask and answer questions about a reading selection.

Name ____________________

Look at the examples of questions.

Use them when speaking with classmates and your teachers.

Read clues in the word box for help.

right	wrong	again	slower	louder	help
what	where	when	how	first	next

"Is this right?"

"Can you please help me?"

"What should I do next?"

Use these sentence frames to ask questions. Use the sentence frames to answer questions, too.

Who is ________? That person is ________.

What is ________? That is ________.

When did ________ happen? It happened ________.

Where is ________? The ________ is ________.

Why did ________ happen? It happened because ________.

Use Classroom Resources

Teaching Tip
Place labels on various classroom resources (maps, dictionaries, calendar, computers, and others you may have in the room) to help children remember the names of the resources. Model using various resources as you read, write, and look for locations. Think aloud to demonstrate how to use these resources.

Preteach *I was reading a story, and I found a word I didn't know. I tried to figure out what the word meant from reading the words around it, but I still needed help. I asked my friends, but they didn't know either. So I used this.* (Show a dictionary.) *A dictionary is a classroom resource. It's a tool I can use to find out word meanings.* Model how to use a dictionary and its features: guide words, pronunciations, and definitions.

Teach/Model Draw attention to the worksheet with the list of classroom resources. Start with the first one. *A map shows the locations of places. I'll circle the answer about a place. Why would I use a map? I'd use a map to find the capital of our state. I'd use a map to figure out how to get somewhere. I'd use a map to locate lakes, oceans, or countries.*

Practice As you consider the calender, dictionary, and clock with children, have children consider how and why they use the resources. The worksheet can be completed as an ongoing activity. Be sure to think aloud as you use various resources and demonstrate how and why to use them. Children can add resources that are particular to your classroom.

Assess Assess children's ability to choose appropriate resources. For example, they would use a computer to find out more information on a topic or a calendar to find an important date or holiday.

Beginning Have children work in pairs to find a holiday or important date on a calendar, or find their home state on a map.

Intermediate/Advanced Have children work in pairs to use a picture dictionary to find a word from a reading selection. Help them restate the definition in their own words.

Advanced High Have small groups of children use a classroom resource such as a map to locate directions, cities, and physical features.

Name ____________________

Read the name of the resource.
Think about why you would use it.
Circle the correct answer.

Classroom Resources

map
I use this to find a place.
I use this to find a word.

calendar
I use this to find a word.
I use this to tell what day it is.

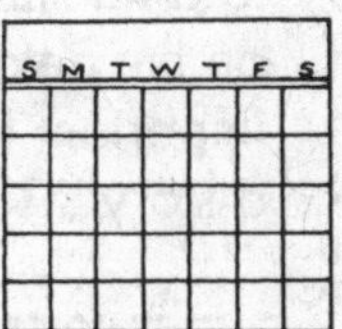

dictionary
I use this to find a place.
I use this to find a word.

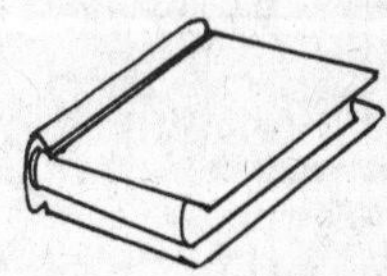

clock
I use this to tell the time.
I use this to call a friend.

What else do you use in your classroom?
List ideas here.

Retell in Your Own Words

Teaching Tip
Remind children that when we explain something in our own words, we don't need to tell all the details, just the important ones. Help children sort details into categories: *need to know* and *nice to know.* Help children summarize both written material and spoken messages. You can apply the same to a retelling: focus on the details that are important in telling a story.

Preteach *I saw a movie yesterday. When my friends asked me about it, I didn't tell every detail from the beginning to end. Instead, I told the most important things. This is called summarizing. I summarize things I see, things I read, and things I hear. When I summarize, I know that I have sorted out the most important details. A summary includes important things, not everything. I do the same thing when I tell a story. I tell important things about the people or animals in the story and the things they do. Some details are not as important in helping us understand the whole story.*

Teach/Model Ask children to listen carefully as you read a short passage aloud. After you read, ask children to contribute to a summary of the passage. Help frame their thinking as you list their ideas to create a summary. Help them distinguish between the need-to-know details and the nice-to-know details. Have pairs of children read the complete summary together. Then reread the passage. Have pairs decide if the summary lists the most important details. What should be added or changed? Discuss and clarify answers. Repeat this process with a story to focus on retelling.

Practice Have children use the graphic organizer on the worksheet to list details from a written or spoken passage or story. In the box at the bottom, children can write summaries. Their summaries should be short. Ask children to read their summaries aloud and compare them with their classmates. The worksheet can also be used to retell a story. Details might be characters and events. If necessary, have children use the details to dictate a summary. They can copy the summary that you have written.

Assess Assess children's summaries and retellings to be sure that children have included only important details. Ask questions to guide their thinking for example, *Why is this detail important? Do we need to know this information? Will we be able to understand the story without it?*

Beginning Have children orally summarize a simple spoken message or a simple text, such as a comic strip. They can work in pairs to practice, then share oral summaries with the group.

Intermediate Provide a simple text and a sample summary or retelling that is missing some information. Ask children to read and discuss in pairs. *What details are missing?* Next, provide a sample summary or retelling that includes too much information. *What details don't need to be included?*

Advanced/Advanced High Ask children to work in pairs to create directions for summarizing or retelling. Have them share their directions and sample summaries with other children.

Name ___________________________________

Use the graphic organizer to list important details.

Write a summary in the box.

Say the summary aloud.

Use the summary starters if you need to.

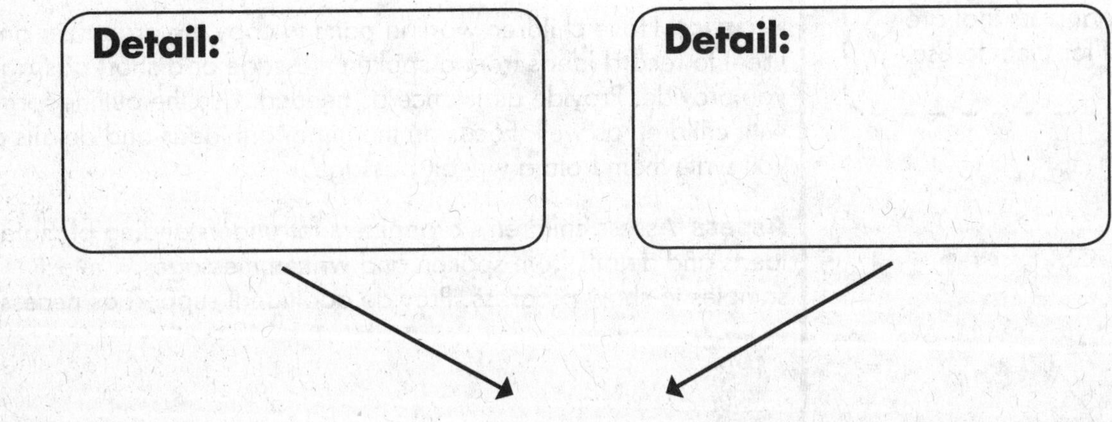

Summary language:

In summary, . . .

The most important ideas are . . .

What we need to remember is . . .

Take Notes/ Create an Outline

Teaching Tip
Provide graphic organizers for taking notes, such as concept webs, T-charts, outline forms, and other organizers you plan to use with children. As children work with different types of note taking, they will find the organizers that are easiest for them to use.

Preteach *When I meet with other teachers, I listen for important ideas and take notes. You do the same thing in class. When you listen you write down important ideas. When you read you write down important ideas too. Writing down ideas, or taking notes, helps you remember them later.*

Teach/Model Model using the web graphic organizer on the worksheet. Tell children that the web organizer is great for writing down details about one idea. Think aloud as you differentiate between main idea and details and place them on the web organizer.

Practice Have children work in pairs to copy the organizer and use it to record ideas from a spoken message or a short passage you provide. Provide assistance as needed. Use the outline form with children as well. Focus on the important ideas and details as you write them from a written passage.

Assess Assess children's organizers for understanding of main ideas and details from spoken and written messages. Collect samples to show progress. Provide additional support as necessary.

Beginning Guide pairs to create a web organizer about a simple passage. Have them use the organizer to retell the important ideas of the passage to a partner.

Intermediate Write important ideas and details from a familiar passage on index cards. Have children sort the cards before they record details in the outline. Then they can use their outlines to summarize the important ideas of the passage for a partner.

Advanced/Advanced High Ask children to work on organizers independently. They can share with partners and summarize their notes.

Name ____________________

Concept Web

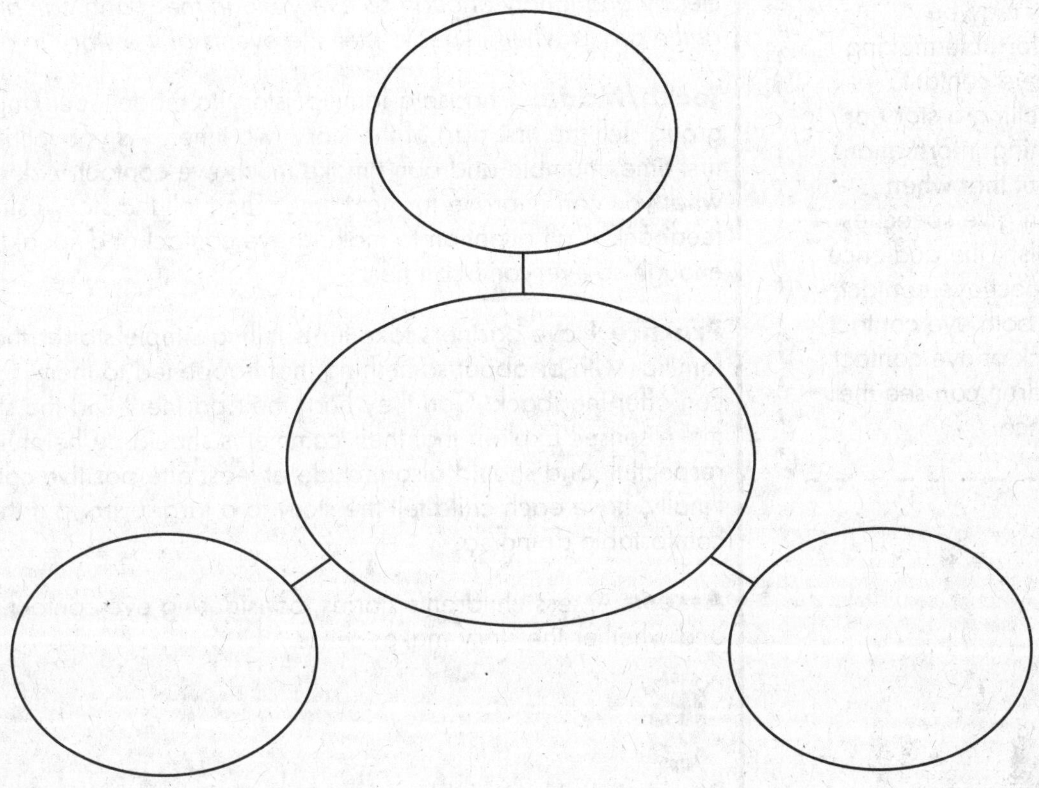

Outline

I. Main idea ____________________

A. Detail ____________________

B. Detail ____________________

II. Main idea ____________________

A. Detail ____________________

B. Detail ____________________

Give a Speech

Transfer Skills
Children of some cultures may be uncomfortable making direct eye contact when telling a story or explaining information. Point out that when children give speeches in English, the audience will expect eye contact. Model both eye contact and lack of eye contact so children can see the difference.

Preteach *When I am telling a story to a group, the voice I use is different than the voice I use when talking to a friend. I speak clearly and loudly enough so everyone in the group can hear. I look at the group when I speak. I tell the events of the story in order.*

Teach/Model Choose a familiar story to model speaking to a group. Tell the first part of the story two times. As you tell it the first time, mumble and don't make much eye contact. Ask children what you can improve for next time. Then tell the story using the feedback. Call attention to making eye contact and speaking loudly enough so everyone can hear.

Practice Have partners take turns telling simple stories they are familiar with or about something that happened to them. Partners can offer feedback. Can they hear their partner? Did the story make sense? Explain that their comments should be helpful and respectful, and should also include at least one positive comment. Finally, have each child tell the story to a larger group if they feel comfortable doing so.

Assess Assess children's stories, considering eye contact, volume, and whether the story makes sense.

Beginning Have children work on telling simple stories, speaking aloud. Give children a chance to plan what they will say. Talk to them about the sequence of events in the story so they can think about how they will tell it.

Intermediate Have children work on elaborating. Lead them by explaining that stories are more interesting if they use describing words that tell us what something looked, felt, smelled, or sounded like. Help them think of adjectives to describe the people, places, or things in their stories.

Advanced/Advanced High Give children time to plan, and guide them to add dialogue to their stories. Model how to use words to introduce dialogue, such as "and then the wolf said . . ." Help them to use different voices that show the personalities of the different characters in the story.

Name ________________________________

Use the planner to organize ideas for telling a story.

Write the title of the story.

Draw how you will introduce your speech.

Use your drawings to tell the story.

Title:

____

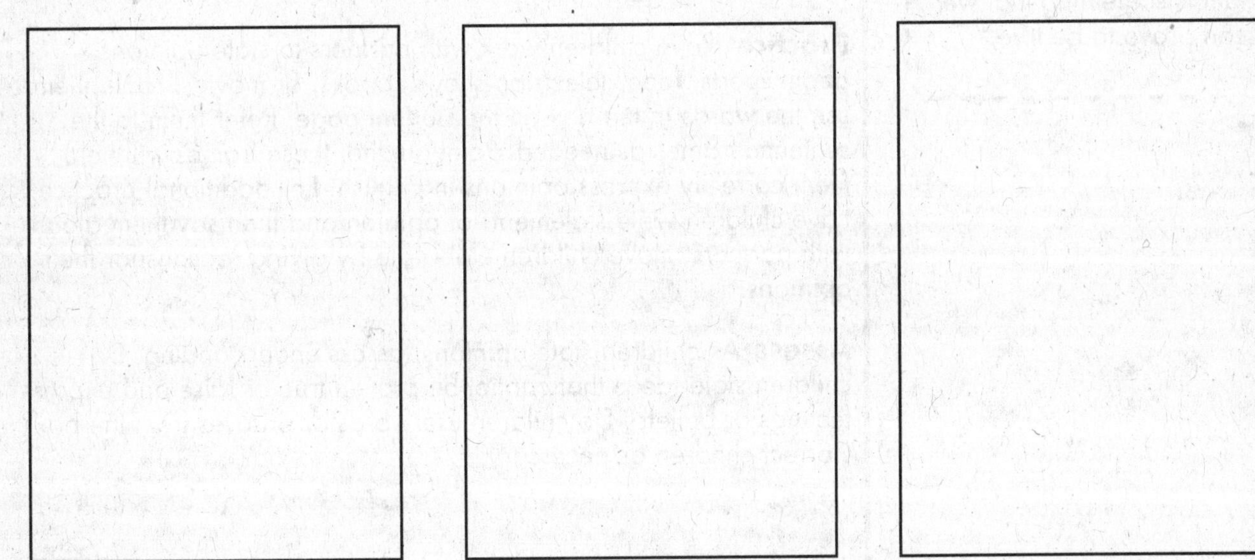

Rate your story telling.

People could hear me.   

People could understand my words.   

I told the ideas in order.   

My story made sense.   

Express Opinions

> **Teaching Tip**
> Children sometimes have difficulty distinguishing facts from opinions. Explain to them that sometimes we tell about our own ideas and feelings, but others may not agree with us. If someone doesn't agree with us, it doesn't mean we are "wrong," it just means someone else has a different idea. But a fact is something that we can prove to be true.

Preteach Explain to children: *We tell our opinions to show what we think or believe. We cannot prove if an opinion is true or false. A fact is something that we can prove is true. If I say, "It is raining outside," that's a fact. I can look outside and see rain falling. If I say, "Rainy weather is the best weather," that's an opinion. I like rainy weather because it helps my flowers grow in the garden. But some people don't like rain. They have different ideas or feelings. We can listen to other people's opinions and respect them, even if we don't agree.*

Teach/Model Display the words and phrases from the student page. *We use these words to tell what we think or believe.* Model creating an opinion using one of the words or phrases. *I think baseball is the best sport. I am saying what I think or believe, but others may not agree. This is an opinion.*

Practice Have children work with partners to state opinions about sports, food, television shows, books, or movies. Have them use the words in the box on the student page. Refer them to the sentence frames as needed. Point out that these frames will help them correctly express opinions in English. For additional practice, have children write statements of opinion and then say them aloud with partners. Have children elaborate by giving reasons for their opinions.

Assess As children state opinions, assess understanding. Do children state ideas that cannot be proven true or false and express feelings or beliefs? Do children use words or phrases from the box? Correct children as necessary.

Beginning Write sentence frames on index cards and distribute them to children. Have them work in pairs to state opinions using the frames.

Intermediate When calling on children to give oral opinions, have them use phrases such as *I like* or *I do not like*, rather than single words. Have pairs ask each other why he or she has that opinion. Report answers to the class.

Advanced/Advanced High Challenge children to add other opinion words or phrases to the box and write additional sentence frames. They can use the frames to state opinions.

Name ______________________________

Opinion Words

I think	I believe	my opinion is	I agree
I disagree	I like	I do not like	
best	worst	good	bad

Complete opinions using these sentence frames:

I like ______________________________.

I think ______________________________.

I believe ______________________________.

I do not like ______________________________.

My opinion is ______________________________.

Challenge! Add more details to your sentence.

I like ______________ because ______________.

Her opinion is ______________ because ______________.

Express Feelings

Transfer Skills
All people experience feelings, yet the "correctness" of expressing those feelings varies from culture to culture. Work with children to understand the appropriate times to openly express feelings and the social norms associated with the process.

Preteach *If you see someone with a frown on his or her face* (demonstrate for children), *you know that person might be sad or angry. Anger and sadness are feelings. We often express our feelings with our faces and our actions, but we can also use words to show feelings. Finding the right words isn't always easy!*

Teach/Model Use exaggerated facial expressions and body language to express a feeling, such as happiness or confusion. Model by speaking: *I am happy. I feel happy.* Model another feeling and have children use the frames after you model:

You feel ________________. *You are* ________________.

Practice Explain a situation to children that would elicit a feeling, such as *Your favorite cousin is coming to a family party. You haven't seen your cousin in a long time. How do you feel?* (excited, happy) *You came to school without your homework. You know your teacher is going to ask for it.* (worried, guilty) Have children gesture to show the emotion and then work with partners to express that feeling in words. As children suggest more feeling words, write them on a chart for reference so that children can include them on their worksheets.

Assess As children express their feelings, assess the sentences they use as well as their ability to identify feelings. Correct any misconceptions as children use sentence frames to express feelings.

Beginning Have children draw or make faces to show a facial expression that expresses a feeling. Partners can identify the feeling and create a sentence: *He/she feels* ____________.

Intermediate Have children look for pictures in magazines or newspapers that show a situation that would elicit feelings. Have them speak about the picture.

Advanced/Advanced High Challenge children to think of specific words for feelings, such as *joyful, excited, lively, positive, pleased, thrilled,* or *upbeat* instead of *happy.*

Name ______________________________

Feeling Words

glad	afraid	proud	angry
lonely	confused	surprised	

Record words that express feelings in the box. A few words are already in the box. Add more.

Speak a sentence using one of the frames below. Choose words from the box.

I feel ______________________________.

I am ______________________________.

He/She is ______________________________.

They felt ______________________________.

They are ______________________________.

He/She was ______________________________.

They were ______________________________.

Challenge! Add more details to your sentence.

I feel ______________ because ______________.

They felt ______________ when ______________.

Discuss with Classmates

Teaching Tip
Consider setting roles for class discussions, such as a word finder (picks out new or important words in the text), a highlighter (points out important or interesting events or features), and a summarizer. Model how to do each of these roles and provide guided practice before assigning these roles for children to do independently.

Preteach *When do we have discussions? I discuss lessons and games with children. I talk with my family at the dinner table. I discuss ideas with other teachers at school. In a discussion, we speak and we listen. We respect other people's ideas.*

Teach/Model Create a fishbowl, in which you and a few children are in the center while others are around you watching. Introduce an easy discussion topic such as a question about a selection you have just read. Model the discussion behaviors from the rubric on the next page. As you model these behaviors, pause to think aloud. You might say *I repeated back what Tommy said to me. He knows that I have understood him. He also knows I was listening. Now it is my turn to speak. It is important to take turns being a good listener and a good speaker.*

Practice Have children work in small groups. Introduce a topic such as: *What is your favorite thing to do after school?* As children discuss, monitor and encourage the positive behaviors you observe. Share these positive behaviors with the class and have children identify others they know.

Assess Use the rubric on the page to have children assess their discussion skills. Follow up with your own observations of child discussions.

Beginning Model for children examples of nonverbal communication skills that a good listener uses: nodding, making eye contact, and making appropriate expressions. Have them mimic you as you model them.

Intermediate Offer children an example of a conversation that could occur at the lunch table. Have the children mimic you, each partner playing another role. Stress the importance of active listening and behaviors that go with it.

Advanced/Advanced High Have children model discussion scenarios and demonstrate behaviors of listening and speaking for other groups.

Name ______________________________

Rate what you do during discussions with your classmates.

I share ideas.			
I answer questions.			
I listen to other people.			
I look at people when I talk.			
I repeat back what other people say.			
I am friendly to classmates.			

What do you want to talk about?

Make a list.

Pick something to talk about!

____

____

____

____

____

____

Act Out or Draw Meaning

Teaching Tip
Drawing what a word means helps etch the meaning of that word into the brain, making it a part of our active vocabularies. Children may think they cannot draw pictures because they are not artistic. Help them devise symbols or other ways to illustrate meaning when they are "stuck" for picture ideas.

Preteach Choose a content-area or lesson word that children recently learned. *When I learn new words, I want to remember them. Drawing a picture of what the word means helps me remember a word. Acting it out also helps me remember a word. I just learned a new word in science:* solar. *If something comes from the sun, it is* solar. *For example, energy that comes from the sun is* solar energy. *I can draw a picture of the sun with arrows showing the energy coming from it.* (Show picture.) *I can also act out the meaning by standing up like the rising sun. I can move my arms in a circle to show the energy coming from the sun.*

Teach/Model Introduce words from a recent story or from content-area studies. Place children in small groups, and give each group a word. Have children work together to create a picture and/or gestures to demonstrate meanings of the words. Groups can share with other groups as you monitor for understanding.

Practice Play a guessing game with children. Distribute words on index cards that children have learned in class. Children can take turns drawing pictures or acting out word meanings for other classmates to guess. Use the worksheet for children to create dictionaries of word meanings. Distribute copies of the drawing frames when children learn new words. Have children keep and add to their own personal word books.

Assess Assess children's drawings to clear up any misconceptions about the words. Discuss with children how drawing words may help them remember word meanings.

Beginning Ask children to follow up their drawings or gestures by explaining word meanings orally.

Intermediate Ask children to use each word in a sentence to describe what they drew or acted out.

Advanced/Advanced High Have children look up the definitions of words in a dictionary to supplement their understanding. They can write definitions in their own words to show understanding.

Name ______________________________

Word: ______________________________

Drawing

This word means ______________________________

Word: ______________________________

Drawing

This word means ______________________________

Read the Words Around You

Teaching Tip
Engage children by asking them each to bring in something from home with words on it that they can read: a cereal box, a milk carton, an advertisement from a magazine, for example. Create a display. Ask children what information they get from reading the words on each of these items.

Preteach Before starting, draw a stop sign on the board and ask what it means. Children may answer *stop. Everywhere are words and signs that can help us.* We need to learn what these signs tell us. Point out that the name of the school is on the front of the building. The sign tells people what this building is. It helps people find the school. Then, point out that the classrooms have numbers. These help children find their way around the school.

Teach/Model Walk around the classroom until you find an example of instructional environmental print. Model reading the word, and figuring out what it means: *A sign on this door reads P-U-L-L. I know that word is* pull. *This sign tells me how to open the door.* Then, model opening the door.

Practice Tell children that their task is to keep a log of the signs they notice and can read throughout the school day. They must keep track of the words in the table on their worksheets. At the end of the day, have children share one word they recognized in a sign, and one they did not. Discuss as a class. Help them understand the meanings of words they did not recognize. As you discuss children's examples, talk about the information they get from reading the signs or other environmental print. Children can keep a running log of environmental print they see and learn. Discuss the words regularly.

Assess Assess children's understandings of environmental print by questioning them as they share their results, for example: *Why do you think the sign "office" was placed in that spot?* (The sign tells us where the principal's office is.) Explain the meanings of unknown words to children.

Beginning Have children only keep track of words they recognize and know.

Intermediate Have children organize their words by category, such as *foods, signs, rooms, clubs,* and so on.

Advanced/Advanced High Provide environmental print for children, such as store advertisements, posters, and additional signs. Children can discuss with partners what they learn from reading these signs.

Name ____________________

Write the words you see around you.

Practice saying each word aloud.

Date	Words I Know	Words I Do Not Know Yet

Use Nouns in Your Speaking

Transfer Skills
In some languages, such as Chinese and Vietnamese, there are no distinctions between singular and plural nouns. Help children understand that even when adding a number to modify a noun, we still use the plural form: *five apples* rather than *five apple*.

Preteach *Nouns are words that name people, places, or things. Nouns can name one thing, or they can name more than one thing. I have one pencil in my hand. But I have three pencils on my desk.*

Teach/Model Select an item from the classroom and say the noun. Then give the plural form of that noun. *This is a desk. If there are three of them, I have three desks.* Repeat for other objects around the room. Invite children to identify other nouns they can see. Guide children to use both singular and plural forms.

Practice Have children complete the sentence frames on the worksheet. Invite them to think of other nouns that might fit the frames and add them to the noun bank. Use images or illustrations to help them identify the nouns.

Assess As children complete their worksheets, circulate to assess their work and clear up any misconceptions.

Beginning Write words on index cards, one word per card, with a combination of verbs, adjectives, and nouns. Have children identify which words are nouns. Have children choose a noun to use in a sentence. Check for understanding.

Intermediate/Advanced Give index cards to children with singular and plural nouns. Have them sort the words according to whether they are singular and plural. Ask them to choose a word and give the singular form for plural or plural form for singular.

Advanced High Provide a variety of illustrated books and magazines to children. Have children identify nouns from the pictures. Assist them in writing the words and adding them to the noun bank. Have children use words in sentences. Check for understanding.

Name ______________________________

Look at the picture.
Read the sentence.
Write a noun in the sentence.

Noun Bank					
finger	apple	book	house	sound	sun
fingers	apples	books	houses	sounds	suns

Say the sentences aloud.

1. We need ______________ for our pie.

2. Hold up two ______________.

3. The ______________ is hot.

4. We heard a ______________.

5. There are three ______________ on this block.

6. Please put those ______________ on the shelf.

Use Prepositions and Adjectives in Your Speaking

Teaching Tip
Follow a similar routine for teaching prepositions. Focus on prepositions that tell position and time by modeling and demonstrating: *I push the chair under the table. I put my coat on the hook. When I describe where I put things, I use special words to tell where. These words, on and under, are called prepositions. We can use prepositions to tell locations. We can also use prepositions to tell when things happen. We eat lunch after our math class. In that sentence, after is a preposition that helps us tell time.*

Preteach Demonstrate as you describe adjectives. *The soup was hot, chunky, and delicious. When I was describing the soup, I used special words to give details about it:* hot, chunky, *and* delicious. *These words are called adjectives, and they tell more about what something is like. They tell us what something looks, feels, smells, or sounds like.*

Teach/Model Choose an adjective from the list on the child worksheet. Demonstrate how the adjective can be used to describe a noun. *The bird had soft, smooth feathers.* Choose another subject and invite children to match it with an adjective. *What adjectives could be used to describe a car?*

Practice Have children use the space on the bottom of the worksheet to draw a picture. They can write about the picture using adjectives. Model if necessary: *I drew a picture of myself riding my bicycle. The bicycle is fast, shiny, and new. What adjectives would you use to describe something outdoors, like a tree?* Children can also use this sheet to work with prepositions. Have them list prepositions in the second column. They can use prepositions to talk about locations or time. *My bicycle is on the sidewalk. The helmet is on my head.*

Assess Assess children's pictures and sentences for understanding of how to use adjectives and prepositions. Provide extra support as necessary.

Beginning Write words on index cards, one word per card, with a combination of verbs, adjectives, and nouns. Have children identify which words are adjectives. Have children use each word in a sentence. Check for understanding.

Intermediate/Advanced Provide a variety of illustrated books and magazines. Have children use adjectives to describe pictures. Assist them in writing the words and adding them to the adjective bank. Have children use each word in a sentence. Check for understanding.

Advanced High Challenge children to find prepositions and adjectives from their reading or from other sources. They can add them to the worksheet and to a chart for class reference. Have them practice using prepositions that tell time in addition to location.

Name ______________________________

Write adjectives in the first column.

Write prepositions in the second column.

ADJECTIVES	PREPOSITIONS
soft	in
smooth	on
big	over

Draw a picture.

Write about it. Use adjectives and prepositions.

____

____

____

____

Use Verbs in Your Speaking

Teaching Tip
Use the worksheet as a basis for a chart to which you can add verbs as children encounter them in their reading and listening. As you add them to the chart, have children draw pictures to illustrate their meanings, discuss their meanings, and use them in sentences.

Preteach *Verbs are words that show action, or something you do. I walk across the classroom* (model walking across the classroom). *The word* walk *is a verb. It describes something I do. I write on a piece of paper* (model writing). *The word* write *is also a verb, because it is also an action.*

Teach/Model Show a picture of a person doing something, such as running, eating, or some other action that is easy to identify. Then provide a sentence frame represented by a picture with the verb replaced with a blank: *The woman __________ a bottle of water.* Add the verb shown in the picture. *The woman drinks a bottle of water.* Drink *is the verb because it tells what she is doing. What other things could she do with the bottle of water?* Invite children to provide other verbs, such as *pour, spill,* or *fill.*

Practice As a class, create a verb bank at the front of the class listing verbs to draw from. Begin by providing a few verbs. Brainstorm other verbs to add to the bank. Distribute sentence frames for children to complete with verbs. Add additional verbs to the verb bank as children come up with more actions.

Assess Assess children's answers on the worksheet. Correct any errors, and explain misunderstandings children may have.

Beginning Assist children by reading the sentence and showing a picture that illustrates the verb. After children use the verb to choose the correct answer, they can reread the sentence to reinforce their understanding of the concept in English.

Intermediate/Advanced Ask children to choose a verb and work in pairs to write a new sentence that includes the phrase. They can illustrate their sentences to show meaning.

Advanced High Have children search for verbs in their reading selections or other printed material, share them in small groups, and discuss their meanings.

Name ______________________________

Read each sentence.

Choose the right word for the sentence.

Write the word on the line.

Verb Bank

shops swims rides eats play

1. The girl ____________ in the lake.

2. Marta ____________ her bicycle on the sidewalk.

3. The family ____________ dinner together.

4. We love to ____________ outside.

5. My mother ____________ in the city.

Can you think of other verbs you can use in these sentences? Add them to the verb bank.

Part 6
Multilingual Vocabulary

Introduction to Multilingual Vocabulary

The story words are arranged by unit and week to coincide with the reading selections. Each story word is translated into Spanish, Chinese, Vietnamese, Korean, and Hmong. Use the translated story words to build children's background knowledge before reading a selection. Frontloading the vocabulary will allow children to access the content and will aid their comprehension of the text.

Table of Contents

Multilingual Vocabulary
Unit 1

English	Spanish	Chinese	Vietnamese	Korean	Hmong
Week 1: The Twin Club					
cousins	primos	堂兄弟	anh/chị/em bà con	사촌	Cov kwv tij kuv npawg thiab viv ncaus
meadow	prado	草地	đồng cỏ	초원	tiaj nyom
parents	padres	父母	cha mẹ	부모	niam thiab txiv
promise	promete	承諾	hứa hẹn	약속	cog lus
Week 2: Exploring Space with an Astronaut					
astronaut	astronauta	太空人	phi hành gia	우주비행사	tus neeg tsam dav hlau mus saum qaum ntuj
experiment	experimento	實驗	thí nghiệm	실험	sim ua
gravity	gravedad	重力	trọng lực	중력	luj sib luag
shuttle	transbordador	太空梭	phi thuyền con thoi	왕복선	dav hlau mus saum qaum ntuj
telescope	telescopio	望遠鏡	kính viễn vọng	망원경	koob xoom
Week 3: Henry and Mudge and the Starry Night					
drooled	babeó	流口水	chảy nước miếng	침을 흘리다	los qaub ncaug, siv qaub ncaug
lanterns	linternas	燈籠	lồng đèn	랜턴	teeb
shivered	tiritaba	顫抖	rùng mình	벌벌 떠는	tshee
snuggled	se acurrucaron	舒適地蜷伏	ôm quấn quít	다가붙다	sib puag sib qawg

English	Spanish	Chinese	Vietnamese	Korean	Hmong
Week 4: A Walk in the Desert					
cactus	cactus	仙人掌	cây xuong rồng	선인장	tsob ntoo pos
climate	clima	天气	khí hậu	기후	ntuj siab
coyote	coyote	北美土狼	chó rừng	코요테	hma
harsh	severo (áspero)	严峻	khắc nghiệt	가혹한	phem heev
desert	desierto	沙漠	sa mạc	사막	chaw moj siab qhua
Week 5: The Strongest One					
dangerous	peligroso	危險	nguy hiểm	위험한	phom sij
gnaws	roe	咬	gặm nhấm	갉아먹다	tom, xo
narrator	narrador	敘事人	người kể chuyện	이야기하는 사람 내레이터	tus phiav zaj dab neeg
relatives	parientes	親戚	thân nhân họ hàng	친척	txheeb ze

Unit 2

English	Spanish	Chinese	Vietnamese	Korean	Hmong
Week 1: Tara and Tiree, Fearless Friends					
brave	valiente	勇敢	can đảm	용감한	tsis ntshai
collar	collar	衣領	cổ áo	칼라,깃	tsho ntsej
slipped	se resbalaron	滑倒	bị trượt	미끄러진	nplua
Week 2: Abraham Lincoln					
fault	culpa - culpable	過失	lầm lỗi	잘못	txhaum
honest	el honesto	誠實	thật thà	정직한	ncaj ncee
lawyer	abogado	律師	luật sư	변호사	kws lij choj
noticed	se dio cuenta	注意到	được thông báo	알아챘다	qhia tas lawm
Week 3: Scarcity					
hurricanes	huracanes	暴風	bão	허리케인	Ntwv Khauv Zeeg Cuab Loj
resources	recursos	資源	nguồn tài nguyên	자원	tej qhov qho
scarce	escasear	不足	hiếm	부족한	tsawg tsawg li
scarcity	escasez	缺乏	thiếu thốn	부족함	muaj tsawg kawg
trade-off	hacer un sacrificio	交換	trao đổi	거래	Sib-Pauv xwb
Week 4: The Bremen Town Musicians					
excitement	emoción	興奮	sự hứng thú	흥분	zoo siab
mill	molino	磨坊	cối xay	방앗간	tshuab zom txhu
monsters	monstruos	妖怪	quái vật	괴물	pab laib
musician	músico	音樂家	nhạc sĩ	음악가	cov neeg ntau nkauj
robbers	ladrones	強盜	tên trộm cướp	강도	tub sab

English	Spanish	Chinese	Vietnamese	Korean	Hmong
Week 5: One Good Turn Deserves Another					
armadillo	armadillo	犰狳	con tatu	아르마딜로	Tus Kum Zaug
creature	creatura	生物	sinh vật	생물	tshiaj
grateful	agradecido	感激	biết ơn	감사하는	zoo siab heev li
groaned	gruñó	嘆息	rên rỉ	끙끙거렸다	ntsaj
snorted	resopló	噴鼻息	tiếng khịt khịt	콧방귀 뀌다	ua qaj

Unit 3

English	Spanish	Chinese	Vietnamese	Korean	Hmong
Week 1: Pearl and Wagner: Two Good Friends					
electricity	electricidad	電力	điện	전기	hluav taws xob, faim fab
robot	robot	機械人	người máy	로봇	robot
trash	basura	垃圾	rác rưởi	쓰레기	khib nyiab
wad	bolita	一團	cuộn vải hoặc cuộn giấy để chèn	작은 뭉치	lub hau ntsaws
Week 2: Dear Juno					
envelope	sobre	信封	bao thư	봉투	hnab ntawv
persimmons	caquis	柿子	trái hồng	감	txiv qab nplaig
photograph	fotografía	照片	tấm ảnh chụp	사진	duab
smudged	emborronada	弄髒	bị bẩn, bị lem	더러워진	ua kom plooj
Week 3: Anansi Goes Fishing					
delicious	delicioso	美味	ngon	맛있는	qab heev
justice	justicia	正義	công lý	공정, 공평	caj ncees
lazy	perezoso	懶惰	lười biếng	게으른	tub nkeeg
weave	tejer	織	dệt	짜다, 엮다	ua ntos
Week 4: Rosa and Blanca					
chiles	chiles	番椒	ớt	칠리	kua txob (hmoov)
luckiest	más afortunada	最幸運的	may mắn nhất	운이 좋은	muaj hmoo tshaj
tortillas	tortillas	未經發酵的玉米餅	bánh tráng mỏng bằng bột mì hoặc bột bắp	토티야(멕시코 지방의 빵)	ncuav pob kws

English	Spanish	Chinese	Vietnamese	Korean	Hmong
Week 5: A Weed Is a Flower					
agriculture	agricultura	農業	nông nghiệp	농업	ua liaj ua teb
college	universidad	大學	đại học	대학	tsev kawm ntawv qib siab
greenhouse	invernadero	溫室	nhà kính để trồng cây	온실	tsev yug paj ntoos
laboratory	laboratorio	實驗室	phòng thí nghiệm	연구실	chav tsev sim khoom los yog ua tshuaj

Unit 4

English	Spanish	Chinese	Vietnamese	Korean	Hmong
Week 1: A Froggy Fable					
clearing	claro	空地	dọn sạch	개간지	hav nyom du du
crashed	estrellarse	倒塌	đổ sầm xuống	무너졌다	tsoo
perfect	perfecto	完美	hoàn toàn	완벽한	tab tom
pond	estanque	池塘	cái ao	연못	pag dej tauv
spilling	derramar	溢出	tràn ra	엎지름	txeej
splashing	salpicadura, salpicar	戏水	lội bì bõm	(물을) 튀기기	kov dej txaws
traveled	viajó	旅行	du hành	여행했다	mus ncig
Week 2: Life Cycle of a Pumpkin					
bumpy	desiguales	果實	dằn xốc	울퉁불퉁한	thawv thawv
fruit	fruta	收穫	trái cây	과일	txiv
harvest	cosecha	根	thu hoạch	수확	caij sau noob loos
root	raíz	平滑	gốc rễ	뿌리	cag (ntoo)
smooth	lisas	泥土	bằng phẳng, êm ái	부드러운	du du
soil	tierra	藤蔓	đất	토양	hmoov av
vine	enredadera	高低不平	dây leo	포도나무	hmab
Week 3: Soil					
grains	granos	穀物	hột	알갱이	Ntsiav
material	material	材料	vật liệu	재료	qhov qho
particles	partículas	粒子	hạt lấm tấm	입자들	Khoom
seep	se filtra	滲漏	thấm	스며들다	qus
substances	sustancias	物質	hóa chất	물질	tej yam
texture	textura	材質	kết cấu	조직	daim tawv

English	Spanish	Chinese	Vietnamese	Korean	Hmong
Week 4: The Night the Moon Fell					
balance	equilibrio, equilibrar	平衡	cân bằng	균형	nyob nreg nreg
canyons	cañones	峡谷	hẽm núi	깊은 골짜기	kwj ha tob tob
coral	coral	珊瑚	san hô	산호	txhaa av
rattle	traqueteo, traquetear	发嘎嘎声	kêu lách cách	방울뱀	nchos
slivers	astillas	缝隙	mảnh nhỏ	은화	ntshiv
sway	vaivén	摆动	đong đưa	(앞뒤로) 흔들리다	co mus mus los los
whisper	susurro, susurrar	耳语	thì thầm	속삭이다	hais lus ntxhi
Week 5: The First Tortilla					
awaken	despertar	苏醒	thức dậy	깨다	tsa sawv
cliffs	acantilados	绝壁	vách đá	낭떠러지	tsag tsua
mountain	montaña	山	núi	산	roob
prize	premio	奖赏	giải thưởng	상품	nqi zog
rainbow	arco iris	彩虹	cầu vồng	무지개	zaj sawv
suffer	sufren	受苦	đau khổ	고통을 받다	raug txom nyem
volcano	volcán	火山	núi lửa	화산	roob hluav taws

Unit 5

English	Spanish	Chinese	Vietnamese	Korean	Hmong
Week 1: Fire Fighter!					
building	edificio	燃燒	tòa nhà	건물	tsev
burning	ardiente	面罩	đang cháy	불타는	kub nyhiab
masks	máscaras	迅速	khẩu trang, dụng cụ che mặt	가면	daim looj ntsej muag
quickly	rápidamente	呼叫	mau lẹ	빨리	tsuag tsuag
roar	rugido	站	gầm thét	고함치다	qw nrov nrov
station	estación	緊緊	trạm	역, 정거장	tshooj
tightly	bien	建築物	một cách chặt chẽ	단단히	nruaj nruaj
Week 2: Carl the Complainer					
annoy	fastidioso	惹惱	làm phiền	불쾌하다	Laj mloog
complain	me estoy quejando	抱怨	than phiền	투덜거리다	foob tas li
mumbles	hablando entre dientes	咕噥	lầm bầm	중얼거리다	hais li ub li no
P.M.	p. m.	下午	buổi chiều	오후	Tav Su Rov Yav
shrugs	se encoge de hombros	聳肩	nhún vai	으쓱하다	nroj tsuag
signature	firmas	簽名	chữ ký	서명	ko npe

English	Spanish	Chinese	Vietnamese	Korean	Hmong
Week 3: Bad Dog, Dodger!					
chased	persiguieron	咀嚼	rượt đuổi	뒤쫓다	caum
chewing	mordiendo	滴下	nhai	씹다, 깨물다	xo
dripping	goteando	抓取	chảy nhỏ giọt	(젖어서) 물방울이 떨어지는	(dej) los ib teem ib teem
grabbed	agarró	訓練	chộp lấy	잡다, 잡아채다	tuav
practice	entrenamiento	款待	tập dợt	연습	xyaum
treat	galleta (de perro)	搖擺	món ăn đặc biệt ưa thích	다루다	qhaub noom
wagged	meneó	追逐	vẫy đuôi	흔들다	co tw
Week 4: Horace and Morris but mostly Dolores					
adventure	aventura	爬	cuộc phiêu lưu	모험	mus loj leeb
climbed	subieron	社團小屋	đã leo	기어오르다	nce
clubhouse	casa del club	探險	nhà ở câu lạc bộ	클럽 회관	tsev koos haum
exploring	explorando	最偉大	thám hiểm	탐험하는	soj ntsuam
greatest	mejores	最真實	vĩ đại nhất	최고의	zoo tshaj
truest	más verdaderos	驚異	thật nhất	진실의	ntseeg tau
wondered	se preguntaba	冒險	tự hỏi	놀라운	xav txog
Week 5: The Signmaker's Assistant					
afternoon	tarde	下午	buổi chiều	오후	tav su
blame	culpen	責備	đổ tội	비난하다	liam
ideas	ideas	主意	ý kiến	아이디어, 생각	tsw yim
important	importante	重要	quan trọng	중요한	tseem ceeb
signmaker	rotulista	招牌師父	thợ làm bảng hiệu	간판 제작자	tu ua daim sign
townspeople	ciudadanos	市民	dân ở phố	마을 사람	neeg zos

Unit 6

English	Spanish	Chinese	Vietnamese	Korean	Hmong
Week 1: Just Like Josh Gibson					
bases	bases	方法	vị trí để bắt được quả bóng (trong bóng chày/dã cầu)	베이스	cov base
cheers	gritos de entusiasmo	歡呼	lời reo mừng cổ võ	격려하다, 응원하다	qw quas
field	campo	場地	sân	필드	teb
plate	base meta	板	vị trí đứng đánh quả bóng	홈 플레이트, 마운드	daim plate
sailed	volaban	航行	lướt	날리다	ya puag saum ntuj
threw	tiró	投擲	ném liệng	던지다	txawb
Week 2: Red, White, and Blue: The Story of the American Flag					
America	Estados Unidos	美國	Hoa Kỳ	미국	teb chaws mis kas
birthday	cumpleaños	生日	sinh nhật	생일	hnub yug
flag	bandera	國旗	lá cờ	깃발	chij
freedom	libertad	自由	tự do	자유	kev ywj pheej, kev ywj siab
nicknames	apodos	綽號	biệt danh	별명	sis npe
stars	estrellas	星星	những ngôi sao	별	hnub qub
stripes	franjas	條紋	các đường sọc	줄무늬	kab txaij

English	Spanish	Chinese	Vietnamese	Korean	Hmong
Week 3: A Birthday Basket for Tía					
aunt	tía	姑母	cô, dì	이모, 고모	ntsaum
bank	alcancía	堤	ngân hàng	은행	tsev rau nyiaj
basket	cesta	籃子	cái rổ	바구니	pob tawb
collects	recoge	收集	thu thập	수집하다	khaws cia
favorite	favorito	特別喜愛	thích nhất	좋아하는	nyiam tshaj
present	regalo	禮物	món quà	선물	khoom plig
Week 4: Cowboys					
campfire	fuego (de campamento)	營火	lửa trại	모닥불	cub ntawg
cattle	ganado	牛	trâu bò	소	ib pab nyuj
cowboy	vaquero	牛仔	người chăn bò	카우보이	neeg yug nees thiab nyuj
galloped	galoparon	疾馳	phi nước đại	질주하다, 서두르다	dhia (nees dhia ya)
herd	manada	群	đàn, bầy	무리	ib pab tsiaj
railroad	ferrocarril	鐵路	đường rầy xe lửa	철로	kev luv train
trails	sendas	足迹	đường mòn	끌고 가다	kab kev
Week 5: Grace for President					
assembly	asamblea	集会	hội họp	집합, 집회	sablaj
election	elección	选举	tuyển cử	선거	kev xaiv
microphone	micrófono	扩音器	máy vi âm	마이크	maivkausfoos
rallies	reuniones políticas	集会	tập họp	(정치적) 모임, 집회	sablaj
slogan	eslogan, lema	标语	khẩu hiệu	구호, 슬로건	qauv lus
speeches	discursos	演说	diễn văn	연설	hais lus

Part 7
Linguistic Contrastive Analysis, ELL Teaching Routines, Graphic Organizers, and High-Frequency Words

Contents

Linguistic Contrastive Analysis

Use these pages to find out more about challenges in pronunciation and grammar that your English language learners may face as they produce spoken English. The Linguistic Contrastive Analysis chart compares sounds in English with sounds in Spanish, Vietnamese, Cantonese, Hmong, Filipino, Korean, and Mandarin.

English Language Learner Teaching Routines

These routines support systematic and scaffolded instruction in using core lesson materials.

Graphic Organizers

Graphic organizers provide visual support important to English language learners' comprehension.

High-Frequency Words

The High-Frequency Words section includes activities that allow students to use these words in speaking and writing to build their competency and fluency.

How People Speak

All languages have consonant and vowel sounds. Consonants are made with some obstruction of the vocal tract, either a complete stoppage of air or enough constriction to create friction. Vowels are produced with a more open vocal tract; there is no constriction that might cause friction.

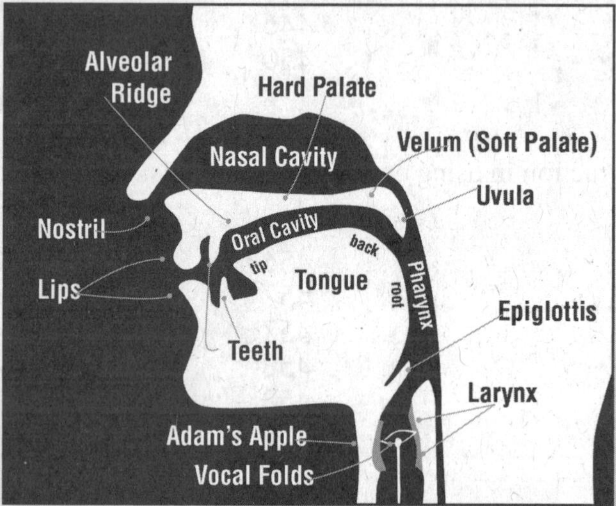

Figure 1: The human vocal tract makes the sounds of speech.

Consonants

Every consonant can be described by noting three characteristics: voicing, place of articulation, and manner of articulation.

Voicing

Many sounds of language, including all vowels, employ vibration of the vocal folds in the larynx. This creates more resonance and energy for the sound. All speech sounds are characterized as either voiced (with vocal fold vibration) or voiceless (with no vocal fold vibration). Feeling the vibration around the Adam's apple can help you understand this difference. If you say "sssss" and then "zzzzz," you can feel the distinction: /s/ is voiceless and /z/ is voiced.

Place of Articulation

This is the location in the vocal tract where the air stream may be constricted. The /s/ sound, for example, is made with the tongue tip close to the alveolar ridge (see Figure 1).

Place of Articulation Terms

Alveolar: tongue tip and ridge behind teeth

Bilabial: using both lips

Glottal: produced at the larynx

Interdental: tongue tip between upper and lower teeth

Labio-dental: upper teeth and lower lip

Labio-velar: rounding of lips; tongue body raised toward velum

Palatal: body of tongue and high part of palate

Palato-alveolar: tongue tip and palate behind alveolar ridge

Velar: body of tongue and velum (soft palate)

Manner of Articulation

This is the type or degree of constriction that occurs in an articulation. For example, the /t/ sound completely stops the airflow with the tongue tip at the alveolar ridge, but /s/ allows air to pass noisily through a small opening.

Manner of Articulation Terms

Affricate: complete constriction followed by slow separation of the articulators resulting in friction

Approximant: close constriction, but not enough for friction

Fricative: narrow constriction; turbulent airflow causing friction

Glottal: produced at the larynx

Lateral: air passes over sides of tongue

Nasal: lowered velum to let air escape through the nose

Stop: complete constriction, closure so that air cannot escape through the oral cavity

Tap: brief contact between tongue tip and alveolar ridge

Vowels

Vowels are open, sonorous sounds. Each vowel can be uniquely described by noting the position of the tongue, the tension of the vocal tract, and the position of the lips. Vowels are described by ***height,*** where the tongue is relative to the roof of the mouth. They can be high, mid, or low. Tongue backness tells if the tongue articulation is in the front or back of the mouth.

Tense vowels are more common around the world. In English, they are longer and include an expansion of the throat at the pharynx. Lax vowels are shorter with a more neutral pharynx. An example is the tense long *e* as in *meet*

Speaking English

versus the lax short *i* as in *mitt*. The lips either can be in a spread or neutral position, or they can be rounded and protrude slightly.

English is the third most widely spoken native language in the world, after Mandarin and Spanish. There are about 330 million native speakers of English and 600 million who speak it as a foreign language.

English Consonant Sounds

The following chart gives the International Phonetic Alphabet (IPA) symbol for each English consonant along with its voicing, place, and manner of articulation. This information can be used to understand and help identify problems that non-native speakers may encounter when learning to speak English.

CONSONANTS OF ENGLISH		
IPA	Articulation	Example
p	voiceless bilabial stop	**p**it
b	voiced bilabial stop	**b**it
m	voiced bilabial nasal stop	**m**an
w	voiced labio-velar approximant	**w**in
f	voiceless labio-dental fricative	**f**un
v	voiced labio-dental fricative	**v**ery
θ	voiceless interdental fricative	**th**ing
ð	voiced interdental fricative	**th**ere
t	voiceless alveolar stop	**t**ime
d	voiced alveolar stop	**d**ime
n	voiced alveolar nasal stop	**n**ame
s	voiceless alveolar fricative	**s**oy
z	voiced alveolar fricative	**z**eal
ɾ	voiced alveolar tap	bu**tt**er
l	voiced alveolar central approximant	**l**oop
ɹ	voiced palato-alveolar affricate	**r**ed
ʃ	voiceless palato-alveolar fricative	**sh**allow
ʒ	voiced palato-alveolar affricate	vi**s**ion
ʧ	voiceless palato-alveolar affricate	**ch**irp
ʤ	voiced palato-alveolar affricate	**j**oy
j	voiced palatal approximant	**y**ou
k	voiceless velar stop	**k**ite
g	voiced velar stop	**g**oat
ŋ	voiced velar nasal stop	ki**ng**
h	voiceless glottal fricative	**h**ope

English Vowel Sounds

Most languages in the world have around five vowel sounds. English has 13 common vowel sounds, which means that many students of English must learn more vowel distinctions than there are in their native language. The lax vowels are most difficult. Some vowels are diphthongs, meaning the tongue is in one position at the beginning of the sound, and it moves to another position by the end of it.

VOWELS OF ENGLISH		
IPA	Sound	Example
i	ē	b**ea**t
ɪ	ĭ	b**i**t
e	ā	b**ai**t
ɛ	ĕ	b**e**t
æ	ă	b**a**t
u	ōō	b**oo**t
ʊ	ŏŏ	c**ou**ld
o	ō	b**oa**t
ɔ	aw	l**aw**
ɑ	ŏ	h**o**t
ə	ə	**a**bout
ʌ	ŭ	c**u**t
ɝ	er	b**ir**d
ɑ ʊ	ow	h**ou**se
ɔ ɪ	oy	b**oy**
ɑ ɪ	ī	b**i**te

Figure 2 is a schematic of the mouth. The left is the front of the mouth; the right is the back. The top is the roof of the mouth and the bottom is the floor. Placement of the vowel shows where the tongue reaches its maximum in the English articulation.

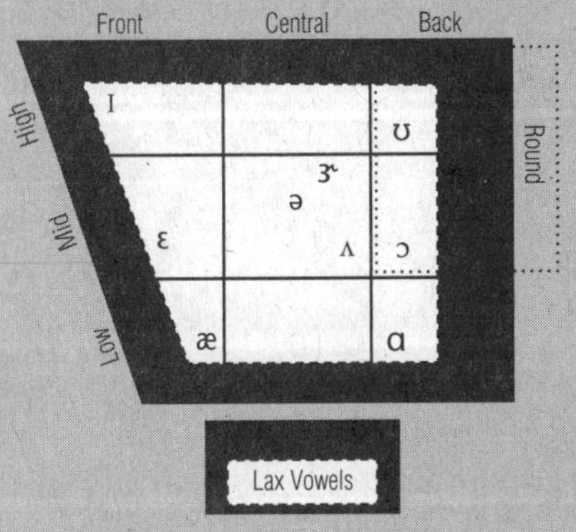

Figure 2: English vowel sounds

Transference

Pronunciation

All languages build on the same fundamentals. All languages contrast voiced and voiceless sound and have stops and fricatives. Many languages use the same places of articulation for consonants as well. The majority of sounds will easily transfer from another language to English.

However, there will always be some sounds that are not found in a person's native language that can pose a challenge to the English language learner. English has a few relatively rare sounds, such as the interdental sounds spelled with *th,* /ɵ/ and /ð/. The /r/ sound in English is also a very rare type of sound. Most other languages use a tap or trill articulation for an /r/ sound.

In some languages, the /l/ and /r/ sounds belong to one psychological category. This means that they count as the same sound in that language. In this case, it is not the articulation that is difficult, but the perception of the difference and consistent use of one versus the other in any word context. This type of psychological category is called a *phoneme,* and multiple speech sounds all can be categorized as the same phoneme in that language.

This is true for English as well, where, for example, the alveolar lateral /l/ as in *lob* and the velarized lateral /ɫ/ as in *ball* are both counted as the same sound—an *l*—to native speakers of English. It is important to keep in mind that both the phonetic articulation of a sound and its psychological, phonemic category factor into the learning of a new language.

Grammar

Pronouncing English is not the only stumbling block for English learners. The grammar and usage, or syntax, of English may present distinctions that are unique to the language. For example, English syntax requires adjectives to precede the nouns they modify, as in *the tall girl.* In other languages, such as Spanish, Hmong, and Vietnamese, adjectives follow nouns, as in *la chica alta* (literally *the girl tall* in Spanish). This may cause word-order problems, particularly for less advanced English learners.

Other syntactic differences are less obvious and may cause problems even for advanced learners. For example, many East Asian languages (such as Mandarin, Cantonese, and Korean) do not mark agreement between subject and verb. Speakers of these languages may therefore leave out agreement markers, such as the *-s* in *The girl like cats.*

The use of articles varies across languages. For instance, Spanish uses the definite article more often than English, while Mandarin and Cantonese do not have articles. A Spanish-speaking English learner might say *The girl likes the cats* instead of *The girl likes cats,* and a Mandarin or Cantonese speaker might say *Girl like cat.*

Plural marking is another potential trouble spot: Vietnamese, Filipino, Cantonese, and Mandarin do not add plural markers to nouns. Learners speaking these languages may have difficulty with English plurals, saying *cat* instead of *cats.*

Grammar Hot Spots

Look for Grammar Hot Spots on the following pages for tips on the most common syntax errors by speakers of languages other than English.

Common First Languages

In the Common First Languages section, you will find details of some common non-English languages spoken in the United States. They are:

- Spanish
- Vietnamese
- Cantonese
- Hmong
- Filipino
- Korean
- Mandarin

You can use the fundamentals of speech articulation already covered to help you understand where the languages differ from English. Differences in the spoken language and in the writing systems are explored as well. These sections pinpoint common trouble spots specific to learners of English.

Culture Clues

Look to Culture Clues for insights into the cultural differences of each language learner as well as ideas for ways to embrace students' diversity.

Linguistic Contrastive Analysis

The Linguistic Contrastive Analysis Charts provide a quick reference for comparing English sounds with those of other languages. The charts allow you to check at a glance which sounds have equivalents in other languages. For those sounds that don't have equivalents, you can find the closest sound used as a substitute and suggestions for helping someone gain a native English articulation.

In these charts, the sounds are notated using the International Phonetic Alphabet (IPA). This is the most widely recognized and used standard for representing speech sounds in any language. A guiding principle of the IPA across all languages is that each sound is uniquely represented by one symbol, and each symbol represents only one sound.

The chart has columns for each native language with rows corresponding to each English phoneme. Each cell in the chart gives an example word using that sound in the native language, a definition in parentheses, and transference tips below. If there is no sound equivalent to English, a common substitution used by speakers of that language may be provided.

Transference Tips

Transference tips give you ideas of how the sound will be produced by the learner. Cells in bold print indicate where the English learner may have particular difficulty with the English sound.

Common First Languages

Spanish

Background

Spanish is the second most widely spoken language in the world. There are more than 400 million native Spanish speakers in 20-plus countries on three continents. Spanish vocabulary and pronunciation differ from country to country. While most dialect differences in English are in vowel sounds, Spanish dialects differ in their consonants.

Spoken

Spanish sounds are similar to those found in English, so there is a strong foundation for the native Spanish speaker learning English. However, there are three key differences between English and Spanish consonants:

1. Most of the alveolar sounds in English, such as /t/, /d/, and /n/ are produced farther forward in the mouth in Spanish. Instead of the tongue touching the alveolar ridge as in English, in Spanish it touches the back of the teeth.
2. Another difference is that the /r/ sound in English is not found in Spanish. There are two /r/ sounds in Spanish. One is the tap /ɾ/, which occurs in English as the quick sound in the middle of the name *Betty*. Psychologically, this tap sound is a kind of /t/ or /d/ sound in English, while in Spanish it is perceived as an /r/. The other /r/ sound in Spanish is a trill, or series of tongue taps on the alveolar ridge. This does not occur in English.
3. The third key difference between English and Spanish can be found in the English production of the voiceless stops /p/, /t/, and /k/. In English these sounds are aspirated, with an extra puff of air at the end, when the sound occurs at the beginning of a word or stressed syllable. So, /p/ is aspirated in *pit.* Learners can add a puff of air to such sounds to sound more like native English speakers.

There are five vowels in Spanish, which are a subset of the English vowels. Spanish vowels include tense vowel sounds a, e, i, o, u. Lax vowel sounds in English are the problematic ones for native Spanish speakers.

Written

Like English, written Spanish uses the Roman alphabet, so both writing systems are similar. There are a few orthographic differences to note, however:

- The letter *h* in Spanish is silent, but the sound /h/ is written as *j* or *g.*
- A single letter *r* in Spanish represents a tap, while the double *rr* represents a trill.
- Accents are used to show the stress on a syllable when the stress is different from the usual rules. In some cases, words change meaning according to the accents. For example, *el* means *the* while *él* means *he.*

Written Spanish vowels are pronounced like the symbols in the IPA. So, the Spanish *i* is pronounced with the long *e* as in the word *beat*. The IPA and Spanish symbol for this letter is the same: *i.*

Grammar Hot Spots

- Double negatives are part of standard grammar in Spanish. Stress the single negative construction in English.
- English prepositions are a common stumbling point for Spanish speakers.

Culture Clues

The Spanish language covers many countries, dialects, and cultures. Always encourage students to share special things about their culture, such as foods, festivals, or social customs.

Vietnamese

Background

Approximately 80 million people in Vietnam speak Vietnamese. The northern dialect is the standard, though central and southern dialects also exist. Most Vietnamese speakers in the United States are from southern Vietnam and speak the southern dialect.

Spoken

Vietnamese is a tonal language, so each syllable is pronounced with a distinctive tone that affects meaning. Vietnamese has a complex vowel system of 12 vowels and 26 diphthongs. Its consonants are simpler, but Vietnamese syllable structure allows few possibilities for final consonants.

Students may need help noticing and learning to reproduce final consonant sounds in English words and syllables. Vietnamese syllable structure allows for limited combinations of initial consonants. Students also may need help with the more complex initial consonant clusters of English words and syllables.

Culture Clues

In traditional Vietnamese education, there is a strict division between the roles of student and teacher. Students may be confused if asked to direct a part of their own study, so encourage group work.

Written

Since the 1600s, Vietnamese has used a Romanized alphabet. Many characters written in Vietnamese have sounds different from their English counterparts, such as *d, x, ch, nh, kh, g, tr, r,* and *e.*

Grammar Hot Spots

- Like English, Vietnamese uses Subject-Verb-Object (SVO) syntax, or word order.
- Vietnamese does not use affixes; instead, syntax expresses number, case, and tense.

Cantonese

Background

Cantonese is one of the seven major Chinese languages, not all of which are mutually intelligible. Cantonese is mostly spoken in China's southern provinces, Hong Kong, and Macau by about 66 million people. It is a tonal language, and the same sequence of letters can have different meanings depending on their pitch.

Spoken

Cantonese has six stops, aspirated and non-aspirated /p/, /t/, /k/; three fricatives /f/, /s/, /h/, and two affricates /ts/, /tsʰ/. Some that do not exist in Cantonese can be difficult for the English language learner. The /v/ often gets pronounced as /f/ or /w/; the /z/ is often said as /s/; the sounds spelled with *th* are often said as /t/, /d/, or /f/. Cantonese speakers have difficulty distinguishing between /l/ and /r/, since /r/ is not present in their language. They tend to produce an /l/-like sound for both English sounds in words such as *ride* and *lied.*

Cantonese has 11 vowels and 10 diphthongs. One of the major problems for Cantonese speakers is distinguishing between English tense and lax vowels because the distribution of Cantonese short and long vowels is determined by the sound context.

Syllables in Cantonese don't have consonant clusters. English consonant clusters are often deleted or broken up by vowel insertion (e.g., *list* becomes *lis*). This may be especially problematic when producing English past tense (e.g., *baked*).

Written

Cantonese is written with standard Chinese characters known as *Hànzi* where each character represents a syllable and has a meaning. Additional Cantonese-specific characters were also added. Cantonese speakers may have difficulty with sound-letter correspondences in English.

Grammar Hot Spots

- English articles and prepositions are difficult for Cantonese speakers. *In, on,* and *at,* for instance, can be translated as the same preposition in Cantonese.
- Plurals, tenses, and gerund endings are difficult for Cantonese speakers to transfer to English.

Common First Languages

Hmong

Background

Hmong is a group of approximately 18 languages within the Hmong-Mien family. There are roughly four million speakers of Hmong, including 200,000 in the United States. They are mainly from two groups with mutually intelligible dialects—Hmong Daw and Mong Leng.

Spoken

Hmong vowels are few and simple, but its consonants are complex and differ from those of English. Notable features of Hmong phonology absent from English include consonantal pre-nasalization (the /m/n/ŋ/ sound before a consonant) and the contrast between nasalized and non-nasalized vowels. Hmong is tonal. Each syllable is pronounced with a distinctive pitch.

Culture Clues

In traditional Hmong culture, learning takes place through hands-on experience. Students may find it difficult to adjust to the use of graphics or print media. Competition, personal achievement, and self-directed instruction may be unfamiliar concepts, so students may prefer group work.

Written

The Romanized Popular Alphabet (RPA), developed in the 1950s, is the usual way of transcribing Hmong. Syllable-final consonants are absent in pronunciation but are used to orthographically represent the tonal value of a given syllable. Students may need particular help in identifying and learning to reproduce the final consonant sounds of English words and syllables.

Grammar Hot Spots

- Like English, Hmong is an SVO language. Personal pronouns are marked for number, including inflection for singular, dual, and plural, though they are not marked for case.
- Because Hmong and English prepositions often have different semantic qualities, students may need help mastering uses of English prepositions. For example, it is correct to say "think <u>about</u> [something]" rather than "think <u>on</u> [something]."

Filipino

Background

Filipino and English are the official languages of the Philippines, where 175 languages are spoken. There are about 24 million native speakers of Filipino, and more than 50 million people speak Filipino as a second language. You may hear the terms *Filipino* and *Tagalog* being used interchangeably. Another term is *Pilipino.*

Spoken

Filipino has many similar speech sounds to English. The notable exceptions are the lack of the consonant sounds /f/, /v/, and those spelled with *th.* Of these, the English /f/ and /v/ cause the most difficulty for learners. For /f/, they may substitute /p/. The distinction between long *e* (as in *beat*) and short *i* (as in *bit*) is also a trouble spot. Filipino does not allow consonant clusters at the end of syllables, so *detect* may be simplified to just one final consonant *(detec)*.

Culture Clues

Most people from the Philippines can speak Filipino, but for many it is not their first language. Ask Filipino students about other languages they speak. Because English is used alongside Filipino as the language of instruction in the Philippines, most Filipinos are familiar with English.

Written

The Filipino alphabet has 28 letters and is based on the Spanish alphabet, so the English writing system poses little problem.

Grammar Hot Spots

- Filipino word order is Verb-Subject-Object (VSO), which does not transfer well to English.
- Inflectional verb endings, such as *-s, -en, -ed,* and *-ing* do not exist in Filipino, so it is common to leave out the third person singular verb marker (*"He walk,"* not *"He walks"*).

Korean

Background

Korean is spoken by 71 million people in North and South Korea. Standard Korean is based on the speech in and around Seoul.

Spoken

Korean does not have corresponding sounds for English /f/, /v/, /θ/, /ð/, and /ʤ/. In word-initial position, all Korean stops are voiceless. Voiced stops /b/, /d/, and /g/ are only produced between two vowels. Korean speakers may have difficulty producing /s/, /ʃ/, and /z/ in some contexts, in addition to English /r/ and /l/ sounds (e.g., *rock* and *lock*). They may have problems in producing English consonant clusters (e.g., *str-, sk-*). These problems can often be eliminated by vowel insertion or consonant deletion. In addition, the distinction between English tense and lax vowels (e.g., long *e* as in *beat* vs. /ɪ/ as in *bit*) may be problematic for Korean speakers.

Culture Clues

Korean uses a complex system of honorifics, so it is unusual for Korean students to use the pronoun *you* or call their teachers by their first name.

Written

Modern Korean uses the Korean alphabet *(Hangul)* or a mixed script of *Hangul* and Chinese. *Hangul* is an alphabetic script organized into syllabic blocks.

Grammar Hot Spots

- In contrast to English, Korean word order is Subject-Object-Verb (SOV). The verb always comes at the end of a sentence.
- Korean syllable stress is different, so learners may have difficulties with the rhythm of English.

Mandarin

Background

Mandarin Chinese encompasses a wide range of dialects and is the native language of two-thirds of China. There are approximately 870 million Mandarin speakers worldwide. North Mandarin, as found in Beijing, is the basis of the modern standard language.

Spoken

Mandarin Chinese and English differ substantially in their sound structure. Mandarin lacks voiced obstruent consonants (/b/, /d/, /g/, /ʤ/), causing difficulty for speakers in perceiving and producing English voiced consonants (e.g., *buy* may be pronounced and perceived as *pie*). The sounds spelled with *th* are not present in Mandarin, so they are often substituted with /s/ or /t/ causing, for example, *fourth* to be pronounced as *fours.* Mandarin Chinese has five vowels. Due to the relatively small vowel inventory and contextual effects on vowels in Mandarin, many English vowels and tense/lax distinctions present problems for speakers of Mandarin Chinese. Mandarin allows only a very simple syllable structure, causing problems in producing consonant clusters in English. Speakers may drop consonants or insert vowels between them (e.g., *film* may become /filəm/). The use of tones in Mandarin may result in the rising and falling of pitch when speaking English.

Written

Chinese is written with characters known as *Hànzi.* Each character represents a syllable and also has a meaning. A Romanized alphabet called *Pinyin* marks pronunciation of characters. Chinese speakers may have problems mastering letter-sound correspondences in written English, especially for sounds that are not present in Mandarin.

Grammar Hot Spots

- The non-inflected nature of Chinese causes Mandarin speakers to have problems with plurals, past tense markers, and gerund forms *(-s, -ed, -ing).*
- Mastering English tenses and passive voice is difficult. Students should be familiarized with correct lexical and syntactic features as well as appropriate situations for the use of various tenses and passives.

Linguistic Contrastive Analysis Chart

The Consonants of English

IPA	ENGLISH	SPANISH	VIETNAMESE	CANTONESE
p	*pit* Aspirated at the start of a word or stressed syllable	*pato* (duck) Never aspirated	*pin* (battery)	*pʰa (to lie prone)* Always aspirated
b	*bit*	*barco* (boat) Substitute voiced bilabial fricative/ɞ/ in between vowels	*ba* (three) Implosive (air moves into the mouth during articulation)	**NO EQUIVALENT** **Substitute /p/**
m	*man*	*mundo* (world)	*mot* (one)	*ma* (mother)
w	*win*	*agua* (water)	**NO EQUIVALENT** **Substitute word-initial /u/**	*wa* (frog)
f	*fun*	*flor* (flower)	*phu'o'ng* (phoenix) Substitute sound made with both lips, rather than with the lower lip and the teeth like English /f/	*fa* (flower) Only occurs at the beginning of syllables
v	*very*	**NO EQUIVALENT** Learners can use correct sound	*Việt Nam* (Vietnam)	**NO EQUIVALENT** **Substitute /f/**
θ	*thing* Rare in other languages. When done correctly, the tongue will stick out between the teeth.	**NO EQUIVALENT** Learners can use correct sound	**NO EQUIVALENT** **Substitute /th/ or /f/**	**NO EQUIVALENT** **Substitute /th/ or /f/**
ð	*there* Rare in other languages. When done correctly, the tongue will stick out between the teeth.	*cada* (every) Sound exists in Spanish only between vowels; sometimes substitute voiceless θ.	**NO EQUIVALENT** **Substitute /d/**	**NO EQUIVALENT** **Substitute /t/ or /f/**
t	*time* Aspirated at the start of a word or stressed syllable English tongue-touch. Is a little farther back in the mouth than the other languages.	*tocar* (touch) Never aspirated	*tám* (eight) Distinguishes aspirated and non-aspirated	*tʰa* (he/she) Distinguishes aspirated and non-aspirated
d	*dime* English tongue-touch is a little farther back in the mouth than the other languages.	*dos* (two)	*Đồng* (Dong = unit of currency) Vietnamese /d/ is implosive (air moves into the mouth during articulation)	**NO EQUIVALENT** **Substitute /t/**
n	*name* English tongue-touch is a little farther back in the mouth than the other languages.	*nube* (cloud)	*nam* (south)	*na* (take)
s	*soy*	*seco* (dry)	*xem* (to see)	*sa* (sand) Substitute *sh–* sound before /u/ Difficult at ends of syllables and words
z	*zeal*	**NO EQUIVALENT** Learners can use correct sound	*rồi* (already) In northern dialect only Southern dialect, substitute /y/	**NO EQUIVALENT** **Substitute /s/**
ɾ	*butter* Written 't' and 'd' are pronounced with a quick tongue-tip tap.	*rana* (toad) Written as single *r* and thought of as a /r/ sound.	**NO EQUIVALENT** **Substitute /t/**	**NO EQUIVALENT** **Substitute /t/**
l	*loop* English tongue-touch is a little farther back in the mouth than the other languages. At the ends of syllables, the /l/ bunches up the back of the tongue, becoming velarized /ɫ/ or dark-l as in the word *ball.*	*libro* (book)	*cú lao* (island) /l/ does not occur at the ends of syllables	*lau* (angry) /l/ does not occur at the ends of syllables

HMONG	FILIPINO	KOREAN	MANDARIN
peb (we/us/our) Distinguishes aspirated and non-aspirated	*paalam* (goodbye) Never aspirated	*pal* (sucking)	*pʰei* (cape) Always aspirated
NO EQUIVALENT **Substitute /p/**	*baka* (beef)	**NO EQUIVALENT** **/b/ said between vowels** **Substitute /p/ elsewhere**	**NO EQUIVALENT**
mus (to go)	*mabuti* (good)	*mal* (horse)	*mei* (rose)
NO EQUIVALENT **Substitute word-initial /u/**	*walo* (eight)	*gwe* (box)	*wen* (mosquito)
faib (to divide)	**NO EQUIVALENT** **Substitute /p/**	**NO EQUIVALENT** **Substitute /p/**	*fa* (issue)
Vaj ('Vang' clan name)	**NO EQUIVALENT** **Substitute /b/**	**NO EQUIVALENT** **Substitute /b/**	**NO EQUIVALENT** **Substitute /w/ or /f/**
NO EQUIVALENT **Substitute /th/ or /f/**	**NO EQUIVALENT** Learners can use correct sound, but sometimes mispronounce voiced /ð/.	**NO EQUIVALENT** **Substitute /t/**	**NO EQUIVALENT** **Substitute /t/ or /s/**
NO EQUIVALENT **Substitute /d/**	**NO EQUIVALENT** Learners can use correct sound	**NO EQUIVALENT** **Substitute /d/**	**NO EQUIVALENT** **Substitute /t/ or /s/**
them (to pay) Distinguishes aspirated and non-aspirated	*takbo* (run) Never aspirated	*tal* (daughter)	*ta* (wet) Distinguishes aspirated and non-aspirated
dev (dog)	*deretso* (straight)	**NO EQUIVALENT** **Substitute /d/ when said between vowels and /t/ elsewhere.**	**NO EQUIVALENT** **Substitute /t/**
noj (to eat)	*naman* (too)	*nal* (day)	*ni* (you) May be confused with /l/
xa (to send)	*sila* (they)	*sal* (rice) Substitute *shi*– sound before /i/ and /z/ after a nasal consonant	*san* (three)
NO EQUIVALENT Learners can use correct sound	**NO EQUIVALENT** Learners can use correct sound	**NO EQUIVALENT** Learners can use correct sound	**NO EQUIVALENT** **Substitute /ts/ or /tsʰ/**
NO EQUIVALENT **Substitute /t/**	*rin/din* (too) Variant of the /d/ sound	Only occurs between two vowels Considered a /l/ sound	**NO EQUIVALENT**
los (to come) /l/ does not occur at the ends of syllables	*salamat* (thank you)	*balam* (wind)	*lan* (blue) Can be confused and substituted with /r/

The Consonants of English (continued)

IPA	ENGLISH	SPANISH	VIETNAMESE	CANTONESE
ɹ	*red* Rare sound in the world Includes lip-rounding	**NO EQUIVALENT** **Substitute /r/ sound such as the tap /ɾ/ or the trilled /r/**	**NO EQUIVALENT** **Substitute /l/**	**NO EQUIVALENT** **Substitute /l/**
ʃ	***sh**allow* Often said with lip-rounding	**NO EQUIVALENT** **Substitute /s/ or /ʧ/**	*sieu thị* (supermarket) southern dialect only	**NO EQUIVALENT** **Substitute /s/**
ʒ	*vision* Rare sound in English	**NO EQUIVALENT** **Substitute /z/ or /ʤ/**	**NO EQUIVALENT** **Substitute /s/**	**NO EQUIVALENT** **Substitute /s/**
ʧ	***ch**irp*	***ch**ico* (boy)	***ch**ính phủ* (government) Pronounced harder than English *ch*	**NO EQUIVALENT** **Substitute /ts/**
ʤ	*joy*	**NO EQUIVALENT** **Sometimes substituted with /ʃ/ sound** **Some dialects have this sound for the *ll* spelling as in *llamar***	**NO EQUIVALENT** **Substitute /ch/, the equivalent sound, but voiceless**	**NO EQUIVALENT** **Substitute /ts/** **Only occurs at beginnings of syllables**
j	*you*	*cielo* (sky) Often substitute /ʤ/	*yeu* (to love)	*jau* (worry)
k	***k**ite* Aspirated at the start of a word or stressed syllable	***c**asa* (house) Never aspirated	***c**om* (rice) Never aspirated	*kʰa* (family) Distinguishes aspirated and non-aspirated
g	***g**oat*	***g**ato* (cat)	**NO EQUIVALENT** **Substitute /k/**	**NO EQUIVALENT** **Substitute /k/**
ŋ	*ki**ng***	*ma**ng**o* (mango)	***Ng**ŭyen* (proper last name)	*phaŋ* (to cook)
h	***h**ope*	***g**ente* (people) Sometimes substitute sound with friction higher in the vocal tract as velar /x/ or uvular /χ/	***h**oa* (flower)	***h**a* (shrimp)

HMONG	FILIPINO	KOREAN	MANDARIN
NO EQUIVALENT **Substitute /l/**	**NO EQUIVALENT** **Substitute the tap /ɾ/**	**NO EQUIVALENT** **Substitute the tap or /ɾ/ confused with /l/**	*ran* (caterpillar) Tongue tip curled farther backward than for English /r/
sau (to write)	*siya* (s/he)	Only occurs before /i/; Considered a /s/ sound	*shi* (wet)
zos (village)	**NO EQUIVALENT** Learners can use correct sound	**NO EQUIVALENT**	**NO EQUIVALENT** **Substitute palatal affricate /tþ/**
cheb (to sweep)	*tsa* (tea)	*cʰal* (kicking)	*cheng* (red)
NO EQUIVALENT **Substitute *ch* sound**	*Dios* (God)	**NO EQUIVALENT** **Substitute *ch* sound**	**NO EQUIVALENT** **Substitute /ts/**
Yaj (Yang, clan name)	*tayo* (we)	*je:zan* (budget)	*yan* (eye)
Koo (Kong, clan name) Distinguishes aspirated and non-aspirated	*kalian* (when) Never aspirated	*kal* (spreading)	*ke* (nest) Distinguishes aspirated and non-aspirated
NO EQUIVALENT **Substitute /k/**	*gulay* (vegetable)	**NO EQUIVALENT** **Substitute /k/** **Learners use correct sound between two vowels**	**NO EQUIVALENT** **Substitute /k/**
gus (goose)	*angaw* (one million)	*baŋ* (room)	*tang* (gong) Sometimes add /k/ sound to the end
hais (to speak)	*hindi* (no)	*hal* (doing)	**NO EQUIVALENT** **Substitute velar fricative /x/**

Linguistic Contrastive Analysis Chart

The Vowels of English

IPA	ENGLISH	SPANISH	VIETNAMESE	CANTONESE
i	*beat*	*hijo* (son)	*di* (to go)	*si* (silk)
ɪ	*bit* Rare in other languages Usually confused with /i/ (*meat* vs. *mitt*)	**NO EQUIVALENT** **Substitute /i/**	**NO EQUIVALENT** **Substitute /i/**	*sik* (color) Only occurs before velars Substitute /i/
e	*bait* End of vowel diphthongized—tongue moves up to /i/ or /ɪ/ position	*eco* (echo)	*kê* (millet)	*se* (to lend)
ɛ	*bet* Rare in other languages. Learners may have difficulty distinguishing /e/ and /ɛ/: *pain* vs. *pen*	**NO EQUIVALENT** **Substitute /e/**	**NO EQUIVALENT** **Substitute /e/**	*seŋ* (sound) Only occurs before velars; difficult to distinguish from /e/ in all positions
æ	*bat* Rare in other languages Learners may have trouble getting the tongue farther forward in the mouth	**NO EQUIVALENT** **Substitute short *o* or short *u***	*ghe* (boat)	**NO EQUIVALENT** **Hard to distinguish between /æ/ and long *a***
u	*boot*	*uva* (grape)	*mua* (to buy)	*fu* (husband)
ʊ	*could* Rare in other languages Learners may have difficulty distinguishing /u/ and /ʊ/: *wooed* vs. *wood*	**NO EQUIVALENT** **Substitute long *u***	**NO EQUIVALENT** **Substitute long *u* (high back unrounded)**	*suk* (uncle) Only occurs before velars Difficult to distinguish from /u/ in all positions
o	*boat* End of vowel diphthongized – tongue moves up to /u/ or /ʊ/ position	*ojo* (eye)	*cô* (aunt)	*so* (comb)
ɔ	*law*	**NO EQUIVALENT** **Substitute /o/ or /ɑ/** **Substituting /o/ will cause confusion (*low* vs. *law*); substituting /ɑ/ will not**	*cá* (fish)	*hok* (shell) Only occurs before velars Difficult to distinguish from /o/ in all positions
ɑ	*hot*	*mal* (bad)	*con* (child)	*sa* (sand)
ɑ ʊ	*house* Diphthong starts /ɑ/ and moves to /ʊ/	*pauta*	*dao* (knife)	*sau* (basket)
ɔ ɪ	*boy* Diphthong starts at /ɔ/ and moves to /ɪ/	*hoy* (today)	*ròi* (already)	*soi* (grill)
ɑ ɪ	*bite* Diphthong starts at /ɑ/ and moves to /ɪ/	*baile* (dance)	*hai* (two)	*sai* (to waste)
ə	*about* Most common vowel in English; only in unstressed syllables Learners may have difficulty keeping it very short	**NO EQUIVALENT** **Substitute short /u/ or the full vowel from the word's spelling**	*mua* (to buy)	**NO EQUIVALENT**
ʌ	*cut* very similar to schwa /ə/	**NO EQUIVALENT** **Substitute short *o***	*giờ* (time)	*san* (new)
ɝ	*bird* Difficult articulation, unusual in the world but common in American English Learners must bunch the tongue and constrict the throat	**NO EQUIVALENT** **Substitute short *u* or /er/ with trill**	**NO EQUIVALENT** **Substitute /ɨ/**	*hæ* (boot)

HMONG	FILIPINO	KOREAN	MANDARIN
ib (one)	*ikaw (you)* This vowel is interchangeable with /ɪ/; hard for speakers to distinguish these	zɪːʃaŋ (market)	*ti* (ladder) Sometimes English /i/ can be produced shorter
NO EQUIVALENT **Substitute long *e***	*limampu* (fifty) This vowel is interchangeable with /i/; hard for speakers to distinguish these	**NO EQUIVALENT** **Substitute long *e***	**NO EQUIVALENT**
tes (hand)	*sero* (zero)	*be:da* (to cut)	*te* (nervous) Sometimes substitute English schwa /ə/
NO EQUIVALENT **Substitute long *a***	*sero* (zero) This vowel interchanges with /e/ like *bait*; not difficult for speakers to learn	*thɛ:do* (attitude)	**NO EQUIVALENT**
NO EQUIVALENT **Substitute short *e***	**NO EQUIVALENT** **Substitute short *o* as in *hot***	**NO EQUIVALENT**	**NO EQUIVALENT** **Substitute /ə/ or short *u***
kub (hot or gold)	*tunay* (actual) This vowel interchanges with /ʊ/ like *could*; not difficult for speakers to learn	*zu:bag* (watermelon)	*lu* (hut) Sometimes English /u/ can be produced shorter
NO EQUIVALENT **Substitute a sound like long *e* (mid central with lips slightly rounded)**	*gumawa* (act) This vowel interchanges with /u/ like *boot*; not difficult for speakers to learn	**NO EQUIVALENT**	**NO EQUIVALENT**
NO EQUIVALENT	*ubo* (cough)	*bo:zu* (salary)	*mo* (sword) This vowel is a little lower than English vowel
Yaj (Yang, clan name)	**NO EQUIVALENT** **Spoken short *o* as in *hot***	**NO EQUIVALENT**	**NO EQUIVALENT** **Substitute long *o***
mov (cooked rice)	*talim* (blade)	*ma:l* (speech)	*ta* (he/she) Sometimes substitute back /o/ or /u/
plaub (four)	*ikaw* (you)	**NO EQUIVALENT**	**NO EQUIVALENT**
NO EQUIVALENT	*apoy* (fire)	**NO EQUIVALENT**	**NO EQUIVALENT**
qaib (chicken)	*himatay* (faint)	**NO EQUIVALENT**	**NO EQUIVALENT**
NO EQUIVALENT	**NO EQUIVALENT** **Spoken as short *o* as in *hot***	**NO EQUIVALENT** **Difficult sound for learners**	**NO EQUIVALENT**
NO EQUIVALENT	**NO EQUIVALENT** **Spoken as short *o* as in *hot***	**NO EQUIVALENT**	**NO EQUIVALENT**
NO EQUIVALENT **Substitute diphthong /əɪ/**	**NO EQUIVALENT** **Spoken as many different vowels (depending on English spelling) plus tongue tap /ɾ/**	**NO EQUIVALENT**	**NO EQUIVALENT**

ROUTINE 1 • ELL VOCABULARY ROUTINE

1 Introduce the Word Say the word, and then relate the word to children's prior knowledge and experience. When possible, also relate the word to the weekly concept. Supply a child-friendly definition and have children say the word.

Example: Ask the children if they have ever seen a turtle. Say *shell*. Explain that a shell is the hard covering on some animals' bodies. Then, relate the word *shell* to the text, explaining how it is used in that context.

2 Demonstrate Provide examples to show meaning. When possible, use gestures, pictures, realia, or other visuals to help convey the meaning.

Example: Show the children pictures of different kinds of shells. *Where might you find shells?* Explain that many animals have shells covering their bodies.

3 Apply Have children demonstrate understanding of the word. Include opportunities for both verbal and nonverbal responses, such as using the word in a sentence, drawing, or physical gestures to show understanding.

Example: What animals have shells? Draw a picture of one you know.

4 Display the Word Display the word in the classroom along with visual support to show meaning.

Example: Say the word *shell*. Have children identify the sound-spellings that make the word and write the word on a sheet of paper. Have children draw a picture of a shell under the word.

ROUTINE 2 • STORY WORDS

1 Before Reading

INTRODUCE THE WORD MEANING Provide a simple, child-friendly definition. Relate the word to the children's prior knowledge.

Example: What do firefighters wear? Uniforms are special clothes that you wear to work.

INTRODUCE THE WRITTEN WORD Divide the word into syllables, if appropriate, and blend the syllables to read the word. Have children repeat each word after it is read.

Example: Write *uniform*. Read the word aloud: *uniform*. Read the word: u-ni-form. *Say the word after me:* uniform. *We will read this word in our story today.*

GUIDE PRACTICE To build deeper knowledge of word meaning, children listen to the word in a context sentence. If possible, provide a picture, visual, or gesture to help them understand the word.

Example: Show a picture of a police officer in a uniform. *Listen as I use the word* uniform *in a sentence: The police officer wears a uniform to work.*

ON THEIR OWN Children use the selection vocabulary in their own sentences. If needed, provide a sentence frame to guide them.

Example: A _______ wears a uniform to work.

CORRECTIVE FEEDBACK If children do not use the word correctly, model the correct use of the word in a sentence and have them try again.

2 During Reading

Children:

- use vocabulary strategies to figure out the meanings of unknown words.
- get clarification from others, if necessary.
- refer to a word wall or other reference.

3 After Reading

Children:

- use words to discuss the selections.
- use the words in writing.
- add words to a word wall or word bank.

ROUTINE 3 • WHOLE-WORD BLENDING

1 Introduce Whole-Word Blending Write the word. When possible, use visuals or gestures to help convey meaning. *We will use sounds and letters we know to read words.*

2 Connect Sounds to Spellings

MODEL Point to each spelling and say its sound. Emphasize any letter combinations that should be considered together such as digraphs and diphthongs, and vowel combinations.

Example: Point out that the double *s* only makes one sound, /s/. Say /m/ /i/ /s/ as you touch under *m*, *i*, and *s*.

m i s s

GUIDE PRACTICE Have children say the sounds as you touch under the letter(s). *When I touch under the letter(s), you say the sound.*

Example: Children say /m/ /i/ /s/ as you touch under *m*, *i*, and *ss*.

CORRECTIVE FEEDBACK If children say an incorrect sound, refer them to the appropriate Sound-Spelling Card. Provide examples of other words with this sound-spelling. Point out any sounds that may be different or new to the children's native language.

3 Blend Sounds

MODEL Blend the word by saying the sound for each spelling, with no pause between sounds, as you move your hand in a continuous motion from one letter to the next. Stretch continuous sounds.

Example: Blend /mmmiiisss/.

GUIDE PRACTICE Run your hand below the word as the children blend the sounds with you and without you.

CORRECTIVE FEEDBACK If children stop between sounds, then model how to say the whole word.

4 Read the Word

MODEL Blend the word by pronouncing it as you quickly run your hand beneath it.

GUIDE PRACTICE Have children say it quickly.

CORRECTIVE FEEDBACK Model how to say the word, first slowly and then quickly.

ROUTINE 4 • SOUND-BY SOUND BLENDING

1 Introduce Blending Write and say the word. When possible, use visuals or gestures to help convey the meaning.

2 Connect Sounds to Spelling

MODEL Say the first sound in the word and write the letter(s) that spell that sound. Tell children to watch your mouth and emphasize any letter combinations such as vowel combinations, diphthongs, and digraphs. Touch under the letter(s) as you say the sound.

GUIDE PRACTICE Have children say the sound as you touch under the letter(s).

CORRECTIVE FEEDBACK If children say an incorrect sound, refer them to the appropriate Sound-Spelling Card. Provide them with other words with that sound-spelling.

3 Add a Sound-Spelling

MODEL Say the next sound in the word and add the letter(s) for that sound. Touch under the letter(s) as you say the sound.

GUIDE PRACTICE Have children say the sound as you touch under the letter(s).

CORRECTIVE FEEDBACK Use corrective feedback as shown above.

4 Blend sounds

MODEL Run your hand from letter to letter as you say the sounds without pausing between them. Repeat until all sounds have been added and blended.

Example: Blend /nnnaaa/, and /nnnaaap/.

GUIDE PRACTICE Have children repeat each sound. Then have children blend the sounds with you and then without you.

CORRECTIVE FEEDBACK If children stop between sounds, then model how to say the sounds without stopping between them. Have children blend the sound again.

5 Read the Word

MODEL Blend the whole word. Run your hand under the letters as you say the sounds quickly.

GUIDE PRACTICE Have children blend the sounds quickly to read the word.

CORRECTIVE FEEDBACK Model how to say the sounds first slowly and then quickly.

ROUTINE 5 • NONDECODABLE WORDS

1 Introduce Nondecodable Words
Some English words do not sound like their spellings. We learn how to say them by remembering the letters. We will say and spell the words together.

Example: Write *do.*

2 Connect Letters to Words

MODEL Point to the word on the board. Say the word. Identify the letters in the word and indicate the number of letters in the word.

Example: This is the word *do.* It has two letters. The letters are *d* and *o.*

GUIDE PRACTICE Have children repeat with you the word, the letters of the word, and the number of letters in the word. Then, have the children do this on their own.

CORRECTIVE FEEDBACK If children pronounce the word incorrectly, model again the sounds in the word. Remind children to watch how you move your mouth. Point out any letters that do not follow the standard rules or may be different from their native language patterns.

Example: This is the letter d. *It makes the sound /d/. The letter* o *in this word does not make its usual sound. It makes the /ü/ sound. Let's try the word again:* do.

3 Demonstrate Usage

MODEL Use the nondecodable word in a sentence to demonstrate usage of the word. Provide an example that relates to their experience and uses the word in the same context as the text.

Example: Listen to this sentence: *Mom said to do my homework.*

GUIDE PRACTICE Have children use the word in a sentence. Provide a sentence frame if necessary.

CORRECTIVE FEEDBACK If children are not using the word correctly, model again the correct usage. Provide pictures, examples, or visual clues to help them understand its usage.

ROUTINE 6 • MULTISYLLABIC WORD STRATEGY

Use this routine for multisyllabic words that do not have prefixes, suffixes, or roots.

1 Introduce the Strategy *We're going to use word parts to help us read words. Breaking words into smaller parts, or chunks, can help us to read longer words.*

Example: Write *yellow.*

When possible, use visuals or gestures to demonstrate the meaning of the word.

2 Connect to Sound-Spellings

MODEL One way to break a word into chunks is to divide it into syllables. In this word, I divide the word into syllables by separating the two *l*'s.

Example: Yellow *has two syllables:* yel *and* low. *Breaking the word into smaller chunks helps you to read the word. Now, you can sound out the parts.*

GUIDE PRACTICE Have children say each syllable as you run your hand underneath the letters in that syllable. Point out any letters or syllables that may be different from the child's native language.

CORRECTIVE FEEDBACK If children have difficulty understanding syllables, have them place their hands underneath their chin. Then, have the children repeat the word. Explain that each time their chin touches their hand, it indicates a syllable. Then write the words on the board to show them how the words are divided into syllables.

3 Read the Word

MODEL Read the syllables as you run your hand beneath them, and then read the syllables together as you say the word.

Example: This is how I read this word. First I read each syllable, and then I read the syllables together: yel/low—yellow.

GUIDE PRACTICE Have children read the syllables, and then read the word as you run your hand beneath the parts.

CORRECTIVE FEEDBACK If children have difficulty using sound-spellings and syllabication to read word parts, then read one part at a time as you cover the remaining parts.

ROUTINE 7 • WORD PARTS STRATEGY

Use this routine to teach word structure skills: base words and inflected endings, prefixes, suffixes, contractions, compound words, and syllables.

1. **Introduce the Strategy** *We will break longer words into smaller parts. Word parts help us read the word. Some word parts help us understand what a word means.* When possible, use visuals, gestures, or examples to demonstrate its meaning.

2. **Introduce the Word Parts** Discuss the word part that is the focus of the lesson, and, if appropriate, describe its relationship to the base word. Help children make any connections between suffixes or prefixes in English and their native language. Then check the children's understanding.

   Example: Look at the word pigpen. *Let's break the word into two smaller words. What word do you see at the beginning? What word do you see at the end?*

3. **Use Word Parts for Meaning** Explain the meaning of prefixes, suffixes, and inflected endings when introducing them. For compound words, demonstrate how you can sometimes, but not always, tell the meaning from its parts. Provide examples. Then check understanding.

   Example: Have you ever seen a pig? Some pigs live in pens. Pens have fences around them to keep the pigs in. What do you think a pigpen is? Draw or show children a picture of a pig in a pigpen.

4. **Read the Word**

   MODEL Read the word parts as you run your hand beneath them, and then read the parts together to say the word.

   Example: This is how I read compound words. First, I read the first chunk, pig; *next, I read the second chunk,* pen. *Then I read the two chunks together:* pig, pen—pigpen.

   GUIDE PRACTICE Have children identify the word parts and then read the word as you run your hand beneath the parts.

   CORRECTIVE FEEDBACK If children have difficulty reading word parts, have them identify one part at a time. It may be necessary to have them blend the base word or individual syllables before reading the whole word.

ROUTINE 8 • VOWEL-FIRST BLENDING

This routine can be used for children who have difficulty identifying vowel sounds in words. This routine is also useful for ELL children who may associate different sound-spellings to vowels.

1. **Introduce Vowel-First Blending** *When we read these words, we will say the sound of the vowel before we read the whole word.*

2. **Connect to Sound-Spellings**

   MODEL Write the letters that spell the vowel sound. Touch under the letters as you say the sound.

   Example: Touch under the letters as you say /ā/.

   GUIDE PRACTICE Have children say the sound as you touch under the vowels.

   CORRECTIVE FEEDBACK If children do not say the correct sound, then refer them to the appropriate Sound-Spelling Card. Provide children with examples of other words with this sound-spelling.

3. **Add Sound-Spellings and Blend Sounds**

   MODEL Add the remaining sound-spellings one at a time. Touch under the letter(s) while saying each sound. After each sound-spelling is added, model blending the sounds, running your hand from letter to letter as you say the sounds.

   GUIDE PRACTICE Have children repeat each sound as its spelling is added. After adding a sound-spelling, have children blend the sounds with you.

   CORRECTIVE FEEDBACK If children stop between sounds, then model how to say the sounds without stopping between them.

4. **Read the Word**

   MODEL Blend the whole word. Run your hand under the letters as you say the sounds quickly to read the word.

   GUIDE PRACTICE Have children say the words quickly to read the word.

   CORRECTIVE FEEDBACK If children have difficulty saying the sounds quickly, then model how to say the sounds first slowly and then quickly.

ROUTINE 9 • PAIRED READING

1. **Select the Text** Select a text or passage that is at the children's reading level. If possible, pair the ELL child with a child who reads fluently.
2. **First Reading** Children read the selected text, switching readers at a logical breaking place—for example, at the end of a sentence, paragraph, or page. Choose a smaller segment of text for children needing more support. Reader 1 begins while Reader 2 follows along, tracking the print with his or her fingers or eyes when the partner is reading.
3. **Second Reading** Partners reread, but Reader 2 begins so that each child is reading different text.
4. **Reread** For optimal fluency, children should reread the text three or four times.
5. **Provide Corrective Feedback** Listen to the children read and provide corrective feedback regarding their oral reading (stress, rhythm, and intonation) and use of blending strategies. Keep in mind that English language learners can read fluently in English with an accent.

ROUTINE 10 • FLUENCY: CHORAL READING

1. **Select a Passage** Select a grade-level passage.
2. **Model** Have the children track the print as you read. While you read, pay attention to the elements of fluency. Read at an appropriate rate and rhythm. Emphasize the correct stress and intonation for each sentence, such as phrasing a question and stressing the important words in the sentence.
3. **Guide Practice** Have children read along with you.
4. **On Their Own**
   - Have the class read aloud with you.
   - For optimal fluency, children should reread three or four times.

ROUTINE 11 • FLUENCY: WORD READING

Use this routine to build automaticity for reading words.

1. **Review Skills** Begin by reviewing previously learned phonics or word structure skills. For sound-spellings, refer to the Sound-Spelling Cards to identify the sound(s) and spelling(s). For word parts, write a sample word and identify its parts.

2. **Introduce the Strategy** Tell children that they will practice reading words quickly in their head. Then they will read the words aloud together.

   MODEL *When I see a new word, I think about the sound for each letter. I say the sounds in my head. Then I blend the sounds quickly to read the word.*

   GUIDE PRACTICE Have children blend the word in their head and then read it aloud when you point to it.

   CORRECTIVE FEEDBACK If children have difficulty, have them whisper-read the sounds before reading the word aloud together.

3. **Build Automaticity** Write a list of words for the skill that is being reviewed. Ask children to blend sounds in their head and then read aloud each word when you point to it. Allow about two seconds per sound for previewing a word. Decrease the previewing time with practice.

ROUTINE 12 • FLUENCY: ORAL REREADING

1. **Read** Select text that is specific to the child's reading level. Model reading a part of the text. As you read, follow the words with your finger and then have the child do so. Then have the child read the selected text orally.

2. **Ask** Ask the child to point out words that he or she is unfamiliar with. Sound out the words together. Provide a simple definition or visual support.

3. **Reread** After confusing words are cleared up, have the child reread the text until he or she can do so fluently.

   CORRECTIVE FEEDBACK If the child is still struggling after three or four rereads, provide corrective feedback.

ROUTINE 13 • FLUENCY: TIMED READING

❶ **Select a Passage**
- Select a passage at the child's reading level.
- Have two copies of the passage.
- Read the passage aloud while the child follows with his or her finger on the other copy.

❷ **Timed Reading**
- Have the child read the text aloud.
- On your copy, mark any errors the child makes.
- Mark where the child is after one minute.

❸ **Figure Words Correct per Minute (WCPM)** To figure WCPM, subtract the number of mistakes from the number of words the child read in one minute. Tell the child his or her WCPM, and explain that by practicing, he or she can do even better.

❹ **Review** Review with the child mistakes he or she made. Help the child reread unknown words until he or she can do so without errors.

❺ **Timed Reading**
- Challenge the child to reread the passage now that he or she is comfortable with the difficult words.
- Figure out his or her WCPM during the second round. Let the child know how much he or she has improved. Point out the importance of practicing.

❻ **Provide Corrective Feedback:** Remind children that the goal is not to read as quickly as possible, but to read accurately and quickly.

❼ **Extra Time** Invite children to set their own WCPM goal for another section. Help them to reach that goal.

ROUTINE 14 • RETELLING/SUMMARIZING: NARRATIVE

❶ **Introduce Retelling** *When we retell a story, we tell the story in our own words. Before we can retell a story, we need to know the parts of the story. We need to remember what happened first, next, and last.*

❷ **Identify Plot** Explain that every story has a beginning, middle, and end. The parts of the story are called the plot. Have children write *Beginning, Middle,* and *End* at the top of three sheets of paper. Provide an example of a familiar story, such as *Little Red Riding Hood*, or *Jack and the Beanstalk.* Then, ask children *What event happens at the beginning of the story?* Have children draw a picture to tell. Continue with each section until children have drawn three pictures. Explain that they drew the plot.

❸ **Introduce Sequence Words** Explain that certain words are used to tell when things happen. Examples of these words are *first, next,* and *last.* Model using the words *first* and *next* to describe the beginning and middle of the story.

Example: First, Jack sold the family's cow and bought a bag of magic beans. Next, Jack planted the beans in the ground, and the beans began to grow.

Invite a volunteer to explain the last part of the story, using the word *last.*

❹ **Practice Retelling** Ask a child to explain his or her own drawing, using the words *first, next,* and *last.* After, tell the child, *You just retold the story!* As time permits, repeat the lesson with other familiar stories.

CORRECTIVE FEEDBACK Allow children to review text and pictures as needed to remind them of parts of the plot. They can then use what they remember to retell the story.

As an extension, children can create a chart based on a story they know. Then, they can cut apart the three sections and exchange with a partner. The partner will then try to put the steps in order based on the pictures or what the child has written.

ROUTINE 15 • RETELLING/SUMMARIZING: NONFICTION

1. **Introduce Summarizing** Explain to children that summarizing a passage means telling what it was about. Summarizing does not include details. It just includes the most important parts.

2. **What Happened?**

   MODEL Before reading, ask a child to tell you about his or her favorite pet or animal. Then, model summarizing what the child told you. *When I summarized, I didn't include all the details. I just told you about the important parts.*

   GUIDE PRACTICE After children have read the selections, help them make a concept web. In the center, write a few words about the selection. Then have children write or draw the most important parts in the outer circles.

   CORRECTIVE FEEDBACK If children have difficulty telling the important parts, model how to find them by pointing to pictures and talking about what you see.

3. **When Did It Happen?**

   MODEL *I can also summarize by telling when things happened. I tell what happened first, next, and last.*

   Example: First, the bird collects twigs. Next, it builds a nest. Last, the bird lays its eggs.

4. **Review** Review with the child mistakes he or she made. Help the child reread unknown words until he or she can do so without errors.

   GUIDE PRACTICE Help children make a sequence chart. Write the words *first*, *next*, and *last* and fill in the first event. Have children draw pictures to show what happened first, next, and last in the reading.

   CORRECTIVE FEEDBACK If children have difficulty tracking the sequence, have them use the pictures and point to what happens first, next, and last.

ROUTINE 16 • SPELLING

1. **Introduce Spelling** *We will use the sounds and letters we know to spell words. First, listen to the word. Then, say its sounds and write the letters.*

2. **Dictate the Word** Say the word, use it in a sentence, and say the word again.

   Example: dig; *I dig with a shovel.* dig

3. **Segment the Sounds**

   MODEL Sound out the word. Have children echo each sound. *The word is* dig. *The sounds in* dig *are* /d/ /i/ /g/. Have children echo each sound.

   CORRECTIVE FEEDBACK If children are having difficulty saying each sound correctly, drag each sound out: /d/ /i/ /g/. Remind children to watch how you move your mouth. Emphasize any sounds that may be different than the children's native language.

4. **Spell the Sounds**

   MODEL Say the first sound and write its spelling.

   GUIDE PRACTICE Ask a volunteer what letter or letters make the first sound. Write the letter or letters. Repeat with the other sounds. Have children say each sound with you, and then write its spelling after you.

   CORRECTIVE FEEDBACK If children have difficulty spelling a sound, have them refer to a Sound-Spelling Card to identify the spelling.

5. **Proofread Spelling** Continue the dictation until all words have been spelled. Then display the correct spelling for each word. Help children proofread their work, circle any misspelled words, and write them correctly.

ROUTINE 17 • CONCEPT TALK VIDEO

1. **Introduce Talk Video** Explain to children that they will be watching a video. Explain that the video will introduce the Question of the Week.
2. **Assess Understanding** Once the video ends, write three different questions on the board. Only one is the correct Question of the Week. Ask children, "Which is the question of the week?" Then, replay the section of the video that answers this question. Pause it when done.
3. **Access Prior Knowledge** Invite children to discuss any prior knowledge they have about the weekly question or concept. Encourage them to share their experiences or stories. Invite struggling speakers to draw a picture that illustrates their story.
4. **Summarize** Begin the video again. Pause it at critical points, such as when new information is taught. Have children draw a picture that illustrates a part of the video. Have them write a title for their picture.

   CORRECTIVE FEEDBACK If children are unable to draw a picture, rewind and watch the video again. Ask questions that will guide them to understand the main idea of the section.

ROUTINE 18 • AUDIOTEXT CD

1. **Before Listening** Have children open their Student Edition to the selection you choose. Tell them they are going to read along while listening to the selection on a CD.
2. **During Listening** Ask children to look at the pictures as they listen to the CD. Then, play the CD again. This time, have children follow along with their finger as they listen.
3. **Model** Replay the CD, this time allowing children to watch you choral read along with it. Make sure you imitate not only the words but the expression with which they are read.
4. **After Listening** Have children choral read sections of the passage with you at a slower pace. Pause and make a note of hard words or phrases. When the passage has been reread once, write the difficult words and phrases on the board. Help children to understand each word by sounding it out. Explain the meanings of any difficult phrases.
5. **Reread** Reread the passage. Have children echo read with you until they read the passage fluently. Then, play back the CD. Have children read along with the CD, without you. Finally, have them take turns reading aloud to a partner without even the CD to guide them. Ask one partner to follow along in their student edition as the other partner reads.

   CORRECTIVE FEEDBACK Make sure children do not sacrifice accuracy for speed. Difficult sections can be replayed until children understand them.

ROUTINE 19 • GRAMMAR JAMMER

1. **Introduce Grammar Jammer** As you plan instruction, preview the Grammar Jammer song or rhyme to select examples of the language conventions topic of the week. Then tell children that you will play a song or rhyme; identify the topic (such as nouns, adjectives, verbs, or sentences). View and listen to the Grammar Jammer with children. Repeat an important concept.

   Example: *The song is about nouns. Nouns are words that we use to name people, places, animals, or things. What nouns do you remember hearing in the rhyme? Did you hear the plural nouns?*

2. **Display the Concept** Use a Grammar Jammer image, or write and display examples of two words or sentences to represent the conventions skill. Explain the concept.

   Example: *One noun is* girl. *Is a girl a person or a thing?* (a person) *Yes, the word* girl *is a noun that names a person. What noun identifies more than one girl?* (girls)

   MODEL Play the Grammar Jammer song or rhyme again. Identify more examples, such as (for nouns) a few common nouns and proper nouns, singular and plural nouns, and possessive nouns. Explain as needed. For each noun, verb, or adjective (for those Grammar Jammer topics), use the word in a sentence.

   GUIDE PRACTICE Have children view and listen to Grammar Jammer again, and have the group identify several examples. Have volunteers make up and say short sentences.

   CORRECTIVE FEEDBACK Clarify any examples that children do not say or use correctly. Acknowledge correct responses, and positively point out improvements in children's understanding or language production.

3. **On Their Own** As children's literacy skills and ability to view electronic images emerge, have partners revisit the Grammar Jammer song or rhyme. As appropriate, guide children to write or dictate responses to the Grammar Jammer journal prompt. Then invite children to make up their own rhymes using words and sentences that exhibit the conventions skill.

ROUTINE 20 • MODELED PRONUNCIATION AUDIO CD

1. **Before Listening** Tell children that they will be listening to a CD to help with sound pronunciation. Have them take out the Sound-Spelling Cards that they will be learning about.

2. **During Listening** After each pronunciation, hit pause. Repeat each sound and exaggerate your mouth movements. Use your fingers to guide children to watch your mouth. Then have children repeat each sound. Rewind, and play the sound again. Write the letters that make the sound on the board. Repeat it again, and have children do the same.

   Example: The sound is /bl/. The letters that make the sound are b *and* l. *Listen as I say the sound again: /bl/.*

   Before continuing, write the sound-spelling on the board. Have children find the card that matches it, and hold it above his or her head.

   CORRECTIVE FEEDBACK If a child picks the wrong card, offer corrective feedback. Explain how the card he or she chose should sound. Press play again. Repeat the exercise for each sound learned.

3. **After Listening** Write each sound-spelling on the board. Have children repeat each one after you. Pair children. Have them practice their pronunciation using their Sound-Spelling Cards as guides.

   CORRECTIVE FEEDBACK Walk around the room listening to children. If children have difficulty remembering what each spelling sounds like, replay the CD, pointing out each example on the board as it plays.

Table of Contents

K-W-L Chart

Topic ____________________

What Do I **K**now?	What Do I **W**ant to Learn?	What Did I **L**earn?

Word Rating Chart

Word	Know	Have Seen	Don't Know

Story Predictions Chart

Title____

What might happen?	What clues do I have?	What did happen?

Story Map A

Title ________________________________

Beginning

Middle

End

Story Map B

Title

____

Characters

Who is in the story?

____

Setting

Where does the story happen?

____

When does the story happen?

____

Events

What happens in the story?

____

____

____

____

____

____

____

Story Comparison

Title A ______________________

____

Characters

Who is in the story?

Setting

Where and **when** does it happen?

Events

What happens in the story?

Title B ______________________

____

Characters

Who is in the story?

Setting

Where and **when** does it happen?

Events

What happens in the story?

Web

Main Idea

Main Idea

Details

Venn Diagram

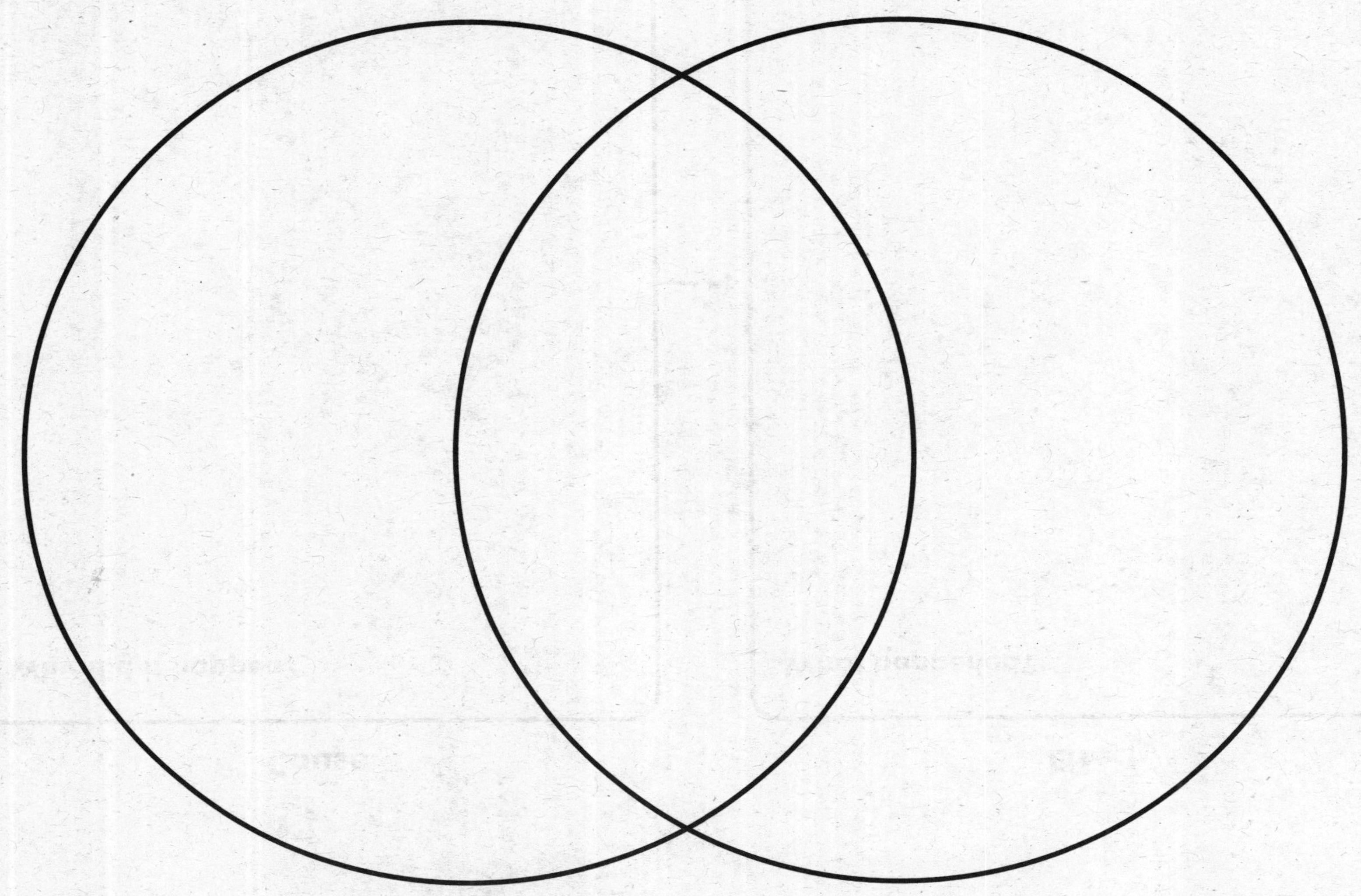

Cause and Effect

Cause

Why did it happen?

→

Effect

What happened?

Problem and Solution

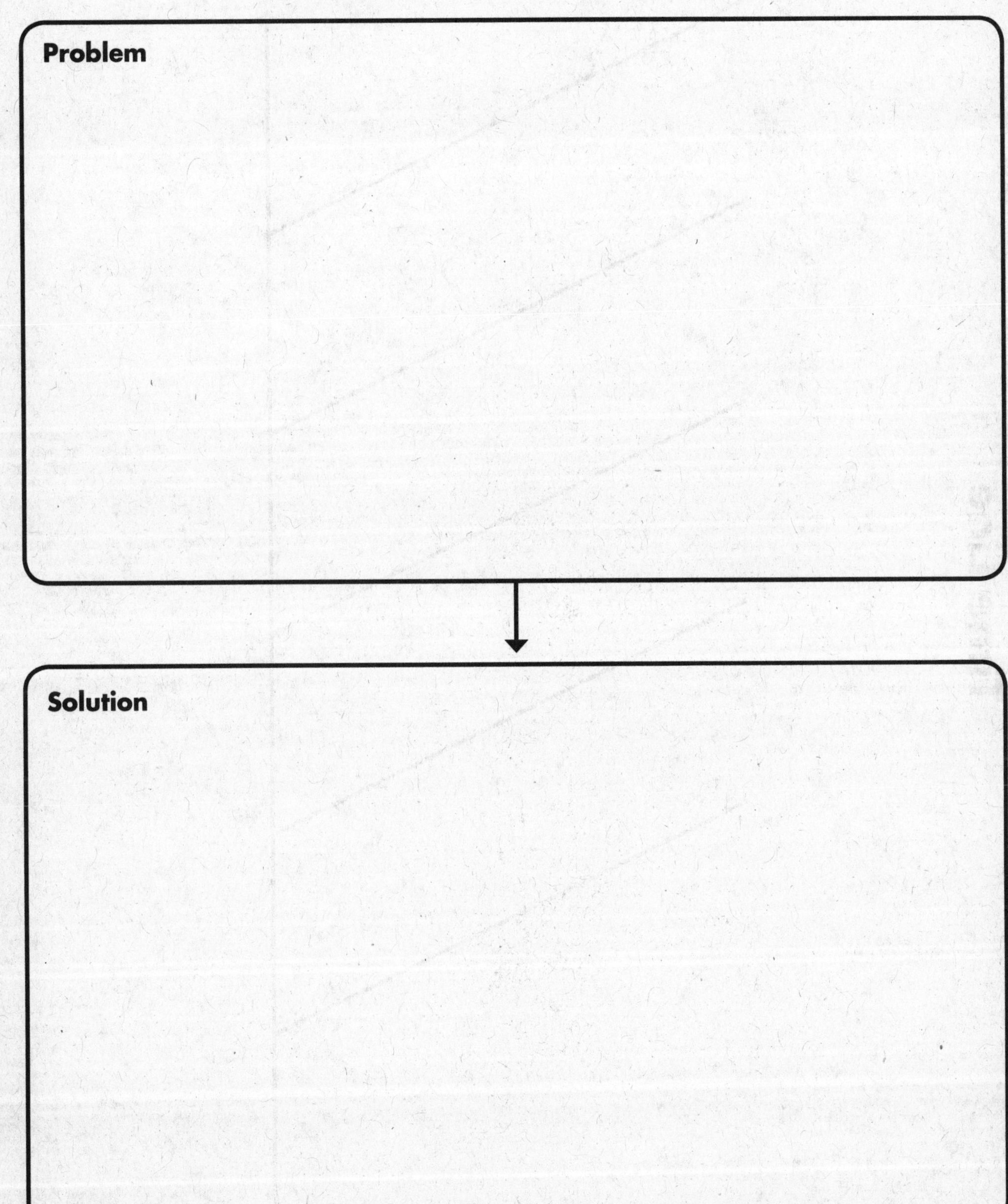

Time Line

Steps in a Process

Process ________________________________

Step 1

Step 2

Step 3

T-Chart

Three-Column Chart

Outline Form

Title ______________________________

A ______________________________

1. ______________________________

2. ______________________________

B ______________________________

1. ______________________________

2. ______________________________

K-W-L CHART

About the Graphic Organizer

Children build prior knowledge about a selection, ask questions to set purposes for reading, and record what they learn as they read.

Instructional Routine

The K-W-L chart works well with expository text. Display the chart for children.

- Identify a topic to model using the chart (e.g., dogs). Write the word *Know* on the board. Underline the *K*. Tell children that the *K* stands for "What Do I Know?" Ask children what they know about dogs and record their responses.
- Write *Want* on the board and underline *W*. Tell children that the *W* stands for "What Do I Want to Learn?" Ask children what they want to know about dogs. Model recording their responses in the form of questions. *(Is it hard to train a dog? Do some dogs make better pets than other dogs?)*
- Write *Learn* on the board. Underline the *L*. Tell children that the *L* stands for "What Did I Learn?" As you read, ask children what they are learning. They should try to answer the questions in the *W* column.

Teaching Tips

- After modeling, children can complete the K-W-L chart in pairs or small groups. You might brainstorm as a class ideas for the *K* column and have children work together to write questions.
- Model how to write a question with a capital letter and a question mark.
- Modify the chart if necessary by changing the headings into sentence frames: *I know* ________ *I want to know* ________ *I learned* ________

Extensions

- Create K-W-L charts that you can post in the room as you learn about different topics in content areas, such as social studies and science. Children can add to the *L* columns of the charts as they learn more.
- Have children work in pairs to read an article at their reading level or to listen to an article you read aloud. They can use K-W-L charts to organize their thinking.

Skill and Strategies

- Activate Prior Knowledge
- Set Purpose
- Summarize

WORD RATING CHART

About the Graphic Organizer

The word rating chart helps children explore what they already know about words.

Instructional Routine

You can use this chart with any list of words that children are learning. The chart is a great tool for ongoing assessment.

- Model how to use the chart. Display the chart for children and list words for a selection.
- Explain that the word *Know* means that children know and can use the word. Choose a word and model: *I know the word* ________. *It means* ________. *I can use it in a sentence:* ________ Place a check in the correct column.
- Explain that column 3, *Have Seen*, means that children have seen or heard the word, but they aren't sure what it means. Choose a word and model: *I have seen this word before. I read it in the newspaper. But I'm not sure if I know how to use it.* Place a check in the column.
- Explain that column 4, *Don't Know,* means that children don't know the word at all. Think aloud about a word you don't know and place a check in the correct column.

Teaching Tips

- After modeling, children can complete a word rating chart on their own. You might write the words in the chart and copy before distributing.
- Use the chart as a diagnostic tool to determine on which words you'll focus in classroom studies.

Extensions

- Have children revisit their chart after they have read a selection or studied the words. They can adjust their ratings.
- Consider adding a column to the chart in which children can write sentences with words they know.
- You might create a visual for each word in the chart before you distribute it to children.
- Encourage children to state meanings of words in their own words.

Skill and Strategies

- Activate Prior Knowledge
- Recall and Retell
- Context Clues

STORY PREDICTIONS CHART

About the Graphic Organizer

Children preview the selection title and illustrations and then predict what might happen in the selection.

Instructional Routine

This graphic organizer works well with any selection in which the title and/or pictures suggest predictions about the events in a story. Consider using it for content-area selections as well.

- Preview the selection with children. Read the title and lead a picture walk. Ask children what they think will happen in the selection. Remind them to use what they know about the topic of the story. Record their predictions in the chart.
- Ask children how they figured out what would happen. Ask *Have you read a story like this before? What did you see in the pictures that helped you figure out what would happen next?* Record the clues they used in the chart.
- After reading, look back at the predictions. Write what actually happened in the third column. Ask children if their predictions were different. Why do they think the story turned out differently?

Teaching Tips

- Focus on clues in illustrations. What details in the illustrations help children make predictions?
- Model sentence frames for predicting. *I think ________ will happen. I think this will happen because ________.*

Extensions

- After completing this activity as a class exercise, have children use the chart in pairs, small groups, or independently.
- Use the chart with content-area selections. Focus on the content, giving children a sentence frame to use: *I think I will learn about ________ because ________.*

Skill and Strategies

- Predict
- Activate Prior Knowledge
- Draw Conclusions

STORY MAP A

About the Graphic Organizer

Children use this chart to record the sequence of events in a selection.

Instructional Routine

This organizer works well with any selection with a clear sequence of events.

- Display the organizer. Write the title of the selection.
- Start reading. Pause to ask *What happens first?* Record what happens first on the organizer.
- Focus on events in the middle of the story, pausing for children to identify them. Record them in the chart.
- As you finish the selection, record important events from the end.

Teaching Tips

- Make a list of words that tell time order, such as *after, later, first,* or *next.* Provide sentences frames to help children use them.
- Encourage children to use story maps to retell the events to partners.

Extensions

- Have children draw pictures of events in the organizer. They can label the pictures.
- Use the story map with events in social studies or with steps in a sequence.

Skill and Strategies

- Sequence/Plot
- Recall and Retell
- Text Structure
- Summarize

STORY MAP B

About the Graphic Organizer

Children record the characters and setting of a story and track a sequence of events.

Instructional Routine

This graphic organizer works well with any selection that has a clear series of events. It can help children identify different story elements.

- ○ Display the organizer. Write the title of the selection on the organizer.
- ○ Read the selection. Pause to ask children where and when the story takes place. Record those details in the *setting* section.
- ○ As you read, pause to think aloud and record information about characters on the organizer.
- ○ As you read, pause to record information about the sequence of events.

Teaching Tips

- Model sentence frames for talking about characters and setting: ________ *is a person/animal in this story. This story takes place in [the future/the past/today].*
- Children can identify events in the organizer and describe those events.
- Children may not need all the lines, or they may need more. Help them modify the organizer depending on the story.

Extensions

- After completing this activity as a class exercise, have children use the chart in pairs, in small groups, or independently.
- Help children look for clue words for sequence. Make a list of clue words to display for children's reference.
- Help children think of words to use to describe characters. Make a list and have children add to it.

Skill and Strategies

- Story Elements: Character, Setting, Plot
- Recall and Retell
- Summarize

STORY COMPARISON

About the Graphic Organizer

Children use this chart to record how two selections are similar and different.

Instructional Routine

This organizer works well with selections that have something in common. It's a great tool for comparing texts by the same author or about the same topic or texts in the same genre.

- ○ Choose two stories to compare. Write their titles on the organizer.
- ○ Ask questions to elicit characters, setting, and plot events. Record details on the chart.

Teaching Tips

- After modeling how to use the organizer, children can work on the organizer with partners or in small groups.
- Provide sentence frames for comparison and model how to use them, such as: *The characters in this story are* ________ *but the characters in that story are* ________.
- Invite children to use the chart to retell stories.

Extensions

- Children can use the chart to compare a story and a nonfiction text about the same topic.
- Have children use one half of the chart to plan the writing of their own story.
- If the comparison is too difficult for children, they might simply use one half of the organizer to complete a story map.

Skill and Strategies

- Story Elements: Character, Setting, Plot
- Text Structure
- Summarize
- Compare and Contrast

WEB

About the Graphic Organizer

Children explore their prior knowledge as they brainstorm related ideas, recognize concept relationships, and/or organize information. They can highlight a central concept and connect it to related words, ideas, or details.

Instructional Routine

This graphic organizer has multiple uses and is appropriate for all levels of learners. Use different approaches to the web as you develop the organizer with children.

- Display the organizer. Write a central idea or topic in the middle of the web.
- Ask children for ideas that are related to the central idea. Record those ideas in the circles attached to the middle circle.
- Point out that the lines show connections. If you wrote *kinds of texts,* for example, in the middle oval, you might write *fantasy, fairy tale, article,* and *poem* in the outer circles. Those are all types of texts.

Teaching Tips

- Once you have modeled how to use the organizer, have children complete the organizer independently, in pairs, or in small groups.
- Encourage children to explain how the ideas on the web are related to the central ideas. Provide sentence frames to help children talk about the web. *The important idea is* ________ *Some ideas related to this are* ________
- Use this web to explore main ideas and details, character names along with their traits, vocabulary words and their synonyms, and so on.

Extensions

- Children can use the organizer to record ideas about a topic in content-area reading, such as things plants need to grow.
- Have children use the web to record background knowledge about a topic. Use the webs to assess gaps in understanding as you plan instruction.

Skill and Strategies

- Classify
- Summarize
- Main Idea and Supporting Details

MAIN IDEA

About the Graphic Organizer

Children recognize a main idea and distinguish between the main idea and the supporting details.

Instructional Routine

This organizer works especially well with nonfiction selections that are organized around main ideas and details.

- Record a main idea in the top box. Define main idea as the most important idea. A main idea, for example, might be: Many things happen in the spring.
- Model by recording a detail that supports, or tells more about, the main idea (such as flowers blooming, days getting longer, days getting warmer, animals having babies). Have children supply additional supporting details as you record them.

Teaching Tips

- Supply a sentence frame about main ideas: *The most important idea is* ________ Supply a sentence frame about supporting details. *One detail about this idea is* ________
- Display part of a selection and model highlighting important ideas. Record the important ideas in the organizer.
- Extend or add additional boxes if necessary to add more supporting details.

Extensions

- Have children use the organizer to record ideas for writing pieces of their own.
- Have children use the chart in pairs or small groups to record important ideas from content area reading, such as in social studies or science.

Skill and Strategies

- Main Idea and Supporting Details
- Summarize

VENN DIAGRAM

About the Graphic Organizer

Children use this organizer to record similarities and differences between places, ideas, characters, or other elements of fiction or nonfiction.

Instructional Routine

A Venn diagram works well in any situation that lends itself to comparing and contrasting.

- Start by comparing and contrasting something simple and familiar, such as cats and dogs. Write the subjects you are comparing over the circles of the Venn diagram.
- Point to where the circles overlap. Let children know that in this section, you'll write similarities, or how the two things are alike. Ask how the two subjects are alike (e.g., both have tails, both have four legs). Record children's responses.
- Point to an individual circle and let children know that, in this section, you'll write details that describe only what is labeled at the top of the circle. Ask children to list details as you record them.

Teaching Tips

- It might help children if you ask questions that lead to details to write in the diagram, such as *Are both of these objects blue? Do both of them have four legs?* and so on.
- Help children with sentence frames: *These two things are alike because* ________ *These two things are different because* ________
- List words that signal comparing and contrasting, such as *alike, different, but,* and so on. Children can point to those words in the text.

Extensions

- Children can create Venn diagrams to compare themselves to characters in fictional texts.
- Children can use Venn diagrams to compare topics in content areas, such as two plants, two animals, or two different games.

Skill and Strategies

- Compare and Contrast
- Summarize

CAUSE AND EFFECT

About the Graphic Organizer

Children identify cause-and-effect relationships in either fiction or nonfiction.

Instructional Routine

This graphic organizer works well with any selection that has clear cause-and-effect relationships.

- Tell children that something that happens is an effect. Record an effect on the graphic organizer (*I got out an umbrella*).
- Then ask children "Why did it happen?" Tell them the reason something happens is a cause. Record the cause on the graphic organizer (*It started to rain*).
- Restate the cause and effect: *It started to rain, so I got out an umbrella.*

Teaching Tips

- Remind children to ask themselves *What happened?* and *Why did it happen?* to identify effects and causes. It is usually easier to identify effects first, before the causes.
- List clue words that signal causes and effects, such as *because* and *so.* Look over the clue words with children, but remind them that not all causes and effects in selections have clue words.

Extensions

- Children can write causes and effects in their content area classes. They could record, for example, something about animals or the weather. (*The puppy ate healthy food, so it grew up into a big dog! It started raining, so we had recess indoors.*)
- If children need extra assistance, fill in either causes or effects before distributing the organizer. Ask children to work in pairs to find the corresponding causes or effects.

Skill and Strategies

- Cause and Effect
- Summarize
- Text Structure

PROBLEM AND SOLUTION

About the Graphic Organizer

Children identify problems and solutions presented in fiction or nonfiction.

Instructional Routine

This graphic organizer works well with any selections with clear problems and solutions.

- Tell children that a problem is something that needs to be solved. Give an example of a simple problem. (*I forget to bring my lunch to school.*) Record it in the organizer.
- Ask children what they might do to "fix" the problem. Tell children that fixing a problem is solving a problem. Ask children how they might solve the problem. (*I can put my lunch in the same place every night. I can ask my brother to remind me.*) Record their ideas in the solution section.

Teaching Tips

- Once children understand how to use the organizer, focus on a problem and solution from a piece of text.
- Provide sentence frames to help children discuss problems and solutions. *One problem is* ______ *I can solve the problem by* ______

Extensions

- Write a problem in the school, classroom, or community in the first box and distribute organizers to pairs or small groups. Children can brainstorm solutions.
- Children can draw problems and solutions in the organizer and then label them with words or phrases.

Skill and Strategies

- Plot
- Summarize
- Text Structure

TIME LINE

About the Graphic Organizer

Children organize events from fiction or nonfiction in sequential order along a continuum.

Instructional Routine

This organizer helps children organize events or ideas from a text in time order.

- After reading a short text, ask children what happened first. Record the first event on the chart.
- Continue asking children to name events in order, placing them on the continuum. Point out that they use this chart the same way they read: from left to right.

Teaching Tips

- Remind children to look for clues in the text to the order in which things happen. They might find dates or clue words such as *first, next, then,* and *last*.
- If children need extra support, write events from the text on sentence strips. Have children work in pairs or small groups to place the strips in order and then write the events on the time line.

Extensions

- Children can create time lines about things that have happened in their school or community or in their own lives.
- Have children interview partners and create time lines based on important events in their partners' lives.
- Have children use the time lines to retell the stories.

Skill and Strategies

- Summarize
- Text Structure
- Sequence/Plot

STEPS IN A PROCESS

About the Graphic Organizer

Children break down a process into simple steps or directions.

Instructional Routine

This graphic organizer works well with any procedure that has relatively few steps. If children need more or smaller steps, help children redesign the organizer.

- Display the organizer. Write the title on the organizer, such as *Making a Peanut Butter Sandwich.*
- Ask children what the first step is. Record the first step in the organizer.
- Write the remaining steps in the organizer in order as children supply them.

Teaching Tips

- Once children can contribute to a steps in a process chart, have them work in pairs or small groups to write the steps of a simple process.
- Tell children to look for clue words to sequence in a text such as *first, next,* and *later* to help them sequence the steps.

Extensions

- Children may draw the steps in the organizer and label them with words or phrases.
- Have children use the organizer to show steps in a recipe, steps for doing a science project, steps for playing a game, or steps in another content area.

Skill and Strategies

- Steps in a Process
- Sequence
- Visualize

T-CHART

About the Graphic Organizer

Children can explore and compare ideas, story elements, or vocabulary words. They can also chart ideas within and across texts, or between prior knowledge and new ideas.

Instructional Routine

This is a multipurpose graphic organizer that is helpful when exploring two concepts. It works well with all types of selections.

- Model using the chart. Display the chart and write two topics being studied on the chart, one topic per column. Start with a simple topic, such as *vowels* and *consonants.*
- Elicit responses from children based on the topics chosen. Model how to list ideas or examples in the correct columns.

Teaching Tips

- Children can write in the chart, but they can also draw and list or label.
- Children can use the T-chart to compare story elements, such as the traits of two characters.
- Use a T-chart to organize ideas gathered in a class brainstorming session.
- Use a T-chart to explore two vocabulary words. Write the words at the tops of the columns. Then under each word, children can sketch the word, write a quick definition, or write the word used in a simple sentence.

Extensions

- Children can work with partners, each partner completing one half of the chart.
- Children can use T-charts for topics related to math, science, or health, such as fruits/vegetables, numbers > 10/numbers < 10, plants with leaves/ plants with needles, animals that walk/animals that swim, games with balls/games with sticks, and so on.

Skill and Strategies

- Compare and Contrast
- Main Idea and Supporting Details
- Summarize
- Activate Prior Knowledge

THREE-COLUMN CHART

About the Graphic Organizer

The chart can be used to explore or classify ideas, story elements, genres, or vocabulary features. It can also help children recognize comparisons and contrasts, or chart ideas within and across texts.

Instructional Routine

This is a multi-purpose organizer that works well for exploring and organizing ideas for three concepts, words, or ideas. It works well with many selections.

- Display the organizer. Choose three simple headings and write them on the chart, such as *red, yellow,* and *blue*.
- Ask children for details for each heading and record them on the chart (for example, things that are red, things that are yellow, and things that are blue). Point out that this chart helps organize information.

Teaching Tips

- Once you have modeled how to use the organizer, children can complete organizers independently or in pairs or small groups.
- Children can draw in the charts as well as list ideas.
- Children can use the three-column chart to explore story characteristics, such as three different characters in a story.
- Children can use the chart to organize ideas they generate during brainstorming.
- Children can use the chart to organize ideas about three different vocabulary words.

Extensions

- Children can use the organizer to record ideas that follow the idea of *before, during,* and *after.*
- Children can use the chart to organize ideas in any curricular area. For example, in social studies, children could list three different holidays and list details about them. In science, children could list three different animals and use the chart to describe their traits.

Skill and Strategies

- Classify
- Summarize
- Main Idea and Supporting Details
- Activate Prior Knowledge

OUTLINE FORM

About the Graphic Organizer

Children use a simplified outline form to take notes on the organization of print materials or to organize their own thoughts before writing.

Instructional Routine

Writers can change the outline form to suit their own purposes, but this form gets children started with the basic outline organization.

- Model using the outline form by creating an outline about a simple topic, such as "People in Our Class." Place the title on the top line.
- Show children how to record the main ideas. You might display the text to point out where to find the main ideas in the text. The main ideas for this outline might be *girls, boys,* and *adult helpers.*
- Break down the main ideas into smaller details on the secondary lines. You could list some boys' names, some girls' names, and the names of adult helpers in the class.
- Model the same form as the basis for a class writing about something that you are currently studying.

Teaching Tips

- Depending on English proficiency, children can use words, phrases, or sentences in their outlines. Encourage them to be consistent throughout the entire outline.
- Model using an outline to plan writing. Point out that outlines are tools that can be changed before and during writing if the organization will make more sense.

Extensions

- Create an outline by doing a class outline on a piece of content-area text, such as an article from a science book.
- Show children text features in a content area book, such as titles, heads, subheads, labels, and captions. Ask how these features might help them create an outline.

Skill and Strategies

- Text Structure
- Summarize
- Main Idea and Supporting Details

High-Frequency Words

The high-frequency words are words that appear most often in written English, words of the greatest general service to English language learners. Many of the words are part of word families that are useful for students to know as they learn English.

Each week, provide the list of high-frequency words for students' reference for speaking and writing. Choose strategies from this bank of activities to ensure students' mastery.

Cloze Activity

Create a passage that includes high-frequency words. Display the passage, covering high-frequency words, for example with sticky notes. Ask students to read the passage with you, substituting the missing words. Have them explain how they figured out which words to use.

Play Bingo

After students have learned at least 25 words, provide a 5 × 5 grid with a high-frequency word written in each square. Read aloud high-frequency words as you draw them randomly. Students cover words they hear with markers to create a row. When a student has created a row, have him or her read the words aloud.

Semantic Map

For words with richer meanings, create semantic maps. Place the word in the middle of a web and ask students to supply related words for the "arms." Discuss word relationships.

High-Frequency Scavenger Hunt

Have students keep the word lists on their desks for the week. Ask them to tally how many times they see each word in their reading selections, science or social studies books, magazine articles, and so on. They can tally how often they say the word.

Realia and Visuals

Use both hands-on experiences and visuals to reinforce meanings of the words.

- Provide realia that evokes meanings of high-frequency words. For *year,* for example, you might show a calendar. For *see,* you might show a pair of eyeglasses. Discuss the items, using the high-frequency words.
- Use visuals to teach abstract high-frequency words. For *of,* for example, you could show pictures: a basket of laundry, a slice of bread, a glass of water.

Word Sorts

Have students sort the words. Provide index cards with words, one word per card. Students can sort them into categories you provide *(words that show action, words that name things, words in the same family,* and so on) or sort them and explain the rationale behind their categories.

Flashcard Activities

- Post high-frequency words on a word wall as you introduce them. From time to time, hand students flashcards with the words on them, one word per card. Students match the card to the word on the wall, then use the word in a sentence.
- Hand out flashcards, one word to each pair of students. Students work together to create two sentences using the word.
- Make up simple sentences using the high-frequency words. Write the sentences on cards, one word per card. Hand the cards out to students. Have them unscramble the words to make a sentence and read it aloud chorally.
- Pair students and give one student in each pair a card. The student with the card gives clues about the word for the other student to guess.